Profiles of
People in Power:
the World's Government Leaders

Profiles of
People in Power:
the World' s Government Leaders

Roger East and Richard J. Thomas

FIRST EDITION

Europa Publications
Taylor & Francis Group

LONDON AND NEW YORK

First Edition 2003

Published by Europa Publications Limited
11 New Fetter Lane, London EC4P 4EE, United Kingdom
(A member of the Taylor & Francis Group)

ISBN 1-85743-126-X

Printed and bound by TJ International Ltd, Padstow, Cornwall

FOREWORD

PROFILES OF PEOPLE IN POWER is being published for the first time in 2003. Its primary purpose is to provide, in a single volume, a comprehensive set of succinct biographical portraits of the heads of state and government of every sovereign country in the world as at 1 January 2003. Where appropriate, the leaders of ruling parties, presidents-elect and outgoing presidents are also included.

A number of additional features have been included to enhance the value of this book as a work of reference.

The biographical profiles—arranged by country—are preceded by a concise description of the constitutional structure of the country's leadership, executive branch and legislature. These descriptions are drawn from *People in Power*, a bimonthly publication compiled by Cambridge International Reference on Current Affairs (CIRCA) Ltd, which provides up-to-date listings of government membership around the world.

Each country entry also contains a table listing the names of all those who have held the office of head of state, head of government or ruling party leader since 1 January 2000, with their dates of taking (and, where relevant, leaving) office.

The book is fully indexed by personal names and by dates of taking power. A further index lists countries by type of political regime, and an appendix provides address and contact data.

Roger East and Richard J. Thomas
Cambridge, January 2003.

ACKNOWLEDGEMENTS

The authors gratefully acknowledge the assistance received with the compilation of this book from many of the governments concerned, and the co-operation of international organizations in providing us with photographs. We are also greatly indebted to Helen Hawkins, Rosemary Payne and the staff of Cambridge International Reference on Current Affairs (CIRCA) Ltd, in particular Catherine Jagger, for their painstaking work in collecting and revising data. Special thanks are also due to Catherine Jagger for copy editing and project management.

We have made extensive use of material from the bimonthly *People in Power*, published by CIRCA Ltd. *The Europa World Year Book* and *The International Who's Who* have both been used extensively for the cross-checking of detailed factual information.

CONTENTS

Contents

Contents

Contents

Contents

PHOTOGRAPHS

OF

WORLD LEADERS

United Nations (UN) Millennium Summit

New York, USA, 2000

African Union (AU) Inaugural Summit

Durban, South Africa, 2002

Asia–Pacific Economic Co-operation (APEC) Summit

Los Cabos, Mexico, 2002

European Union (EU) Enlargement Summit

Copenhagen, Denmark, 2002

United Nations Millennium Summit (New York, USA, 2000)

(Front row) 1: Obasanjo, Nigeria. 2: Lukashenka, Belarus. 3: Ragheb, Jordan. 4: Abdullah II, Jordan. 5: Aliyev, Azerbaijan. 6: Kocharian, Armenia. 7: Blair, UK. 8: Chirac, France. 9: Clinton, USA. 10: Halonen, Finland. 11: Annan, UN. 12: Nujoma, Namibia. 13: Jiang, China. 14: Putin, Russia. 15: de la Rúa, Argentina. 16: Klestil, Austria. 17: Turnquest, Bahamas. 18: Harald V, Norway. 19: Stoltenberg, Norway. 20: Kim Dae Jung, South Korea. 21: Wahid, Indonesia.

(Second row) 22: Sassou-Nguesso, Rep. Congo. 23: Pastrana, Colombia. 24: Monteiro, Cape Verde. 25: Bolkiah, Brunei. 26: Mogae, Botswana. 27: Rawlings, Ghana. 28: Schröder, Germany. 29–30: Representatives, UN. 31: Gurirab, Namibia. 32: Mori, Japan. 33: Castro, Cuba. 34: Izetbegović, Bosnia & Herzegovina. 35: Stoyanov, Bulgaria. 36: Mbeki, South Africa. 37: Lagos, Chile. 38: Azali, Comoros.

(Third row) 39: Shevardnadze, Georgia. 40: Bongo, Gabon. 41: Obiang Nguema, Equatorial Guinea. 42: Noboa, Ecuador. 43: Guelleh, Djibouti. 44: Chrétien, Canada. 45: Clerides, Cyprus. 46: Rodríguez, Costa Rica. 47–49: Various representatives. 50: Mesić, Croatia. 51: Havel, Czech Republic. 52: Amato, Italy. 53: Mejía, Dominican Republic. 54: Flores, El Salvador. 55: Afewerki, Eritrea. 56: Jammeh, Gambia. 57: Portillo, Guatemala.

(Fourth row) 58: Chissano, Mozambique. 59: Falcam, Micronesia. 60: Khouna, Mauritania. 61: Konaré, Mali. 62: Muluzi, Malawi. 63: Adamkus, Lithuania. 64: Tito, Kiribati. 65: Nazarbayev, Kazakhstan. 66: Flores, Honduras. 67: Jagdeo, Guyana. 68: Dowiyogo, Nauru. 69: Préval, Haiti. 70: Mádl, Hungary. 71: Moi, Kenya. 72: Vike-Freiberga, Latvia. 73: Ratsiraka, Madagascar. 74: Gayoom, Maldives. 75: Note, Marshall Islands. 76: Zedillo, Mexico. 77: Bagabandi, Mongolia.

(Fifth row) 78: Trajkovski, Macedonia. 79: Bashir, Sudan. 80: Kučan, Slovenia. 81: Wade, Senegal. 82: Trovoada, São Tomé & Príncipe. 83: Mitchell, St Vincent & the Grenadines. 84: Constantinescu, Romania. 85: Hamad, Qatar.

86: Estrada, Philippines. 87: Bolaños, Nicaragua. 88: Mswati III, Swaziland. 89: Kwaśniewski, Poland. 90: Lucinschi, Moldova. 91: Michelotti, San Marino. 92: Marcucci, San Marino. 93: Kabbah, Sierra Leone. 94: Salat Hassan, Somalia. 95: Rakhmanov, Tajikistan. 96: Eyadéma, Togo.

(Sixth row) 97: Bird, Antigua & Barbuda. 98: Representative, Paraguay. 99: Representative, Oman. 100: Bouteflika, Algeria. 101: Burhanuddin Rabbani, Afghanistan. 102: Tran, Viet Nam. 103: Batlle, Uruguay. 104: Howard, Australia. 105: Ben Ali, Tunisia. 106: Representative, UAE. 107: Sezer, Turkey. 108: Kuchma, Ukraine. 109: Chávez, Venezuela. 110: Saleh, Yemen. 111: Mugabe, Zimbabwe. 112: Mejdani, Albania. 113: Representative, Monaco. 114: Representative, Panama. 115: Ajodhia, Suriname.

(Seventh row) 116: Oddsson, Iceland. 117: Mitchell, Grenada. 118: Meles, Ethiopia. 119: Yamassoum, Chad. 120: Zimba, Bhutan. 121: Verhofstadt, Belgium. 122: Representative, Bahrain. 123: Fenech Adami, Malta. 124: Arafat, Palestine. 125: Patterson, Jamaica. 126: Sodano, Vatican City. 127: Barak, Israel. 128: Hasina, Bangladesh. 129: Musa, Belize. 130: Representative, Egypt. 131: Laar, Estonia. 132: Simitis, Greece. 133: Sidimé, Guinea. 134: Ahern, Ireland.

(Eighth row) 135: Sope, Vanuatu. 136: Panday, Trinidad & Tobago. 137: Persson, Sweden. 138: Dzurinda, Slovakia. 139: Douglas, St Kitts & Nevis. 140: Guterres, Portugal. 141: Musharraf, Pakistan. 142: Kok, Netherlands. 143: Mosisili, Lesotho. 144: Forné, Andorra. 145: Frick, Liechtenstein. 146: Koirala, Nepal. 147: Clark, New Zealand. 148: Morauta, Papua New Guinea. 149: Anthony, St Lucia. 150: Goh, Singapore. 151: Aznar, Spain. 152: Lavaka, Tonga. 153: Ionatana, Tuvalu.

(Back row) 154–171: Various representatives. 172: Juncker, Luxembourg. 173–180: Various representatives.

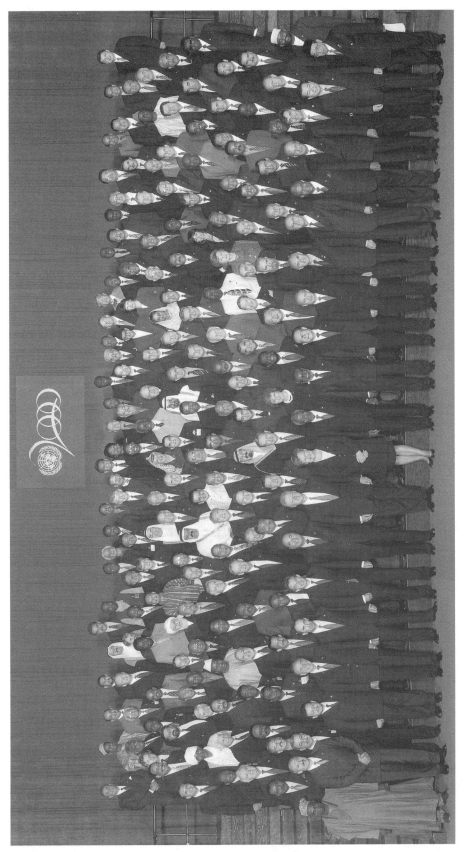

African Union Inaugural Summit (Durban, South Africa, 2002)

© Government of South Africa/African Union

(Front row) 1: Moi, Kenya. 2: Kadhafi, Libya. 3: Eyadéma, Togo. 4: Mwanawasa, Zambia. 5: Representative, AU. 6: Mbeki, South Africa. 7: Chissano, Mozambique. 8: Representative, Lesotho. 9: Bongo, Gabon. 10: Obiang Nguema, Equatorial Guinea. 11: Representative, Egypt. 12: Unknown.

(Second row) 13: Bouteflika, Algeria. 14: de Menezes, São Tomé & Príncipe. 15: Nujoma, Namibia. 16: Mugabe, Zimbabwe. 17: Compaoré, Burkina Faso. 18: Khouna, Mauritius. 19: Biya, Cameroon. 20: Museveni, Uganda. 21: Representative, Tunisia. 22: Bashir, Sudan. 23: Deby, Chad. 24: Representative, Mauritius.

(Third row) 25: Kérékou, Benin. 26: Representative, Liberia. 27: Buyoya, Burundi. 28: Mkapa, Tanzania. 29: Muluzi, Malawi. 30: Afewerki, Eritrea. 31: Toumani Touré, Mali. 32: Patassé, Central African Republic. 33: Jammeh, Gambia. 34: Sassou-Nguesso, Republic of the Congo. 35: Mogae, Botswana. 36: Azali, Comoros.

(Back row) 37: Representative, Western Sahara. 38: Pires, Cape Verde. 39: Kufuor, Ghana. 40: Representative, Côte d'Ivoire. 41: Wade, Senegal. 42: Tandja, Niger. 43: Obasanjo, Nigeria. 44: Guelleh, Djibouti. 45: Unknown. 46: Kagame, Rwanda. 47: Salat Hassan, Somalia. 48: Kabila, Dem. Republic of the Congo. 49: Meles, Ethiopia.

Asia–Pacific Economic Co-operation Summit (Los Cabos, Mexico, 2002)

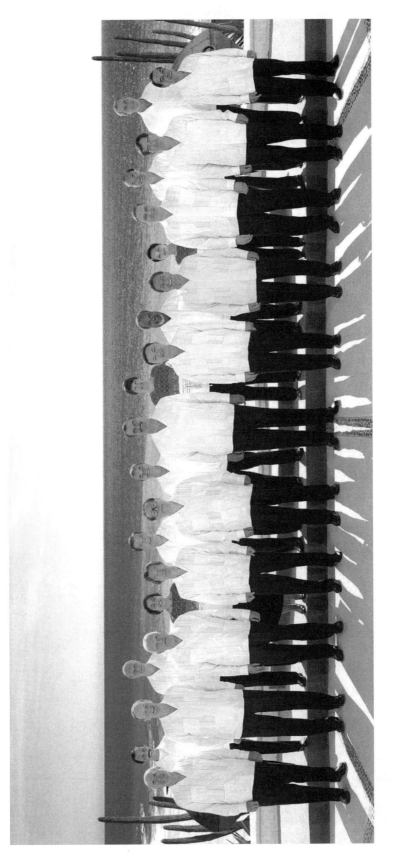

© Government of Mexico/APEC

(Front row) 1: Howard, Australia. 2: Chrétien, Canada. 3: Representative, Hong Kong. 4: Koizumi, Japan. 5: Jiang, China. 6: Fox, Mexico. 7: Thaksin Shinawatra, Thailand. 8: Toledo, Peru. 9: Kasyanov, Russia. 10: Representative, Taiwan. 11: Phan, Viet Nam.

(Back row) 12: Bolkiah, Brunei. 13: Lagos, Chile. 14: Megawati Sukarnoputri, Indonesia. 15: Kim Dae Jung, South Korea. 16: Representative, Malaysia. 17: Clark, New Zealand. 18: Somare, Papua New Guinea. 19: Arroyo, Philippines. 20: Representative, Singapore. 21: Bush, USA.

European Union Enlargement Summit (Copenhagen, Denmark, 2002)

(Front row) 1: Berlusconi, Italy. 2: Simitis, Greece. 3: Prodi, EU. 4: Rüütel, Estonia. 5: Unknown. 6: Halonen, Finland. 7: Representative, Denmark. 8: Anders Fogh Rasmussen, Denmark. 9: Chirac, France. 10: Clerides, Cyprus. 11: Vike-Freiberga, Latvia. 12: Adamkus, Lithuania. 13–14: Representatives, EU. 15: Gül, Turkey.

(Second row) 16: Nastase, Romania. 17: Dzurinda, Slovakia. 18: Repše, Latvia. 19: Kallas, Estonia. 20: Brazauskas, Lithuania. 21: Saxecoburggotski, Bulgaria. 22: Špidla, Czech Republic. 23: Drnovšek, Slovenia. 24: Ahern, Ireland. 25: Balkenende, Netherlands. 26: Juncker, Luxembourg. 27: Blair, UK. 28: Schüssel, Austria. 29: Schröder, Germany. 30: Durão Barroso, Portugal. 31: Miller, Poland.

(Third row) 32–36: Various representatives. 37: Aznar, Spain. 38: Fenech Adami, Malta. 39: Medgyessy, Hungary. 40: Persson, Sweden. 41: Verhofstadt, Belgium. 42–46: Various representatives.

(Back row) Various representatives.

AFGHANISTAN

Full name: The Islamic State of Afghanistan.

Leadership structure: Most foreign countries did not recognize the 1996–2001 *taliban* regime, continuing to recognize the former government of President Burhanuddin Rabbani until a new interim post-*taliban* regime was created. The chairman of this interim government, Hamid Karzai, appointed by agreement at the UN-brokered Bonn conference in November–December 2001, retained this function after his election by the Loya Jirga in June 2002 as transitional president.

Official President: Burhanuddin Rabbani   28 June 1992—22 Dec. 2001
(ousted by *taliban* on 27 Sept. 1996)

Leader of the *Taliban*: Mohammad Omar   3 April 1996—13 Nov. 2001

Transitional President: Hamid Karzai   Since 19 June 2002
(chairman of interim government from 22 Dec. 2001)

Chairmen of the Interim Council (under the *Taliban*):
Mohammad Rabbani   27 Sept. 1996—16 April 2001

Mawlawi Abdul Kabir   16 April 2001—13 Nov. 2001

Legislature: Since the abolition in 1992 of the bicameral Meli Shura (National Assembly), no new legislature has yet been established. A Loya Jirga was convened on 11 June 2002. It comprised 1,051 delegates, with 160 seats reserved for women and six for religious leaders.

Profile of the Transitional President:

Hamid **KARZAI**

Hamid Karzai, educated outside Afghanistan and with strong family links in the USA, is leader (khan) of the Popolzai tribe of ethnic Pashtuns—the largest single ethnic group in Afghanistan. Having grown disillusioned with the post-Soviet-occupation government of Burhanuddin Rabbani, Karzai initially lent his support to the Islamic taliban *movement before turning against them in the late 1990s. He was chosen to head the post-*taliban *government by a conference of Afghan notables held in Germany in December 2001.*

Hamid Karzai was born into the Popolzai tribe on 24 December 1957 in the southern Afghan city of Kandahar, the Popolzai stronghold. His father, Abdul

Ahad Karzai, was khan of the Popolzai (from which almost all of Afghanistan's kings were drawn from the 18th century onward), and served as a prominent member of the government before the fall of King Zahir Shah (also a member of the Popolzai clan) in 1973. The Karzai family fled the Soviet invasion of Afghanistan and moved to Quetta, Pakistan, in 1983. Most of Hamid's seven brothers and his sister emigrated to the USA where they now head the successful Helmand franchise of Afghan restaurants. However, Hamid remained in the south Asian region and attended college in India.

During the struggle of the various *mujahideen* factions in the 1980s against Soviet domination, Karzai acted as an adviser and diplomat for the resistance forces. However, throughout this time he maintained a low profile, and is even said to have run a small hotel in Peshawar, Pakistan. His connection with the *mujahideen* movements brought him to prominence in 1992 when newly appointed President Rabbani chose him as deputy foreign minister. He was the most prominent Pashtun member of this regime.

The *mujahideen* government quickly fell into internal disputes which were reflected in violent struggle throughout the country. Various warlords held de facto dominion over their own territories and Karzai grew disaffected with the inability of the government to maintain control. He left the government in 1994 having been approached by the new *taliban* (Islamic student) movement which was drawn mostly from the Pashtuns. He gave his full support to the movement, supplying them with arms and advice. The *taliban* seized Kabul in 1996 and effectively controlled the majority of the country. In return for his backing the *taliban* nominated Karzai to be their representative to the UN—although the UN's refusal to recognize the regime made this nomination ineffective.

Within a year, Karzai had grown concerned at the extent to which the regime had fallen under what he saw as the dominant influence of 'foreign' Islamic fundamentalists, principally Arabs such as Osama bin Laden, and the Pakistani secret service. In 1998 he began to foment an anti-*taliban* opposition based in Quetta, along with his father, and looked unsuccessfully to the West for assistance. In 1999 Abdul Ahad Karzai was shot dead by unknown assailants on his way home from mosque. Hamid Karzai immediately blamed the *taliban* regime, and anti-*taliban* sentiment gathered pace among the horrified Popolzai and other Pashtuns. Hamid was appointed khan of the clan ahead of his older, but US-based brothers. In defiance of the *taliban* and the Pakistani authorities he arranged a 300-vehicle convoy to take his father's body from Quetta to be buried in their ancestral home of Kandahar. The *taliban* are thought to have allowed the funeral for fear of creating further division within their own Pashtun stronghold.

Karzai continued to press for Western assistance from his base in Pakistan. He was not rewarded until international attention was focused on his home country following the 11 September 2001 attacks in the USA, committed by followers of Afghan-based Osama bin Laden. Karzai slipped back into Afghanistan in October 2001 as the US bombing campaign got under way, and this time received overt logistical and even military support from the USA in his attempts to build on anti-*taliban* sentiment among the Pashtuns. In a celebrated event he escaped a heavy-handed assassination attempt by the *taliban* with the assistance of US warplanes.

Karzai was named as a prime candidate to lead the post-*taliban* government during talks held in Bonn, Germany, despite the fact that he himself remained in Afghanistan. His dominant position among the Pashtuns, and his close relationship with ex-king Zahir Shah, increased Karzai's standing and he was chosen to be interim leader on 5 December 2001. One day later he was at the centre of negotiations which saw the handover of the last *taliban* stronghold, Kandahar.

The interim government was installed in Kabul on 22 December and was formalized as a permanent administration with Karzai as president by a Loya Jirga in June 2002. It is supported in Kabul by an international UN peacekeeping force. Karzai's government immediately sought to reverse the social prohibitions of the *taliban*, notably those against women, and set about planning to encourage private investment and market reforms in the war-ravaged country. In his efforts to strengthen central authority, he faces strong resistance from Northern Alliance commanders keen to maintain their hard-won power but has the almost unconditional support of the international community. He has been the subject of several assassination attempts. Presidential elections are scheduled for 2004.

Hamid Karzai married Zinat, a doctor, late in life and they have no children. He speaks six languages, including English.

ALBANIA

Full name: The Republic of Albania.

Leadership structure: The head of state is a president indirectly elected by the People's Assembly. The president's term of office is five years, with a maximum of two successive terms. The head of government is the prime minister, who is appointed by the president. Under the terms of the 1998 Constitution, the prime minister's appointment must be approved by the People's Assembly. The Council of Ministers is elected by the Assembly.

Presidents:	Rexhep Mejdani	24 July 1997—24 July 2002
	Gen. (retd) Alfred Moisiu	Since 24 July 2002
Prime Ministers:	Ilir Meta (acting from 29 Jan. 2002)	29 Oct. 1999—22 Feb. 2002
	Pandeli Majko	22 Feb. 2002—31 July 2002
	Fatos Nano	Since 31 July 2002

Legislature: The legislature is unicameral. The sole chamber, the People's Assembly (Kuvendi Popullor), has 140 members under the 1998 Constitution, directly elected for a maximum of four years.

Profile of the President:

Gen. (retd) Alfred **MOISIU**

Alfred Moisiu is an independent politician who has served in both communist and postcommunist governments. As president of the Albanian North Atlantic Association (ANAA), he has been at the forefront of the country's attempts to integrate with the West. Indeed his personal motto reads, "West, Peace, Justice and Development". He was appointed president in June 2002 as a compromise candidate designed to end years of political infighting within the ruling Albanian Socialist Party (Partia Socialiste e Shqipërisë—PSS). He took office in July.

Alfred Moisiu, a widower with four children, was born on 1 December 1929 in Shkodër, northern Albania. He joined the communist-led Albanian partisans in 1943 in their two-year struggle to liberate the country from Nazi forces, and afterwards went to St Petersburg (then Leningrad in the Soviet Union) to attend the Soviet military engineering school, from which he graduated in 1948. He went on to study at the Academy of Military Engineering in Moscow where he was awarded the Golden Medal. A legacy of his Soviet education is a fluency in Russian.

Returning to Albania in 1948, Moisiu began his military career at the Joint Officers School in Tirana and worked as an instructor at the city's Military Academy. He eventually attained the rank of general. When he returned from Moscow in 1958 he began to diversify his military career with assignments at the engineering directory of the ministry of defence until he was made a full director of engineering and fortification at the ministry in 1971. He served as deputy defence minister for a year from 1981 before leaving government service.

As Albania underwent its transition to democracy, Moisiu was appointed defence minister in the technical government from October 1991 until April 1992. After his term in office he acted as adviser to his successor at the ministry before becoming deputy minister once again in 1994. In the same year he founded the Albanian North Atlantic Association which aims to promote Albania's ultimate membership of the North Atlantic Treaty Organization (NATO). He left office in 1997.

His election five years later as president of Albania came as the supposed climax of a drawn-out battle within the PSS between the then prime minister Pandeli Majko and his predecessor Ilir Meta on the one hand, and the long-time PSS leader and next prime minister, Fatos Nano, on the other. Moisiu's candidacy arose after the country's ambassador to the European Union (EU), Artur Kuko, had declined to stand. Moisiu was inaugurated on 24 July 2002.

Profile of the Prime Minister:

Fatos **NANO**

Fatos Nano is leader of the ruling Albanian Socialist Party (Partia Socialiste e Shqipërisë—PSS). Originally a lecturer in economics under the communist-era regime, he first became prime minister for a short period in 1991. Between then and 2002 he was imprisoned for three years for corruption, and returned as premier in 1997–98. Immediately prior to his reappointment in July 2002 he led internal party opposition to the incumbent government.

Fatos Thanas Nano, who is married with two children, was born on 16 September 1952 in Tirana. He studied political economy at Tirana University and graduated in 1975. After a period working in the management of the state steelworks in Elbasan, southeast of Tirana, he went on to pursue a career as economic researcher and lecturer at the faculty of economy and at the Institute of Marxist–Leninist Studies in Tirana. In the late 1980s he was one of the first individuals publicly to criticize the policies of the ruling Party of Labour of Albania (Partia e Punës e Shqipërisë—PPS).

With the collapse of the communist regime in December 1990, Nano became secretary-general of the Council of Ministers, and by the following January had become deputy prime minister for economic reforms. In March 1991 he assumed the leadership of the provisional government formed in advance of the first multiparty elections held on 31 March. His election as chairman of the PSS followed his appointment as prime minister for a second term in May 1991. Nano committed his government to the introduction of a free-market economy. However, a wave of anti-communist strikes obliged his government to resign within a month, although Nano continued to sit as a deputy in the People's Assembly.

On 30 July 1993 Nano was arrested and stripped of his parliamentary immunity from prosecution to face charges of embezzlement. In April 1994 he was convicted of mishandling US$8 million of aid from the Italian government, of dereliction of duty and of falsifying state documents. His detention and the arrest of several other ministers prompted protests against alleged gross violations of legal procedure. Sentenced to serve 12 years in prison, he was nevertheless re-elected to the PSS leadership and continued to be regarded as the main political opponent of the then president, Sali Berisha.

The 1997 rebellion in the south of the country, precipitated by economic collapse, resulted in the release of many prison detainees. Nano, one of those released in this way, was formally pardoned by Berisha on 17 March. The PSS went on to win a general election held in two rounds in June–July 1997; PSS Secretary-General Rexhep Mejdani replaced Berisha as president, and immediately called on Nano to form a government. On 25 July Nano took office at the head of a coalition government but was forced to step down in October 1998 amid a return of popular protest against economic reforms.

Having been re-elected leader of the PSS, Nano led a campaign within the party against the next PSS prime minister, Ilir Meta, accusing him and his government of corruption. The struggle reached a head in January 2002 when Meta resigned. The resulting deadlock over who should succeed as head of government prompted international financial agencies to withhold payments from Albania. Nano's supporters within the party were finally included in the next government, headed by Pandeli Majko, which lasted from February until the party voted in July to merge the position of party leader with prime minister, guaranteeing Nano's return to power.

ALGERIA

Full name: The People's Democratic Republic of Algeria.

Leadership structure: The head of state is a president, directly elected by universal adult suffrage. The president's term of office is five years. The president appoints a prime minister, who has the formal status of head of government and who appoints the Council of Ministers. The president, not the prime minister, presides at meetings of the Council.

President:	Abdelaziz Bouteflika	Since 27 April 1999
Prime Ministers:	Ahmed Benbitour	23 Dec. 1999—27 Aug. 2000
	Ali Benflis	Since 27 Aug. 2000

Legislature: The legislature, the Parliament (Barlaman), is bicameral. The lower chamber, the National People's Assembly (Majlis al-Chaabi al-Watani), has 389 members (eight of them representing Algerians abroad), directly elected for a five-year term. The upper chamber, the National Council (Majlis al-Oumma), has 144 members; one-third of the members are appointed by the president, the other two-thirds indirectly elected for six-year terms, half of the seats being elected every three years.

Profile of the President:

Abdelaziz **BOUTEFLIKA**

Abdelaziz Bouteflika was a long-serving member of the National Liberation Front (Front de libération nationale—FLN) and foreign minister for much of the 1960s and 1970s, but then spent some seven years in exile as the tide turned against those closely associated with the government of the late President Houari Boumedienne. 'Rehabilitated' in 1988, he kept a relatively low profile until emerging as the regime's preferred consensus candidate for the April 1999 presidential election, leading the National Democratic Rally (Rassemblement national démocratique—RND). Bouteflika is well connected in Algeria's upper social strata, and has a strong support base among the urban elite and the military.

Abdelaziz Bouteflika was born on 2 March 1937 in Oujda, on the Algeria–Morocco border, where he was also educated. In 1956 he joined Algeria's National Liberation Army, the military wing of the FLN, and was promoted to the rank of major, although he did not take part in any fighting. By the early 1960s he was working in the headquarters of military commanders of the southern regions and his administrative career was greatly boosted when he joined a secret Algerian delegation to France in 1961.

Following national independence in 1962, Bouteflika was appointed by President Ahmed Ben Bella as minister of youth, sport and tourism. He went on to become foreign minister from 1963 to 1979 under Ben Bella and his military successor, Col. Boumedienne. In this capacity Bouteflika was a key figure, overseeing the international recognition of the country's territorial borders and forging strong ties with the rest of the Arab world notably at the conference of Khartoum in 1967 and during the Arab–Israeli war in 1973. In 1971 he helped to ride out the embargo imposed by France following the nationalization of Algeria's hydrocarbon reserves, and from 1974 to 1975 he was president of the UN General Assembly. On the global stage, Bouteflika has also been a strong supporter of decolonization.

The death of Boumedienne in 1978 was followed by a power struggle and a backlash against the 'Boumediennists'. Bouteflika, charged with corruption, went into exile in 1980, and, although the case against him was later dropped, he did not return permanently to Algeria until January 1987. His rehabilitation into national politics followed the signing of the 'motion of the 18' in protest at the violence unleashed by the government against reformist protestors in October 1988. At a party congress the following year he was appointed to the central committee of the FLN.

During the violence of the 1990s Bouteflika kept a low profile. Bloodshed followed the nullification of election results in 1992 which would have led to an Islamic government. Bouteflika rejected an offer to sit on the High Council of State which was formulated as an interim presidency. In 1994 he even refused the presidency itself, but in the somewhat more promising circumstances of December 1998 he did announce his candidacy for the April 1999 presidential elections. Dubbed the 'candidate of consensus', he realized this unfortunate title when all six of his opponents stepped down from the competition at the last minute, accusing him of large-scale electoral fraud. Unopposed, Bouteflika easily swept the board at the polls with nearly 80% of the vote. He is backed in the National People's Assembly by a majority coalition which includes his own authoritarian RND, the FLN and two moderate Islamic parties.

The long-running civil conflict was high on the national agenda and Bouteflika was quick to act towards its resolution. A referendum showed massive public support for his 'civil reconciliation' programme which included an amnesty for Islamic militants until January 2000, which was followed by the release of 5,000 political prisoners. By the deadline of the amnesty, 1,500 militants had handed themselves over including the major paramilitary organization, the Islamic Salvation Army, which voluntarily decommissioned its arms in July 1999. Although this decommissioning received the backing of the main Islamist movement, the Islamic Salvation Front, Bouteflika maintained the political ban on the latter. Two other insurrectionary forces ignored the amnesty, but despite the continuing violence Bouteflika remained keen to talk of peace.

Since becoming president, Bouteflika has made several firebrand speeches against outside interference in Algerian affairs aimed both at other Arab nations and the West, whom he accused in February 2000 of "rubbing Africa off the map" through its economic imperialism. The former colonial power, France, had renewed diplomatic ties in 1999, having broken off relations in 1992.

Profile of the Prime Minister:

Ali **BENFLIS**

Ali Benflis is a lawyer by training, with a particular interest in human rights. Married with four children, he had followed a legal career, apart from three years in government as minister of justice from 1988, until he was appointed prime minister by President Abdelaziz Bouteflika in August 2000. Given the strong executive role of the president and the considerable influence wielded by the armed forces, the prime minister has a relatively limited role.

Ali Benflis was born on 8 September 1944 in Batna, in northeast Algeria. After leaving school he studied at the University of Algiers, and started a career in the law, becoming a tribunal judge at Blida in 1968. The following year he was appointed deputy director of the committee on infant delinquency at the ministry of justice, and in 1970 he returned to Batna as public prosecutor. In 1971 he became procurator-general of Constantine, a post he held until 1974. He was a member of the Bar of East Algeria from 1974 until 1983, and its president in that last year. Four years later he became president of the Bar in Batna. Since 1983 he has held the post of head of legal finances.

In the 1980s he turned his attention in particular to human rights, and was a founding member of the Algerian League for Human Rights, which was constituted in 1987. In the same year he became president of the league's eastern region. He entered the cabinet in 1988, serving as minister of justice until 1991. For the rest of the decade, amid the turbulence and violence which followed the armed forces' intervention to prevent the election of an Islamist government, he kept a low profile. Recalled to government as prime minister in August 2000, he was confirmed in this post after the legislative elections of May 2002. He had also been appointed secretary-general of the FLN on 20 September 2001, having served on the party's central committee and political bureau since 1989.

ANDORRA

Full name: The Coprincipality of Andorra.

Leadership structure: Under the 1993 Constitution, the titular heads of state are the president of France and the bishop of Urgel (in Spain), whose powers relate solely to relations with France and Spain. The head of government is the president of the Executive Council, which is appointed by the General Council. There is a permanent delegation for Andorran affairs in Andorra headed respectively by the prefect of the Pyrénées-Orientales department in France and a vicar-general from the Urgel diocese.

Coprince (Bishop of Urgel):   Joan Martí Alanis   Since 31 Jan. 1971

Coprince (President of France):   Jacques Chirac   Since 17 May 1995

President of the Executive Council: Marc Forné Molné   Since 7 Dec. 1994

Legislature: The legislature is unicameral. The sole chamber, the General Council of the Valleys (Consell General del Valles), has 28 members, directly elected for a maximum four-year term.

Profile of the Coprince (Bishop of Urgel):

Joan **MARTÍ** Alanis

Joan Martí Alanis is a bishop of the Roman Catholic Church in Spain. Having studied classics he entered the priesthood in 1951. He was invested as bishop of Seo de Urgel, and consequently coprince of Andorra, on 31 January 1971.

Joan Martí Alanis was born on 29 November 1928 in El Milà, in the archdiocese of Tarragona. He graduated from the University of Salamanca with a degree in classical humanities and was then ordained as a priest on 17 June 1951. He remained in his native archdiocese for 19 years as an episcopal vicar of doctrine of the faith and teaching; he was also director of the Colegio Episcopal de la Mare de Déu de la Mercè in Montblanc and founding director of the Colegio Menor de Sant Pablo in Tarragona. Two years after he became bishop of Urgel in 1971, he and the then French president Georges Pompidou held in 1973 the first ever personal meeting between two coprinces to discuss matters affecting the future of Andorra. Since 1989 he has also been a member of the pontifical council on social communication.

Profile of the Coprince (President of France):

Jacques **CHIRAC**—*see France.*

Profile of the President of the Executive Council:

Marc **FORNÉ** Molné

Marc Forné was first appointed as head of government of the principality of Andorra by the General Council in December 1994, and re-elected to the post twice, after general elections in February 1997 and March 2001. Forné is a former lawyer and political journal director, and leads the Liberal Party of Andorra (Partit Liberal d'Andorra—PLA).

Marc Forné Molné was born on 30 December 1946 in La Massana, Andorra. He studied firstly in Andorra la Vella and then in Spain, at Seo de Urgel, before graduating in law from the University of Barcelona. From 1969 he worked for three years as a civil servant in the department of public services. In 1973 he founded *Tribune*, a political journal aimed at Andorran youth and a vehicle for the discussion of reforms on such issues as the electoral system and the responsibilities of the coprinces. In 1978 he founded (and directed for 11 years) a political weekly called *Andorra-7*. Meanwhile, from 1974 until his appointment as head of government he practised law in the family firm, with his father and brother. He was one of the first Andorran lawyers to practise in English.

Between 1966 and 1972 Forné campaigned for changes in the law to grant Andorran-born people full political rights. As his father was Spanish, he himself had no political rights, until the law was changed in 1970 to give rights to children of an Andorran mother, and to all those born in Andorra whose parents were also born there.

In 1984 he was part of a group which became the Liberal Party. In the December 1993 elections he was the third-placed candidate on the Liberal Union list, and was thus elected to the General Council, in which he became head of the commission on internal affairs and vice president of the commission on territorial organization. He drew up legislation on civil marriage and divorce, on the civil register and reforms to the penal code.

When the then head of government Oscar Ribas Reig resigned after being defeated over his proposed budget, Forné was chosen on 7 December 1994 to succeed him, with the formal title of president of the Executive Council. He formed a coalition, since his own party controlled only 13 of the 28 seats in the General Council. The following year he was elected president of the PLA.

The PLA secured an absolute majority in early elections held in February 1997 and held onto its position in March 2001. Forné was re-elected head of government on both occasions.

ANGOLA

Full name: The Republic of Angola.

Leadership structure: The head of state is a president, directly elected by universal adult suffrage. The president's term of office is five years, but elections have not been held since 1992. The president is head of government and appoints the prime minister, a post reintroduced in December 2002. The president also appoints and presides over the Council of Ministers.

President:	José Eduardo dos Santos (acting from 10 Sept. 1979)	Since 21 Sept. 1979
Prime Minister:	Fernando da Piedade	Since 5 Dec. 2002

Legislature: The 223-member unicameral National Assembly (Assembléia Nacional) is directly elected for a four-year term, but elections have not been held since 1992. The Assembly extended its own mandate for the second time on 17 October 2000. No date was set for the end of the mandate.

Profile of the President:

José Eduardo **DOS SANTOS**

José Eduardo dos Santos was involved from his youth in the struggle to end Portuguese colonial rule, as a member of the Marxist–Leninist guerrilla Popular Movement for the Liberation of Angola (Movimento Popular de Libertação de Angola—MPLA). He succeeded to the presidency four years after independence, but his regime remained dogged until 2002 by a protracted civil war against Jonas Savimbi's National Union for the Total Independence of Angola (União Nacional para a Independência Total de Angola—UNITA).

Born in Luanda on 28 August 1942, the son of a bricklayer, José Eduardo dos Santos joined the MPLA in 1961 while still a student in Luanda, and set up a youth organization within it. In November of that year he fled north across the Congolese border, initially to Léopoldville (now Kinshasa) to escape the Portuguese colonial authorities. Enlisting in the MPLA guerrilla army the following year, he soon became the organization's chief representative in Brazzaville.

In 1963 he went to study in the Soviet Union at the Baku Petroleum and Gas Institute, receiving degrees in petroleum engineering and in radar communications. After completing his studies in 1969 he did a one-year military communications course before returning to Angola in 1970 to resume his role in the anti-colonial struggle. He was head of the MPLA's principal communications centre on the northern front, where he became in 1974 a member of the readjustment commission and also head of finances. In September 1974 he was elected to the MPLA central committee.

In June 1975 he was named as the MPLA's foreign affairs secretary, and after the proclamation of independence on 11 November he was appointed minister of external relations, later transferring to become minister of planning. He also held the office of first deputy premier until it was abolished in 1978, and was put in charge of national reconstruction on the party central committee.

After President Neto's death in 1979, dos Santos moved up to take over the MPLA leadership, which carried with it the roles of state president and commander-in-chief of the armed forces, to which he was sworn in on 21 September 1979. The dos Santos succession marked a setback for hard-line pro-Soviet elements within the embattled party leadership, and the ascendancy of those who favoured a sustained attempt to negotiate an end to the civil war with UNITA. For most of the next decade this proved unattainable, however, with the Reagan administration in the USA and the South African apartheid government (itself also embroiled in Namibia) both increasingly committed to backing and arming UNITA. The MPLA regime for its part remained militarily reliant on the Cuban forces which had helped avert its defeat in the months after independence.

Prospects for peace apparently improved with two sets of agreements in which dos Santos played a major part—those signed in New York in 1988 to end South African and Cuban involvement, and the 1991 Bicesse accord with UNITA which provided for a peace process, a UN presence and a transition to multiparty democracy. Elections held in September 1992 were dominated by the presidential contest between dos Santos (who won 49.6% of the vote) and Savimbi (who won 40%). UNITA responded by launching an intensified civil war, however, which prevented the holding of a second-round runoff. Peace negotiations resumed in 1994, but fighting continued and a power-sharing formula remained largely unimplemented until the death of Savimbi in February 2002, after which progress became more evident.

Dos Santos is generally credited with supporting the peace process, and with having overseen the reorientation of the MPLA away from its Marxist–Leninist ideological foundation in the wake of the collapse of communism in Eastern Europe and the Soviet Union. At successive party congresses in December 1990 and May 1992, reforms were adopted and he was re-elected as party chairman. A more hard-line element in the party, however, backed the election of Lopo do Nascimento as secretary-general in 1993, and reflected concern that the party's forces had weakened themselves dangerously vis-à-vis UNITA by observing the terms of the peace process. Moreover, the war has left the economy crippled, with rampant inflation and growing signs of discontent in the capital, Luanda, in spite of the deployment of special forces to forestall public protest. The president, his family and his immediate circle of advisers have been accused by critics of lacking answers to the country's pressing problems, and of corruption and preoccupation with their own business interests, while dos Santos himself has suffered serious illness, believed to be prostate cancer.

Profile of the Prime Minister:

Fernando **DA PIEDADE**

Fernando 'Nandó' da Piedade is a very close ally of President José Eduardo dos Santos. A former active participant in the liberation struggle, he is a member of the politburo of the Popular Movement for the Liberation of Angola (Movimento Popular de Libertação de Angola—MPLA), and was interior minister before being chosen to fill the resurrected post of prime minister in December 2002 as part of the country's peace process.

Fernando da Piedade Dias dos Santos was born on 5 March 1952 in Luanda, then the administrative capital of the Portuguese overseas province of Angola. Drafted into the colonial army he was briefly imprisoned for his pro-independence views. In June 1974 he deserted and joined the MPLA, in Cabinda, in its struggle against the Portuguese. He eventually reached the rank of major. Angola became an independent country in November 1975 amid a civil war between the MPLA and the US-backed National Union for the Total Independence of Angola (União Nacional para a Independência Total de Angola—UNITA).

In the early 1970s da Piedade occupied posts in the now defunct People's Army for the Liberation of Angola and the national police force. He entered direct government service as deputy interior minister in 1984 and studied law at the newly opened Agostinho Neto University. President dos Santos appointed him deputy minister of state security in 1986 and chose him to head the commission for reorganization of the ministry of state security later that year. Under da Piedade's guidance the commission purged the ministry of several senior members, jailing them for corruption. The commission was disbanded in 1988.

Da Piedade was elected to the MPLA's politburo in 1998 and in February 1999 he was made full interior minister in a cabinet reshuffle which saw President dos Santos take over the functions of prime minister. In the meantime the attempts of the early 1990s to end the civil war had given way to renewed violence. As part of the government's effort to find a resolution of the apparent impasse, da Piedade was made co-ordinator of the peace process and national reconciliation. In 2002 the death of UNITA leader Jonas Savimbi opened up the way for peace and a lasting ceasefire was signed in April. By December the country was beginning to restructure itself after 27 years of war. UNITA members were inducted into government and President dos Santos appointed da Piedade to the resurrected post of prime minister.

14

ANTIGUA AND BARBUDA

Full name: Antigua and Barbuda.

Leadership structure: The head of state is the British sovereign, styled 'Queen of Antigua and Barbuda and of Her other Realms and Territories, Head of the Commonwealth', represented by a governor-general who is appointed on the advice of the prime minister of Antigua and Barbuda. The head of government, the prime minister, is the leader of the majority in the House of Representatives and is appointed by the governor-general. The governor-general also appoints, on the prime minister's advice, the cabinet, which is responsible to Parliament.

Queen:	Elizabeth II	Since 6 Feb. 1952
Governor-General:	Sir James B. Carlisle	Since 10 June 1993
Prime Minister:	Lester Bird	Since 9 March 1994

Legislature: The legislature, the Parliament, is bicameral. The lower chamber, the House of Representatives, has 17 members, directly elected for up to five years. The upper chamber, the Senate, has 17 members, appointed by the governor-general on the advice of the prime minister and the leader of the opposition, for the life of the Parliament.

Profile of the Governor-General:

Sir James B. **CARLISLE**

Sir James Carlisle has been governor-general of Antigua and Barbuda since 1993. He represents the monarch, Queen Elizabeth II, as titular head of state. His appointment came after a long career in dentistry.

James Carlisle was born on 5 August 1937 and has been married three times. He most recently married Nalda Amelia Meade in 1984 and he has a total of five children. He attended Bolans Public School, Antigua, between 1946 and 1954, and afterwards worked as a primary school teacher. In 1960 he went to the UK, joining the Royal Air Force while also pursuing courses at North West London Polytechnic and (in 1963–64) at Singapore University. Returning to the UK he did an 'A-level' course at Northampton College of Technology and then attended the University of Dundee in 1967–72, qualifying as a dentist.

From 1972 to 1992 he worked in general practice in Scotland, Wales, England and Antigua, and was also a part-time school dental officer in Scotland and Antigua. Between 1981 and 1983 he was a volunteer dentist at the Baptist Dental Clinic, and from 1983 to 1986 was manager of the fluoride programme with the Catholic Dental Centre. In 1990–91 he studied laser dentistry at Orlando, Florida. In 1993 he instituted a free dental care programme for children and the elderly. He was also chairman of the National Parks Authority (1986–90) and chairman of the Tabitha Senior Citizen's Home (1987–90). He took up his appointment as governor-general in June 1993 and was created a Knight Grand Cross of the Most Distinguished Order of St Michael and St George in November of that year.

Profile of the Prime Minister:

Lester **BIRD**

Lester Bird was sworn in as prime minister of Antigua and Barbuda on 9 March 1994, and formed a government the next day. The country's second prime minister since independence in 1981, he succeeded his father, veteran politician and 'father of the nation' Vere Bird.

Lester Bryant Bird was born on 21 February 1938. Brought up as a Methodist and educated at Antigua Grammar School, he also distinguished himself at sports, playing cricket for the Leeward Islands and representing his country at long jump. He continued to shine as an athlete during his studies at the University of Michigan, where he graduated in 1962. After completing his studies in law in the UK, where he was called to the Bar at Gray's Inn in 1969, he returned to Antigua and worked as a lawyer in private practice (1969–76). He is married with four daughters and one son.

His political career began with his nomination to the Senate in 1971, when his father's Antigua Labour Party (ALP) began a rare five-year period in opposition. Lester was named as ALP chairman and as leader of the opposition in the upper house, fulfilling the latter role until the party returned to government at the 1976 elections. Elected to the House of Representatives himself on this occasion (and re-elected at successive elections ever since), he joined his father's government as deputy prime minister. He was also minister of economic development, tourism and energy, and after independence in 1981 he added the external affairs portfolio. In this capacity he was the first chairman of the Organization of Eastern Caribbean States (OECS) in 1982 and held the OECS chairmanship again in 1989.

No longer designated as deputy prime minister from 1991 onward, he retained the post of minister of external affairs, together with responsibility for planning and trade. He received a boost to his hopes for eventual succession to the leadership when in November 1990 an inquiry recommended that his elder brother Vere Bird Jr, like him a cabinet minister, be banned from holding public office over the issue of supplying Israeli-made weapons to drugs cartel leaders in Colombia. When his father announced in March 1992 that he would be stepping down at the next election, the ALP convened a special convention to elect a successor, but the voting on 24 May showed an equal split between Lester Bird and the information minister John St Luce, and it was not until the ALP's 1993 convention in September of the following year that Lester Bird was able to secure the leadership, defeating St Luce by 169 votes to 131.

In the March 1994 general election, the ALP, under attack over corruption issues, promised more open government, an ombudsman to handle complaints, and the creation of new jobs by the expansion of tourism in particular. The ALP won 11 of the 17 seats. It was noted that Lester Bird found a place in his cabinet for St Luce but not for his brother Vere Jr, although he did later appoint him as a special adviser. Lester himself assumed the portfolios of external affairs, planning, social services and information. In a reshuffle of the cabinet in 1996 he took on in addition the responsibility for communications, civil aviation, international transport and gaming.

Elections in March 1999 saw the ALP's majority increased to 12 seats and Bird was reconfirmed as prime minister. In a new cabinet Bird at last found room to rehabilitate his brother fully, appointing him minister of agriculture. He also changed his own portfolio collection and by December 2002 he was in control of the ministries of foreign affairs, finance, national security and justice and legal affairs, in addition to being prime minister.

ARGENTINA

Full name: The Republic of Argentina.

Leadership structure: The head of state is a president, normally directly elected by universal adult suffrage. The president's term of office, under the 1994 Constitution, is four years, renewable once only. The head of government is the president. The cabinet is appointed by the president.

Presidents:	Fernando de la Rúa	10 Dec. 1999—21 Dec. 2001
	Ramón Puerta (acting)	21 Dec. 2001—23 Dec. 2001
	Adolfo Rodríguez Saá (interim)	23 Dec. 2001—31 Dec. 2001
	Eduardo Camaño (acting)	31 Dec. 2001—2 Jan. 2002
	Eduardo Alberto Duhalde	Since 2 Jan. 2002
Cabinet Chiefs:	Rodolfo Terragno	10 Dec. 1999—5 Oct. 2000
	Chrystian Colombo	5 Oct. 2000—21 Dec. 2001
	Humberto Schiavoni	21 Dec. 2001—23 Dec. 2001
	Luis Lusquiños (acting)	23 Dec. 2001—31 Dec. 2001
	Antonio Cafiero	31 Dec. 2001—3 Jan. 2002
	Jorge Capitanich	3 Jan. 2002—3 May 2002
	Alfredo Atanasof	Since 3 May 2002

Legislature: The legislature, the National Congress (Congreso de la Nación), is bicameral. The lower chamber, the Chamber of Deputies (Cámara de Diputados), has 257 members, directly elected for four-year terms (with half of the seats renewed every two years). The upper chamber, the Senate (Senado), has 72 members, who until December 2001 were indirectly elected. The terms of all sitting senators ended in December 2001. The whole Senate was directly elected for the first time in October 2001 and thereafter the senators will hold their seats for six-year terms, with one-third renewable every two years.

Profile of the President:

Eduardo Alberto **DUHALDE**

Eduardo Duhalde is a stalwart of the Peronist party, known officially as the Justicialist Party (Partido Justicialista—PJ), and has a reputation as a populist firebrand. He has been particularly active in anti-drugs campaigns. Vice president to President Carlos Menem in 1989–91, he then left the central executive to govern the country's largest administrative province, Buenos Aires. When he stepped down from that post in 1999 his administration was mired in accusations of corruption and the province was facing large-scale debts. Elected to the Senate in 2001, he took over the presidency on 2 January 2002 with the whole country in economic and social turmoil.

Eduardo Alberto Duhalde Maldonado was born on 5 October 1941 in Lomas de Zamora, just south of Buenos Aires. He graduated in law from Buenos Aires University in 1970. In July 1971 he married Hilda Beatriz González, who has given strong support to her husband's political career, as well as pursuing her own within the PJ. They have five children.

Duhalde entered the local council in his home city of Lomas de Zamora in 1973. He was forced from his post in the left-wing municipal administration in 1976 by the country's new military rulers, and blocked from public office, but re-entered the city council seven years later, following the return of democracy. In 1987 he was elected to the Chamber of Deputies as a member of the PJ, and for two years he was the first vice president (i.e. deputy speaker) of the chamber. In 1989 he was the running mate of the PJ's successful presidential candidate Carlos Saúl Menem, but Duhalde abandoned the post of vice president in 1991 in order to run for the governorship of Buenos Aires province.

For the remainder of Menem's ten-year presidency Duhalde was Buenos Aires governor, where his populist policies included massive spending on projects to help the province's poorest residents, and a penchant for public works schemes. By the time he left office in 1999 he was plagued by accusations of corruption. His successor as governor found the province's funds so depleted that employees there had to be paid in government bonds. During this time he had faced competition from the powerful mayor of Buenos Aires, the right-wing Fernando de la Rúa of the Radical Civic Union (Unión Cívica Radical—UCR).

Chosen as the PJ candidate for the presidential elections in October 1999, Duhalde again came up against de la Rúa, and was defeated by a substantial margin (taking only 38% of the vote to his rival's 49%). Duhalde was later elected to the Senate in October 2001, as part of the PJ's increased majority.

As the de la Rúa government struggled to cope with a spiralling economic crisis, rising popular discontent led to street protests calling for the president's dismissal. De la Rúa finally agreed to step down on 21 December 2001. In his wake three more presidents came and went in quick succession before Congress turned to Senator Duhalde. He accepted the post and agreed to take over de la Rúa's moribund presidency, which is set to expire in September 2003. Duhalde has since announced that early presidential elections will be held in spring 2003.

With banking processes frozen and foreign investors and creditors withholding vital funds, Duhalde was faced with an uphill task. Having been granted special economic powers by Congress, he had the peso removed from its ten-year-old peg to the US dollar and expedited financial transparency laws requested by the IMF. Although he has remained in office thus far, popular discontent continues as the Argentinian economy degrades further.

Profile of the Cabinet Chief:

Alfredo **ATANASOF**

Alfredo Atanasof is a member of the Justicialist Party (Partido Justicialista—PJ) and a renowned trade union activist based in the Buenos Aires region. Head of the Argentinian Confederation of Municipal Workers (Confederación de Obreros y Empleados Municipales de la Argentina—COEMA) since 1991, he managed the government's relations with the unions throughout the 1990s. He was appointed to the government of President Eduardo Duhalde in January 2002 and was made chief of the cabinet in May.

Alfredo Néstor Atanasof was born on 24 November 1949 in La Plata. He is married and has two children. He began his working life as a secretary for a regional trade union based in La Plata in 1972. Within two years he was made secretary-general of La Plata Workers' Union, a post he held for 23 years.

Throughout the 1970s and 1980s Atanasof worked with a number of trade union movements. In 1983–85 he was an executive member of the La Plata branch of the umbrella General Confederation of Labour (Confederación General del Trabajo—CGT). From 1984 he served as secretary of the Buenos Aires federation of municipal workers' unions, and then stepped up to the national level in 1991 when he was first elected secretary-general of COEMA. In that year he also became secretary of parliamentary relations for the CGT, and entered government service as adviser to the minister of labour. It was also in 1991 that Atanasof began his connection to the PJ, and in 1995 was elected to the Chamber of Deputies as a PJ deputy. He was re-elected in 1999, when he was the only trade union activist to win a seat, and has sat on various parliamentary commissions.

The end of 2001 saw the collapse of the Argentinian economy and successive presidential administrations. On 2 January 2002 Duhalde was inaugurated as president, and Atanasof, recognized as a close ally, was appointed to the new cabinet as labour minister. His determination to reduce rising unemployment was undermined by the continuing economic malaise. In a cabinet reshuffle in April he was repositioned as cabinet chief and was sworn in at the beginning of May.

ARMENIA

Full name: The Republic of Armenia.

Leadership structure: The head of state is a president, directly elected by universal adult suffrage. The president's term of office is five years, renewable once only. The president appoints the prime minister, and the other members of the cabinet as proposed by the prime minister. The prime minister is head of government, and directs and co-ordinates its work.

President:	Robert Kocharian (acting from 3 Feb. 1998)	Since 9 April 1998
Prime Ministers:	Aram Sarkissian	3 Nov. 1999—2 May 2000
	Robert Kocharian (acting)	2 May 2000—12 May 2000
	Andranik Markarian	Since 12 May 2000

Legislature: The legislature is unicameral. The sole chamber, the National Assembly (Azgayin Joghov), has 131 members, directly elected for a four-year term.

Profile of the President:

Robert **KOCHARIAN**

Robert Kocharian was once a member of the Soviet-era communist party. In the last years of the Soviet Union he became prominent in the pro-independence movement in the Armenian-dominated enclave of Nagorno-Karabakh, of which he is a native. His term as the enclave's first 'president' (1994–97) was followed by a one-year spell as prime minister of Armenia. He was elected president of Armenia after the incumbent's surprise resignation in early 1998, and seeks a second term in 2003.

Robert Kocharian, who is married with three children, was born on 31 August 1954 in Stepanakert (now known as Xankändi), Nagorno-Karabakh, and joined the Soviet army in 1972 for three years. He then studied electronics and technology at the Polytechnic Institute in Yerevan, the Armenian capital, graduating in 1982. The previous year he had begun a job as an engineer and electrotechnician at the Karabakh silk production factory in Stepanakert. In 1987 he became secretary on the committee of the factory's communist party. The following year he began campaigning for the formation of a unified Republic of Armenia, to include Nagorno-Karabakh. He founded Unification (Miatsum), an ostensibly nonpolitical movement which became the leading faction in the Karabakh movement.

In 1989, the year in which he left the communist party, Kocharian became a deputy in the Armenian Supreme Council. Towards the end of the year the council declared an Armenian republic which included Nagorno-Karabakh, although the Soviet government declared this move unconstitutional. On 2 September 1991 Nagorno-Karabakh declared itself a republic, then the Communist Party of Armenia dissolved itself and on 23 September Armenia voted for independence from the Soviet Union. At this time Kocharian was elected a deputy to the Supreme Council of Nagorno-Karabakh. From August 1992, when a state of emergency was declared, he became chairman of the defence committee which effectively governed the region. In December 1994 he was elected the first president of the Republic of Nagorno-Karabakh by the Supreme Council, his position being confirmed in a direct election in the enclave in November 1996.

Kocharian was appointed prime minister of Armenia on 19 March 1997 by Armenian president Levon Ter-Petrossian, who hoped to use this nationalistic gesture to relieve popular discontent at the high unemployment and rising poverty brought about by recent economic reforms. Kocharian expressed hopes that his appointment might speed up the resolution of the status of his war-ravaged home territory. In Azerbaijan, however, it was regarded as an insult and as evidence of de facto Armenian annexation of the Nagorno-Karabakh enclave.

The two men's close relationship soon soured, with Kocharian critical of any attempts to dilute the enclave's claims. Ter-Petrossian unexpectedly resigned in February 1998 amid disagreements with the government over a proposal from the Organization for Security and Co-operation in Europe (OSCE) to end the dispute. Kocharian was successfully elected in his place and was inaugurated on 9 April.

His term as president has been fraught with conflict between himself and the government. He clashed in particular with Aram Sarkissian, who was prime minister for six months after the incumbent, his brother Vazgen Sarkissian, was killed in a shoot-out in the parliament in October 1999. Sources of friction included the enclave, alleged corruption, and Kocharian's authoritarian approach. There have been several unsuccessful attempts to have Kocharian impeached, including one for his refusal to allow the military prosecutor-general to testify in the 1999 parliament massacre. Consequently, his rule is frequently protested by large demonstrations in Yerevan, where over 10,000 people rallied in September 2001 against his declared intention to run for a second term in 2003. There remains no end in sight for the Nagorno-Karabakh dispute.

Profile of the Prime Minister:

Andranik **MARKARIAN**

A computer specialist and career politician who was briefly detained for seditious nationalism under Soviet rule, Andranik Markarian is seen as a close ally of President Robert Kocharian, and has pledged to stop the chronic infighting between the executive and government. Markarian heads the large Unity (Miasnutiun) parliamentary bloc but relies on smaller factions and nonpartisans to establish a working majority.

Andranik Markarian was born in the early 1950s in what was then the Soviet Socialist Republic of Armenia. From an early age he became involved with nationalist activists. In the early 1970s he joined the banned National Unity Party and was arrested by the Soviet authorities in 1974. After two years in a penitential gulag he returned to Armenia. His prisoner-of-conscience past is renowned in Armenia where he insists it does not equate with modern-day anti-Russian sentiment.

Following the assassination of Prime Minister Vazgen Sarkissian in a shoot-out in the parliament building in October 1999, his brother Aram took on the position only to be dismissed in May 2000 after months of political wrangling with President Kocharian. The president filled the vacuum with Markarian, who had become the new head of the Armenian Republican Party which was the leading member of the powerful Unity parliamentary bloc.

Upon his appointment Markarian faced hostility from large factions of the Unity bloc and promptly relieved himself of dissident ministers mostly from the Yerkrapah Union of Veterans of the Karabakh War. Despite resistance from parliament Markarian pledged to continue the policies of his immediate predecessors and to rule a government of accord. A major part of his new policy revolved around an ending of conflict between the government and Kocharian. Although he also reiterated that there would be no land swap with Azerbaijan over the Nagorno-Karabakh enclave, relations with the Caucasian neighbour are mostly conducted through the president.

AUSTRALIA

Full name: The Commonwealth of Australia.

Leadership structure: A Constitutional Convention voted by an overwhelming majority, on 14 February 1998, to hold a referendum on whether Australia should become a republic. The referendum, held on 6 November 1999, rejected the suggested format, involving replacement of the monarchy by a president selected by Parliament. The head of state thus remains the British sovereign, styled 'Queen of Australia and Her other Realms and Territories, Head of the Commonwealth', and represented by a governor-general who is appointed on the advice of the Australian prime minister. The head of government is the prime minister, who is appointed by the governor-general and responsible to Parliament. The cabinet is selected by the prime minister and appointed by the governor-general. Members of the cabinet must be members of the federal Parliament.

Queen:	Elizabeth II	Since 6 Feb. 1952
Governors-General:	Sir William Deane	16 Feb. 1996—29 June 2001
	Peter Hollingworth	Since 29 June 2001
Prime Minister:	John Howard	Since 11 March 1996

Legislature: The legislature, the Parliament, is bicameral. The lower chamber, the House of Representatives, has 150 members, directly elected for a maximum of three years. The upper chamber, the Senate, has 76 members (12 members for each of the six states, directly elected for a maximum of six years, and two each for the Northern Territory and the Australian Capital Territory, directly elected for three years). Half of the Senate is normally elected at the same time as the House of Representatives.

Profile of the Governor-General:

Peter HOLLINGWORTH

Peter Hollingworth has been a serving member of the Anglican Church in Australia since 1960. A high-profile member of the clergy, he had attained the position of archbishop of Brisbane before he was appointed governor-general. His term in office has been shrouded in controversy since allegations that as archbishop he did not do enough to investigate charges of sexual abuse within the Church.

Peter Hollingworth was born in Adelaide, South Australia, on 10 April 1935. After attending schools in Melbourne, Victoria, where his parents had moved, he began his national service in 1953. It was during his time in the armed forces that he first experienced life working within the Church as he was assigned as a secretary to the padre's office. Once demobbed he studied theology at Trinity College, University of Melbourne, and graduated in 1960. He married Kathleen Ann Turner, whom he had met while on national service, on 19 May 1960. She had trained as a physiotherapist and practised throughout her married life, eventually retiring from the Royal Women's Hospital in Brisbane in 1998. They have three children.

Hollingworth became deacon-in-charge and then priest-in-charge of St Mary's Church in the north of Melbourne, before joining the administration of the anti-poverty Brotherhood of St Laurence movement as a chaplain in 1965. By the time he left the Brotherhood in 1990 he had become its executive director. During this time he wrote several books, including *The Powerless Poor* (1972) and *Australians in Poverty* (1979). He was elected canon of St Paul's Cathedral in 1980 and was consecrated bishop of the Inner City in 1985.

Hollingworth was elected archbishop of Brisbane in 1989 and took up his post the following year. He used his new high-profile position to further highlight the plight of the urban poor. He was honoured as Australian of the Year for 1992, using the position to focus attention on the young unemployed. His high standing made him a prime candidate to take over the position of governor-general and he was selected in May 2001 by Queen Elizabeth II to assume the role; he took office on 29 June.

His term in office has been dogged by accusations that he himself, and the Anglican Church in general, had failed to react adequately to cases of child abuse within the Church. Hollingworth has even been accused of actively covering up incidents. An investigation was officially launched by his successor as archbishop of Brisbane, Phillip Aspinall, in 2002. Despite the controversy Hollingworth has received unqualified backing from the Australian political establishment and from within the Church itself.

Profile of the Prime Minister:

John **HOWARD**

John Howard is a former lawyer and a member of parliament since 1974. He was Liberal leader from 1985 to 1989, and the party turned to him once again in early 1995, by which time he had moved from his former 'radical conservative' stance to redefine himself as a 'tolerant conservative'. He became prime minister the following March, after leading a Liberal–National coalition to a general election victory, defeating the Australian Labor Party (ALP) which had been in government for the previous 13 years.

John Winston Howard was born in Earlwood, New South Wales, in 1939, and was educated locally at Canterbury Boys' High School. He graduated in 1961 from Sydney University with a degree in law, and was admitted as a solicitor of the New South Wales Supreme Court the following year, becoming a partner in a Sydney law firm (1968–74). He married Alison Janette Parker in 1971 and they have two sons and one daughter.

From 1972 to 1974 Howard was the vice president of the New South Wales Liberal Party, and in May 1974 he was elected to the federal Parliament as a Liberal MP for Bennelong, a suburb of Sydney. For a brief period in 1975 he served as a member of the opposition shadow ministry, speaking on consumer affairs.

When Gough Whitlam's ALP government was ousted in late 1975, and Liberal leader Malcolm Fraser was invited to form a government in his place, Howard became a government minister for the first time, serving as minister for business and consumer affairs, then briefly as minister of state for special trade negotiations in 1977. He was treasurer in Fraser's government from November 1977 to March 1983. After the electoral defeat for the Liberal–National coalition in 1983, Howard was chosen to be deputy leader of the Liberal Party (and of the opposition), with Andrew Peacock as the new party leader. A rivalry between these two saw the party leadership change hands several times during a long period in opposition. Howard became leader in September 1985, adopting a right-wing stance against a range of ALP policies, including increased Asian immigration. In May 1989 he was ousted as party leader by Peacock. Howard held several shadow cabinet posts, especially in the field of industrial relations and employment. He also chaired the manpower and labour market reform group, and made an unsuccessful bid for the party leadership again after the general election in 1993.

Having redefined himself as a 'tolerant conservative', Howard made his political comeback in January 1995, and was re-elected leader of the Liberal Party unanimously on 30 January when Alexander Downer stood down after only eight months in the post. As leader of the opposition, Howard confirmed his party's retreat from proposals to raise indirect taxes. He refrained from making a clear commitment, however, on the issue of the proposed move from a monarchy to a republican system which was a key part of the ALP government's pre-election position. Howard led the Liberal Party in its strong showing in the general election of 2 March 1996, enabling him to claim the post of prime minister as head of a Liberal–National coalition government sworn in on 11 March.

The Howard government was re-elected in early elections held in October 1998 but over the course of his first two terms as prime minister Howard's popularity declined, despite progress on the management of the economy. He was criticized for weak handling of a challenge from the far right, while he risked a major rural–urban split on the race issue by advocating legislation to make it more difficult for aborigines to claim native title rights over lands leased from the state by white farmers. His referendum on whether Australia should become a republic produced a 'no' vote on the basis that the alternatives offered, such as an indirectly elected president, were unacceptable. By 2001 it was generally expected that the Liberal–National coalition would be resoundingly ousted in the next election, and the ALP surged to victory in local elections, taking all but one state by February.

However, public opinion took a sudden and dramatic swing to the right towards the end of that year based on two issues: international terrorism and immigration. The attempt by 450 Afghan refugees to enter Australia illegally aboard the *Tampa* in August 2001, and the 11 September attacks in the USA, galvanized support for Howard's hard-line stance on these issues. The Liberal–National coalition was consequently re-elected in November 2001 for a third term.

Since then, the government's popularity at the national level has been damaged by discomfort over the conditions in detention camps for asylum seekers, but received a boost after the October 2002 Islamist terrorist bombing in Bali, where Australian tourists were the most numerous of the victims. At the local level, however, the ALP completed its clean sweep of state legislatures in March 2002.

AUSTRIA

Full name: The Republic of Austria.

Leadership structure: The head of state is a federal president, directly elected by universal adult suffrage. The president's term of office is six years, renewable once only. The head of government is the federal chancellor, who is appointed by the president. The federal government is appointed by the president at the chancellor's recommendation.

Federal President:	Thomas Klestil	Since 8 July 1992
Federal Chancellors:	Viktor Klima	28 Jan. 1997—4 Feb. 2000
	Wolfgang Schüssel	Since 4 Feb. 2000

Legislature: The legislature, the Parliament (Parlament), is bicameral. The lower chamber, the National Council (Nationalrat), has 183 members, directly elected for a four-year term. The upper chamber, the Federal Council (Bundesrat), has 64 members elected for various terms by the provincial assemblies. Powers relating to some formal acts of state are vested in the two chambers meeting together as the Federal Assembly (Bundesversammlung).

Profile of the Federal President:

Thomas **KLESTIL**

Thomas Klestil is a former diplomat whose career included posts as Austria's representative at the UN and as ambassador to the USA. When he was elected as president in 1992, as the candidate of the Austrian People's Party (Österreichische Volkspartei—ÖVP), he was seen as a suitably uncontroversial choice after the tempestuous tenure of Kurt Waldheim, the former UN secretary-general and target of persistent allegations over German army atrocities during the Second World War.

Thomas Klestil was only a child during the period of Austria's union with Nazi Germany, having been born in Vienna on 4 November 1932. He attended primary and secondary school in Vienna and then enrolled in the city's University of Commercial Studies, where he gained the degree of Diplomkaufmann and then in 1957 a doctorate in economics. He is married with three children.

From 1957 he worked in the office for economic co-ordination of the federal chancellery, before joining the diplomatic corps in 1959. His first appointment was as a member of the Austrian mission at the Paris-based Organization for Economic Co-operation and Development (OECD). In 1962 he was posted to the Austrian embassy in Washington D.C., before taking up an appointment in 1966 as aide to the ÖVP federal chancellor Josef Klaus, a position he held until 1969. From 1969 to 1974 he was Austrian consul-general in Los Angeles. On his return to Vienna he was appointed head of the department of international organizations in the federal ministry of foreign affairs. He held this post until 1978. In that year Klestil was appointed permanent representative of Austria at the UN in New York. He remained in this post until 1982, when he became Austrian ambassador to the USA and to the Organization of American States (OAS) in Washington D.C. Between 1987 and 1992 he was general secretary for foreign affairs.

Klestil was elected federal president on 24 May 1992, when he secured 56.9% of valid votes cast in a second round of voting against his opponent Dr Rudolf Streicher of the Social Democratic Party of Austria. He took office in July. The resumption of more normal diplomatic relations in the post-Waldheim era was signalled by a visit from the then Israeli foreign minister Shimon Peres in December 1992, while Klestil paid a state visit to Israel in November 1994, the first by an Austrian president. He was emphatically re-elected in April 1998 with 63.5% of the vote against his nearest rival, Lutheran bishop of Burgenland Gertraud Knoll.

Profile of the Federal Chancellor:

Wolfgang **SCHÜSSEL**

Wolfgang Schüssel is a career politician with a background in law, and has led the right-of-centre Austrian People's Party (Österreichische Volkspartei—ÖVP) since 1995. He held various ministerial posts, and was vice chancellor in a socialist-led coalition government from 1995 onward, before becoming federal chancellor on 4 February 2000 at the head of a controversial coalition between the ÖVP and the far-right Freedom Party of Austria (Freiheitliche Partei Österreichs—FPÖ).

Wolfgang Schüssel was born on 7 June 1945 in Vienna. He attended the renowned Schottengymnasium grammar school until graduation in 1963, and went on to obtain a doctorate in law from Vienna University. He is married with two children.

Schüssel became secretary of the parliamentary group of the ÖVP in 1968 and in 1975 he moved to the party's Austrian Business Federation where he served as secretary-general until 1991. He entered Parliament at the 1979 elections and headed the ÖVP's parliamentary economic group from 1987.

In April 1989 Schüssel was appointed as minister of economic affairs in a coalition led by the Social Democratic Party of Austria (Sozialdemokratische

Partei Österreichs—SPÖ). Over the course of the early 1990s, however, the ÖVP suffered from falling popular support, mostly due to the rise of the FPÖ. The October 1994 federal elections saw the ÖVP fall to an all-time low of only 27.7% of the vote. This poor showing brought a change of leadership in 1995, in which Schüssel became party chairman, and therefore federal vice chancellor in the continuing SPÖ-led coalition government. Later that same year the ÖVP scored a slight recovery in a snap election.

Schüssel added the foreign affairs portfolio to his responsibilities from 1996, but the coalition was brought to the point of collapse in 1999, when the far-right FPÖ made further gains in parliamentary elections, achieving parity of seats with the ÖVP, both behind the SPÖ. With the SPÖ unwilling to countenance a coalition with the far right, the then chancellor Viktor Klima stepped down, making way for Schüssel to form a controversial government which included six FPÖ cabinet members on 4 February 2000.

The resulting ostracism of Austria by other EU member states proved relatively short-lived, but Schüssel's government was nevertheless beset by repeated disputes about—and among—its far-right contingent. The FPÖ's popularity began to plummet, and the resignation of its charismatic but controversial leader Jörg Haider did nothing to improve its standing. The coalition reached breaking point in September 2002, over Schüssel's plans to postpone tax cuts in order to cover the damage caused by that year's severe flooding. The FPÖ walked out of government in protest, and fresh elections were called for 24 November.

The ÖVP's impressive 42% of the vote in this poll made it the largest party, and ensured that Schüssel would remain in office as chancellor if he could put together another coalition. By the end of 2002 he had not yet done so, and had not ruled out re-forming the previous alliance with the FPÖ, even though the latter's support in the elections had fallen dramatically to just 10% of the vote.

AZERBAIJAN

Full name: The Republic of Azerbaijan.

Leadership structure: The head of state is a president, who is directly elected by universal adult suffrage. Under the 1995 Constitution the president's term of office is five years, nonrenewable. The incumbent president (Heydar Aliyev), whose re-election in 1998 was the first time he had stood for the post under this 1995 Constitution, nevertheless announced in October 2002 that he would stand again in 2003. Executive power is held by the president. The highest executive body is the cabinet of ministers appointed by the president. The prime minister, appointed by the president, is head of government. There is, in addition, a National Security Council, set up under presidential authority by a decree of 10 April 1997.

President:	Heydar Aliyev	Since 10 Oct. 1993
	(acting from 24 June 1993)	
Prime Minister:	Artur Rasizade	Since 26 Nov. 1996
	(acting from 20 July 1996)	

Legislature: The legislature is unicameral. The sole chamber, the National Assembly (Milli Majlis), has 125 members, directly elected for a five-year term.

Profile of the President:

Heydar **ALIYEV**

A former KGB official and senior communist leader, Maj.-Gen. Heydar Aliyev dominated the political scene in Azerbaijan for most of the last two decades of Soviet rule. He returned to power soon after independence, becoming acting president in June 1993 when a rebellion had forced the incumbent Abulfaz Elchibey to flee the capital, Baku. He was confirmed in office by an election held later that year, and re-elected five years later.

Born on 10 May 1923 in Nakhichevan, an Azeri-populated enclave surrounded by the territory of Armenia, Turkey and Iran, Heydar Alirza oglu Aliyev was the fourth of eight children. He began studies at the Azerbaijan Industrial Institute's department of architecture in Baku, but these were interrupted by the Soviet entry into the Second World War in 1941. He later successfully completed a history degree at the Teacher Training Institute of Azerbaijan, while in his military career he was promoted to the rank of major-general. He married an ophthalmologist, Zarifa-khanum, and had one son and one daughter, but his wife died in 1985.

A member of the Communist Party of the Soviet Union (CPSU) from 1945 to 1991, Aliyev was an official of the security forces and a member of the Council of Ministers of the Nakhichevan Autonomous Republic from 1941 to 1949. In 1949 he joined the staff of the ministry of foreign affairs and the committee of state security (KGB) of the Azerbaijan Soviet Socialist Republic, rising to become vice chairman, then chairman of the Azerbaijan KGB between 1967 and 1969. In July 1969 he was elected first secretary of the central committee of the Communist Party of Azerbaijan.

Taking his party and government career beyond the confines of his own republic, Aliyev became a notable figure in Moscow too, as a member of the politburo of the CPSU in 1982–87 and also first deputy chairman in charge of transport in the Soviet Council of Ministers. However, in 1987 he retired from the CPSU politburo following disagreements with Mikhail Gorbachev, the then general secretary of the party. Aliyev opposed the Soviet reassertion of control in Baku in January 1990, which followed increasing unrest after the 1988 outbreak of hostilities with neighbouring Armenia over the status of Nagorno-Karabakh.

In October 1990 Aliyev was elected to the Azerbaijan Supreme Soviet but in 1991, the year of Azerbaijan's declaration of independence, he resigned from the CPSU. The following year he founded the New Azerbaijan Party (Yeni Azerbaijan Partiyasi—YAP) and became its chairman.

On 15 June 1993, amid a coup attempt to oust President Elchibey, the National Assembly (which had replaced the Supreme Soviet) elected Aliyev as its chairman. Within days Elchibey had fled the capital, and Aliyev assumed the duties of state president. Following an August referendum supporting the removal of Elchibey, presidential elections were held on 3 October 1993. Aliyev won 98.8% of votes in a turnout of 97%. However, no major opposition candidates had stood for election, while human rights monitors described the poll as undemocratic and said that the media had been closely controlled by Aliyev throughout. Aliyev was sworn in on 10 October 1993.

Aliyev's YAP secured an overwhelming majority of seats in legislative elections in both November 1995 and November 2000. On both occasions the conduct of the elections was much criticized.

In March 1995 Aliyev foiled a coup attempt by the interior ministry's militia. That August an assassination attempt against him was uncovered. He has consolidated his power as president, securing re-election on 11 October 1998 (his first election under the 1995 Constitution) and declaring in October 2002 that he intended to seek a further term when elections again became due the following year, despite the constitutional limit of a single term.

Profile of the Prime Minister:

Artur **RASIZADE**

Artur Rasizade is an engineer by training who worked in machine construction for the oil industry before becoming involved in the state planning committee. For the last five years of the communist era (1986–91) he was a deputy prime minister at republican level. He is a member of the New Azerbaijan Party (Yeni Azerbaijan Partiyasi—YAP), a party of former communists founded in September 1992 by the country's current president and dominant political figure, Heydar Aliyev.

Artur Tahir oglu Rasizade was born on 26 February 1935 in Gyandja. He trained as an engineer at the Azerbaijan Institute of Industry and joined the Azerbaijan Institute of Oil Machine Construction when he was 22. He worked there for 21 years, rising to the post of director in 1973. From 1973 to 1977 he was also chief engineer of Trust Soyuzneftemash. In 1978 he left the engineering sector to become deputy head of the Azerbaijan state planning committee for three years. Then he joined the central committee of the Communist Party of Azerbaijan as a head of section from 1981 until 1986, before his appointment as first deputy prime minister. He retained this position until 1992, the year after the independence of Azerbaijan.

When the former communists were defeated in presidential elections in 1992 by the Azerbaijan Popular Front (Azerbaijan Khalq Cabhasi—AKC), Rasizade had to resign and became an adviser to the Foundation of Economic Reforms. Meanwhile Aliyev broke away from the AKC, which had declared a new age limit for presidential candidates which would have disqualified him from contesting elections. He formed the YAP, which Rasizade subsequently joined, and was elected president in 1993.

In February 1996 Rasizade became Aliyev's assistant, before being appointed first deputy prime minister again in May. After the resignation of the prime minister on 19 July, following accusations from Aliyev of bad management of the economy, Rasizade became acting prime minister. He was confirmed in this position on 26 November 1996, and remained in office following the November 2000 legislative elections.

BAHAMAS

Full name: The Commonwealth of the Bahamas.

Leadership structure: The head of state is the British sovereign, styled 'Queen of the Commonwealth of the Bahamas and of Her other Realms and Territories, Head of the Commonwealth', and represented by a governor-general who is appointed on the advice of the Bahamian prime minister. The head of government is the prime minister, appointed by the governor-general. The cabinet is appointed by the governor-general on the advice of the prime minister.

Queen:	Elizabeth II	Since 6 Feb. 1952
Governors-General:	Sir Orville Turnquest	3 Jan. 1995—13 Nov. 2001
	Dame Ivy Dumont (acting from 13 Nov. 2001)	Since 1 Jan. 2002
Prime Ministers:	Hubert Ingraham	21 Aug. 1992—3 May 2002
	Perry Christie	Since 3 May 2002

Legislature: The legislature, the Parliament, is bicameral. The lower chamber, the House of Assembly, has 40 members, directly elected for a maximum five-year term. The upper chamber, the Senate, has 16 members, nominated immediately after the election of the House of Assembly for the same term.

Profile of the Governor-General:

Dame Ivy **DUMONT**

Dame Ivy Dumont is a member of the right-of-centre Free National Movement (FNM). Trained as a teacher, she had served in the cabinet of FNM prime minister Hubert Ingraham before being appointed acting governor-general in November 2001. On 1 January 2002 she was made the country's first ever female full governor-general, acting as the nominal representative of the head of state, Queen Elizabeth II.

Ivy Dumont, née Turnquest, was born on 2 October 1930 at Roses on Long Island in the central Bahamas, which was then a British Crown Colony. On leaving school in 1948 she began a career in education, graduating from the teacher training college in 1951 and receiving the Bahamas Teacher's Certificate in 1954. For the next 21 years she worked as a teacher, gaining a teaching degree in 1970 and ultimately becoming a head teacher. She married Police Inspector Reginald Dumont. They have two children.

In 1975, two years after the Bahamas became independent, Ivy Dumont entered political service as a deputy permanent secretary in the ministry of works and utilities where she stayed until 1978. In this time she gained a master's degree (1977) and a doctorate (1978) in public administration. Between 1978 and 1992 she worked in the human resources department of the Roy West Trust Corporation, a private financial firm.

Following legislative elections held in mid-1992 Dumont was appointed to the Senate to represent the FNM, of which she was also to serve as secretary-general. Prime Minister Hubert Ingraham also brought her into the cabinet, one of its three women members, and she headed the ministry of health and environment for three years. She moved across to the education and training ministry in January 1995. She remained in charge at the ministry when it was transformed into the ministry of education in March 1997 after the FNM was re-elected. She retired from front-line politics in January 2000, retaining her seat in the Senate.

In November 2001 the then governor-general, Sir Orville Turnquest (no relation), stepped down so that his son, FNM leader Tommy Turnquest, could lead the party into the 2002 general elections (which it went on to lose resoundingly). Senator Dumont was drafted in as an interim replacement on 13 November, and was permanently confirmed in the role on 1 January 2002.

Profile of the Prime Minister:

Perry **CHRISTIE**

Perry Christie is leader of the left-leaning Progressive Liberal Party (PLP). A career politician, he became in 1974 the youngest Bahamian appointed to the Senate. He has represented the Centreville constituency in the House of Assembly continuously since 1977, the same year he entered the cabinet. He led the PLP to a sweeping victory in elections in May 2002.

Perry Gladstone Christie was born on 21 August 1943 in Nassau, the capital of the Bahamas, which was then a British Crown Colony. After graduating in law in 1969 from Birmingham University in the UK, he was appointed to the Senate in 1974, one year after the Bahamas gained independence. Three years later he was elected to the House of Assembly and was drafted into the cabinet as minister of health and national insurance. He was assigned to the tourism ministry in 1982.

Having fallen out with the government and the party in 1984, Christie was dismissed from the cabinet. He left the PLP and successfully stood as an independent in the 1987 legislative elections, once again representing Centreville. Following a rapprochement he rejoined the party in March 1990 and was brought back into government, this time as minister of agriculture, trade and industry. Two years later the PLP suffered its first electoral defeat since independence.

Now in opposition, Christie became joint deputy leader of the PLP in 1993 and rose to full leader in 1997 when the PLP was defeated once again by a resurgent Free National Movement. Rallying the party in opposition to Prime Minister Hubert Ingraham's privatization policies, Christie led the PLP to victory in May 2002 taking a clear majority of 28 seats in the 40-seat Assembly.

Perry Christie was a keen athlete in his youth and represented the Bahamas in the triple jump at the 1960 West Indies Federation Games, and in the 1963 Central American and Caribbean Games where he won the bronze medal. He is married to Bernadette Christie, née Hanna, who is a practising lawyer. They have two sons and a daughter.

BAHRAIN

Full name: The Kingdom of Bahrain.

Leadership structure: The head of state is a hereditary monarch. As part of the movement towards a constitutional monarchy, Sheikh Hamad proclaimed himself king on 14 February 2002 and the country's official name became the Kingdom of Bahrain. The king appoints the cabinet. The prime minister is formally the head of government.

King: Sheikh Hamad bin Isa al-Khalifa   Since 6 March 1999
(amir until 14 Feb. 2002)

Prime Minister: Sheikh Khalifa bin Sulman al-Khalifa   Since 19 Jan. 1970
(president of the State Council until 16 Aug. 1971)

Legislature: Under the 2002 Constitution the National Assembly is bicameral. The lower house, the Chamber of Deputies (Majlis al-Nuwab), has 40 directly elected members. The upper house, the Consultative Council (Majlis al-Shura), is a consultative body appointed by the king, and has 40 members. Both houses have a four-year mandate, although the king is able to extend the term of each house for a maximum of two years. All adult Bahrainis, including women, are eligible to vote for the members of the lower house. In preparation for the election of the National Assembly, the process of legalizing political parties was started in September 2001, the 1975 law suspending elections was repealed by the king in February 2002, and the former Consultative Council was dissolved.

Profile of the King:

Sheikh **HAMAD** bin Isa al-Khalifa

Sheikh Hamad bin Isa al-Khalifa has been head of state of Bahrain since the death of his father Sheikh Isa in March 1999. Following a Western military education Sheikh Hamad has had a long association with Bahrain's armed forces. His reign has been characterized by a degree of leniency towards opponents and by the initiation of moves towards a constitutional monarchy. As amir he was absolute ruler, advised by a cabinet. Sheikh Hamad proclaimed himself king in February 2002.

Hamad bin Isa al-Khalifa was born in Riffa on 28 January 1950. After completing his primary education in Bahrain in 1964 he was proclaimed as crown prince and received a British public school education at the Leys School in Cambridge.

Returning briefly to Bahrain in 1967, he then went back to England to be trained as an officer at the Mons Officer Cadet School in Aldershot. After graduating he played a central role in the creation of the Bahrain Defence Force (BDF) and has been its commander-in-chief ever since. From 1972 to 1973 Sheikh Hamad was at the US Army Command and Staff College at Fort Leavenworth, Kansas. He also received the US military honour certificate for his work with the BDF since 1968.

Sheikh Hamad's main interests are sports, especially horse riding, and aviation. In 1975 he was appointed president of the supreme council of youth and sports and in 1977 he established the amiri stables which were welcomed into the World Arabian Horses Organization the following year. He also founded the al-Areen Wildlife Parks Reserve in 1976 and cites falconry as a favourite pastime. As a keen aviator Sheikh Hamad pushed for the establishment of the Bahrain Amiri Air Force and created the Defence Air Wing in 1978. After learning to fly helicopters in the same year he was admitted to the Helicopters Club of the UK in 1979. Another interest is historical research. He founded the Historical Documents Centre at his court in 1978, and from the centre's collection he published *al-Watheqa* magazine as a source of historical documents and photographs. He also founded the Bahrain Centre for Studies and Research in 1981.

As a member of Bahrain's ruling dynasty and its heir apparent, Sheikh Hamad took an active role in politics from early on. Head of the defence directorate and a member of the State Council in 1970, he became minister of defence in the cabinet of the newly independent amirate in 1971, retaining this portfolio until his accession to the throne in 1999. His father made him a member of the al-Khalifa Family Council in 1974.

Since becoming head of state, Sheikh Hamad has maintained continuity with his father's regime by retaining a substantially unchanged cabinet, which includes his uncle as prime minister, while also developing his own liberal image, notably with the holding of legislative elections in October 2002. Measures of clemency towards opponents began early in his reign with the release of 320 prisoners in June 1999 including Bahrain's top Shi'a Muslim opposition leader, Sheikh Abdel amir al-Jamri. Alongside domestic advances, he has tried to improve Bahrain's relations with the outside world. As well as establishing a human rights commission in October 1999 Sheikh Hamad established diplomatic relations with the Vatican City, reiterating his government's tolerance of the country's Christian minority. He also brokered a thawing of tensions between the amirate and neighbouring Qatar, exchanging ambassadors and setting up channels to discuss their long-running border dispute.

Sheikh Hamad married his cousin Sheikha Sabeeka bint Ibrahim al-Khalifa on 9 October 1968. They have six sons (the eldest of whom, the heir apparent Sheikh Salman bin Hamad al-Khalifa, was born in 1969) and four daughters.

Profile of the Prime Minister:

Sheikh **KHALIFA** bin Sulman al-Khalifa

Sheikh Khalifa was appointed head of government of Bahrain on 19 January 1970, the year before Bahrain gained its independence from the UK. Sheikh Khalifa is the brother of the late amir, Sheikh Isa, and uncle of Sheikh Hamad, and heads a cabinet dominated by members of the ruling al-Khalifa dynasty.

Khalifa bin Sulman al-Khalifa was born on 28 November 1935 in Bahrain, the second son of the then heir apparent, Sheikh Sulman. Married with two sons and a daughter, he was educated, like his elder brother Sheikh Isa, at the royal court, but then continued his studies in London, UK. In 1957 he became chairman of the country's education council, and in 1961, the year of his father's death, he was appointed director of finance and president of the electricity board. Between 1966 and 1970 he was also president of the Council of Administration.

On 19 January 1970 the Council of Administration was replaced by a 12-member State Council in moves to make the country appear less of an autocracy. Khalifa became its president, a position equivalent to that of prime minister, and other council members were also given ministerial portfolios.

The following year Bahrain gained its independence. This had little immediate effect on the structure of the ruling body apart from redesignating the State Council as the cabinet and Khalifa as prime minister. Under a new constitution introduced in 1973, a partially elected National Assembly was formed. In August 1975, however, the assembly was abolished because it was considered to obstruct the governing of the country, and only the cabinet, led by Khalifa, was retained, putting power firmly back in the hands of the royal family.

Sheikh Khalifa is chairman of many other official bodies including the board of directors of the Bahrain Monetary Agency and the councils for civil aviation, the civil service, defence, petroleum, projects and water resources.

BANGLADESH

Full name: The People's Republic of Bangladesh.

Leadership structure: The head of state is a president, elected by Parliament. The president's term of office is five years. The head of government is the prime minister, who is the dominant political figure but is nominally appointed by the president, as is the cabinet (on the advice of the prime minister).

Presidents:	Shahabuddin Ahmed	9 Oct. 1996—14 Nov. 2001
	A.Q.M. Badruddoza Chowdhury	14 Nov. 2001—21 June 2002
	Jamiruddin Sircar (acting)	21 June 2002—6 Sept. 2002
	Iajuddin Ahmed	Since 6 Sept. 2002
Prime Ministers:	Sheikh Hasina Wajed	23 June 1996—15 July 2001
	Latifur Rahman (chief adviser)	15 July 2001—10 Oct. 2001
	Khaleda Zia	Since 10 Oct. 2001

Legislature: The legislature is unicameral. The sole chamber, the Parliament (Jatiya Sangsad), has 300 members, directly elected for a five-year term.

Profile of the President:

Iajuddin **AHMED**

Iajuddin Ahmed is the first nonpolitician to be appointed president of Bangladesh. A senior authority in soil sciences, he has been connected with Dhaka University since 1950. He advised the transitional government in 1991 and headed the University Grants Commission in the late 1990s. He was appointed as the country's 17th president on 6 September 2002.

Iajuddin Ahmed was born in the village of Nayagaon, near Munshiganj, on 1 February 1931. He is married to Anwara Begum, a professor of zoology, and they have three children. He graduated in earth sciences from Dhaka University in 1952 and went on to receive a master's degree from the same university in 1954. He then travelled to the USA where he obtained a master's degree (1958) and then a doctorate (1962) from Wisconsin University. His work on soil salinity and rice yields has created a process to better conserve soil nutrients in rice fields.

Returning to what was by then East Pakistan, Ahmed joined the staff of Dhaka University and began a 40-year career at the institution. He began as an assistant professor of soil sciences in 1963, became an associate professor the next year and a full professor in 1973. Administratively he was provost (head) of the university's Salimullah Muslim Hall between 1975 and 1983, and dean of the biological sciences faculty in 1989–90 and 1990–91. He also sat on various councils and committees in the university administration.

In 1991 Ahmed was called to advise the caretaker government of Acting President Shahabuddin Ahmed. A government structure with power centred on the prime minister was then introduced in place of the previous presidential system. Under Prime Minister Begum Khaleda Zia, Ahmed was made chairman of the University Grants Commission. He remained in this position until 1999. In June 2002 the incumbent president, A.Q.M. Badruddoza Chowdhury, elected shortly after the return to power of Prime Minister Zia the previous year, left office amid a dispute with her government, and Ahmed was nominated to fill the position. He came out of retirement to become president in September.

Profile of the Prime Minister:

Khaleda **ZIA**

Begum Khaleda Zia was inaugurated for her third official term as prime minister of Bangladesh on 10 October 2001. Originally a retiring housewife, she came to prominence as the political heir of her assassinated husband, military leader and president Gen. Ziaur Rahman. Hounded by the military regime in the 1980s, she led the right-wing Bangladesh Nationalist Party (BNP) to power in 1991, becoming the country's first female head of government. She led the BNP back to victory in 2001. In her first terms as premier she pushed hard for the reform of the education system, and particularly for women's rights. She currently heads a coalition government which includes hard-line Islamic parties.

Khaleda Zia, née Majumder, was born on 15 August 1945 in Dinajpur district in what was then northern Bengal in British-controlled India. She married Capt. Ziaur Rahman in 1960 and was educated at Surendranath College in Dinajpur. She concentrated on bringing up her two sons while her husband rose through the Pakistani army to reach the rank of general, and led calls for the secession of East Pakistan in 1971. Bangladesh was born later that year after a brief civil war. In 1975 Gen. Zia seized power in a military coup and proclaimed himself president of Bangladesh in 1977. Even during this period Khaleda Zia kept a very low public profile. However, this was all changed when her husband was murdered in May 1981 during an abortive coup attempt.

Vice President Justice Abdus Sattar, who took over as head of state and chairman of the BNP (which Gen. Zia had founded in 1979), was overthrown by Gen. Ershad in 1982. In opposition he appointed Khaleda Zia as vice chairwoman of the BNP. She inherited the chairmanship of the party on Sattar's retirement in February 1984 and was confirmed in the post by the party in August. As chairman she worked to unify political opposition to the authoritarian Ershad regime, forming a seven-party coalition alongside a similar grouping formed by the BNP's main rival, the Awami League (AL). During the nine years of military rule, Khaleda Zia was arrested on seven separate occasions. Deriding an apparent return to democracy in 1986, the BNP boycotted elections and remained in opposition along with the AL.

By 1990 popular discontent against Ershad and support for the opposition political parties had grown sufficiently to convince the president to step down and organize fresh elections. Khaleda Zia led the BNP to a convincing victory in February 1991 and was appointed the country's first female prime minister. Her BNP government revised the presidential system in favour of a 'parliamentary' system with a more powerful prime minister as head of government (implemented from 19 September 1991). In her first term, Khaleda Zia worked to ensure equality and improvement in education and attempted to achieve autarky in food production while ensuring provision for the needy. However, her courting of the Islamic right and her support for strict free-market economics provoked mass discontent. Riots and popular demonstrations convinced her to organize early elections in 1996.

The polls were boycotted by the AL, ensuring a BNP victory, and Khaleda Zia was inaugurated for her second term in February. However, the agitation continued and she called new elections for June. The BNP was narrowly defeated by the AL and became the largest opposition party in the country's recent history. In opposition Khaleda Zia led an increasingly outspoken voice of dissent against the government. In 1999 she formed a four-party opposition alliance and led a prolonged boycott of Parliament. In return Prime Minister Sheikh Hasina Wajed had charges of corruption levelled at her, and she was forced to appear in court to defend herself in September 2000. The BNP led a series of increasingly aggressive strikes as the country headed into elections in 2001 but failed to bring about a premature collapse of the AL government.

Elections on 1 October 2001 were preceded by high levels of violent unrest and yielded a sweeping victory for the BNP and its coalition allies. The BNP secured 66% of the seats in Parliament leaving the AL with just 20%. Khaleda Zia was inaugurated as prime minister nine days later. Within months of taking power, she had in turn filed corruption charges against Sheikh Hasina, while demonstrations by the AL followed a familiar pattern, descending into violence in January 2002.

BARBADOS

Full name: Barbados.

Leadership structure: The head of state is the British sovereign, styled 'Queen of Barbados and of Her other Realms and Territories, Head of the Commonwealth', and represented by a governor-general who is appointed on the advice of the Barbadian prime minister. The head of government is the prime minister, who is responsible to Parliament and appointed by the governor-general. The cabinet is appointed by the governor-general on the advice of the prime minister.

Queen:	Elizabeth II	Since 6 Feb. 1952
Governor-General:	Sir Clifford Husbands	Since 1 June 1996
Prime Minister:	Owen Arthur	Since 7 Sept. 1994

Legislature: The legislature, the Parliament, is bicameral. The lower chamber, the House of Assembly, has 28 members, directly elected for a five-year term. The upper chamber, the Senate, has 21 members, appointed to office for a five-year term by the governor-general, 12 of them on the advice of the prime minister, two on the advice of the leader of the opposition and seven representing religious, economic and social interests.

Profile of the Governor-General:

Sir Clifford **HUSBANDS**

Sir Clifford Husbands has been governor-general of Barbados since June 1996. He represents the monarch, Queen Elizabeth II, as titular head of state. A British-trained barrister, he was a Supreme Court judge before his appointment as governor-general.

Clifford Straughn Husbands was born on 5 August 1926 at Morgan Lewis Plantation in St Andrew parish. He was educated locally at Harrison College, before travelling to the UK to begin his legal training. He was called to the Bar in 1952, and later that year was admitted to practise in Barbados, working in private practice from 1952 to 1954. For the next six years, he practised in Barbados, Grenada, Antigua, Montserrat and elsewhere, before returning to Barbados in 1960 to work in the attorney general's chambers.

In 1967 Sir Clifford was appointed director of public prosecutions, a year later becoming a Queen's Counsel. In 1976 he was appointed a judge of the Supreme Court in Barbados, and he has held the position of justice of appeal since 1991; he has acted as chief justice of Barbados on a number of occasions. He also acted as governor-general for a brief period in 1990, before his formal appointment as governor-general on 1 June 1996.

Sir Clifford has been chairman of the community legal services commission and the penal reform committee, and also a member of the judicial and legal services commission. He received the Gold Crown of Merit in 1986, and was made a Companion of Honour of Barbados in 1989. Sir Clifford was created a Knight of St Andrew in 1995 in recognition of his outstanding legal and judicial service to Barbados, and upon becoming governor-general in 1996 was made a Knight Grand Cross of the Most Distinguished Order of St Michael and St George.

Profile of the Prime Minister:

Owen **ARTHUR**

Leader of the moderate social-democratic Barbados Labour Party (BLP), Owen Arthur is an economist by training and has been a member of parliament since the early 1980s. When taking office at the age of 44 in 1994, he was the country's fifth prime minister since independence in 1966.

Owen Seymour Arthur was born in Barbados on 17 October 1949, and educated at All Saints' Boys' School and Parry School on a government scholarship. He graduated in economics and history from the University of the West Indies in 1971, gaining a master's degree in economics in 1974. He is married to Beverley, née Batchelor.

He worked at the national planning agency in Jamaica in 1974–79, becoming chief economic planner, then taking up a post as director of economics at the Jamaica Bauxite Institute for three years (1979–81). In 1981 he was appointed as chief project analyst in the ministry of finance and planning, assisting in the preparation of Barbados's 1983–88 development plan, and taking part in negotiations with the International Monetary Fund (IMF). Other positions held by Arthur include membership of the board of directors of the Central Bank of Barbados, and of the Barbados Industrial Development Corporation. He has also served as a member of the board of directors of Jamaica's scientific research council.

Becoming a member of the Senate in 1983, Arthur became chairman of the BLP in the same year. In 1984 he was elected to the House of Assembly as a BLP candidate, the party being then in government. He was parliamentary secretary at the ministry of finance and planning from 1985 until 1986, when the BLP lost the election and began a period of eight years in opposition. During this period

Arthur held a part-time lectureship in management at the University of the West Indies, and worked as a consultant with the Caribbean Community (Caricom) in 1992.

Arthur was elected leader of the BLP, and thus leader of the parliamentary opposition, in July 1993. The September 1994 general election, called early following a revolt within the Democratic Labour Party, resulted in the BLP winning 19 of the House of Assembly's 28 seats, and Arthur became prime minister. The relative success of Arthur's government saw the party go on to win a landslide 26 seats, and a further five-year term in the January 1999 elections.

In addition to the premiership Arthur holds the portfolios of defence and security, finance and information. Committed to equal opportunity, he allocated ministerial portfolios in his first cabinet to all three of his party's women MPs and now has four female ministers. As prime minister, his priorities are the growth of the economy and international competitiveness. In 1995 he set up an advisory commission on constitutional and institutional reform.

BELARUS

Full name: The Republic of Belarus.

Leadership structure: The head of state is a president, directly elected by universal adult suffrage. The president appoints the chairman of the Council of Ministers. The Council of Ministers exercises executive power; it is accountable to the president, and responsible to the National Assembly and its chairman is the head of government.

President:	Aleksandr Lukashenka	Since 20 July 1994
Prime Ministers:	Sergei Ling (acting from 18 Nov. 1996)	19 Feb. 1997—18 Feb. 2000
	Vladimir Yermoshin (acting from 18 Feb. 2000)	14 March 2000—1 Oct. 2001
	Gennady Novitsky (acting from 1 Oct. 2001)	Since 10 Oct. 2001

Legislature: The legislature, the National Assembly (Natsionalnoye Sobranie), is bicameral. The lower chamber, the House of Representatives (Palata Predstaviteley), has 110 members, directly elected for a maximum of four years; the House met for the first time on 17 December 1996, when its members were former members of the previous legislature, the Supreme Council. The upper chamber, the Council of the Republic (Soviet Respubliki), has 56 members elected by regional soviets, and eight members appointed by the president; it first met on 13 January 1997.

Profile of the President:

Aleksandr **LUKASHENKA**

Aleksandr Lukashenka was manager of a collective farm in the Soviet and immediate post-Soviet era. He continues to favour a considerable degree of state regulation of the economy. At the international level he has made close relations with Russia the centrepiece of his presidency, but has become increasingly isolated within Europe as the head of a regime which lacks convincing democratic credentials.

Aleksandr Grigorjevich Lukashenka was born on 30 August 1954 in the village of Kopys in northeastern Belarus. He graduated from the history faculty of the

Mogilev Pedagogical Institute in 1975. He also has a degree in agricultural and industrial economics from the Belarussian Agricultural Academy (1985). During his military service in 1975 and 1977, he worked as a political propagandist with the Soviet border troops in Brest and then in 1977–78 in Komsomol, the communist youth league. From 1980 to 1982 he rejoined the army as a deputy company commander but then moved to various positions within the command economy. He rose to the post of deputy chairman of the collective farm in Shklov and then deputy manager of a construction materials factory in the same town. In 1987 he became head of the Harazdiec farm in the Mogilev region, a post he held until 1994.

In July 1990 Lukashenka was elected as a deputy to the Supreme Soviet of the Belarussian Soviet Socialist Republic and founded a Communists for Democracy deputies' group. At the time of the short-lived coup against Soviet President Mikhail Gorbachev in August 1991 he supported the 'national emergency committee' which briefly seized power in the Kremlin. In December of the same year he was the only deputy in the Belarus Supreme Soviet to vote against the formation of the Commonwealth of Independent States (CIS).

Lukashenka subsequently built up his popularity as chairman of the Supreme Soviet's Commission for the Struggle against Corruption, a post to which he was appointed in April 1993. The commission's allegations played a key role in ousting the reformist Stanislau Shushkevich as chairman of the Supreme Soviet in January the following year. A new constitution providing for a presidential form of government opened the way for direct presidential elections held in two rounds in June and July 1994. In an unexpected result, Lukashenka was elected president for a five-year term, polling 44.8% of the vote in the first round and 80.1% in the second.

During his term of office Lukashenka has promoted increasingly close political relations with Russia. Working closely with the then Russian president Boris Yeltsin, Lukashenka oversaw the drafting of a full union treaty in December 1999, setting 2005 as the deadline for full integration of Belarus and Russia. However, the election of President Vladimir Putin in Russia in 2000 put a brake on the pace of unification and strained relations, weakening Lukashenka's position.

Domestically Lukashenka has come increasingly into conflict with parliament, the judiciary, the media and the wider public, as he has strengthened his hold on power. In August 1996 he announced that a nationwide referendum would be held on proposals to change the 1994 Constitution in order to strengthen his presidential position still further. In this referendum, on 24 November, the results were recorded as a turnout of 84% and a 70.4% 'yes' vote for establishing a bicameral parliament and extending Lukashenka's term of office to the year 2001. The opposition denounced the vote as a 'farce' designed to legitimize a dictatorship and strongly denounced the later extension of Lukashenka's term to 2002.

Nevertheless, Lukashenka was re-elected in 'early' presidential elections on 9 September 2001, with 75% of the vote. The opposition candidate Vladimir Goncharik was backed by the international community in claiming large-scale fraud and intimidation during the election. By late 2002 the EU had responded to Lukashenka's authoritarian regime by banning him and his government from travelling to the Union's member states. He replied by allegedly threatening to help illegal immigrants across the border into Poland in protest at the EU's refusal to compensate Belarus for maintaining its border security.

Profile of the Prime Minister:

Gennady **NOVITSKY**

Gennady Novitsky was nominated as prime minister of Belarus on 1 October 2001 and his appointment was approved by the House of Representatives on 10 October. He trained as an engineer in Soviet-era Belarus before entering the government in 1994. He is an independent, but very much in the shadow of the constitutionally more powerful president.

Gennady Vasilevich Novitsky was born on 2 January 1949 in Mogilev, in the east of what was then the Belarussian Soviet Socialist Republic. He is married with two sons. Like many future post-Soviet politicians he trained as an engineer, graduating from the Belarussian Polytechnic Institute in 1971. He began his career at the Mogilev Construction Trust, rising to become chief engineer by the time he left in 1977.

Combining his knowledge and expertise in the construction industry with public administration, Novitsky joined the construction department of the Mogilev regional committee of the Communist Party of Belarus in 1977. Four years later he moved to the regional Interkolkhoz (collective farms) Construction Trust as chief engineer but returned to the committee in 1985 as head of the construction department. From 1988 until 1994 he served as chairman of the Rural Construction Trust having completed a specialist course at the Soviet Academy of Sciences.

In the recently independent Belarus, Novitsky was summoned by the newly inaugurated president, Aleksandr Lukashenka, to serve as minister of architecture and construction in 1994. He was promoted to deputy prime minister in 1997. His career took a surprising turn in October 2001 when Lukashenka turned to him to be his next prime minister after his own, disputed, re-election. Lukashenka explained that he valued Novitsky as an experienced "team player".

BELGIUM

Full name: The Kingdom of Belgium.

Leadership structure: The head of state is a hereditary constitutional monarch. The head of government is the prime minister, who is appointed by the monarch, and is responsible to the Chamber of Representatives. The cabinet is appointed by the monarch on the prime minister's advice.

King:	Albert II	Since 9 Aug. 1993
Prime Minister:	Guy Verhofstadt	Since 12 July 1999

Legislature: The legislature, the Federal Chambers (Chambres Législatives Fédérales/Federale Wetgevende Kamers), is bicameral. The lower chamber, the Chamber of Representatives (Chambre des Représentants/Kamer van Volks-vertegenwoordigers), has 150 members, directly elected by proportional representation for a four-year term. The upper chamber, the Senate (Sénat/ Senaat), has 71 members, also with a four-year term; 40 senators are elected, and the rest co-opted by the elected members. Regional parliaments have since 1995 been directly elected and elect regional governments.

Profile of the King:

ALBERT II

Albert II took the constitutional oath and ascended the throne as the sixth king of the Belgians on 9 August 1993 after the death of his brother, Baudouin I. Keenly interested in sport, he plays no direct political role as head of state, but is regarded as a key unifying figure in a country with three distinct linguistic and cultural heritages: that of French-speaking Wallonia, Flemish-speaking Flanders, and the small German-speaking minority.

Albert was born prince of Liège in Brussels on 6 June 1934, the son of Léopold III and Queen Astrid. He married Donna Paola Ruffo di Calabria in 1959. They have two sons and a daughter.

As prince of Liège (i.e. before his accession to the throne) he held several posts relating to his academic studies in harbour management and transport policy, as a vice admiral of the navy, and as honorary president (from 1962) of the Belgian office of foreign trade. In this capacity Albert has presided over almost 90 economic missions abroad, seeking to win foreign investment for Belgium.

Between 1954 and 1992 he also served as president of the Caisse Générale d'Epargne et de Retraite. He was president of the Belgian Red Cross from 1958 until 1993, and set up the Prince Albert Fund for the Training of Foreign Trade Experts in 1984. This fund was designed to award grants to young Belgian graduates or executives to undergo training in the branches of Belgian companies located outside western Europe.

In the political sphere, Albert has fulfilled a variety of roles, especially after 1967 when he began to carry out projects in the fields of town planning, housing, environmental protection and management. In 1969 he was appointed president of the conference of European ministers responsible for the preservation of cultural heritage. He represented Belgium at the 1972 UN environmental conference in Stockholm, Sweden, and has presided over the Belgian committee for the European 'year of the renaissance of the city'.

Profile of the Prime Minister:

Guy VERHOFSTADT

Guy Verhofstadt was appointed prime minister of Belgium after the resignation of Jean-Luc Dehaene in June 1999. Verhofstadt is the first liberal premier in 61 years, and heads a multiparty coalition consisting of his own Flemish Liberals and Democrats (Vlaamse Liberalen en Demokraten—VLD), the Walloon liberals, the ecologists and the socialist parties. A career politician who put much energy into pressing for party reforms, Verhofstadt became leader of the Flemish liberal Party for Freedom and Progress (Partij voor Vrijheid en Vooruitgang—PVV) in 1981, and masterminded their metamorphosis into the VLD in 1992.

Guy Verhofstadt was born in Dendermonde, near Ghent, on 11 April 1953. His father, Marcel, was a magistrate and adviser to the leader of the PVV's Ghent branch, Willy de Clercq. At school Guy was noted as a difficult pupil and admits to having done only enough to get by. From 1971 he studied law at the University of Ghent and took an active role in the Flemish Liberal Student Union, and upon graduation in 1975 he immediately threw himself into liberal politics, becoming a town councillor. Two years later he found a mentor in the old family friend de Clercq, who was by now the PVV chairman, and became his political secretary. The position stood him in good stead to re-energize the PVV youth movement (Jongeren) which he chaired from 1979 to 1981—the year of his marriage to Dominique Verkinderen, with whom he has two children. He made a name for himself in party politics as a reformist by producing a radical manifesto advocating a thorough overhaul in the party's structure.

In 1981 the PVV became the right flank to the ruling centre-left coalition. De Clercq was drawn into the cabinet which left the way free for Verhofstadt to become the country's youngest party leader as chairman of the PVV. Verhofstadt became a member of parliament in 1985 and was subsequently appointed as deputy prime minister and minister for the budget. He maintained these positions until 1988 when the ruling Christian People's Party (Christelijke Volkspartij—CVP) reaffirmed their alliance with the socialists, and the liberals were elbowed out of the governing coalition. After re-election as party chairman in 1989 Verhofstadt sat in the Chamber of Representatives as the leader of the opposition, giving him the opportunity to flesh out the reformist politics he had long been conceiving. In November 1992 these policies were put into practice when the PVV transformed into the VLD; the move was, in essence, an exercise in political inclusivism. Verhofstadt put everything behind renewed success in the 1995 elections on the back of his reforms and was bitterly disappointed by the electoral defeat of that year. In response he took a short sabbatical from active politics in Tuscany, Italy.

In 1996 Verhofstadt staged a comeback acting as a reporter on the Rwanda Committee, which had been organized to investigate the 1994 genocide of Tutsis, and by 1997 he had been re-elected as chairman of the VLD in time for the run-up to the 1999 elections. The VLD campaigned on promises to lower taxes and increase morality in policy-making, and following the food contamination scandal that shocked the country two weeks before polling, it became the biggest single party in the 150-seat Chamber of Representatives with 23 seats ahead of the CVP's 22. When the then prime minister Jean-Luc Dehaene resigned over the scandal, Verhofstadt was asked to form a government by King Albert on 23 June 1999 and took office in July, thereupon resigning the chairmanship of the VLD. As prime minister Verhofstadt has introduced a conference aimed at revamping governing bodies, a wave of privatizations and a promise to guarantee social security. He has also paid his debt to his ecologist coalition partners by proposing a gradual phasing out of nuclear power by 2025, despite its major role in the country's current energy mix.

BELIZE

Full name: Belize.

Leadership structure: The head of state is the British sovereign, styled 'Queen of Belize and of Her other Realms and Territories, Head of the Commonwealth', and represented by a governor-general who is appointed on the advice of the Belizean prime minister. The head of government is the prime minister, who is responsible to parliament, and appointed by the governor-general. The governor-general appoints the rest of the cabinet on the prime minister's advice.

Queen:	Elizabeth II	Since 6 Feb. 1952
Governor-General:	Sir Colville Young	Since 17 Nov. 1993
Prime Minister:	Said Musa	Since 28 Aug. 1998

Legislature: The legislature, the National Assembly, is bicameral. The lower chamber, the House of Representatives, has 29 members, directly elected for a five-year term. The upper chamber, the Senate, has eight members, appointed by the governor-general on the advice of the prime minister and the leader of the opposition.

Profile of the Governor-General:

Sir Colville **YOUNG**

Sir Colville Young's background is in linguistics and education, and his career moved from teaching to university lecturing. In 1986 he became president of the University of Belize, a post he held for four years. He was appointed as governor-general in November 1993.

Colville Norbert Young was born in Belize City on 20 November 1932, and was educated at St Michael's College (1946–50) before going on to obtain a first-class teacher's certificate in 1955. He studied for a degree in English at the University of London and then at the University of the West Indies, graduating in 1961. He gained a doctorate in linguistics from York University in 1973, his thesis being based on a study of the creolized English spoken in Belize.

Young, who is married with three sons and one daughter, followed a career in education, and was principal of St Michael's College in 1974–76. Having spent a decade as lecturer in English and general studies at the Belize Technical College, he became president of the University College of Belize in 1986. From 1990 until 1993 he was one of its lecturers. He presented papers at the 1980 and 1990 conferences of the Society for Caribbean Linguistics, and received a citation from the prime minister in 1988 for his contribution to Belizean culture.

Young was appointed governor-general in November 1993, after the prime minister had requested his predecessor's resignation. He is also a trustee of the Belize Urban Development Corporation. Young has written a number of books, including *Creole Proverbs of Belize* (1980), *Caribbean Corner Calling* (1988), *Language and Education in Belize* (1989) and *From One Caribbean Corner* (poems) (1983). He was a founding member of First Belizean Steel Band and of the Beltek Steel Orchestra, and has composed music including *Missa Caribeña*, the first Belizean setting of the mass.

Profile of the Prime Minister:

Said **MUSA**

Said Musa was a successful lawyer before going into politics. He has been a member of the House of Representatives for the People's United Party (PUP) since 1979 and party leader since 1996. As foreign minister he secured a celebrated recognition of Belize's territorial integrity from Guatemala in 1991, only to see Guatemala's claim reopened in 2000 while he was prime minister.

Said Wilbert Musa was born in the border town of San Ignacio on 19 March 1944. A boy from humble origins who improved his prospects through education, he moved on from secondary school in Belize City to study law at the University of Manchester, England, graduating in 1966. He was called to the Bar at Gray's Inn in London and briefly stayed in England (where he married his wife Joan). He returned to Belize in 1967 where he served as a circuit magistrate and then a Crown Counsel in the office of the director of public prosecutions the following year. In 1970 he left public service and set up as an independent partner in law with his associate, Lawrence Balderamos.

In the course of the early 1970s Musa was active in nongovernmental politics joining the United Black Association for Development, and running the People's Action Committee and the Society for the Promotion of Education and Research, both of which he helped to found in 1969. He also cofounded the *Journal of Belizean Affairs* in 1972, but his nonparty political activity ended when he joined the PUP in 1974.

Despite losing the election in the Fort George constituency of Belize City in 1974, Musa was nominated to the Senate, where he sat until 1979, at the request of the PUP prime minister, George Price. He eventually won the Fort George seat in a sensational victory against the opposition United Democratic Party leader Dean Lindo in 1979 and has represented it in government ever since. Between

1979 and 1984 Musa was attorney general and minister of education, sports and culture. As a member of the cabinet Musa was involved with independence negotiations with the UK in 1981, and the drafting of the new constitution. Following independence he represented his country at the Caribbean Community (Caricom), the Commonwealth of Latin American Nations and the UN. In the first postindependence elections in 1984 the PUP suffered a crushing defeat, relegating Musa to the opposition benches in the House of Representatives.

In 1989 the PUP clawed back into power and Musa rejoined the cabinet, this time as foreign minister. The year 1991 was one of particular achievement for Musa when he oversaw Belize's admission to the Organization of American States (OAS) and, most significantly, secured territorial recognition of Belize's borders from Guatemala. Following another electoral defeat for the party in 1993, Musa went on to take first the deputy leadership of the PUP in 1994 and then full leadership in 1996. He led a reinvigorated party to a stunning victory in the elections of August 1998 winning almost 60% of the vote and giving them an overpowering 26 seats in the 29-seat House of Representatives. As prime minister, Musa faced an international crisis in 2000 when Guatemala renewed its territorial claim to half of Belize, severing once again the diplomatic ties established in 1991.

BENIN

Full name: The Republic of Benin.

Leadership structure: The head of state is a president, directly elected by universal adult suffrage. The president's term of office is five years, renewable once only. The president is head of government as well as head of state. The president appoints and presides over the Council of Ministers.

President: Gen. Mathieu Kérékou   Since 24 March 1996

Legislature: The legislature is unicameral. The sole chamber, the National Assembly (Assemblée Nationale), has 83 members, directly elected for a maximum of four years.

Profile of the President:

Gen. Mathieu **KÉRÉKOU**

Gen. Mathieu (Ahmed) Kérékou, a French-trained army officer who ruled Benin from 1972 to 1991, then had the distinction of being the first former dictator in mainland Africa to hand over power after returning his country to multiparty democracy. Five years later, in March 1996, he won back power by the ballot box, and is currently serving a second (and, according to the current constitution, final) five-year term.

Born on 2 September 1933 in Natitingou, in the north of what was then Dahomey, Mathieu (Ahmed) Kérékou was educated initially in Mali and Senegal. He then enrolled at the Saint-Raphaël military school in France, and served in the French army until 1961 when he was appointed second lieutenant in the army of newly independent Dahomey. He was an aide-de-camp to President Hubert Coutoucou Maga between 1961 and 1963. In 1967, when his cousin Maj. Maurice Kouandété led a military coup, Kérékou became chairman of the Military Revolutionary Council. He returned to French military schools between 1968 and 1970, when he became commander of the Ouidah paratroop unit and deputy chief of staff.

In October 1972, following five years of coups and political crises, Maj. Kérékou led a military coup which ousted the then president Justin Ahomadegbé. On coming to power he declared the country a Marxist–Leninist state and appointed a military revolutionary government of army officers who were all under the age of 40, assuming for himself the positions of president, head of government and minister of national defence. He executed some of his political opponents, imprisoned others, dismissed senior army officers and has been accused of human rights abuses. In 1975 he changed the country's name from Dahomey to Benin. Four years later, when his power base was sufficiently strong for him to be confident of retaining the presidency, he staged elections, nominally returning the country to civilian rule.

During nearly two decades in power he nationalized private business and expanded government control but by the late 1980s began to be accused of destroying the economy, while public pressure grew for him to introduce reforms reversing these policies. In 1989, facing further mass protests and pressure from the French government, he dropped single-party Marxism for multiparty politics. A national conference in February 1990 appointed former finance minister Nicéphore Soglo as interim prime minister and Kérékou reluctantly agreed to hold free elections. In the ensuing March 1991 presidential election he won only 32.2% of the vote. Conceding victory to Soglo, Kérékou stepped down in what was the first example in mainland Africa of a former dictator relinquishing power following a democratic election. Kérékou was given immunity from prosecution, made a public apology for the mistakes and abuses of his term, and was allowed to remain active in politics.

In the next presidential election, in March 1996, Kérékou was returned to power. Although he polled only one-third of the total vote and trailed Soglo in the first round, he picked up support from the eliminated candidates and won 52.5% of the vote in the second round. Soglo, whose popularity had suffered both from his perceived autocratic attitudes and his economic austerity policies, contested the result before the Constitutional Court, but conceded defeat when the court on 24 March formally declared Kérékou the winner.

His first term in office as an elected president was a relative success, despite a dip in the country's economic growth prompted by drought in 1998. In February 2001 Kérékou announced that he would stand for re-election. He led with 47% in the first poll, and was left to face a token candidate after his main opponents boycotted the second round. They claimed widespread fraud but Kérékou countered by claiming that democracy was "alive and kicking" in Benin.

BHUTAN

Full name: The Kingdom of Bhutan.

Leadership structure: The head of state is a hereditary monarch, who until 1998 was also automatically the head of government. On 6 July 1998, however, the king dissolved his cabinet (Lhengyal Shungtshog) for the first time in 26 years, instituting a system whereby it is headed by an annually rotating chairman. The king's role is now reserved to matters of sovereignty and national security.

Druk Gyalpo (Dragon King):   Jigme Singye Wangchuk   Since 24 July 1972

Chairmen of the Cabinet:	Sangay Ngedup	9 July 1999—31 July 2000
	Yeshey Zimba	31 July 2000—8 Aug. 2001
	Khandu Wangchuk	8 Aug. 2001—14 Aug. 2002
	Kinzang Dorji	Since 14 Aug. 2002

Legislature: The legislature is unicameral. The sole chamber, the National Assembly (Tshogdu), has 154 members, of whom 105 are directly elected by universal adult suffrage for three-year terms. There are 12 seats reserved for representatives of religious bodies and 37 nominated by the government.

Profile of the Druk Gyalpo (Dragon King):

JIGME Singye Wangchuk

King Jigme acceded to the throne of Bhutan in 1972 at the age of 16 on the death of his father, Jigme Dorji Wangchuk. As king he has followed the cautious modernizing approach of his father, although he remains firmly rooted in Bhutan's traditional heritage, which he has sought to protect against being overwhelmed by outside cultural influences.

Jigme Singye Wangchuk was born in Dechenchholing Palace, Thimphu, on 11 November 1955. He was initially educated by private tutors, and later at St Joseph's School in Darjeeling, India. He studied in England from 1965 to 1969, returning to Bhutan in 1970 to complete his education at the Wangchuk Academy in Paro. He was named crown prince in March 1972, after which he began participating in cabinet meetings, and was appointed chairman of the planning commission. Installed formally as crown prince on 5 May 1972, he acceded to the throne as Druk Gyalpo (the Dragon King) only just over two months later, on 24 July, on the sudden death of his father. His coronation took place in June 1974.

As king of Bhutan he chaired the cabinet until the political reforms of 1998, and is commander-in-chief of the armed forces. He has also retained the chairmanship of the planning commission and regularly tours the country, attempting to combine the ideals of technological development with principles of continuity in a traditional society. He has, however, taken a strong stance against the growth of political opposition, especially from those of Nepalese descent in the banned left-wing Bhutan People's Party. In 1988 he imposed a code of conduct, and his attempt to forge a new national identity has alienated the ethnic Nepalese of the south, inspiring a fierce minority rights campaign. Partly to counter the threat of cross-border dissident activity, he has worked to promote diplomatic links with India (from which Bhutan receives most of its aid) and with China.

A regular participant in summit meetings of the Non-Aligned Movement and the South Asian Association for Regional Co-operation (SAARC), King Jigme has been instrumental in the very gradual opening up of Bhutan to economic development and to strictly limited tourism.

Profile of the Chairman of the Cabinet:

Kinzang **DORJI**

Lyonpo Kinzang Dorji was educated as a vet, and had a long career in government agencies involved in protecting and developing the environment, prior to becoming speaker of the National Assembly in 1997 and a government minister in 1998. He assumed the office of prime minister in August 2002.

Kinzang Dorji was born in Chhali, in the east of Bhutan, in 1951. After attending school locally he travelled to Calcutta (now Kolkata) in India to study veterinary medicine and animal husbandry. On graduation he returned to Bhutan to begin work for the government as a vet in 1976. Dorji rose rapidly through the national animal husbandry administration, becoming successively an assistant director, deputy director (in 1979) and joint director (in 1983) before his appointment as full director of animal husbandry in 1986. As a fully fledged government administrator he was nominated in 1989 to be zonal administrator (*dzongda*) for Sarpang, Zhemgang, Trongsa and Bumthang districts (*dzongkhags*).

In government from 1991, Dorji was director-general of agriculture and then a government secretary from 1994. As the country began to undergo limited democratic reforms, Dorji was elected speaker of the National Assembly in June 1997. King Jigme devolved effective day-to-day power to the government in 1998 and Dorji was appointed to the cabinet as deputy minister before being elected full minister by the National Assembly on 1 July. He assumed the annually rotating role of cabinet chairman (prime minister) on 14 August 2002.

BOLIVIA

Full name: The Republic of Bolivia.

Leadership structure: The head of state is a president, directly elected by universal adult suffrage, but chosen by Congress if no candidate gains a majority of the vote. The presidential term is five years. The incumbent may not seek re-election. The head of government is the president, who appoints the cabinet.

Presidents:	Gen. Hugo Bánzer Suárez	6 Aug. 1997—7 Aug. 2001
	Jorge Quiroga Ramírez	7 Aug. 2001—6 Aug. 2002
	Gonzalo Sánchez de Lozada	Since 6 Aug. 2002

Legislature: The legislature, the National Congress (Congreso Nacional), is bicameral. The lower chamber, the Chamber of Deputies (Cámara de Diputados), has 130 members, directly elected for a five-year term. The upper chamber, the Chamber of Senators (Cámara de Senadores), has 27 members, also directly elected for a five-year term.

Profile of the President:

Gonzalo SÁNCHEZ DE LOZADA

Gonzalo Sánchez de Lozada heads the right-of-centre Nationalist Revolutionary Movement (Movimiento Nacionalista Revolucionario—MNR) and became famous in Bolivia for successfully tackling the country's hyperinflation in 1985. He served as president from 1993 to 1997 and introduced a raft of social and political reforms as well as an extensive privatization programme. Elected for a second term on 4 August 2002, after heading the first round of polls in June, he faces a country once again suffering economic decline and social unrest.

Gonzalo Sánchez de Lozada was born on 1 July 1930 in Bolivia but moved while he was still a small child to the USA where his father was a Bolivian diplomat in Washington D.C. Consequently his entire education was in US schools, giving him a fluency in English which is said to surpass his knowledge even of Spanish. He graduated from the University of Chicago with a degree in philosophy and English literature in the early 1950s. He is married to Ximena Iturralde Monje and they have two children.

In the thirty years following his graduation, Sánchez de Lozada founded and managed successive companies, beginning with the film production company

59

Telecine in 1953, followed by the petroleum firm Andean Geo-Services (1957–62) and then the mining concern Compañía Minera del Sur (Comsur, 1962–79), which is now one of the largest mining companies in Bolivia.

In 1979 he turned his full attention to Bolivian politics and was elected to the Chamber of Deputies to represent the constituency of Cochabamba. After another two years spent at the helm of Comsur (1980–82), Sánchez de Lozada returned to the Chamber in 1982, again representing Cochabamba. He graduated to the Chamber of Senators in 1985. A year later, as the country suffered under massive hyperinflation, outspoken reformist Sánchez de Lozada was called into the cabinet of President Víctor Paz Estenssoro as minister of planning and co-ordination. He quickly launched his New Political Economy, a plan to combat the spiralling inflation, which had hit 25,000%. Within a year the programme of structural adjustment and tight fiscal control had brought inflation down to double figures. His success catapulted him to the presidency of the MNR in 1988, and saw him chosen as the party's candidate for the 1989 presidential elections.

Although Sánchez de Lozada won the greatest single share of seats in the first-round, popular vote, he was overtaken in the second, congressional poll by a coalition of opposition parties which gave its support to social-democrat Jaime Paz Zamora. Sánchez de Lozada led the MNR into opposition and rallied his supporters for the next presidential elections in 1993. This time his popularity paid off and he was elected president with the backing of former military dictator Hugo Bánzer.

As president, Sánchez de Lozada unveiled a comprehensive Plan de Todos (Plan for Everyone) which included constitutional and educational as well as economic reforms. Government control over budgets and low-level decisions was devolved to local authorities while a sweeping privatization programme aimed at slashing government expenditure and encouraging foreign investment. Although his economic policies were fruitful in the short term—the government earned US$1,700 million from privatization—external debt had rocketed to US$5,000 million. Left-wing opposition to his austerity measures culminated in violent protests and the arrest of the leaders of the Central Bolivian Workers union followed by a 90-day state of emergency in mid-1995.

In 1997 Sánchez de Lozada handed over office to Hugo Bánzer who had won that year's presidential poll. He retired temporarily from front-line politics and returned to his private business and political interests. His connection to Comsur had made him one of the richest men in Bolivia. As the country's economy continued to struggle, Sánchez de Lozada saw an opportunity to return to the political stage. Bánzer had retired due to ill health in 2001 and Sánchez de Lozada registered his candidacy at the head of the MNR for the 2002 presidential elections. Although he led the polls from the outset, he faced a stiff challenge from Aymaran protest leader Evo Morales and was only elected with the strong congressional support of the MNR and its allies. He promised in his second term to reappraise the government's pro-Western financial approach.

BOSNIA AND HERZEGOVINA

Full name: Bosnia and Herzegovina.

Leadership structure: The head of state is a collective presidency, with one member representing each ethnic group (Bosniac, Serb and Croat). The chair of the presidency rotates among its members every eight months. Both the (Bosniac-Croat) Federation and the Republika Srpska (RS) also have their own directly elected presidents. The executive consists of a central Council of Ministers and separate executives for the two entities. Appointments to the executives must be in consultation with, and can be vetoed by, the UN's international high representative. From December 2002 the post of prime minister became fixed, with a four-year term, rather than rotating every eight months.

Chairmen of the Presidency:

	Ante Jelavić (Croat)	15 June 1999—14 Feb. 2000
	Alija Izetbegović (Bosniac)	14 Feb. 2000—14 Oct. 2000
	Zivko Radišić (Serb)	14 Oct. 2000—14 June 2001
	Jozo Križanović (Croat)	14 June 2001—14 Feb. 2002
	Beriz Belkić (Bosniac)	14 Feb. 2002—28 Oct. 2002
	Mirko Sarović (Serb)	Since 28 Oct. 2002

Prime Ministers:	Haris Silajdžić & Svetozar Mihajlović	4 Feb. 1999—6 June 2000
	Spasoje Tusevljak	6 June 2000—18 Oct. 2000
	Martin Raguz (acting)	18 Oct. 2000—11 Nov. 2000
	vacant	11 Nov. 2000—22 Feb. 2001
	Bozidar Matić	22 Feb. 2001—18 July 2001
	Zlatko Lagumdžija	18 July 2001—15 March 2002
	Dragan Mikerević	15 March 2002—23 Dec. 2002
	Adnan Terzić	Since 23 Dec. 2002

International High Representatives:

	Wolfgang Petritsch	18 Aug. 1999—27 May 2002
	Paddy Ashdown	Since 27 May 2002

Legislature: The legislature of Bosnia and Herzegovina, the Parliamentary Assembly (Parlamentarna Skupština), is bicameral. The House of Representatives (Predstavnički Dom/Zastupnički Dom) has 42 members who are directly elected to the two constituent chambers, the Chamber of Deputies of the (Bosniac-Croat) Federation, with 28 members, and the Chamber of Deputies of the Republika Srpska, with 14 members. The House of Peoples (Dom Naroda) has 15 members, ten of them appointed from the Federation and five from the Republika Srpska. Both houses have two-year terms.

The Federation also has a bicameral Assembly (Skupština), including a House of Representatives (Predstavnički Dom/Zastupnički Dom) with 140 directly elected members, and a House of Peoples (Dom Naroda) with 74 indirectly elected members. The Republika Srpska has a National Assembly (Narodna Skupština) with 83 directly elected members. All of these houses have two-year terms.

Profile of the Chairman of the Presidency:

Mirko **SAROVIĆ**

Mirko Sarović is a founding member of the ultranationalist Serbian Democratic Party (Srpska Demokratska Stranka—SDS). A prominent politician in Sarajevo's municipal institutions, he has courted controversy for his outspoken support for war criminal, and cofounder of the SDS, Radovan Karadžić. He was president of the Republika Srpska (RS) before being elected as the Serb member of the tripartite federal presidency in 2002. Under the rotation system he was made the first chairman of the new presidency in October that year.

Mirko Sarović was born on 16 September 1956 in Rogatica, eastern Bosnia, which was then an integral part of a socialist Yugoslavia. He graduated in law from the University of Sarajevo in 1979 and worked for ten years for the commercial companies Famos and Unis. Elected to the Sarajevo Municipal Assembly in 1989, he was among the first members of the far-right SDS when it was founded by Karadžić in the early 1990s as the collapse of Yugoslavia loomed.

After the war Sarović was elected to the Parliamentary Assembly in 1996 and appointed vice president of the RS in 1998. He was elected full president on 26 January 2000 but was refused official recognition by the International High Representative, and was forced from office on 2 February. He returned to the post, for the second time, in December 2000. His unashamed admiration for Karadžić caused international controversy when in March 2002 he described the indicted war criminal as "a symbol of freedom" for Bosnian Serbs. He also attacked the centrist idea of eventually scrapping the separate ethnic entities in Bosnia, declaring that "there is no Bosnia without the Republika Srpska".

Nationalist parties representing all three of the country's main ethnic groups performed well in the October 2002 legislative elections and Sarović was elected as the Serb representative to the tripartite federal presidency. He stepped down from his role in the RS and was inaugurated as the first chairman of the new presidency on 28 October that year. His term as chairman will last for eight months.

Profile of the Prime Minister:

Adnan **TERZIĆ**

Adnan Terzić is vice president of the Bosniac-nationalist Party of Democratic Action (Stranka Demokratske Akcije—SDA). Based in the central Bosnian town of Travnik, he has been an integral part of the Bosniac-nationalist movement since the 1992–95 civil war. However, on his appointment as federal prime minister on 23 December 2002 he promised to oversee a multi-ethnic and liberal government.

Adnan Terzić was born in 1960 into the Muslim Bosniac community in Bosnia and Herzegovina, which was then a constituent republic of socialist Yugoslavia. Trained as a geodetic engineer, he was a prominent advocate of the Bosniac-nationalist movement from the early 1990s.

While serving as mayor of the town of Travnik in 1996, Terzić officially denied that ethnic Croat families in the region had been banished following the Dayton Peace Accord. In the new cantonal structure adopted after the war, Terzić soon rose to prominence and was elected governor of the Central Bosnia canton for 1997–98, and again for 2000–01. During his governorships he oversaw the return of refugees and the implementation of redevelopment plans.

The SDA took on a more liberal stance at its congress in October 2001 and Terzić was elected its vice president as part of these changes. He was key in leading the party to electoral success in the 2002 general elections which saw gains for the three traditional nationalist parties. Under new constitutional arrangements he was confirmed by a majority in parliament on 23 December as the country's first prime minister to have a fixed four-year term.

Profile of the International High Representative:

Paddy **ASHDOWN**

Paddy Ashdown is a liberal democrat from the UK. During the wars of the Yugoslav succession he was a very vocal advocate of international military intervention. He was nominated to be the UN's high representative in Bosnia and

Herzegovina in early 2002. Ashdown's position is constitutionally the most powerful in the country.

Jeremy John Durham Ashdown was born on 27 February 1941 in Delhi, India. His family returned to Northern Ireland, in the UK, in 1945. Ashdown enlisted with the Royal Marines while still studying at Bedford School in east England, and joined the military full-time in 1959. He married Jane Courtenay in 1961; they have two children.

A commander in the elite Special Boat Service from 1965, Ashdown saw active service in Borneo, the Persian Gulf and Belfast. He left the army in 1972 and took up a position at the UK's mission to the UN in Geneva, Switzerland. Many have since speculated that this post acted as cover for an assignment as a member of MI6, the UK foreign secret service. In 1976 Ashdown settled in England working with local industries. Having joined the then Liberal Party in 1975 he unsuccessfully stood for election in 1979. After two years as a local youth worker (1982–83), Ashdown was elected to the House of Commons, the lower house of the UK parliament, in 1983.

When the Liberals merged with the Social Democratic Party in 1988, Ashdown was elected leader of the resultant Liberal Democratic Party (LDP). In this position he pressed the government to take direct military action to try and halt the bloodshed in the disintegrating Yugoslavia and later in Kosovo. In August 1999 he stepped down as LDP leader and announced that he would retire from parliament at the next election. He was knighted in 2000 and was made Baron Ashdown of Norton-sub-Hamdon in 2001 when he left the House of Commons. As a life peer he is now a member of the House of Lords, the upper house of the UK parliament.

Ashdown was nominated to be international high representative in Bosnia in February 2002 to replace Wolfgang Petritsch, who stepped down in May. In his new role Ashdown has been notably proactive. In June 2002 he dismissed the federal finance minister, citing corruption, and in December that year he restructured the federal government to increase its power and create a prime ministerial post that no longer rotated every six months.

BOTSWANA

Full name: The Republic of Botswana.

Leadership structure: The head of state is a president, who is elected by parliament. A limit of two terms, to apply from 1999, was confirmed by referendum on 4 October 1997. The president's term of office is five years. The head of government is the president. The vice president and the cabinet are appointed by the president.

President: Festus Mogae   Since 1 April 1998

Legislature: The legislature is unicameral. The sole chamber, the National Assembly, has 46 members (40 directly elected for a five-year term, four co-opted members and two ex officio members (the president of the republic and the attorney general). A 15-member House of Chiefs acts as an advisory body on tribal matters and on alterations to the constitution.

Profile of the President:

Festus **MOGAE**

Festus Mogae, who took over as president of Botswana in 1998 and was elected to a full five-year term by the National Assembly the following year, is an Oxford-educated economist with an illustrious previous career within the national bank and the International Monetary Fund (IMF). He leads the Botswana Democratic Party (BDP), which has maintained a parliamentary majority since the country's first general election in 1965.

Festus Gontebanye Mogae was born on 21 August 1939 in Serowe in eastern Botswana. After receiving his initial education in Botswana, he travelled to the UK to study economics, first at the North West London Polytechnic, and then at the universities of Oxford and Sussex. He returned to newly independent Botswana in 1968 to become a planning officer at the ministry of development planning. He married Barbara Gemma Modise that year and together they have three daughters.

In 1971 Mogae was appointed as senior planner at the ministry and was attached to the Botswanan branch of the IMF as an alternate governor. He also worked with the African Development Bank and the International Bank for Reconstruction and Development. In 1972 he was made director of economic affairs at the ministry and was permanent secretary from 1975. During the early

1970s he was also on the board of various companies, including De Beers Botswana diamond mining company among others. In 1976 he moved to a permanent position with the IMF first as an alternate executive director. From 1978 he moved to Washington D.C. to work as a full executive director with responsibility for anglophone Africa.

Mogae returned to Botswana in 1980 to take up the governorship of the national bank and begin his high-level political career. In 1982 he was appointed as permanent secretary to President Ketumile Masire, a position he held for seven years in all. After Masire began his third term in 1989 he appointed Mogae to head the same ministry of finance and development planning where he had begun his career. As a trusted member of Masire's government Mogae was appointed as vice president in 1992. He contested, and won, a seat in the National Assembly representing the Palapye constituency in 1994.

In November 1997 President Masire announced his desire to retire at the end of March the following year. Mogae, as his deputy, took over the remainder of the presidential term from 1 April 1998. On taking office he made no changes to his predecessor's cabinet apart from the introduction of Lt.-Gen. Ian Seretse Khama, the son of Botswana's first president, as minister of presidential affairs and ultimately his vice president. The move began a rift between the executive and the ranks of the ruling BDP as the party chairman, Ponatshego Kedikilwe, had been groomed for the position.

In legislative elections held in October 1999 Mogae's BDP managed to reverse a recent downward trend in its popularity and increase its number of seats in the National Assembly, which duly re-elected Mogae as president. Mogae provoked outrage from the opposition and public alike in December when he agreed to grant Khama a one-year sabbatical. The leave of absence was cut short in August 2000 when Mogae recalled his deputy and, despite removing his ministerial position, installed him as his ministerial co-ordinator—effectively the head of government. Mogae explained that he had brought Khama back to give momentum to the eighth national development plan, current mid-term reviews of which had shown that it was lagging behind schedule. The move prompted criticism from his own cabinet who had little personal affection for the abrasive Khama.

BRAZIL

Full name: The Federative Republic of Brazil.

Leadership structure: The head of state is a president, directly elected by universal adult suffrage. The term of office is four years. A president is permitted to stand for re-election once only. The head of government is the president. The cabinet is appointed by the president.

Presidents:	Fernando Henrique Cardoso	1 Jan. 1995—1 Jan. 2003
	Luiz 'Lula' da Silva	Since 1 Jan. 2003

Legislature: The legislature, the National Congress (Congresso Nacional) is bicameral. The lower chamber, the Chamber of Deputies (Câmara dos Deputados), has 513 members, directly elected for a four-year term. The upper chamber, the Federal Senate (Senado Federal), has 81 members, elected for eight-year terms, one-third and two-thirds alternately every four years.

Profile of the President:

Luiz 'Lula' **DA SILVA**

Luiz da Silva, popularly known simply as 'Lula', was a metalworker-turned-trade unionist who cofounded the socialist Workers' Party (Partido dos Trabalhadores—PT) and came to symbolize left-wing opposition to the military-backed regimes of the 1970s and 1980s. Having failed in successive challenges for the presidency in 1989, 1994 and 1998, he toned down his socialist rhetoric in order to win elections in October 2002, and embraced liberal economics, but still maintains that globalization should be tempered by truly fair trade.

Luiz Inácio da Silva, whose nickname 'Lula' translates as 'squid', was born in October 1945; official records and his mother differ on the exact date. His impoverished family lived near Garanhuns, in the northeastern state of Pernambuco, but his father left to seek a way out of poverty in the southern state of São Paulo. The rest of the family—mother and six siblings—followed in 1952, moving to São Paulo city itself in 1956. Lula soon lost his 'northern' accent, sparing him the discrimination often suffered by northern Brazilians in mainstream society.

Lula was put to work as a street vendor as soon as he arrived in the south, peddling newspapers and shining shoes. At the age of 14 he became a metalworker, a full-time job which brought his schooling to an end, although he did a night-school course on metalworking until 1963. He lost a finger while working as a lathe operator. He married Maria de Lourdes in 1966 but was widowed three years later when Maria, and their child, died in childbirth. In 1974 he remarried, to Marisa Letícia Rocco, with whom he has three children; Lula also has two other children.

In 1966 Lula began working at Villares Industries and threw himself into trade union activism in the face of a recently installed autocratic military regime. In 1969 he was elected as an executive member of the São Bernando do Campo and Diadema Metalworkers' Union. By 1975 he had become its president. During his presidency he led two major industrial strikes against the Vauxhall motor company. His activities were gravely noted by the regime and he was briefly imprisoned.

Party politics was liberalized in 1979 and on 10 February 1980 Lula became one of the founder members of the PT. Its support for the radical movement of the landless, and industrial action, played a key role in toppling the military-backed government in 1985. During that period Lula helped create the Workers' Central Union in 1983 and led the 'Direct Elections Now' campaign in 1984 in an ultimately successful bid to press for direct presidential elections. In 1986 he was elected to the National Constituent Assembly with 650,000 votes—the largest personal mandate in the election. In 1987 he stepped down as PT president and put his popularity to the test as a presidential candidate for the 1989 poll.

Lula was beaten into second place by Fernando Collor de Mello, but formed a 'parallel government' in 1990 and successfully campaigned to have Collor de Mello impeached in 1992. He stood for the presidency two more times but was defeated on both occasions by the conservative Fernando Henrique Cardoso.

As the economy in neighbouring Argentina collapsed and began to impact on Brazil, Lula stepped up once more in 2002. This time he distanced himself from the landless movement and watered down his socialist rhetoric, replacing a promise to default on Brazil's international debts with a pledge to maintain the liberal economic policies of his predecessor. He also smartened his image and courted big business by sharing his candidacy with running mate José Alencar, a textile magnate and a champion of capitalism from the small Liberal Party.

Lula's popularity in pre-election polling alarmed international investors, who went so far as to devalue the country's credit rating and warn of bleak times ahead. Nonetheless he secured victory in the second round of voting on 27 October 2002, against José Serra, the candidate favoured by the incumbent President Cardoso, who was constitutionally barred from standing again himself. Lula's mandate rests on an unprecedented popular base as he received 61% of the vote, a record 52.7 million ballots in his favour. He was inaugurated for a four-year term on 1 January 2003.

Profile of the Previous President:

Fernando Henrique **CARDOSO**

A sociologist with an international academic reputation, Fernando Cardoso was the only Brazilian head of state of the 20th century to secure a second term of office, having opened the way to seek re-election by means of a constitutional amendment in 1997. Actively involved in politics with centrist parties since the early 1980s, he first claimed credit as saviour of the economy after the success of his 'real plan', establishing a stable currency, when he was economy minister in 1993–94. His second term ended on 1 January 2003.

Fernando Henrique Cardoso was born on 18 June 1931 in Rio de Janeiro, the son of a general. He has been married since 1952 to Ruth Corrêa Leite, who, like him, became a distinguished sociologist, and they have three children. He gained a doctorate from the University of São Paulo in 1961, and in 1962/63 studied industrial sociology at the University of Paris in France.

Becoming known as a leading young leftist academic in Brazil, Cardoso was forced into exile in 1964 when the military dictatorship took power, but he continued teaching abroad, while writing critical articles about the military regime. During this period he was professor of developmental sociology in Chile and deputy director of the UN's Latin American Centre for Economic and Social Planning (1964–67) and then taught sociological theory at the University of Paris-Nanterre (1967–68).

On his return to Brazil in 1968 he set up a social sciences think tank, and took over the directorship of the department of social sciences at the University of São Paulo (1968/69). During this period his research centre was bombed by right-wing terrorists, and he was banned from teaching in 1969, arrested, and interrogated by military intelligence agents. In 1972 he left Brazil again for a lengthy period, holding professorships notably at Stanford, USA, (1972), Cambridge, UK, (1976/77) and Paris (1977 and 1980/81).

In 1980 Cardoso revived his São Paulo think tank, the Brazilian Centre for Analysis and Planning (Centro Brasileiro de Análise e Planejamento—CEBRAP), of which he was president until 1982. Also in 1980 he helped found the Christian-democratic centrist Party of the Brazilian Democratic Movement (Partido do Movimento Democrático Brasileiro—PMDB), which pursued a broad pro-democracy campaign, and in 1982 he entered the Federal Senate as a PMDB senator for the state of São Paulo. After the end of the era of military rule, and the PMDB's success in the 1986 elections, Cardoso rose to the position of government leader in the Senate, and took part in the work of the National Constituent Assembly to frame the more liberal 1988 Constitution.

Cardoso resigned as leader of the PMDB in June 1988 in order to found (with others) the new Brazilian Social Democratic Party (Partido da Social Democracia Brasileira—PSDB), which condemned the then President José Sarney for clinging to office without a real mandate and for indulging in what Cardoso called "corruption with impunity". After several years in opposition, and the eventual impeachment of Sarney's successor President Fernando Collor de Mello, Cardoso was appointed as minister of foreign affairs in October 1992, then minister of finance and economy in May 1993. Cardoso made his political reputation with the success of his plan to regain control over the economy, tackling Brazil's rampant inflation and implementing a currency reform, the so-called 'real plan'.

In the presidential elections of 3 October 1994 he overcame a strong challenge from the Workers' Party candidate, who had a massive early opinion poll lead, and took over 54% of the vote on the first round. His three-party centrist coalition also established a strong position in the concurrent legislative elections.

Cardoso was sworn in as president for a four-year term on 1 January 1995. He vowed to democratize the country, to limit human rights abuses within the police force, and to reduce the sharp disparities of wealth characteristic of Brazilian society. His free-market economic philosophy made him an enthusiastic proponent of the privatization of state-run monopolies and the removal of trade restrictions, but his social welfare promises ran into difficulties, and on human rights and environmental protection his government made limited real progress beyond the framing of policies and programmes.

In June 1997 the Senate finally approved a constitutional amendment to allow an incumbent president to stand for re-election. The price Cardoso paid for getting this through Congress was to soft-pedal on some of the more politically sensitive aspects of his programme to cut the cost of Brazil's overstaffed bureaucracy.

A collapse in confidence among international investors spread from Asia and Russia to place Brazil's currency and economy in danger by the latter part of 1998. Since this crisis coincided with the federal elections, Cardoso took the courageous decision to make it clear to the voters that he saw no alternative to the introduction of greater budgetary austerity. He was returned for a second term of office in October 1998 with just over 53% of the vote, while his PSDB did better than expected in the simultaneous elections to Congress and the five-party government coalition retained a three-fifths majority. Within a fortnight after beginning his new presidential term on 1 January 1999, however, and despite having secured international backing for his economic programme, Cardoso was compelled by international speculative pressure to abandon his long-standing hostility to devaluation of the currency, the real.

Cardoso has retained an active interest in the study of political and sociological issues and alternative paths to development, having first established his reputation internationally in the late 1960s as coauthor of *Dependency and Development in Latin America*. He is president of several foundations and has been a member since 1990 of the New World Dialogue initiative at the World Resources Institute in Washington D.C.

BRUNEI

Full name: The Sultanate of Brunei (Negara Brunei Darussalam).

Leadership structure: The head of state is the sultan. The head of government is the sultan, who presides over and is advised by a Council of Cabinet Ministers, a Religious Council and a Privy Council. The cabinet is appointed by the sultan.

Sultan: Sir Hassanal Bolkiah   Since 5 Oct. 1967
                          (also prime minister from 1 Jan. 1984)

Legislature: There is no elected legislature.

Profile of the Sultan:

Sir Hassanal **BOLKIAH**

Sir Hassanal Bolkiah, who trained at the UK's Sandhurst military academy and succeeded to the throne at the age of 21 following his father's abdication, is frequently cited as one of the richest people in the world, thanks to his tiny country's oil wealth. He has placed increasing emphasis in recent years on Brunei's Islamic identity, putting behind him his earlier image as something of a 'jet-setter' and playboy.

Hassanal Bolkiah was born on 15 July 1946 in Brunei Town (now known as Bandar Seri Begawan), and was educated privately in Brunei and in Kuala Lumpur, Malaysia. In 1961 he was installed as the crown prince and heir apparent. From 1963 he attended the Royal Military Academy, Sandhurst, as an officer cadet and gained his captain's commission in 1967, before succeeding to the throne on 5 October. He was crowned as the 29th sultan and *yang di-pertuan* (ruler) on 1 August 1968. He has ten children by his two wives—four sons and six daughters.

In 1978 the sultan led a diplomatic mission to London to discuss with the British government a change of status for Brunei. A Treaty of Friendship and Co-operation was drawn up, whereby the British government relinquished its responsibilities for the conduct of Brunei's foreign affairs and its defence. The treaty confirmed that Brunei would, at the end of 1983, "assume its full international responsibilities as a sovereign and independent state". On the day Brunei formally became fully independent, 1 January 1984, the sultan appointed himself prime minister. He also took on the portfolios of finance and home affairs, swapping these in 1986 for the defence portfolio.

Brunei: *Sir Hassanal Bolkiah*

His status as the richest man in the world has slipped in recent years and in 2000 he was knocked from the top spot even in Asia. Indeed money scandals tarnished his family's reputation when in that year he launched a lawsuit against his younger brother, Prince Jefri, who had been finance minister from 1986 until 1997, for the alleged embezzlement of more than US$35,000 million. The suit was dropped and Jefri's assets frozen and returned to the state.

BULGARIA

Full name: The Republic of Bulgaria.

Leadership structure: The head of state is a president, directly elected by universal adult suffrage. The president's term of office is five years. The head of government is the prime minister, who is responsible to the National Assembly. The cabinet is appointed by the prime minister.

Presidents:	Petar Stoyanov	22 Jan. 1997—22 Jan. 2002
	Georgi Purvanov	Since 22 Jan. 2002
Prime Ministers:	Ivan Kostov	21 May 1997—24 July 2001
	Simeon Saxecoburggotski	Since 24 July 2001

Legislature: The legislature is unicameral. The sole chamber, the National Assembly (Narodno Sobranie), has 240 members, directly elected for a four-year term.

Profile of the President:

Georgi **PURVANOV**

Georgi Purvanov is a former chairman of the reformed-communist Bulgarian Socialist Party (BSP). A communist-era historian and a member of the old Bulgarian Communist Party (BCP), he became a key leader of the reformist wing of the renamed BSP in the 1990s. Following the defeat of the party in the 2001 elections, Purvanov was an unexpected victor in presidential elections in November 2001. He took office in January 2002.

Georgi Sedefchov Purvanov was born in Sirishtnik in western Bulgaria on 28 June 1957. He served two years in the army from 1975 before studying history at Sofia University. After graduating in 1981 he joined the BCP and worked as a researcher in the party's Institute of History, specializing in the emergence of the modern Bulgarian state at the turn of the 20th century. He is married to the academic Zorka Purvanova and they have two sons.

In 1991 Purvanov was elected to the recently renamed BSP's Supreme Council and championed the realignment of the party towards a more centrist approach in the newly democratic Bulgaria. The BSP was returned to power in elections in 1994, but faced increasing political and economic problems. Although his faction within the party gained the ascendancy, and he was elected party chairman in December 1996, Purvanov realized how untenable the government's position had become, and he and the new prime minister, Nikolai Dobrev, refused a further mandate in February 1997, instead leading the BSP into opposition.

From here Purvanov worked to transform the party in line with other social-democratic parties elsewhere in Europe. Although he led its opposition to the bombing in Yugoslavia by the North Atlantic Treaty Organization (NATO) in 1999, the following year he pledged its support for Bulgaria's campaigns to join both NATO and the European Union (EU).

The personal prestige of the incumbent president Petar Stoyanov, who also had the full backing of the hugely popular and newly elected prime minister, Simeon Saxecoburggotski, made Purvanov's electoral victory in presidential elections in November 2001 all the more surprising. He was inaugurated as president on 22 January 2002 and consequently stood down from the leadership of the BSP. He has vowed to pursue his predecessor's policies of promoting Bulgaria's ties to the West, but has also expressed a desire to deepen relations with former allies of the East.

Profile of the Prime Minister:

Simeon **SAXECOBURGGOTSKI**

Simeon Saxecoburggotski shares an unusual distinction with Cambodia's King Sihanouk as an erstwhile hereditary monarch turned politician. In his case he was on the throne only as a young child and was then exiled, spending most of his life as a west European-based businessman, and not returning to the land of his birth until 1996. He has not officially renounced the throne, but has effectively rejected its restitution by swearing allegiance to the republic. He led a newly formed centrist National Movement–Simeon II (NMS II) to electoral victory in June 2001 and governs in coalition with the minority-based Movement for Rights and Freedoms.

Prince Simeon Borisov Saxe-Coburg-Gotha was born in Sofia on 16 June 1937 and was immediately named prince of Tirnovo and next in line for the throne. He was proclaimed King Simeon II when aged only six, on the death of his father, King Boris III, on 28 August 1943. Royal authority was exercised by a three-member Council of Regency, headed by his uncle, Prince Kyril, whose members were executed along with most other senior leaders of the regime following the Soviet-inspired communist coup in September 1944. After the end of the Second World War the new government quickly organized a stage-managed referendum on 6 September 1946 which overwhelmingly rejected the monarchy; Simeon and his remaining family were exiled. The contentious nature of that plebiscite forms the basis of Saxecoburggotski's claim to the vacant throne.

After studying at the British Victoria College in Alexandria, Egypt, Simeon was offered asylum with his family in 1951 in Franco's Spain. He graduated from the Lycée Française in Madrid in 1956 before attending the Valley Forge Military Academy in Pennsylvania, USA, until 1959. For the next 40 years he worked in various business ventures based mainly in Spain and Morocco, including the Omnium holding company, the Casablanca-based Consumar sugar producer and the Eurobuilding hotel chain. He travelled extensively around the Mediterranean, and claims proficiency in eight languages. He married Margarita Gómez-Acebo y Cejuela in 1962 and they have five children, the eldest of whom, Kardam, took the title prince of Tirnovo as heir to the throne.

Following the collapse of European communism, Simeon returned to Bulgaria in 1996. He received massive popular acclaim, but maintained his professional career in Madrid as it became clear he would not soon be allowed a smooth transition into Bulgarian politics. Having been barred from running in presidential elections, he returned again to his homeland in April 2001 and announced the formation of a new political party, the NMS II. Although Bulgarians remain steadily in favour of republicanism, the NMS II's promise of an end to economic insecurity, coupled with the image of the former king, untainted by either the communist or the troubled postcommunist regimes, proved a highly successful formula. The movement attracted many prominent figures from the incumbent centre-right administration, and the NMS II won 43% of the vote in the elections in June and exactly half of the seats in the National Assembly.

Despite initially signalling that he would not seek the premiership, the extremely popular ex-king was invited to form a government by President Petar Stoyanov on 15 July and took office on 24 July. In a concession to Bulgarian national pride, and a further acknowledgement of the insolubility of the republic, he exchanged his royal, Germanic name for the more Slavic version Simeon Saxecoburggotski. The NMS II resisted transformation into a political party, capitalizing instead on its image as a broad-based political movement. Saxecoburggotski appointed a distinctly pro-Western technocratic cabinet and has retained the outgoing government's stated aims of closer integration into Europe and securing the transition to a free-market economy.

BURKINA FASO

Full name: Burkina Faso.

Leadership structure: The head of state is a president, directly elected by universal adult suffrage. A parliamentary vote on 11 April 2000 fixed the presidential mandate at five years, with a maximum of two terms. Executive authority is vested jointly in the president, who is responsible to Parliament, and in the Council of Ministers, which is headed by the prime minister (appointed by the president) and which is also responsible to Parliament.

President:	Capt. Blaise Compaoré (seized power on 15 Oct. 1987)	Since 31 Oct. 1987
Prime Ministers:	Kadré Désiré Ouédraogo	6 Feb. 1996—7 Nov. 2000
	Paramanga Ernest Yonli	Since 7 Nov. 2000

Legislature: The legislature, the Parliament (Parlement), is bicameral. The lower chamber, the National Assembly (Assemblée Nationale), has 111 members, directly elected for a five-year term. The upper chamber, the House of Representatives (Chambre des Représentants), is a consultative body with 178 members, appointed or indirectly elected by provincial councils and a variety of interest groups, for a three-year term.

Profile of the President:

Capt. Blaise **COMPAORÉ**

Capt. Blaise Compaoré has been president since the 1987 military coup which overthrew his former fellow parachute officer Thomas Sankara. Compaoré's military regime gave way to a multiparty system in 1991, when a new constitution was approved by referendum. He was elected in December 1991, under controversial circumstances and re-elected in 1998. Constitutional changes in 2000 established that this should be his final term in office.

Born on 3 February 1951 in Ouagadougou, Blaise Compaoré joined the army and was sent as a parachute trainee to the Yaoundé military school in Cameroon, where he first met fellow trainee Sankara. He graduated as an officer in 1978, going on to become a commander at the National Commando Training Centre in the town of Po in southern Burkina. When Sankara took power in a 1983 coup, establishing an avowedly Marxist–Leninist government, he appointed Compaoré as minister of state to the presidency and as a member of the National Revolutionary Council. Compaoré subsequently became minister of justice, holding this post from 1984 to 1987.

In October 1987, following disagreements with Sankara, Compaoré mounted his own coup. Together with up to 100 others, Sankara was killed in fighting in the capital during the struggle. Compaoré declared himself chairman of the Popular Front (Front Populaire—FP) and head of state, and formed a new government on 31 October. Over the succeeding years he followed policies of 'rectification' which, although nominally socialist, in fact featured economic reforms including the privatization of state-run industry. In 1989 he founded the Organization for Popular Democracy–Labour Movement (Organisation pour la Démocratie Populaire–Mouvement du Travail—ODP–MT).

In June 1991 Compaoré retired from the army under public pressure and announced multiparty elections. On 1 December he was elected president in a direct election in which he was the sole candidate. Opposition parties boycotted the contest (in which there was a turnout of only 28%) after the breakdown of tripartite talks, complaining of the lack of any prospect of a national conference. Violent protests followed, and a leading opposition figure was killed in a bomb explosion.

Condemning this violence as the work of the enemies of democracy, Compaoré postponed legislative elections due in January 1992 and announced that a national reconciliation forum would be convened forthwith to consider democracy, human rights and development. When the legislative elections did take place, in May 1992, opposition parties claimed that massive fraud had occurred. Compaoré's ODP–MT won three-quarters of the seats, and repeated this success five years later, having in the meantime absorbed several opposition groupings and restyled itself as the Congress for Democracy and Progress (Congrès pour la Démocratie et le Progrès—CDP).

Although Compaoré's personal hold on power appears to remain strong, his CDP government has suffered from continuing accusations of human rights abuses. The death of journalist Norbert Zongo in 1998 caused particular discontent. A variety of opposition parties chose to compete in the 2002 legislative elections, having boycotted previous polls, and the CDP was reduced to a narrow overall majority.

Profile of the Prime Minister:

Paramanga Ernest **YONLI**

Paramanga Ernest Yonli is an economist by training, with a university education completed in France, and a background in agricultural development, on which he has written extensively. Fluent in English as well as French, he worked in

Burkina as a researcher on regional food-related issues before entering government in 1996.

Paramanga Ernest Yonli was born in 1956 at Tansarga, Tapoa province. He moved to the capital for his secondary education in 1969, and in 1976 he entered the University of Ouagadougou to study economics, graduating in 1979. Two years later he gained a master's degree in economics, specializing in planning and development, from the University of Benin (Togo). In 1981 he moved to France for further study at the Sorbonne in Paris, gaining a diploma in international economy and development in 1984, and a doctorate from the University of Paris in agricultural development in 1985. He is married with three children.

An association with the Netherlands, marked by the award of a doctorate from the University of Ouagadougou/University of Gronigen (Netherlands) in 1987, led to his involvement in the latter part of the 1980s with agricultural development studies and projects in Burkina Faso undertaken with Dutch co-operation and financing. Between December 1988 and October 1990 his work was based at the Dutch embassy in Ouagadougou. In 1990 the focus of his work moved to the Centre d'Etudes, de Documentation, de Recherches Economique et Sociales (CEDRES) at the University of Ouagadougou and the University's faculty of economics and management, where he stayed until 1994. During this time he was a member of a Dutch–Burkinabé–Ghanaian research group on regional food security and sustainable development and gained a bursary from the Dutch Foundation for the Advancement of Tropical Research (WOTRO).

Yonli was appointed to the government in February 1996 by President Compaoré, serving firstly as director of the prime minister's office, and subsequently as minister of public office and institutional development, before becoming prime minister in November 2000.

BURUNDI

Full name: The Republic of Burundi.

Leadership structure: The 1998 transitional Constitution provides for a president, but abolished the post of prime minister. The Council of Ministers is appointed by the president.

President: Maj. Pierre Buyoya   Since 11 June 1998
(head of military junta from 25 July 1996)

Legislature: Under the 1998 Constitution, a seven-member Constitutional Court led by President Buyoya was appointed on 24 June 1998. A transitional National Assembly (Assemblée Nationale) was inaugurated on 18 July 1998, composed of 117 members from most political parties and civilian society. A further 53 members of the National Assembly were elected on 1 January 2002. A transitional Senate (Sénat) with 51 co-opted members was inaugurated on 4 February 2002, in accordance with the Arusha peace deal.

Profile of the President:

Maj. Pierre **BUYOYA**

Maj. Pierre Buyoya has been head of state of Burundi since July 1996, when troops loyal to him overthrew the government of interim President Sylvestre Ntibantunganya in a bloodless coup. A member of the Tutsi ethnic group, and a former career soldier who had already seized power once a decade earlier, Buyoya justified his 1996 military intervention as a move to avert ethnic violence between majority Hutus and minority Tutsis.

Pierre Buyoya was born on 24 November 1949. Pursuing a military career, he trained in Belgium, at the Royal Military Academy in Brussels, and in France and the then West Germany, before returning to become an officer in Burundi, where successive military regimes had been in place since 1966. In 1982 Buyoya became a member of the central committee of the ruling and sole party, the ostensibly left-wing Union for National Progress (Union pour le Progrès National—Uprona). He rose to the rank of major, but was nevertheless little known until September 1987, when he led the military coup in which President Jean-Baptiste Bagaza was deposed.

For the next five years Buyoya ruled as head of the Military Committee for National Salvation. Relying on the support of the small Tutsi elite, he nevertheless attempted to aid Tutsi–Hutu reconciliation, releasing hundreds of political prisoners and appointing Hutus to ministerial posts.

In March 1992 Buyoya approved a constitution providing for the country's first multiparty elections. The resulting June 1993 presidential election saw his defeat by Melchior Ndadaye, who thus became Burundi's first Hutu president.

As ethnic tension persisted, with clashes between the largely Tutsi army and Hutu militants, Ndadaye and several of his ministers were murdered in a Tutsi coup attempt in late 1993, and his Hutu successor, Cyprien Ntaryamira, was killed in a helicopter crash in April 1994. (It was the death of the Rwandan president, a passenger in the same helicopter, which precipitated the attempted genocide by Hutus against Tutsis in neighbouring Rwanda.) Interethnic tension continued to bedevil the supposed four-year transition period which was then initiated under a power-sharing interim government formula.

Buyoya's second coup, on 25 July 1996, was followed up by the suspension of the parliament and a ban on political parties. These measures were lifted two months later, while the civilian cabinet appointed by Buyoya featured members of the rival parties and a Hutu prime minister. However, Buyoya's attempts to establish democratic credentials (with presidential and legislative elections originally scheduled for June 1998) were dealt a serious blow when a UN report published in 1996 named him and other senior army officers as instigators of the murder of Ndadaye in 1993. The international community shunned his regime, with neighbouring states imposing an economic boycott which seriously damaged the economy. Meanwhile fighting continued.

Former South African president Nelson Mandela led renewed international efforts to talk peace in Burundi in 2000 and a peace deal was eventually wrung out in Arusha, in neighbouring Tanzania. A joint Hutu–Tutsi transitional government was finally established in late 2001 with Buyoya scheduled to hand over the presidency to his new Hutu vice president Domitien Ndayizeye after 18 months. However, fighting continued as various Hutu rebel groups repeatedly shunned the talks.

CAMBODIA

Full name: Kingdom of Cambodia.

Leadership structure: The head of state under the 1993 Constitution is the king. The head of government is the prime minister, responsible to the Parliament but appointed by the king. The Royal Government of Cambodia is appointed by the prime minister.

King: Norodom Sihanouk   Since 24 Sept. 1993
(head of state from 20 Nov. 1991)

Prime Minister: Hun Sen   Since 26 Nov. 1998
(head of government from 14 Jan. 1985)

Legislature: The legislature, the Parliament, is bicameral. The lower chamber, the National Assembly (Radhsphea Ney Preah Recheanachakr Kampuchea), has 122 members, directly elected for a five-year term. A 61-member Senate was approved by the National Assembly on 4 March 1999, and held its first session on 25 March. Its membership was determined in proportion to the results of the 1998 legislative elections, with senators serving a five-year term.

Profile of the King:

SIHANOUK

King Sihanouk has been Cambodia's head of state since the 1991 UN-sponsored peace agreement. First crowned king at 18 in 1941, under French colonial administration, he subsequently went into exile as a national figure campaigning for independence, and returned to lead Cambodia along the path of nonalignment. Ousted in a US-backed coup in 1970, he allied himself with Chinese-backed communist insurgents, but was effectively a prisoner of the murderous Khmer Rouge regime between 1975 and 1979, and spent the 1980s as head of an anti-Vietnamese coalition government-in-exile.

Norodom Sihanouk was born on 31 October 1922 in Phnom Penh, the capital of Cambodia. The country was at that time under French colonial rule as part of Indochina, and the young prince's early education was in Paris. He returned to Indochina to attend secondary school in Saigon in Viet Nam, later returning to France for military training.

Upon the death of his grandfather, Sihanouk was proclaimed king of Cambodia, for the first time, on 26 April 1941. The Vichy government in France supported this choice, anticipating that his inexperience and reputation for high living would make him easy to manipulate. However, Sihanouk proved to be no mere jazz-loving playboy but a subtle and astute political operator, and increasingly significant as a national independence leader. In 1953–54 he mounted a protest against French rule by going into exile, returning only when independence was achieved. By abdicating the throne in favour of his father in 1955 he freed himself to play an unfettered political role. Retaining the title of prince, he effectively controlled internal affairs through his political movement Sangkum (Popular Socialist Community—Sangkum Reastr Niyum), while holding office as prime minister and minister of foreign affairs until 1956, and then as ambassador at the UN. On his father's death in 1960 he became once again head of state, but he declined to take up the title of king.

A participant at the founding conference of the Non-Aligned Movement in Belgrade, Yugoslavia, in 1961, Sihanouk demonstrated great skill in getting aid from both superpowers at the height of the Cold War, but ultimately was unable to keep Cambodia isolated from the region's dominant confrontation, the Viet Nam War. The US government suspected him of complicity with the North Vietnamese and of allowing them the use of Cambodian territory, and in 1970 he was driven into exile by Lon Nol's US-backed right-wing military coup. Controversially, as Cambodia was being shattered in what the US military cynically regarded as a 'sideshow' to their Viet Nam War, Sihanouk then allied himself with the Cambodian communist Khmers Rouges. Concluding a national unity front agreement (Front Uni National du Kampuchéa—FUNK) in Beijing, he became a figurehead in their insurgency, and was named head of state of Democratic Kampuchea when they took control of Phnom Penh in 1975. Virtually a prisoner in the royal palace, however, Sihanouk resigned the following year, finding to his enduring shame that he had no power to restrain the Pol Pot government's genocidal policies. Among perhaps as many as two million Cambodians killed by the Khmers Rouges were five of Sihanouk's own children.

Sihanouk managed to flee in 1979 when the Khmers Rouges were ousted by intervention from Viet Nam. He spent the next decade in exile, living mainly in Beijing and in the North Korean capital Pyongyang. The Khmers Rouges, driven out of Phnom Penh, struck back at the new regime from border areas, in uneasy alliance with noncommunist guerrillas. To Sihanouk, the Vietnamese domination of his country was so great an evil that he was tempted back into the expediency of alliance with the Khmers Rouges once again. Accordingly, if reluctantly, he agreed in 1982 to join a tripartite anti-Vietnamese coalition, the so-called 'coalition government of Democratic Kampuchea' (CGDK). The government-in-exile over which he presided received wide international recognition, with Western backing, notwithstanding the fact that the Khmers Rouges were militarily its strongest element.

During this period Sihanouk worked to build up the credibility of his own guerrilla forces, founding a National United Front for an Independent, Neutral, Peaceful and Co-operative Cambodia (Front Uni National pour un Cambodge Indépendant, Neutre, Pacifique et Co-opératif—Funcinpec). In 1989 the CGDK was superseded by a so-called National Government of Cambodia, with Sihanouk again its president.

Viet Nam pulled its forces out in 1989, and in 1991 a UN-brokered peace accord was concluded between the three anti-Vietnamese factions and the Hun Sen government in Phnom Penh. Sihanouk took on the presidency of a new Supreme National Council of Cambodia in July 1991, which recognized him as the legitimate head of state in November, and elections went ahead in 1993 despite a Khmer Rouge withdrawal from the peace process. The May polls were dominated by Sihanouk's royalist supporters on the one hand, and the former Phnom Penh government led by Hun Sen on the other, an outcome which Sihanouk recognized in putting together a power-sharing agreement between them. This formula, in which Sihanouk was confirmed as head of state on 14 June, created a joint premiership between Hun Sen and Sihanouk's son Prince Norodom Ranariddh. (Sihanouk has married six times and has fathered, by his count, 14 children.) A vote in the Parliament approved a proposal to restore the monarchy, and Sihanouk thus became king once again, on 24 September 1993.

Suspecting that royalists were promoting reconciliation with the remaining Khmer Rouge rebels to tilt the balance of power, Hun Sen in mid-1997 tightened his own grip in what was effectively a coup, driving out Ranariddh and naming a replacement himself. Sihanouk's response was equivocal, neither outright condemnation nor acquiescence. He was by now old and ill, a distant figure living mainly in Beijing, and once again his behaviour reflected his appreciation of the realities of power. Remaining aloof from the political fray as Hun Sen pushed through the holding of elections in July 1998, he then offered to mediate to resolve the postelection stalemate, and managed to broker a deal which eventually led to a renewed coalition government.

Profile of the Prime Minister:

HUN SEN

Hun Sen is vice chairman of the socialist Cambodian People's Party (CPP). A one-time Khmer Rouge guerrilla who fell out with that movement's 1975–79 regime, he returned from exile as part of the Vietnamese-backed government when the Khmers Rouges were driven out, and then led one side of the coalition government formed after the UN-sponsored May 1993 elections. Ousting his copremier in 1997, he was effectively re-elected in 1998 and heads a surprisingly durable coalition with the royalists.

Hun Sen was born in Kampong Cham province on 5 August 1952, although his official birth date is given as 4 April 1951. He studied in Phnom Penh before joining the Khmer Rouge guerrillas in 1970, eventually rising to commandant, and losing an eye in 1975 in the successful Khmer Rouge attack on Phnom Penh which ended their long insurgency. That year Hun Sen married Bun Sam Hieng, and they have three sons and three daughters.

In 1977, alienated from the genocidal new regime, and facing the threat of a purge, Hun Sen fled to Viet Nam, becoming leader of an anti-Pol Pot group there and founding in 1978 the Kampuchean National United Front for National Salvation (KNUFNS). This formed a nucleus for the government installed in Phnom Penh after the Vietnamese-backed military operation which drove the Khmer Rouge regime from the capital in 1979.

Hun Sen was foreign minister between 1979 and 1985 in this government, which renamed the country the People's Republic of Kampuchea (PRK), but was denied wide international recognition, the West backing instead an exile coalition government including both Prince Sihanouk's royalists and the Khmers Rouges. Heavily involved in the fighting, mainly against Khmer Rouge forces, Hun Sen became in addition deputy prime minister in 1981 and prime minister, despite his youth, in January 1985. He was thus a signatory of the October 1991 Paris accords which allowed for the return of Sihanouk and the holding of elections. That same month the PRK's ruling party, the Kampuchean People's Revolutionary Party (KPRP), renounced Marxism–Leninism and adopted the new CPP name. Hun Sen, a moderate in party terms, became deputy party leader with hard-liner Chea Sim as president.

The elections held in May 1993 under UN supervision (but boycotted by the Khmers Rouges) resulted in a victory for the royalist National United Front for an Independent, Neutral, Peaceful and Co-operative Cambodia (Front Uni National pour un Cambodge Indépendant, Neutre, Pacifique et Co-opératif—Funcinpec). Hun Sen's government, however, refused to relinquish power, and the compromise coalition formula, with two copremiers—Hun Sen and Prince Ranarridh—was eventually agreed in June. Under the new constitution, adopted in September, Ranarridh became 'first' prime minister and Hun Sen 'second' prime minister. In the ensuing years (until the events of July 1997) the government, still dogged by a Khmer Rouge insurgency in the northwest, moved gradually to introduce free-market economic reforms. However there were growing signs of authoritarianism and a Hun Sen personality cult, fostered in the face of tensions within the coalition (and factional differences within both of its constituent halves). Assessments of Hun Sen stressed his hard work, tactical astuteness and continual drive to extend his power base, while also noting the fear he inspired in opponents, and his displays of anger when crossed.

In July 1997 Hun Sen ousted Ranariddh. Despite some attempts to explain this as a pre-emptive strike against a royalist deal with remaining elements of the Khmers Rouges, Hun Sen's move was generally portrayed as a cynical consolidation of his power, encouraged also by personal animosities. Despite the misgivings of the international community, elections held in July 1998 were described as 'free and fair' by the UN Joint Inspection Team. Hun Sen, having initially refused to stand in the election, emerged as the power broker in coalition negotiations which were increasingly dogged by violence. Four months later a coalition was finally agreed between the CPP and the royalist Funcinpec, with Hun Sen as sole prime minister and Ranarridh as speaker of the National Assembly.

Since then Hun Sen has overseen a relatively liberal government. He stepped down as commander-in-chief of the armed forces in January 1999 and the government has promoted its environmental policies. He is still in discussion with the UN on setting up trials of the former members of the Khmer Rouge.

CAMEROON

Full name: The Republic of Cameroon.

Leadership structure: The head of state is a president, directly elected by universal adult suffrage. The president's term of office is seven years. The president appoints the ministers, including the prime minister, who is head of government.

President:	Paul Biya	Since 6 Nov. 1982
Prime Minister:	Peter Mafany Musonge	Since 19 Sept. 1996

Legislature: The unicameral legislature, the National Assembly (Assemblée Nationale), has 180 members, directly elected for a five-year term.

Profile of the President:

Paul **BIYA**

Trained in France in law and public administration, Paul Biya became president of Cameroon in 1982 on the resignation of Ahmadou Ahidjo, whom he had previously served under as prime minister. A Roman Catholic and a southerner, he oversaw a transition from single-party rule to multiparty politics in the early 1990s. He was elected for further presidential terms in 1992 and again for a seven-year term in 1997. However, his swearing-in ceremony on 3 November 1997 was boycotted by opposition deputies in a protest over what they alleged was massive electoral fraud.

Paul Biya was born on 13 February 1933 in Mvomeka'a, in the south of Cameroon. He is the father of three children, and married his second wife in April 1994.

He was educated at local Catholic schools and at the Lycée Général Leclerc in Yaoundé, before going to France in 1956 to study for a degree in public law at the University of Paris. Graduating in 1960, he spent the subsequent two years at the Institut d'Etudes Politiques and the Institut des Hautes Etudes d'Outre-mer. He returned to Cameroon in 1962, going into the postindependence civil service as a *chargé de mission* in the department of foreign aid (1962–63). In 1963 he obtained a postgraduate diploma in public law. In 1964 he moved to the ministry of national education, youth and culture. Biya also served on a goodwill mission to Ghana and Nigeria.

In December 1967 he was appointed director of the civil cabinet of Cameroon. Early the next year he was also made general secretary to the president, and in 1970 he became a minister of state in the president's office. He was appointed prime minister in June 1975, but was regarded as still having a relatively low-profile advisory role until November 1982, when Ahidjo stepped aside for health reasons and handed over the presidency to Biya as his designated successor.

The appointment of Biya, a francophone Catholic from southern Cameroon, directly challenged the political hegemony of the northern Muslims. Several revolts seriously threatened his rule in 1983–84, the first of them blamed on Ahidjo himself, who fled the country and resigned his remaining post as head of the ruling party, the Cameroon National Union (Union Nationale Camerounaise—UNC). Biya consolidated his position, taking over the party leadership himself and having his role as president confirmed by an overwhelming majority in the January 1984 election. Promising some gradual steps towards greater democratization, he restyled the ruling party in 1985 as the Cameroon People's Democratic Movement (Rassemblement Démocratique du Peuple Camerounais—RDPC), and initiated some measures of social and economic liberalization.

Presidential elections in April 1988 were held on the basis that he was the sole candidate, producing the required near-unanimous endorsement, but pressure for political pluralism ultimately led to the drafting of a new constitution, which was formalized in November 1990 and opened the way for multiparty elections. When these took place in 1992 the RDPC won most seats, but not an overall majority, in the legislature. Biya himself only narrowly won the presidential poll in October, claiming almost 40% of the vote against almost 36% officially credited to John Fru Ndi of the Social Democratic Front (SDF).

Thereafter the SDF mounted a sustained campaign for an all-party national conference and an interim government to supervise fresh elections. Biya refused to cede authority from his own government in this way, but his re-election as president on 17 May 1997, when he was recorded as having won 92.5% of the vote, was marred by opposition claims of fraud, and a low turnout in the north and west of the country in response to boycott calls. Nonetheless, Biya has remained in power, despite vocal and often physical opposition from the SDF, which accuses Biya and his government of corruption and sanctioning extrajudicial killings. Biya's regime also faces growing calls for autonomy from the anglophone west.

Profile of the Prime Minister:

Peter Mafany **MUSONGE**

Paul Mafany Musonge is a qualified civil engineer, who became prime minister in September 1996, with no previous direct political experience.

Paul Mafany Musonge was born on 3 December 1942 at Buea, Fako department, in the southwest of the country. He received his secondary education at St Joseph's College in Buea between 1957 and 1961, and then travelled to the USA, where he graduated in civil engineering from the Drexel Institute of Technology, Philadelphia, in 1967, and gained a master's degree in structural engineering from Stanford University, California, in 1968.

He returned to Cameroon, and from March 1969 worked as an engineer in the west of the country. From 1970 until 1980 he was employed as an engineer by the ministry of transport, and subsequently by the ministry of housing and roads. In 1980 he was appointed director of the Laboratoire National de Génie Civil, a post he held until 1984, when he became director of the Parc National de Matériel de Génie Civil (MATGENIE). In 1988 he moved to the post of director-general of the Cameroon Development Corporation (CDC), where he worked for eight years until President Biya picked him to become prime minister. Musonge is married with four children.

CANADA

Full name: Canada.

Leadership structure: The head of state is the British sovereign, styled 'of the United Kingdom, Canada and Her other Realms and Territories, Queen, Head of the Commonwealth, Defender of the Faith', and represented by a governor-general who is appointed on the advice of the Canadian prime minister. The head of government is the prime minister, who is appointed by the governor-general. The cabinet is appointed by the governor-general on the recommendation of the prime minister.

Queen:	Elizabeth II	Since 6 Feb. 1952
Governor-General:	Adrienne Clarkson	Since 7 Oct. 1999
Prime Minister:	Jean Chrétien	Since 4 Nov. 1993

Legislature: The legislature, the Parliament, is bicameral. The lower chamber, the House of Commons, has 301 members, directly elected for a five-year term. The upper chamber, the Senate, has 105 members appointed by the governor-general on the recommendation of the prime minister. Senators retain their seats until age 75.

Profile of the Governor-General:

Adrienne **CLARKSON**

Adrienne Clarkson has a long history as one of Canada's leading television journalists, producing and presenting many shows for the Canadian Broadcasting Corporation (CBC) since 1965. Her appointment in October 1999 as governor-general broke with the recent trend of ex-politicians, and her Chinese birth makes her the first immigrant to hold the post.

Adrienne Clarkson (née Poy) was born to Chinese parents in Hong Kong in 1939. Her family fled the Japanese advance in the Second World War, arriving as refugees in Canada in 1942. She received a public school education in Ottawa and graduated with a master's degree in English literature from the University of Toronto. She studied as a postgraduate at the Sorbonne in Paris, France, and as a member of the Chinese-Canadian minority she is notable for her ability to speak both English and French fluently. From 1965 to 1982 she forged her career as a producer, writer and host of a number of successful CBC television programmes including *Take Thirty* and *Adrienne at Large*. She has also written a number of articles and three books. During this period she was married (from 1963 to 1975), to the political scientist Stephen Clarkson, and they had two daughters. She married her current husband, the political writer John Ralston Saul, in 1999 after a 15-year romance.

From 1982 to 1987 Clarkson was the first agent-general for the state of Ontario in Paris. Her duties in this post were to promote Ontario's business and cultural interests to Europe, foreshadowing her role as governor-general. In 1987 she became the president of the Canadian publisher McClelland & Stewart until returning to broadcasting in 1988. For the next ten years she was executive producer, writer and host for the programmes *Adrienne Clarkson's Summer Festival* and *Adrienne Clarkson Presents*. As well as these achievements she also wrote and directed several films, receiving various television industry awards from Canada and the USA. From 1998 until her appointment as governor-general, Clarkson served as chair of the Board of Trustees of the Canadian Museum of Civilization in Hull, Québec, and as president of IMZ (an international association of cultural programmers based in Vienna, Austria) as well as continuing her work as a television presenter and producer.

In 1999 she was taken by surprise at her nomination to be governor-general in succession to the retiring Roméo LeBlanc. She became the second female holder of this office. She promised to travel extensively in Canada to meet the populace during her five-year tenure, and announced her desire to spend more time in the governor-general's second official residence, La Citadelle in Québec City.

Profile of the Prime Minister:

Jean **CHRÉTIEN**

Jean Chrétien, a francophone Québécois from a working-class background with a populist 'little man' image, is a lawyer by training. He has spent 40 years in active politics, and has extensive government experience at federal level. Now in a record third consecutive term of office as prime minister, he first came to power following the Liberal Party's landslide victory in the 1993 general election, but has seen the party progressively lose support outside its Ontario heartland as regional considerations have come to dominate the federal political picture. He publicly announced in August 2002 that he would not seek a fourth term and would step down as party leader in 2004.

Jean Chrétien was born in Shawinigan, Québec, on 11 January 1934. His father was a machinist in a paper mill and an organizer for the Liberal Party. The 18th of 19 children in the family, he contracted polio at a young age, which left him with a distorted mouth and one deaf ear. He was educated at local schools and at the age of 12 began attending party rallies and working for the Liberal Party. He studied law at Laval University (Québec), where he ran the Liberal club and promoted the party in the 1956 elections. He married Aline Chaine in 1957, and they have three children. He was called to the Bar in 1958, and practised law for several years thereafter. In 1962 he worked as a director with the Shawinigan senior chamber of commerce.

In 1963 Chrétien was elected to the House of Commons for the first time, representing the constituency of St-Maurice-Lafleche, a seat which he held at successive elections for over 20 years. He began to rise through the ranks of the Liberal Party and gained wide ministerial experience in the 1960s, as parliamentary secretary to Prime Minister Lester Pearson in 1965, secretary to the minister of finance from 1966 to 1967, minister without portfolio from 1967, and minister of Amerindian affairs and northern development from July 1968 in the new government of Pierre Trudeau. He later became president of the treasury board (1974–76). By 1976 he had been appointed minister of trade, industry and commerce. He was the first French Canadian to be minister of finance, a post he held from 1977 to 1979, by which time he was considered a senior figure in the Liberal Party.

Becoming minister of justice, attorney general and minister of state for social development in 1980, Chrétien was made responsible for constitutional negotiations. As such he was a strong advocate of Canadian unity, and led the 'no' campaign in the 1980 referendum on the independence of Québec. The culmination of his work in this ministry was the repatriation of Canada's constitution in 1982. In September 1982 he was named as minister of energy, mines and resources.

In 1984 Chrétien failed in his first bid for the leadership of the Liberal Party, which, following the announcement of Trudeau's resignation, was defeated in a general election. After two years Chrétien resigned from the House of Commons and returned to private legal practice. He also became a senior adviser with Gordon Capital Corporation in Montreal.

Chrétien succeeded in a second bid for the party leadership in 1990, was re-elected to Parliament, and became leader of the opposition in December of that year. In part because of his work in rebuilding the party between 1990 and 1993, but largely because of the massive unpopularity of the Progressive Conservative government, he led the Liberals to a landslide victory in the November 1993 elections.

Initially Chrétien was a popular prime minister. He pushed through policies on cutting the defence budget, and stressed Canada's independence from its US neighbour, notably on environmental issues and foreign policy, while seeking renegotiation of the terms of the recently concluded North American Free Trade Agreement (NAFTA). The threat of secessionism in Québec, which he steadfastly opposes, has however dogged his government, along with the broader constitutional issues of relations between the federal government and the provinces. A referendum on Québec sovereignty was almost carried in late 1995, despite concessions to the province which gave it the status of a 'distinct society' and which risked provoking resentment in provinces which did not get equivalent treatment. The regional backlash at the June 1997 elections greatly weakened Chrétien's position, effectively confining the Liberal Party's power base to Ontario (a paradoxical situation when its leader is from Québec) and leaving it with only a narrow parliamentary majority.

The party's fortunes were revived in 2000, however, when Chrétien announced a large public spending programme directly before calling snap elections. Profiting also from the internal chaos of the recently renamed conservative opposition Canadian Alliance, the Liberals were able to win an unprecedented third consecutive term in office in the November elections with an increased majority in the lower house.

Chrétien has since begun to voice concern over the unilateral approach to foreign and environmental policy taken by the new right-wing US government of George W. Bush. He was forced in 2002 to announce that George Bush "is not a moron at all" after an aide disparaged the US leader's intelligence, but has repeatedly urged caution over US plans to launch a war against Iraq. Nevertheless he has strengthened the government's position on forging the world's largest trading bloc across the Americas by 2005. Facing rumours of a leadership challenge, Chrétien announced in August 2002 that he would step down as Liberal Party leader in February 2004 to allow a new leadership to take it into elections due by 2005.

CAPE VERDE

Full name: The Republic of Cape Verde.

Leadership structure: The head of state is a president, directly elected by universal adult suffrage. The president's term of office is five years. The head of government is the prime minister, who is responsible to the National Assembly. The Council of Ministers is appointed by the prime minister.

Presidents:	António Mascarenhas Monteiro	22 March 1991—22 March 2001
	Pedro Pires	Since 22 March 2001
Prime Ministers:	Carlos Veiga (acting from 28 Jan. 1991)	4 April 1991—5 Oct. 2000
	António Gualberto do Rosário (acting from 29 July 2000)	5 Oct. 2000—1 Feb. 2001
	José Maria Neves	Since 1 Feb. 2001

Legislature: The legislature is unicameral. The sole chamber, the National Assembly (Assembléia Nacional), has 72 members, directly elected for a five-year term.

Profile of the President:

Pedro **PIRES**

Pedro Pires is a veteran of the armed struggle against Portuguese colonialism in Africa, and was independent Cape Verde's first prime minister in 1975. He led the ruling left-wing African Party for the Independence of Cape Verde (Partido Africano da Independência de Cabo Verde—PAICV) into multipartyism, and ultimately defeat in 1991, but returned to the limelight in 2001, riding the wave of the party's electoral revival. Although long seen as on the political left, he now champions a more pragmatic, liberal approach. As president his influence is overshadowed by the constitutional power of the prime minister.

Pedro Verona Rodrigues Pires was born on 29 April 1934 on the island of Fogo (Fire Island) in what was then the Portuguese colony of Cape Verde and Portuguese Guinea (modern-day Guinea-Bissau). He was educated in the islands before heading for Lisbon, Portugal, in 1956 to attend the faculty of science at the city's university. On graduation he was drafted into the Portuguese Air Force where he met with other people from Portugal's scattered colonies. He was already dedicated to the liberation of his homeland, and deserted from the air force in June 1961 in order to join the burgeoning anti-colonial movement back in Africa.

After taking an indirect route through Spain and France, Pires arrived in Ghana in September 1961. There he met the pro-independence leader Amilcar Cabral and joined his African Party for the Independence of Guinea and Cape Verde (Partido Africano da Independência de Guiné e Cabo Verde—PAIGC). The independence struggle in lusophone Africa was interconnected and Pires travelled to Morocco to join the secretariat of the Conference of the Nationalist Organizations within the Portuguese Colonies. The movement took up arms in Guinea in 1963 and Pires was appointed to the central committee of the PAIGC in 1965, and to its Council of War in 1967.

As the PAIGC forces gained ground, Pires served from 1971 in the administration of the liberated areas in the south of what is now Guinea-Bissau and was appointed assistant state commissioner in the first government of that country in 1973. In the same year he was also elected president of the National Committee of the PAIGC for Cape Verde and was at the centre of successful negotiations for the independence of the two connected African territories in 1974. Cape Verde and Guinea-Bissau separated and Pires returned to his country of origin to serve as director of party policy in the transitional government of Cape Verde, before being elected to the newly created National Popular Assembly in June. In the country's first postcolonial government he was appointed prime minister. In the same year he married Adélcia Maria da Luz Lima Barreto; they have two daughters.

During Pires's three consecutive prime ministerial terms (1975–91), Cape Verde was run as a left-wing single-party state. Following a coup in Guinea-Bissau and the abandonment of the idea of reunifying the two states, the Cape Verdian branch of the PAIGC separated to form the PAICV in 1981. Pires served as its deputy secretary-general, under the leadership of the then President Aristides Pereira.

As part of a trend towards multipartyism throughout Africa, the PAIGC agreed in 1990 to free elections. Pires replaced Pereira as secretary-general, but in the first free polls in February 1991 the PAICV was resoundingly beaten by the Movement for Democracy. Pires stayed at the helm of the defeated party for another three years.

The PAICV was beaten again in 1996 but saw its popularity return in the late 1990s. In legislative elections in January 2001 it secured a safe majority and nominated Pires as its presidential candidate for the following month. Despite the party's renewed vigour, Pires won the race by only 17 votes. He took office on 22 March.

Profile of the Prime Minister:

José Maria **NEVES**

José Maria Neves, a Brazilian-trained administrator, became leader of the African Party for the Independence of Cape Verde (Partido Africano da Independência de Cabo Verde—PAICV) in time to lead it back to power in the 2001 elections after a ten-year stint in opposition. He is seen as a champion of the younger, more technocratic generation of Cape Verdian politicians now taking over from the veterans of the anti-colonial struggle.

José Maria Pereira Neves was born on 28 March 1960 in Santa Catarina, on the island of São Tiago (Santiago). He was educated in public administration at the Getúlio Vargas Foundation in São Paulo, Brazil. He has worked specifically on organizational development and management of human resources and was director of the National Centre of Public Administration.

Neves's political career began in local government in Santa Catarina. Going on to win election to the National Assembly, he became its vice president. He was appointed prime minister and minister of defence in February 2001 after leading the PAICV back to power in January.

CENTRAL AFRICAN REPUBLIC

Full name: The Central African Republic.

Leadership structure: The head of state is a president, directly elected by universal adult suffrage. The president's term of office is six years. The head of government is the prime minister, who is appointed by the president and appoints the Council of Ministers.

President:	Ange-Félix Patassé	Since 22 Oct. 1993
Prime Ministers:	Anicet Georges Dologuélé	4 Jan. 1999—1 April 2001
	Martin Ziguélé	Since 1 April 2001

Legislature: The legislature is unicameral. The sole chamber, the National Assembly (Assemblée Nationale), has 109 members, directly elected for a five-year term.

Profile of the President:

Ange-Félix **PATASSÉ**

Ange-Félix Patassé is a former agronomist and one-time communist militant, whose turbulent political career includes a spell as prime minister under the notorious regime of self-styled Emperor Bokassa. Patassé was founding president (in exile) of the Movement for the Liberation of the Central African People (Mouvement pour la Libération du Peuple Centrafricain—MLPC) in 1979 and spent most of the 1980s in detention or in exile. His election as president in 1993 marked the end of the military dictatorship of Gen. André Kolingba.

Born on 25 January 1937 in Paoua, Ange-Félix Patassé was educated at the higher school of tropical agriculture in Nogent-sur-Marne in France. An agricultural inspector from 1959 to 1965, he then began a political career, initially as director of agriculture, then as minister of development in 1965. The following year Jean-Bédel Bokassa seized power in a military coup.

In 1969, after several years out of government, Patassé returned to the cabinet, and over the next seven years held a variety of ministerial positions under the Bokassa regime. These included responsibility for transport and power, for development and tourism, for agriculture and forests, for transport and commerce, for rural development and for health and social affairs. From 1974 to 1976 he was minister of state for tourism, waters, fishing and hunting.

In 1976 Bokassa appointed Patassé as prime minister of the Central African Republic (CAR). Later in the year, when Bokassa declared himself emperor, Patassé's post was restyled 'vice president of the Council of the Central African Revolution', a new body which took the place of the government. However, within two years he had fallen out of favour with Bokassa, who dismissed him in 1978, ostensibly for embezzlement of public funds.

Having fled to Paris, where he founded the MLPC in 1979, Patassé returned when Bokassa was ousted with the help of French troops in September of that year. However, he was immediately put under house arrest, and although he escaped he was soon recaptured and detained for a further year. In 1981 he was a candidate in the presidential election, but lost to the incumbent David Dacko, who was ousted by Gen. Kolingba a few months later. Patassé, accused in April 1982 of plotting against Kolingba, took refuge in the French embassy before fleeing to Togo.

Patassé remained in exile for the next ten years before returning to the CAR, when as the MLPC candidate he successfully contested the presidential elections held in two rounds in August and September 1993. Sworn in on 22 October, he ruled in conjunction with a government in which a number of parties accepted representation (the MLPC having failed to win an overall Assembly majority in the legislative elections), but significantly increased his own powers under constitutional amendments introduced from the beginning of 1995.

Despite the 1993 elections being held under French supervision, French officials later expressed dissatisfaction over corruption and ethnic bias in Patassé's administration. A member of the Baya ethnic group himself, Patassé faced particular opposition within the Yakoma-dominated military, and he had to rely on intervention by French troops (garrisoned in the CAR) on several occasions to restore order when civilian strikes were followed by army mutinies during his first term.

Patassé's re-election in September 1999 was instantly rejected by the nine main opposition parties, who claimed widespread fraud. Patassé was awarded 52% of the vote against his nearest rival, Kolingba, who received 19%. Patassé was inaugurated for his second six-year term on 22 October 1999. Public demonstrations against Patassé and the state of the economy ended in the arrest of some opposition deputies in December 2000, prompting their parties to boycott the National Assembly.

Discontent turned into open insurrection in May 2001 when soldiers loyal to Kolingba were defeated in pitched battles in Bangui by loyalist troops and Chadian, Congolese and Libyan allies. The situation was complicated when the army chief of staff Gen. François Bozize led another mutiny in November that year. Patassé was forced to rely once more on Libyan support. Fighting reignited in October 2002 and there was a public outcry when Libyan planes bombed areas of Bangui in their efforts to put down this latest mutiny, which had spread to the northern hinterland. Bozize was eventually exiled to France, via Chad, while Kolingba remains a wanted man.

Profile of the Prime Minister:

Martin **ZIGUÉLÉ**

Martin Ziguélé had no government experience or political profile when he was appointed as prime minister in 2001. He is a financial administrator whose career in insurance and reinsurance had been boosted by periods working in Europe with British, French and German companies, and shortly before becoming prime minister he had reached the position of national director for the Central African Republic (CAR) within the Cameroon-based Bank of Central African States (Banque des Etats de l'Afrique Centrale—BEAC).

Martin Ziguélé was born on 12 February 1957 in Paoua. He attended primary school there and completed his secondary education in the capital, Bangui, where he went on to do a degree in English—complemented by obtaining a higher diploma in 1976–78 from the International Insurance Institute in Yaoundé, Cameroon. He is married with six children.

Having worked initially in the ministry of finance, and then completed his national service, he did the first of his several European 'stages' or work placements in July 1981 with the reinsurers Golding Stewart Wrightson in London. He also spent time with Munich Re in April–May 1984 and on other placements in Casablanca and Paris. From September 1988 he held progressively more senior posts in Bangui during a seven-year stint with the CAR state insurance and reinsurance service (SIRIRI). He then worked for a spell of four and a half years as head of the life policies division with CICA-RE, the joint reinsurance company for the west African member states of the International Conference on Insurance Control (Conférence Internationale des Contrôles d'Assurances—CICA), based in the Togolese capital Lomé. In July 2000, when he was appointed to the BEAC post as national director for the CAR, he went initially to BEAC's Yaoundé headquarters, and had been back in Bangui in his new role for less than two months when the unexpected call came on 1 April 2001 for him to become prime minister.

On 12 July 2002 Ziguélé took on the finance and budget portfolios in addition to his prime ministerial responsibilities.

CHAD

Full name: The Republic of Chad.

Leadership structure: The head of state is a president, directly elected by universal adult suffrage. The president's term of office is five years. The head of government is the prime minister, who is appointed by the president. The cabinet is appointed by the prime minister.

President:	Idriss Deby	Since 4 March 1991
	(seized power on 4 Dec. 1990)	
Prime Ministers:	Nagoum Yamassoum	13 Dec. 1999—12 June 2002
	Haroun Kabadi	Since 12 June 2002

Legislature: The legislature is unicameral. The sole chamber, the National Assembly (Assemblée Nationale), has 155 members, directly elected for a four-year term.

Profile of the President:

Idriss **DEBY**

Idriss Deby has been in power in Chad since his 1990 coup, and was elected president for successive five-year terms in July 1996 and May 2001. A French-trained soldier, he was the leader of the forces which enabled his fellow Muslim, northerner Hissène Habré, to take power in the capital, N'Djamena, in 1982. He turned against Habré in 1989 and subsequently mounted a successful Libyan-backed invasion from bases in Sudan.

Deby was born in 1952 in Fada, Ennedi, in eastern Chad, into the Muslim Zaghawa tribe. He trained as a soldier, attending the Aeronautic Institute in Amaury de la Grange in France in 1976–78. He quickly rose to become chief of staff in 1982 of the Armed Forces of the North (Forces Armées du Nord—FAN), the supporters of Habré. In the ongoing civil war Deby led the FAN forces and captured N'Djamena, declaring Habré head of state in June 1982. Habré then promoted him to colonel and appointed him commander-in-chief of the armed forces and his military adviser. In 1985 Deby returned to France, this time attending the higher military academy in Paris.

Deby tried unsuccessfully to oust Habré from power on 1 April 1989, subsequently escaping into Sudan, where he founded a Patriotic Salvation

Movement (Mouvement Patriotique du Salut—MPS) and launched a number of attacks into Chadian territory. In November 1990 he led a successful invasion backed by Libyan troops, putting Habré to flight and proclaiming himself head of state and chairman of the interim council of state in December. He was inaugurated as president in March 1991, as fighting continued against troops loyal to Habré and against other tribal groups.

Since taking power Deby has sought progressively to bring the many rival factions in Chad into a 'national reconciliation' process, as part of which he eventually conceded the introduction of a multiparty system. A new constitution was approved by referendum in March 1996, which is secular in form (ostensibly to avoid closing the door to reconciliation with southern-based Christian opponents), although Deby's regime has in practice introduced many elements of Islamic *shari'a* law.

Presidential elections on 2 June 1996 saw Deby head a field of 15 candidates in the first round, and in the runoff on 3 July he won 69% of the vote. He suffered something of a setback when his MPS failed to win an overall majority in legislative elections in early 1997. Deby again managed, however, to bring in more former opposition groups to support his regime, which has been greatly bolstered by the prospect of exploiting the country's enormous recently discovered oil resources. A harsh policy of shooting criminals on sight, and other human rights violations, brought criticism from abroad, with European countries becoming increasingly attentive to the Chadian situation. Deby's re-election for a further presidential term on 27 May 2001, when he was credited with 67% of the vote, prompted opposition candidates to protest over targeted state violence, ballot-rigging and fraud. The ensuing demonstrations were met with a firm crackdown and a spate of arrests, and the Deby government's hold on power was underlined when the MPS won two-thirds of the seats in the legislature in elections in April 2002.

Profile of the Prime Minister:

Haroun **KABADI**

Haroun Kabadi is a senior member of the ruling Patriotic Salvation Movement (Mouvement Patriotique du Salut—MPS). Born in 1949, he was first brought into the government in January 1998 as communications minister, in which capacity he also served as government spokesman. He was withdrawn from the cabinet in July 1998 and took up a position as managing director of the state-run cotton-processing Société Cotonnière du Tchad. After the MPS victory at the polls in 2002 he returned to government in June as prime minister of an expanded cabinet. He has close links with President Idriss Deby.

CHILE

Full name: The Republic of Chile.

Leadership structure: The head of state is a president, directly elected by universal adult suffrage. The president's term of office is six years. The head of government is the president, who is responsible to the National Congress. The cabinet is appointed by the president.

Presidents:	Eduardo Frei Ruiz-Tagle	11 March 1994—11 March 2000
	Ricardo Lagos Escobar	Since 11 March 2000

Legislature: The legislature, the National Congress (Congreso Nacional), is bicameral. The lower chamber, the Chamber of Deputies (Cámara de Diputados), has 118 members, directly elected for a four-year term. The upper chamber, the Senate (Senado), has 38 members elected for an eight-year term (half of which are renewed every four years), and another nine appointed directly by the outgoing government and the Supreme Court. In addition, former presidents who filled that position for six uninterrupted years are ex officio life senators. Eduardo Frei, president until March 2000, is the only current life senator under this provision, the former military dictator Gen. Augusto Pinochet having resigned his senatorial seat on 20 August 2002.

Profile of the President:

Ricardo **LAGOS** Escobar

Ricardo Lagos is an eminent academic, who has written five texts on Chilean politics and economics since 1969. He was inaugurated as president on 11 March 2000. He founded the Party for Democracy (Partido por la Democracia—PPD) in 1987 as a vehicle for the outlawed Socialist Party (Partido Socialista—PS). He now heads the Coalition of Parties for Democracy (Concertación de Partidos por la Democracia—CPD), which includes the PPD and the PS.

Ricardo Lagos Escobar was born on 2 March 1938 in Santiago to Emma Escobar and Froilán Lagos. He attended the law school of the University of Chile in Santiago from 1955 to 1960, and was president of the students' union there. He went to Duke University in North Carolina, USA, in 1961 to study for a doctorate in economics. On returning to Chile Lagos was appointed a professor of the University of Chile, eventually becoming its secretary-general in 1969. While remaining a prominent academic in the field of social sciences throughout the

1970s, in 1971 he held his first political post when he was sent as ambassador to the UN. In the same year he married Luisa Durán de la Fuente. They have two children each from previous marriages, and one daughter born in 1975.

Following the military coup which overthrew and killed the socialist president Salvador Allende in 1973 and installed Gen. Augusto Pinochet as head of state, Lagos spent some years abroad as a visiting academic, first in Buenos Aires in Argentina, and then at the University of North Carolina in Chapel Hill, USA. In 1982 he sat on the executive committee of the PS, and was president between 1983 and 1984 of the Democratic Alliance, a coalition of opponents of the Pinochet dictatorship. In 1987, following the legalization of non-Marxist political parties, he founded the PPD and, as part of the CPD, he canvassed the nation in support of the 'no' campaign against Pinochet's confirmation for a new term as president.

The 'no' vote won in the plebiscite held in October 1988 and Pinochet was forced to hold elections in 1989. The Christian Democratic Party (Partido Demócrata Cristiano—PDC) candidate, Patricio Aylwin Azócar, became president and Lagos's PPD was included in the ruling CPD coalition. In the legislative elections the PPD became the third-largest party in Congress despite a residual anti-left bias in the electoral law. President Aylwin appointed Lagos as minister of education in 1990 where he worked until 1992 to improve equality of access and raise teaching standards.

Lagos ran for president in 1993 against the official CPD candidate, Eduardo Frei of the PDC who went on to a convincing win. Under Frei, Lagos was given the portfolio of the public works ministry which he ran from 1994 to 1998, investing around US$2,000 million in various projects designed to reinvigorate Chile's deprived sectors.

In 1999 Lagos stood once again as the PPD's presidential candidate and received the endorsement of the CPD. A close-fought election in December led to a runoff against the conservative Independent Democratic Union candidate, Joaquín Lavín, on 16 January 2000. Victory for Lagos made him the country's first socialist president since Allende.

CHINA

Full name: The People's Republic of China.

Leadership structure: The head of state is a president, indirectly elected by the National People's Congress (NPC). The president's term of office is five years, renewable once only. The head of government is the premier, who is responsible to the NPC. The State Council is elected by the NPC on the nomination of the premier.

President: Jiang Zemin   Since 27 March 1993

Premier: Zhu Rongji   Since 17 March 1998

General Secretary of the Chinese Communist Party:

Jiang Zemin   24 June 1989—15 Nov. 2002

Hu Jintao   Since 15 Nov. 2002

Legislature: The legislature is unicameral. The sole chamber, the NPC or National People's Congress (Quanguo Renmin Daibiao Dahui), has 2,979 members, indirectly elected for a five-year term.

Profile of the President of the Republic:

JIANG Zemin

Jiang Zemin established himself in the 1990s as China's most powerful leader, having risen to the top under the patronage of former 'elder statesman' leader Deng Xiaoping. Regarded as a reformist, he identified himself with the rapid opening of the economy to private enterprise, but repeatedly made it clear that the 'Chinese road' involved no corresponding liberalization in the political sphere.

Jiang Zemin was born on 17 August 1926 in Yangzhou city, northwest of Shanghai, in Jiangsu province, which remained under Japanese occupation until 1945. The adopted son of a communist revolutionary martyr, he attended an American missionary school, joined the Chinese Communist Party (CCP) himself in 1946, and graduated with a degree in electrical engineering from Jiaotong University in Shanghai in 1947. He is married to Wang Yeping and they have two sons.

In the initial years of the People's Republic of China (proclaimed by Mao Zedong in 1949 after the communist victory in the long civil war), Jiang Zemin was CCP party secretary in a soap factory in Shanghai. In 1955 he went to Moscow as a trainee, working in the Stalin Automobile Plant. Returning to China in 1956, he moved into the power industry and machine-building, rising through a series of party posts to membership of the central committee in 1982. That year he also became a first deputy minister in the electronics ministry, and he was promoted in 1983 to the rank of minister in the same department, holding the portfolio for two years.

Jiang Zemin first came to wider public notice as mayor of Shanghai, a post he held from 1985 to 1989, and he also became a member of the party politburo during this period (in 1987). When Zhao Ziyang was dismissed as party general secretary and from all his other party posts as a dangerous liberal, in the clampdown which accompanied the June 1989 Tiananmen Square massacre, Jiang was picked to replace him. This was partly on the strength of his own handling of student demonstrations in Shanghai in December 1986, when he had taken a firm line but defused the situation without recourse to military force. He had also endeared himself to the hard-liners by his measures in April 1989 to prevent student demonstrations from developing, while impressing others in the party by his record of effective economic management in the relatively go-ahead environment of Shanghai. In November 1989 and April 1990, when Deng stepped down as chairman of the central state and party military commissions, Jiang's appointment confirmed his status as Deng's unofficial heir apparent.

The notion that Jiang might prove no more of a political heavyweight than Deng's previous protégés was dispelled by the success of economic reforms under his leadership, his clarity and determination that there should be no concomitant political liberalization process, and his steady accumulation of leadership positions. This culminated in his election (with the usual unanimity) by the NPC on 27 March 1993 as president of the People's Republic for a five-year presidential term, a post to which he was re-elected (for a second and constitutionally final term) in March 1998.

Following the death of Deng in February 1997, Jiang Zemin paid particular attention to his relationship with the army, where support for him was apparently less firmly established than among party cadres. On the other hand, at the September 1997 party congress (when he was re-elected as party general secretary) he announced plans to cut the armed forces by 500,000 men, and by mid-1998 he was sufficiently confident of his position to initiate a major and unprecedented attack on members of the armed forces who engaged in smuggling, following this up with an order in July of that year that the armed forces, police and judiciary were to renounce all involvement in business activities.

Jiang's ascendancy, vis-à-vis the more conservative faction associated with Li Peng, had been established in the context of China's rapid economic growth and a reduction in inflation. His promotion of market reforms, including far-reaching privatization measures approved by the 1997 congress, was accompanied by a firm line against dissident activity, and a campaign against corruption. With the thrust of economic policy clearly established by the time of the party congress, Jiang appeared willing to cede much of the responsibility for economic management to Zhu Rongji, who like Jiang was a technocrat, a reformist and a former mayor of Shanghai.

Conversely, a series of high-profile meetings with foreign leaders during 1998 (notably including visits to China by then US president Bill Clinton and UK prime minister Tony Blair, and visits by Jiang to both Russia and Japan) marked Jiang's increasing personal control over foreign affairs. The cementing of better relations with the USA was seen as his particular objective, and considerable coverage was given to a speech made by Clinton in Beijing when he praised Jiang as a "man of vision". The desire to foster China's connections with the USA also apparently encouraged Jiang to appear more conciliatory in his stance on the treatment of dissidents. In December 1998, however, there was a fresh crackdown, with Jiang making a distinctly hard-line speech in which he stressed that "the Western mode of political systems must never be copied" and pledged to smash opposition to the party.

Recognizing a shift towards a new generation in the upper echelons of the party, Jiang began cultivating a protégé of his own, Vice President Hu Jintao, while remaining determined to make his own indelible mark on Communist China. The year 2000 saw a major crackdown on government corruption with more executions in China than in the rest of the world put together. The following year Jiang unveiled his 'Three Represents' theory, which sought to make his economic liberalization a permanent tenet of CCP ideology, embracing business as the party's third component after culture and agriculture. The doctrine was accepted as official party ideology in April 2001.

At the 16th CCP congress, held in November 2002, the formal process of handing over power from Jiang to Hu began. Jiang surrendered his role as CCP general secretary on 15 November. Pending the approval of a new government lineup by the NPC in early 2003, Jiang remained president of China and head of the armed forces.

Profile of the Premier of the State Council:

ZHU Rongji

Zhu Rongji, like President Jiang Zemin a former mayor of Shanghai, is known as 'the Boss' and noted for his successful economic management, bringing China's raging inflation under control in the mid-1990s while continuing to deliver rapid growth. He is also renowned for his dislike of bureaucracy and corruption, and a relatively frank and relaxed approach to politics which encouraged the media to present him as 'China's Gorbachev'. His 'rightist' politics twice led to his rural-exile from the Chinese Communist Party (CCP) in the reign of Chairman Mao.

Zhu Rongji was born in 1928 and joined the CCP in 1949. His first experience of political isolation as a farm labourer in the Chinese hinterland came in 1957 when, while serving as an official at the State Planning Commission, he unwisely made use of Chairman Mao's campaign to encourage criticism and condemned the government policy of 'irrational growth'. He returned to the commission in 1962 but was purged once more during Mao's Cultural Revolution, this time to feed pigs and tend goats in the countryside. Only under Deng Xiaoping's administration in the 1970s did Zhu find full political rehabilitation.

In 1988 he was appointed as mayor of Shanghai and soon established a reputation as an economic reformist, overseeing the city's rapid regeneration through foreign investment and a crackdown on corruption. He received national praise in 1989 when he personally defused a volatile student protest, contrasting notably with the coinciding massacre in Beijing's Tiananmen Square. In the 1990s Zhu enjoyed the fruits of his success when he was appointed as deputy prime minister in 1991 and then served as the governor of the Central Bank of China between the years 1993 and 1995. His legacy to the 1990s was to reduce China's racing inflation to 1% from a destructive high of 25%. At the Communists' 15th party congress in September 1997 he was promoted to third place in the ruling standing committee and, when Li Peng came to the end of his term in March 1998, Zhu received a glowing endorsement from the party to succeed him as prime minister.

At the 16th CCP congress in November 2002 Zhu retired from his senior post within the party in preparation for the formation of a new government structure, in which the new CCP general secretary, Hu Jintao, was expected to take over the presidency.

Profile of the General Secretary of the Chinese Communist Party:

HU Jintao

Hu Jintao joined the Chinese Communist Party (CCP) while still a student, and quickly worked through the ranks to become leader of its youth wing, the Communist Youth League (CYL), the youngest ever alternate member of its central committee and the youngest ever provincial governor. When he took over from Jiang Zemin as CCP general secretary in 2002 it was widely assumed that he would also succeed him as president of China in 2003. Some observers suggest that he will then show his full reformist colours, whereas others point to his brutal suppression of separatists in Tibet and his quick support for the government's bloody handling of the 1989 Tiananmen Square demonstrations.

Hu Jintao was born in December 1942 in Jixi in the eastern province of Anhui. He moved to Taizhou, in neighbouring Jiangsu province, in about 1948 after the death of his mother, and was raised by his great aunt Liu Bingxia. Hu travelled to Beijing in the 1960s to study hydraulic engineering at the respected Tsinghua University, where he joined the CCP, met his future wife Liu Yongqing (with whom he has two children), and continued to work as a researcher and political instructor after graduating.

The Cultural Revolution (1966–76) targeted the new political class and Hu was sent to rural Gansu province in 1968 to be 're-educated' as a farm labourer. He was rehabilitated later that year and rejoined party work as party secretary at the engineering bureau of the ministry of water resources and electrical power. In 1974 he became secretary of the Gansu provincial construction commission and developed ties with senior CCP member Song Ping. Song was to play a major part in abetting Hu's subsequent rapid climb up the party hierarchy.

In 1982 Hu became the youngest ever alternate member of the CCP central committee, at age 39, and joined the secretariat of the Gansu CYL. The following year he returned to Beijing to work at the headquarters of the generally reformist CYL and became head of its secretariat in 1984. He left the CYL and headed back out west to Guizhou province in 1985 as the youngest ever provincial party chief, and cultivated a reputation as a compassionate reformer. While there he was also made a full member of the CCP central committee in 1987.

Pushed further west, Hu was made the first nonmilitary party chief of Tibet in 1988. He dropped his tolerant attitude in his new position when, within a month of his arrival, separatist activists began organizing bigger and more violent demonstrations. In March 1989 over 40 Tibetans were killed by police during rioting and Hu organized the deployment of 100,000 troops to suppress the separatists. His ability to maintain order in Tibet thereafter, even during the Tiananmen Square demonstrations in June, earned him special notice within the central CCP machinery. He was the first provincial leader to express support for the government's actions. In 1990 he returned once more to Beijing, claiming altitude sickness, and began to build the most powerful support network in the party.

China's then paramount leader Deng Xiaoping nominated Hu in 1992 to organize the 14th CCP congress and Hu replaced Song as a member of the politburo's standing committee—the party's highest organ. Over the course of the 1990s he moved into a number of high-profile positions and worked closely with President Jiang Zemin on his largely reformist agenda. He was appointed vice president in March 1998 and vice chairman of the central military commission in September 1999. However, he has made a point of not disclosing his own political leanings.

By 2002 he was being identified worldwide as China's president-in-waiting. It surprised no one when on 15 November, at the conclusion of the 16th CCP congress, Hu was appointed general secretary of the party and recognized as the leading figure in the politburo. For the time being he remains vice president of China and second-in-command of the military.

COLOMBIA

Full name: The Republic of Colombia.

Leadership structure: The head of state is a president, directly elected by universal adult suffrage. The president's term of office is four years. The head of government is the president, who is responsible to parliament. The cabinet is appointed by the president.

Presidents:	Andrés Pastrana Arango	7 Aug. 1998—7 Aug. 2002
	Álvaro Uribe Vélez	Since 7 Aug. 2002

Legislature: The legislature, the Congress (Congreso), is bicameral. The lower chamber, the House of Representatives (Cámara de Representantes), has 166 members, directly elected for a four-year term. The upper chamber, the Senate (Senado), has 102 members, directly elected for a four-year term, including two senators representing indigenous people in specific areas.

Profile of the President:

Álvaro **URIBE** Vélez

Álvaro Uribe Vélez is an independent but is associated with right-wing politics and accused by his detractors of intimate ties to right-wing paramilitaries and the infamous Medellín drugs cartel. A career politician in the region of his birth, Antioquia, Uribe served as both a senator for the region and as its governor before successfully being elected president of Colombia in 2002.

Álvaro Uribe Vélez was born on 4 July 1952 in Medellín. His father is popularly believed to have been associated with the Medellín cartel and was the subject of unsuccessful extradition requests from the USA. Uribe is married to Lina Moreno and they have two sons. He graduated in law from the University of Antioquia and began work in the public works department of the Medellín city council in 1976.

The following year Uribe moved up to national government level as secretary-general of the labour ministry before being appointed director of civil aeronautics in the Colombian aviation agency in 1980. During his time at the agency he is accused of corruption, particularly of providing the Medellín cartel with private airstrips. Four years later he was appointed mayor of Medellín. His detractors accuse him of gaining influence through illegal channels, claiming that he received the post after his father made significant donations to the president of the day. Medellín was renowned worldwide at the time as the base for the powerful drugs cartel of the same name, which was then headed by Pablo Escobar. Uribe was publicly linked to Escobar several times, but was still sufficiently popular to be elected to the Senate in 1986.

During two consecutive terms in the upper chamber Uribe proved consistently popular with both the public and his colleagues, polling among the top five in opinion polls and even winning the Best Senator award in 1993. That same year he studied for a postgraduate course in management and conflict resolution at Harvard University, USA.

On leaving the Senate Uribe was appointed governor of the Antioquia province in 1995 for a one-year, nonrenewable term. His tenure has been shrouded in controversy. On the one hand he is praised for slashing government spending in the province, and providing an increase in education and welfare payments. He is also credited with greatly improving the region's road network. On the other hand he was the patron of a number of right-wing paramilitary groups under his Rural Vigilance Committee scheme. The resultant Convivir groups were condemned by Amnesty International among others as government-sanctioned death squads. They were scrapped by the national government in 1997 at the end of Uribe's governorship. It is alleged that the Convivir gunmen simply shifted their allegiance to the Self-Defence Forces of Colombia (Autodefensas Unidas de Colombia—AUC) which was responsible for an escalation in the country's civil conflict until its official disbandment in 2002. From 1998 to 1999 Uribe worked as an associate professor at Oxford University, UK, on a British Council fellowship.

Uribe returned to high-profile political life in his campaign for the 2002 presidential elections. In his bid to replace the right-of-centre incumbent Andrés Pastrana Arango, he pledged to abandon the previous peace negotiations with the powerful left-wing rebel groups, and to revitalize the government's campaign with massive injections of funds into the defence and police budgets. He won the election with an unprecedented first-round victory, claiming 53% of the vote. Many observers predicted that his rise signalled the end of the country's traditional two-party system.

Uribe's inauguration on 7 August 2002 was met, as promised by left-wing guerrillas, with a concerted bombing campaign in Bogotá. Thirteen people were killed and Uribe introduced a state of emergency. Under the decree greater powers were soon granted to the police force. As president Uribe is accused of maintaining his links with right-wing paramilitaries while abandoning previous connections to the narcotics industry in favour of a close relationship with the USA. He is a keen supporter of the US-backed Plan Colombia and has welcomed an intensification of the USA's military campaign against narcotics growers. He also intends to bring his Community State initiative to the national level, by encouraging a system of government informers among the public to tackle the left-wing guerrillas.

COMOROS

Full name: The Union of the Comoros.

Leadership structure: Under the 2002 Constitution the Union president is elected from each of the three islands in turn, for a four-year term. Each island also has its own regional president. The head of government of the Union is the president. Each island's president is also head of its government.

Presidents:	Col. Assoumani Azali (seized power 30 April 1999)	6 May 1999—21 Jan. 2002
	Hamada Madi 'Boléro' (interim)	21 Jan. 2002—26 May 2002
	Col. Assoumani Azali	Since 26 May 2002
Prime Ministers:	Bianrifi Tarmidi	1 Dec. 1999—11 Dec. 2000
	Hamada Madi 'Boléro' (post then abolished)	11 Dec. 2000—15 April 2002

Legislature: Under the 2002 Constitution, the islands will each have a local parliament. The Union will have a legislative assembly with 33 members, five members appointed by each of the three local parliaments and 18 elected through direct universal suffrage.

Profile of the President:

Col. Assoumani **AZALI**

Assoumani Azali has a military background and, like many previous heads of state in the Comoros, assumed power in a coup in 1999. He justified his action on the grounds that the government was not taking adequate measures to control the current unrest stemming from separatist demands by the island of Nzwani. Having framed a new constitution for the newly entitled Union of the Comoros, Azali was declared its president and sworn in on 26 May 2002, after a complex process of elections in each of the Union's main constituent islands.

Assoumani Azali was born in Mitsoudjé on the island of Njazidja (formerly Grande Comore) on 1 January 1959. A career soldier, he was chief of staff when in April 1999 he led a bloodless coup to overthrow President Tadjidine Ben Saïd Massoundi and the elected government. Under a new constitutional charter Azali was declared head of state and government and commander-in-chief of the armed forces, and he also assumed legislative authority. Initially he announced his intention to stay in power for only one year, pending new constitutional arrangements.

The basis for the constitutional changes was the Antananarivo agreement, a document drawn up at a conference held in Antananarivo (Madagascar) in April 1999 (before the coup), providing for greater autonomy for the islands of Nzwani and Mwali (formerly known as Anjouan and Mohéli) within a new Union of the Comoros. The unrest which provided the occasion for Azali's coup broke out when the Nzwani delegates refused to sign the accord, which continued to be obstructed by the separatists there, who went on to form a 'government of national unity' on the island, and held a referendum in January 2000 to demonstrate support for full Nzwani independence.

The problem appeared intractable with Azali backtracking on a pledge to return the country to civilian rule by April 2000. However, with the backing of the Organization of African Unity (the precursor to the African Union), an accord known as the Fomboni Declaration was signed in August 2000. It took a further 18 months before Azali finally agreed to step down as 'president' of the Comoros on 21 January 2002 in order to run for the new post of union president in March–April. A long process of elections, annulments and political manoeuvring was finally resolved on 26 May when Azali was inaugurated as the new union president. Also elected in the first half of 2002 were the regional presidents of each of the three Comoran islands who quickly sought to assert their powers in the new structure.

DEMOCRATIC REPUBLIC
OF THE CONGO

Full name: The Democratic Republic of the Congo.

Leadership structure: The head of state is the president. The succession to office of the current incumbent, Maj.-Gen. Joseph Kabila, was approved unanimously by parliament on 24 January 2001, eight days after the assassination of his father Laurent Kabila. On 26 January Joseph Kabila was sworn into office as president. The head of government is the president, who appoints the cabinet.

Presidents:	Laurent Kabila	29 May 1997—16 Jan. 2001
	(seized power on 17 May 1997)	
	Joseph Kabila	Since 26 Jan. 2001
	(interim from 17 Jan. 2001)	

Legislature: A Constituent and Legislative Assembly was inaugurated on 21 August 2000. It has 300 members appointed by the president.

Profile of the President:

Joseph **KABILA**

Joseph Kabila was trained as a military officer in Rwanda and China. When he succeeded his assassinated father in January 2001 he raised hopes of revitalizing the country's neglected peace process, but a resolution of the complex regional conflict centred on his Democratic Republic of the Congo (DRC) remained elusive until late 2002.

Joseph Kabila was born on 4 December 1971 in Hewa Bora, in the eastern province of South Kivu, to an ethnic Tutsi woman from Rwanda while his father was in exile in Tanzania as an opponent of the Mobutu regime. He is believed to be the eldest of ten children fathered by Laurent Kabila, almost all born to different mothers. Joseph, who is himself now married with one daughter, received his early education in Tanzania and went on to study in neighbouring Uganda. He began his military training in Rwanda in around 1995.

As his father began to press for an armed overthrow of the Mobutu regime in what had become known as Zaïre, Joseph Kabila entered the country for the first time in 1996 as a commander in his father's rebel army. Gaining support from almost all regional powers, the rebels and their allies swept across the country and entered Kinshasa in 1997. Laurent was installed as the new president of the renamed DRC and Joseph was sent to China to receive a further six months of military education. On his return his father promoted him to major-general and placed him at the head of the Congolese armed forces.

Initial hopes of a swift return to democracy were thwarted, however, and Laurent Kabila soon lost the support of his Rwandan and Ugandan allies. As army chief of staff, and with the experience gained in the 1996–97 conflict, Joseph Kabila was despatched to the eastern front line and led the campaign there until 2001. During this time Joseph Kabila, who has the reputation of being painfully shy, remained firmly out of the international limelight, which was entirely taken up by his charismatic father. While his supporters applauded his command as instrumental in holding back the rebel advance, his detractors suggest that any victories by government forces were won mostly with the use of foreign assistance, and that Joseph would not arrive in 'liberated' areas until after they had fallen to his troops.

On 16 January 2001 Laurent Kabila was shot by a bodyguard at his offices in Kinshasa. The authorities denied initial reports while Joseph was rushed back to the capital. On the following day he was overwhelmingly accepted as interim leader, and was appointed president straight after his father's funeral. Analysts at the time suggested that he was a wholly unsuitable choice as head of state, pointing to his less-than-glorious career on the front line, his lack of political experience and even his alleged Rwandan heritage. However, he worked quickly to repair the damage done by his increasingly authoritarian father and talked the talk of a leader committed to achieving peace. He met with his Rwandan counterpart within days and UN-brokered peace talks were under way by February. Political parties were unbanned and the Congo River was reopened to commercial traffic in August.

Nevertheless, despite promising to hold fresh elections as soon as all foreign troops had left Congolese soil, Kabila then let the impetus of his first few months slowly slip away. A long-awaited inter-Congolese dialogue between warring factions was suspended within days of opening and by early 2002, although large-scale withdrawals had begun, many thousands of foreign soldiers remained in the DRC and countries such as Angola and Uganda reiterated their intention to maintain their presence in the aim of attaining regional security. While Kabila's hold on power no longer appeared tenuous, his commitment to a peaceful solution had grown ever more suspect.

Over the course of 2002, however, pressure for an end to the conflict finally seemed to be having an effect. Kabila met with his Rwandan and Ugandan counterparts, and oversaw continuing negotiations with rebel factions. Tens of thousands of Rwandan, Ugandan and Zimbabwean troops began withdrawing in August and 15,000 left in the last three weeks of September alone. Meanwhile, Kabila secured aid for his war-ravaged country worth US$410 million, and US$4,600 million of old debt was cancelled in September.

A power-sharing peace deal initially touted in April was finally signed on 16 December 2002, with Kabila as president and four major factions represented by vice presidents. However, the UN noted that the country's resources had been recklessly pillaged by invading forces and exploited by corrupt government officials, painting a bleak picture of the country's economic security. Elsewhere the vacuum created by departing soldiers prompted turf wars between local militias, resulting in all too frequent massacres and massive displacement of local populations.

REPUBLIC OF THE CONGO

Full name: The Republic of the Congo.

Leadership structure: The head of state under the 2002 Constitution is a president, directly elected by universal adult suffrage for a term of seven years. The head of government under the 2002 Constitution is the president, who appoints the cabinet.

President: Denis Sassou-Nguesso   Since 25 Oct. 1997
                         (in de facto control from 15 Oct. 1997)

Minister of State in charge of Co-ordination of Government Action:
                    Isidore Mvouba   Since 18 Aug. 2002
                    (first holder of this post)

Legislature: Under the 2002 Constitution, the legislature, the Parliament (Parlement), is bicameral. The lower chamber, the National Assembly (Assemblée Nationale), has 137 members, directly elected for a five-year term. The upper chamber, the Senate (Sénat), has 66 members, indirectly elected for a six-year term (one-third of members every two years).

Profile of the President:

Denis SASSOU-NGUESSO

Gen. Denis Sassou-Nguesso, who returned to power in 1997, had dominated the Congolese political scene prior to the country's first multiparty elections in 1992. He was a prominent member of the military committee which took over the running of the then Marxist regime in 1977, and was president from 1979 to 1992, under a single-party structure. Defeated in the 1992 elections, he took his party (and its militia) into opposition. His return to power was assisted by Angolan forces in a decisive military offensive which ended five months of effective civil war.

A member of the Mboshi ethnic group, Denis Sassou-Nguesso was born in 1943 in Oyo in the territory then known as the Middle Congo, which was part of French Equatorial Africa. He joined the army of the newly independent Republic of the Congo and as a young junior officer he supported the self-declared Marxist regime established after a military coup in 1968. He has been married twice and is the father of seven children, one of whom is married to Gabonese president Omar Bongo.

Regarded in the 1970s as strongly pro-Soviet, Sassou-Nguesso headed the political police from 1974, and in late 1975, when he had reached the rank of major, he was appointed to a nine-member ruling Council of State. The military leadership sought to tighten its grip on the ruling Congolese Labour Party (Parti Congolais du Travail—PCT) after the assassination of the president, Maj. Ngouabi, in March 1977. Ngouabi's successor, Gen. Yhombi-Opango, set up a military committee in which Sassou-Nguesso was first vice president 'responsible for co-ordinating PCT activities' as well as minister of defence.

Using his party role as a power base, Sassou-Nguesso was within two years able to challenge Yhombi-Opango for power, forcing him to resign when he criticized the PCT in February 1979. A newly formed PCT presidium thereupon appointed Sassou-Nguesso as interim president. He was confirmed in this post, as well as becoming party chairman, at a special PCT congress on 27 March.

Although the single-party structure ensured Sassou-Nguesso's unopposed re-election at five-year intervals (in July 1984 and 1989), economic difficulties led his regime to turn increasingly away from state socialism and towards free-market policies which could satisfy the criteria for attracting International Monetary Fund (IMF) support. In October 1990 an extraordinary party congress (at which Sassou-Nguesso was elected president of a new central committee) formally abandoned Marxism–Leninism and endorsed the creation of a multiparty political system.

A national conference was convened from February 1991, and by June of that year had secured the role of interim head of government for the prime minister rather than the president. Legislative elections in June–July 1992 established the recently formed Pan-African Union for Social Democracy (Union Panafricaine pour la Démocratie Sociale—UPADS) as the leading party, and when presidential elections were held in August 1992, Sassou-Nguesso as the PCT candidate was knocked out in the first-round ballot, finishing third with under 17% of the vote. Conceding defeat with what he claimed to be "serenity", he thereupon called on his supporters to vote for the UPADS leader Pascal Lissouba, who won the runoff and was sworn in on 31 August.

In the five years of the Lissouba regime, however, Sassou-Nguesso maintained a high profile within a series of alliances that combined parliamentary opposition with extraparliamentary protest and militia activity. Talks on a possible all-party coalition, and the integration of rival militias into the national army, produced a short-lived agreement in late 1994 on ending hostilities, and a similarly unimplemented peace pact a year later. With the approach of presidential elections due in July 1997, Lissouba tried unsuccessfully to disarm the PCT militia, and large-scale fighting broke out in the capital, Brazzaville, in June of that year. Attempts at external mediation failed to resolve the conflict, and were rendered irrelevant when a successful offensive by Sassou-Nguesso's forces, backed by Angola, left him in full control by mid-October.

Sassou-Nguesso was inaugurated as president on 25 October 1997. The following month, when his takeover was still not widely accepted internationally, his position was boosted by his long meeting with French President Jacques Chirac (with whom he shares membership of a French Masonic order) at a francophone summit in Hanoi, Viet Nam. An executive National Transitional Council was created in January 1998, but fighting and violence continued throughout the year, culminating in an inconclusive battle for Brazzaville itself in December. Sassou-Nguesso pursued talks with rival militias but remained at loggerheads with their key leaders, Lissouba and his former prime minister Bernard Kolelas.

By late 1999 a peace deal had been forged and the process of rehabilitation had begun. The civil war was officially declared over in February 2000 and a new draft constitution was proffered by Sassou-Nguesso in November that year, under which the president would hold considerable executive power as head of government. The document was approved by 84% in a referendum on 20 January 2002, and Sassou-Nguesso went on to win 90% of the vote in presidential elections on 10 March, but only after the main opposition candidate, André Milongo, had pulled out of the poll and called for a boycott. Less than a month later the fragile peace was shattered with renewed fighting between government forces and so-called Ninja rebels in the turbulent southern Pool region. Thousands of people were displaced and fighting spilled over into the outskirts of Brazzaville once again.

Profile of the Minister of State in charge of Co-ordination of Government Action:

Isidore **MVOUBA**

Isidore Mvouba, who comes from the Pool region in the south of the country, is a member of the ruling Congolese Labour Party (Parti Congolais du Travail— PCT). He first joined the government following President Denis Sassou-Nguesso's takeover of power in late 1997, as cabinet director and permanent undersecretary at the presidency. In a reshuffle in January 1999 he was appointed minister of transport, civil aviation and merchant navy.

Campaign director for President Sassou-Nguesso in the March 2002 presidential elections, Mvouba retained his existing ministerial responsibilities, but ceased to be head of the president's office, when he was nominated to fill the new role of minister of state and co-ordinator of government action in August 2002. In his new capacity it was Mvouba who formally presented the newly reshuffled ministerial team to parliament on 18 August. His prominence is particularly significant in view of the problems of violent conflict in his native Pool region in 2002.

COSTA RICA

Full name: The Republic of Costa Rica.

Leadership structure: The head of state is a president, directly elected by universal adult suffrage. The president's term of office is four years, not renewable. The head of government is the president, who appoints the cabinet.

Presidents: Miguel Ángel Rodríguez Echeverría   8 May 1998—8 May 2002

Abel Pacheco de la Espriella   Since 8 May 2002

Legislature: The legislature is unicameral. The sole chamber, the Legislative Assembly (Asamblea Legislativa), has 57 members, directly elected for a four-year term.

Profile of the President:

Abel **PACHECO** de la Espriella

Abel Pacheco is a leading figure in the right-wing Social Christian Unity Party (Partido Unidad Social Cristiana—PUSC). Although trained as a psychiatrist he achieved fame in Costa Rica as a television commentator and writer. He was elected president in an unprecedented second-round vote held on 7 April 2002, and took office on 8 May.

Abel de Jesús Pacheco de la Espriella was born in the capital, San José, on 22 December 1933. His family moved to Mexico when he was still young and he graduated in medicine from the Independent National University there before studying psychiatry at Louisiana State University in the USA. He has been married twice and has six children.

In the 1960s Pacheco worked at the National Psychiatric Hospital in San José, becoming director. He later resigned claiming that the hospital provided insufficient care to its patients. From medicine Pacheco moved into television. His first notable documentary *National Legends and Traditions* won him a prize from the University of Latin America. Later he became a well-known face on Costa Rican television as a political and social commentator. Other career directions included ventures in commerce and, most notably, writing. He has had seven books of poetry and short stories published and has received a National Prize for his works.

Pacheco's centre-right conservatism and popular renown enabled him to become leader of the PUSC in 1996, the same year he was elected to the Legislative Assembly, representing a constituency in San José. After recovering from a minor stroke in 2000, he was selected to represent the party in presidential elections in 2002, which, for the first time ever, required a second round to determine a clear result. In the runoff poll, marked by an unprecedented low turnout, Pacheco won with 58% of the vote against the candidate from the National Liberation Party, Rolando Araya. Despite his conservatism, Pacheco disagrees with the privatization of key state-owned industries and is a staunch supporter of environmental programmes.

CÔTE D'IVOIRE

Full name: The Republic of Côte d'Ivoire.

Leadership structure: The head of state is a directly elected president serving a five-year term, renewable once only. Under the 2000 Constitution the head of government is the president, who appoints the prime minister, and also appoints the cabinet on the proposal of the prime minister.

Presidents:	Gen. Robert Guéï (seized power on 25 Dec. 1999)	4 Jan. 2000—26 Oct. 2000
	Laurent Gbagbo	Since 26 Oct. 2000
Prime Ministers:	*vacant*	25 Dec. 1999—18 May 2000
	Seydou Elimane Diarra	18 May 2000—26 Oct. 2000
	Pascal Affi N'Guessan	Since 26 Oct. 2000

Legislature: The legislature is unicameral. The National Assembly (Assemblée Nationale) has 225 members, directly elected for a five-year term.

Profile of the President:

Laurent **GBAGBO**

Laurent Gbagbo was prominent in opposition politics in the 1980s and 1990s before eventually being elected president in 2000. During the early part of his period in opposition he spent six years as a political refugee in France. He stood against the long-established President Félix Houphouët-Boigny in the presidential elections of October 1990, when his party, the Popular Ivorian Front (Front Populaire Ivoirien—FPI), challenged the official outcome awarding Houphouët-Boigny over 80% of the vote. Although Gbagbo was nominated FPI presidential candidate in 1995, the party did not contest that election.

Laurent Gbagbo was born on 31 May 1945 at Gagnoa, in the south of the country. He studied at the Petit Séminaire St-Dominique Savio in Gagnoa, before moving to the Lycée Classique in Abidjan from 1962, receiving his baccalauréat in 1965. He went to university in Abidjan, before moving to the Université de Lyon, France, to study classics and French. He returned to Côte d'Ivoire to study history in 1968, then went back to France to complete his studies at the Sorbonne with a master's degree in history in 1970. In the same year he became a teacher of geography and history at the Lycée Classique in Abidjan. He is married with four children.

In March 1971 Gbagbo was arrested and sent to military camps in Akoué, Séguéla and Bouaké. On his release in January 1973 he was appointed to the education directorate, where he worked until 1977. He resumed his history studies in Paris in 1979, and the following year he was elected director of the Institut d'Histoire.

In 1982 Gbagbo created the FPI, before going into exile in France, where he was granted political asylum in 1985. He returned to Côte d'Ivoire for the FPI Constitutional Congress, at which he was elected the party's secretary-general. He stood in the presidential elections of October 1990 as the FPI candidate against incumbent President Houphouët-Boigny. When Houphouët-Boigny was awarded over 80% of the vote, the FPI challenged the result.

In November 1990 Gbagbo was elected deputy to the National Assembly for Ouragahio, and was the president of the FPI parliamentary group between 1990 and 1995. He was among over 100 people arrested in February 1992 in the wake of a violent anti-government protest in the capital. He was convicted under a new presidential decree making political leaders liable for any offences committed during demonstrations by their supporters, and was given a two-year prison sentence and a fine. In June 1995 he was again nominated FPI presidential candidate, but did not run as the FPI boycotted the election in protest over the electoral code in a vain attempt to get the elections postponed. In 1996 he became president of the FPI.

Gbagbo was a candidate in the presidential election held in October 2000. When President Henri Konan Bédié was overthrown in December 1999 in a coup led by Gen. Robert Guéï, it was anticipated that Alassane Ouattara would become president. Bédié had tried to ban Ouattara from standing as a presidential candidate on the grounds of the status of his Ivorian nationality. By October 2000, however, Gen. Guéï had ceased to support Ouattara, and the main contenders in the election were Guéï and Gbagbo. After the poll both claimed victory, but a popular outcry forced Guéï to concede defeat. Gbagbo had not only favoured the banning of Ouattara, but had adopted an anti-northerner (and thereby anti-Muslim) stance in his election campaign. Although Gbagbo reached an agreement with Ouattara once in power and stressed the importance of national unity, the treatment of Ouattara prompted a sense of racial and religious division between the north and south of the country. Legislative elections in December, preceded by widespread violence, were won by the FPI.

A culture of fear, and frequent racist attacks on 'foreigners' in Abidjan and other major cities, continued throughout 2001 and 2002. For his part, Gbagbo made overtures to Ouattara's Rally of the Republicans (Rassemblement des Républicains—RDR) while openly accusing Ouattara himself of attempting to destabilize the country. A 'reconciliation forum' intended to ease relations between Gbagbo, Ouattara and Guéï was abandoned in September 2001 as neither of the main guests accepted the president's invitation.

A breakthrough in August 2002, when the RDR joined the government, was followed by a major setback, as Guéï led an army mutiny in Abidjan in September. Although Guéï died in early fighting, Gbagbo's position as civilian president became effectively only that of a factional leader, as the rebellion quickly escalated into a full-scale civil war between the north and the south of the country. By the end of 2002 Gbagbo's forces were in control of just the southern half of the country, with at least three separate 'patriotic' movements holding sway over the north and west, and French peacekeepers attempting to stabilize the situation.

Profile of the Prime Minister:

Pascal **AFFI N'GUESSAN**

Pascal Affi N'Guessan trained as a telecommunications engineer. He had little previous national political experience prior to his appointment in 2000 to the transitional cabinet. Having directed Laurent Gbagbo's successful campaign for the presidency, he was rewarded by promotion to prime minister after the October election (whereas his elder brother supported Alassane Ouattara's rival and ultimately outlawed bid as a candidate for the presidency in 2000).

Pascal Affi N'Guessan was born in 1953 at Bouadikro, east of Abidjan, an area inhabited by Agni-speaking people within the broader Akan ethnic group. He was educated locally before going to the Institut National des Télécommunications in Eury, France, to study telecommunications engineering, for which he also holds an Ivorian diploma. He is married with seven children.

Having held the tourism portfolio in Gen. Guéï's transitional regime prior to the October 2000 presidential elections, Affi N'Guessan was appointed prime minister by the incoming President Gbagbo (whose campaign Affi N'Guessan had directed). He is also minister of planning and development. A low-profile premier, he is something of a rarity in the upper echelons of Gbagbo's Ivorian Popular Front (Front Populaire Ivoirien—FPI) as an ethnic Akan from central Côte d'Ivoire. The Akan are more generally associated with the former ruling party of Presidents Houphouët-Boigny and Konan Bédié, whereas the FPI's power base lies more in the (also mainly Christian) west of the country. Affi N'Guessan was made president of the FPI in July 2001, taking over from Gbagbo himself.

CROATIA

Full name: The Republic of Croatia.

Leadership structure: The head of state is a president, directly elected by universal adult suffrage for a five-year term. The head of government is the prime minister, who, under the 2000 constitutional amendments, is appointed by and responsible to the Croatian Assembly. The cabinet is appointed by the prime minister.

Presidents:	Vlatko Pavletić (acting up to and following the death of President Franjo Tudjman on 10 Dec. 1999)	26 Nov. 1999—2 Feb. 2000
	Zlatko Tomčić (acting)	2 Feb. 2000—18 Feb. 2000
	Stipe Mesić	Since 18 Feb. 2000
Prime Ministers:	Zlatko Matesa	7 Nov. 1995—27 Jan. 2000
	Ivica Račan	Since 27 Jan. 2000

Legislature: The legislature, the Croatian Assembly (Hrvatski Sabor), is unicameral. The sole chamber, the House of Representatives (Zastupnički Dom), currently has 151 members (increased from 127 to at most 160 under a law of October 1999), directly elected for a four-year term. In the enlarged House, 140 deputies are elected in ten constituencies, five elected by ethnic minorities, and a variable number (not more than 15) chosen to represent Croatians abroad (six in the 2000 elections). The Assembly was formerly bicameral, but became unicameral on the expiry in May 2001 of the then current mandate of the upper house, the House of Counties (Županijski Dom), after the House of Representatives voted in late March 2001 to abolish the House of Counties.

Profile of the President:

Stipe **MESIĆ**

Stipe Mesić's election as president in February 2000 marked a major shift for Croatia following the death the previous December of the stridently nationalistic Franjo Tudjman. Mesić was especially popular among female and younger voters due to his relaxed style. A career politician, Mesić was the last chairman of the joint presidency of the Socialist Federal Republic of Yugoslavia before Croatian independence and civil war in 1991. In 1994 he split with Tudjman over the government's growing authoritarianism and its pursuit of Croat nationalist ambitions in war-torn neighbouring Bosnia.

Stjepan Mesić was born in the eastern town of Slavonska Orahovica on 24 December 1934. A prominent student activist, he graduated from the University of Zagreb with qualifications in law, and served in the early 1970s as a member of the Croatian republican parliament (within what was then Yugoslavia) before being sentenced to one year in jail for his involvement in the 'Croatian Spring', the 1971 uprising against Yugoslav central control from Belgrade. He is married with two daughters.

In 1989 Mesić joined Tudjman in the newly formed nationalist Croatian Democratic Union (Hrvatska Demokratska Zajednica—HDZ) and following success at the polls in 1990 was appointed as president of the Executive Council—effectively the republic's prime minister. In an effort to sustain the Zagreb-Belgrade relationship, Mesić was appointed to the joint Yugoslavian presidency in May 1991, becoming its chairman on 1 July. As the federation disintegrated beneath him the position became increasingly untenable; Croatia officially pronounced itself independent on 8 October, and on 5 December he resigned as president, famously declaring: "Yugoslavia no longer exists."

The ensuing war abated in 1992 and Mesić was elected as speaker of the Croatian parliament. From this position he led the growing criticisms of the HDZ's authoritarianism and especially the rising cult of personality surrounding the president. From 1993 tensions spiralled, with the war in neighbouring Bosnia raising the possibility of a 'greater Croatia' carved out of Bosnian territory, and in 1994 Mesić was relieved from his post as speaker after he formed the Croatian Independent Democrats (Hrvatski Nezavisni Demokrati—HND). Despite a renewed pact with the Bosnian Muslim-Croat federation Mesić remained in defiance of the HDZ and fared poorly at the polls following the Croat military successes of 1995. Mesić subsequently abandoned the HND to join the Croatian People's Party (Hrvatska Narodna Stranka—HNS) in 1997 and was soon promoted to its vice presidency.

In the autumn of 1999 President Tudjman's health deteriorated rapidly. His death on 10 December gave rise to an urgent race to fill the vacancy. Mesić, who stood as the HNS candidate, was at first seen as an outsider, but quickly rose in opinion polls, contrasting himself to Tudjman's authoritarian approach. He swept the polls to take 56% of the vote in the second round on 7 February 2000. He took office on 18 February. Part of his manifesto had been to reduce the role of president to that of a 'guarantor of balance' in the republic, and on taking office he immediately entered into a dialogue with the Assembly to define the new presidential remit.

Profile of the Prime Minister:

Ivica **RAČAN**

Ivica Račan, who became prime minister when his Social Democratic Party (Socijaldemokratska Partija Hrvatske—SPH) won 47% of the vote in the January 2000 legislative elections, is a career politician and former member of the League of Communists of Yugoslavia (Savez Komunista Jugoslavije—SKJ). As Yugoslavia's disintegration began to take hold, he led the party's Croatian branch (Savez Komunista Hrvatske—SKH) in a declaration of independence from Belgrade in 1990. Keenly aware of the need to deradicalize, he transformed the party into the SPH and helped to guide Croatia through its transition from communism to democracy.

Ivica Račan was born on 24 February 1944 in a Nazi labour camp in Edersbach, near Leipzig in Germany, where his family had been deported. He grew up in the town of Slavonski Brod in eastern Croatia, joining the ruling communist party at 16 and winning election to the Slavonski Brod municipal committee. In 1965 he started work as a researcher at the Zagreb Institute for Social Research and, after studying law at Zagreb University in 1970, sat on the party central committee from 1974 to 1982, subsequently becoming a member of the presidency of the central committee of the SKJ in 1986.

In December 1989 Račan was elected as president of the SKH and headed its delegation at the SKJ's 14th party congress in Belgrade, where he led the rebellion against the authoritarianism of Serbia's Slobodan Milošević. Račan led a walkout of the congress by the SKH, together with the Slovenian delegation, which for many signalled the start of the collapse of the Socialist Federal Republic of Yugoslavia. As one of Croatia's de facto leaders he oversaw the holding of democratic elections in 1990 which led to victory for Franjo Tudjman's nationalist Croatian Democratic Union (Hrvatska Demokratska Zajednica—HDZ) as well as a parliamentary seat for Račan.

Račan worked to transform the old League of Communists, dropping its name and pre-independence connotations to create the SPH in 1991, and building a solid support base in nine years as the main opposition to the HDZ. He was himself re-elected to parliament in 1995 and 1997. For the 2000 elections, seeking to break the HDZ's hold on power, he signed a coalition pact with the social liberal leader Dražen Budiša and together they pushed the nationalists into second place. With Račan's SPH confirmed as the biggest single party, he became prime minister on 27 January at the head of what was to prove over the next two years a fractious coalition (no longer including the social liberals after July 2002). Although the Croatian People's Party of Stipe Mesić was not part of this coalition, Račan worked with Mesić after the latter's election to the presidency in February 2000 to curb the powers of the executive and complete the democratic transformation of Croatia.

CUBA

Full name: The Republic of Cuba.

Leadership structure: The head of state is a president, indirectly elected by the National Assembly. The president's term of office is five years. The head of government is the president. The Council of Ministers is appointed by the National Assembly.

President of the Council of State and Council of Ministers:

Fidel Castro Ruz	Since 2 Dec. 1976
(prime minister since 16 Feb. 1959,	
having taken power on 1 Jan. 1959)	

Legislature: The legislature is unicameral. The sole chamber, the National Assembly of the People's Power (Asamblea Nacional del Poder Popular— ANPP), has 601 members, directly elected for a five-year term. It elects the Council of State, which represents it between its sessions.

Profile of the President of the Council of State and Council of Ministers:

Fidel **CASTRO** Ruz

Targeted as an object of particular hatred by successive US administrations, Fidel Castro survives in power as a lone remnant from the gallery of internationally known communist figures of the Cold War era. The leader of the Cuban revolution in 1959, he has been in power longer than any other current nonhereditary ruler in the world, although despite his age he still presents himself as the fatigue-clad, bearded revolutionary. He still runs a one-party state, but the pope's visit in January 1998 marked the beginning of an improvement in his regime's international relations, and its partial emergence from the isolation it had suffered since the collapse of communism elsewhere.

Fidel Alejandro Castro Ruz was born on 13 August 1926 in Birán in the Oriente region of southeast Cuba. His father Angel Castro, who had arrived as an immigrant farm labourer from Galicia, Spain, owned a 23,000-acre sugar plantation. One of seven children, Fidel Castro had a strict upbringing in a large Roman Catholic family, although he was later to be excommunicated. After attending the local primary school he went to Jesuit schools in Santiago and Havana, and graduated in law from the University of Havana in 1949. He practised as a lawyer in Havana, and planned to stand for parliament, until Gen. Batista seized power in 1952.

After first attempting unsuccessfully to use the law to oppose Batista, by bringing a suit against the dictator for contravening the constitution, Castro became involved in underground resistance. On 26 July 1952 he led an assault on the Moncada barracks in Oriente. Half of his force were killed and both Fidel Castro and his brother Raúl were captured and sentenced to 15 years in prison. Defending himself at the trial, Castro closed his defence with the much-quoted words "History will absolve me". His marriage to Mirta Díaz-Bilart, with whom he had one son, ended with her divorcing him while he was in prison.

Released under a general amnesty in May 1955, Castro fled to Mexico and then on to the USA. He returned to Cuba aboard the *Granma* on 2 December 1956 as leader of an 82-man group of Cuban exiles calling themselves the 26 July Revolutionary Movement. Batista's troops killed 70 of them soon after they landed, leaving the Castro brothers, Che Guevara and just nine others to form the nucleus of a guerrilla movement in the mountainous Sierra Maestra region. Gathering strength over the next two years, the guerrilla army marched on Havana and put Batista to flight on 1 January 1959. The USA recognized Castro's government on 7 January and on 16 February Castro declared himself prime minister.

It was the expropriation of US-owned firms which underlay the rapid deterioration in relations with the USA. Castro responded to Soviet overtures by concluding deals on trade, oil, food and credit, while the USA retaliated on the expropriation issue by imposing an economic embargo. Fearing a Marxist and pro-Soviet state 'in its back yard', the new Kennedy administration in the USA gave the go-ahead for a disastrous attempted invasion of Cuba by CIA-backed Cuban exiles, who were wiped out at the Bay of Pigs in April 1961. In 1962 Castro agreed to a Soviet nuclear weapons base being established on the island. Global nuclear war seemed imminent as the USA imposed a naval blockade to stop the missiles reaching their new base. Superpower negotiation between Presidents Kennedy and Khrushchev ended the crisis, with the Soviet ships turning back with their cargo of missiles, but from then on Castro's government was viewed with even more hostility by the USA and several attempts were made to assassinate Castro.

Castro had declared Cuba a communist single-party state in December 1961, the year in which he was awarded the Lenin Peace Prize. His regime pressed ahead with the nationalization of industry, setting up farm collectives and appropriating property from the wealthy or from foreigners. Thousands of opponents of his regime were imprisoned or executed and many of the middle and upper classes left Cuba, forming a substantial community of exiles in Miami.

In 1963 Castro became first secretary of the United Party of the Cuban Socialist Revolution which became the Cuban Communist Party (Partido Comunista de

Cuba—PCC) in 1965. He did not formally join the party's politburo, however, until 1976. Cuba approved its first constitution in that year and, instead of prime minister, Castro officially became head of state and government as president of the Council of State and the Council of Ministers. Since then he has been re-elected to the presidency a number of times, most recently by the National Assembly in February 1998 when he began a new five-year term in office. He also retains the leadership of the PCC as its first secretary, and in 1992 became, in addition, chairman of the National Defence Council.

From the 1960s until the 1990s Castro governed Cuba on strict Marxist lines. Within Cuba he pointed with particular pride to achievements in the national education and health services. Keen to export the Cuban example, he was active in the Non-Aligned Movement and supported revolutions in Latin America, Ethiopia and Angola, with substantial commitments of military hardware, training and troops.

Through the 1990s Castro insisted on maintaining Cuba's Marxist identity, and came under criticism for the suppression of dissent (with a strong clampdown as late as 1999) as well as for his cautious approach on economic reform. The loss of the once substantial Soviet aid and the ending of preferential trade deals contributed to the problems of the economy, as did, above all, the maintenance of the US trade embargo. Concessions to free enterprise included the introduction of farmers' markets, and a foreign investment law in 1995. In March 1996, however, at a rare meeting of the PCC's central committee, Castro announced stronger measures to restrict private business ventures, emphasizing again his hard-line stance. (The previous December, during a visit to China, he had praised his hosts for holding out against capitalism, thereby reinforcing his own reputation for last-ditch resistance, if not for perceptive analysis of Chinese affairs.) The emergence of a dollarized tourist sector has nevertheless become a major factor in changing the nature of the economy.

On the issue of religious freedom, the unprecedented visit to Cuba by Pope John Paul II in January 1998 helped to encourage the regime's loosening of controls over the Roman Catholic Church, which was even given time for broadcasts on state television, and Christmas was reinstated as a national holiday.

Reports continued to emerge of plots among Cuban exiles to assassinate Castro, while in July 1998 the matter of his health hit the headlines. Officials strongly denied claims made by a Cuban surgeon and recent defector that she had been part of a team which had operated on him for a serious brain condition the previous October. Castro's habits have long frustrated his doctors. His habit for making long-winded speeches in the blazing Cuban sun wearing no hat led to a public collapse in 2001, and in late 2002 an insect bite that he had scratched forced him to take bed rest for a number of days, causing him to miss his first National Assembly session in 25 years. Castro's age and increasing infirmity have made the issue of the succession one of the main focuses of political life, especially with presidential elections due once again in February 2003.

CYPRUS

Full name: The Republic of Cyprus.

Leadership structure: The head of state is a president, directly elected by universal adult suffrage. The president's term of office is five years. The head of government is the president, who appoints the Council of Ministers.

President: Glafcos Clerides   Since 28 Feb. 1993

Legislature: The legislature is unicameral. The sole chamber, the House of Representatives (Vouli Antiprosopon), has 80 members (56 seats for Greek-Cypriots, 24 seats nominally reserved for Turkish-Cypriots), directly elected for a five-year term.

Profile of the President:

Glafcos **CLERIDES**

Glafcos Clerides is a British-trained barrister and parliamentarian, and a veteran of Greek Cypriot politics since pre-independence days. He leads the conservative Democratic Rally (Dimokratikos Synagermos—DISY), which he founded in 1976, and has been president since February 1993.

The eldest son of a lawyer, Glafcos Clerides was born in Nicosia on 24 April 1919, when Cyprus was still under British rule, and received his early education in Cyprus and in the UK before the outbreak of the Second World War in 1939. He joined the Royal Air Force, was shot down over Germany in 1942 and spent the rest of the war in a prison camp. He then resumed his studies in law at King's College, London, gaining a degree in 1948. He was called to the Bar in 1951, after which he returned to Cyprus to practise law (1951–60). During this time he defended numerous fighters of the National Organization of Cypriot Combatants who had been arrested by the British authorities, and also prepared a dossier on British human rights' violations in Cyprus, which was submitted to the Human Rights Commission of the Council of Europe.

When agreement on the basis for independence was eventually reached in 1959, Clerides joined the transitional government as minister of justice. He also led the Greek Cypriot delegation in the joint constitutional committee, which drafted the island's new constitution. Following independence in August 1960, Clerides was elected to the House of Representatives and became president (speaker) of the house the same year, holding this post until 1976. His daughter Katharine Clerides is also politically active and holds a seat in the House of Representatives.

Head of the Red Cross in Cyprus in 1961–63, Clerides led the Greek Cypriot delegation to the London conference on the Cyprus problem the following year, and from 1968 to 1972 he was the chief Greek negotiator in intercommunal talks between the two halves of the island. As president of the House of Representatives Clerides often acted as deputy to President Makarios, most notably in July 1974 when a coup forced Makarios to flee and Turkish troops invaded the northern part of the island. Clerides acted as head of state until Makarios returned at the end of the year.

Clerides founded the Unified Party in February 1969. He went on to create the more conservative DISY in 1976, drawing members from the Unified Party, the Progressive Front, and the Democratic National Party. Although DISY won no seats in the 1976 elections, it has since grown to be the largest party in the House of Representatives. Clerides sat in the house between 1981 and 1991 as a member for Nicosia, and led the DISY party campaign in general elections in 1981, 1985 and 1991, but failed in his 1983 and 1988 bids for the presidency. However, in the 1993 presidential election he eventually succeeded in winning a narrow second-round victory over businessman and incumbent president Georgios Vassiliou. Clerides thus became the first head of state of Cyprus to be elected since independence without the backing of the communist Progressive Party of the Working People. Clerides was re-elected in 1998 for a further term and was widely expected to achieve victory once again in polls scheduled for February 2003.

During the early part of Clerides's presidency there were intermittent outbursts of intercommunal violence. UN mediation resulted in direct talks between Clerides and Rauf Denktaş, president of the self-proclaimed Turkish Republic of Northern Cyprus, ostensibly aimed at resolving the long-standing division of the island. Occasionally giving rise to optimistic speculation in the media, this protracted process was given greater urgency by the approach of the date in 2004 when Cyprus—with or without its Turkish-occupied sector—was to join the European Union. Nevertheless, the negotiations were still stalled at the end of 2002, amid a growing sense that the veteran protagonists Clerides and Denktaş had themselves become obstacles to agreement.

TURKISH REPUBLIC OF NORTHERN CYPRUS

The internationally unrecognized Turkish Republic of Northern Cyprus (TRNC) adopted a constitution in May 1985 creating an executive presidency, directly elected by universal adult suffrage for a five-year term. The TRNC also has an Assembly (Cumhuriyet Meclisi), with 80 members directly elected for a five-year term.

Profile of the TRNC 'President':

Rauf **DENKTAŞ**

A British-trained barrister whose role in representing the Turkish Cypriots dates back to before the ending of British rule in 1960, Rauf Denktaş presided over the TRNC's predecessor, the Turkish Federated State of Cyprus, from 13 February 1975, after the island was partitioned de facto between Greek Cypriot and Turkish Cypriot communities following Turkish military intervention the previous year. Since 15 November 1983 Denktaş has been president of the self-proclaimed TRNC, which is recognized only by Turkey.

Rauf Denktaş was born in Baf (Paphos) on 27 January 1924 and was educated at the English School in Nicosia and then as a barrister at Lincoln's Inn, London. A teacher from 1942 to 1943, he practised law in Nicosia from 1947 to 1949, becoming a Junior Crown Counsel to the attorney general's office in that year, Crown Counsel in 1952 and then acting solicitor general from 1956 to 1958.

In 1948 he had become a member of the Consultative Assembly seeking Cypriot independence from the UK and a member of the Turkish Cypriot affairs committee. As chairman of the Federation of Turkish Cypriot Associations he attended the UN General Assembly in 1958 and led the Turkish Cypriot delegation at the 1959 London conference, at which it was agreed that Cyprus should be a bicommunal partnership state; the rights of the Turkish Cypriot minority, and the independence of the country as a whole, were to be guaranteed by Greece, Turkey and the UK. Denktaş headed the Turkish Cypriot delegation on the constitutional committee drafting the constitution under which Cyprus became independent on 16 August 1960.

As president of the Turkish Communal Chamber from 1960 Denktaş led the opposition to Greek Cypriot proposals to modify the constitution, an issue which led to intercommunal conflict (and the interposition of a UN peacekeeping force) in 1964. Exiled from the island for four years, Denktaş became interlocutor at intercommunal talks which followed a fresh upsurge of violence in 1967, and was re-elected as president of the Turkish Communal Chamber in 1970. The nominal position of vice president of Cyprus, to which he was elected unopposed in February 1973, was increasingly irrelevant to the real situation, however, with talks achieving nothing and the Turkish Cypriots focusing instead on organizing their own government within the area in which they were the majority population.

A short-lived extreme right-wing coup backed by the Greek military junta on 15 July 1974, and the Turkish response of sending troops to occupy northern Cyprus, crystallized the partition of the island. A Turkish Federated State of Cyprus was proclaimed in the Turkish-occupied north in February 1975. Denktaş was designated as its first president, and won an overwhelming victory when presidential elections were held in June 1976, with his National Unity Party (Ulusal Birlik Partisi—UBP) dominating that year's elections to a Turkish Cypriot Assembly. He retained this post until 15 November 1983, when the federated state was replaced by a Turkish Republic of Northern Cyprus (TRNC), whose 'declaration of full independence' was recognized only by Turkey.

Although indisputably the leading figure in Turkish Cypriot politics, Denktaş has seen his share of the vote in successive TRNC presidential elections fall from over 70% in 1985 to only 44% in 2000. The decline in his popularity reflects concern over the deteriorating economic situation in the internationally isolated north, the perceived dangers of being left out of Cypriot membership of the European Union (due in 2004), and the absence of any breakthrough in the protracted talks on a negotiated Cyprus settlement. Denktaş has continued with these talks under UN auspices, but without contributing any real new ideas. The UBP split in 1992 when he rejected the idea of abandoning the talks and formalizing the partition. His supporters set up a breakaway Democratic Party (Demokrat Parti—DP) which he subsequently joined; like the UBP it is essentially a centre-right formation, committed to a secularist approach and ostensibly inspired by the example of Atatürk as founder of modern Turkey.

Rauf Denktaş is married to Aydın Münür. They have had two daughters and three sons, one of whom has died; Serdar Denktaş led the DP between 1996 and 2000 and again from 2002, and has held various ministerial posts.

Profile of the TRNC 'Prime Minister':

Derviş **EROGLU**

Derviş Eroglu was prime minister from 1985 to 1993, and again since August 1996, of the government of the self-styled Turkish Republic of Northern Cyprus (TRNC), which declared its independence in 1983 but has won recognition only from Turkey. A former doctor, he leads the right-wing National Unity Party (Ulusal Birlik Partisi—UBP) established in 1975. Eroglu challenged TRNC President Rauf Denktaş unsuccessfully in the 1995 presidential election, but his current government is a coalition between his UBP and the pro-Denktaş Democratic Party (Demokrat Parti—DP).

Derviş Eroglu was born in Ergazi, Famagusta, on the eastern coast of Cyprus, in 1938. Having studied medicine at Istanbul University, Turkey, he worked as a medical doctor before resuming his medical studies in 1969, specializing as a urologist at Ankara University. He is married with four children.

Following the Turkish invasion and occupation of northern Cyprus in 1974, Eroglu entered the Assembly of the self-proclaimed Turkish Federated State of Cyprus in 1976 and has been re-elected four times. Between 1976 and 1977 he served as the territory's minister of education, culture, youth and sports and, following the TRNC's declaration of independence, became a member of the Constituent Assembly in November 1983. He first became chairman of the UBP that year, after its split between pro- and anti-Denktaş elements, and was prime minister of four successive governments between 1985 and 1993.

Eroglu went into opposition from the beginning of 1994, the TRNC Assembly elections the previous month having brought to power a coalition of the pro-Denktaş DP and the leftist Republican Turkish Party. In the territory's presidential elections in April 1995 Eroglu went through to a second-round runoff against Denktaş (who on previous occasions had won outright in the first round of voting). Although Eroglu took only 37.5% of the second-round vote, the unprecedented strength of his challenge reflected the TRNC's growing economic problems as a result of its political isolation and concerns about Denktaş's increasing personal power. When the DP-led coalition government collapsed on 4 July 1996, Eroglu went on to form a new coalition between the UBP and the DP six weeks later.

In elections on 6 December 1998 the UBP fell only two seats short of a majority itself and Eroglu formed a new coalition with the leftist Communal Liberation Party (Toplumcu Kurtuluş Partisi—TKP). With talks with the Greek Cypriot government continuing to founder into the new century, Eroglu was able to claim 30% in the first round of presidential elections in April 2000, but withdrew from the second round against Denktaş. The UBP–TKP coalition collapsed in May 2001 after disagreeing over whether to support continuing talks with the Greek Cypriots, and Eroglu returned to his earlier coalition formula with the DP, commanding 37 seats in the 50-seat TRNC Assembly and thus a powerful majority in favour of the talks.

CZECH REPUBLIC

Full name: The Czech Republic.

Leadership structure: The head of state is a president, indirectly elected by a joint session of both houses of Parliament. The president's term of office is five years, with a maximum of two consecutive terms. The head of government is the prime minister, who is responsible to the Chamber of Deputies. The Council of Ministers is appointed by the prime minister.

President:	Václav Havel	Since 2 Feb. 1993
Prime Ministers:	Miloš Zeman	17 July 1998—12 July 2002
	Vladimír Špidla	Since 12 July 2002

Legislature: The legislature, the Parliament (Parlament), is bicameral. The lower chamber, the Chamber of Deputies (Poslanecká Sněmovna), has 200 members, directly elected for a four-year term. The upper chamber, the Senate (Senát), has 81 directly elected members. All members of the Senate were first elected in November 1996; one-third of the seats come up for re-election every two years, and senators now serve six-year terms.

Profile of the President:

Václav **HAVEL**

Václav Havel, the renowned playwright and former leading dissident, provided Czechoslovakia's 1989 'velvet revolution' with leadership of unusual moral authority. Described as a 'philosopher king', with an unassuming and informal manner which belies the strength of his influence, he was president from 1989 but resigned in disappointment as Czechoslovakia prepared to dissolve in 1992. In January 1993 he became president of the new Czech Republic. In this primarily ceremonial role, despite his own serious illness, he has proved influential in cementing relations with western Europe and in matters affecting civil rights.

Václav Havel was born on 5 October 1936 in Prague. Because of his bourgeois family background (his father was a prominent businessman), the postwar communist regime initially denied him a university place and he worked instead as a chemical laboratory technician, while studying at evening classes and eventually graduating in 1954. From 1954 to 1957 he attended the economics faculty of the Czech Technical University in Prague. He did his military service from 1957 to 1959.

In 1960 he started working as a stagehand, first at the ABC Theatre and then at the Theatre on the Balustrade in Prague, where he rose to be literary manager and assistant director by 1968. His plays were first performed while he was studying dramatic art theory at the Prague Academy of Performing Arts from 1962 to 1966; he won international acclaim with *The Garden Party* (1963) and subsequent work such as *The Increased Difficulty of Concentration* (1968), *Audience* (1975) and *The Mountain Hotel* (1976).

In 1968, caught up in enthusiasm for the promise of a new liberal communism in the so-called 'Prague Spring', Havel chaired the Circle of Independent Writers, and was a fierce opponent of the invasion by Warsaw Pact forces that August. The subsequent period of repression saw his work banned in Czechoslovakia, although it circulated as *samizdat* (illegal 'self-published' manuscripts) and was published to widespread acclaim in the West. Forced to move to the country and work as a labourer in a brewery, he organized a petition in 1972 pressing for the release of political prisoners, and in 1975 he wrote a critical open letter to President Gustáv Husák. On 1 January 1977 Havel was a founding signatory of what became the rallying call of the human rights movement, Charter 77.

The spokesperson for the small group of dissident intellectuals behind this original initiative, Havel also helped set up the Committee for the Defence of the Unjustly Prosecuted in 1978, and wrote his influential essay *The Power of the Powerless*. His sustained dissident activity led to his house arrest in 1978–79, and he spent a long period in prison from 1979 to 1983 on a charge of sedition, during which he wrote the famous series of *Letters to Olga* to his wife. (Olga Šplíchalová, whom he married in 1964, died in January 1996. A year later Havel was remarried, to the acclaimed Czech actress Dagmar Veškrnová.)

In January 1989 Havel was again arrested, with a group of human rights demonstrators, and sentenced to nine months' imprisonment for incitement and obstruction. This aroused a major international protest, which embarrassed the regime into releasing him in May.

The astonishingly rapid collapse of communist rule in Czechoslovakia—and elsewhere across central and eastern Europe—in late 1989 propelled Havel into a national leadership role, despite his own ambivalence about direct political involvement. Informally identified as the leader of Civic Forum (Občanská Fórum—OF), which he helped set up in November, he was at the forefront of the protest movement and massive popular demonstrations which swept the old regime from power. On 29 December Havel was elected by the parliament as interim president, pending the holding of general elections the following June; the new Federal Assembly, meeting on 5 July 1990, then confirmed him in office for two years.

The 1990 elections underlined Havel's problems in establishing a neutral nonparty presidential role, given his close connections with Civic Forum, his attendance at their rallies and his controversial comment during the campaign that he would be voting for Civic Forum candidates. During his subsequent term, Havel's relations with Slovak nationalist leader Vladimír Mečiar were often difficult, while it was common knowledge that he differed with the finance minister and later Czech prime minister Václav Klaus over the speed and uncompromising radicalism of the switchover to a free-market economy.

Havel stood down as Czechoslovakia's president at the end of his two-year term in July 1992, when his federalist constitutional proposals had been rejected and it was becoming increasingly unlikely that any form of Czech and Slovak federation would survive the pull of Slovak separatism. When the separation of the two states had been formalized, the Parliament of the Czech Republic elected him unopposed to the presidency on 26 January 1993. He took office on 2 February. In May of that year several foreign nationals were arrested after a suspected assassination attempt against him.

Although the presidency was required to be nonpartisan, Havel's moral stature gave his role considerable weight in Czech public life and in promoting the country's interests in integration within a democratic Europe. Unexpectedly, it took two rounds of voting (by the members of both houses of Parliament) for him to win re-election for a further, and constitutionally final, five-year term of office in January 1998. This was principally because of the hostility of supporters of Klaus, angered by Havel's appointment of a nonparty prime minister and the relegation of Klaus to an opposition role after his government collapsed in late 1997. Havel's backing of the temporary nonparty administration continued until the passage of a constitutional amendment compelled him to call a general election for June 1998. Meanwhile, he took the opportunity of his inaugural speech at the beginning of his second term in February 1998 to rededicate himself to the development of democracy and civic society and to combating the growth of nationalism and xenophobia. On several occasions since then he has decried prejudice and discrimination against the Roma minority, calling for greater tolerance and the renewal of the 'spirit of 1989'.

Havel's health has on several occasions caused serious alarm. A heavy smoker, he had surgery for lung cancer in December 1996, and suffered a serious bout of pneumonia in October–November 1997. In April 1998 he had surgery again in Austria, and in July–August 1998 an operation to remove his temporary colostomy was followed by emergency surgery to deal with the consequences of the collapse of his right lung. Since then he has been in relatively better health although he has fought through recurring bronchial infections, usually worsened by winter weather at the beginning of each year. Concerns that he might not see his last term in office through to its conclusion proved groundless, however, and by the end of 2002 he was preparing to step down from public life for the last time on 2 February 2003 to make way for his successor.

Profile of the Prime Minister:

Vladimír **ŠPIDLA**

Vladimír Špidla has led the left-of-centre Czech Social Democratic Party (Česká Strana Sociálne Demokratická—ČSSD) since April 2001. Having worked as an archaeologist among other jobs during the communist era, he entered politics in 1990 and was appointed to the cabinet as a deputy prime minister in 1998. He became prime minister in July 2002 after steering the ČSSD to re-election.

Vladimír Špidla was born in Prague on 22 April 1951 in what was then the capital of communist Czechoslovakia. He began his studies in history at the Charles University in the city in 1970 and received his doctorate in the subject in 1976. He has been married twice and has two children from his first marriage, as does his second wife.

Between 1976 and 1989 Špidla took on various roles. These included working to preserve historic monuments, straightforward archaeology fieldwork and even jobs as a worker in a wood-processing plant, a dairy and a building materials store. Shying away from politics until the 'velvet revolution' brought down the communist regime in 1989, he then joined the Jindřichův Hradec District National Committee as vice chairman with responsibilities for education, health, social affairs and culture. From here he moved to the local labour office in 1991. He was elected to the ČSSD's executive in 1992 and, having entered the Chamber of Deputies in 1996, was made vice chairman of the party in March 1997.

In the ČSSD government of Prime Minister Miloš Zeman, Špidla was appointed deputy prime minister and minister of labour and social affairs in July 1998. His political abilities were duly noted and in April 2001 the party voted to make him its new chairman with the remit of heading its re-election campaign the following year. The party received 30% of the vote in the June 2002 elections and Špidla was nominated by President Václav Havel to form a new ČSSD-led coalition. Špidla's government quickly ran into complications, however, when in September 2002 one of the junior coalition partners, the Freedom Union, rejected a proposed 'flood tax' designed to pay for recent severe flood damage.

DENMARK

Full name: The Kingdom of Denmark.

Leadership structure: The head of state is a hereditary monarch. The head of government is the prime minister, who appoints a cabinet.

Queen:	Margrethe II	Since 15 Jan. 1972
Prime Ministers:	Poul Nyrup Rasmussen	25 Jan. 1993—27 Nov. 2001
	Anders Fogh Rasmussen	Since 27 Nov. 2001

Legislature: The legislature is unicameral. The sole chamber, the Parliament (Folketing), has 179 members, directly elected for a four-year term.

Profile of the Queen:

MARGRETHE II

Queen Margrethe II succeeded to the Danish throne in January 1972 upon the death of her father Frederik IX. An amendment to the Danish constitution, adopted in 1953 through a referendum, permitted female descendants of the reigning monarch to ascend the throne as long as there were no male heirs. As is the rule with Scandinavian monarchs Queen Margrethe has no personal political power. Her titular roles include that of supreme commander of the Danish defence forces.

Margrethe II was born on 16 April 1940 at Amalienborg. Given the names Margrethe Alexandrine Thorhildur Ingrid, she is the eldest daughter of King Frederik IX (1899–1972) and Queen Ingrid (1910–2000). Having completed her secondary education in Denmark at Zahles Skole, she took the philosophy examination at Copenhagen University in 1960, studied prehistoric archaeology at Cambridge University in 1960–61, and later specialized in political science at Århus (1961–62), the Sorbonne (1963) and the London School of Economics (1965). In her youth she took part in several archaeological excavations in Greece, Sudan and Rome.

In April 1958 Margrethe first began attending the weekly meetings of the Council of State between the monarch and the cabinet. Since ascending the throne on 15 January 1972 she has taken an active interest in matters of state, meeting her ministers weekly and representing Denmark abroad.

Margrethe illustrated Tolkien's *The Lord of the Rings* in 1977 and as an artist she has also worked with handicrafts and textiles and designed seals, calendars, and costumes for television and theatre productions. In 1981, with her French husband, she translated Simone de Beauvoir's *All Men Are Mortal*. She was awarded the Danish Language Society Prize in 1989 and is an honorary member of the Swedish Royal Academy of Science, History and Antiquities.

Margrethe married on 10 June 1967 the French diplomat Count Henri-Marie-Jean-André de Laborde de Monpezat, who took the courtesy title Prince Henrik of Denmark. They have two sons, Crown Prince Frederick and Prince Joachim.

Profile of the Prime Minister:

Anders Fogh **RASMUSSEN**

Anders Fogh Rasmussen was originally an outspoken right-winger within the Liberal Party (Venstre), but softened his style on taking over the party leadership in 1998. Remodelling himself along the lines of the so-called 'third way' associated with UK prime minister Tony Blair and German chancellor Gerhard Schröder, Rasmussen has earned the nickname 'Mr Perfect'. He combines his recently developed support for Denmark's welfare state with stricter rules on immigration, heading a minority coalition that depends on support in Parliament from the far-right Danish People's Party (Dansk Folkeparti—DF).

Anders Fogh Rasmussen was born on 29 January 1953 in Ginnerup, east Jutland. He grew up on the family farm and completed his secondary education in 1972 at the Viborg Cathedral School, where he had already begun his career in right-wing politics, founding and chairing the school branch of the Young Liberals. He went on to Århus University to study economics, graduating in 1978 with a master's degree. While at university he headed the Young Liberals Party from 1974 and joined the Danish Youth Council in 1976. In the year of his graduation he was successfully elected to Parliament as a member of Venstre, and married his wife Anne-Mette, with whom he has three children.

Since 1978 Rasmussen has been re-elected to Parliament at every election. At first he combined his rapid political career with a professional line as an economics consultant, beginning at the Danish Federation of Crafts and Small Industries. His work also included positions with the Building Council's Mortgage Credit Fund, the insurance company Østifterne and the investment firm Andelsinvest. During these early years in Parliament he was a strident critic of the postwar welfare state, and wrote a number of vehement articles against it, including *From Social State to Minimal State* which prompted much discussion. In the meantime he was also sitting on parliamentary fiscal affairs and housing committees.

Following Venstre's electoral successes in the 1980s Rasmussen rose high and fast. From 1987 to 1992 he was minister of taxation and from 1990 he combined that portfolio with the ministry for economic affairs. His meteoric career was threatened in 1992 when he was forced to step down from the cabinet after opposition claims that he had misled Parliament. With his own downfall came that of the party and Venstre was voted into opposition in 1993. For five years Rasmussen remained vocally prominent in Parliament as vice chairman of the economic and political affairs committee, while also resuming some consultancy work.

In 1998 Rasmussen was elected leader of Venstre ahead of legislative elections. The party's failure to oust the incumbent Social Democrat government that year was largely put down to the electorate's fear that under Rasmussen Venstre would dismantle the welfare state. The defeat prompted a rethink and the beginning of Rasmussen's remarkable transformation. In just three years he distanced himself from the right-wing rhetoric of his past, learning to embrace both welfare state and Denmark's membership of the EU. Seeking to dominate the middle ground of Danish politics, he mixed these newer philosophies with some mainstream conservatism, support for lower taxation, and an even harsher approach to immigration. He struck a populist chord when he referred to unemployed immigrants, of whom there are few in Denmark, as "scroungers".

In the November 2001 elections a positive response among voters to Rasmussen's new image, combined with widespread disappointment with the pro-EU Social Democrats, gave Venstre the largest share of the vote, for the first time since the 1920s. However, the party still lacked an overall majority, with only 31% of the seats in Parliament. Rasmussen formed a minority coalition with the Conservative People's Party, which left him dependent on the far-right DF for support in Parliament.

DJIBOUTI

Full name: The Republic of Djibouti.

Leadership structure: The head of state is a president, directly elected for a six-year term. The president appoints the Council of Ministers, which is responsible to the president. The prime minister presides at meetings of the Council of Ministers and is formally head of government.

President:	Ismaïl Omar Guelleh	Since 8 May 1999
Prime Ministers:	Barkat Gourad Hamadou (acting since 6 Feb. 2001)	30 Sept. 1978—7 March 2001
	Dileita Mohamed Dileita	Since 7 March 2001

Legislature: The legislature is unicameral. The sole chamber, the National Assembly (Assemblée Nationale), has 65 members, directly elected for a five-year term.

Profile of the President:

Ismaïl Omar **GUELLEH**

Ismaïl Omar Guelleh was handpicked as successor by his uncle, the aging president Hassan Gouled Aptidon, whom he served as chief of staff for 22 years. As he was seen as the regime's strongman, his election to the presidency, as the candidate of the ruling Popular Rally for Progress (Rassemblement Populaire pour le Progrès—RPP), was hotly contested by the rebel Front for the Restoration of Unity and Democracy (Front pour la Restauration de l'Unité et de la Démocratie—FRUD). Since becoming president in May 1999, however, he has overseen the end of the civil war and encouraged the FRUD's participation in politics.

Ismaïl Omar Guelleh, who is now married with four children, was born into the ethnic Issa community in 1947 in the Ethiopian town of Dire Dawa. His parents sent him to a French religious school there for his primary studies, and then to secondary school in neighbouring Djibouti, which was under French colonial rule as French Somaliland. After leaving school he joined the French administration's police force in 1968 and was promoted to inspector in 1970. Despite his chosen profession within the colonial social structure, Guelleh became involved in the illegal Issa-dominated separatist movement, the African Popular League for Independence (Ligue Populaire Africaine pour l'Indépendance—LPAI).

When the authorities discovered Guelleh's connection with the LPAI in 1975 he was suspended from the police force. Over the next two years he participated in several LPAI missions overseas, seeking support in Libya and Mogadishu, and entering discussions with the French government over independence for Djibouti, which finally came in 1977. Guelleh played an active role in the foundation of the separatist newspaper *Populaire*, which was run by his colleague Ahmed Dini, and his own publication *Djibouti Aujourd'hui*.

The newly independent Djibouti was run from 1977 to 1999 by President Gouled, Guelleh's uncle, and Guelleh was throughout this period head of the president's office with special remit over national security. As a prominent member of the LPAI he was included in the 1979 transformation of the League into the RPP which then ran the country as a single-party state until 1992. In 1983 Guelleh was elected to the party's central committee and directed a cultural commission to Paris before becoming a member of its executive from 1987. After a referendum in 1992 the country adopted a multiparty constitution but in practice the RPP still utterly dominated national politics. Political tensions mingled with ethnic divisions to fuel the fierce civil war which had erupted in 1991. The breakaway FRUD, headed by Guelleh's old LPAI comrade Ahmed Dini, backed an Afar uprising and rejected a power-sharing deal offered by the government in 1993.

As Gouled's heir apparent, Guelleh was elevated to be the third vice president of the RPP in 1996 before being nominated as its presidential candidate when Gouled finally announced his resignation in February 1999. He faced as little apparent opposition at the polls as his uncle had, and swept into office with 74% of the vote in the April elections. The results were immediately questioned by the FRUD candidate Moussa Ahmed Idriss and the international community at large.

Guelleh's greatest achievement after becoming president was the conclusion in February 2000 of a peace agreement to end the country's bitter ethnic-fuelled conflict. Later that same year he expanded his role as peacebroker to the Horn of Africa region, inviting political leaders from neighbouring Somalia to Djibouti to negotiate the restoration of centralized government to that troubled state.

Profile of the Prime Minister:

Dileita Mohamed **DILEITA**

Dileita Mohamed Dileita is a member of the ruling People's Rally for Progress (Rassemblement Populaire pour le Progrès—RPP). A career diplomat, he served as ambassador to Ethiopia before being appointed prime minister in March 2001.

Dileita Mohamed Dileita was born on 12 March 1958 in Tadjoura in what was then French Somaliland. He is married and has one child. He was sent to Cairo,

Egypt, and later Reims, France, for his education before attending the Centre for Vocational Training in Médéa, Algeria. He graduated in 1981 and returned to Djibouti where he worked at the ministry of foreign affairs, subsequently becoming an adviser to the country's embassies, and going back to France in 1986 to study diplomacy at the French foreign ministry.

Continuing his diplomatic career, Dileita returned to Djibouti to become chief of protocol. He had a further spell in France from 1992, as an adviser to the Djibouti embassy there, and in 1997 he was made full ambassador to Ethiopia. In this role he also represented the country at the Organization for African Unity (OAU) and played a key part in brokering peace talks between Ethiopia and Eritrea at the end of their two-year border war.

In February 2001 the aging veteran prime minister, Barkat Gourad Hamadou was allowed to retire. President Ismaïl Guelleh appointed Dileita in his place in March.

DOMINICA

Full name: The Commonwealth of Dominica.

Leadership structure: The head of state is a president, elected by the legislature. The president's term of office is five years, renewable once only. The head of government is the prime minister, who is appointed by the president from among the members of the House of Assembly.

President:	Vernon Shaw	Since 6 Oct. 1998
Prime Ministers:	Edison James	14 June 1995—3 Feb. 2000
	Roosevelt 'Rosie' Douglas	3 Feb. 2000—1 Oct. 2000
	Pierre Charles (acting from 1 Oct. 2000)	Since 3 Oct. 2000

Legislature: The legislature is unicameral. The sole chamber, the House of Assembly, has 21 directly elected members and nine appointed senators who sit for a five-year term.

Profile of the President:

Vernon **SHAW**

Vernon Shaw, a committed Methodist and freemason, earned a reputation as a diligent and hardworking civil servant during a 42-year career in a variety of government offices. Although unaffiliated to any party, he was elected president in 1998 as the nominee of the then ruling United Workers' Party (UWP).

Vernon Lorden Shaw was born on 13 May 1930 on Dominica, then a part of the British Leeward Islands federation. He was educated at the Dominica Grammar School, and taught there as a temporary master for a period after completing his own schooling in 1947, before going to Trinity College, Oxford, UK, to study development administration. He began his civil service career at the central housing and planning authority, working as an accountant. Vernon Shaw is married to Eudora, also a civil servant, and they have four children.

After a series of increasingly senior posts in the treasury, the post office and the department of trade, he was appointed in 1967 as permanent secretary in the newly independent Dominica's ministry of education and health. He went on to work at the external affairs ministry and as chief establishment officer from 1971.

In 1977 Shaw was made secretary to the cabinet of Prime Minister Patrick John, of the Dominica Labour Party, and remained in this post until his retirement from the civil service in June 1990. During this period he served as ambassador-at-large for an independent Dominica—at the UN, the Organization of American States (OAS) and the high commission in London.

Between 1990 and 1998 Shaw had various posts, including tutoring at the University of the West Indies and chairing the Dominica Broadcasting Corporation. Up to his election he worked at the public service board of appeal. Shaw was nominated by the UWP to replace incumbent President Crispin Sorhaindo in October 1998 and was elected by the House of Assembly for a five-year term in a vote that closely followed party lines.

Profile of the Prime Minister:

Pierre **CHARLES**

Pierre Charles was appointed prime minister in October 2000 after the sudden death of the previous incumbent, Roosevelt 'Rosie' Douglas, two days earlier. Charles had hitherto served as deputy leader of the ruling Dominica Labour Party (DLP) and communications and public works minister under Douglas.

Pierre Charles was born on 30 June 1954 on Dominica which by then had been a member of the British Windward Islands federation for 14 years. He was educated in various island institutions and graduated from St Mary's Academy in 1972. After leaving school he became involved in the national youth council, of which he was president from 1977. He completed his professional education at a teacher training college between 1978 and 1979. After working briefly as a teacher he was elected as a senator in the first postindependence parliament.

Between 1979 and 1988 Charles ran Farm-to-Market, a banana exporting business. During this time he ran for public office as a village councillor for Grand Bay in 1984 and entered the House of Assembly to represent the district in 1986. He has served this same constituency ever since. On leaving Farm-to-Market Charles devoted his time to politics as a member of the opposition DLP. He was appointed deputy party leader in 1991.

Following legislative elections in January 2000, won by the DLP after more than ten years in opposition, Charles was appointed to the cabinet by Douglas as minister of communications and works. As deputy leader he was best placed to step in as premier and party leader when Douglas died of a heart attack in October of that year. He has also taken on Douglas's clutch of portfolios.

Pierre Charles is married and enjoys playing basketball as well as listening to Creole and folk music. Between 1973 and 1979 he was an active member of La Jeune Etoile Chorale music group, and as manager of the Midnight Groovers Band he produced two albums between 1995 and 1998.

DOMINICAN REPUBLIC

Full name: The Dominican Republic.

Leadership structure: The head of state is a president, directly elected by universal adult suffrage. The president's term of office is four years. A president may serve at most two consecutive terms. The head of government is the president, who appoints and presides over the cabinet.

Presidents:	Leonel Fernández Reyna	16 Aug. 1996—16 Aug. 2000
	Hipólito Mejía Domínguez	Since 16 Aug. 2000

Legislature: The legislature, the National Congress of the Republic (Congreso Nacional), is bicameral. The lower chamber, the Chamber of Deputies (Cámara de Diputados), has 150 members, directly elected for a four-year term. The upper chamber, the Senate (Senado), has 30 members, also directly elected for a four-year term.

Profile of the President:

Hipólito **MEJÍA** Domínguez

Hipólito Mejía heads the leftist Dominican Revolutionary Party (Partido Revolucionario Dominicano—PRD), but is generally seen as a party moderate. Known as 'El Guapo de Gurabo' (the tough guy from Gurabo), he has a down-to-earth style which has drawn criticism for its popularism. Like many Dominicans he is a devout Christian, and headed the Christian Family Movement in the mid-1960s. He won elections in 2000 campaigning on a promise to redirect the benefits of economic growth towards the country's many poor.

Rafael Hipólito Mejía Domínguez was born on 22 February 1941 in a peasant farming family in Gurabo, near Santiago, in the country's rural heartland. He was educated at grammar schools in the region until he entered the Jesuit-run San Cristóbal Polytechnic Institute in 1957 where he studied agronomy. Graduating in 1964, he married Rosa Gómez that same year and they have four children. He then attended the University of North Carolina, USA, to study the workings of the tobacco industry.

On his return in 1965 Mejía was appointed as director of the country's tobacco institute before joining the US-based company Rohm and Haas as area representative for the Caribbean. In this role he worked to promote new agricultural technologies throughout the islands. His work refocused on the

Dominican Republic from 1973 when he worked as a representative of various international companies.

The presidential victory of the PRD's Antonio Guzmán Fernández in 1978 brought Mejía into politics. He served as Guzmán's secretary of agriculture for the entire four-year term and applied his agricultural background to the role with general success. Guzmán's defeat at the polls in 1982 took them both out of government and Mejía returned to private affairs. Alongside his previous role of regional agricultural consultant, he took up the running of his family's agricultural company. However, he retained his affiliation to the PRD, having been appointed the party's deputy leader, and made a brief return to the national stage when the popular PRD leader José Peña Gómez chose Mejía as his running mate in the 1990 presidential contest. The election was won by four-time president Joaquín Balaguer Ricardo, and Mejía returned to his family business once again.

The death of Peña Gómez from cancer in 1998 is thought to have secured a large sympathy vote in elections later that year which gave the PRD a large majority in both houses of Congress. On the back of this success Mejía stood in the presidential campaign for 2000. Leonel Fernández Reyna's administration had done much for the GDP of the Dominican Republic, but had had little effect on the living conditions of the rural poor, and was domestically criticized for being aloof. Mejía's promises of greater investment in the country's social infrastructure secured him 49.9% of the vote in May. A runoff was avoided when his main opponents, Danilo Medina Sánchez of the Dominican Liberation Party and the 93-year-old Balaguer,—each with around 25%—both conceded defeat. Mejía was inaugurated on 16 August.

As president, Mejía has worked to cut back on the unwieldy government apparatus constructed under Fernández. One of his first acts in promoting government austerity was to reduce his own pay by 40%. He went on to dismiss 70,000 government workers, but then filled many of the posts with loyalist PRD supporters.

EAST TIMOR

Full name: The Republic of East Timor.

Leadership structure: The head of state is a president, directly elected by universal adult suffrage. The president's term of office is five years. The head of government is the prime minister, who is appointed by the president and nominates the Council of Ministers.

UN Administrator: Sérgio Vieira de Mello   25 Oct. 1999—19 May 2002

President: José Alexandre 'Xanana' Gusmão   Since 20 May 2002

Prime Minister: Mari Alkatiri   Since 20 May 2002
(chief minister from 20 Sept. 2001)

Legislature: The Constituent Assembly (Assembléia Constituinte), with 88 members, was elected in August 2001 and inaugurated on 15 September. In December 2001 the Assembly began debating the details of a constitution for a fully independent state in preparation for presidential elections. The Assembly voted on 31 January 2002 to convert itself into a full parliament without further elections. The parliament's term of office was not announced.

Profile of the President:

'Xanana' **GUSMÃO**

Active in the resistance from the time of the Indonesian invasion in 1975, 'Xanana' Gusmão was leader of the Revolutionary Front for an Independent East Timor (Frente Revolucionária do Timor Leste Independente—Fretilin) from the early 1980s, and a founder member of the broader-based National Council of Maubere Resistance (Conselho Nacional da Resistência Maubere—CNRM). He was captured by the Indonesian authorities in 1992 and imprisoned until September 1999, his release following Indonesian acceptance of the need to prepare a transition to independence. As the principal surviving hero of the resistance, he became a popular choice for the new state's presidency once he had overcome his initial reluctance to take on the task.

José Alexandre Gusmão was born in Manatuto, East Timor, on the night of 20–21 June 1947. His father was a schoolmaster and part-time factory inspector. Gusmão attended a Jesuit seminary for his secondary education, and spent the subsequent years either unemployed or in construction and low-grade clerical

148

jobs. He married Emilia Baptista in 1970 and they had two children together. In 1974 political tensions in East Timor escalated, as Portuguese sovereignty came increasingly to be questioned and internecine conflict threatened, causing Gusmão to contemplate emigration to Australia. He remained in the country, however, and joined Fretilin after the Democratic Union of Timor (União Democrática Timorense—UDT) tried to seize power from the Portuguese in August 1975, precipitating a civil war.

In 1975 Gusmão helped organize Fretilin, working at the Fretilin department of information and later gaining election to the Fretilin central committee. Gusmão also helped set up the Armed Forces for the National Liberation of East Timor (Forças Armadas de Libertação Nacional de Timor Leste—Falintil). On 28 November 1975 Fretilin declared East Timor independent, but on 7 December Indonesian troops invaded, crushing Fretilin and leaving Gusmão separated in far-eastern Timor. After this Gusmão was given responsibility for a handful of resistance fighters in the far-eastern part of East Timor and he set about rebuilding the movement there.

In 1986 Gusmão presided over the formation of the CNRM which drew on much broader support within East Timor than just Fretilin. By 1988 he was the commander of a pan-East Timorese underground army, uniting several underground resistance movements, including Fretilin, the UDT and the youth movement Renetil. During this period he continued to seek a peaceful resolution to the conflict, pushing for negotiations with the Indonesian government and a UN presence on the island. He also tried to promote international awareness of the political situation in East Timor.

Gusmão was captured in November 1992 in a western suburb of Dili. Between February and May 1993 an Indonesian court tried him for rebellion, possession of firearms and causing death to villagers. He was sentenced to life imprisonment, later reduced to 20 years. Gusmão continued to appeal to the international community from his prison cell, and to demand UN involvement in East Timor. He received a high-profile visit from the world's most famous ex-prisoner, South Africa's Nelson Mandela, in July 1997, and was appointed president of the National Council of Timorese Resistance (Conselho Nacional da Resistência Timorense—CNRT), the successor to the CNRM, in April 1998. The accession of B.J. Habibie as Indonesian president in May 1998 raised hopes of a breakthrough, but in the event Gusmão's sentence was only reduced by four months.

January 1999 proved to be a key month in East Timor's history. Gusmão was permitted to serve the rest of his sentence under house arrest (although he was not moved until April) and the Indonesian government surprisingly gave its consent to a referendum on Timorese independence. Tragically, this news prompted a dramatic increase in violence on the island and Gusmão urged Falintil to resume its struggle. Nonetheless, on 30 August 1999, an overwhelming 79% of voters endorsed independence. The violence increased following the announcement of the 'yes' result as anti-independence militias ravaged the territory. Gusmão was released from house arrest on 7 September, but, fearing for his safety, travelled to exile in Australia.

Once relative peace had been restored by a UN force, Gusmão made a triumphant return to Dili in October 1999. Although clearly the most popular figure in the country, he startled observers by declaring in February 2000 that he would not seek the presidency when independence was granted. He resigned as leader of Falintil in August 2000 in order to concentrate on the political path to independence, and was appointed head of the transitional National Council (advisory assembly) in October. Becoming increasingly disillusioned with the whole process, however, he stepped down in March 2001, with a parting shot at the UN administration. In the meantime he had divorced his wife and married former Australian secret agent Kirsty Sword in July 2000. They now have two infant children.

By August 2001 he had succumbed to growing public pressure and announced that he would, after all, stand for the presidency. His popularity was such that the only other candidate stood merely in order to provide voters with a choice. He was elected with 83% of the vote on 14 April 2002. East Timor became independent a month later on 20 May, on which day Gusmão was inaugurated.

Profile of the Prime Minister:

Mari **ALKATIRI**

Mari Alkatiri was one of the founders of the Revolutionary Front for an Independent East Timor (Frente Revolucionária do Timor Leste Independente— Fretilin) independence movement which now governs East Timor. Noted in the past for his international left-wing connections, he was effectively exiled in Mozambique from 1975 until 1999, when he was appointed economics minister in the first interim government, and then chief minister in the second. He went on to become prime minister upon independence in May 2002, making him the most prominent member of the country's small Muslim community, while his brother is Dili's leading Islamic cleric.

Mari bin Hamud Alkatiri was born on 26 November 1949 in Dili, in what was then the Portuguese colony of East Timor. He is one of ten children. His family had moved to the East Indies in the 19th century from the al-Khatiri sultanate in what is now Yemen. He travelled to the then Portuguese colony of Angola in the late 1960s where he graduated as a surveyor from the Angolan School of Geography. Alkatiri is married to Marina Ribeiro and they have three children.

Returning to East Timor, Alkatiri found work as a chartered surveyor in the colonial administration's public works department. Almost immediately he became active in the community's independence struggle and was a cofounder of the Movement for the Liberation of East Timor in January 1970. This secretive group was allowed to come into the open in 1974 following political revolution and liberalization in Portugal. Thus the movement was transformed first into the Timorese Social Democratic Association and then merged with other groups to form Fretilin on 11 September 1974.

With Indonesia rapidly seeking to incorporate East Timor, the local government sought to garner international support for the country's self-declared independence. Alkatiri was appointed state minister of political affairs in November 1975 and was despatched to Africa along with other prominent politicians to canvass world leaders. He left East Timor three days before the Indonesian invasion and did not return for almost 24 years. He lived in exile in Mozambique and continued to promote the Timorese cause. He was among the statesmen who managed to secure the UN's condemnation for the invasion and was subsequently appointed as East Timor's foreign minister-in-exile in 1977. In the following decades he found work in Mozambique as an academic and has said that he intends eventually to return to academia.

Alkatiri finally went back to East Timor in 1999, just before the UN-sponsored referendum on independence. As the violence which followed the resounding 'yes' vote died down he was appointed economics minister in the first interim, UN-supervised government. His most important task in this role was to secure an agreement with neighbouring Australia over sharing the significant mineral resources hidden beneath the Timor Sea. Although the agreement was hailed as a future boon to the Timorese economy it has since been sharply criticized for overly favouring Australia. Alkatiri has defended his work, citing the need to maintain good relations with the fledgling country's more powerful neighbours. Following elections to the Consituent Assembly in August 2001, a second transitional government was formed in September with Alkatiri as chief minister.

On 20 May 2002 East Timor emerged as the world's youngest independent country and Alkatiri was elected prime minister at the head of the Fretilin government. His position, however, is precarious. His relationship with the immensely popular president, Xanana Gusmão, is famously stormy. Alkatiri refused to vote in the presidential election himself. One of the major divisions between the two leaders is their attitude regarding the need to prosecute the militiamen responsible for the 1999 violence. Alkatiri has fervently called for justice, while Gusmão proposes a more forgiving approach to reconciliation. Alkatiri is also under pressure from the Timorese opposition for his apparently authoritarian style of government. He is accused of trying to create a one-party state after refusing to create a 'unity' government and instead relying on the absolute majority enjoyed by Fretilin in the parliament. Furthermore he is derided for being one of the large number of politicians who stayed away from East Timor following the invasion and is criticized for filling his cabinet with other former exiles.

ECUADOR

Full name: The Republic of Ecuador.

Leadership structure: The head of state is a president, who is directly elected by universal adult suffrage. The president's term of office is four years. The head of government is the president, who appoints the cabinet.

President:	Jamil Mahuad	10 Aug. 1998—21 Jan. 2000
Head of Military Junta:	Lucio Gutiérrez Borbúa	21 Jan. 2000—22 Jan. 2000
President:	Gustavo Noboa Bejarano	Since 22 Jan. 2000

Legislature: The legislature is unicameral. The sole chamber, the National Congress (Congreso Nacional), currently has 121 members; 101 members elected on a provincial basis, and 20 members directly elected on a national basis, all for four-year terms. Under the 1998 Constitution, the number of deputies will be adjusted to allow for increasing population, with two elected for each province, plus one more for each 200,000 inhabitants of a province.

Profile of the President:

Gustavo **NOBOA** Bejarano

Gustavo Noboa was appointed as president of Ecuador on 22 January 2000 during a bloodless coup which ousted his predecessor Jamil Mahuad, under whom he had been vice president. A lifelong teacher, Noboa had served one year as a regional governor and then only 17 months as Mahuad's deputy before becoming president. In office he has pursued a highly controversial policy of dollarization of the Ecuadorian economy.

Gustavo Noboa Bejarano was born on 21 August 1937 in Guayaquil. A committed Catholic, he spent two decades as a teacher in Ecuador's Catholic high schools before being appointed as dean of the law school of Guayaquil University. He went on to become the university's rector, a position he held for ten years. In parallel with his teaching career he was involved in industry as personnel manager of a sugar refinery from 1972 onward. Apart from a period as governor of Guayas province from March 1983 to August 1984, and involvement in negotiations over Ecuador's border dispute with Peru, he had little political experience when he stood as Mahuad's vice-presidential running mate in the May 1998 elections.

Sworn in as vice president on 10 August 1998, Noboa found his time largely taken up with battling against a cash-starved government for funds to help repair the considerable damage caused by the exceptional storms which visited Ecuador in 1997 and 1998 due to the infamous El Niño phenomenon. He was greatly respected in the government administration for his personal intelligence and anti-corruption stance.

In January 2000 disgruntled Amerindians were joined by police officers and the armed forces in a peaceful revolution that ousted the Mahuad government for its inability to address the concerns of the poor or to cope with Ecuador's increasingly weak economy. As the incumbent vice president, Noboa was chosen to succeed Mahuad, and was popularly appointed by the leaders of the short-lived coup, who then transferred power into his hands.

As president, Noboa pursued two main avenues of policy—tracking down corrupt officials from the country's recent past, and dollarizing the economy as part of a plan to stabilize the nation's worsening finances. For his anti-corruption commitment he has been largely praised, but the process of replacing the Ecuadorian sucre with the US dollar has caused serious discontent.

Profile of the President-elect:

Lucio **GUTIÉRREZ** Borbúa

Col. Lucio Gutiérrez is the founder of the socialist Patriotic Society Party 21 January (Partido Sociedad Patriótica 21 de Enero—PSP). A military man from the age of 15, he was imprisoned for his role in the January 2000 coup and left the military to pursue his political ambitions with the PSP. His overt leftist rhetoric, open admiration of the Venezuelan soldier-turned-socialist president Hugo Chávez and support for the Amerindian rebels in 2000 made him an unexpected winner of presidential elections in 2002. He is set to be inaugurated on 15 January 2003.

Edwin Lucio Gutiérrez Borbúa was born on 23 March 1957 in the town of Tena on the Amazonian side of the Andes. In 1972, at the age of just 15, Gutiérrez joined the Ecuadorian army. He received his further education through the military and has qualifications in business management and civil engineering. He also studied international relations and continental defence at the Inter-American Defense College in Washington D.C., USA. During his military career he rose to the rank of colonel and served in the UN peacekeeping force in Nicaragua as well as in the presidential guard back in Ecuador. He is married to Ximena Bohórquez, a congresswoman in her own right, and they have two daughters.

As the country entered its worst financial crisis in history in the 1990s, so Gutiérrez became increasingly vocal in his opposition to the incumbent president, Jamil Mahuad. In a celebrated incident he controversially ignored the president at a military ceremony in 1999, and on 21 January 2000 he led the army in supporting a coup by militant Amerindian demonstrators. Mahuad was forced to flee the capital and for one day Gutiérrez headed a military junta before handing power back to a civilian government led by Vice President Gustavo Noboa. The military hierarchy and the new government denounced the coup and Gutiérrez spent six months in jail for his efforts.

After his release Gutiérrez resigned his commission and formed the PSP. His growing popularity was based on his role in the coup, his military background, his non-elite upbringing and even his dark, Amerindian-like, complexion. Another major factor was increasing disaffection with the mainstream political parties. In the first round of presidential elections, held on 20 October 2002, Gutiérrez came a surprise first with 20% of the vote. He immediately set about watering down his leftist rhetoric, and even travelled to the USA to convince international donors that he would not seek an end to the country's dollarization or renege on its debt commitments. In a runoff on 24 November against banana magnate Alvaro Noboa (no relation to Gustavo), Gutiérrez scored 59% of the vote. He pledged to form a government of national unity on his inauguration in January 2003.

EGYPT

Full name: The Arab Republic of Egypt.

Leadership structure: The head of state is a president, nominated by the People's Assembly and confirmed by popular referendum. The president's term of office is six years. The president appoints all the members of the Council of Ministers. The prime minister chairs meetings of the Council of Ministers and is head of government.

President:	Mohammed Hosni Mubarak (acting from 6 Oct. 1981)	Since 14 Oct. 1981
Prime Minister:	Atif Mohammad Obeid	Since 5 Oct. 1999

Legislature: The legislature is unicameral. The sole chamber, the People's Assembly (Majlis al-Sha'ab), has 444 members directly elected by universal adult suffrage, and ten members appointed by the president, all for a five-year term. There is also a Consultative Council (Majlis al-Shoura), which has advisory powers. It has 264 members, 88 appointed by the president and 176 directly elected, for a six-year term.

Profile of the President:

Mohammed Hosni **MUBARAK**

Hosni Mubarak has been president of Egypt and its dominant political figure for more than two decades. A former air force commander and hero of the 1973 war with Israel, Mubarak had become vice president, and was standing next to President Anwar al-Sadat at the military parade at which Sadat was assassinated by Islamic militants in 1981. Mubarak, while maintaining Sadat's controversial 1979 treaty with Israel, has based his policies on achieving a rapprochement with other Arab states, while clamping down on dissent.

Mohammed Hosni Mubarak was born on 4 May 1928 in Kafr al-Musailha, within the al-Menoufiyah governorate. From 1947 until 1949 he studied for a degree in military sciences at the Egyptian Military Academy. Specializing in aviation sciences, he then attended the Air Force Academy and went on to join the Egyptian air force in 1950. Between 1952 and 1959 he lectured at the air force academy, while he also briefly attended the Frunze Military Academy in the Soviet Union.

In the 1950s and 1960s Mubarak was a successful air force pilot, seeing action in the Yemen civil war as a bomber squadron commander and in the 1967 Arab–Israeli war. Later in 1967 he took up a two-year post as director of the aeronautical academy. He was appointed successively air force chief of staff in 1969 and then commander in 1972 (a post he held until 1975). Acclaimed as a war hero after leading a successful air offensive against Israel in the 1973 war, he was promoted in that year to the rank of lieutenant-general. Mubarak is married with two sons.

Mubarak's political rise under the Sadat regime was an exceptionally rapid one. Within three years of his first government appointment, as deputy minister for military affairs in 1972, he was made vice president by Sadat. Taking up this post in 1975, he was also given special responsibilities for state security. In 1978 he took charge of the organization of the newly formed National Democratic Party (NDP), acting as vice president of the party until 1981 and thereafter as its chairman.

A smooth transfer of power to Mubarak took place following Sadat's assassination on 6 October 1981. He was nominated as the NDP's presidential candidate that same day and endorsed by a nationwide referendum a week later with an approval rating recorded as 98.4%.

When he took office Mubarak was seen as a political moderate, who promised a degree of continuity with Sadat's policies. In the event, his presidency has been notable particularly for the gradual rebuilding of relations with the Arab states which had ostracized Sadat over his Camp David accords with Israel. He has maintained a degree of independence in Egypt's foreign policy, despite heavy reliance on US aid, and has been notably cool in dealings with Israel, which he has visited only once, in 1995. Even this was a condolence call rather than an official visit, on the occasion of the funeral of the Israeli prime minister Yitzhak Rabin, on whom many of the hopes for an Israeli–Palestinian peace agreement had rested. His credit with the US government was boosted by his leading role among Arab states in opposing the Iraqi invasion of Kuwait in 1990 and by his decision to commit Egyptian troops to join the US-led forces in the 1991 Gulf War.

Mubarak has been re-elected no less than three times for further presidential terms, in 1987, 1993 and 1999, despite having earlier proclaimed that no president should serve more than two terms. In each case he has been nominated as the sole candidate by the National Assembly and endorsed overwhelmingly by national referendum.

He described the central themes of his third term as economic reform and the promotion of a free-market system, combating unemployment and fighting terrorism. He has proved uncompromising in his attitude towards Muslim militant groups in Egypt, and there have been several attempts on his life, most notably on 26 June 1995 when he narrowly escaped assassination during a visit to Addis

Ababa, Ethiopia. His clampdown on fundamentalist activity, while incurring criticism from human rights groups over reprisal killings, political trials and the use of torture, has not succeeded in doing more than containing a situation that remains tense and potentially explosive.

In foreign affairs, Mubarak has leaned closer to his Arab contemporaries. In June 2000 he ended the 21-year-old deadlock between Egypt and Iran by calling President Mohammad Khatami to congratulate him for Iran's entrance to the G15 group of developing countries. Conversely he has increasingly criticized Israel, accusing it in April 2002 of state-sponsored terrorism against the Palestinians.

Profile of the Prime Minister:

Atif Mohammad **OBEID**

Atif Mohammad Obeid had an academic background, before entering the cabinet in 1985, serving in two portfolios before being appointed prime minister in October 1999.

Atif Mohammad Obeid was born in 1932. He studied at the faculty of commerce, Cairo University, and the University of Illinois, USA, gaining both a master's degree and a doctorate. In 1970 he became a member of the Arab League's media policy co-ordinating committee, and he also held the posts of professor at the business administration faculty of commerce, Cairo University, and president of the International Management Centre. He is married and has two children.

In 1985 President Hosni Mubarak appointed Obeid minister of cabinet affairs and minister of state for administrative development, and he held these posts until 1993, when he became minister of the public enterprise sector. It was from this portfolio that he was promoted to become prime minister in 1999.

EL SALVADOR

Full name: The Republic of El Salvador.

Leadership structure: The head of state is a president, directly elected by universal adult suffrage. The president's term of office is five years. The head of government is the president, who appoints a Council of State.

President: Francisco Flores Pérez   Since 1 June 1999

Legislature: The legislature is unicameral. The sole chamber, the Legislative Assembly (Asamblea Legislativa), has 84 members, directly elected for a three-year term.

Profile of the President:

Francisco **FLORES** Pérez

Francisco Flores, known affectionately as 'paco', is one of El Salvador's youngest ever presidents, aged only 39 when he took office on 1 June 1999. A former member of the Legislative Assembly, and its speaker in 1997–99, he is a member of the right-wing Nationalist Republican Alliance (Alianza Republicana Nacionalista—ARENA). As president he has to contend with an Assembly in which the left-wing former guerrilla movement, the Farabundo Martí National Liberation Front (Frente Farabundo Martí para la Liberación Nacional— FMLN), is the largest single party.

Francisco Guillermo Flores Pérez was born on 17 October 1959. After a secondary education in El Salvador, Flores spent the 1980s attending various universities both at home and in the USA including the University of Chicago and a year at the prestigious Harvard University in Cambridge, Massachusetts. During these years he acquired degrees in political science and economics and a master's degree in philosophy. He is married to Lourdes Rodríguez and they have two young children.

In 1991 Flores began his political career as a junior minister of planning during the presidency of Alfredo Cristiani Burkard and soon rose to a position in the executive office itself, acting as a presidential adviser. Following the ceasefire with the FMLN rebels in 1992, Flores was deeply involved in the rewriting of the national constitution, and in 1994 he was appointed to the position of secretary of information under the presidency of Armando Calderón Sol.

From 1995 to 1999 Flores sat as a member of the Legislative Assembly and in June 1997 he was elected to be its speaker, in which role he became known as 'paco' (peacemaker). In March 1998 he received the ARENA nomination as presidential candidate and fought a strong campaign against the leftist opposition. His refusal to attend a US-style debate earned him criticism for his apparent arrogance, but he captured a conclusive 51.4% of the vote in the first round of elections on 7 March 1999, convincingly outpacing his nearest rival Facundo Guardado of the FMLN who received only 29%. In legislative elections in March 2000 the ARENA hegemony was cracked when, for the first time since the end of the civil war, it was overtaken (by the FMLN) as the largest single party.

EQUATORIAL GUINEA

Full name: The Republic of Equatorial Guinea.

Leadership structure: The head of state is a president, directly elected by universal adult suffrage. The president's term of office is seven years. The president appoints the Council of Ministers. The prime minister is head of government.

President: Brig.-Gen. Teodoro Obiang Nguema Mbasogo   Since 12 Oct. 1982 (seized power on 3 Aug. 1979)

Prime Ministers: Angel Serafin Dougan   29 March 1996—4 March 2001

        Cándido Muatetema Rivas   Since 4 March 2001

Legislature: The legislature is unicameral. The sole chamber, the House of Representatives of the People (Cámara de Representantes del Pueblo), has 80 members, directly elected for a five-year term.

Profile of the President:

Brig.-Gen. Teodoro **OBIANG NGUEMA** Mbasogo

Brig.-Gen. Teodoro Obiang Nguema, having deposed and executed his brutal and despotic uncle Francisco Macías Nguema in 1979, went on to create his own single-party structure, and in the last decade has paid little more than lip service to the notion that Equatorial Guinea had made a transition to multiparty democracy. In the most recent presidential elections, in 1996, he was the sole candidate.

Teodoro Obiang Nguema Mbasogo was born on 5 June 1941 in Acó Acam near Mongomo, on the eastern border with Gabon. He is a member of that region's Esangui ethnic group, a small subgroup of the country's Fang majority. He went to school in Bata, the principal mainland port, and then received military training at the Zaragoza Military Academy in Spain from 1963 to 1965. In 1968 under his uncle's regime he was appointed deputy minister of defence and then military governor of the island of Fernando Póo (now known as Bioko). In the early 1970s he worked in government service, in the planning department and in the ministry of education. From 1975 he was defence minister and aide-de-camp to the president. The 11-year dictatorship of Macías was known for its brutality and

Obiang Nguema's own brother was among victims who were executed, in his case for complaining about unpaid wages.

On 5 August 1979 Obiang Nguema led a coup against Macías, ordered his execution and declared himself president. Despite the release of many political prisoners, Obiang Nguema continued to rule despotically as his uncle had done, surrounding himself in the same way with Esangui relatives. Since 1980 Obiang Nguema has also held the positions of minister of defence and supreme commander of the armed forces.

After a number of coup attempts in the years immediately following his takeover, a new constitution was adopted in 1982 which provided for a handover to civilian rule after a seven-year period during which Obiang Nguema was to rule as president.

In 1987 Obiang Nguema founded the Equatorial Guinea Democratic Party (Partido Democrático de Guinea Ecuatorial—PDGE) as the sole legal political party and, having meanwhile arrested his opponents, was the only candidate for the presidential elections held in June 1989.

External pressure, including the withholding of foreign aid and funds from the International Monetary Fund (IMF), eventually induced him to allow a nominal change to multipartyism, with six parties legalized in 1992. Most of the opposition leaders remained in exile, however; those who were allowed back returned only at real personal risk, and there was frequent violent disruption of opposition meetings. In 1993 the USA withdrew its diplomatic representation, citing the government's abuse of human rights. In November of that year the PDGE won all but 12 seats in legislative elections which were boycotted by the opposition following more arrests. The results were disputed by the US and Spanish governments and the latter withdrew aid to the country. The 1999 elections were equally unsatisfactory, with the official results giving the PDGE an even more overwhelming parliamentary majority.

The presidential elections held in February 1996 had similarly been denounced by opposition parties, who had been given only six weeks notice of the poll. Among the instances of election malpractice was the fact that the electoral list supplied by the UN was replaced by a government one, omitting many voters from the register in the areas where opposition groups commanded most support. The official results, which gave Obiang Nguema nearly 98% of the vote, showed many more votes cast than there were registered voters.

In June 1997 a coup attempt was foiled and a spate of arrests followed. Another clampdown in 2002 saw 68 opposition leaders jailed in connection with this same 1997 coup attempt. Obiang Nguema has already been nominated by the PDGE to stand again as the party's presidential candidate for the elections due in 2003.

Profile of the Prime Minister:

Cándido **MUATETEMA RIVAS**

Cándido Muatetema Rivas is secretary-general of the ruling Equatorial Guinea Democratic Party (Partido Democrático de Guinea Ecuatorial—PDGE). Educated in Cuba, he served in the cabinet of Prime Minister Silvestre Siale Bileka in 1992–96, then concentrated on his career within the party before being chosen by President Teodoro Obiang Nguema to head the new government in 2001.

Cándido Muatetema Rivas was born on 2 February 1960 in the village of Batete in the southwest corner of Bioko island (then known as Fernando Póo). He studied economy and finance at the University of Pinar del Río, Cuba. Returning to Equatorial Guinea on graduating in the mid-1980s, he found work in the country's economy ministry.

Muatetema Rivas entered the cabinet for the first time as minister of youth and sports in 1992. He held the post for the duration of Bileka's administration, and stepped down with him in 1996. During the next five years he rose through the party's ranks to become deputy secretary-general.

Underlying tensions between President Obiang Nguema and the then prime minister Angel Serafin Seriche Dougan erupted in February 2001 and the cabinet resigned. Muatetema Rivas was appointed on 26 February (and sworn in on 4 March) as prime minister at the head of a largely unchanged government, and was promoted to secretary-general of the PDGE at the same time.

ERITREA

Full name: The State of Eritrea.

Leadership structure: The head of state is a president, elected by the National Assembly, of which he is chairman. Under the new constitution the president's term of office is five years. The head of government is the president, who appoints and presides over a State Council which includes ten provincial governors.

President: Issaias Afewerki   Since 24 May 1993
                                     (headed provisional government
                                     before independence, from 29 May 1991)

Legislature: The legislature is unicameral. Once the legislative election process is completed the 150-member National Assembly (Hagerawi Baito) will be elected directly for a four-year term. In March 1994 it was decided that for the rest of the transitional period 75 Assembly members should be the members of the ruling central committee of the People's Front for Democracy and Justice (PFDJ) and 75 should be elected, but no mechanism was provided for such elections.

Profile of the President:

Issaias **AFEWERKI**

Issaias Afewerki is the first president of the State of Eritrea, elected one month after the April 1993 referendum which overwhelmingly endorsed secession from Ethiopia. He had come to prominence as a military leader in the three decades of struggle against Ethiopian occupation, helping to found the Eritrean People's Liberation Front (EPLF) under whose leadership the country was liberated when the Mengistu regime in Ethiopia was overthrown in 1991.

Born on 2 February 1946 in Asmara, Issaias Afewerki completed one year as an engineering student at the University of Addis Ababa before going underground in 1966 and joining the Eritrean Liberation Front (ELF), which had begun an armed liberation struggle in 1962. Part of his military training was undertaken in China. From 1967 to 1970 he was regional and then general commander of the ELF, which merged with other groups in 1970 to form the EPLF. As a founding EPLF member he held various leading positions, becoming deputy secretary-general in 1977 and secretary-general in 1987. Part of his contribution to the liberation struggle was his success in obtaining support for the movement in the Islamic world.

The EPLF's military victories played a major role in the downfall of the Mengistu regime in Ethiopia in May 1991. Afewerki immediately set up a provisional government, and at a conference in London, UK, in August he secured recognition of his administration as the legitimate provisional government of Eritrea, while agreeing to hold a referendum on independence within two years. When this took place, in April 1993, there was a 99.8% vote recorded in favour of secession. As a result of the close links maintained between Afewerki and Meles Zenawi, the Ethiopian prime minister, Ethiopia accepted Eritrea's secession on 3 May. A provisional assembly, composed of the EPLF's central committee and an equal number of elected members, confirmed Afewerki as president on 22 May, two days before independence was formally declared.

In February 1994 the EPLF changed its name to the People's Front for Democracy and Justice (PFDJ), since when Afewerki has been chairman of the National Assembly and of the PFDJ. He has made it his priority to develop and modernize the infrastructure of Eritrea and lead the country out of its many years of warfare and famine. A national constitution was adopted in May 1997, but multiparty elections, due to have been held within four years of independence, have yet to be arranged. Even a promise to schedule polls in December 2001, made just after the end of hostilities with Ethiopia in late 2000, did not come to pass. In the meantime Afewerki has clamped down on opposition, arresting a number of former government ministers and pro-democracy activists in September 2001.

ESTONIA

Full name: The Republic of Estonia.

Leadership structure: The head of state is a president, elected by the Parliament. However, if no candidate receives the votes of at least 68 of the 101 members of Parliament in up to three rounds of voting, an electoral assembly is convened, which includes 266 local government representatives in addition to the members of Parliament. In the voting by the electoral assembly a simple majority is sufficient to elect the new president. The president's term of office is five years. The head of government is the prime minister, who is appointed by the president and who nominates the Council of Ministers.

Presidents:	Lennart Meri	6 Oct. 1992—8 Oct. 2001
	Arnold Rüütel	Since 8 Oct. 2001
Prime Ministers:	Mart Laar	25 March 1999—28 Jan. 2002
	Siim Kallas	Since 28 Jan. 2002

Legislature: The legislature is unicameral. The sole chamber, the Parliament (Riigikogu), has 101 members, directly elected for a four-year term.

Profile of the President:

Arnold **RÜÜTEL**

Arnold Rüütel is a respected agronomist and is also active on environmental issues. A former senior member of the communist hierarchy, he was briefly (until 1992) Estonia's first postcommunist head of state, but it was as leader of the right-of-centre Estonian People's Union (Eestimaa Rahvaliit—ERL) that he was elected to the country's presidency nine years later.

Arnold Rüütel was born on 10 May 1928 on the island of Saaremaa during Estonia's brief period of interwar independence. Still only a child when the country came under Soviet control in the Second World War, he graduated from an agricultural college in 1949 and began a long career in the Soviet agricultural sector as head of the agronomic department on Saaremaa. He moved to the Estonian Institute of Cattle Breeding in 1957 as head zootechnician. A year later he married Ingrid; they have two daughters. By the time he left the institute in 1963 he had become its assistant director. For the next six years he directed work at the Tartu Model State Farm. He also studied at the Estonian Agricultural Academy, graduating in 1964. From 1969 he acted as rector of the academy.

From 1977 Rüütel began combining his scientific and administrative work with politics. In 1983 he was elected chairman of the Supreme Soviet of the Estonian Soviet Socialist Republic (SSR). In this capacity he played a vital role in the emergence of a separate Estonian state in the late 1980s and the drafting of the 1988 *Resolution on the Sovereignty of the Estonian SSR*. He was re-elected in 1990 as the country began separating itself from the Soviet Union. He was de facto head of state until 1992, when he failed to win presidential elections.

In the Parliament Rüütel headed the Estonian Rural People's Party (later to merge to form the ERL) from 1994. He was elected vice speaker in 1995 and headed the regional Baltic Assembly. He continued to promote agricultural issues and established a number of agricultural and environmental bodies, including the Estonian Society for Nature Protection and the Estonian Green Cross. Parliament elected him president on 21 September 2001 and he took office on 8 October.

Profile of the Prime Minister:

Siim **KALLAS**

Siim Kallas is chairman of the Estonian Reform Party (Eesti Reformierakond— ER) and a career economist. After four years as president of the Bank of Estonia he entered the cabinet as foreign minister in 1995. He became prime minister in January 2002 after the collapse of the previous government through mistrust.

Siim Kallas was born in Tallinn on 2 October 1948, in what was then the Estonian Soviet Socialist Republic. He graduated in economics from the Tartu State University in 1972, the same year that he married Kristi Kartus, who is now a doctor; they have one son and one daughter. After postgraduate studies he entered the Estonian Soviet finance ministry in 1975 and was made director of the Estonian Central Board of Savings Banks in 1979.

Moving out of finance in 1986, Kallas supported the growing Estonian pro-democracy movement in his new role as deputy editor of the *Rahva Hääl* (People's Voice) newspaper. He left the publication in 1989 and, following the country's independence from the Soviet Union in 1991, returned to public finance as the new president of the Bank of Estonia.

Kallas entered government in 1995 when he was appointed foreign minister and founded and led the ER in the Parliament. Out of the cabinet from 1996 to 1999, he was appointed finance minister in March 1999 when the ER joined the coalition of Prime Minister Mart Laar. Although his administration was praised internationally for its privatization drive, Laar felt unsupported within his own government and announced he would resign in January 2002. Kallas negotiated a coalition with the Estonian Centre Party and was duly appointed prime minister.

ETHIOPIA

Full name: The Federal Democratic Republic of Ethiopia.

Leadership structure: The head of state is a president, elected by a joint session of the House of People's Representatives and the House of the Federation. The president's term of office is six years, renewable once only. The head of government is the prime minister, who is appointed by the House of People's Representatives, and appoints the Council of Ministers.

Presidents:	Negaso Gidada	22 Aug. 1995—8 Oct. 2001
	Lt. Girma Wolde Giorgis	Since 8 Oct. 2001
Prime Minister:	Meles Zenawi	Since 23 Aug. 1995
	(transitional president from 28 May 1991)	

Legislature: The legislature, the Federal Parliament, is bicameral. The lower chamber, the House of People's Representatives (Yehizb Tewokayoch Mekir Bet), has 548 members, directly elected for a five-year term. The upper chamber, the House of the Federation (Yefedereshn Mekir Bet), has 108 members, indirectly elected for a five-year term by the government councils of the nine states which make up the federation.

Profile of the President:

Lt. Girma **WOLDE GIORGIS**

Girma Wolde Giorgis is an independent politician with a long but low-profile career in government service. Heading the country's aviation department in the 1950s, he went on to lead the Red Cross in the then Ethiopian province of Eritrea. He was chosen by the Federal Parliament to be president of Ethiopia in 2001.

Girma Wolde Giorgis was born in December 1925 in Addis Ababa, into the majority Oromo ethnic group. He is married and has five children. After studying at an Italian school in the city in the late 1930s, he was enlisted in the UK-established Ethiopian Military Radio Communication in 1941 in the midst of the Second World War. Towards the end of that conflict he graduated from the Genet Military School as a lieutenant, in 1944, and transferred to the Ethiopian air force in 1946.

Wolde Giorgis travelled abroad between 1950 and 1952 to complete his education in air traffic management in the Netherlands, Sweden and Canada. When he returned he taught the subject in Ethiopia. In 1955 he was appointed director of the government's new civil aviation department and became a board member of Ethiopian Airlines in 1958.

Wolde Giorgis switched from aviation to more direct government service in 1959 when he became director-general of the ministry of trade, industry and planning. He was elected to parliament for the first time in 1960 and was appointed speaker. Between 1965 and 1974 he worked in commerce, both as manager of the Import and Export Enterprise (IMPEX) and as a representative for the business community at various nongovernmental organizations. Under the Dergue military regime which came to power in 1974, and its successors, Wolde Giorgis worked for the regional branch of the International Red Cross in what was then the Ethiopian northern province of Eritrea. Amid increasing civil conflict in the country, and especially in Eritrea, Wolde Giorgis returned to Addis Ababa in 1991 and established Lem Ethiopia, an environmental protection agency.

After a 35-year absence from parliament, Wolde Giorgis returned in 2000 when he was elected to the House of People's Representatives as an independent candidate. A year later he was selected by the government of Prime Minister Meles Zenawi as the presidential nominee. His appointment was seen as a tactical move by the government, as he was a largely unknown figure, and particularly as his ethnic Oromo background contrasted with the predominance of Tigrayans in Ethiopia's principal positions of power. He took over from the outgoing head of state, the increasingly combative President Negaso Gidada, on 8 October 2001. Just six days later Wolde Giorgis was taken to hospital with a serious heart condition, raising doubts about his ability to fulfil his full six-year term.

Profile of the Prime Minister:

MELES Zenawi

Meles Zenawi has been prime minister of Ethiopia since August 1995, following a general election dominated by the Ethiopian People's Revolutionary Democratic Front (EPRDF). For the preceding four years he had headed an interim government formed after the overthrow of the Marxist military dictatorship of Mengistu. Meles had risen to prominence through the Tigray People's Liberation Front (TPLF), which, apart from its Eritrean counterpart, had been the most effective of the anti-Mengistu forces during the long armed struggle. Having accepted that the Eritreans should proceed to separate independence, the Tigrayans are a dominant element in the ruling EPRDF coalition.

Meles Zenawi, who is now married with three children, was born on 9 May 1955 in Adwa, in Tigray in northern Ethiopia. He went to the prestigious Gen. Wingate High School in Addis Ababa and entered the University of Addis Ababa Medical

School. In 1975, however, he left to help found a rebel Marxist–Leninist League of Tigray, a core element in the TPLF alliance ten years later. As TPLF secretary-general, Meles became a figure of real national significance when TPLF forces, encouraged by military successes by the Eritrean secessionist movement, turned the tide of their own war against Mengistu's troops and overran most of Tigray between 1988 and 1989. An alliance with other guerrilla groups in September 1989 brought into being the broader multi-ethnic EPRDF coalition of guerrilla movements, with Meles as its chairman. The Mengistu regime, having failed to reach a negotiated settlement, was swept away by military defeat in May 1991, and in July Meles was elected president of a transitional government of Ethiopia and chairman of the Council of Representatives.

Although the transition process was affected by disputes and violence, mainly between rival groups organized along ethnic lines, the EPRDF dominated both the Constituent Assembly elections in June 1994, and the general election held under the new federal constitution in May 1995—and marred by opposition boycotts and allegations of intimidation. Meles was elected unanimously as prime minister by the House of People's Representatives on 23 August 1995, the day after the formal establishment of the Federal Democratic Republic of Ethiopia.

Meles Zenawi's role in Ethiopia's transition to democracy and federalism won him the 'good governance award' of the Washington D.C.-based intergovernmental Global Coalition for Africa, although his administration has been criticized on human rights grounds for its harsh measures against those expressing opposition or discontent. In October 1996 Meles dismissed one of the deputy prime ministers, Tamirat Layne, accusing him of abuse of power, and this and other changes enabled him to consolidate his own position ahead of the May 2000 legislative elections, when the EPRDF retained an overwhelming majority of seats. He was re-elected by acclamation in parliament on 10 October 2001 to another five-year term as prime minister.

FIJI

Full name: The Republic of the Fiji Islands.

Leadership structure: The head of state is a president, appointed by the Great Council of Chiefs. The president's term of office is five years. The head of government is the prime minister, who is appointed by the president and responsible to the Parliament. The cabinet is appointed by the prime minister.

President: Ratu Sir Kamisese Mara   18 Jan. 1994—29 May 2000
(acting from 29 Nov. 1993)

Head of Interim Military Government:
Commodore Josaia Voreqe 'Frank' Bainimarama   29 May 2000—18 July 2000

President: Ratu Josefa Iloilo   Since 18 July 2000
(interim until 15 March 2001)

Prime Ministers: Mahendra Chaudhry   19 May 1999—27 May 2000

vacant   27 May 2000—3 July 2000

Laisenia Qarase   3 July 2000—14 March 2001
(interim)

Ratu Tevita Momoedonu   14 March 2001—16 March 2001

Laisenia Qarase   Since 16 March 2001
(interim to 10 Sept. 2001)

Legislature: The legislature, the Parliament, is bicameral. The lower chamber, the House of Representatives, has 71 members, directly elected for a five-year term. Under the 1997 Constitution, 25 of the 71 seats are open to all races, but elected in single-member constituencies; the other 46 seats are allocated for election by Fiji's various ethnic communities. The upper chamber, the Senate, has 32 members, appointed by the president for five-year terms, following recommendations from the political parties, in proportion to their seats in the House of Representatives, and from the Great Council of Chiefs.

Profile of the President:

Ratu Josefa **ILOILO**

A prominent western chief, Ratu Josefa Iloilo had been vice president before the May 2000 Fijian nationalist coup, but he had not held any other government position. The coup overthrew the ethnic Indian prime minister and brought about the resignation of the incumbent president. Iloilo's appointment as president by the Great Council of Chiefs in July 2000 was repeated eight months later, after a court decision that the 1997 Constitution scrapped by the coup leaders actually remained in force. Ill health prevented him from taking on the full powers of the presidency but he did nominate a pro-military government after the end of the crisis.

Josefa Iloilo was born on 29 December 1920 on Taveuni island. From 1939 to 1968 he worked as a schoolteacher on the islands. During these 30 years he helped to introduce the Boy Scout movement to the country, establishing scout troops on many islands.

As Tui Vuda (high chief of Vuda, on the main westerly island of Viti Levu) Iloilo represents the interests of the western isles. In the late 1990s he was appointed as vice president by the then president Ratu Sir Kamisese Mara. Having established a reputation as a corruption-free administrator, Iloilo was nominated in 1999 as a candidate for chairman of the Great Council of Chiefs, but was defeated in the body's first secret ballot by the incumbent prime minister Ratu Sitiveni Rabuka.

In May 2000 Fijian supremacist and local businessman George Speight took Mahendra Chaudhry, the country's first ever ethnic Indian prime minister, and his cabinet hostage, and demanded the revocation of the 1997 Constitution. In the ensuing crisis martial law was imposed and President Mara stepped down at the rebels' insistence. Iloilo, whose daughter (now dead) had been married to Speight's brother, was Speight's second choice as an acceptable candidate for president and was offered the position by the Great Council of Chiefs.

From the outset it was clear that Speight had miscalculated in expecting Iloilo to be amenable to his own objectives. In his acceptance speech Iloilo called for a multiracial country, and he defied the nationalists by appointing the military-backed Laisenia Qarase as prime minister. Speight was arrested soon afterwards. However, Iloilo's ill health—giving rise to speculation that he might have Parkinson's disease—cast a shadow over his inauguration. Qarase, meanwhile, has failed to reinstate the multiracial 1997 Constitution and considers the country's Indian population as permanently disenfranchised.

Less than a year after the coup the Constitutional Court threw the country into political chaos when it ruled on 1 March 2001 that the dissolution of the 1997 Constitution and the removal of the government in 2000 had both been illegal. Iloilo's position came directly into question until he was renominated by the Great Council of Chiefs a few days later. On 14 March Iloilo officially dismissed

Chaudhry and appointed his own nephew (Ratu Tevita Momoedonu) as prime minister. Iloilo was re-inaugurated the following day, along with Momoedonu, and then accepted Momoedonu's resignation 24 hours later. Closing the loop, Iloilo reappointed Qarase as prime minister.

Profile of the Prime Minister:

Laisenia **QARASE**

Laisenia Qarase was appointed as interim prime minister of Fiji by the military authorities on 3 July 2000, confirmed in the position by President Ratu Josefa Iloilo later in the month, and formed a new government after his party's success in elections just over a year later. His initial appointment followed a nationalist coup, led by Fijian supremacist George Speight, which overthrew the government of ethnic Indian Mahendra Chaudhry. Qarase has been a prominent champion of Fijian rights in the Indian-dominated economic sector and since being premier he has done nothing to rehabilitate the large Indian minority disenfranchised in the coup.

Laisenia Qarase was born in 1941 into the Tota clan in Mavana on Vanua Balavu, in the Lau group of eastern islands. After attending local schools he travelled to the country's main island, Viti Levu, to enrol at Suva Boys' Grammar School. He left Fiji in 1959 and studied commerce and co-operative development at Auckland University in New Zealand. Now married with five children, he is described as a quiet and modest man.

From his first job with the Fijian Affairs Board until becoming prime minister, Qarase has worked for the advancement of the country's ethnic Fijian population. His career as a civil servant included posts at the ministries of finance, commerce and industry and public services before he was appointed as the first ethnic Fijian managing director of the Fiji Development Bank (FDB) in 1983. While at the bank he has admitted he felt angered by the dominance of ethnic Indians in the financial sector.

Following the pro-Fijian coups of 1987 the new government turned to Qarase for help in rebuilding the damaged economy. His suggested policies centred on promoting the economic involvement of native Fijians. He introduced a nine-point plan which extended government assistance to Fijians and oversaw the creation of Fijian Holdings. However the plan mostly resulted in bankruptcies and large debts and he was embroiled in scandal at Fijian Holdings over the acquisition of shares by members of his family. From 1994 he was chairman of Fiji Television and clashed with the government of Prime Minister Sitiveni Rabuka over its plans to introduce US investment into the company without consulting him. In 1998 he quit both the television company, and the FDB, to take up a new position at the Merchant Bank of Fiji.

In the new regime inaugurated by the multiracial 1997 Constitution, Qarase was nominated to the Senate in 1999 by the powerful Great Council of Chiefs as a candidate for the opposition Fijian Political Party. From the Senate he became a vocal critic of the government's policies towards the indigenous islanders. He also sat on the boards of several indigenous Fijian investment companies.

George Speight's two-month coup in 2000 drew great sympathy from conservative Fijians anxious to turn back the advance of multiracialism. Qarase was nominated by the military to head an interim government, and won the backing of the Great Council of Chiefs for his appointment. Although this disappointed Speight's own political ambitions, Qarase proved a stalwart supporter of Speight's pro-Fijian policies, saying openly that the people "were not ready" for an ethnic Indian prime minister. He initially rejected calls to convene new elections, while the initial international pressure to reinstate Chaudhry subsided to demands to restore the 1997 Constitution.

Although this demand was met by the Constitutional Court ruling of 1 March 2001, Qarase has resolutely resisted court pressure to incorporate Chaudhry and his opposition Fijian Labour Party (FLP). The direct result of the ruling saw Qarase temporarily dismissed in mid-March, but he returned to office in a complex manoeuvre within just two days as President Ratu Josefa Iloilo officially dismissed Chaudhry, nominally appointed his own nephew at the head of a new FLP government, and then accepted its resignation so as to allow Qarase to take back the reins of power.

Fresh elections were called for May 2001 and Qarase led his new United Fiji Party (Soqosoqo Duavata ni Lewenivanua—SDL) to a narrow victory. In defiance of the 1997 Constitution, which grants parties with more than eight seats at least one cabinet ministry, Qarase went on to completely ignore the FLP (which had gained 27 seats) in his new, nationalist government. He was sworn in for his first legitimate full term in office on 11 September 2001. Repeatedly refusing to accept that the FLP is entitled to cabinet representation, Qarase has even weathered an August 2002 amendment of the election results which put the SDL on a level footing in the House of Representatives with the FLP.

FINLAND

Full name: The Republic of Finland.

Leadership structure: The head of state is a president, directly elected by universal adult suffrage. The president's term of office is six years. The head of government is the prime minister, who is elected by Parliament and appointed by the president. The Council of State is appointed by the president as proposed by the prime minister.

Presidents:	Martti Ahtisaari	1 March 1994—1 March 2000
	Tarja Halonen	Since 1 March 2000
Prime Minister:	Paavo Lipponen	Since 13 April 1995

Legislature: The legislature is unicameral. The sole chamber, the Parliament (Eduskunta), has 200 members, directly elected for a four-year term.

Profile of the President:

Tarja **HALONEN**

Tarja Halonen is the country's first female head of state, a career politician, left-winger and feminist. She appealed to Finnish voters to redress the imbalance of the sexes in politics through her election, and—having raised her daughter Anna on her own—caused some surprise when she married her subsequent partner Pentti Arajärvi six months after her election to the presidency. The role of president is an active one in Finnish politics, especially in foreign affairs, the portfolio she held as a minister from 1995 until her election in 2000.

Tarja Kaarina Halonen was born in Helsinki on 24 December 1943. She studied law and foreign languages, and speaks several European languages fluently. As a law graduate, she worked for the firm Lainvalvonta from 1967 to 1968. Strengthening her trade union credentials, she worked as social affairs secretary and then general secretary of the National Union of Finnish Students between 1969 and 1970, and as a lawyer with the Central Organization of Finnish Trade Unions from 1970 until 1974. She became parliamentary secretary to Prime Minister Kalevi Sorsa of the Social Democratic Party (Suomen Sosiali-demokraattinen Puolue—SDP) in the years 1974 to 1975.

In the late 1970s and early 1980s Halonen expanded her political life by joining many nongovernmental organizations as well as beginning a so-far unbroken career as a deputy in Parliament in 1979. Since 1975 she has been a member of the representative body of the co-operative retail company Elanto, and in 1977 she joined the Helsinki city council, on which she served until 1996. She also sat on the supervisory board during this time. On top of these roles she was a director of the International Solidarity Foundation and, reflecting her passion for the theatre, chaired the TNL theatre organization.

The late 1980s saw Halonen hold a number of government posts. She chaired the parliamentary social affairs committee from 1984 until her appointment as a minister at the ministry of social affairs and health in 1987. From 1989 she was also minister for Nordic co-operation, and in 1990 she took on the justice portfolio as well. She lost all three positions following the defeat of the SDP in the March 1991 legislative elections. Following four years in opposition the party's popularity returned to a postwar high in March 1995 and Halonen was appointed as minister of foreign affairs, where she remained until her election as president in 2000. She won a closely fought second-round victory on 6 February over the Finnish Centre Party candidate Esko Aho, gaining 51.6% to his 48.4%. In her electoral address she outlined her socialist principles of high government spending and heavy taxation while maintaining a realist approach to funding.

Profile of the Prime Minister:

Paavo **LIPPONEN**

Paavo Lipponen has been Finland's prime minister since April 1995. A former journalist and long-standing member of the Social Democratic Party (Suomen Sosialidemokraattinen Puolue—SDP), which he has chaired since 1993, he had ten years of experience as a deputy in Parliament, and was briefly its speaker, but had not held ministerial office before he became prime minister. His SDP is the largest single party in Parliament, dominating the ruling coalition.

Paavo Tapio Lipponen was born on 23 April 1941 in Turtola (now Pello), near the border with Sweden. He studied political science and was editor of the student newspaper *Ylioppilaslehti* from 1963 until 1965, and continued to work in journalism as a freelance reporter for the Finnish broadcasting company YLE between 1965 and 1967, before moving into politics.

Within the SDP Lipponen worked first as research and international affairs secretary and then as head of the political section between 1967 and 1979. He was appointed in 1979 as private secretary to the then prime minister and future president, Mauno Koivisto, and continued in this role until 1982. Consolidating his position within the party, he was a member of the SDP committee from 1987 to 1990 and of the party's council from 1990 to 1993, and was in addition chairman of the SDP Helsinki district from 1985 to 1992. He was a member of Parliament from 1983 until 1987 and again from 1991, the year in which the SDP went into opposition for the first time for a quarter-century.

Outside the political sphere, Lipponen was managing director of the Viestintä Teema Oy company from 1988 to 1995, and head of the Finnish Institute of International Affairs from 1989 to 1991. He also worked as chairman of the supervisory board of the major metal and engineering conglomerate Outokumpu Oy from 1989 to 1990.

In June 1993 he was elected to succeed Ulf Sundqvist as SDP chairman, a post he still holds. In the face of considerable opposition among party members, he succeeded in taking the party into the October 1994 European Union (EU) membership referendum on the pro-EU side, and received a boost to his own standing as a result. In 1995 he was briefly speaker of the Parliament until the general election on 19 March 1995. In this election Lipponen's SDP won 28.3% of the vote and 63 of the 200 parliamentary seats, the party's best result since 1945. Stressing the need for strong government, he formed a five-party 'rainbow' coalition, which took office on 13 April 1995.

Although Finland only joined the EU in January 1995, Lipponen was determined that Finland should be among the countries participating in EU economic and monetary union (EMU) from the outset. Having led Finland into the exchange rate mechanism (ERM) in October 1996, and ensured that it met the criteria for EMU membership by late 1997 (continuing the tight budgetary policies of his centre-right predecessor, while also succeeding in bringing unemployment down), he remained a strong supporter of the adoption of the single European currency, the euro, which fully replaced the markka with effect from January 2002.

At the March 1999 general election the SDP dropped to a 51-seat share but remained the largest party. Lipponen regrouped the rainbow coalition. In November 2000, however, the government's unity began to crack. A plan to build a fifth nuclear reactor was published, prompting the Greens to eventually split from the grouping in May 2002. Their departure did not remove the government's majority and the reduced rainbow continued in office, with fresh elections due in March 2003.

Paavo Lipponen married Päivi Hiltunen, a schoolteacher, in January 1998 and they have two infant children. He also has one fully grown daughter from a previous relationship. He has famously championed the importance of proper provisions for paternity leave, and himself took six days' leave from heading the government after the birth of each of his children.

FRANCE

Full name: The French Republic.

Leadership structure: The head of state is a president, directly elected by universal adult suffrage. The president's term of office was reduced from seven years to five years with effect from 2002, under legislation passed by both chambers of Parliament in June 2000, and approved by a referendum on 24 September 2000, although the referendum attracted a turnout of only around 30%. The head of government is the prime minister, who is appointed by the president. The Council of Ministers is appointed by the prime minister.

President:	Jacques Chirac	Since 17 May 1995
Prime Ministers:	Lionel Jospin	2 June 1997—6 May 2002
	Jean-Pierre Raffarin	Since 6 May 2002

Legislature: The legislature, the Parliament (Parlement), is bicameral. The lower chamber, the National Assembly (Assemblée Nationale), has 577 members, directly elected for a five-year term. The upper chamber, the Senate (Sénat), has 321 members, indirectly elected for a nine-year term. One-third of the membership is renewed every three years.

Profile of the President of the Republic:

Jacques **CHIRAC**

Chirac has become western Europe's elder statesman since the departure from office of former German chancellor Helmut Kohl. As president of France since 1995, Chirac has far-reaching political powers under the constitution framed by de Gaulle in 1958, in particular with regard to external relations, holding referendums, issuing decrees and declaring a state of emergency. He has been a prominent Gaullist politician for 30 years. He is strongly identified with Paris, where he was mayor from 1977 to 1995, and was twice prime minister during that time. The workings of the French political system obliged him to share power in 1997 in a so-called 'cohabitation' with the socialists, until the 2002 elections delivered him a strong pro-presidential majority.

Jacques Chirac was born in the fifth *arrondissement* of Paris on 29 November 1932. His father François was a bank clerk and later a company director. Jacques Chirac attended two prestigious Parisian *lycées*, went on to the Institut d'Etudes

Politiques in Paris, and attended Harvard University summer school in 1953. As a junior officer with the French army he was wounded in Algeria in the mid-1950s. In 1956 he married Bernadette Chodron de Courcel; they have two daughters, Laurence and Claude.

Between 1957 and 1959 Chirac was a student at France's elite civil service training institution, the Ecole Nationale d'Administration. Upon graduation he began his political career as an auditor in the government's finance office. In 1962 he became *chargé de mission* within the government of Georges Pompidou, soon moving from the government secretariat to a three-year spell as adviser in Pompidou's private office. He became a junior minister in 1967, with responsibility first for employment and, from 1968 to 1971, for economy and finance. He was also public auditor at the Cour des Comptes from 1965, a member of the Corrèze municipal council from 1965 to 1967, was first elected National Assembly deputy for Corrèze in 1967, and chaired the Corrèze general council from 1970 to 1979.

Chirac gained ministerial experience in the early 1970s at the ministry of agriculture and rural development (1972–74) and briefly as minister of the interior. When Valéry Giscard d'Estaing won the presidency in May 1974, Chirac at first prospered, as a leading Gaullist in Giscard's centre-right alliance. In addition to the post of prime minister from May 1974, he took on the general secretaryship of the Gaullist party, the Union of Democrats for the Republic (Union des Démocrates pour la République—UDR) from December. The two fell out, however, less over policy than because of friction between their two dominant personalities. Chirac resigned from the government in August 1976, and in December established his dominance within the Gaullist movement, transforming the UDR into the Rally for the Republic (Rassemblement pour la République—RPR) with himself as its president. The following March he won election for the first time as mayor of Paris, using this power base to keep himself in the political forefront; he retained both the RPR leadership and the Paris mayorship until he launched his successful bid for the presidency in the mid-1990s.

In the run-up to the 1981 presidential election, Chirac increasingly distanced the RPR leadership from the Giscard government, seeking to project himself rather than the president as the leader of the centre-right 'majority'. In the election, the first of his three bids for the presidency, he split the centre-right vote on the first round but finished a poor third behind the incumbent Giscard and the eventually successful François Mitterrand.

The honeymoon of the left in government soon gave way to acrimonious divisions and a reversal of direction on the economy, and in 1986 the centre-right came back strongly in the legislative elections. Chirac's RPR, its leadership rejuvenated by him in the years in opposition, performed so well that Mitterrand had little option but to make him prime minister. Thus began the first so-called 'cohabitation', a two-year test of some hitherto unexplored aspects of the division of powers under the Fifth Republic's constitution. The experiment was made to work, but Chirac's economic policies—based on a radical privatization programme—proved less successful with the electorate, and his party was divided on how to deal with the challenge of the National Front from the extreme right, a minority favouring some form of alliance.

Challenging Mitterrand for the presidency in April–May 1988, Chirac this time went through to the runoff, but finished second, with just under 46% of the vote. The general election the following month restored a centre-left majority, while also tilting the balance on the right away from Chirac towards Giscard.

Chirac favoured a 'yes' vote in the 1992 referendum on the Maastricht Treaty on European Union. Although his RPR was divided on this issue, it gained fresh momentum in the 1993 legislative elections, again becoming the largest party in a united centre-right grouping which won a landslide victory. Chirac, remaining aloof to prepare a third presidential bid, put forward fellow party member Edouard Balladur as prime minister for the second 'cohabitation' government, little expecting that his loyal colleague would emerge as a rival for the presidency in 1995. Balladur's candidacy was backed by the centre-right Union for French Democracy, Giscard having decided against standing himself. Chirac overtook Balladur by campaigning strongly with populist calls to tackle unemployment and 'social exclusion'. Second in the first ballot in April, with socialist Lionel Jospin unexpectedly leading the poll, Chirac picked up most of the Balladur votes in the second round on 7 May, ending with 52.6%, and was sworn in as president for a seven-year term on 17 May 1995.

Two years into his own first presidential term, Chirac found himself in another 'cohabitation', this time on the other side, when the pendulum in the legislative elections (called early by Chirac in the hope of a vote of confidence) swung back to the left. With Jospin as prime minister, the new socialist-led government in office between June 1997 and May 2002 was in the forefront of dealing with tensions over the state of the economy. To some extent this took the spotlight off Chirac, who had been criticized for neglecting his presidential campaign promises in pursuit of austerity policies to prepare for European monetary union.

It also turned out to be the socialists who paid a heavy price in electoral popularity at the 2002 elections. On this occasion, following constitutional changes to bring the president's term of office into line with that of the Assemblée Nationale, the presidential poll took place in April–May and the legislative elections followed in June. The shock result of the first round of the presidential election, where the far-right candidate Jean-Marie Le Pen came second—behind Chirac but ahead of Jospin—left pro-democracy voters no alternative but to rally around Chirac in the second round. The outcome of this was to deliver him a massive majority, where once he had been thought fatally compromised by mounting accusations of financial impropriety and political skulduggery. Moreover, it enabled his RPR to build a coalition known as the

Union for a Presidential Majority (Union pour la Majorité Presidentielle—UMP) which swept to an overall majority in the ensuing legislative elections.

In a Gaullist gesture asserting French independence on the world stage, Chirac caused particular controversy soon after taking office for the first time in 1995, with a six-month programme of nuclear tests in the Pacific. On controversial issues such as relations with Iraq, he has shown a marked unwillingness to accept any notion of US leadership. Fundamentally, however, his approach to foreign policy is based around the Franco-German alliance at the core of European Union integration, and the improvement in France's relations with North Atlantic Treaty Organization (NATO) countries was marked by its full involvement as a NATO member country in military action against Yugoslavia when the crisis over Kosovo erupted in early 1999.

Profile of the Prime Minister:

Jean-Pierre **RAFFARIN**

Jean-Pierre Raffarin is a member of the centre-right Liberal Democracy (Démocratie Libérale—DL) party. A career politician in his home region of Poitou, he has also been a public relations manager in the commercial sector. He was in the cabinet as a junior minister from 1995–97, and a member of the European Parliament (MEP) before that. He was appointed as interim prime minister following the defeat in presidential elections of the left-wing incumbent, Lionel Jospin, in May 2002, and was confirmed in office after the June legislative elections.

Jean-Pierre Raffarin was born on 3 August 1948 in Poitiers. His father, Jean Raffarin, was a noted radical politician. Jean-Pierre Raffarin graduated from the Ecole Supérieure de Commerce in Paris and began work in the marketing department of Cafés Jacques Vabre in 1973. Three years later he entered politics as an adviser to the minister of labour, a post he held for five years. During this period he wrote his first book, *Life in Yellow* (1977), and in 1980 he married Anne-Marie Perrier, with whom he has one daughter.

For most of the 1980s Raffarin was occupied with regional politics in Poitou and with running the consultancy firm, Bernard Krief Communications. Between 1979 and 1988 he also lectured at the Institut des Sciences Politiques in Paris and wrote a further three books on politics. By 1988 he had left the commercial sector and had been elected chairman of the Poitou–Charentes regional council. The following year he was elected as an MEP, representing the conservative republicans.

Raffarin returned to mainstream national politics in 1995 when the presidential victory of Jacques Chirac gave the centre-right control of both the government and the presidency. Raffarin became a member of the Union for French

Democracy (Union pour la Démocratie Française—UDF) and was elected as a senator for Vienne. Prime Minister Alain Juppé brought him into his cabinet as minister of small and medium-sized businesses and also minister of commerce and craft industry. However, his period on the front line was short-lived as the right-wing coalition was ousted from power in the 1997 general elections. Thrust into opposition, Raffarin split from the UDF and joined the reorganized DL while concentrating on his local role as deputy mayor of Chasseneuil-du-Poitou, a post he had held since 1995.

The country's most recent period of cohabitation was brought to an end in 2002 when the increasingly unpopular and divided centre-left coalition was defeated in both presidential and legislative polls. Raffarin was appointed interim prime minister by the newly re-elected Chirac on 6 May and began building up support for a galvanized centre-right bloc. He has coined the term 'creative humanism' for his own particular brand of conservative politics. The Union for a Presidential Majority (Union pour la Majorité Presidentielle—UMP) coalition proved successful and won a majority in the June 2002 legislative elections, with Raffarin at its head. Raffarin has benefited from his down-to-earth, regionalist approach, contrasting strongly with the media-savvy personalities prominent in the previous government. As prime minister he has pledged to push through greater privatization and a reduction in income tax.

GABON

Full name: The Gabonese Republic.

Leadership structure: The head of state is a president, directly elected by universal adult suffrage. The constitution was amended in 1997 to extend the presidential term of office from five to seven years, but the next election was nevertheless held within five years. The head of government is the prime minister, who is appointed by the president. The Council of Ministers is appointed by the prime minister.

| **President:** | Omar Bongo | Since 2 Dec. 1967 |
| | (acting from 28 Nov. 1967) | |

| **Prime Minister:** | Jean-François Ntoutoume-Emane | Since 24 Jan. 1999 |

Legislature: The Parliament (Parlement) is bicameral. The lower chamber, the National Assembly (Assemblée Nationale), has 120 members, directly elected for a five-year term. The upper chamber, the Senate (Sénat), has 91 members, elected for a six-year term by municipal and regional councillors.

Profile of the President:

Omar **BONGO**

Omar Bongo, head of state in a single-party regime for 25 years, continued in office after winning the country's first multiparty presidential elections in December 1993. This term was extended by constitutional amendment from five to seven years, but he nevertheless went to the polls in December 1998 and secured a further term. Before first becoming president he had held a number of posts in government service and had been a close adviser to his predecessor, President Léon M'Ba.

Albert-Bernard Bongo (he renamed himself Omar when he converted to Islam in 1973) was born in Lewai, Franceville, in the southeast of Gabon, on 30 December 1935. He gained a diploma in commerce from Brazzaville Technical College in the Congo. From 1958 he worked briefly in the civil service and was in the French Air Force for two years prior to independence. In 1960 he entered the ministry of foreign affairs.

Appointed as assistant director in the Gabonese cabinet in 1962, he was director of President M'Ba's private office by that October. In the succeeding years he held a variety of positions in government administration and became one of the president's closest advisers. In 1965 he entered the cabinet, as minister-delegate to the presidency. By November the following year he was vice president, and he became president in 1967 following the death of President M'Ba. In 1968 he founded the Gabonese Democratic Party (Parti Démocratique Gabonais—PDG), introducing a single-party system.

Bongo was elected to a new seven-year term in February 1973, confirmed in office in 1980, and re-elected to a further term in 1986. His government was generally regarded as pro-Western, maintaining close relations with France in particular. His role in international organizations included chairing the Organization of African Unity (OAU) in 1977, and he was active as a mediator in regional disputes. Bongo married his second wife Edith Lucie Nguesso, the daughter of the president of the Republic of the Congo, in August 1990.

In 1990 Bongo announced proposals to establish a multiparty democratic system. Parliamentary elections took place in late 1990 and early 1991. When the presidential elections were held on 5 December 1993, Bongo topped the poll with 51.18% of the vote, and he was sworn in for his new term on 22 January 1994. Although international observers endorsed the conduct of the poll, dissatisfied opposition supporters formed a 'parallel administration'; protracted political disputes led eventually to constitutional amendments and the holding in 1996–97 of fresh elections to the National Assembly and Senate. In March 1997 a constitutional amendment was approved extending future presidential terms from five to seven years.

Bongo was re-elected with 67% of the vote on 6 December 1998, an easy victory over his nearest rival, Pierre Mamboundou, who received only 17%. Bongo was re-inaugurated in January 1999 despite opposition claims of fraud. In October 2000 Bongo secured lifetime immunity from prosecution. He has sought to conciliate the political opposition and invited the Rally for Gabon to join the government, which it did in January 2002.

Profile of the Prime Minister:

Jean-François **NTOUTOUME-EMANE**

Jean-François Ntoutoume-Emane is a member of the ruling Gabonese Democratic Party (Parti Démocratique Gabonais—PDG). A career politician, he held a number of different portfolios simultaneously in the late 1990s before he was appointed prime minister.

Jean-François Ntoutoume (he took on the suffix Emane later in life) was born on 6 November 1939. He has a doctorate in political science from the University of Jussieu, Paris. He joined the government for the first time in February 1996 as the minister of state for habitat, lands and urban planning and welfare, and in 1997 he was appointed minister of state, minister of land registry, town planning and housing and minister of state control, decentralization, territorial administration and regional integration. Alongside his nomination as prime minister in January 1999, he retained the lands and urban planning portfolio.

President Omar Bongo found reason to berate Ntoutoume-Emane in August 2000 for his government's "comatose" performance. Despite this reproach, Ntoutoume-Emane oversaw the PDG's re-election in December 2001 and remained at the helm of the new government. His wife Sophie has occasionally acted as a deputy to First Lady Edith Lucie Bongo at diplomatic occasions.

GAMBIA

Full name: The Republic of The Gambia.

Leadership structure: The head of state is a president, directly elected by universal adult suffrage. The president's term of office is five years, with no limit on re-election. The head of government is the president. The cabinet is appointed by the president.

| President: | Col. (retd) Yahya Jammeh
(seized power on 22 July 1994) | Since 26 July 1994 |

Legislature: The legislature is unicameral. The sole chamber, the National Assembly, has 53 members, 48 of them directly elected by universal adult suffrage, and five appointed by the president, for a five-year term.

Profile of the President:

Col. (retd) Yahya **JAMMEH**

Yahya Jammeh has held power in The Gambia since his bloodless coup in 1994, and was elected as president in a poll held under controversial circumstances in September 1996. His re-election in 2001 was similarly contentious. Before taking power he was a military police officer, trained in part in the USA.

Yahya Alphonse Jamus Jebulai Jammeh was born on 25 May 1965 in Kanilai village in Foni Kansala district, and educated locally at the Kanilai and Bwiam primary schools and then at Gambia high school. Joining Gambia's national police force in 1984, he was promoted to sergeant two years later. Then, in 1989, he was commissioned as an officer and was put in charge of the presidential escort of the presidential guard. He joined the military police unit in 1991. Promoted to lieutenant in 1992, he became commander of the National Military Police that year and was made a captain in 1994. His military training has taken him abroad to the USA, where he attended the military police officers' basic course in Fort McClellan, Alabama.

In July 1994 he led a coup organized by a small group of five young army lieutenants aged between 25 and 30. The coup ousted the veteran President Dawda Jawara, who had headed a succession of democratically elected governments since independence in 1965, and suspended the constitution. Jammeh headed a five-member Armed Forces Provisional Ruling Council, and assumed the title of 'president', although this was not recognized internationally.

185

Under pressure both from within the country and from abroad, Jammeh drew up a revised constitution providing for a return to civilian rule and multiparty politics, which was approved in a referendum in August 1996. However, within a week of the referendum Jammeh banned the three main opposition parties and announced that anyone who had held presidential or ministerial office in the 30 years preceding the 1994 coup would not be permitted to stand in the forthcoming presidential election. Foreign observers refused to attend the poll because of the circumstances under which it was being held. When it took place, on 26 September, Jammeh was elected president with 56% of the vote. The Alliance for Patriotic Reorientation and Construction (APRC), which Jammeh had formed in August to back his presidential candidacy, won 33 of the 45 elected seats in the new National Assembly the following January.

Two separate coup attempts against Jammeh were foiled in January and July 2000 while public confidence in the police force plummeted and violent demonstrations over police brutality rocked the country later that year. Jammeh's political stance grew ever more conservative and in June 2001 he publicly admitted that he was seriously considering introducing Islamic *shari'a* law in The Gambia. In order to legitimize his position, however, he lifted his previous ban on political parties in July that year, prompting ex-president Jawara to promise a swift return, but he was not in time to prevent Jammeh's re-election, with 53% of the vote, in October.

Soon after his re-inauguration Jammeh faced stiff criticism from international human rights bodies. Amnesty International, in particular, felt that the supposed liberalism engendered before the election was hollow, as a number of Jammeh's opponents suddenly found themselves incarcerated. The APRC was ensured victory in legislative elections in January 2002 as an insufficient number of opposition candidates registered to compete against it—33 APRC politicians were entirely unopposed. Jammeh's consolidation of power seemed complete in June 2002, when he welcomed Jawara's eventual return from exile and promised him a future role as a respected 'elder statesman'.

GEORGIA

Full name: Georgia.

Leadership structure: The head of state is a president directly elected by universal adult suffrage. The president's term of office is five years, renewable once only. The head of government is the president, who is responsible to Parliament. The Council of Ministers is appointed by the president.

President:	Eduard Shevardnadze (head of state from 10 March 1992)	Since 26 Nov. 1995
State Ministers:	Vazha Lortkipanidze (acting from 1 May 2000)	7 Aug. 1998—11 May 2000
	Giorgi Arsenishvili	11 May 2000—21 Dec. 2001
	Avtandil Jorbenadze	Since 21 Dec. 2001

Legislature: The legislature is unicameral, but is to become bicameral "following the creation of appropriate conditions". The sole existing chamber, the Parliament (Sakartvelos Parlamenti), has 235 members, 85 elected in single-member constituencies and the rest from party lists, for a four-year term.

Profile of the President:

Eduard **SHEVARDNADZE**

Among national leaders in postcommunist countries who had also held high office under communism, Eduard Shevardnadze stands out. Once the police chief and head of the communist security apparatus in Georgia, and since independence the pre-eminent statesman of that small and crisis-riven country, he enjoys an international reputation derived from his role between 1985 and 1990 as Soviet foreign minister under Mikhail Gorbachev, helping to engineer the Soviet Union's withdrawal from the Cold War arms race and from regional hegemony in eastern Europe.

Eduard Amvrosiyevich Shevardnadze was born on 25 January 1928, the son of a teacher in the village of Mamat in the Lanchkhuti region of Georgia not far from the Black Sea. Heavily involved in youth work and as a teacher and activist in Komsomol, the communist youth league, he became first secretary of Komsomol at republic level in Georgia in 1957. Two years later he was first elected to the Supreme Soviet in the republic, and also in 1959 completed a correspondence degree in history at the Kutaisi Pedagogical Institute. A devoted family man, Shevardnadze and his wife Nanuli had one son and one daughter, and later became proud grandparents.

Drafted into the civilian police in Georgia, Shevardnadze began to make a name for himself as head of the republic's ministry of public order from 1965 onward, tackling both unrest and corruption, and clamping down on self-enrichment by government and party officials. He was promoted to minister of the interior and, from 1972, became first secretary of the Georgian communist party. He held this post, the top leadership position in Georgia under Soviet rule, for over a decade and was noted among other things for a relatively sympathetic attitude towards Jews seeking to emigrate to Israel.

Shevardnadze was a member of the central committee of the Communist Party of the Soviet Union (CPSU) from 1976. However, his rapid elevation at central level in 1985, to the CPSU politburo and simultaneously to the post of foreign minister, despite his lack of experience in foreign affairs or central government, came as a result of his political association and growing personal friendship with the new CPSU general secretary Gorbachev.

Over the next five years Shevardnadze worked as Gorbachev's right-hand man in transforming Soviet foreign relations. Beginning with the bilateral Soviet–US summits of 1985 and 1986, the new Soviet leadership backed away progressively from the economically ruinous effort to sustain the superpower rivalry of the Cold War. Soviet troops had pulled out of Afghanistan by 1989, while a series of agreements on arms control and arms reduction coincided with a loosening of the Soviet grip on what had been the communist bloc. The crowds who welcomed the collapse of communism across the countries of central and eastern Europe hailed Shevardnadze, like Gorbachev, as a hero of democratization.

At home, however, Shevardnadze felt the growing danger of a military and hard-line backlash. Resigning as foreign minister in December 1990, he delivered a dramatic speech warning that "dictatorship is coming", and the August 1991 Moscow coup attempt proved his warnings justified. Joining in efforts to rally support for Gorbachev, he returned briefly to the post of Soviet foreign minister as the Soviet Union was disintegrating in 1991.

He returned in March 1992 to newly independent Georgia, where open conflict between nationalist factions was threatening to destroy a country that was already in serious economic disarray. Appointed within four days as chairman of a military-dominated State Council, he was pitched into a period of overt conflict with the ousted former president Zviad Gamsakhurdia and more seriously with secessionists in Abkhazia, which borders Russia on the Black Sea coast. On 11 October 1992 he was elected chairman of the Parliament of Georgia, and a referendum endorsed him as head of state and commander-in-chief of the armed forces. Under a new constitution three years later, the office of president was reintroduced, with executive powers, and Shevardnadze was elected for a five-year term in a nationwide ballot on 5 November 1995. He won more than three-quarters of the votes cast, ahead of the former communist party first secretary and four minor candidates, and welcomed the outcome as showing that "democracy and reforms have triumphed". Shevardnadze had formed the Citizens' Union of Georgia (CUG) in 1993 as a pro-democracy and free-market-oriented alliance with a strong environmentalist element and it won a large majority in the November/December 1995 legislative elections.

Meanwhile, the threat of the disintegration of Georgia remained Shevardnadze's most acute and recurring problem. In February 1994 he and Russian President Boris Yeltsin signed a treaty of friendship and co-operation, especially controversial in that it allowed for the continuing existence of Russian military bases on Georgian soil. His pro-Russian line, and his decision to take Georgia into the Russian-dominated Commonwealth of Independent States (CIS), reflected his perception of how vulnerable Georgia's position had become, especially after rebel forces gained the upper hand in the northern separatist republic of Abkhazia (where he himself came under heavy shelling during one visit).

The stabilization of the Abkhazia situation, with a Russian-backed ceasefire in March 1994 and the presence of a Russian-dominated international peacekeeping force thereafter, still left the issue of what to do about a flood of ethnic Georgian refugees. Meanwhile the country faced economic problems so severe that Shevardnadze was forced to announce unpopular food rationing measures. Over the next few years, however, he began to be able to claim some success in tackling chronic instability, although there were renewed flare-ups of the conflict with Abkhazia, and other separatist struggles in different parts of the country. Relations with Russia have become complicated by the Chechen independence struggle just on Georgia's border. Russia has claimed that the Pankisi Gorge area in northern Georgia is a safe haven and training ground for Chechen guerrillas. Shevardnadze has since cultivated a new relationship with the USA, and agreed to have US special forces train Georgian troops in anti-terrorist operations in 2002.

Shevardnadze's own life remains under threat from would-be assassins, his regime having struggled to control the private armies of various nationalist leaders. In August 1995 he survived a car bombing in Tbilisi, and a second attempt was made to kill him in February 1998. Brittle signs of the beginning of economic recovery were damaged in 1998 by drought and a currency crisis, but the long-heralded opening in April 1999 of a pipeline to take oil from the Caspian Sea across Georgia to the Black Sea brought a promise of substantial and much-needed revenue to his beleaguered government.

While political opposition to Shevardnadze continues, his public popularity remains high. He was re-elected, for what he later promised would be his final term, on 9 April 2000 with 79% of the vote. The opposition claimed widespread fraud. During this term he has sought to pull the feuding parties together and has backed calls for an executive prime minister, whom the president would have the power to appoint and dismiss. However, the CUG itself became riven with internal divisions, and a large section of the party defected to the opposition in March 2002.

Profile of the State Minister:

Avtandil **JORBENADZE**

Avtandil Jorbenadze is leader of the ruling Citizens' Union of Georgia (CUG). Trained as a physician, he worked in the capital's health care system before being appointed to government for the first time in 1992. He was made state minister on 21 December 2001 after President Eduard Shevardnadze had dismissed the previous administration in November.

Avtandil Jorbenadze was born on 23 February 1951 in the village of Chibati in western Georgia, which was then an integral part of the Soviet Union. He graduated as a doctor from the Tbilisi State Medical University in 1974, and was later awarded a doctorate in social hygiene and health management from the Moscow Physicians' Postgraduate Institute in 1991. He married Nino Vepkhvadze in the early 1970s and they now have two children.

Having worked after graduating as an intern at the main hospital and small clinics in Tbilisi, Jorbenadze was called to military service in 1976. He was given the rank of senior lieutenant in the Soviet army and worked as a military doctor until 1978. He returned to civilian work once he had been demobbed and was made deputy chief doctor of the main Tbilisi hospital in 1982, and first deputy of the capital's health department in 1986.

In 1992 Jorbenadze was brought into the government of a recently independent Georgia as deputy minister of health. He left the cabinet the following year to work in the office of the state consultant, before returning that October as health minister. In December 1999 he was given the added responsibility of social security, and in 2000 he was also made labour minister.

On 1 November 2001 President Shevardnadze dismissed the entire cabinet after a political outcry over the storming of a television station by security agents. After almost two months of deliberation, the president appointed Jorbenadze to head a new cabinet on 21 December. Jorbenadze was elected leader of the pro-Shevardnadze CUG in June 2002. Since 2001 Shevardnadze has been suggesting that he would like to create an executive prime ministerial post.

GERMANY

Full name: The Federal Republic of Germany.

Leadership structure: The head of state is a president, elected by the Bundesversammlung—a specially constituted body comprising the members of the lower chamber of the federal legislature and an equal number of representatives elected by the state legislatures. The president's term of office is five years. The head of government is the federal chancellor, who is elected by the Bundestag on the proposal of the federal president. The federal government is appointed by the president on the proposal of the federal chancellor.

Federal President: Johannes Rau   Since 1 July 1999

Federal Chancellor: Gerhard Schröder   Since 27 Oct. 1998

Legislature: The legislature is bicameral. The lower chamber, the Federal Assembly (Bundestag), has 603 members, directly elected for a four-year term. The upper chamber, the Federal Council (Bundesrat), has 69 members appointed by the states (*Länder*) for variable terms.

Profile of the Federal President:

Johannes **RAU**

Johannes Rau's mainly symbolic presidential role has, as he puts it, "only the force of words, little more". A deeply religious man, Rau has been a member of the Social Democratic Party of Germany (Sozialdemokratische Partei Deutschlands—SPD) since 1957, and reached the summit of his career when he was chosen as its candidate for the federal chancellorship, but lost that election in 1987. For two decades he was the most prominent politician, and minister-president, in his home state (Land) *of North Rhine-Westphalia.*

Johannes Rau was born in the western city of Wuppertal-Barmen on 16 January 1931, the son of a Protestant pastor. His religious convictions have played a strong part in his career, earning him the nickname 'Brother Johannes'. He was a member of the Evangelical Church of the Rhineland from 1965 to 1999. He first began work at a theological publishing firm in 1949, rose to become managing director by 1954, and stayed with the company until 1967.

It was in 1957 that Rau became a member of the SPD. His political mentor was Gustav Heinemann, who went on to become the first SPD president of Germany from 1969 to 1974, and whose granddaughter Christina Delius married Rau in 1982; they have one son and two daughters.

A member of the State Parliament (Landtag) in North Rhine-Westphalia for over 40 years, from 1958 until his election to the federal presidency in 1999, Rau was also chairman of the SPD in North Rhine-Westphalia from 1977, and minister-president there from 1978, until he stepped down from both these posts in May 1998. He had previously been a member of the Wuppertal city council (1964–78), head of the city's SPD faction (1964–67) and mayor of Wuppertal (1969–70).

Having left the publishing business in 1967 to devote himself to politics on a full-time basis, Rau became a member of the SPD national executive that year, and party deputy chairman in 1982. Nominated as the party's candidate for federal chancellor in the 1987 election, he was defeated by the incumbent chancellor Helmut Kohl of the Christian Democratic Union (Christlich Demokratische Union—CDU). This represented a major setback. Rau was widely seen as having contributed to the loss of his party's popular mandate, and as a representative of an 'old school' socialism.

In 1994, after four years chairing the parliamentary mediation committee, Rau was nominated as the SPD candidate for the post of federal president. Losing unexpectedly to the CDU candidate Roman Herzog, he returned to the Federal Council, serving for a second time as its speaker for a year (as he had in the parliamentary year 1982/1983).

In November 1998 (six months after he had stepped down as state premier and SPD leader in North Rhine-Westphalia) Rau was nominated once more as SPD candidate for federal president. At last successful, in the ballot of the electoral council held in May 1999, he showed his characteristic restraint, saying that it represented "neither a coronation or the accomplishment of a lifelong dream" but the chance "to serve democracy".

Profile of the Federal Chancellor:

Gerhard **SCHRÖDER**

Gerhard Schröder is the moderate leader of Germany's Social Democrats (Sozialdemokratische Partei Deutschlands—SPD), heading a government coalition with the environmentalist Greens. He came to power at the 1998 election, ending Helmut Kohl's 16 years as federal chancellor. Schröder completed his transition from radical young socialist to proponent of the 'new centre' as head of the regional government in the northwest German state (Land) of Lower Saxony from 1990 to 1998. Ambitious, designer-suited and business-friendly, he is frequently cited with UK prime minister Tony Blair as representative of a new centrist politics in western Europe.

Gerhard Fritz Kurt Schröder was born in Mossenberg near Detmold, North Rhine-Westphalia, on 7 April 1944. His father was killed a few days later as German troops withdrew from Romania. His mother Erika, a Protestant and staunch social democrat, did cleaning work to support him and his elder sister; she went on to have three more children by a second marriage.

Schröder was obliged to leave school at the age of 14 and work as an apprentice in a china shop. He went to night school to gain his school-leaving certificate, going on to study law at the University of Göttingen, and financing his studies by working on a building site. He joined the SPD in 1963, and has been a member of the public service union ÖTV since 1973.

Upon qualifying he set up a legal practice in Hanover in 1978 and in the same year was elected chairman of the Young Social Democrats (Jusos). He gained an early reputation as a radical firebrand, opposing the stationing of US nuclear weapons on West German soil, courting conservative criticism by appearing without a tie to deliver his maiden speech in the Federal Assembly (where he became a deputy on the SPD list in the October 1980 elections) and, in his law practice, defending former terrorists. A widely circulated—though possibly apocryphal—story told to illustrate Schröder's personal ambition describes him rattling the gates of the chancellor's residence in Bonn after a drinking spree, shortly after Helmut Kohl became federal chancellor in 1982, and shouting, "I want in there!".

Although still a Federal Assembly deputy until 1986, it was in regional politics in Lower Saxony that Schröder first really made his mark. In 1984 he was SPD candidate for minister-president (i.e. regional head of government); two years later, in June 1986, he became a deputy in the State Parliament (Landtag), for which he had to give up his Federal Assembly seat; and he finally became minister-president after the 1990 state election by forming a 'red–green' coalition with the environmentalist Greens.

During this period Schröder moved away from the radical stance of his early years in politics, alienating some on the left of his own party but cultivating broader contacts and, importantly, winning the confidence of key business figures. The conservative daily *Frankfurter Allgemeine Zeitung* wrote that he had "undergone an astonishing personality change" after coming to power in Lower Saxony. "The wounded aggressiveness of the opposition leader has become relaxed joviality, the stilted wish to impress has been replaced by the cool, governing style of an unassailable office holder." He dropped the Greens from government in Lower Saxony when the SPD gained a majority of one seat in the 1994 state election.

Although he joined the SPD presidium in 1989, he had an ambivalent relationship with the party apparatus and especially with his contemporaries and rivals, Oskar Lafontaine, the former minister-president of Saarland who was later to become his minister of finance, and Rudolf Scharping, who was leader of the SPD group in the Federal Assembly and later became defence minister. By turning the tide of a run of poor party results in state elections, and winning 47.9% of the vote and an absolute majority of seats in the Lower Saxony poll on 1 March 1998, Schröder demonstrated that he had the credentials to succeed at federal level, and he secured election the following day as the SPD candidate for chancellor.

The federal election on 27 September 1998 was Schröder's hour of triumph. As a proponent of the 'new centre' he campaigned as a 1990s politician seeking a 'third way' between old conservative and socialist values. Having determinedly made this move to the centre ground to gain electoral support, like his UK counterpart Tony Blair, he encountered criticism during the campaign from observers who questioned where the substance of his policies lay. His detractors portrayed him as a wheeler-dealer and telegenic showman, who had discarded his radical image in favour of centrist rhetoric, fashionable Italian designer clothes and a penchant for fine cigars and champagne. His image as a modern leader, however, capable of both bold and pragmatic decisions and seeking to reconcile liberal capitalism with social values, appealed to an electorate which was eager for change after 16 years of Chancellor Kohl.

The SPD emerged from the 1998 elections as the largest party, but needed a coalition partner to command a majority in parliament. Schröder put together an agreement with the Greens, who thus entered the federal government for the first time. When Schröder's cabinet was formed in October, however, its image was immediately dented by the withdrawal of his most controversial and business-oriented nominee, computer entrepreneur Jost Stollmann, and by debate about the amount of power he had conceded to Lafontaine, the SPD chairman and standard-bearer of the left, as head of a new financial superministry.

In its first six months the Schröder government had a rude awakening. Battered by disagreements with the Greens, particularly over phasing out nuclear power plants, the SPD suffered badly in state elections in Hesse in early 1999. Bigger drama followed when Lafontaine resigned, following disagreements about monetary issues within the new European single currency, about tax policy, and indeed about the overall direction the SPD was taking in government. Although many still regarded Lafontaine as representing the heart and soul of the party, Schröder assumed the SPD chairmanship himself; his formal election in April 1999 was unopposed, but, unusually, a quarter of the delegates still failed to back him. This early hesitation was replaced by overwhelming party support at his re-election to the post in November 2001.

Following the 11 September 2001 attacks in the USA, Schröder's popularity began to fall as he gave his backing to US president George W. Bush's 'war on terrorism'. In November 2001 he survived a parliamentary vote against the deployment of German troops in the 'war' only by turning it into a confidence vote in his government. His stance forced his Green coalition partners to move further away from their traditional pacifistic stance. More important perhaps was the global economic slowdown, which had been accelerated by the 11 September attacks. Unemployment in Germany slipped past the symbolic four million mark in December and continued to hover around that level. In opinion polls leading up to the September 2002 elections Schröder trailed the Christian Democrat candidate Edmund Stoiber.

Floodwaters came to Schröder's rescue. The dramatic inundation of Dresden in August 2002, and his own swift response, was a boon to his popularity, along with his confident handling of television debates. The SPD did lose seats in the election but maintained a majority with the help of its Green partners in the face of an overall swing to the right. In his second term, Schröder has begun to lean away from alliance with Bush and has turned instead to the, by now historic, Franco-German alliance. When campaigning for re-election he insisted that he would serve for no longer than ten years, unlike his predecessor Helmut Kohl.

Gerhard Schröder has had four marriages. The first, in 1968, was with librarian Eva Schubach, his childhood sweetheart. After leaving her, he married schoolteacher Anne Taschenbach in 1971. He benefited during his rise to power from his partnership with his third wife, political scientist Hiltrud 'Hillu' Hampel, whom he married in 1984 and whose two daughters he helped to bring up. In early 1997 he married his fourth wife, the Bavarian journalist Doris Köpf, who also has a daughter.

GHANA

Full name: The Republic of Ghana.

Leadership structure: The head of state is a president, directly elected by universal adult suffrage. The president's term of office is four years, renewable once only. A 25-member Council of State, appointed by the president, and a similarly appointed 20-member National Security Council, have advisory functions. The head of government is the president, who is responsible to Parliament. The Council of Ministers is appointed by the president.

Presidents:	Jerry Rawlings (seized power on 31 Dec. 1981)	7 Jan. 1993—7 Jan. 2001
	John Kufuor	Since 7 Jan. 2001

Legislature: The legislature is unicameral. The sole chamber, the Parliament, has 200 members, directly elected for a four-year term.

Profile of the President:

John **KUFUOR**

John Kufuor was a founding member of the New Patriotic Party (NPP). The successor from early 2001 to Ghana's head of state for 20 years Jerry Rawlings, Kufuor is a lawyer by training who came to political prominence in the 1990s. He ran unsuccessfully against Rawlings in the 1996 presidential elections.

John Agyekum Kufuor was born on 8 December 1938 in Kumasi, to a respected family of chiefs and professionals. After attending Prempeh College in Ghana he travelled to the UK to study law at Lincoln's Inn in London and was called to the Bar in 1961. After this he attended Oxford University, graduating in politics, philosophy and economics (PPE) in 1964. He is married to Theresa Mensah and they now have five children. Kufuor is a Roman Catholic and is known as the 'gentle giant'.

Returning to Ghana (which had experienced an army coup in 1966), Kufuor entered local government as chief legal officer and town clerk in Kumasi in 1967. While the country swung between democracy and military government in the 1960s–80s Kufuor played a humble role in the country's politics as a founding member of the Progress Party in 1969, the Popular Front Party in 1979 and ultimately the NPP in 1992. He was thrown in jail by military regimes on two separate occasions, but during this period also served as deputy foreign minister and secretary for local government. He resigned the latter post after just seven months in 1982 in disillusion with the newly installed government of President Jerry Rawlings. He was instrumental in the establishment in 1994 of the country's District Assemblies. These assemblies were designed to defuse certain racial and regional conflicts by granting a measure of decentralization.

Kufuor was defeated by President Rawlings in the November 1996 presidential elections, but his real opportunity came with Rawlings's retirement from the presidency four years later. Rawlings's preferred successor was John Atta Mills, whose nomination as candidate of the National Democratic Congress he had approved in 1999, well ahead of the December 2000 ballot. The election campaign, which contained the country's first ever debate between the seven presidential candidates, rapidly resolved itself into a contest between the two leading contenders, Atta Mills and Kufuor. The resulting win for Kufuor (with 48% against 45% for Atta Mills), and the simultaneous albeit narrow victory of Kufuor's NPP in the parliamentary elections, confirmed that Rawlings's popularity had been more of a personal than a party matter. Kufuor took office on 7 January 2001.

GREECE

Full name: The Hellenic Republic.

Leadership structure: The head of state is a president, elected by Parliament. The president's term of office is five years, renewable once only. The head of government is the prime minister, who is appointed by the president. The cabinet is appointed by the president on the recommendation of the prime minister.

President: Costas Stephanopoulos   Since 10 March 1995

Prime Minister: Costas Simitis   Since 22 Jan. 1996

Legislature: The legislature is unicameral. The sole chamber, the Parliament (Vouli), has 300 members, directly elected for a four-year term.

Profile of the President:

Costas **STEPHANOPOULOS**

Costas Stephanopoulos, now in his second five-year term in the largely ceremonial post of head of state, is a former lawyer who spent seven years in exile in Paris during the colonels' dictatorship (1967–74), returning to become a junior member of the 1974 national unity government. He founded the short-lived Democratic Renewal (Komma Dimokratikis Ananeosis—DIANA) grouping in 1985 as an offshoot from the conservative New Democracy (Nea Dimokratika) party. His election as president was made possible, however, by support from deputies of the Panhellenic Socialist Movement (Panellinion Socialistikon Kinima—PASOK).

Constantinos 'Costas' Stephanopoulos was born on 15 August 1926 in Patras. He graduated from the University of Athens with a law degree and practised law in Patras from 1954. In 1964 he was elected a member of parliament for Achaia, representing the National Radical Union, but went into exile in Paris when the colonels seized power in 1967. Returning to Greece in 1974, he became deputy trade minister in the government of national unity which was formed after the fall of the military regime. In subsequent elections in 1977, 1981 and 1985 he stood successfully for parliament as a New Democracy candidate in Achaia.

Stephanopoulos held three cabinet posts during the latter half of the 1970s, that of the interior in 1974–76, of social services in 1976–77 and of minister of state in 1977–80. After two failed attempts to win the leadership of New Democracy, he resigned from the party in 1985, setting up his own splinter group, DIANA, on whose platform he won a seat in parliament representing Greater Athens in the 1989 general election.

In 1994 Stephanopoulos dissolved DIANA, after it had failed to win any seats in the European Parliament elections of that year, and withdrew from active politics. He coauthored a work entitled *The National Interest and Security Policy* in 1995.

An uncharismatic but respected figure, and a widower with two sons and one daughter, Stephanopoulos was nominated to stand for the presidency in 1995 as successor to the 88-year-old Constantinos Karamanlis. Although his nomination was sponsored by the small right-wing Political Spring (Politiki Anixi) party, his erstwhile New Democracy colleagues had not forgiven his defection a decade earlier, so the crucial factor for Stephanopoulos was the support of PASOK. He was eventually elected, on 8 March 1995, polling 181 votes out of 300. His re-election victory on 8 February 2000 was somewhat more convincing as he gained 269 votes, while his only rival claimed just ten.

Profile of the Prime Minister:

Costas **SIMITIS**

Costas Simitis, a founder member of and since June 1996 the leader of the Panhellenic Socialist Movement (Panellinion Socialistikon Kinima—PASOK), is a lawyer by training. He taught law abroad after escaping the colonels' regime, and held a variety of ministerial posts in PASOK governments from 1981 onward before becoming prime minister. His leadership of PASOK marks something of a generation change and represents a shift away from the party's traditional left-wing policies.

Constantinos 'Costas' Simitis was born on 23 June 1936 in Piraeus, Athens, the son of a lawyer who distinguished himself in the resistance to German occupation in the Second World War. He studied law and economics at the University of Marburg, West Germany, where he gained a doctorate in 1959. A qualified lawyer from 1961, he was at the London School of Economics between 1961 and 1963. He is married to Daphne Arkadiou and has two daughters.

Simitis's active involvement in politics began in 1965 when he cofounded the Alexandros Papanastasiou Society, a society for political study and research. Between 1967 and 1969 he was involved in clandestine action against the military regime of the colonels. He only avoided arrest by escaping abroad, and was court-martialled in absentia, while his wife was arrested by the regime and kept in isolation. Living in Germany and teaching law at the University of Konstanz and the Justus Liebig University in Giessen, Simitis remained active in the opposition to the colonels until the eventual demise of the military regime in 1974, attending public meetings and writing articles. In 1970 he became a member of the national council of the Panhellenic Liberation Movement, which a few years later was to become part of PASOK.

Simitis was among the founding members of PASOK in 1974, and held positions on its central committee and executive committee. He also continued teaching law, at the Pantios University of Athens where he has been a full professor since 1977. During PASOK's first period in government from 1981 to 1985 he was minister of agriculture. Simitis was first elected to Parliament as a representative of the port of Piraeus in 1985, and has been re-elected at every election since then. He held the ministerial portfolio of national economy between 1985 and 1987, of education and religious affairs between 1989 and 1990, and of industry, energy, technology and trade from 1993 to 1995. However, he resigned in September 1995 in protest at the failure of the ailing prime minister Andreas Papandreou to address the question of his succession.

When Papandreou was eventually persuaded to resign as prime minister on 15 January 1996, the PASOK parliamentary party elected Simitis to the premiership in two rounds of voting and he was sworn in as prime minister on 22 January. He was elected chairman of PASOK on 30 June of the same year, following Papandreou's death on 2 June.

Regarded as a modernizer within the party, Simitis promised tax and welfare reforms. He led PASOK to an unexpectedly convincing victory in the general election on 22 September 1996, thereby strengthening his hand in moving the party away from its traditional left-wing orientation, although allowing as a result the growth of support for the communist left and for a splinter group of former PASOK members. In office he retained his main party leadership rivals within his government in prominent ministerial posts, while introducing tough reforms to ensure Greece's entry into the eurozone in 2001. The drachma, Europe's oldest currency, was replaced in Greece by the euro on 1 January 2002. In the meantime PASOK had been re-elected on 9 April 2000, with only 1% more of the total popular vote than the opposition New Democracy, which was nevertheless enough to give it an overall majority in Parliament.

GRENADA

Full name: Grenada.

Leadership structure: The head of state is the British sovereign, styled 'Queen of the United Kingdom of Great Britain and Northern Ireland and of Grenada and Her other Realms and Territories, Head of the Commonwealth', and represented by a governor-general who is appointed on the advice of the Grenadian prime minister. The head of government is the prime minister, who is responsible to Parliament. The cabinet is appointed by the governor-general on the advice of the prime minister.

Queen:	Elizabeth II	Since 6 Feb. 1952
Governor-General:	Sir Daniel Williams	Since 8 Aug. 1996
Prime Minister:	Keith Mitchell	Since 22 June 1995

Legislature: The legislature, the Parliament, is bicameral. The lower chamber, the House of Representatives, has 15 members, directly elected for a five-year term. The upper chamber, the Senate, has 13 members all appointed by the governor-general after the election of the House of Representatives (seven on the advice of the prime minister, three on the advice of the leader of the opposition and three on the advice of the prime minister after consulting various interests).

Profile of the Governor-General:

Sir Daniel **WILLIAMS**

Sir Daniel Williams, a former teacher and lawyer, was a member of Parliament and government minister in 1984–89, and then returned to legal practice for seven years until being appointed governor-general.

Born on 4 November 1937 in Grenada, Daniel Charles Williams began his working life early, teaching in a school in Grenada from 1952 to 1958, during which time he was promoted to deputy principal. Moving to London in 1959, he was briefly an assistant machine operator before joining the civil service, working in 1960–64 as a postal and telegraph officer. Entering further education, he became a student at London University and graduated in law in 1967. He then entered Lincoln's Inn to train as a barrister, and was called to the Bar in Grenada in 1969, after which he started in private practice. He served as a magistrate in St

Lucia between 1970 and 1974 and then returned to private practice for the next ten years. He is married with four adult children.

Williams first entered politics in 1984, after the US intervention and the removal of the left-wing revolutionary government. He was a successful New National Party (NNP) candidate in the legislative elections of 3 December. Between 1984 and 1989 he served as minister of health, housing and the environment, of community development and women's affairs, and of legal affairs and as attorney general. In 1988 he acted briefly as prime minister, deputizing for the ailing Herbert Blaize.

Retiring from active politics at the time of the NNP's heavy electoral defeat in 1989, he returned to practising law, becoming a Queen's Counsel in 1996. That same year, following his appointment as governor-general, he was made a Knight Grand Cross of the Most Distinguished Order of St Michael and St George. He has published several works on law and public affairs. He also founded the Grenada, Carriacou and Petite Martinique Foundation for Needy Students, registered in 1996.

Profile of the Prime Minister:

Keith **MITCHELL**

Keith Mitchell became prime minister following the general election in June 1995. A former university lecturer in mathematics, and captain of the Grenada national cricket team in 1973, he has been the leader of the centre-right New National Party (NNP) since 1989.

A Roman Catholic like most Grenadians, Keith Claudius Mitchell was born on 12 November 1946 in Happy Hill, St George's. He attended local primary schools and the Presentation Boys' College, and played cricket for Grenada for several years before going to Barbados to study mathematics and chemistry at the University of the West Indies (1968–71). He returned to Grenada to work as a teacher at the Presentation Boys' College for two years, and captain the island's cricket team, before going to Washington D.C. in 1973. He obtained a master's degree in mathematics at Howard University and a doctorate in mathematics and statistics from the American University, and taught at Howard from 1977 to 1983. Mitchell has written several textbooks on mathematics for Caribbean students. He and his wife Marietta have one son.

In Grenada's last pre-independence elections in 1972 Keith Mitchell stood unsuccessfully as a candidate for the Grenada National Party. He set up the Systems Technology and Research consultancy in 1979, running this business for five years and not returning to active politics until 1984. By this time Grenada's experiment with left-wing socialism under the New Jewel Movement had come to a violent end and a US-led force had intervened to oust a self-styled revolutionary council in 1983.

Mitchell was elected to Parliament in December 1984 as a member of the NNP, a merger of a number of centre and conservative parties brought together with US encouragement by their shared hostility to former prime minister Sir Eric Gairy's Grenada United Labour Party. Between 1984 and 1989 Mitchell was secretary of the NNP, becoming its leader in January 1989. He held government office during this period as minister of works, communications and public utilities, and also dealt with civil aviation, energy, community development and women's affairs.

Increasingly at odds with prime minister and former NNP leader Herbert Blaize, Mitchell was dismissed from the government in mid-1989 by Blaize, who then exacerbated the fragmentation which the party had suffered in recent years by forming a new party himself. The election eventually held the following March (after the death of Blaize) left the NNP with only two seats in the 15-member Parliament, one of them held by Mitchell himself as party leader. He built up the party's credibility again in opposition and led it to victory on 20 June 1995, this time winning eight seats. In addition to becoming prime minister, Mitchell took on the portfolios of finance, external affairs, information and national security.

The NNP lost its one-seat majority in November 1998 when one of its parliamentarians, Raphael Fletcher, resigned from the party. Fresh elections were called for January the following year. Mitchell's popularity was confirmed when the NNP won 62% of the vote and all 15 seats in the House of Representatives. In his second term, Mitchell has discussed the idea of reintroducing hanging to tackle growing levels of violent crime. He has also re-established diplomatic links with communist Cuba, in October 2002. He now holds, in addition to the post of prime minister, the portfolios of national security and information.

GUATEMALA

Full name: The Republic of Guatemala.

Leadership structure: The head of state is a president, directly elected by universal adult suffrage. The president's term of office is four years, not renewable. The head of government is the president, who is responsible to the Congress. The cabinet is appointed by the president.

Presidents:	Álvaro Arzú Irigoyen	14 Jan. 1996—14 Jan. 2000
	Alfonso Portillo Cabrera	Since 14 Jan. 2000

Legislature: The legislature is unicameral. The sole chamber, the Congress of the Republic (Congreso de la República), has 113 members, directly elected for a four-year term.

Profile of the President:

Alfonso **PORTILLO** Cabrera

Alfonso Portillo is an economist by training, and his politics are not easily defined. He spent some years in exile for supporting the left-wing guerrillas in the country's civil conflict, and promises to end class discrimination. On the other hand, he has repeated calls to crack down on crime and is closely linked to the former military dictator and fundamentalist Christian Gen. (retd) José Efraín Ríos Montt, who is accused of many human rights violations during his time in power in the 1980s. The Guatemalan Republican Front (Frente Republicano Guatemalteco—FRG), to which Portillo belongs, commands a large majority in the Congress where it is headed by its founder, Ríos Montt.

Alfonso Antonio Portillo Cabrera, the son of a rural teacher, was born on 24 September 1951 in Zacapa province and trained as an economist. His support for the left-wing guerrillas battling against the military dictatorship in the 1970s led to his exile to Mexico where he was appointed a professor at the Guerrero Autonomous University. His career there came to an abrupt end in 1982 when he killed two men in a brawl at a private party in the Mexican town of Chilpancingo and went into hiding fearing prosecution for murder. The incident, which he admitted to but claimed self-defence, prompted difficult questions for him during his later political campaigns, but also raised his profile among a Guatemalan electorate hardened by a 36-year civil war.

After the return of civilian rule to Guatemala, Portillo was elected to the Congress of the Republic as a candidate of the Christian Democracy Party in 1990. Five years later he switched allegiance to join the FRG. When Gen. Ríos Montt was disqualified as a presidential candidate, Portillo was nominated by the party to run in his place. His campaign slogan for the 1996 election, 'Portillo the presidency, Ríos Montt the power', highlighted his unashamed manipulation of Ríos Montt's popular appeal. The contest was close and Portillo was only defeated by Álvaro Arzú Irigoyen by 30,000 votes in a second round.

For his second attempt at the presidency, in 1999, Portillo maintained his links with Ríos Montt, but emphasized his own independent strengths. His platform combined elements of both right and left with the focus on redressing social imbalances while reforming the ineffective police force. He almost won the vote in the first round, falling just short of the necessary 50%, and outstripped his remaining opponent with an impressive 68% victory in the runoff. He was inaugurated on 14 January 2000. The FRG went on to win a similar victory in the Congress.

As president Portillo appointed a broad-based administration including some prominent left-wing opponents of Ríos Montt. His promises to fight poverty have yielded few tangible results, but on the issue of crime he has instigated joint police–army patrols on the streets of major towns. His calls for closer regional integration were realized when he signed an integration pact with Nicaragua and El Salvador in May 2000. The fears of human rights activists over his links with Ríos Montt have apparently proved unfounded. However, his electoral "commitment to the downtrodden" appeared somewhat hollow when farm labourers began a fierce strike protest, demanding a fairer distribution of land, in October 2000.

Alfonso Portillo Cabrera's popularity received a dent in June 2000 when he sent his close family to Canada amid fears of a plot to have them kidnapped.

GUINEA

Full name: The Republic of Guinea.

Leadership structure: The head of state is a president, directly elected by universal adult suffrage. The president's term of office is five years. An amendment to the constitution to allow the president to stand for a third, longer, term was approved in a referendum held on 11 November 2001. The president is head of government and appoints the members of the Council of Ministers.

President:	Maj.-Gen. Lansana Conté	Since 5 April 1984
	(seized power on 3 April 1984)	
Prime Minister:	Lamine Sidimé	Since 8 March 1999

Legislature: The legislature is unicameral. The sole chamber, the National Assembly (Assemblée Nationale), has 114 members directly elected for a five-year term.

Profile of the President:

Maj.-Gen. Lansana **CONTÉ**

Maj.-Gen. Lansana Conté has been president since April 1984, following a military coup. He was confirmed in office at elections in December 1993, and again in 1998. A soldier in the French army prior to Guinea's independence in 1958, he had risen through the Guinean armed forces to be chief of army staff by 1975, and took power nine years later following the death of the country's leftist and increasingly dictatorial leader since independence, President Sekou Touré.

Lansana Conté, who is from the Soussou ethnic group, was born in 1934 in Koya. He went to military schools in Bingerville, Côte d'Ivoire, and Senegal, where he graduated from the St Louis Military School, joining the French army in 1955. After Guinea's independence in 1958 he rose to become regional commander in the north and northwest, was promoted to the rank of colonel in 1975, and for the next nine years was chief of army general staff.

In April 1984, ten days after the death in office of President Sekou Touré, Conté and Col. Diarra Traoré led a successful bloodless military coup. Conté assumed the presidency and the portfolios of defence and security, while Traoré became prime minister. They abolished the constitution and set up the Military

Committee of National Recovery with Conté as its chairman. Hundreds of political prisoners were released and freedom of speech was restored.

By December 1984 disagreements between Conté and Traoré led to the latter's demotion. Conté's popularity fell amid resentment of tough austerity measures which he had introduced at the instigation of the World Bank and International Monetary Fund (IMF). In July 1985 Traoré took advantage of Conté's absence abroad to denounce the regime and try to seize power, but the coup was halted within a day and over 200 prisoners were taken. Traoré and other leaders were executed, although this was not officially confirmed for two years. Those prisoners who survived were released in 1988.

In October 1988 Conté agreed to the drafting of a new two-party constitution which would return the country to civilian rule and this was overwhelmingly approved by a referendum in December 1990. Meanwhile he promoted himself to general and in February 1991 a new Transitional Council of National Recovery was established under his chairmanship. More parties were legalized in 1992 but unauthorized public meetings were banned to avoid further violence.

Presidential elections were set for late 1993 and were eventually held on 19 December after riots had resulted in their postponement by two weeks. Conté secured 51.7% of the vote, in a poll marred by violence, at least 12 fatalities, and opposition claims of widespread irregularities.

In June 1995, in the country's first multiparty legislative elections, Conté's Party of Unity and Progress (Parti de l'Unité et du Progrès—PUP) won 71 out of 114 seats, although opposition parties again alleged electoral fraud. The same accusations were levelled at Conté's successful re-election on 14 December 1998. He gained 56% of the vote against 25% for Mamadou Bâ and 17% for Alpha Condé. It was Condé who proved to be Conté's biggest subsequent rival and he was charged with plotting a coup soon afterwards.

Opposition anger at electoral irregularities was deflected by the worsening security problem on the country's southern border. Conté accused the country's immigrant Sierra Leonean population of aiding cross-border attacks. Legislative elections were postponed indefinitely due to the 'state of war' in the south of the country. To try and control internal security, Conté launched a new 'pitiless' era in February 2001, bringing back capital punishment after a seven-year absence.

Relative peace was eventually restored in the south and Conté began to look to the future in late 2001. Legislative elections were called and a referendum was organized to approve constitutional changes to allow Conté a third term. The opposition condemned the approval of these changes in the November vote, claiming that the government's estimation of an 87% turnout was a gross exaggeration of the 20% of the electorate that had actually bothered to take part. The PUP increased its majority to 85 seats in legislative elections which were eventually held in June 2002 and were boycotted by the opposition.

Profile of the Prime Minister:

Lamine **SIDIMÉ**

Lamine Sidimé is a member of the ruling Party of Unity and Progress (Parti de l'Unité et du Progrès—PUP). A lawyer trained in France and Senegal, he was appointed to the Transitional Council of National Recovery which oversaw the country's return to democracy in the early 1990s. He was head of the Supreme Court before he was picked to lead a new government as prime minister in March 1999.

Lamine Sidimé was born in 1944 in Mamou, centre-west Guinea. He is married and now has three children. He travelled to France in the late 1960s to study law and received his degree in 1970 from the University of Paris II, and a diploma in criminology from the same institute in 1971. After graduating he left for north Africa where he taught law at the University of Algiers, Algeria.

In 1980 Sidimé was awarded a doctorate in private law from the University of Dakar, Senegal, and five years later he qualified to teach. He spent the end of the 1980s conducting research in Burkina, Niger and Burundi. In 1990, as Guinea headed towards democracy, Sidimé returned to take up a position at the University of Conakry. As a prominent lawyer he was consulted as the military regime attempted to overhaul the country's body of laws and in 1991 he was appointed to the Transitional Council of National Recovery. His work was rewarded the following year when he was appointed president of the Supreme Court.

When President Lansana Conté dismissed the cabinet on 8 March 1999, he turned to Sidimé to be his new prime minister. He remained in office through successive cabinet reshuffles and the legislative elections of June 2002, at which his party won a large majority of the seats.

GUINEA-BISSAU

Full name: The Republic of Guinea-Bissau.

Leadership structure: The head of state under the constitution is a president, directly elected by universal adult suffrage for a five-year term. The president is the head of government, and appoints the Council of Ministers including the prime minister.

Presidents:	Malam Bacai Sanhá (acting)	14 May 1999—17 Feb. 2000
	Kumba Yallá	Since 17 Feb. 2000
Prime Ministers:	Francisco Fadul (acting from 3 Dec.1998)	20 Feb. 1999—19 Feb. 2000
	Caetano N'Tchama	19 Feb. 2000—21 March 2001
	Faustino Imbali	21 March 2001—9 Dec. 2001
	Alamara Nhassé	9 Dec. 2001—17 Nov. 2002
	Mário Pires	Since 17 Nov. 2002

Legislature: The legislature is unicameral. The sole chamber, the National People's Assembly (Assembléia Nacional Popular), has 102 members, directly elected for a four-year term.

Profile of the President:

Kumba **YALLÁ**

Kumba Yallá, who was elected president in 2000 with 72% of the votes, is a former teacher. His stated priorities include national reconciliation, boosting the economy and curbing corruption in the government. In foreign relations he declared upon taking office that he would seek good relations with Senegal, in view of the 11-year border dispute between the two countries.

Kumba Yallá was born around 1953 and trained as a teacher. In 1992 he split from the Social Democratic Front, of which he had been vice chairman, to found the Social Renewal Party (Partido para a Renovação Social—PRS).

In July 1994 he was the PRS candidate in the presidential election, and after the first round Yallá received the support of all the opposition parties. He was, however, narrowly defeated in the runoff ballot held in August by João Bernardo Vieira of the African Independence Party of Guinea and Cape Verde (Partido Africano da Independência da Guiné e Cabo Verde—PAIGC). He tried unsuccessfully to challenge the election results, and announced that the PRS would not take part in the new government. Yallá contested the November 1999 presidential elections, and in the runoff held in January 2000 he beat the acting president Malam Bacai Sanhá, the PAIGC candidate. He took office on 17 February. The Council of Ministers he formed drew its members from several former opposition parties.

One initial difficulty for Yallá was the matter of the loyalty of the armed forces, as many members retained allegiance to Gen. Ansumane Mané, leader of the military junta that held power up to May 1999. Gen. Mané issued a challenge to Yallá in November 2000, by declaring himself head of the army, but he was killed in an exchange of gunfire a few days later.

Profile of the Prime Minister:

Mário **PIRES**

Mário Pires is a founder member of the ruling Social Renewal Party (Partido para a Renovação Social—PRS). Born in 1950, he was an economist and general director of Pesca Artesanal before the defeat of the long-ruling African Independence Party of Guinea and Cape Verde in legislative elections in 1999. From early 2000 he was chief of staff to newly elected President Kumba Yallá before being appointed prime minister in November 2002 for the few months leading up to elections due in early 2003.

GUYANA

Full name: The Co-operative Republic of Guyana.

Leadership structure: The head of state is a president, nominated by the majority party in the National Assembly after legislative elections. The president's term of office is five years. The president appoints the prime minister and the cabinet. The president is head of government.

President: Bharrat Jagdeo   Since 11 Aug. 1999

Prime Minister: Sam Hinds   Since 9 Oct. 1992
(except 17 March 1997—22 Dec. 1997
and 9 Aug. 1999—11 Aug. 1999)

Legislature: The legislature is unicameral. The sole chamber, the National Assembly, has 65 members (53 elected and 12 regional representatives) with a five-year term.

Profile of the President:

Bharrat **JAGDEO**

Bharrat Jagdeo first took over the presidency from Janet Jagan when she was taken ill in 1999, and was re-elected to the post on 19 March 2001. Educated in economics in the Soviet Union, Jagdeo had served People's Progressive Party (PPP) governments as Guyana's representative at the World Bank and International Monetary Fund (IMF) among other posts. He was minister of finance between 1995 and 1999 before being handpicked by Jagan as her successor. His appointment prompted dissent from the mostly Afro-Guyanese opposition People's National Congress (PNC) but was considered by many as the start of a new era in Guyanese politics.

Bharrat Jagdeo was born on 23 January 1964 to ethnically Indian-Guyanese parents in the small farming community of Unity, Mahaica, just east of the capital Georgetown. Bharrat means India in Hindi. His father worked on the railways and his mother was a peasant farmer. After attending the local primary and secondary schools, Jagdeo spent a short time as a teacher before winning a scholarship to study economics at the Patrice Lumumba University in Moscow, then the capital of the Soviet Union, in 1984. Having received a master's degree in 1990 he returned to Guyana and began work at the state planning secretariat in 1992. He had joined the PPP's youth wing in 1980 and became a member of the party itself in 1983.

Between October 1992 and 1999 Jagdeo was attached to the ministry of finance, first as a special adviser to the minister, and then as junior minister himself from October 1993. Within this role he was given responsibility in a number of key institutions including the Guyana Water Authority, and as a director of the regional Caribbean Development Bank (CDB). His reputation in these positions earned him the posting as Guyana's governor to the World Bank and secured his promotion to full minister of finance in March 1995. However, his hard-line attitude to negotiations is credited with prolonging a strike by civil servants in 1999. Bharrat Jagdeo married his wife Varshnie in 1998.

When President Janet Jagan, herself a controversial appointment, fell increasingly ill with a heart condition in 1999 she turned to Jagdeo as her chosen heir. A few days before the hand over of power in August the then Prime Minister Sam Hinds (a member of the Afro-Guyanese community) agreed to resign to allow Jagdeo's nominal appointment to the post to secure his succession as president under Guyana's constitutional practice. This process caused unrest among Afro-Guyanese, led by the PNC which already disputed the validity of the 1997 elections and Jagdeo's consequent selection as head of state. However, from the start Jagdeo has attempted to overcome the country's long history of race-driven politics and unsuccessfully suggested co-operation with the PNC. Coming from a much younger generation of politicians his appointment was accompanied with keen speculation of imminent change.

The presidential term expired in early 2001 and Jagdeo was selected to run for another term by the PPP. His success at the polls in March was again contested by the PNC which initiated a series of violent demonstrations in Georgetown and across the country in the following month. After extensive talks with PNC leader and former president Desmond Hoyte, Jagdeo's government was able to begin its second term in early May.

Profile of the Prime Minister:

Sam **HINDS**

Sam Hinds is an engineer who spent 25 years working in the bauxite industry and came late to politics. He emerged through his involvement in the human rights movement in the last years of the People's National Congress regime, and became prime minister when former president Cheddi Jagan's left-wing People's Progressive Party (PPP) finally won power at the October 1992 elections. Elevated temporarily from the premiership to the presidency in March 1997 when Cheddi Jagan died, he was passed over as the party's presidential candidate for the December 1997 elections in favour of Jagan's wife, Janet.

Samuel Archibald Anthony Hinds was born on 27 December 1943 in Mahaicony, on the east coast in the Demerara region. He was educated at Queen's College in Georgetown, the capital, and then went on to study at the University of New Brunswick in Canada, where he graduated with a degree in chemical engineering in 1967. He worked for DEMBA, the bauxite operations subsidiary of Alcan in Linden, Guyana, from 1967 to 1992.

Hinds, who is married with three children, did not enter politics until 1989. He made his name as a prominent member and cofounder of Guyanese Action for Reform and Democracy (GUARD), a pressure group launched in 1990 by the Guyana Human Rights Association to demand free and fair elections. Not formally a member of the PPP, he was elected to the National Assembly on 5 October 1992 as leader of the Civic movement of business and professional people, standing in an electoral alliance with the PPP. He was appointed as first vice president and prime minister when the new PPP government came to office under President Cheddi Jagan in October 1992.

Hinds's succession to the presidency on 6 March 1997 was in accordance with the provisions of the constitution, but it was not generally thought likely that he would retain this top political post for long, even if he were to be re-elected on the PPP ticket in the end-of-year elections. In the event the party turned instead to Jagan's wife Janet (whom Hinds had appointed as his successor as prime minister in March) as its more charismatic standard bearer. Two days before Janet Jagan's resignation due to ill health in August 1999, Hinds temporarily stepped down from his post as prime minister. This was merely a formality to allow Bharrat Jagdeo to hold this office momentarily, a manoeuvre which then allowed Jagdeo to move on to the vacant presidency, according to the constitution.

HAITI

Full name: The Republic of Haiti.

Leadership structure: The head of state is a president, directly elected by universal adult suffrage. The president's term of office is five years, not immediately renewable. The president appoints the prime minister, who must be approved by the National Assembly. The prime minister is head of government and chooses the cabinet, in consultation with the president.

Presidents:	René Préval	7 Feb. 1996—7 Feb. 2001
	Jean-Bertrand Aristide	Since 7 Feb. 2001
Prime Ministers:	Jacques Edouard Alexis (nominated on 15 July 1998)	11 Jan. 1999—2 March 2001
	Jean-Marie Chérestal (acting from 21 Jan. 2002)	2 March 2001—15 March 2002
	Yvon Neptune	Since 15 March 2002

Legislature: Under the 1987 Constitution, the legislature, the National Assembly (Assemblée Nationale), is bicameral. The lower chamber, the Chamber of Deputies (Chambre des Députés), has 83 members, directly elected for a four-year term. The upper chamber, the Senate (Sénat), has 27 members, directly elected for a six-year term, with one-third of senators elected every two years.

Profile of the President:

Jean-Bertrand **ARISTIDE**

Jean-Bertrand Aristide returned to the presidency of Haiti in 2001 after the controversial elections of 26 November 2000, which were boycotted by the opposition. A former Catholic priest who was first elected president in 1991, Aristide heads the controversial Lavalas Family (Fanmi Lavalas—FL) political bloc. He had been a champion of socialism in the 1980s against the much-hated Duvalier regime, but, in power, his motives have increasingly been questioned as the FL's governance continues to breed discontent and economic depression.

Jean-Bertrand Aristide was born on 15 July 1953 in Port-Salut on the country's southwestern peninsula. Soon after his birth his father died and his family moved to the capital, Port-au-Prince, where he was educated by Catholic priests of the influential Salesian order. He completed his education at the College Notre Dame in the northern town of Cap-Haïtien before beginning his noviciate studies at the Salesian seminary, in La Vega in the neighbouring Dominican Republic, in 1974. As a novice he pursued postgraduate studies in philosophy and psychology back in Haiti. In 1979 he travelled to Rome and Israel where he spent two years studying the bible and added Hebrew to his canon of languages, which also include English as well as his native French and Creole. Throughout his studies Aristide found common cause with Latin American liberation theology which advocated active religious involvement in socialist politics.

In 1983 Aristide was ordained in Haiti. After a further postgraduate degree in biblical theology in Canada, he taught the subject to novices in Port-au-Prince. From the start of his religious career he preached activism to his economically deprived congregations. He continued in this vein when he was sent to the church of St Jean Bosco in one of the capital's largest slums, La Saline, where he taught at the National School for Arts and Crafts. He quickly became associated with *ti legliz*, a Catholic pressure group, and used his sermons and his position to criticize the corrupt regime of the Duvalier family. His prominence in the opposition movement was confirmed with the broadcasting of his sermons on the Catholic radio station, Radio Soleil. In 1986 he continued a broadcast while the military opened fire on his congregation during a demonstration outside the Duvaliers' notorious Fort Dimanche prison. His prominence within the *ti legliz* movement earned him the murderous attentions of the later Haitian military dictators and several attempts on his life have been made since the late 1980s.

Among Aristide's critics, however, was the Catholic Church, which after 1987 turned its disapproval on liberation theology and the political activity of priests. Having ignored commands to stop blurring the boundaries between the spiritual and the temporal, he was finally expelled from the Salesian order in 1988, and after the fall of the military ruler Gen. Henri Namphy, he retired from the forefront of Haitian politics. He spent much of 1988–90 working with the Lafanmi Selavi home for street children he had founded in 1986. His political ambition was not held back for long, however, and in 1990 he announced his candidacy for the presidential elections. After a mere six weeks of campaigning Aristide was elected president at the head of the National Front for Change and Democracy (Front National pour le Changement et la Démocratie—FNCD) with a popular 67% of the vote, defeating the more conventional candidate, former World Bank official Marc Bazin. Aristide was sworn in as president in February 1991 at the head of a minority FNCD government.

President Aristide's socialist policies and attempts to bring the Duvaliers to justice met with immediate resistance from the conservative former powers and the legislature itself. In September 1991 he was ousted in a military coup led by the commander-in-chief of the armed forces Lt.-Gen. Raoul Cédras. Aristide was forced into exile, first in Venezuela, and then to the USA, from where he gathered international support against the military regime. The USA and the UN applied strong diplomatic pressure to force the Haitian government to reinstate Aristide and in 1994 20,000 US troops entered the country to supervise the reluctant resignation of the junta. Aristide was reinstated as head of state and completed his original term's final 16 months. In this period he worked to dismantle the oppressive infrastructure constructed by the military government and established a new civilian police force under the auspices of the newly formed Lavalas group. However, the new security force met with increasing criticism as civil unrest at the high cost of living increased.

On completing his presidency in 1996 Aristide defied popular support and stood down from the presidential race, enabling his close associate and former prime minister René Préval to stand and win for the Lavalas coalition. The two men's relationship soured, however, as Aristide opposed President Préval's privatization policy. Aristide split away from the ruling Lavalas bloc and formed the Lavalas Family in November 1996. Two years later the governing Lavalas movement changed its name to the Organization of the People's Struggle (Organisation du Peuple en Lutte—OPL), while the Aristide Foundation for Democracy evangelized its founder's trademark blend of grass-roots socialist democracy and opposition to the government. Accusations of Aristide's involvement in a political assassination failed to reduce his popularity as Préval began effectively ruling by decree, postponing elections into 2000.

After a series of disputed legislative elections in 2000 Aristide announced to cheering supporters in October that he would stand in the following month's presidential poll. Accusations of irregularities that had dogged the parliamentary elections resurfaced for the presidential contest in November but failed to prevent Aristide assuming victory as the only major candidate, with an official 92% of the vote. Opposition claims put the turnout as low as 5%. Aristide took office on 7 February 2001. The debatable majority for the FL in parliament has left Aristide's government internationally isolated. The opposition OPL rejected Aristide's overtures to join his government.

Jean-Bertrand Aristide, having been forced to renounce the priesthood following Vatican disapproval of his role as head of state in 1994, was free to marry the Haitian-American lawyer Mildred Trouillot in 1996. They have two daughters. Trouillot had served as an adviser to both the military government and Aristide's own post-1994 administration. Aristide is a keen musician and writer. His first book, *Why*, was published in 1978. Recent books include *Dignity* (1995) and *Eyes of the Heart* (2000).

Profile of the Prime Minister:

Yvon NEPTUNE

Yvon Neptune is a leading member of the ruling Lavalas Family (Fanmi Lavalas—FL) political bloc. A close associate of the FL's founder, President

Aristide, for whom he acted as spokesman in the mid-1990s, Neptune was a key figure in the bloc's foundation. He was elected senator in one of the disputed legislative elections in 2000. He was appointed prime minister on 4 March 2002, six weeks after Jean-Marie Chérestal had resigned from the post, and took office on 15 March.

Yvon Neptune was born on 8 November 1946 in Cavaillon, near Les Cayes in the south of the country. After a local education he travelled to New York City and Paris, France, to study architecture in the 1970s. Although in his later career he has piled abusive rhetoric on the USA, which he refers to as 'the laboratory', he spent much of the 1980s and 1990s working for an architectural firm in Long Island, New York. He is married and has two children.

Neptune became closely associated with Jean-Bertrand Aristide from 1991 during the former president's exile in the USA. He returned to Haiti with Aristide in 1994 and from November of that year, until the end of Aristide's term in office in February 1996, he was the president's official spokesman. Neptune stayed loyal to his patron in his subsequent split from the governing Lavalas movement. He was a leading player in the foundation of the FL in November 1996. During the late 1990s Neptune added to his political work by teaching English to students at the Aristide Foundation for Democracy in Port-au-Prince.

Representing the FL, Neptune was easily elected senator as part of the bloc's landslide electoral victory in May 2000. His prominence within the movement secured his appointment as speaker of the Senate. In this capacity he defended the Senate's immunity during the investigation into the murder of journalist Jean Dominique, famously taunting the "insignificant little judge" who was attempting to question Senator Dany Toussaint. Neptune became interim leader of the FL when Aristide took office as president in February 2001, continuing to lead the party until March 2002.

In January 2002 the embattled prime minister, Jean-Marie Chérestal, resigned to pre-empt a vote of no confidence. The country was left with a caretaker government until Neptune was called upon in March to support Aristide as the sixth prime minister of the latter's two (interrupted) terms.

217

HONDURAS

Full name: The Republic of Honduras.

Leadership structure: The head of state is a president, directly elected by universal adult suffrage. The president's term of office is four years, and is not renewable. The head of government is the president, who appoints the cabinet.

Presidents:	Carlos Roberto Flores	27 Jan. 1998—27 Jan. 2002
	Ricardo Maduro	Since 27 Jan. 2002

Legislature: The legislature is unicameral. The sole chamber, the National Congress (Congreso Nacional), has 128 members, directly elected for a four-year term.

Profile of the President:

Ricardo **MADURO**

Ricardo Maduro is leader of the right-wing Nationalist Party (Partido Nacional—PN). Head of the country's central bank in the 1990s, he champions the neoliberal economic approach and has spearheaded an effort to crack down on the country's rising levels of violent crime. He was forced to prove his Honduran nationality in order to run for president in 2001.

Ricardo Maduro Joest was born on 20 April 1946 in Panama City. His maternal grandmother had been born in Honduras and it was to there that the family moved in 1952. After attending primary school in Tegucigalpa, Maduro travelled to Pennsylvania, USA, to complete his secondary education and graduated in economics from the renowned Stanford University, California, in 1969. He married the Salvadoran Miriam Andreu in 1971 and they had four children before divorcing in 1996.

Returning to Honduras in the early 1970s, Maduro began his career there as general manager for the photocopying company Xerox. In 1976 he left the multinational to form his own firm, Inversiones La Paz, an investment holding company which financed and bought a variety of different concerns and currently has many interests in the Honduran commercial sector. Maduro's business career was widely praised and he won awards for Businessman of the Year in 1983 and even Man of the Year from *El Heraldo* newspaper in 1991.

When Honduras returned to democracy in 1984 Maduro became involved in centre-right politics and finally took on Honduran citizenship. He headed the presidential campaigns of PN candidate Rafael Callejas. Although unsuccessful in 1985, Callejas was victorious in 1989 and was inaugurated in January 1990. On his appointment he rewarded Maduro by nominating him as director of the Honduran Central Bank and as co-ordinator of the government's economic office. From this position Maduro was able to put his economic training into practice and pushed through the country's first major economic reforms, for which he is now vilified by the liberal opposition. At the end of Callejas's term in office and following the PN's electoral defeat in 1994, Maduro returned to his business interests.

In 1997 Maduro's only son, 24-year-old Ricardo Ernesto, was kidnapped and murdered. The attack had a deep effect on the former banker who had become leader of the PN and he sought to win the presidential elections in 2001 on the back of a strong anti-crime platform. The opposition Liberal candidate, Rafael Piñeda, tried to derail Maduro's campaign with a legal challenge to his nationality, and therefore his right to run. The Honduran birth of Maduro's grandmother in 1888 vindicated his cause and he resumed campaigning after a brief pause. He secured victory in the first round of the vote on 25 November, with 52% against Piñeda's 44%, and was sworn in the following January at the head of a PN government.

HUNGARY

Full name: The Republic of Hungary.

Leadership structure: The head of state is a president, elected by the National Assembly. The president's term of office is five years, renewable once only. The head of government is the prime minister, who is appointed by the president and appoints a cabinet.

Presidents:	Árpád Göncz (acting from 2 May 1990)	3 Aug. 1990—4 Aug. 2000
	Ferenc Mádl	Since 4 Aug. 2000
Prime Ministers:	Viktor Orbán	6 July 1998—27 May 2002
	Péter Medgyessy	Since 27 May 2002

Legislature: The legislature is unicameral. The sole chamber, the National Assembly (Országgyűlés), has 386 members, directly elected for a four-year term.

Profile of the President:

Ferenc **MÁDL**

Ferenc Mádl has no official party affiliation, and held ministerial posts in both conservative and socialist–liberal governments in the early 1990s. He was a founder and president of the centrist Hungarian Civic Co-operation Association (Magyar Polgári Együttműködés Egyesület—MPEE) in the late 1990s. A professor of law by training, he has been popularly referred to in the National Assembly as 'Mr Professor' and indeed he instructed a fair number of current parliamentary deputies while teaching at the law department of Budapest's Eötvös Loránd University.

Ferenc Mádl was born on 29 January 1931 to a poor peasant family in the small western village of Bánd, Veszprém county. He attended Pécs University before graduating in law from the Eötvös Loránd University in 1955, which was also the year of his marriage to Dalma, with whom he has one son. He had a further period of academic study at the faculty of international comparative law at Strasbourg University from 1961 to 1963.

On his return to communist Hungary Mádl worked at the Institute of State and Legal Sciences at the Hungarian Academy of Sciences until 1971. From then until the fall of communism in 1990 he pursued a career as a teacher of law at Eötvös Loránd University, receiving his doctorate in 1974 and heading the university's Institute of Civil Law from 1978. Seven years later he took charge of the faculty of international private law and became a corresponding member of the Hungarian Academy in 1987 (he achieved full membership in 1993). From 1989 he served as a judge for the international arbitration centre in Washington D.C, USA.

Following the first free elections in Hungary in over 50 years in 1990 Mádl was appointed to the conservative-dominated cabinet as minister without portfolio and worked on the government's science policy. Despite a change of ruling parties in the next election in 1993 he was kept in the government, as minister of culture and education, until July 1994.

In the following year's presidential elections Mádl was praised by the incumbent Árpád Göncz, a man consistently voted the most popular politician in the country since 1990, for agreeing to stand against him to provide a genuine choice to the National Assembly. Mádl, who had been nominated by three centrist parties, received only 20% of the vote. He went on to become president of the MPEE, which provided membership to centrist-oriented professionals, from its foundation in 1996.

From 1999 Mádl returned to political activity under the conservative administration of Prime Minister Viktor Orbán, to whose government he became a scientific adviser. In the same year he was honoured with Hungary's highest civilian award, the Széchenyi Prize for his academic work, having authored many texts and developed his own approaches to the study of law.

In 2000, when Göncz was reaching the end of his second, and constitutionally final, term in office, Mádl was nominated as the ruling coalition's presidential candidate by the right-wing Independent Smallholders' and Civic Party. Intended to be an apolitical consensus candidate, he unexpectedly failed to win election in the first two rounds of voting, despite cross-party support from all but the small far-right Hungarian Justice and Life Party. His conservative connections, particularly his involvement with the MPEE seemed to be counting against him with leftist politicians, but he finally secured the necessary majority in a third round of voting on 6 June.

After his election Mádl called for a strengthening of the moral power of the presidency, and urged greater equality for the country's minority populations, especially the Roma. He was inaugurated for a five-year term of office on 4 August.

Profile of the Prime Minister:

Péter **MEDGYESSY**

Péter Medgyessy, an economist who worked for the communist-era government within several departments of the finance ministry, does not belong to any particular party, but was selected by the centre-left Hungarian Socialist Party (Magyar Szocialista Párt—MSzP) to head its new government after the April 2002 legislative elections. Revelations of his secret agent past—he controversially passed information to the covert intelligence agencies in the late 1970s—emerged just two months after his election.

Péter Medgyessy was born in Budapest in 1942. He graduated from the city's University of Economics in 1966 and received his doctorate in the subject from the same institution. As well as learning about finances, Medgyessy learned to speak a number of foreign languages including English, French, Romanian and Russian. Following his graduation in 1966 he began work straight away in the communist government's ministry of finance. In the course of the next 20 years he worked for various departments within the ministry including the economy department, the department of prices and the international finance department, rising to be head of the department of state budget and deputy finance minister.

As the country moved towards democracy at the end of the 1980s Medgyessy was to play an important role in reforming the economy. He was appointed minister of finance in 1987. His greatest achievement from his one-year term was to establish a new banking system that would allow Hungary to reintegrate with the international financial community. He was rewarded for his efforts with a promotion to deputy prime minister with responsibility for economic affairs in 1988 in the interim administration of Prime Minister Miklós Németh. The (former communist) MSzP was forced into opposition in the country's first postcommunist elections held in 1990 and Medgyessy moved out of government service for the first time in 24 years to become chairman and chief executive of Magyar Paribas—the Hungarian branch of the French-based financial services firm. He switched over to head the Hungarian Bank for Investment and Development in late 1994.

In March 1996 Medgyessy was asked to return to the cabinet as finance minister under the MSzP government of Gyula Horn. In this second term at the head of the ministry Medgyessy introduced, among other things, a revised pension system which won the praise of the Organization for Economic Co-operation and Development (OECD). Nevertheless the MSzP failed to maintain the affections of the wider public and were returned to opposition in 1998. From October that year Medgyessy worked as chairman of the Inter-Európa Bank. He also sat on the board of the Atlasz Insurance Company, led the Hungarian Economic Association and held the post of professor at the Budapest College of Finance and Accounting.

Medgyessy accepted the nomination of the MSzP in June 2001 to be the party's candidate for prime minister, and resigned from Inter-Európa the following September. He led the party to victory at the polls in April 2002, scraping together a coalition with the Alliance of Free Democrats (Szabad Demokraták Szövetsége—SzDSz) to displace the ruling coalition led by the conservative Federation of Young democrats, which remained nonetheless the largest party in the National Assembly.

Medgyessy took office on 27 May, but just two months into his term he offered to resign when the right-wing newspaper *Magyar Nemzet* disclosed that he had passed information to the communist-era secret service while he worked at the finance ministry between 1977 and 1982. He admitted that he had supplied information regarding the alleged attempt by foreign governments to block Hungary's membership of the International Monetary Fund (IMF) but justified his actions as patriotism. He eventually won the support of the SzDSz and the MSzP and secured his place as premier.

ICELAND

Full name: The Republic of Iceland.

Leadership structure: The head of state is a president, directly elected by universal adult suffrage. The president's term of office is four years. The head of government is the prime minister, appointed by the president, who also appoints a cabinet.

President:	Ólafur Ragnar Grímsson	Since 1 Aug. 1996
Prime Minister:	Davíd Oddsson	Since 30 April 1991

Legislature: The legislature is unicameral. The sole chamber, the Parliament (Althing), has 63 members, directly elected for a four-year term.

Profile of the President:

ÓLAFUR RAGNAR GRÍMSSON

Ólafur Ragnar Grímsson, who was returned unopposed for a second presidential term beginning on 1 August 2000, is the former leader of the left-wing People's Alliance (PA). He originally made his name as a broadcaster and political scientist. He gave up the PA leadership in 1995, the year before he first stood for the state presidency—a post held in the recent past by nonparty figures, notably Ólafur Ragnar's immediate predecessor, four-term president Vigdís Finnbogadóttir.

Born on 14 May 1943 in Ísafjördur in northwest Iceland, the son of a barber, Ólafur Ragnar went to the capital, Reykjavík, to complete his secondary education and then to university in England. He graduated in economics and political science at Manchester University in 1965 and completed a doctorate there in political science, working on a research project on smaller European democracies, while becoming known at home through radio and television work. He then took up a lectureship at the University of Iceland, where he became professor of political science in 1973. The following year he married Gudrún Katrín Thorbergsdóttir, the executive director of the Icelandic Post Office Workers' Union, and their twin daughters were born in 1975. His wife died in 1998.

Initially a member of the Progressive Party, Ólafur Ragnar first stood for Parliament in 1974 for the Liberal and Left Alliance, whose executive board he chaired in 1974–75. Moving over to a prominent role in the left-wing PA, he was a PA member of Parliament from 1978, first for Reykjavík and then for Reykjanes. Between 1980 and 1983 he chaired the PA parliamentary party and in 1987 he was elected as PA leader, a post he held for eight years but relinquished at the 1995 national convention. In 1988–91 he was a member of the coalition government led by Steingrímur Hermannsson, and as minister of finance was credited with having brought the problem of rampant inflation under control.

A member of the parliamentary assembly of the Council of Europe in 1980–84, and again in 1995, Ólafur Ragnar was active particularly on north–south issues. Between 1984 and 1990 he was chairman and later international president of the international association of Parliamentarians for Global Action (PGA). In this capacity he was actively involved with the 'six nations peace initiative', which included among others the late premiers Olav Palme of Sweden and Rajiv Gandhi of India. He accepted the Indira Gandhi Peace Prize on behalf of the PGA in 1987.

Ólafur Ragnar was elected on 29 June 1996 as the fifth president of Iceland, heading the nationwide poll with 40.9% of the vote against three other candidates, and taking office in August. His second term, to which he acceded without having to contest an election, began on 1 August 2000.

Profile of the Prime Minister:

DAVÍD ODDSSON

Davíd Oddsson had never held a parliamentary seat before the 1991 elections which brought him into office as prime minister. A trained lawyer and ex-journalist and dramatist, he had made his name in politics as mayor of the capital, Reykjavík, and took over the leadership of the liberal-conservative Independence Party (IP) only shortly before the 1991 elections. The IP's coalition partners in his first term, the Social Democratic Party (SDP), were replaced after the 1995 elections by the right-wing liberal Progressive Party (PP), a formula which Davíd Oddsson retained for his third term as prime minister after the May 1999 elections.

Davíd Oddsson was born on 17 January 1948 in Reykjavík. He graduated from Reykjavík College in 1970, the year in which he married Ástridur Thorarensen, a nurse, with whom he has one son. While studying for a law degree at the University of Iceland, which he completed in 1976, Davíd Oddsson worked as chief clerk at the Reykjavík Theatre (1970–72), then as a parliamentary reporter for the newspaper *Morgunbladid* (1973–74) and then for a publishing company. He has written four television dramas and is coauthor of two plays for the theatre, and he was chairman of the executive committee of the Reykjavík arts festival (1976–78). In 1976 he joined the Reykjavík Health Insurance Fund, initially as office manager and, from 1978, as managing director, a position he held until 1982.

Davíd Oddsson's political career is based on municipal politics in Reykjavík and a long association with the IP. He has been a member of the Reykjavík city council since 1974, including a nine-year tenure as mayor of Reykjavík (1982–91). He has sat on the IP executive committee since 1979 (having been on the board of directors of its youth federation from 1973 to 1975), was party vice chairman between 1989 and 1991, and took over in March 1991 as party chairman, replacing Thorsteinn Pálsson.

The April 1991 elections were a triumph for Davíd Oddsson and his party, which increased its parliamentary representation to 26 out of 63 seats. This placed him in a strong position in coalition negotiations, and on 30 April he was sworn in as prime minister in a government comprising IP and SDP members. The severe economic austerity measures of the ensuing years, with two currency devaluations, were relaxed somewhat in 1994 to encourage an upturn in the economy, although Davíd Oddsson's SDP coalition partners suffered a damaging party split as the strain of unpopularity began to tell.

In the elections held on 8 April 1995 the IP vote held up reasonably well, the party finishing with 25 seats in the Parliament, but heavy losses by the SDP left Davíd Oddsson keen to find a stronger coalition partner. The PP, with 15 seats, agreed to join a right-of-centre coalition, and Davíd Oddsson was sworn in as prime minister with a new cabinet on 23 April. The coalition was re-established after the IP's victory in the May 1999 elections, in which it gained one more seat in Parliament, although the PP dropped to just 12. Davíd Oddsson was re-elected IP chairman in October 2001. In office he has sought to strengthen relations with the European Union, but his government has been involved in lengthy fishing disputes with Russia, Norway and Denmark.

INDIA

Full name: The Republic of India.

Leadership structure: The head of state of the Union is a president, elected by an electoral college consisting of members of the upper and lower Houses of Parliament. The president's term of office is five years. The president is head of the Union, and formally exercises all executive power on the advice of the government. In practice, the head of government is the prime minister, who chairs the Council of Ministers and is responsible to the Parliament.

Presidents: Kocheril Raman Narayanan   25 July 1997—25 July 2002

                     A.P.J. Abdul Kalam   Since 25 July 2002

Prime Minister: Atal Bihari Vajpayee   Since 19 March 1998
                     (acting from 17 April 1999—13 Oct. 1999)

Legislature: The legislature, the Houses of Parliament (Sansad), is bicameral. The lower chamber, the House of the People (Lok Sabha), has 545 members, 543 of them directly elected for a five-year term by universal adult suffrage and two nominated by the president to represent the Anglo-Indian community. The upper chamber, the Council of States (Rajya Sabha), has 245 members, 233 of them elected by the State Legislative Assemblies (one-third being replaced every two years), and 12 nominated by the president.

Profile of the President:

A.P.J. Abdul **KALAM**

A.P.J. Abdul Kalam, popularly known as the 'Missile Man', was closely associated with India's drive to produce indigenous missiles and other weaponry, both as engineer and as advocate. He is also the 'father' of India's nuclear weapons programme and masterminded the controversial underground tests in 1998. A practising Muslim from southern India, he was nominated as a presidential candidate by the ruling Bharatiya Janata Party (BJP) in a successful move to win consensus support.

Avul Pakir Jainulabdeen Abdul Kalam was born on 15 October 1931 near the southern port of Rameswaram in what is now the state of Tamil Nadu. Coming from a lower middle class background he took on part-time jobs to earn enough to pay for his education. He graduated from the Madras Institute of Technology in

1958 with a degree in aeronautical engineering and immediately applied to both the Indian Air Force (IAF) and the defence ministry's directorate of technical development and production. While the IAF rejected his application to be a pilot, he was successfully assigned to a hovercraft project in the directorate's Defence and Research Development Organization (DRDO). Five years later he moved to Bangalore, to the new Indian Space Research Organization (ISRO).

Throughout the 1960s Kalam was a powerful advocate of India's need to design and produce its own technology. Within the ISRO he was made director of the satellite launch vehicle (SLV) project. The SLV-III carried the first Indian Rohini satellite into near-earth orbit in 1975. He also worked on projects to create an indigenous battle tank (the Arjun) and the still-in-production Light Combat Aircraft. In 1982 he went to Hyderabad to become director of the DRDO itself, overseeing during the next ten years the implementation of his newly created Integrated Guided Missile Development Programme—producing the *Prithvi*, *Trishul*, *Akash* and *Nag* missiles and most notably the *Agni* long-range missile which is capable of delivering a nuclear warhead.

In July 1992 Kalam was appointed scientific adviser to the defence minister and secretary of the department of defence research and development, supervising the programme which led to India's Pokhran-II nuclear tests in May 1998. The controlled underground explosion of nuclear weapons confirmed India as one of the few nuclear-capable countries of the world and seriously threatened already tense relations with neighbouring Pakistan, which carried out its own tests later that year. From December 1999 until November 2001 Kalam served as chief scientific adviser to the Indian government.

Kalam's presidential candidacy in 2002, as the nominee of the ruling BJP, soon received the backing of most major parties. He faced only a single left-wing candidate, Lakshmi Sahgal, and received 90% of the vote in the election held by the Houses of Parliament on 18 July 2002. He took office on 25 July. A devout Muslim, he was seen as a figurehead who could help heal some of the scars of the country's recent intercommunal violence, which had flared up in murderous conflict between Hindus and Muslims in Gujarat earlier in the year. His election was also welcomed by Pakistan, despite his intimate connection with the Indian nuclear weapons programme and the ensuing tension between the two countries.

Profile of the Prime Minister:

Atal Bihari **VAJPAYEE**

When A.B. Vajpayee became Indian prime minister in March 1998, dire warnings abounded about intercommunal tensions being stirred up by right-wing Hindu chauvinism. Vajpayee, the so-called 'acceptable face' of the Bharatiya Janata Party (BJP) and its most distinguished parliamentary orator, nevertheless commanded respect for his personal qualities and political experience, and the victory of a BJP-led coalition in the 1999 elections gave him a more stable platform for government.

Atal Bihari Vajpayee was born on 25 December 1926 in Gwalior, now in Madhya Pradesh, in a high-caste Brahmin family. His elder brother was a member of the Hindu militant Rashtriya Swayamsevak Sangh (RSS), which he himself joined through its youth network in 1939. He was arrested in 1942 for his participation in the Quit India movement directed against British rule. He subsequently completed his first degree at Victoria (now Laxmibai) College in Gwalior, and a master's degree in law at DAV College in Kanpur, but his progress towards qualification in law was interrupted by partition in 1947, when he decided to work full-time with the RSS, the parent organization from which right-wing Hindu parties and paramilitary groups developed over the subsequent decades.

In 1951 he helped found the Jan Sangh party, of which he was parliamentary leader for 20 years from 1957, president from 1968 to 1973, and representative on the National Integration Council, revived by Prime Minister Indira Gandhi in 1968 "to counter the menace of communalism". First elected to the House of the People in 1957, he has remained a member ever since except for two terms when he sat in the Council of State (1962–67 and 1986–91). A former journalist, author of books on foreign policy and on the caste system, and poet with several well-known publications to his name, Vajpayee is one of the most compelling orators in the Indian parliament. He has never married, but has two adopted children.

Detained along with many other opposition politicians during the period of emergency rule declared by Mrs Gandhi and her Congress (I) regime in 1975, Vajpayee was the leading Jan Sangh representative in the broad Janata coalition which ousted Congress (I) from power in the 1977 elections. He was minister of external affairs for the three years of Janata rule, until 1980. In that year he cofounded the BJP, and was its president for six years until 1986, helping it project a relatively moderate image. Then he moved over to be general secretary, with the more confrontationalist veteran Lal Krishna Advani becoming BJP president.

The leader of the parliamentary opposition from 1993, Vajpayee found himself on the threshold of power after the general election of April/May 1996. The BJP had campaigned for an independent nuclear weapons policy, a more restrictive stance on foreign investment (by contrast with the outgoing government's recent liberalization), and the building of a Hindu temple at Ayodhya, on the disputed site where a mosque had been destroyed by Hindu militants over three years previously. Its main rival, the Congress (I) party, accused it of anti-Muslim bigotry and stirring up intercommunal tension. Having won 30% of the seats in the House of the People, the BJP claimed the right as the largest party to try to form a government. Named as prime minister on 13 May 1996, Vajpayee was unable to build a coalition which could command a parliamentary majority, and resigned in advance of a no-confidence motion on 28 May. A United Front coalition government was then formed by the left-wing and regional alliance, headed by Deve Gowda as prime minister, with Congress (I) promising its backing (but not participating) to keep the BJP out of power.

Vajpayee got his second chance to form a government in early 1998, when Congress (I) withdrew its support from the United Front and thereby precipitated an inconclusive early general election. This time around, although the BJP increased its own representation only slightly, Vajpayee had a sufficient coalition, albeit an unstable one ranging from Shiv Sena to the right of the BJP to regional parties which did not share its nationalist agenda. He was sworn in as prime minister on 19 March 1998.

The central tenet of Vajpayee's political philosophy is a nationalism in which Hindu customs and culture represented the defining features of the Indian national identity. This culture, the Hindutva, should, he believes, command the allegiance of all Indians, whether they are by religion Hindu, Muslim or any other creed. In his own words, "Mecca can continue to be holy for the Muslims but India should be holier than the holy for them". His government, however, with its dependence on secular parties for a majority, did little to implement a nationalist cultural programme, apart from an unsuccessful attempt to modify the secular curriculum for state schools to include study of the Sanskrit language and Hindu scripture. Nor was its slogan of "India shall be built by Indians" translated into a vigorous programme of *swadeshi* (self-reliance); only token restrictions were introduced on foreign investment, within a context which effectively continued the process of opening up the economy.

On international affairs, Vajpayee did play the high-risk card of assertiveness on nuclear weapons policy, carrying out five nuclear tests just two months after taking office. He gained considerable popularity within India as a result but triggered 'tit-for-tat' tests by Pakistan which caused great alarm across the world and resulted in international sanctions on both countries. Later, however, Vajpayee sent out an unexpectedly conciliatory message towards Pakistan by a visit there in late February 1999, disregarding the opposition of the so-called 'saffron fringe' of Hindu fundamentalists to any negotiation. This visit followed the successful sporting reconciliation of a tour of India by the Pakistani cricket team, but was itself soon put into a gloomier perspective by the outbreak of tension and shooting incidents along the Line of Control, the de facto border, in disputed Kashmir.

Always at the mercy of his quarrelsome and personality-fraught coalition partners, Vajpayee lost his majority when one of the southern regional parties pulled out in April 1999. Defeated in an ensuing vote of no confidence, he resigned on 17 April, but remained in office in a caretaker capacity (his Congress (I) rivals having attempted unsuccessfully to form a new coalition government) pending yet another general election. The BJP retained its status as the largest single party in the September–October poll and gained a majority at the head of the National Democratic Alliance (NDA) coalition. Vajpayee was made leader of the NDA and was sworn in for his third term as prime minister.

Since then, Vajpayee's policies have done little to improve relations with Pakistan. Indeed, following the initiation of the US 'war on terrorism' in late 2001, relations across the Line of Control in Kashmir have entered a new, even more delicate, stage. Accusations of warmongering have been traded liberally and the world held its breath as the two nuclear-armed rivals appeared only just to avoid war in late 2001–early 2002. Within India interethnic relations have suffered. In December 2000 Vajpayee angered Muslims and moderates when he asserted that the Ayodhya temple project was "an expression of national yearning". Over 500 people, mostly Muslims, were killed in race riots in Gujarat in February 2002. Economically, Vajpayee's government has been criticized by the international community for failing to curb spending. He has since backed further privatizations.

INDONESIA

Full name: The Republic of Indonesia.

Leadership structure: The head of state is a president, elected to date by the People's Consultative Assembly. In August 2002 the Assembly voted to introduce direct elections for the president and vice president. The president's term of office is five years. The head of government is the president, who appoints a cabinet.

Presidents:	Abdurrahman Wahid	20 Oct. 1999—23 July 2001
	Megawati Sukarnoputri	Since 23 July 2001

Legislature: The legislature, the unicameral House of Representatives (Dewan Perwakilan Rakyat), has 500 members serving a five-year term: 462 directly elected and 38 military appointments. The 700-member People's Consultative Assembly (Majelis Permusyawaratan Rakyat), which comprises the 500 members of the House of Representatives and 200 government appointees (135 delegates of the regional assemblies and 65 representatives of parties and groups), is the highest authority of the state. It determines the constitution, and until August 2002 elected the president and the vice president.

Profile of the President:

Megawati **SUKARNOPUTRI**

Megawati Sukarnoputri heads the centrist Democratic Party of Indonesia–Struggle (Partai Demokrasi Indonesia Perjuangan—PDI–P). The daughter of the country's first president, the charismatic Sukarno, Megawati served as a rallying point in the 1990s for opposition to the regime of her father's successor, President Suharto. After his fall, her party emerged as the largest in parliament at the 1999 elections. Having initially settled for the position of vice president, she assumed many of the powers of the presidency a year later, and eventually took over the post itself in 2001, when parliament finally ousted her infirm and increasingly isolated predecessor Abdurrahman Wahid.

Megawati Sukarnoputri was born in Yogyakarta, Java, on 23 January 1947. Her father, Sukarno, had declared himself president of an independent Indonesia two years previously. Megawati was Sukarno's eldest daughter by his second wife, Fatmawati. Her privileged upbringing came to an abrupt end in 1967 when her father was ousted by Suharto. At the time she was studying agriculture at

Pajajaran University in Bandung. She dropped out of the course and never returned.

In the following years she endured a series of personal tragedies and failures. In 1970 her first husband, a fighter pilot known as Surendro, disappeared in action over the province of Papua, known then as Irian Jaya. A year later her father died, and in 1972 Megawati pulled out of another degree course, abandoning her studies in psychology at the University of Indonesia in Jakarta. Her marriage that same year to the Egyptian diplomat Hassan Gamal Ahmad Hassan soon collapsed, and he left her and Indonesia before their union was annulled, in 1973, on the grounds that Surendro was still technically considered alive. Before that year was out she had remarried again, to businessman Taufik Kiemas to whom she is still married. She has had three children, all with Kiemas. Their joint ownership of a string of petrol stations in Java has ensured them a sizable personal fortune.

Recognizing the political asset Megawati represented, President Suharto brought her, and the politically ambitious Kiemas, into the political limelight in 1987. They were made members of the government-sponsored PDI and both won seats in the House of Representatives. Despite her initial reluctance to engage in national politics, Megawati became a symbol of Sukarnoism—and quickly fell out of favour with the Suharto government as her popularity rocketed.

In 1993 Megawati was elected chairman of the PDI at the head of a growing and increasingly outspoken faction within the party. Her main rival, her predecessor as party leader, Suryadi, received the full weight of government support and attempted to have her ousted as PDI leader three years later. The resulting confrontation within the party and state-sponsored violence towards her served only to increase her public standing. Pressured by the increasingly autocratic government she organized the PDI–P as a splinter from the PDI in 1996.

In 1998 popular protests culminated in Suharto's resignation. Legislative elections held in June 1999 resulted in a popular victory for the PDI–P, which became the largest single party in the House of Representatives with 31% of the seats. Megawati claimed that this gave her a clear mandate to become president. A collection of mostly Islamic parties, many of whom objected to the principle of a female head of state, disagreed. Abdurrahman Wahid of the National Awakening Party, another popular figure, was appointed president in October 1999 and Megawati was made his deputy.

Within a year the frailty and suspect financial dealings of Wahid had lost him the support of parliament. His unilateral dismissal of cabinet ministers provoked a hostile reaction which effectively compelled him to devolve the everyday running of government to Megawati on 9 August 2000. Her already confirmed popularity, and her constitutional position as vice president, secured her place as the viable alternative to Wahid. The two disagreed irreconcilably and by May 2001 Wahid was vehemently denouncing attempts by parliament to further devolve his powers to her. Just two months later the House of Representatives ousted Wahid and elevated Megawati to the post of president for the remainder of his five-year term.

Since she became president, Megawati's critics have implied that she has proved to be little more than a figurehead, unsuited and unwilling to hold the reins of power. After a year in office she was forced to defend her government's close association with the International Monetary Fund (IMF). Her policies towards those provinces struggling for independence have done little to reduce tensions. She has also, unsuccessfully, opposed plans to introduce direct presidential elections in time for the next poll in 2004. Nonetheless, her tenure has shown considerably greater stability than that of her predecessor.

IRAN

Full name: The Islamic Republic of Iran.

Leadership structure: The head of state is a president, who is directly elected by universal adult suffrage. The president's term of office is four years, renewable once only. Overall authority is exercised by the country's spiritual leader, the *wali-e faqih*. The president is head of government and appoints the Council of Ministers, subject to approval by the Majlis.

Spiritual Leader (*Wali-e Faqih*):

	Ayatollah Ali Khamenei	Since 4 June 1989
President:	Mohammad Khatami	Since 3 Aug. 1997

Legislature: The legislature is unicameral. The sole chamber, the Islamic Consultative Assembly (Majlis-e Shura-e Islami), known as the Majlis, has 290 members, directly elected for a four-year term, on a nonparty basis. An 83-member Assembly of Experts (Majlis-e Khobregan), also elected by universal suffrage but consisting entirely of clerics, decides on religious and spiritual matters, notably including the election of the *wali-e faqih*. The Council of Guardians of the Constitution (Shura-ye Negahban-e Qanun-e Assassi) is a 12-member judicial body empowered among other things to exercise a supervisory role for elections.

Profile of the Spiritual Leader (*Wali-e Faqih*):

Ayatollah Ali **KHAMENEI**

Ali Khamenei, a follower of the Ayatollah Khomeini since the 1960s, in 1981 became Iranian president effectively by default, there being a dearth of potential candidates for a post which combined lack of powers with risk of assassination. He moved up in 1989 to succeed as the country's 'spiritual leader' following Khomeini's death. Khamenei was generally regarded at the time as a comparatively nonpartisan figure. He relinquished the presidency just as that office took on real powers as head of state and government, but he has latterly proven to be a conservative influence, restraining the introduction of a more liberal stance by the government of President Mohammad Khatami.

Ali Hoseini Khamenei was born in 1939 in Mashhad, in the northeastern province of Khorasan. He entered a theological school in Mashhad at the age of ten, graduating in 1957 and continuing his studies at Najaf (in Iraq) and in the Iranian holy city of Qom. At the theological school there he studied religious science and came under the influence of Ayatollah Khomeini, who later led the Islamic Revolution of 1979. Becoming an outspoken opponent of the regime of the shah, Khamenei was active in the anti-shah campaigns led by Khomeini in 1962 and 1963, and was first arrested and briefly detained at this time. Involved thereafter in a combination of religious teaching, pro-Islamic agitation and clandestine militant organization, he was arrested several more times in the next 15 years, spending a total of three years in prison, and in 1977–78 he was exiled to the town of Iranshahr in the far southwest. As a religious authority Khamenei had attained the second-rank religious title of *hojatolislam* by the time of the 1979 revolution. He has written several books on Islam and history, such as *The Role of Muslims in the Independence Struggle of India*. He speaks Farsi, Arabic and Azeri, and is married with six children.

From 1978 Khamenei led the anti-government movement in Mashhad. Moving to Tehran early the following year, he was a founder member of the Foundation of the Oppressed, and joined the central council of the Tehran Militant Clergy Association.

After the 1979 revolution Khamenei was appointed Revolutionary Council representative for the army. He was deputy for, and then head of, revolutionary affairs at the national ministry of defence, becoming commander of the Islamic Revolutionary Guard for a relatively brief period (until February 1980). Elected in 1980 to the Majlis, he was secretary-general of the government-sponsored, but now defunct, Islamic Republican Party, of which he had been a cofounder, and was increasingly seen as one of Ayatollah Khomeini's closest associates. He also held, from January 1980, the influential position of leader of the Friday prayers in Tehran.

Khamenei was wounded in the right hand in an assassination attempt in June 1981, part of a spate of terrorist violence affecting the Islamic regime. In October of that year, following the ousting of President Abolhassan Bani-Sadr and the assassination of his successor Mohammad Ali Radjai, Khamenei was picked as the regime's candidate to fill the vacant presidency, winning the predictable overwhelming majority against four other candidates in the nationwide poll. He was re-elected, against two opponents, in August 1985.

Generally seen as a conservative rather than a hard-line radical in the context of postrevolutionary Iranian politics, Khamenei on occasion came under strong criticism from radical rivals, but as president he avoided identifying himself with any particular faction. He also managed to distance himself from the 1983 defection of his sister to Iraq, where she joined his estranged brother-in-law Sheikh Ali Tehrani, who had fled to Baghdad in 1981 where he had begun making broadcasts hostile to the Khomeini regime.

In May 1989 Khamenei was made chairman of the secretariat of the *imam* (Khomeini), and on 4 June, the day after Khomeini's death, was elected by the

Assembly of Experts to succeed him as Iran's new 'spiritual leader' (*wali-e faqih*). He was also given the religious title of ayatollah, as being more compatible with his status than the less elevated title *hojatolislam*. Constitutional amendments approved the following month removed the requirement that the 'spiritual leader' should hold the religious status of a grand ayatollah or *marja* (source of emulation), Khamenei himself being only a jurist or *motjahed*.

The 'spiritual leader' combines supreme religious power with overall political authority, although since the death of Khomeini it is not the 'spiritual leader' but the president (previously a mainly ceremonial post) who heads the executive and combines the functions of head of state and head of government. Khamenei's elevation to the post of 'spiritual leader' opened the way for the election as president of Ali Akbar Rafsanjani, seen as a relative moderate. Rafsanjani and to a greater extent his successor since 1997, Mohammad Khatami, have steered Iran towards a policy of greater liberalization and openness to the West.

Khamenei, for his part, while presenting himself as generally nonpartisan, has on key occasions been identified as more pro-conservative (such as taking a firm stand against the reformist-dominated press in 2000–01). It was Khamenei who reaffirmed and maintained Khomeini's notorious February 1989 *fatwa* or death sentence against the British writer Salman Rushdie over the publication of a novel held to be blasphemous against Islam, in a confrontation with Western liberal values which cast a long shadow until the eventual lifting of the *fatwa* in 1998. Beneath him the reformists have gained strength in the Majlis—with significant victories in the February 2000 legislative elections and with Khatami's re-election in June 2001. In October 2002 Khamenei, amid continuing power struggles between the reformist government and the conservative judiciary, grandly announced that Iran would never accept "so-called democracy".

Profile of the President:

Mohammad **KHATAMI**

Mohammad Khatami, who has studied western philosophy and speaks both English and German, is widely regarded in the West as a moderate in the context of the Islamic revolutionary regime. Within months of his becoming president, new initiatives in foreign policy, notably the successful hosting of an Islamic summit in Tehran, had begun to reduce Iran's international isolation, while relative liberals inside Iran were emboldened in their still unresolved confrontation with the conservative religious and judicial authorities of the theocratic state.

Mohammad Khatami was born at Ardakan, in the central Yazd province, in 1943. His father was well known as a member of the Islamic clergy. He left high school in 1961, after which he went to Qom in order to study theology. In 1965 he moved to Isfahan, and obtained a degree in 1969, followed by a master's degree in education from the University of Tehran (1970). He then returned to the Qom seminary to complete his philosophical studies and courses on *ijtihad* (practice of religious leadership), attaining the religious status of *hojatolislam*. He is now married and has three children.

While a student, Khatami was involved in the anti-shah campaign. After a period in Germany in 1978–79 as head of the Islamic Centre in Hamburg, he returned to Iran in the wake of the 1979 revolution, and was elected in 1980 to the Majlis, representing the constituencies of Ardakan and Meybod. In 1981 he was appointed head of the Kayhan Institute and its newspaper. From 1982 he held responsibilities variously as minister of culture and Islamic guidance, and as head of the joint command of the armed forces and chairman of the war propaganda headquarters. In 1992, however, he was severely criticized for using his role as minister of culture to promote 'decadent' ideas, and the hard-line mullahs successfully pressed for his removal from office. Regarded at this time as a 'moderate' close to President Ali Akbar Rafsanjani, he was appointed instead as the president's cultural adviser and head of Iran's national library, taking a stand in promoting the free circulation of books and films. In 1996 a decree from the 'spiritual leader', Ayatollah Khamenei, made him a member of the High Council of Cultural Revolution. Following the presidential elections of 1997, he now sits as head of this Council.

Khatami's election to the presidency, in a nationwide ballot on 23 May 1997, signalled a surprise defeat for the hard-line candidate Ali Akbar Nateq-Nouri. Khatami won by a considerable margin, receiving approximately 21 million out of 30 million votes, his candidacy having become the rallying point for a wide-ranging coalition supported in particular by industrialists, technocrats, the urban middle classes, students and women. He took office on 3 August. The pace of his reformist agenda has been necessarily slow as he is strongly opposed at almost every turn by the Council of Guardians, and even by Ayatollah Khamenei. His liberal supporters have gained in strength, with victory in the February 2000 elections, but have been subjected to harassment and obstruction. Khatami's brother Mohammad Reza heads the reformist Islamic Iran Participation Front. Khatami himself responded to popular support to stand for re-election in June 2001 and received a resounding 77% of the vote. The tone of his next term was set when Ayatollah Khamenei successfully had Khatami's re-inauguration temporarily postponed in order to reselect members of the Council of Guardians who had been opposed by the Majlis.

IRAQ

Full name: The Republic of Iraq.

Leadership structure: The head of state is a president, nominated by the Revolutionary Command Council, endorsed by parliament and approved by referendum. The president's term of office is seven years. The head of government is the president.

President: Saddam Hussein Since 16 July 1979
(also prime minister from 29 May 1994)

Legislature: The legislature is unicameral. The sole chamber, the National Assembly (Majlis Watani), has 250 members, directly elected for a four-year term. It shares legislative authority with the Revolutionary Command Council, which is appointed by the president.

Profile of the President:

SADDAM HUSSEIN

Saddam Hussein rose within the Arab Ba'ath Socialist Party from 1956 to become party leader and president of Iraq in 1979. He was initially seen by the West as a useful counterbalance to the Islamic revolutionary regime in Iran, but from the time of his invasion of Kuwait in 1990 he has come to be portrayed as the world's most dangerous dictator and the most serious threat to peace and stability. He has remained defiantly in power, surviving defeat by US-led forces in the 1991 Gulf War, but by the end of 2002 was under intense pressure to comply with UN requirements on openly eliminating any weapons of mass destruction.

Saddam Hussein was born on 28 April 1937 in the city of Tikrit, 200 km north of Baghdad. Once in power he was to become increasingly reliant on the loyalty of his Tikriti clan, Sunni Muslims bound together by family ties and patronage. Accounts of his childhood suggest that a forceful uncle was the strongest adult influence, and that violence was the key to making a mark within his group of cousins. In 1956 he joined the Iraqi branch of the Arab Ba'ath Socialist Party, involving himself over the next decade in its revolutionist activity and being arrested several times for involvement in attempted coups. Involved in the attempted assassination of the then Iraqi prime minister Gen. Abd al-Karim Kassem in 1959, he fled the country (later being sentenced to death in absentia) and lived in Syria and Egypt until 1963, studying law in 1961 at Cairo University. In 1963 he married Sajida Khairallah; he has two sons and three daughters.

Arrested again in 1964 for plotting the overthrow of President Abd al-Rahman Aref, Saddam Hussein was elected as a member of the Ba'ath leadership while in prison, and in 1966, still only in his twenties, became deputy secretary of its Iraqi branch. He played an active role in the two Ba'athist coups of July 1968 which brought fellow Tikriti Gen. Ahmad Hassan al-Bakr to power, and he was rewarded with the vice chairmanship of the Revolutionary Command Council (RCC) the following year. He built up an elaborate network of secret police, aimed at uncovering and suppressing dissent, but also providing the power base which enabled him to oust Gen. Bakr and take over the presidency and party leadership himself in 1979. Turning on those whom he could not count on for loyalty, he purged any possible opponents from within the ruling circle, and crushed a Kurdish rebellion in northern Iraq, gaining international notoriety by the use of chemical weapons against Kurdish villagers.

The Iran–Iraq war was launched by Saddam Hussein in September 1980 ostensibly in an effort to regain territory occupied by Iran since 1973. It developed, however, into a protracted (and in human terms immensely costly) eight-year struggle for ascendancy between the two principal regional powers, setting his Iraqi Arab nationalism against Iran's Shi'a Muslim clerical leaders and their Islamic revolution. Of these two, Western countries feared Iran most, and supplied much military equipment to Iraq until the war finally ended in a stalemate.

On 2 August 1990 Saddam Hussein provoked a wider crisis when he ordered the occupation of Kuwait, again based on a dispute over territory but offering the opportunity of extending his country's oil wealth. UN demands for a complete withdrawal were ignored, and a US-led alliance initiated heavy air strikes followed up by a land war. This had wide support from Western countries, Soviet acceptance, and backing in the Arab world not just from the conservative monarchies but also from Egypt, Syria and other governments. Saddam Hussein nevertheless invoked the ideas of Muslim *jihad* or holy war, making much of his defiance of the West, and launching missiles at Israel to substantiate the view of himself as a true supporter of the Palestinian cause.

Iraqi forces were overwhelmingly defeated in the field in the January–February 1991 Gulf War, driven out of Kuwait, but saved from the apparent prospect of annihilation when the US-led alliance declared a ceasefire at the end of February, thus rejecting the temptation to expand their limited war aims and press on to take Baghdad. Saddam Hussein had to accept the conditions stipulated by UN resolutions for the ending of hostilities, including the requirement that his regime disclose and destroy any nuclear, chemical and biological warfare facilities and stockpiles. A UN inspections regime was set up to monitor this, with economic sanctions in place pending the certification of Iraqi compliance. The severe impact of these sanctions on the economy, and on the Iraqi people, were only slightly alleviated by a humanitarian provision agreed in late 1996 under which some Iraqi oil could be sold internationally to pay for imports of food and medicine.

Defeat in the Gulf War left Saddam Hussein apparently vulnerable, but he quickly gained the upper hand against rebellions by the Kurdish population in the north and the Shi'a so-called 'marsh Arabs' in the south, and followed up various government reshuffles with purges and executions of military officers in early 1992 and August 1993. In August 1995 divisions opened up within his own family, apparently prompted by the growing power of his son Uday Hussein. Two of his daughters and his sons-in-law Hussein Kamel and Saddam Kamel sought political asylum in Jordan, and called for the overthrow of the regime. When a supposed reconciliation was effected they returned to Iraq in February 1996, indicating the reassertion of Saddam Hussein's control over any real internal dissent—and shortly afterwards the two sons-in-law were shot and killed by another close family member.

Saddam Hussein maintains a close grip on power, surrounding himself with an elite republican guard and advisers drawn mainly from his own Tikriti clan. He holds a monopoly of top state and party offices—adding the role of prime minister in 1994 to the positions he had held since 1979 as head of the RCC, president, head of the party and head of the armed forces—and has been reconfirmed in the presidency for seven-year terms by referendums held in October 1995 and October 2002. In the latter vote he notoriously received a 100% endorsement.

Internationally, Saddam Hussein survived repeated confrontations in the decade following the Gulf War. US and British air power has been used from 1992 to enforce 'no-fly zones' in southern and northern Iraq, while air strikes were mounted against the Baghdad intelligence headquarters in 1993 to punish an alleged assassination plot against former US president George Bush (senior), and US troops and air power were mobilized in quantity in late 1994 to forestall an apparent renewed threat of Iraqi intervention in Kuwait. A serious confrontation in late 1997–98 led to the withdrawal of UN weapons inspection teams, and the growing crisis over Iraqi noncompliance took Iraq back towards the brink of triggering the military action threatened by the USA and the UK. These allies thereupon launched a series of air strikes, claiming success in inflicting serious damage on Iraqi military installations, but finding themselves diplomatically isolated as the international community became divided on how Saddam Hussein's regime should be handled. Air strikes continued sporadically, usually against anti-aircraft installations in the no-fly zones, but Saddam Hussein's defiant declaration that weapons inspectors would not be allowed to return went unchallenged.

Although Saddam Hussein could claim this had been something of a victory, his position became increasingly threatened after the election of Bush's son, George W. Bush, in 2000 as the next US president and specifically following the 11

September 2001 attacks on the USA. Bush launched a 'war on terror' against the al-Qaida network believed responsible for the 11 September attacks, but soon turned his attention to Iraq on the basis of his charge that it was prepared to supply terrorists with weapons of mass destruction. Saddam Hussein's refusal to allow weapons inspectors back into the country became the focus of apparent preparations for all-out war. UN resolution 1441 was passed on 8 November 2002 demanding the return of inspectors and promising "serious consequences" if Saddam Hussein's regime continued to "breach" earlier resolutions. By the end of the year the inspectors were back on Iraqi soil and receiving some outward co-operation in their work. However, Saddam Hussein's position remained threatened as both the USA and the UK insisted that he was harbouring weapons of mass destruction, despite growing international opposition to the idea of another Gulf War. In his defence Saddam Hussein once again appealed for a *jihad* (holy war) against the West's aggression.

IRELAND

Full name: Ireland.

Leadership structure: The head of state is a president (*uachtarán na hÉireann*), directly elected by universal adult suffrage. The president's term of office is seven years. The head of government is the prime minister (*taoiseach*), who is elected by the House of Representatives and appoints the cabinet. The prime minister and the cabinet are both responsible to the House of Representatives.

President (*Uachtarán na hÉireann*):   Mary McAleese   Since 11 Nov. 1997

Prime Minister (*Taoiseach*):   Bertie Ahern   Since 26 June 1997

Legislature: The legislature, the National Parliament (Oireachtas), is bicameral. The lower chamber, the House of Representatives (Dáil Éireann), has 166 Deputies (Teachtaí Dála or TDs), directly elected for a five-year term. The upper chamber, the Senate (Seanad Éireann), has 60 members with a five-year term. Eleven members are nominated by the prime minister, six elected by the universities and 43 elected from five panels of candidates representing various sectoral interests.

Profile of the President (*Uachtarán na hÉireann*):

Mary **McALEESE**

Mary McAleese became the eighth president of Ireland on 11 November 1997, succeeding Mary Robinson who had held the post since 1990. McAleese, a Belfast-born barrister, broadcaster and academic, was previously pro-vice chancellor at Queen's University, Belfast, and is the first person from Northern Ireland to be elected as Irish head of state. She was nominated by the conservative nationalist Fianna Fáil (FF) party and by the Progressive Democrats (PD) as a candidate for the presidency, which is a largely ceremonial role.

Born on 27 June 1951 in Belfast, Mary Lenaghan (as she was until her marriage to Martin McAleese) was the eldest of nine children in a Roman Catholic family. She and her dentist husband now have three children.

She went to secondary school on the Falls Road in Belfast and then read law at Queen's University, Belfast, graduating in 1973. She studied to be a barrister and was called to the Bar in 1974 where she practised mainly in criminal and family law. In 1975 she was appointed Reid professor of criminal law, criminology and penology at Trinity College, Dublin. She held this position until 1979 when she joined the Irish national broadcasting corporation RTE as a journalist and presenter.

In 1981 she returned to the Reid professorship at Trinity, continuing part-time with RTE. In 1987 she was appointed director of the Institute of Professional Legal Studies, which trains barristers and solicitors for the legal profession in Northern Ireland and is regarded as one of the most pioneering departments in Queen's University. In 1994 she was appointed as a pro-vice chancellor of Queen's, the first woman in history to hold such a position at the university.

In 1995 she was a delegate to the conference on trade and investment in Ireland held at the White House, Washington D.C., and then to the Pittsburg conference in 1996. She was also a member of the Roman Catholic Church delegation in 1996 to the North Commission on Contentious Parades, and is a founder member of the Irish Commission for Prisoners Overseas. Before becoming president in 1997 she also held the positions of director of Channel 4 Television, director of Northern Ireland Electricity and director of the Royal Group of Hospitals Trust.

Her election as president of Ireland in October 1997 broke the record for the greatest margin of victory when she took 42.2% of votes in the first round and 58.7% in the second round. She was inaugurated on 11 November.

Profile of the Prime Minister (*Taoiseach*):

Bertie **AHERN**

Bertie Ahern became Ireland's youngest ever prime minister in June 1997, at the age of 45. A member of parliament since the age of 25 and a prominent figure in Dublin city politics, the man once seen as heir apparent to Charles Haughey as head of the conservative, nationalist Fianna Fáil (FF) party has proven that his elevation to the leadership marked a decisive change of the generations in Irish politics. Having signed the Good Friday agreement on Northern Ireland in April 1998, he has shown both patience and determination through the subsequent difficulties in implementing that historic accord.

Bartholomew 'Bertie' Patrick Ahern was born on 12 September 1951, in a working-class Dublin family. Educated at the local national school and by the Christian Brothers, he became an accountant after graduating from Rathmines College of Commerce and University College, Dublin. Bertie Ahern married Miriam Kelly in 1975 and they have two daughters. Ahern is now separated from his wife and lives with his partner Celia Larkin, a Fianna Fáil party worker.

He was first elected to the House of Representatives as an FF deputy at the age of only 25, in 1977. Since 1979 he has combined his career in parliament, where he represents Dublin Central, with membership of Dublin city council. He was lord mayor of Dublin from 1986 to 1987.

Ahern first held government office as an assistant whip from 1980 to 1981. In 1981 he was appointed party spokesperson on youth, and in 1982 became minister of state in the office of the prime minister and the department of defence, and government chief whip. After the defeat of FF in the November 1982 general election he became opposition chief whip and FF's leader of the house. Party vice president from 1983 to 1994, Ahern was also director of by-elections for FF in the 1980s and chaired the party's constituency and organization committee from 1987 to 1992.

With FF back in government after the 1987 general election, Ahern began a seven-year spell as a cabinet minister. His first portfolio was as minister of labour, making his name as architect of a social consensus, which was embodied in a programme for national recovery and a programme for economic and social progress. At the European level, Ireland's turn in the rotating presidency of the European Union (EU) Council of Ministers meant that in the first half of 1990 he was president of the EU Council of social affairs ministers.

In November 1991 Ahern moved to the finance ministry, filling a gap caused by the departure of Albert Reynolds, who left the government after challenging the leadership of the then prime minister, Charles Haughey. The resignation the following February of the discredited Haughey gave rise to a leadership contest from which Ahern, hitherto seen as Haughey's heir apparent, withdrew his own candidacy so that the party could unite behind Reynolds. Ahern retained the post of finance minister in the Reynolds government. He was also a member of the board of governors at the European Investment Bank (which he chaired in 1991/92), the International Monetary Fund (IMF), the World Bank and the European Bank for Reconstruction and Development (EBRD).

In the November 1992 general election a poor result made FF's coalition with the Progressive Democrats (PD) unviable. Ahern, adept at bridge building, eventually succeeded in negotiating a new coalition agreement with the greatly strengthened Labour Party. In the resulting government, which took office in January 1993, he once again took up the finance portfolio under Reynolds.

This coalition collapsed in November 1994 when Reynolds ignored Labour objections and pushed through his favoured appointee for the post of president of the High Court (the country's second-highest judicial post). Reynolds was forced to resign in the uproar which followed. Ahern, now free to seek what was widely regarded as his rightful place as party leader, was elected to that post by FF on 19 November, but found himself on the opposition benches rather than in power, because FF was excluded from a new three-party coalition government headed by John Bruton of Fine Gael.

During the ensuing period the Northern Ireland question loomed large in Irish politics. Bruton, as prime minister, was noted for his conciliatory approach. He pursued a joint initiative with the UK government which was intended to bring the representatives of the province's rival political traditions into an inclusive peace process. FF was traditionally more nationalist. Under Haughey in the mid-1980s, its pro-republican stance on Northern Ireland had been a major factor in driving out a group of party dissidents, who had split away to form the PD. Ten years on, Ahern was aware that maintaining such a stance could mean missing an opportunity for a lasting settlement. Thus, although he was frequently critical of Bruton for bending too far towards the British line, he nevertheless led his party into the June 1997 general election declaring that he would seek to form a coalition with the PD.

Ahern's high personal popularity rating helped boost the otherwise lacklustre performance of FF, which emerged from the election with 77 seats. This was eight more seats than in 1994, although the party won only a fractionally increased share (39.3%) of the vote. After two weeks of negotiations on the formation of a government, Ahern was sworn in on 26 June at the head of an FF–PD coalition, which nevertheless lacked a parliamentary majority.

Declaring it to be his primary objective to work to achieve a settlement in the talks on Northern Ireland, Ahern formed an effective working relationship with the new UK prime minister Tony Blair, both of them being representatives of a younger generation of political leaders. The momentum which they sustained in driving the Northern Ireland peace process forward had its moment of apparent triumph with the Good Friday agreement concluded in April 1998. Throughout the subsequent protracted difficulties involved in moving that agreement forward from signature to implementation, Ahern has remained committed to making it work and has sought to resolve the particularly thorny issue of the decommissioning of weapons held by paramilitary groups.

Domestically, Ahern survived a vote of no confidence in June 2000 and weathered the embarrassment of a 'no' vote in a referendum on the EU's crucial Nice Treaty on enlargement in June 2001. His minority government struggled through to the end of its term, overseeing the introduction of euro notes and coins in January 2002. In the May 2002 general elections FF increased its share of the vote to 41.5% and gained 81 seats. Although it still lacked its long-hoped-for simple majority, it at least gained parliamentary dominance in a renewed coalition with the PD. In October 2002 the Nice Treaty was finally endorsed and Ahern quickly assured the EU that future treaties would not require a referendum to receive Ireland's consent.

ISRAEL

Full name: The State of Israel.

Leadership structure: The head of state is a president, elected by the Parliament. Under an act approved by the Parliament on 21 December 1998, the president's term of office, hitherto five years, is extended to a seven-year nonrenewable term. The head of government is the prime minister, who is appointed nominally by the president, but is in practice responsible to Parliament, and who appoints the cabinet. (The present prime minister was first elected directly, in a nationwide ballot separate from the parliamentary elections, but this short-lived innovation was discontinued under an amendment to the Basic Law on Government passed by the Parliament in March 2001.)

Presidents:	Ezer Weizman	13 May 1993—10 July 2000
	Avraham Burg (interim)	10 July 2000—1 Aug. 2000
	Moshe Katsav	Since 1 Aug. 2000
Prime Ministers:	Ehud Barak (acting from 17 May 1999 until inauguration, and from 9 Dec. 2000)	6 July 1999—6 Feb. 2001
	Ariel Sharon	Since 6 Feb. 2001

Legislature: The legislature is unicameral. The sole chamber, the Parliament (Knesset), has 120 members, directly elected for a maximum four-year term.

Profile of the President:

Moshe **KATSAV**

Moshe Katsav surprised even himself when he defeated former prime minister Shimon Peres in the ballot for a successor to President Ezer Weizman in 2000. The presidency had never previously gone to a Sephardic Jew (originating from communities in Muslim countries) or to a political right-winger. Katsav first joined Likud (Unity) in the 1970s, held cabinet office in Likud-led coalitions of the late 1980s and early 1990s, and several times stood unsuccessfully for the party leadership. As president, however, he promised to stay out of contentious politics.

Moshe Katsav was born in Iran as the eldest of eight children in 1945 and moved to Israel with his parents six years later. His family lived in an immigrant tent camp named Kiryat Malachi, just south of Tel Aviv. Many such communities sprang up amid the large influx of Jews in the first years of the new state. Katsav wrote as a reporter for the locally based *Yediot Aharonot* daily paper from 1966 and was president of the nationalist B'nai B'rith Youth group in 1968 in the camp, which soon grew to become a town. After serving out his national service as a corporal in the Israeli Defence Force he attended the Hebrew University of Jerusalem to study economics and history.

While still a student at university in 1969, Katsav, who was already chairman of the Gahal (forerunner of Likud) student council, campaigned in the mayoral elections for Kiryat Malachi becoming Israel's youngest ever mayor. After completing his studies he returned to the mayor's office in 1974 and held the position for another six years. During this time he joined the newly formed Likud and it was under their banner that he turned his attention to the legislative elections in 1977. Likud swept to power under the leadership of Menachem Begin and Katsav sat in Parliament for the first time.

From 1977 to 1984 Likud dominated the Israeli government and Katsav worked on various parliamentary committees before being appointed as deputy minister of housing and construction in 1981. He joined the coalition cabinet as a full minister in 1984 with the labour and social affairs portfolio. Likud's electoral dominance faded throughout the 1980s. Following the 1988 elections the cabinet was reshuffled once more and Katsav was handed the transportation ministry as well as membership of the ministerial committee on defence. In the course of the government's fourth term it became chronically dependent on smaller right-wing groupings and eventually in 1992 it was voted out of office.

In opposition from 1992 to 1996 Katsav served as Likud's parliamentary leader and also chaired the parliamentary friendship league established with China. He was one of the first right-wing politicians to lend his support to the Oslo Peace Accords signed with the Palestinian Liberation Organization (PLO) in 1993 by the Labour prime minister Yitzhak Rabin. Direct prime ministerial elections were held for the first time in 1996 and Likud party leader Binyamin Netanyahu was elected on the back of widespread anger at a spate of Palestinian attacks in Israel. Netanyahu appointed Katsav as his deputy and together they headed a broad-party coalition with Katsav doubling up as the minister of tourism and the minister in charge of Arab–Israeli affairs. However the government's dilatory approach to the peace process proved extremely unpopular and Netanyahu's coalition splintered apart in the run-up to general elections in 1999.

Katsav was returned to Parliament for a seventh time but found himself in opposition once again. Up until the middle of 2000 he remained a low-profile politician described by his colleagues as "unassuming" and by the media as "surprisingly normal". It was not until President Ezer Weizman stepped down, following scandalous revelations of huge cash gifts, that Katsav was propelled into the limelight. Running against the former prime minister Shimon Peres in the presidential election seemed to be a hopeless task and Katsav was first to point this out, playing instead on his relaxed, moderate personality. However, Peres's clear intention to use the constitutionally powerless presidency to back the increasingly unpopular peace efforts of Prime Minister Ehud Barak's government proved indigestible in the Parliament. Katsav's very public religious devotion apparently swung the contest in his favour giving him 63 parliamentary votes to Peres's 57 in the July election. On his inauguration he pledged to avoid interfering in domestic politics and to serve instead as a figurehead for all Israelis.

Moshe Katsav is married and has five children.

Profile of the Prime Minister:

Ariel SHARON

Before beginning a political career in 1973, Ariel Sharon spent 25 years in the Israeli Defence Force (IDF), winning especial fame as a tank commander in the 1973 war. Subsequently notorious for the invasion of southern Lebanon in 1982, while he was defence minister, and the massacres of Palestinians at Sabra and Chatila, Sharon's 'hawkish' right-wing stance was one of the sparks which began the second Palestinian uprising (intifada) *in 2000 at a time when a lasting peace had seemed to be a possibility. As prime minister he has been forced to soften his hard-line approach, but has reacted to public opinion by demanding an end to violence before talks, while escalating Israel's military offensive.*

Ariel Sharon was born as Ariel Scheinerman on 27 September 1928 in Kfar Malal, an impoverished farming community in what was then British-ruled Palestine. He joined the Jewish resistance movement Haganah at the age of 14 and changed his surname to Sharon ('lion of God') during the 1948 Israeli war of independence, in which he led an infantry company. After the war, and the following Arab–Israeli conflict (1948–49), he was promoted into the IDF's newly created intelligence unit. While studying history and oriental studies at the Hebrew University in Jerusalem in 1952, he was appointed to head the specialist anti-terrorist Unit 101 which carried out covert attacks on the Arab *fedayeen* militia and their supporters. He went on to lead Unit 101 through a series of punitive raids between 1952 and 1956. He led a paratroop brigade during the Sinai campaign in 1956, before being sent to Staff College in Camberley, UK, the following year. He received his second degree, in law, from Tel Aviv University in 1962.

From 1958 to 1967 Sharon worked in the infantry as a brigade commander and as head of the IDF's Northern Command and its training school. He led an armoured division during the Six-Day War of 1967 and headed the Southern Command from 1969. In the latter role he worked to secure Israel's new southern border along the Suez Canal. He attempted to enter politics in 1972 but was recalled to

249

the IDF at the outbreak of the Yom Kippur war in 1973. In this conflict he famously defied his superiors and led an armoured division across the Suez Canal into Egypt in a manoeuvre which hastened the end of the war. He resigned from the IDF again after peace returned later that year to launch his career in politics.

As a candidate for Likud, Sharon was elected to Parliament in December 1973 but stepped down a year later to serve as security adviser to Prime Minister Yitzhak Rabin. After Rabin resigned in 1976 Sharon chose to form his own party, Shlomzion, which won two seats in Parliament the following year. However, Likud had been returned to power in the elections and Sharon opted to disband Shlomzion in favour of rejoining the right-wing establishment. In return Prime Minister Menachem Begin appointed him minister of agriculture and chairman of the ministerial committee for settlements. From this vantage point he advanced the cause of the Gush Emunim settlement movement, and backed an extensive building programme.

As minister of defence from 1981, Sharon spearheaded Operation Oranim in June 1982 as part of the 'peace for Galilee' war. The project aimed to end 'terrorist' attacks in northern Israel and to establish a pro-Israeli, anti-Syrian government in Lebanon. On 16 September that year Christian militiamen massacred around 2,000 Palestinian refugees in camps at Sabra and Chatila. The Kahan Inquiry into the killings ruled that Sharon had not done enough to prevent the murders, and consequently found him indirectly responsible for them. He was forced to resign but remained in the cabinet as minister without portfolio.

Political rehabilitation was swift and from 1984 to 1990 Sharon served as trade and industry minister. In 1990 he was appointed housing minister and in this capacity he ordered the biggest settlement construction drive in the Palestinian areas of the West Bank and the Gaza Strip since they had been occupied by Israel in 1967. Between 1992 and 1996 Likud was forced into opposition but Sharon's popularity among the extreme right continued to grow and he came third and second in consecutive party leadership contests. Following the party's electoral success in 1996 Sharon returned to the cabinet under Prime Minister Binyamin Netanyahu after pressure from the extreme right of the party. He was promoted to the foreign ministry in 1998.

The electoral defeat of Likud in 1999 prompted Netanyahu to resign as party chief; Sharon took over the reins in September that year. As leader of the opposition, Sharon was fiercely critical of the peace initiatives pursued by Labour prime minister Ehud Barak. Progress towards peace with the Palestinian National Authority (PNA) led to a steady stream of compromises on control of the occupied areas over the course of 2000, prompting hope of a lasting peace in the international community, but bitterness among the Israeli far right. On 28 September that year Sharon made a high-profile visit to the Temple Mount/al-Haram al-Sharif site in Jerusalem. His visit provoked widespread anger among the Palestinian community which rapidly escalated into a full-blown *intifada*. While Sharon's critics accused him of purposefully inciting the violence in order to destabilize the Labour government's peace initiatives, Sharon himself blamed Palestinian extremists for using it as an excuse to launch the *intifada*.

As violence continued, public support for Barak's government collapsed and he turned to Likud in an effort to form a national unity coalition. This move in itself prompted further anger among the Palestinians. Although initially Sharon rejected the idea, he reversed his stance by November when Barak called a surprise prime ministerial election for the following February. Sharon immediately began his election campaign, boldly announcing that the 1993 Oslo Peace Accords were dead. His cause was boosted when popular former premier Netanyahu refused to challenge him for the Likud leadership. On 6 February 2001 Ehud Barak was forced to accept defeat in the face of 62% support for Sharon. Once elected Sharon secured parliamentary approval for the abolition of the five-year-old system of direct elections for the premiership.

Unable to command a majority alone, Sharon turned to Labour and other parties to form a 'government of national unity'. Immediately Sharon outlined what was to become the backbone of his policy towards the *intifada*: that there could be no talks before all violence by Palestinian militants had ceased. Despite increasingly powerful retaliations against attacks, and pleas from the Palestinian leadership for militants to end suicide bombings, the cycle of violence rapidly became entrenched. The Labour party under Binyamin Ben-Eliezer began to pull away from Sharon's uncompromising approach and put up a final defence in October 2002 when it unsuccessfully resisted a budget which included funding for the controversial Jewish settlements in the occupied territories. The unity coalition collapsed and Sharon was forced to call fresh legislative elections for January.

Sharon now faced a leadership challenge within Likud from Netanyahu. On 28 November he was comfortably re-elected, but by the close of the year he was plagued by corruption scandals involving himself and his son Omri, who had been linked by the press to organized crime. Nonetheless, opinion polls suggested that Likud would still make significant gains in the upcoming elections.

As prime minister, Sharon has consistently followed a much harder approach to the *intifada* than Barak. Punitive and even pre-emptive air strikes against Palestinian positions precede destructive raids on Palestinian settlements. However, in the face of strong international pressure he has had to instigate a poorly maintained 'policy of restraint'. In the process he has been vilified by the same Jewish settlers' movement he once championed. But, despite the earlier efforts of the more conciliatory Labour members of his cabinet, he has continued to escalate tension in the region, even ordering attacks on Syrian targets in Lebanese territory. Moves in foreign courts to begin a legal case against Sharon for the 1982 massacres in Lebanon are persistently dismissed.

Ariel Sharon is twice a widower. His first wife, Margalit, was killed in a car accident, and his second, Lily, died in 2000. He has two surviving sons, Omri and Gilad, but a third, Gur, was killed in a childhood shooting accident.

ITALY

Full name: The Italian Republic.

Leadership structure: The head of state is a president, who is elected by an electoral college comprising both houses of Parliament and 58 regional representatives. The president's term of office is seven years. The head of government is the prime minister, who is appointed by the president, as is the cabinet, but on the prime minister's recommendation.

President:	Carlo Azeglio Ciampi	Since 18 May 1999
Prime Ministers:	Massimo D'Alema	21 Oct. 1998—26 April 2000
	Giuliano Amato	26 April 2000—11 June 2001
	Silvio Berlusconi	Since 11 June 2001

Legislature: The legislature, the Parliament (Parlamento), is bicameral. The lower chamber, the Chamber of Deputies (Camera dei Deputati), has 630 members, directly elected for a five-year term. The upper chamber, the Senate of the Republic (Senato della Repubblica), comprises 315 senators directly elected for five years on a regional basis, and a variable number of life senators, who include ex-presidents and senators appointed by incumbent presidents.

Profile of the President of the Republic:

Carlo Azeglio **CIAMPI**

Carlo Ciampi, the governor of the Bank of Italy from 1979 to 1993 and briefly prime minister thereafter, was elected as president in 1999 as a consensus candidate and a symbol of Italy's much-hoped-for stability. Almost all of the many political parties from right to left backed his nomination. Old enough to have fought in the Italian army in the Second World War, he spent effectively his whole working life in the Bank of Italy.

Carlo Azeglio Ciampi was born on 9 December 1920 in Livorno, Tuscany. He attended university in the nearby city of Pisa, graduating from the Scuola Normale Superiore with a degree in law. He fought in the Italian army from 1941 to 1944. Joining the Bank of Italy in 1946 (the year of his marriage to Franca Pilla, with whom he has one son and one daughter), he spent 14 years in various branches of the bank as an administrator and inspector of commercial banks, until his appointment to the economic research department in 1960.

In the course of the 1970s Ciampi raced up the bank's hierarchy with astonishing speed. In 1970 he was appointed as the head of the research department, in 1973 he became the bank's secretary-general, and in 1976 he was nominated as deputy director-general. Two years later he was full director-general, and in 1979 was made the governor of the Bank of Italy, a position he fulfilled for 14 years until 1993. In his tenure as governor Ciampi has been credited with drastically reducing the public deficit and overseeing Italy's qualification for first-round entry into the European single currency, his most lauded achievement.

Despite a lack of political experience he was nominated as prime minister in 1993 and served as premier for a single year. From prime minister, Ciampi moved on to become vice president of the Bank for International Settlements from 1994 to 1996 before being appointed as minister for the treasury and the budget. In 1998 he moved to the International Monetary Fund committee which he chaired until 1999 when he was reappointed to the treasury.

Ciampi is one of the few quickly elected presidents in Italy's history, winning in the first round of the voting in Parliament on 13 May 1999, whereas the selection process has been known to take up to 23 rounds. He won 70% of the available votes from across the political divide, with only the Communist Refoundation Party and the secessionist Northern League voting against him. His popularity lay in his political neutrality and his international renown following his economic accomplishments. With such a broad support base it was thought that work would begin straight away to reform many of Italy's political processes. Two successive referendums called to approve changes, however, met with such public apathy that they were rendered invalid.

Profile of the Prime Minister:

Silvio **BERLUSCONI**

Silvio Berlusconi first made his name as Italy's foremost media magnate, then built a political career on the back of his business success, and first became prime minister in 1994 within months of forming his right-wing Forza Italia party. That government lasted a mere eight months, collapsing in disputes with his neofascist coalition partners. Having presented Forza Italia as a fresh and dynamic alternative to the corrupt old party system, Berlusconi was himself caught up in the web of political-funding corruption and in fighting a conviction for bribery and other criminal charges. His return to power in June 2001 was followed by highly controversial legislation which benefited both his own legal position and his business interests.

Silvio Berlusconi was born on 29 September 1936 in Milan, the son of a banker. His entrepreneurial skills were already evident at school where he did homework for fellow pupils, charging for his services on a sliding scale depending upon the marks awarded. As a student of law at the University of Milan, his close friends included Bettino Craxi, who was later to become leader of the Italian Socialist Party and prime minister. Milan remains Berlusconi's home, where he now lives with his second wife, the actress Veronica Bartolini; he has three children by this marriage and two from his first marriage.

After graduation Berlusconi established his own construction and property companies, Cantieri Riuniti Milanesi and Edilnord, in the early 1960s. With these he built up significant property holdings, including the Milan suburb known as Milano 2, on which he began construction in 1969 and which eventually housed 10,000 people.

In the 1970s Berlusconi's business career began to focus increasingly on the media interests for which he was to become best known. In 1974 he founded the cable television company Telemilano, which serviced Milano 2, and the following year he set up Fininvest as the holding company for his growing empire. To circumvent legislation under which only the state-run television service RAI was permitted to broadcast nationally, he set up a network of regional companies, which achieved de facto nationwide coverage by broadcasting the same programmes simultaneously. His own television channel, Canale 5, began broadcasting in 1980. He bought Italy's other two main private television stations, Italia 1 and Rete 4, in 1983 and 1984 respectively.

Having also moved successfully into the advertising business and built up Publitalia to make it the largest advertising agency in Europe, Berlusconi diversified his holdings during the 1980s to include the print media, publishing (including the country's largest publishing concern, Mondadori), the film industry (including the largest cinema chain, Cinema 5), retailing (including the largest chain of department stores, La Standa), insurance, financial services and the football team A.C. Milan. His success in business was based on the combination of commercial acumen and ruthlessness, backed up by an ability to operate the political system to advantage and good high-level connections. His opponents allege that this extended to exploiting links with the freemasons and the Mafia. Berlusconi was a member of the notorious clandestine P-2 masonic lodge, uncovered in 1981 and subsequently outlawed, although he has denied being actively involved in its dealings.

The opportunity for Berlusconi the business phenomenon to become Berlusconi the political leader came with the upheavals of the early 1990s. Ever-widening judicial investigations, mounted by magistrates into kick-back payments and related scandals, began to unravel the web of endemic corruption and bribery through which the traditional parties, both socialist and Christian democratic, had wielded power at the local and national level. The impact of the so-called *mani pulite* (clean hands) operation was to discredit the old parties and thus to transform the political landscape. Berlusconi entered the fray with the formation in January 1994 of Forza Italia, a political party named after the Italian football supporters' chant, which translates loosely as "Come on, Italy!". He proceeded to form a right-wing Freedom Alliance for the March 1994 general election, embracing Forza Italia, the separatist Northern League, the neofascist National Alliance and other smaller right-wing parties.

Berlusconi's successful populist campaign was greatly strengthened by his ownership of 85% of commercial television and 20% of the domestic publishing market. The Freedom Alliance secured a majority of seats in the Chamber of Deputies and Berlusconi, as leader of its largest party, was able to form a coalition government in May 1994. His coalition proved divisive and short-lived, however. He was criticized for appointing his own nominees to key public positions. In July he was obliged after a public outcry to withdraw a decree which ended the preventive detention of corruption and bribery suspects (who by then included Berlusconi's brother and a Fininvest director).

Berlusconi also failed to tackle economic problems, including reducing the public debt and reorganizing the public sector. The draft budget, which focused on cuts in pensions and health care and thus penalized the lower paid, provoked widespread protests and a sharp fall in the value of the lira and of the Milan stock exchange in November. Further, Berlusconi received a summons in November in connection with his alleged bribery of tax inspectors, finally prompting the increasingly disaffected Northern League to withdraw from the coalition and obliging Berlusconi to resign in December 1994. He remained at the head of Forza Italia, whose support fell slightly in the April 1996 general election, which brought to power a centre-left coalition of the Olive Tree Alliance led by the moderate Romano Prodi.

Berlusconi's political position was undermined further by the progress of corruption investigations implicating him personally. In December 1997 he was convicted on charges of false accounting over a 1987 film company deal and given a 16-month suspended sentence. In two judgments delivered in July 1998 he was found guilty of bribing tax inspectors and of illegally funding Craxi's socialists during the 1980s to the tune of 22,000 million lire. He was sentenced to over five years' imprisonment and a fine of 10,000 million lire (US$6 million) but remained free pending the outcome of appeals—and still faced other corruption charges, as well as allegations of money laundering for the Mafia. In 2000 accusations had spread abroad with a Spanish judge demanding the lifting of the immunity from prosecution enjoyed by Berlusconi as a member of the European parliament (since 1999) in order to press charges over fraud at a Spanish television station. He was saved by his victory in general elections in Italy on 13 May 2001.

Heading a new right-wing coalition, the so-called House of Liberties (Casa delle Libertà) which again included the National Alliance and the Northern League, Berlusconi was inaugurated for his second term as prime minister on 11 June 2001. Immediately he began preparing bills to effectively quash outstanding charges against him. One law halved the period before a statute of limitations prevents prosecution on charges of false accounting. A number of bribery charges were dropped in October 2001. Another law in July 2002 eliminated the conflict of interest debate over his media empire. Perhaps most significantly in November 2002 a law was passed allowing defendants to move their trial if they can prove a bias in the court. Using this bill Berlusconi hopes to switch a Milan-based trial against him to another, less biased, court. This will probably have the effect of prolonging the case until it becomes null and void under the previously agreed statute of limitations bill.

Such manipulations and Berlusconi's full support for the USA's 'war on terror' have produced a rapid drop in his popularity. Rallies against the pro-war stance, labour reforms and immigration laws have attracted up to two million people at a time. Berlusconi lost credibility in the eyes of the world when he casually described Western culture as superior to Islam within two weeks of the 11 September attacks. He was forced to apologize and claim misrepresentation. In July 2002 he announced that he supported the idea of a directly elected, executive president, adding that he would be keen to stand for the role himself. From January 2001 to November 2002 Berlusconi took on the additional role of foreign minister.

JAMAICA

Full name: Jamaica.

Leadership structure: The head of state is the British sovereign, styled 'of Jamaica, and of Her other Realms and Territories Queen, Head of the Commonwealth', and represented by a governor-general who is appointed on the advice of the Jamaican prime minister. The head of government is the prime minister, the leader of the majority party in the House of Representatives. The cabinet is appointed by the governor-general on the advice of the prime minister.

Queen:	Elizabeth II	Since 6 Feb. 1952
Governor-General:	Sir Howard Cooke	Since 1 Aug. 1991
Prime Minister:	Percival J. Patterson	Since 30 March 1992

Legislature: The legislature, the Parliament, is bicameral. The lower chamber, the House of Representatives, has 60 members, directly elected for a five-year term. The upper chamber, the Senate, has 21 members, appointed by the governor-general, 13 on the advice of the prime minister and eight on that of the leader of the opposition.

Profile of the Governor-General:

Sir Howard **COOKE**

Sir Howard Cooke, a teacher by profession, was a founding member of the People's National Party (PNP) before the Second World War, and a government minister in the 1970s. He took office as governor-general on 1 August 1991.

Born on 13 November 1915 at Goodwill in the parish of St James, Howard Felix Hanlan Cooke was educated at Mico College and at London University. During his long teaching career he spent over 20 years at Mico College, was headmaster at Belle Castle All-Age School, Port Antonio Upper School and Montego Bay Boys' School, and was at one time president of the Jamaica Union of Teachers. Cooke has also held various managerial positions in the insurance industry with Standard Life, Jamaica Mutual Life, and the American Life Insurance Company (ALICO).

Cooke's political career began in 1938, when he was a founding member of the People's National Party (PNP). Within the party he has been a member of the national executive, chairman of the regional executive and chairman of the party. He sat in the West Indies Federal Parliament as the representative for St James from 1958 until 1962, was a senator in the Jamaican Parliament in 1962–67, and a member of the House of Representatives in 1972–80. His government posts included ministerial responsibilities for pensions and social security, education, public service and labour. He also served on the executive of the Commonwealth Parliamentary Association.

An accomplished cricketer and footballer in his youth, Cooke has also been group scoutmaster and secretary of the St Andrew Boys' Scout Association, and is chief scout of the Scout Association of Jamaica. He is a lay pastor, a senior elder of the United Church of Jamaica and Grand Cayman, and a member of the Ancient and Accepted Order of Masons.

Cooke married Ivy Tal in 1939, and they have two sons and one daughter.

Profile of the Prime Minister:

Percival J. **PATTERSON**

Before becoming prime minister himself in 1994, Percival Patterson, a lawyer who became a Queen's Counsel in 1984, had been for 14 years the loyal deputy to Michael Manley, both in government and in opposition. Securing his position by leading the People's National Party (PNP) to a convincing victory in the March 1993 general elections, Patterson moved the party further away from the radical socialism of the 1970s. His government struggled to bring inflation under control and to reduce the fiscal deficit, and remained preoccupied with the high rate of violent crime, but was re-elected in December 1997 and October 2002.

Percival Noel James Patterson was born on 10 April 1935 at Cross Roads in the parish of St Andrew. He studied English at the University College of the West Indies (UCWI), graduating in 1958, and went on in 1960 to study law at the London School of Economics. He was called to the Bar in 1963, and returned to Jamaica to practise as a lawyer. He is now divorced and has one son and one daughter.

Patterson began his political career while he was still at UCWI, as founder and first president of the UCWI's political club. He joined the PNP in 1958 and was a member of the party executive between 1964 and 1969. In 1967 he was nominated to the Senate, and between 1970 and 1980 he held a seat in the House of Representatives, representing South East Westmoreland as a PNP member. He was campaign director for the PNP for the general elections of 1972, 1976 and 1989.

Starting his cabinet career in 1972 as minister of industry, foreign trade and tourism, Patterson became deputy prime minister and minister of foreign trade in 1978. The government was decisively rejected by the electorate in 1980 and the

PNP was in opposition for over eight years thereafter, during which time Patterson returned to his legal career, becoming a Queen's Counsel in 1984. He was also engaged as a consultant by the Commonwealth Secretariat to assist in drafting the constitution under which Belize became independent in 1981.

The PNP boycotted the 1983 elections, but swept back to power in February 1989, when Patterson was appointed deputy prime minister and minister of development, planning and production. As minister of finance and planning from 1990 to 1991, he supervised the drafting of a new Banking Act, modernized the tax system, and introduced a general consumption tax (GCT).

Having succeeded Michael Manley as prime minister in March 1992, Patterson led the PNP to victory in the 1993 general election. In the ensuing years his government became embroiled in a lengthy dispute over whether it was appropriate, in a state which was not a UK dependency, to continue to have legal appeal procedures going ultimately to the Privy Council. The issue arose over a Privy Council recommendation that life sentences on two convicted murderers should be commuted because they had spent so long on 'death row'; it thus touched not only on Jamaica's independent status but also on the government's determination to fight violent crime. An agreement with the USA in May 1997 allowed greater scope for action in Jamaica by US drug enforcement officers in the battle against trafficking.

Patterson, who was one of the main protagonists of a free trade agreement covering the Caribbean, is acknowledged to have been during his ministerial career one of the chief architects of the Lomé Convention, governing relations between the European Union (EU) and the African, Caribbean and Pacific countries (ACP). After becoming prime minister he sought to introduce more stable relationships between key sectors in the economic sphere, proposing in early 1996 a tripartite 'social contract' between workers, employers and the government.

A mysterious scandal enveloped the government in October 2000 when Patterson announced that he had not authorized the 'bugging' of his own and other ministers' offices, and that an investigation into police connections to the drugs trade was "interlocked" with the bugging plot. However, it was the unsolved problem of increasing political violence on the streets of Kingston which did most to undermine his popularity. Patterson and the PNP were returned with a much reduced majority in the October 2002 elections, now holding just 34 seats in the 60-seat House of Representatives.

JAPAN

Full name: Japan.

Leadership structure: The head of state is a constitutional monarch. The head of government is the prime minister, formally elected by the House of Representatives, who appoints the cabinet.

Emperor:	Akihito	Since 7 Jan. 1989
Prime Ministers:	Keizo Obuchi	30 July 1998—5 April 2000
	Mikio Aoki (acting)	3 April 2000—5 April 2000
	Yoshiro Mori	5 April 2000—26 April 2001
	Junichiro Koizumi	Since 26 April 2001

Legislature: The legislature, the Diet (Kokkai), is bicameral. The lower chamber, the House of Representatives (Shugiin), has 480 members, directly elected by universal adult suffrage for a maximum four-year term. The upper chamber, the House of Councillors (Sangiin), now has 247 members, elected for six-year terms, with half being due for re-election every three years. Under an amendment passed in October 2000 the membership of the upper house will be reduced to 242 at the elections due in 2004.

Profile of the Emperor:

AKIHITO

Emperor Akihito has been head of state since January 1989. The role of emperor, while accorded the highest respect, is primarily a ceremonial one, and in all political matters he acts only as advised by the government. Before his accession Akihito had been crown prince for nearly four decades during the long reign of his father, Emperor Hirohito.

Akihito Tsegu no Miya was born in Tokyo on 23 December 1933. He is the fourth child, and eldest son, of Emperor Hirohito and Empress Nagako. His education, interrupted by evacuation to provincial cities during the Second World War, was partly by private tutors. Akihito also attended the Gakushuin School, which covers the whole range from kindergarten to university, and was originally set up specifically for the imperial family and aristocracy, but opened to the

260

public from 1947. He graduated from Gakushuin University in politics and economics in 1956.

In 1952 Akihito was officially named crown prince, and spent the years before his accession engaged in a mixture of official duties and private interests. His public duties included many overseas visits and tours within Japan. In private life a keen ichthyologist, he is a particular expert on the goby fish, and has made numerous contributions to the Journal of the Ichthyological Society of Japan; he has also been a research associate at the Australian Museum, and in 1985 he was honorary secretary at the International Conference on Indo-Pacific Fish.

In 1987 Akihito became acting head of state. Acceding to the throne on 7 January 1989, he was formally crowned on 12 November 1990.

In 1959 Akihito married Michiko Shoda, the first nonaristocrat to be elevated to royal status. The couple have three children: Naruhito (born in 1960), Fumihito (born in 1965) and Sayako (born in 1969).

Profile of the Prime Minister:

Junichiro **KOIZUMI**

Junichiro Koizumi, who became prime minister in April 2001 following the premature resignation of his deeply unpopular predecessor Yoshiro Mori, is himself exceptionally popular with the Japanese public, although his nationalistic tendencies have led to a cooling in relations with the country's east Asian neighbours. A 'maverick' with an unconventionally enthusiastic style, Koizumi comes from a political family background, and has sat in the House of Representatives as a member of the Liberal Democratic Party (LDP) since 1972.

Junichiro Koizumi was born on 8 January 1942 in Yokosuka, just southwest of Tokyo. His grandfather, Matajiro Koizumi, and his father, Junya Koizumi, both held ministerial posts. Junya was minister of defence in the 1960s. Junichiro graduated from Tokyo's Keio University in 1967 with a degree in economics and travelled to the UK to further his studies at the London School of Economics. However, he returned to Japan after only a year following his father's death from cancer. He unsuccessfully campaigned for his father's seat in the House of Representatives and found work instead as secretary for the LDP member, and future prime minister, Takeo Fukuda.

After two years as a junior secretary Koizumi campaigned again in 1972 for election in the Kanagawa-11 constituency, which covers his home city of Yokosuka. This time he won the seat, and he has been re-elected in ten consecutive polls. Between 1980 and 1988 he served on several parliamentary committees before entering the reshuffled cabinet of Prime Minister Noboru Takeshita as minister of health and welfare. In 1992 he was moved to the posts and telecommunications ministry by Prime Minister Kiichi Miyazawa.

It was during the 1990s that Koizumi was given his 'weirdo' tag. His unusually outspoken rhetorical style was backed by treatises suggesting radical reforms, such as the privatization of the postal savings system. At the same time he was careful not to talk himself out of favour within the guarded and strongly traditional Japanese political system. He even headed one of the internal factions of which the LDP has traditionally consisted, despite later pledging as premier to do away with this patronage-based system.

When the LDP was knocked from its almost permanent position as the ruling party in 1993 by a seven-party coalition led by Shinshinto, it continued its internal wrangling in opposition. Koizumi stood as a candidate for the party leadership in 1995 and 1998—the latter competition was effectively for prime minister as the LDP had returned to power in 1994. In the meantime Koizumi had been returned to the health and welfare ministry in 1996 by Prime Minister Ryutaro Hashimoto.

Prime Minister Keizo Obuchi, who had defeated Koizumi to the party presidency in 1998, led the country through a period of worsening economic prospects and attempted to stave off the trend with record public spending. On his sudden death in April 2000 he was replaced by Yoshiro Mori who stuck closely to Obuchi's policies. The economy did not recover and Mori, helped by a proneness to public gaffes, eventually stepped down from the party leadership, and consequently the premiership, after just one year. In the complex internal voting system, former prime minister Hashimoto appeared to be the main contender in the race but Koizumi capitalized on massive grass roots appeal to score an impressive and unexpected victory. His plain-speaking reformist agenda centred on the promise of "change the LDP, change Japan".

As prime minister, Koizumi has seen his remarkable public approval begin to fail. Initially his promises of wide-ranging economic and political reform kept his popularity soaring. He gave offence internationally by visiting the controversial Yasakuni Shrine, which commemorates Japan's war dead, including posthumously convicted war criminals, and by backing revisionist school history text books, but this brand of nationalism did him no harm at home. It was his record-breaking inclusion of five women in his opening cabinet that, in one sense, contained the seeds of trouble for his popularity, as it was when he was forced to dismiss his firebrand, and extremely popular, foreign minister, Makiko Tanaka, in January 2002, that his ratings began to slide.

The downward momentum gathered as the lacklustre pace of his economic reforms became apparent. In August 2002 he admitted that his timescale for reform had been overambitious. Unemployment rose, exacerbated by falling consumer spending, By the end of the year the restructuring of banks had put many of Japan's major financial institutions on the rocks. In politics critics suggested that, rather than 'changing' the faction system within the LDP, Koizumi had been forced to pander to it, further retarding his reforms.

Junichiro Koizumi has publicly vowed to remain a bachelor, having decided that he is "better off alone". His one and only marriage, to Kayoko Miyamoto, a woman 14 years his junior and the daughter of a pharmaceutical magnate, ended in divorce in 1982 after only four years. He then raised his two eldest sons alone and only later met his third son, with whom Kayako had been pregnant when they divorced. His refusal to ever marry again and his reputation as a keen socialite have not dented his public appeal in the slightest. Indeed his unkempt hairstyle and casual attire have served to improve his popularity. Among his interests he cites *kabuki* (traditional Japanese theatre) as well as karaoke.

JORDAN

Full name: The Hashemite Kingdom of Jordan.

Leadership structure: The head of state is a king. The head of government is the prime minister, who is usually appointed by the king. However, in August 1998, power to appoint and dismiss the prime minister was also given to the crown prince in the event of the king's illness. The Council of Ministers is chosen by the prime minister.

King:	Abdullah II bin al-Hussein (regent from 5 Feb. 1999)	Since 7 Feb. 1999
Prime Ministers:	Abd al-Rauf al-Rawabdeh	4 March 1999—18 June 2000
	Ali Abu al-Ragheb	Since 19 June 2000

Legislature: The legislature, the National Assembly (Majlis al-Umma), is bicameral. The lower chamber, the House of Deputies (Majlis al-Nuwaab), has 80 members, directly elected for a four-year term. The upper chamber, the Senate (Majlis al-Aayan—literally 'House of Notables'), has 40 members, appointed by the king for a four-year term. After the dissolution of the House of Deputies on 16 June 2001, the cabinet introduced temporary legislation, approved by the king on 22 July, to increase the membership of the House to 104, and restructure the electoral districts.

Profile of the King:

ABDULLAH II bin al-Hussein

Abdullah II succeeded to the Hashemite throne of Jordan on the death of his father King Hussein. The son of Hussein's English second wife and educated largely in England, Abdullah is seen as very much in the pro-Western mould of his father with close links to many high-level Israelis giving him an obvious role as peacemaker in the Middle East region. His appointment as heir came only three weeks before Hussein's death, replacing the late king's younger brother Hassan as crown prince and causing brief controversy in Jordan. His succession received praise from across the international community and his continuation of his father's moderate policies has so far proved popular in Jordan.

Abdullah bin al-Hussein was born in Amman on 30 January 1962, the eldest son of eleven children born to the reigning monarch King Hussein and his English second wife Queen Muna. His uncle Hassan was named crown prince and heir to the throne in 1965. After a brief period of preschooling in Amman he was sent to England to be educated at St Edmund's School in 1966 and then to Eaglebrook School in Massachusetts, USA. For his secondary education he attended the Deerfield Academy in the USA before returning to England to enrol in the Royal Military Academy at Sandhurst in 1980. After receiving his commission as a lieutenant in 1981 he studied for a degree in international affairs at Oxford University.

Pursuing a military career interspersed with further studies abroad, he qualified as a helicopter pilot in 1986 while attached to the Royal Jordanian Air Force, then went to Georgetown University in Washington D.C., USA, where he again studied international relations. Returning to Jordan, he commanded tank battalions as a major from 1989. In 1990 he attended the Command and Staff College in Camberley, England. On his return he became armour representative in the office of the inspector-general in 1991 and was promoted in the same year to lieutenant-colonel. In 1993 Abdullah crossed over to the Jordanian special forces as a full colonel, and assumed control of the Royal Jordanian Special Forces as a brigadier-general the following year. In 1997 he was appointed as commander of the Special Operations Command and in 1998 he was promoted to major-general.

In early 1999 the health of Abdullah's father King Hussein deteriorated rapidly. Flying home from hospital in the USA after the failure of a bone marrow operation, he startled Jordanian politics on 25 January by naming his son Abdullah as his heir in place of Prince Hassan.

Abdullah was not a complete stranger to royal duties. He had accompanied his father on many international visits and had made acquaintance with numerous high-ranking regional politicians. However, in Jordan he was largely an unknown quantity. After his father's death on 7 February, he was quickly accepted by the international community. In Jordan he soon won over the stunned population with promises to maintain Jordan's role as Middle East peace broker and a clear desire to continue in his father's populist vein. As king he convened a special parliamentary session to examine possible changes to the controversial press law introduced under his father in September 1998. His first royal decree complied with his father's wishes and nominated his younger half-brother Prince Hamzah, born on 29 March 1980, as crown prince and heir apparent.

King Abdullah married Rania al-Yasin on 10 June 1993 and the couple were crowned on 9 June 1999. Queen Rania was born in Kuwait in 1970 to a notable Jordanian family of Palestinian descent. She had a brief career in private sector banking and information technology before marrying Abdullah, and has since overseen the creation of the Arab world's first child abuse protection project. Together they have one son, Prince al-Hussein born in 1994, and one daughter, Princess Imam born in 1996.

Profile of the Prime Minister:

Ali Abu al-**RAGHEB**

Ali Abu al-Ragheb is a straight-talking, Western-educated economist, whose appointment as prime minister in June 2000 sent a clear message that King Abdullah was eager to press ahead with the country's economic modernization.

Ali Abu al-Ragheb was born in 1946 in Amman. He received a degree in engineering from the University of Tennessee, Knoxville, USA, before returning to Jordan to pursue a career in the business sector.

Ragheb was chairman of Jordan's Contractor's Association from 1986 to 1990 before he headed into politics in 1991 as minister of trade and industry. In the first multiparty elections in 1993 Ragheb was elected to the House of Deputies as an independent candidate, and became chairman of the lower house's finance committee. In 1995, when Sharif Zaid ibn Shaker was appointed prime minister and proceeded to shuffle his cabinet, he appointed Ragheb as minister of energy and mineral resources. In 1996 Ragheb was reappointed to the trade and industry portfolio, only to lose it once more in a further cabinet shake-up under a new prime minister in 1997.

In early 1999 King Hussein died and his successor King Abdullah proceeded to reorganize the government once again. Ragheb had no role in the cabinet formed by the new premier, Abd al-Rauf al-Rawadbeh. He resumed the chairmanship of the parliamentary finance committee and also took a seat on the Economic Consultative Council which was chaired by the new king. In April 2000 Abdullah turned to him to construct a working proposal for the creation of a special economic zone around the southern port of Aqaba. Ragheb's plans did not receive support from the prime minister.

Rawadbeh was dismissed in June, having fallen out of favour in part because of his opposition to the Aqaba project and resistance to the king's reformist plans. The appointment of Ragheb in his place, with his reputation as a 'doer' with a distinctly liberal economic approach, was seen as a clear indicator of the king's political determination on the modernization front. The plans for the Aqaba project were passed by his government the following month. Ragheb remained in power following the dissolution of the House of Deputies ahead of electoral reforms in June 2001 and was reappointed to a new cabinet in January 2002. Elections were repeatedly postponed and are expected in March 2003.

KAZAKHSTAN

Full name: The Republic of Kazakhstan.

Leadership structure: The head of state is a president, directly elected by universal adult suffrage. The president's term of office was extended from five to seven years under constitutional amendments approved by the legislature in October 1998, on the same day as it approved the holding of early presidential elections in 1999. The head of government is the prime minister, who is appointed by the president. The deputy prime ministers and the ministers of foreign affairs, defence, finance and internal affairs are also appointed by the president. The remaining ministers are nominated by the prime minister.

President:	Nursultan Nazarbayev	Since 24 April 1990
	(chairman of the Supreme Soviet from 22 Feb. 1990)	
Prime Ministers:	Kasymzhomart Tokayev	12 Oct. 1999—28 Jan. 2002
	(acting from 1 Oct. 1999)	
	Imangali Tasmagambetov	Since 28 Jan. 2002

Legislature: The legislature, the Parliament, is bicameral. The lower chamber, the Assembly (Majlis), has 77 members, 67 of them directly elected on a single constituency basis, and ten seats allocated proportionately, for five-year terms. The upper chamber, the Senate, has 39 members, 32 indirectly elected and seven appointed, for six-year terms, with half elected every three years.

Profile of the President:

Nursultan **NAZARBAYEV**

Nursultan Nazarbayev rose through the Soviet system to the top post in Kazakhstan before it became independent and has been the country's president ever since. Despite his communist party background, he became an advocate of transforming the economy on free-market lines, strongly influenced by the advice of the Korean-American economist Chan Young Bang. The dominant political personality, he runs an authoritarian regime and has resorted to ruling by decree for substantial periods.

Nursultan Abishevich Nazarbayev was born on 6 June 1940 in the village of Chemolgan, near Almaty. He attended the higher technology course at the Karaganda Metallurgical Combine, and then worked there until 1969, apart from some time spent in Moscow at the Higher Party School of the Communist Party of the Soviet Union (CPSU), which he had joined in 1962. He is married to Sarah Alplisovna Kounakayeva and they have three daughters.

In 1969 Nazarbayev began a career as a party functionary, which took him via district level posts to membership of the CPSU central committee in 1986, and appointment in June 1989 as first secretary of the Communist Party of Kazakhstan (CPK).

Meanwhile, within the government structure, he had been chairman of the Kazakh Council of Ministers since 1984. Changes to the political structure in 1989 saw the creation of a permanent legislature whose chairman took on many of the functions formerly held by the CPK first secretary. Nazarbayev was elected as the first chairman of this reformed body in February 1990—and then in April was elected by the new legislature as the first president of the Kazakh Soviet Socialist Republic.

Nazarbayev was appointed to the CPSU politburo in 1990, but resigned from both the politburo and the central committee in 1991 in protest over the attempted coup in Moscow that August. Independence soon followed and Nazarbayev became first president of the independent Kazakhstan, with the endorsement of a popular vote that December.

As president, Nazarbayev advocated an independent stance while insisting on the importance of relations with the Russian Federation. He committed Kazakhstan to becoming a non-nuclear state, dismantling nuclear warheads and also signing the Nuclear Non-Proliferation Treaty in 1994. In internal affairs, he has used presidential powers to rule by decree to overcome obstacles in the legislature, particularly over the transformation of the economy to a free enterprise model; opposition and human rights groups have accused him of harassing those who express dissent.

On 29 April 1995 95% of the electorate approved Nazarbayev in office for a further five-year term. He then went on to better establish his position with a new constitution which was approved by referendum in August that year and abolished the post of vice president among other measures.

Nazarbayev agreed in October 1998 to hold early presidential elections in January 1999 for a chance at a new, and extended, seven-year term. Several prominent opposition figures were barred from standing in the poll due to prior political infractions. Nazarbayev easily won re-election with around 80% of the vote. The Organization for Security and Co-operation in Europe (OSCE) was in the front line of international critics of the election. On 27 June 2000 Nazarbayev was given special powers for life to address the Parliament and the nation, and advise future presidents after his term expires in 2006.

Profile of the Prime Minister:

Imangali **TASMAGAMBETOV**

Imangali Tasmagambetov is a former communist youth leader and close ally of President Nursultan Nazarbayev (although very much his junior). He owes his elevation to the premiership in 2002 to this relationship, having only relatively brief prior experience of senior government office.

Imangali Nurgaliyevich Tasmagambetov was born in 1956 in what was then the Kazakh Soviet Socialist Republic. He trained as a teacher before beginning political work with Komsomol, the communist youth league. In 1989 he was appointed first secretary of the Kazakh Komsomol and began his close association with Nazarbayev who was then chairman of the Communist Party of Kazakhstan. Nazarbayev had transformed his position into that of president of Kazakhstan by 1991 and Tasmagambetov continued to work closely with him.

After a period as Nazarbayev's assistant, Tasmagambetov was appointed governor of the oil-rich Atyrau *oblast* (region) in 1998. In this role he was criticized by foreign multinationals for attempting to use all means available to extract payment from the prospective investors hoping to make the most of the country's abundant resources. In December 2000 he was moved into the cabinet as deputy prime minister with responsibility for social issues and interethnic relations. Nazarbayev named him as prime minister following the resignation of the incumbent, Kasymzhomart Tokayev, in January 2002.

KENYA

Full name: The Republic of Kenya.

Leadership structure: The head of state is a president, directly elected by universal adult suffrage. The president's term of office is five years. The head of government is the president, who is responsible to the National Assembly. The cabinet is appointed by the president.

Presidents: Daniel arap Moi   14 Oct. 1978—30 Dec. 2002
(acting from 22 Aug. 1978)

Mwai Kibaki   Since 30 Dec. 2002

Legislature: The legislature is unicameral. The sole chamber, the National Assembly (Bunge), has 224 members (210 directly elected for a five-year term, 12 nominated by the president and two, the attorney general and the speaker, ex officio).

Profile of the President:

Mwai **KIBAKI**

Mwai Kibaki is the leader and founder of the Democratic Party (DP) which forms the core of the National Rainbow Coalition (NARC). A veteran politician who had been an integral part of the regime during the 1970s and 1980s, Kibaki left the then ruling Kenya African National Union (KANU) when the country moved to multipartyism in 1991. Twice a failed presidential candidate in the 1990s, he unified opposition against KANU in 2002 and secured the presidency in December that year with a convincing 63% of the vote. Although no new face, he is respected as a politician free from the country's rampant corruption.

Emilio Mwai Kibaki was born into a wealthy family from the Kikuyu tribe, Kenya's largest single ethnic group, on 15 November 1931. He is married to Lucy Muthoni and has four children. After a relatively prestigious education in Kenya, Kibaki went to neighbouring Uganda in 1950 to study economics at Makerere University in Kampala. He then worked briefly for Shell Oil in Uganda, until 1956, when he went to the UK on a Commonwealth scholarship to study public finance at the London School of Economics. He returned to Uganda in 1959 to begin lecturing in economics at Makerere University.

At the height of the Kenyan independence movement Kibaki returned home in 1960 to join the emerging KANU and to help draft the first constitution. He won a seat in the new parliament in 1963, and has been re-elected to the chamber in every successive election, making him the country's second-longest serving deputy after former president Daniel arap Moi.

Kibaki entered government in 1964 when Kenya's first president, Jomo Kenyatta, appointed him assistant minister of economic planning and development. Two years later he was made full minister of commerce and industry and in 1969 began what was to become the longest term in office for a Kenyan minister of finance (1969–82). In this role he oversaw a period of relative economic prosperity. He was also minister of economic planning from 1970 until 1978 and home affairs minister from 1978 to 1988.

In addition to his ministerial posts Kibaki was chosen by Moi to be vice president in 1978, when Moi himself succeeded Kenyatta in the presidency. Kibaki's relationship with Moi began to deteriorate during the 1980s, however. Having lost his responsibilities for the finance portfolio in 1982, he was dismissed as vice president in 1988 and also shunted from the ministry of home affairs to the health ministry, where he remained until 1991.

The introduction of multipartyism in Kenya was forced by popular discontent in 1991 and Kibaki, despite being a former vice president of KANU, took his cue to leave the ruling party. Instead he established the DP in December 1991, but was viewed with great suspicion by some who suggested that he was part of a government plot to split the opposition vote. Indeed, opposition rivalries boosted Moi in his successful re-election bids in 1992 and 1997. In the first of these elections Kibaki came a disappointing third, but rose to a surprising second in 1997, gaining over 30% of the vote. From 1998 he was the official leader of the opposition.

Corruption became the watchword of Moi's final term in office and the popularity of the president and the ruling KANU slumped. Kibaki used his 'clean' image to capitalize on the situation and drew opposition forces into his umbrella NARC just months before the December 2002 elections. In this poll he faced Uhuru Kenyatta, the son of founding president Jomo Kenyatta, whose selection as KANU candidate had been forced through by President Moi to the chagrin of many prominent party members. Kibaki gained a clear 63% victory in the first round and NARC won a majority in simultaneous legislative elections. He was inaugurated on 30 December and promised an end to the country's everyday corruption as his first priority.

Profile of the Previous President:

Daniel arap **MOI**

Daniel arap Moi was president of Kenya for 24 years, following the death in 1978 of Jomo Kenyatta. Originally a teacher, he became a leader of the Kenya

African Democratic Union (KADU), until a postindependence merger into Kenyatta's ruling Kenya African National Union (KANU). Moi was Kenyatta's vice president for 11 years and characterized his policies thereafter as following in Kenyatta's footsteps. Unlike many of the ruling elite of the 1960s and 1970s, however, Moi is not from the largest ethnic group, the Kikuyu. He is a Tigen from the smaller Kalenjin group, and has been criticized for exploiting interethnic rivalries for his own political advantage.

Daniel Toroitich arap Moi was born on 2 September 1924 in the Baringo district in the Rift Valley. Orphaned at the age of four, he was educated at mission school, then in Kabartonjo and finally at the African School in Kapsabet. From 1945 he worked as a teacher, interspersing two spells as head teacher at the African School in Kabarnet with a long period teaching at the Tambach teacher training school there. During his spare time he studied for and passed the London matriculation examinations. He was married from 1951 until 1976, when he divorced his wife Lena. They had five sons and three daughters.

In 1957 Moi became an African representative on the Legislative Council, and from 1960 onward he was chairman of KADU (making him in effect the deputy to party leader Ronald Ngala). He entered the House of Representatives at the 1961 elections. When KANU (the leading nationalist formation) refused to form a pre-independence government until its leader Kenyatta was released from detention, the less radical KADU accepted the opportunity do so, with the backing of the New Kenya Party (representing white voters).

Moi joined this pre-independence government as parliamentary secretary and then minister of education, and in 1962 moved to the ministry for local government. Kenya became independent in December 1963 under a KANU government. A year later, as a new republican constitution came into effect, KADU gave up its opposition role to merge itself into KANU, and Moi was rewarded with the post of minister of home affairs. He held this post until 1967, and thereafter the vice presidency until 1978.

After the sudden death of Kenyatta in August 1978, Moi was sworn in as president and commander-in-chief of the armed forces in October. He held the presidency for 24 years, and for much of this time the home affairs and defence portfolios as well. Some powerful KANU 'barons' and other leading Kikuyu figures initially saw him as only a stopgap, but he tightened his grip after an attempted air force coup in 1982, and won election on his own account in a single-candidate poll in September 1983. Pro-Western on most foreign policy issues and an advocate of private sector business rather than of state socialism, Moi cultivated his support particularly among the Kalenjin and other minority ethnic groups, and among traders of Asian origin who had been the targets of economic nationalism in the latter years of Kenyatta's presidency.

Moi was again re-elected in April 1988 amid accusations of systematic electoral fraud and intimidation. That year's single-party legislative elections purported to offer some element of choice, under a much-criticized system where voters had to line up publicly behind their chosen candidate to cast their vote.

By the end of 1991, continuing pressure, both internally and from foreign donor countries threatening a freeze on aid, compelled the autocratic Moi to concede the need for a multiparty system. He had hitherto opposed this ostensibly on the grounds that it would promote tribalism. Moi won the 1991 poll on 29 December with only 36% of the popular vote, benefiting from the division of the opposition into three main contending factions. Similarly, the December 1997 election, chaotically administered rather than massively fraudulent, gave him a further term of office once again because his opponents could not unite.

Moi's critics accused him of self-enrichment and repression, and complicity in engineering the death of several prominent opponents; they portrayed him as one of the last corrupt and autocratic survivors from his generation of former dictators in Africa. Moi himself, seeking to fend off such charges, denies having accumulated great personal wealth, and pointed to his electoral mandate. By the end of his final term of office, however, in December 2002, he had further eroded both his personal credibility and the electorate's tolerance of increasingly corrupt government. Confronted at last by a unified rather than a fractured opposition, KANU—itself badly internally divided—went down to a crushing defeat at the polls, while Moi's own protracted tenure ended in ignominy with the rejection of his chosen successor, Jomo Kenyatta's son Uhuru Kenyatta.

KIRIBATI

Full name: The Republic of Kiribati.

Leadership structure: The head of state is a president (*beretitenti*), directly elected by universal adult suffrage from candidates selected from members of the legislature. The president's term of office is four years. The head of government is the president, who is responsible to the House of Assembly. The cabinet is appointed by the president.

President: Teburoro Tito   Since 1 Oct. 1994

Legislature: The legislature is unicameral. The sole chamber, the House of Assembly (Maneaba ni Maungatabu), has 40 members directly elected for a four-year term, one appointed representative of the Banaban community (who live on Rabi Island, Fiji), and the attorney general.

Profile of the President:

Teburoro **TITO**

Teburoro Tito is a former education officer, and had been a member of the House of Assembly for seven years before becoming president. He heads a nonparty government, but before coming to power in the 1994 elections he was identified with the Christian democratic opposition.

Teburoro Tito was born on 25 August 1953 at Tabiteuea North, and in 1971 was offered a government scholarship to go to the University of the South Pacific (USP) in Fiji. He studied there for eight years, leaving in 1979 with a science degree and a graduate certificate of education. In 1976 he had become president of the USP students' association, and from 1977 to 1979 was the student co-ordinator. After returning to Kiribati in 1980 he entered the ministry of education as a scholarship officer, and in 1982 was offered a 30-day study tour of the USA intended for future leaders. In 1983 he became senior education officer in Kiribati, a post which he held until 1987. A keen soccer player, he also chaired the Kiribati Football Association from 1980 to 1994. He is married to Nei Keina Tito, and they have one child.

In 1987 Teburoro Tito was elected to the House of Assembly for the constituency of South Tarawa. He was leader of the opposition until 1990 and its deputy leader in 1990–94. He was also a member of the parliamentary public accounts committee from 1987 to 1990, and sat on the Commonwealth Parliamentary

Association executive committee for the Australia–Pacific region in 1988–89, attending numerous conferences and meetings abroad. In 1994, having been nominated for the presidency alongside three other candidates, he won a landslide victory in the national presidential elections, in the wake of a constitutional crisis and claims of misconduct by the outgoing government. He took office on 1 October.

Tito's own government lost seats at the September 1998 election as did the main opposition. Nonetheless, he was re-elected to a second term on 27 November with 52% of the vote. His nearest rival, Harry Tong, claimed 46%. Supporters of Tong made significant gains in legislative elections in November–December 2002 and presidential elections scheduled for early 2003 looked set to be a close race between Tito and opposition nominee Taberannang Timeon.

NORTH KOREA

Full name: The Democratic People's Republic of Korea.

Leadership structure: After the death of Kim Il Sung in 1994, the presidency remained vacant until an amendment to the constitution was approved by the legislature on 5 September 1998. While naming the dead Kim Il Sung as 'eternal president', and designating the chairmanship of the National Defence Commission as 'the highest post of the state', it provided that the chairman of the presidium of the Supreme People's Assembly would represent the state on formal occasions. The premier, elected by the Assembly, is head of government. The other members of the cabinet are appointed by the Assembly on the recommendation of the premier.

'Eternal President':   Kim Il Sung   (deceased)

Chairman of the Presidium of the Supreme People's Assembly:

Kim Yong Nam   Since 5 Sept. 1998

Chairman of the National Defence Commission:

Kim Jong Il   Since 5 Sept. 1998

Premier: Hong Song Nam   Since 5 Sept. 1998
(acting from 21 Feb. 1997)

General Secretary of the Korean Workers' Party (KWP):

Kim Jong Il   Since 8 Oct. 1997

Legislature: The legislature is unicameral. The sole chamber, the Supreme People's Assembly (Choe Go In Min Hoe Ui), has 687 members, elected from a single list of candidates for a five-year term.

Profile of the 'Eternal President':

KIM Il Sung

The late Kim Il Sung dominated North Korea for almost 46 years, as general secretary of the ruling (and sole legal) party, the Korean Workers' Party (KWP), and, from 1972 until his death in 1994, state president. It remains disputed how much he owed his initial leadership role to his Soviet backers, but once confirmed in power after the Korean War he became the object of perhaps the world's most overblown cult of personality, backed by fierce repression. Venerated as the 'great leader', the dictatorial Kim Il Sung even succumbed to the dynastic delusion, setting up his son Kim Jong Il as his intended heir.

Kim Il Sung was born Kim Song Ju on 15 April 1912 in Mangyongdae, Pyongyang, North Korea, the eldest of three sons of a peasant couple, Kim Hyonh Jik and Kang Pan Sok. His nom de guerre is said to have been adopted in memory of a celebrated anti-Japanese guerrilla fighter.

According to official biographies, Kim received his early education at home, and in 1929 attended the Yuwen Middle School in Jilin, Manchuria, where he became active in politics as a member of the South Manchurian Communist Youth Association. He was arrested for his anti-imperialist activities against the Japanese and upon his release in 1930 joined the Korean Revolutionary Army. In 1932 he founded his own Korean People's Revolutionary Army which established bases in the Jiandao region of Manchuria, and from there, official biographers maintain, Kim staged guerrilla raids against Japanese installations. His leading role in this struggle continued until the liberation of Korea north of the 38th parallel by Soviet forces in August 1945.

Other, less flattering accounts of Kim's activities during the 1930s and early 1940s suggest that he spent the war years like a Manchurian 'bandit', preying on poor Korean farmers. Most Western observers believed that he spent most of his time in the Soviet Union training as a spy.

In August 1946 Kim formed the KWP (resulting from the merger of the Communist Party of North Korea and the New Democratic Party of Korea), and with the help of his Soviet allies, proclaimed the Democratic People's Republic of Korea in September 1948. The Korean War (1950–53) perpetuated the division of Korea into two mutually hostile entities, the North supported by the Soviet Union and China and propelled along Kim Il Sung's idiosyncratic 'road to socialism', and the South supported by the USA and determinedly anti-communist. Kim Il Sung took advantage of the environment engendered by this conflict to further consolidate his power, ruthlessly crushing political opponents, and emerged as the undisputed head of North Korea.

Although he was formally elected president in 1972, Kim's real power base lay in the KWP. Using the vehicle of the single-party state, he promoted an intensely nationalistic economic policy. Predicated on his *juche* ideology, an interpretation of Marxism–Leninism, it stressed socialist self-reliance and absolute devotion to the party and nation-state. However, North Korea's international isolation quickly depressed living standards and led to a steady decline in growth. The economic crisis became especially acute towards the very end of Kim's life as he witnessed the collapse of communism in the former Soviet Union and the transformation of the communist regime in his other main erstwhile ally, China.

The most distinctive feature of Kim's regime was the promotion of a quite extraordinary personality cult. Hailed as the 'great leader' and virtually deified by attributes of infallibility and immortality, he was said to have approved the building of more than 50,000 statues of himself as objects of worship. His portraits hung in every house and more than 20 kinds of Kim Il Sung badges were manufactured for people to wear according to their professional and political status. His 38-volume collected *Works* were made obligatory reading, with the North Korean media also regularly publishing evidence purporting to show people avidly studying them across the world, and he designated his own birthday as 'the greatest national holiday'.

Kim died of a heart attack in Pyongyang on 8 July 1994. His death unleashed nine days of national mourning, culminating in a huge state funeral to which no foreign dignitaries were invited. His body was later embalmed by Russian experts and laid in a coffin at his presidential palace (renamed the Kumsuan Memorial Palace). Amendments to the North Korean constitution in 1998 referred to him as 'eternal president' and went so far as to abolish the post of state president, now that he was no longer available to fill it.

Kim Il Sung married twice, according to unofficial sources. Kim Hye Sun, who claimed to be his first wife, was killed by the Japanese in 1940. His second wife, Kim Chong Suk, the mother of Kim Jong Il, died in 1949. Kim Jong Il was groomed for leadership by his father and designated officially as his successor in 1974, acquiring the title 'dear leader' the following year.

Profile of the Chairman of the Presidium of the Supreme People's Assembly:

KIM Yong Nam

Kim Yong Nam has worked in the foreign affairs department of the ruling Korean Workers' Party (KWP) since 1970. A reclusive and media-shy figure, he was appointed as chairman of the presidium of the Supreme People's Assembly in September 1998, making him North Korea's representative on official occasions. However, he is entirely overshadowed by Kim Jong Il.

Kim Yong Nam was born on 4 February 1928 in North Korea. He graduated from the Kim Il Sung University and then continued his studies in Moscow. He joined the KWP in November 1970 and was appointed chairman of the committee for cultural relations and foreign countries. In 1972 he became vice minister of foreign affairs. Rising steadily through the party hierarchy, he became a secretary in 1975, a political commissar in 1977 and a politburo member in October 1980. He then became director of international development in the KWP and chairman of the committee for Korean reunification.

In 1982 he led the country's delegation to the General Assembly of the UN, and in December 1983 he was appointed as deputy prime minister and minister of foreign affairs. He was also chairman of the central committee of the General Federation of Trade Unions of Korea. In July 1997 at a memorial service to mark the third anniversary of the death of Kim Il Sung, it was Kim Yong Nam who announced that the period of mourning was now over. A recluse who rarely gives interviews, he was seen making frequent domestic speeches at this time, and also made a number of foreign visits in an attempt to secure food and aid for the country. His election by the Supreme People's Assembly in September 1998, to chair its presidium, made him the country's representative on formal occasions. He has since travelled even more widely as North Korea's envoy to the outside world. However, his visits are rarely remarked upon while Kim Jong Il's rare trips beyond North Korea have become the focus of international attention.

Profile of the Chairman of the National Defence Commission:

KIM Jong Il

Kim Jong Il is the eldest son of the now deceased 'eternal president' Kim Il Sung. His presumed leadership role, following the death of his father in July 1994, was not immediately reflected in his formal assumption of top posts. It was not until October 1997 that he became general secretary of the ruling Korean Workers' Party (KWP) and nearly a year later that his post as chairman of the National Defence Commission was formally designated as 'the highest post of the state'. Kim Jong Il has championed 'Red Flag ideology', a loosely defined popularist development of the juche ideology which emphasizes national self-reliance and the special role of the leadership.

Kim Jong Il, the eldest son of Kim Il Sung, was born on 16 February 1942. There are two versions of where this took place. The official version is that he was born in an anti-Japanese guerrilla camp at Mt Paektu in North Korea (the site of which is now visited as part of his cult of personality), and grew up lonely because of his father's frequent absences owing to the duties of political leadership. Others say he was born at a Soviet army camp in Vyatsk, near Khabarovsk, the far-eastern region of the former Soviet Union, where his father was being groomed by the Soviet military to set up and lead a communist party in Korea.

Kim Jong Il is said to have attended several schools, including two in China where he was taken for safety during the Korean War. In 1960 he graduated from Namsan Senior High School. He learned to fly in East Germany, graduated in political and economic sciences from Kim Il Sung University in Pyongyang in 1964, and entered politics after spending some time as a guidance worker.

Kim Jong Il's rise was predictably rapid as he was prepared for the succession by his father, who was venerated in the North Korean state and party system as the 'great leader'. Starting as his father's personal secretary, he moved on to the propaganda and agitation department and the party headquarters, was made deputy director of culture and art, and secretary for organization and propaganda in 1973. He was officially designated heir to Kim Il Sung in 1974 when he was put in charge of party operations against South Korea.

In 1975 Kim Jong Il acquired the title 'dear leader'. This remains the best known of his epithets abroad (where he also has a reputation as a playboy), although North Koreans have been encouraged successively to regard him as 'guiding leader' (1983), 'great guiding leader' (1986), 'unprecedented great man' (1994) and latterly 'outstanding leader'.

In October 1980, after the conclusion of what was believed to have been a power struggle over the succession, Kim Jong Il's position was confirmed by his election to a new presidium of the KWP politburo, the innermost leadership circle. He also joined the party secretariat (headed by his father as general secretary) and the military commission, although it was generally believed that he could not rely on the strength of his support within the armed forces. In confusingly vague terminology, he was named in 1991 as leader of the party (and supreme commander of the armed forces, with the rank of marshal).

During the 1980s in particular, Kim Jong Il was linked directly with a number of acts of state-sponsored terrorism, notably the bombing in 1983 which killed 17 members of a top-level South Korean government delegation in Burma (now Myanmar), and the 1987 bombing of a Korean Airlines plane. There was speculation at this time about his health and stability, and suggestions that Kim Il Sung was displeased by unpredictable actions which he had not himself approved.

When Kim Il Sung died in July 1994, the expectation of a dynastic succession was apparently confirmed by the announcement that Kim Jong Il was taking over all his functions. However, there were no formal appointments until he became party general secretary in October 1997, and his public appearances were unexpectedly infrequent. This encouraged the suggestion that he was ill and that a power struggle was under way, masked by the official explanation that posts were not being filled formally out of respect and mourning for Kim Il Sung. The situation was not clarified until September 1998, when the Supreme People's Assembly formally designated his post as chairman of the National Defence Commission as the 'highest post of the state' (although it also provided that the state would be 'represented on formal occasions' not by him but by the chairman of the Assembly's presidium).

Known increasingly as a recluse, Kim Jong Il has had mixed success in his dealings with the outside world. Relations with South Korea entered what at first promised to be a new era in 2000 when Kim met his South Korean counterpart, President Kim Dae Jung, in June in the first North–South summit since the Korean War. Kim Dae Jung was surprised by a personal reception given by Kim Jong Il at a lavish ceremony at Pyongyang airport and the two leaders signed a landmark agreement which stated eventual reunification to be the ultimate goal and set out plans to reunite separated families, and initiate economic and diplomatic ties. However, the path to peace since then has become confused, with meetings cancelled and projects halted through lack of finance and commitment. Since July 2001 Kim Jong Il has made two trips to neighbouring Russia on board special trains; prior to this he had made only one foreign visit since 1997.

The USA has characterized Kim Jong Il as an erratic and dangerous leader. Increasingly perturbed by North Korea's missile development programme and its nuclear research efforts, relations with the USA sank to a new low following the inauguration of US president George W. Bush in 2001. Kim Jong Il and the North Korean government were horrified to be included in Bush's infamous identification of an 'axis of evil' states sponsoring international terrorism. As tensions mounted, Kim Jong Il reacted with a growing attitude of defiance. By the end of 2002 the issue of North Korea's nuclear power programme and the link to nuclear weapons proliferation seemed to overshadow all previous advances in opening up the north of the traditional 'hermit kingdom'.

Kim Jong Il married Kim Yong Suk in 1973, and they have one son and two daughters. He is also believed to have one daughter by a previous marriage and a son by a former mistress, Sung Hye Rim; her reported presence in Europe in 1996 contributed to press speculation about the impact of defections on the ruling elite.

Profile of the Premier:

HONG Song Nam

Hong Song Nam has had a varying career close to the North Korean leadership. Since 1982 he has by turns been a full member and an alternate member of the politburo of the ruling Korean Workers' Party (KWP). He was formally appointed as premier in September 1998.

Hong Song Nam was born in 1924 in the eastern Kangwon Province which is now divided between North and South Korea. He graduated from Kim Il Sung University in Pyongyang and completed his studies in Czechoslovakia. He began his career as an instructor in the heavy industry ministry in 1954 and became manager of the Kusong Machinery Factory in 1957. He entered government as deputy minister for heavy industry in 1964, becoming full minister in 1971.

Rising rapidly in the KWP hierarchy, Hong Song Nam became deputy premier and chairman of the state planning commission in 1973. He has been a member of the KWP central committee since 1980. He was appointed in 1985 as deputy chairman of the state planning committee, and chaired this body from 1986 to 1989. An alternate member of the KWP politburo from 1982, he was listed in 1986 and 1987 as a full politburo member and first deputy premier, but by March 1989 he was being described once again as an alternate member of the politburo, and in government listings after May 1990 he featured as one of the several deputy premiers with no indication of precedence. It was the use of the title 'acting premier' in his telegram of condolence to the Chinese leadership over Deng Xiaoping's death, in February 1997, which fuelled Western press speculation that Premier Kang Song San might have been purged. He was confirmed as premier in the announcements concerning state leadership posts made on 5 September 1998 by the Supreme People's Assembly.

SOUTH KOREA

Full name: The Republic of Korea.

Leadership structure: The head of state is a president, directly elected by universal adult suffrage. The president's term of office is five years, not renewable. The president appoints the prime minister with the approval of the National Assembly and the other members of the State Council. The prime minister is head of government.

President:	Kim Dae Jung	Since 25 Feb. 1998
Prime Ministers:	Kim Jong Pil (acting from 3 March 1998)	17 Aug. 1998—13 Jan. 2000
	Park Tae Joon	13 Jan. 2000—19 May 2000
	vacant	19 May 2000—22 May 2000
	Lee Han Dong (acting from 23 May 2000)	29 June 2000—11 July 2002
	Chang Sang (acting)	11 July 2002—31 July 2002
	vacant	31 July 2002—9 Aug. 2002
	Chang Dae Whan (acting)	9 Aug. 2002—28 Aug. 2002
	vacant	28 Aug. 2002—10 Sept. 2002
	Kim Suk Soo (acting from 10 Sept. 2002)	Since 5 Oct. 2002

Legislature: The legislature is unicameral. The sole chamber, the National Assembly (Kuk Hoe), has 273 members, directly elected for a four-year term.

Profile of the President:

KIM Dae Jung

Kim Dae Jung was hailed as "South Korea's Nelson Mandela" when his December 1997 election triumph completed his political journey from prison to presidency. Renowned for his integrity, he had been repeatedly imprisoned or exiled, and was even sentenced to death (later commuted) after the Kwangju rising in 1980. However, at other times he played an active part in politics and had already contested three presidential elections before 1997. In office, abandoning centre-left populism, he pursued economic reforms, combining austerity with liberal foreign investment rules and a more flexible labour market.

Kim Dae Jung was born in southwest Korea at Mokpo*, near Kwangju* in the Cholla* region, on 3 December 1925 (or by some accounts one or even two years earlier). Raised as a strict Roman Catholic, he excelled at school, winning entry to the local school of commerce, but his education was interrupted by the Second World War. The ending of the 40 years of Japanese rule in 1945 brought de facto partition of Korea, Soviet forces having liberated the north and US troops the south. By the time the Republic of Korea was declared in 1948, Kim was running the local newspaper in Mokpo.

He fought in the Korean War (1950–53), was captured by the forces of the communist North, and upon his release began a political career, managing in 1960 (on his fifth attempt) to win election to the National Assembly. The legislature was abolished after Gen. Park Chung Hee's military coup in 1961, but elections held in 1963 and 1967 saw Kim again elected and, as a gifted orator, becoming spokesman for the opposition to Park's authoritarian regime. During this period he married for the second time—his first wife having died, leaving him with two children. His second wife, the US-educated Lee Hee Ho, a Protestant doctor's daughter, became his most resolute supporter and political conscience. They had a son and now preside over a growing brood of grandchildren. Kim also found time to attend Kyung-Hee University Business School from 1964, and read economics at the graduate school there in 1970.

For the 1971 presidential elections Kim was chosen as the candidate of the left-of-centre opposition New Democratic Party, with a support base among blue-collar workers and students augmented by Kim's personal popularity in his native Cholla region. Despite the Park government's attempts to discredit him as a communist, and a car accident which many believed was really the first of several assassination attempts against him, he mounted an unexpectedly strong challenge, obtaining 45% of the vote. Refusing an ultimatum to join Park's party, he fled instead to Japan, but in 1973 was abducted from Tokyo (allegedly in a CIA-backed secret service operation) and returned to Seoul under house arrest. Imprisoned again from 1976 to 1978 for his criticisms of the Park regime, Kim became the focus of a pro-democracy campaign in which his wife played a key role, organizing choruses of slogans sung after services in the churches by groups of women in hibiscus-coloured shawls.

The May 1980 Kwangju rising, brutally crushed by the army, led to Kim's arrest yet again, this time on charges of plotting to overthrow the government. A death sentence passed on him in September was commuted to life imprisonment as a result of international pressure, and later reduced to 20 years, but in December 1982, due to his ill health, Kim was released in a general amnesty and allowed to travel to the USA for medical treatment.

Effectively exiled in the USA, Kim issued a joint declaration with the other main opposition leader Kim Young Sam committing themselves to work together to end the military regime, now led by President Chun Doo Hwan. He was placed under house arrest when he returned to Seoul in 1985 ahead of legislative elections, in which his supporters performed strongly. A merger with Kim Young Sam's party in April 1987 was reversed, however, just one month before the presidential elections which the regime had unexpectedly agreed to hold by direct ballot that December. This debilitating division in the opposition let Chun's successor Roh Tae Woo retain power; Kim Dae Jung, as leader of his new Party for Peace and Democracy (PPD), polled almost 27% of the vote and finished third, just behind Kim Young Sam.

In 1989, in the latest of many attempts to portray him as 'soft' towards the communist North, Kim was indicted over talks between a PPD representative and the North Korean government. The following year the ruling party achieved a dramatic political coup by absorbing two former opposition groups, co-opting Kim Young Sam on the understanding that he would succeed Roh as the first government-backed civilian candidate for the presidency in 1992. In that election Kim Dae Jung, having helped create a new Democratic Party in 1991 in an effort to rally the remaining opposition, came second behind Kim Young Sam with 34% of the vote.

Although Kim Dae Jung retired from the political arena in 1993, the growing popular disillusionment with Kim Young Sam's government, and the encouragement of his wife, resulted in his return in mid-1995. His National Congress for New Politics (NCNP), despite attracting defectors from the Democratic Party, performed unexpectedly poorly in legislative elections in April 1996, when Kim himself failed to win a seat.

In the run-up to the 1997 presidential elections, the NCNP formed an alliance with the United Liberal Democrats, who had broken away from the ruling party in 1995. Kim became their joint candidate, and in a closely contested campaign he emerged on 18 December as the ultimate winner, just ahead of the ruling party's candidate, who was damaged by a third candidate splitting the vote. Kim's success, which was the country's first ever opposition election victory, was greeted with particular jubilation in Seoul and in Kwangju in his native Cholla region, as tributes poured in to his character and political rectitude. His promises on the release of political prisoners were followed up with a wide-ranging amnesty which included ex-presidents Chun and Roh, who had both persecuted Kim while in power, and were serving long prison terms for corruption and in Chun's case for instigating the 1980 Kwangju massacre.

Celebrations of Kim's election were overshadowed, however, by the need for urgent action on the economy. Caught up in the region-wide crisis as foreign investors pulled out in a collective loss of confidence, South Korea faced calls for major reform, including the restructuring and improved regulation of its powerful industrial–financial conglomerates (*chaebols*), and a heavy dose of austerity measures. It was Kim Dae Jung, rather than the outgoing 'lame duck' Kim Young Sam, who had to put together a package of proposals to meet the conditions required by the International Monetary Fund (IMF) for its support.

General austerity measures, coupled with injections of aid from the IMF, proved early successes for Kim Dae Jung's presidency. However, it was not enough to prevent a number of bankruptcies in late 2000. Kim apologized to the nation on 1 January 2001 for the economy's poor performance but predicted growth in the near future. Relative to the economic slowdown which gripped the world from 2001 the economy has not fared too badly; however, by the end of 2002 the staggering levels of personal debt promised trouble for Kim's successor.

Aside from the economy, Kim's most impressive success came in relations with North Korea. The first North–South summit since the Korean War took place in Pyongyang, North Korea, in June 2000. The meeting was a breakthrough and many projects and cross-border links have been established. Kim was awarded the Nobel Peace Prize on 13 October. However, the climbing cost of maintaining the 'sunshine' policy and the reticence and erratic behaviour of the North Korean government dulled the initial shine. After North Korea was included in the 'axis of evil' by US president George W. Bush in February 2002, it was left to Kim's heir apparent, president-elect Roh Moo Hyun, to take the initiative in pushing forward the North–South détente once again.

Politically Kim has been stymied by his weak parliamentary base. His newly created Millennium Democratic Party (MDP) increased its representation in the April 2000 election but was still overshadowed by the opposition Grand National Party (GNP). Throughout his presidency Kim's choices of prime minister have become a focus of a show of strength by the GNP. In 1998 it tried to block the appointment of Kim Jong Pil and successfully rejected two candidates in 2002 for financial irregularities. Also in 2002 the conviction of Kim's two youngest sons for corruption damaged the popularity of the former people's champion. Nonetheless, his chosen successor Roh Moo Hyun was able to rally support behind the MDP and was elected to take over from Kim when he steps down in 2003.

Profile of the President-elect:

ROH Moo Hyun

Roh Moo Hyun is a member of the ruling Millennium Democratic Party (MDP). Popularly seen as a champion of the poor, he found renown as a human rights lawyer when he prosecuted former top officials during televised corruption trials in 1988. He advocates continuing the policy of negotiation with the erratic North Korean government and rejects demands from the conservative opposition for a more market-oriented economic policy. He won a tight presidential election in

December 2002 with 49% of the vote and is due to be inaugurated on 25 February 2003.

Roh Moo Hyun was born on 6 August 1946 in rural Kimhae*, in southeastern Korea, to a poor peasant family. After graduating from high school in 1966 he was unable to afford formal tertiary education and instead supported himself with menial labour through self-study. He married his childhood sweetheart Kwon Yang Sook in 1971 and they have two children. In 1975 he passed his Bar exam and began his own law practice in Pusan* in 1978.

In 1981 Roh took on the case of one of over 20 students who had been arrested and brutally tortured by the military authorities. Known as the Boolim Incident, the case confirmed Roh as a prominent human rights advocate and as a member of the strengthening pro-democracy movement. In 1987 he was arrested and jailed for three weeks for aiding striking workers during the 'June Struggle' at the Daewoo docks. He moved into the country's newly democratized political sphere in 1988 when he was elected to parliament for the Unified Democratic Party of future president Kim Young Sam. The televised trials that year of former military officials brought Roh to political and public attention for his detailed and thorough questioning. During the 1990s he moved between parliamentary and legal work as he lost his seat in the 1992 election but returned to the chamber in a 1998 by-election.

Despite failing to win a parliamentary seat in the 2000 legislative elections, Roh was made a member of the MDP's Supreme Council and served as maritime affairs and fisheries minister in the cabinet of President Kim Dae Jung between August 2000 and March 2001. Six months later he declared his bid to gain the MDP nomination for the 2002 presidential elections. Once selected, his campaign was boosted when he proved the popular victor of a televised debate with fellow contender Chung Mung Joon and was accepted as the single liberal candidate. However, Chung withdrew his support just hours before polling began in protest over Roh's suggestion that if elected he would seek to mediate between the USA and North Korea, rather than simply backing the USA. In the event Roh won 49% of the vote.

Profile of the Prime Minister:

KIM Suk Soo

Kim Suk Soo is an independent former Supreme Court judge. He has, however, been linked to the opposition Grand National Party. He notably headed the National Election Commission from 1993 to 1997 and was the president's third successive nomination for prime minister when he was accepted by the National Assembly on 5 October 2002.

Kim Suk Soo was born on 20 November 1932 in Hadong in the far south. He was educated in Seoul in the 1950s and graduated from Yonsei University in the capital with a law degree in 1956. Two years later he passed his judicial Bar exam. He is married to Eom Yoon Song and they have four children.

Between 1960 and 1988 Kim served as a judge in a number of courts based largely in either Pusan* or Seoul—beginning as a judge advocate with the military in 1960, entering civilian court service three years later in Pusan, and rising by 1988 to be chief judge at the Pusan district court. With the emergence of the Sixth Republic in 1988 he was appointed to direct government service as vice minister of court administration.

In 1991 Kim was elected to be a Supreme Court judge. He sat on the court for six years until January 1997. He also headed the National Election Commission from 1993, earning a reputation for fairness. Once he stepped down from the Supreme Court, Kim became involved in supervising legal ethics, beginning with the judicial officers' ethics committee of the Supreme Court itself, and including posts with the Korea Press Ethics Committee and the Public Service Ethics Committee in the government. In 1999 he also took up a directorship at the Samsung Electronics Company.

He abandoned all of these positions in September 2002 in an effort to clear himself for parliamentary approval as prime minister. In the two months before that, President Kim Dae Jung had unsuccessfully nominated two other candidates for the position, both of whom had been rejected by the National Assembly on technicalities. Although concerned that the exemption of one of his sons from military service might blight his own candidature, Kim Suk Soo was approved on 5 October. In view of his experience at the election commission, it was thought to be no coincidence that he took up the post of prime minister two months before presidential elections.

---

* Following the revised Romanization of Korean in 2000, Mokp'o became known as Mokpo, Kwangju as Gwangju, Cholla as Jolla, Kimhae as Gimhae and Pusan as Busan.

KUWAIT

Full name: The State of Kuwait.

Leadership structure: The head of state is an amir, chosen from among the ruling family. The amir exercises executive power through the Council of Ministers, which is headed by the prime minister.

Amir: Sheikh Jaber al-Ahmad al-Jaber al-Sabah   Since 31 Dec. 1977

Prime Minister: Sheikh Saad al-Abdullah al-Salim al-Sabah Since 8 Feb. 1978

Legislature: The legislature is unicameral. The sole chamber, the National Assembly (Majlis al-Umma), has 50 members, directly elected for a four-year term. Women do not have the vote. Cabinet ministers who are not already members of the National Assembly are ex officio members of it.

Profile of the Amir:

Sheikh **JABER** al-Ahmad al-Jaber al-Sabah

Sheikh Jaber is the 13th amir chosen from within the al-Sabah family, the Sunni Muslim ruling dynasty since 1756. Ousted by the Iraqi invasion of August 1990, he was restored to power eight months later by the forces of the US-led alliance in the Gulf War. The following year he agreed to an element of liberalization in his autocratic regime, holding legislative elections and bringing some opposition National Assembly members into a cabinet previously made up entirely of members of the royal family.

Jaber al-Ahmad al-Jaber al-Sabah was born in 1928, educated at the Mubarakiya, Ahmadiya and Sharqiya schools, and tutored privately in English, religion and the sciences. He started his public life in 1949 as chief of public security in the oilfields area, a post he held until 1959, when he was made head of the finance department. After Kuwait gained its independence in 1961, the finance department became the ministry of finance and economy, and Sheikh Jaber was appointed its first minister. In 1965 he was appointed prime minister, and on 31 May 1966 he was elected crown prince by the National Assembly. Proclaimed amir of Kuwait on 31 December 1977, he was unanimously given the pledge of allegiance on 1 January 1978.

Since 1986 the amir has been a member of the board of directors of the Kuwait Investment Authority, and since 1987 a member of the higher planning council.

Since 1989 he has been chairman of the committee for measures to activate the economy.

When Kuwait was invaded by Iraq in August 1990 the al-Sabah family went into exile, returning on 14 March 1991 after the country had been liberated and Iraqi forces defeated by a US-led alliance. On 20 April the first cabinet since the liberation of Kuwait was announced by amiri decree, and on 9 July the amir opened the second session of the advisory National Council, relaying his thanks to those countries which had come to Kuwait's aid. In response to pressure for a measure of democratization, elections were held (on a nonparty basis) in October 1992 to the National Assembly, which had been in abeyance since the amir dissolved the previous Assembly in 1986. Some opposition Assembly members were then brought in to the Council of Ministers.

Some concern about the succession was raised in September 2001 when the amir was flown to the UK to receive treatment for a mild brain haemorrhage. However, he soon returned and has since made a full recovery.

Profile of the Prime Minister:

Sheikh **SAAD** al-Abdullah al-Salim al-Sabah

Sheikh Saad, second cousin of the current amir, has been crown prince of Kuwait since January 1978, and was appointed prime minister the following month. Sheikh Saad is also ex officio chairman of the supreme defence council, the supreme petroleum council, the civil service commission and the higher housing council.

Saad al-Abdullah al-Salim al-Sabah was born in 1930, and educated at government schools in Kuwait. In 1951 he went to the UK to attend Hendon College to take a postgraduate course on police and security affairs. Returning to Kuwait in 1954, he held various posts in the police and public security department and was later appointed deputy chief of police and public security. Sheikh Saad is married to Sheikha Latifah Fahd al-Sabah, and has one son and four daughters

Kuwait became fully independent from the UK in June 1961, with Sheikh Saad's father Sheikh Abdullah al-Sabah as amir, and Saad entered the new cabinet as interior minister in January 1962. In 1964 he also became defence minister, retaining both posts on the accession of his uncle Sheikh Sabah the following year. His election as crown prince in 1978, and his appointment as prime minister, followed the accession of his second cousin Sheikh Jaber, only two years his senior, as amir.

Sheikh Saad was reappointed prime minister on 3 March 1985 after the election of a new Assembly. This Assembly was dissolved the following year, reinforcing the concentration of power in the hands of the ruling al-Sabah family, after disputes between elected and ex officio Assembly members over internal security and fiscal issues.

When Kuwait was invaded by Iraq in August 1990 the al-Sabah family went into exile, returning on 14 March 1991 after the country had been liberated and the Iraqi forces defeated by a US-led alliance. Sheikh Saad has been consistently reappointed after elections in October 1992 and 1996 and July 1999, to the disappointment of Kuwaitis hoping for fresh leadership to reflect the election of many of the government's critics to the Assembly. He was also reinstated after he resigned in March 1998 during conflict with the Assembly. Such confrontations have become more regular as the Assembly has voiced its lack of confidence in the ruling family's government.

KYRGYZSTAN

Full name: The Kyrgyz Republic.

Leadership structure: The head of state is a president, directly elected by universal adult suffrage. The president's term of office is five years and is renewable once only, according to the 1994 Constitution. The prime minister is head of government. The president nominates the prime minister (who must be approved by the Supreme Council) and the other members of the government.

President:	Askar Akayev	Since 28 Oct. 1990

Prime Ministers:	Amangeldy Muraliyev (acting from 12 April 1999, and from 11 Dec. 2000)	21 April 1999—21 Dec. 2000
	Kurmanbek Bakiyev	21 Dec. 2000—22 May 2002
	Nikolay Tanayev (acting from 22 May 2002)	Since 30 May 2002

Legislature: The legislature, the Supreme Council (Jogorku Kenesh), is bicameral. The lower chamber, the Legislative Assembly (Myizam Chygaru Palatasy), has 60 members, directly elected for a five-year term, 15 of them elected on a party-list basis and the rest on a constituency basis. The upper chamber, the Assembly of People's Representatives (El Okuldor Palatasy), has 45 members, chosen for a five-year term and representing the different regional and ethnic communities.

Profile of the President:

Askar **AKAYEV**

An applied scientist by training, Askar Akayev had a distinguished academic career under the Soviet regime, as well as heading the science and academic departments of the Kyrgyz Communist Party (KCP). He became Kyrgyz president shortly before the breakup of the Soviet Union and has retained power since then, identifying himself with the objectives of creating a market economy and making his country a financial services centre for central Asia.

Askar Akayevich Akayev was born into a farming family on 10 November 1944, in the village of Kyzyl-Bairak in the Kemin district of Kyrgyzstan. He was an academically gifted student, becoming a doctor of technical science after he graduated from the Leningrad Precision Mechanics and Optics Institute in 1967. He married Mairam in 1970 and they have two sons and two daughters.

Akayev made his early career as a laboratory researcher, engineer, lecturer and professor, and rose to be chairman of what is now the Bishkek Technical University. He was elected vice president of the Kyrgyz Academy of Sciences in 1987, and its president in 1989, and is a member of several such bodies internationally, including the New York Academy of Sciences. His scientific work includes a mathematical study of the problems of heating of computers.

A member of the Communist Party of the Soviet Union (CPSU) from 1981, Akayev headed the KCP central committee's department of science and higher education in 1986–87. In October 1990 the legislature elected him president of the Kyrgyz Soviet Socialist Republic. He was confirmed in a popular poll in October 1991 as the first president of independent Kyrgyzstan, and commander-in-chief of the armed forces.

Having dismissed members of his government's economic team in early 1993 for obstructing the privatization programme, Akayev backed the founding that year of a new Social Democratic Party of Kyrgyzstan, and the following January he won overwhelming support in a referendum on his economic reform programme. Resistance to these far-reaching changes within the legislature persisted, however, in response to which Akayev pushed through, by referendum, changes to both the legislative structure and the distribution of power between president and parliament. In late 1995 he succeeded in getting presidential elections brought forward, to allow him to seek a fresh mandate. This he obtained in the poll on 24 December 1995, claiming the support of over 70% of those voting, and thus overwhelmingly defeating the communist candidate and the one other opposition candidate.

On 13 July 1998 the Constitutional Court ruled that Akayev's re-election as president in 1995 had effectively been his first election under the new constitution. This meant he was permitted to seek a 'second' and final term in office. He won a resounding 74% of the vote on 29 October 2000 despite widespread accusations of irregularities from international observers. In one case a batch of ballot papers marked in Akayev's favour were discovered before the poll had even begun. The chairman of the central election commission admitted that violations had taken place, prompting mass demonstrations. Akayev was inaugurated for his third period in office on 9 December.

Protests against Akayev's rule intensified in 2002 after he was accused of ordering police to open fire on demonstrators on 17 March; five people had been killed. The government of Kurmanbek Bakiyev was forced to resign in May, and anger at Akayev himself continued, with over 1,000 people joining a protest march to Bishkek in September.

Profile of the Prime Minister:

Nikolay **TANAYEV**

Nikolay Tanayev, the first ethnic Russian to be appointed prime minister of Kyrgyzstan, came to the region as an engineer in the Soviet period. Although he has considerable experience in running official bodies in the construction industry, he had been in government for only 16 months when he was asked to take over the premiership.

Nikolay Timofeyevich Tanayev was born on 5 November 1945 in the village of Mikhaylovka in the Penza region of European Russia, near the Volga River. He began his connection with Soviet central Asia when he attended the Jambyl Hydroengineering Institute in the south of Kazakhstan, near the present-day border with Kyrgyzstan. He graduated in engineering in 1969 and began a career involved in infrastructure projects in the region. From 1984 to 1985 he was head of the Osh regional water canal project in western Kyrgyzstan and from 1985 he chaired the Chuy Industrial Construction Trust in Bishkek.

In 2000 Tanayev began working directly for the Kyrgyz government when he became chairman of the state commission on architecture and construction. He was promoted to the cabinet as first deputy prime minister in the government of Prime Minister Kurmanbek Bakiyev in January 2001. The following year the government was plunged into crisis when security forces opened fire on demonstrators killing five people. Accusations that the government had ordered the shooting led to the cabinet's resignation on 22 May. Tanayev was appointed acting prime minister and was confirmed in the post at the end of the month. His new cabinet was mostly unchanged.

LAOS

Full name: The Lao People's Democratic Republic.

Leadership structure: The head of state is a president, elected by the National Assembly. The president's term of office is five years. The head of government is the prime minister, who is appointed by the president, although it is the sole and ruling party, the Lao People's Revolutionary Party (LPRP), which is described as the "leading nucleus" of the political system. The Council of Ministers is appointed by the president.

President: Gen. Khamtay Siphandone Since 24 Feb. 1998

Prime Ministers: Gen. Sisavat Keobounphanh 24 Feb. 1998—27 March 2001

Bounnyang Vorachit Since 27 March 2001

President of the Lao People's Revolutionary Party (LPRP):

Gen. Khamtay Siphandone Since 24 Nov. 1992

Legislature: The legislature is unicameral. The sole chamber, the National Assembly (Sapha Heng Xat), has 109 members directly elected in single-party elections for a five-year term.

Profile of the President:

Gen. **KHAMTAY** Siphandone

Gen. Khamtay Siphandone, a veteran communist fighter and stalwart of the Lao People's Revolutionary Party (LPRP), was elected as prime minister by the National Assembly in 1991. He greatly strengthened his position in the leadership the following year when he became party chairman. It was evident that his authority surpassed that of the then state president, Nouhak Phoumsavanh, and since 1998 Khamtay has combined the party chairmanship with the state presidency.

Khamtay Siphandone was born on 8 February 1924 in Houa Khong village, Champasak Province. He is married to Thongvanh Siphandone. From the early 1950s he was a prominent member of the insurgent Lao Patriotic Front (LPF), chairing its control committee from 1952 until 1954. Between 1955 and 1956 he was a member of the general staff of the Pathet Lao, the LPF's armed forces, and in 1960 he became its commander-in-chief, leading the military struggle in the protracted civil war until the establishment of the communist People's Democratic Republic in late 1975. Between 1975 and 1991 he was deputy prime minister and minister of national defence.

In 1982 Khamtay became part of the nine-member secretariat of the LPRP, the former People's Party of Laos which had been the dominant force in the LPF. His position on the 11-member politburo was confirmed at the party's fifth congress in March 1991. Upon the adoption of the new constitution that August, veteran leader Khaysone Phomvihane moved up from chairing the Council of Ministers to the new executive presidency, leaving the way open for Khamtay to succeed him as prime minister and head of government.

When Khaysone died in November 1992, creating vacancies in both the state and party presidency, the state presidency went to the erstwhile 'number three', Nouhak Phoumsavanh, while Khamtay became LPRP party president. Khamtay was re-elected unanimously to the party presidency at the sixth LPRP congress in March 1996 and became vice president, whereas Nouhak Phoumsavanh was relegated from the politburo to the advisory council of 'old guard' leaders. Khamtay's ascendancy was confirmed in February 1998 when the newly re-elected National Assembly voted him state president. He was reappointed party chairman in March 2001 and state president in April 2002.

Khamtay represents the continuing importance of the civil war generation, holding the top posts while younger cadres compete for position and the country faces the immense challenges of economic restructuring. Khamtay's cautious leadership, and the determination that economic liberalization should not be accompanied by any relaxation of the party's political grip, have not prevented major moves since the 1991 party congress towards opening up the economy to market forces. This trend was accelerated at the international level by the country's admission in 1997 to the Association of South East Asian Nations (ASEAN).

Profile of the Prime Minister:

BOUNNYANG Vorachit

Bounnyang Vorachit was a prominent member of the Pathet Lao armed independence movement, having joined the liberation struggle in 1952 at the age of 14. Later becoming a regional governor and then mayor of the capital, Vientiane, in the mid-1990s, he became a member of the politburo of the ruling Lao People's Revolutionary Party (LPRP) in 1996 and was appointed to the cabinet at the same time. His elevation to the premiership was decided at the LPRP's seventh congress in March 2001.

Bounnyang Vorachit was born on 15 August 1937 in Na village in the Savannakhet region of southern Laos which was then under French colonial rule.

Dropping out of school, he joined the burgeoning communist Lao People's Party in 1952 and was immediately drafted into its armed wing (the basis for the future Pathet Lao). For the rest of the violent struggle to create a communist state in Laos, Bounnyang divided his time between serving in the command structure of the Pathet Lao and studying at military colleges in communist Viet Nam. He is married to Khammeung Vorachit and they have five children.

In 1980 Bounnyang returned from his last study trip to Viet Nam and capped his military career by being appointed political chief of the Central Armed Force. Two years later he switched to civilian administration when he was made governor of Savannakhet province and was promoted to the LPRP's central committee. He held the governorship for ten years before becoming mayor of Vientiane in 1993. In 1996 he climbed further up the LPRP hierarchy and was admitted to the party's politburo as deputy prime minister and chairman of the Laos–Viet Nam co-operation committee. In 1999 he was awarded the additional finance portfolio, confirming his importance within the government structure. At the LPRP's seventh congress in March 2001 Bounnyang was appointed prime minister.

LATVIA

Full name: The Republic of Latvia.

Leadership structure: The head of state is a president, indirectly elected by Parliament. The president's term of office is four years, renewable once only. The head of government is the prime minister, who is responsible to Parliament. The cabinet is appointed by the prime minister.

President:	Vaira Vike-Freiberga	Since 8 July 1999
Prime Ministers:	Andris Škele	16 June 1999—5 May 2000
	Andris Berzinš	5 May 2000—7 Nov. 2002
	Einars Repše	Since 7 Nov. 2002

Legislature: The legislature is unicameral. The sole chamber, the Parliament (Saeima), has 100 members, directly elected for a four-year term.

Profile of the President:

Vaira **VIKE-FREIBERGA**

Vaira Vike-Freiberga is the first female president of Latvia, and indeed of any former-Soviet east European state. Although born in Riga she became a refugee at the end of the Second World War and has spent most of her life abroad, mainly in Canada where she emigrated in 1954 and became a psychology professor.

Vaira Vike (who added the Freiberga suffix once married) was born on 1 December 1937 in Riga. At the end of the Second World War her family fled the Soviet advance through Latvia and she spent her early life in a refugee camp in Lübeck, West Germany. Her family moved on from Germany to Morocco, then under French administration, in 1949 and she attended college in Casablanca from 1950. Four years later she emigrated to Canada.

While working part-time as a supervisor at an all-girls' boarding school in Toronto, she studied for a degree in English language at Victoria College, University of Toronto, graduating in 1958. Along with Latvian and English she is fluent in five European languages. She put her knowledge of Spanish to use as a part-time translator and Spanish teacher at Ontario Ladies' College while studying for her master's degree in psychology at the University of Toronto, graduating in 1960. She is married to Imants Freibergs, a Latvian-born professor of computer science, whom she met while helping to organize a Latvian Youth Festival in Toronto (and with whom she published a book on Latvian folk songs, their shared passion, in 1988). They have two children.

She worked as a clinical psychologist in Toronto's Psychiatric Hospital for a year before returning to full-time education to study for her doctorate in experimental psychology at McGill University in Montréal, Québec, in 1961. In 1965, as a qualified doctor of psychology, she was appointed as an assistant professor at the Université de Montréal, where she worked for the next 33 years until her return to Latvia in 1998. As an academic she has published seven books and over 250 articles and speeches on psychology and research.

Since gaining full professorship in 1979 Vike-Freiberga has served as president of the Social Science Federation of Canada (1980), president of the Canadian Psychological Association, and vice chairman of the Canadian Science Council (1984–89). She was also president of the US-based Association for the Advancement of Baltic Studies in 1984–86.

In 1998 Vike-Freiberga returned to Latvia to become director of the Latvian Institute in Riga. One year later she stood as an independent in the presidential election, defeating six other better known candidates in seven rounds of voting in the Parliament, eventually gaining 53 of the 100 votes. She took office on 8 July 1999. One of her first acts as president was to return to the Parliament a controversial bill to protect and overtly promote the use of Latvian. She also voiced concern over the new aggressive foreign policy seemingly emerging in neighbouring Russia following the election there of President Vladimir Putin in 2000. Relations between the two countries remain strained. During her term Latvia also began official negotiations for membership of the European Union (EU), now scheduled for 2004.

Profile of the Prime Minister:

Einars **REPŠE**

Einars Repše is the founder and leader of the right-of-centre New Era party (Jaunais Laiks—JL). A computer engineer by training, he was prominent in the independence movement and was made governor of the Bank of Latvia in 1991 at the age of just 29. He is now known as the father of the Latvian currency, the lats, and enjoys massive personal popularity. His eight-month-old JL stormed the polls in October 2002, sweeping aside the previous ruling parties. He now heads a four-party conservative coalition.

Einars Repše was born in Jelgava on 9 December 1961 when Latvia still formed an integral part of the Soviet Union. He graduated in physics from the University of Latvia in 1986 and began work as a computer systems designer in the special bureau of scientific instrument design at the Latvian Academy of Sciences. He married Diana Vagale in 1988. They had three children, but are now divorced.

As the Soviet Union headed towards collapse in the late 1980s, Repše helped found the Latvian Independence Movement in 1988 and became a member of the Popular Front in the same year. As the dream of independence became reality, he was elected to the transitional Supreme Council in 1990 and became chairman of the banking and finance subcommittee of the economic committee. In this position he authored plans to reform the country's monetary policy in order to break free from the hold of the Russian rouble. He was elected governor of the Bank of Latvia in September 1991.

During his ten-year tenure Repše oversaw the reform of the monetary laws and the creation of the lats. His work was so successful that he was re-elected by the Parliament in 1997 and awarded the country's highest honour, the Order of the Three Stars. Repše resigned from the bank in November 2001, a year before the end of his six-year term of office. He formed the JL in February 2002 and led it to a significant victory at the polls that October, when it became the largest party with 26 of the 100 seats in the Parliament. He was asked to form a government, and put together his coalition team over the next month.

LEBANON

Full name: The Republic of Lebanon.

Leadership structure: The head of state is a president, elected by the National Assembly. The president's term of office is six years, nonrenewable. The head of government is the prime minister, who is appointed by the president following consultations with the members of the National Assembly.

President:	Gen. Emile Lahoud	Since 24 Nov. 1998
Prime Ministers:	Salim al-Hoss	2 Dec. 1998—23 Oct. 2000
	Rafiq al-Hariri	Since 23 Oct. 2000

Legislature: The legislature is unicameral. The sole chamber, the National Assembly (Majlis al-Nawab), has 128 members, divided equally between Christians and Muslims, directly elected for a maximum four-year term.

Profile of the President:

Gen. Emile **LAHOUD**

Gen. Emile Lahoud is a Maronite Christian and the son of the prominent pro-independence leader Jamil Lahoud. He himself was a naval officer who rose to head the armed forces from the end of the civil war in 1989 until his election as president nine years later, and he is credited with having reformed the military after the destructive conflict. His appointment required a change in the constitution to allow a state official to hold the office, but was assured after he received Syrian backing. Since he has been president, Israel has withdrawn from the occupied southern part of Lebanon.

Emile Jamil Lahoud was born a member of the Maronite Christian community of Beirut on 12 January 1936. His father Gen. Jamil Lahoud is popularly seen as the creator of the national army and a key figure in the country's struggle for independence from France in the 1940s. Jamil Lahoud went on to serve as labour and social welfare minister and earned the nickname 'the Red General' for his concern for the working classes.

Emile Lahoud was educated in Lebanon and joined the country's military academy as a naval cadet in 1956. Two years later he began the first of a number of military training courses abroad, starting with studies in naval engineering in the UK. Foreign training was interspersed with visits home and promotion in the navy. In 1959 he was appointed to command his first ship, the *Beirut*, and by 1966 he had been placed in command of the 2nd division of ships before heading to the USA for further training. He was assigned to the Fourth Bureau of the Army Command as a lieutenant in 1970 and, after attending staff college in Rhode Island, USA, became chief of staff in the office of the Lebanese army in 1973. Meanwhile, in 1967 he had married Andrée Amadouny, with whom he has three children.

Following the outbreak of civil war in Lebanon in 1975, Lahoud was promoted to the rank of commander and was sent back to Rhode Island to complete his training. He returned in 1980 as a captain and was immediately appointed director of personnel in Army Command, later moving to the military office in the embattled government's ministry of defence in 1983. After six more years of destructive conflict, during which the army disintegrated into Muslim and Christian militias, the Syrian-brokered Taïf Agreement brought a long-awaited peace to the country. Lahoud was elevated to commander of the armed forces in November 1989 and took charge of the fractious army, navy and air force with a clear vision of reconstruction in mind.

Early in 1990 Lahoud constituted an emergency plan for the armed forces based on three main principles: that the army be rebuilt with the aid of Syria, that Lebanon concentrate its foreign policy on resisting Israeli aggression, and above all that the army stay firmly out of politics. The restoration of relative stability to the country has been popularly credited to the success of his plan and the unified, apolitical military machine it created. Lahoud's popularity coupled with his proven obedience to Syria and his staunch creed of apoliticism made him a perfect candidate for president (an office traditionally held by a Christian) in 1998, based on the perception that what was achieved in the armed forces could be achieved for the country.

To enable Lahoud's election, his predecessor urged the National Assembly to adopt the necessary alterations to the constitution, which at that time barred military figures from holding the office. The passage of the necessary amendment was assured after Lahoud received the political backing of the Syrian government and he took office in November 1998. Under his presidency Lebanon has battled with corruption and introduced moderate economic liberalization with relative success.

Elections in 2000 toppled the government of Prime Minister Salim al-Hoss. The elections were won by supporters of Rafiq al-Hariri, who had refused in 1998 to continue as prime minister under Lahoud's presidency. Now Hariri was reappointed, leading to a period of 'cohabitation' between the two men. In May 2000 Israel fulfilled its earlier promises and comprehensively withdrew from southern Lebanon although Lahoud protested at the minor infractions of the border still being committed by the former occupiers.

Profile of the Prime Minister:

Rafiq al-**HARIRI**

Rafiq al-Hariri is a Sunni Muslim, as Lebanese prime ministers are required to be under the convention whereby the principal political offices are shared between members of the main religious communities. Hariri is, however, the leader of a nonconfessional bloc, which at both the 1996 and the 2000 elections won a substantial proportion of the seats in the Lebanese parliament. His main distinction is that he is an energetic, successful and immensely wealthy building magnate, who was first appointed prime minister of Lebanon in October 1992 promising policies for economic revival, and who delivered on his promise by encouraging a spectacular construction boom, in Beirut in particular.

Rafiq Bahaa Edine al-Hariri was born in 1944 in Sidon, Lebanon. Interrupting his studies at Beirut University, he emigrated to Saudi Arabia in 1965, subsequently becoming a Saudi national. Supporting himself at first by teaching, he soon became involved with the financial management of an engineering company. Within five years he had established his own construction company, the first of a number of enterprises which he has founded in the course of his successful business career. In 1978 he set up Oger-Saudi Arabia, which later became part of the conglomerate Oger-International, and went on to acquire the MIG group which includes banks in Lebanon and Saudi Arabia, and companies involved in a variety of fields including publishing, computers and insurance. He is married to Nazik Audeh and has five children.

After the Israeli invasion of Lebanon in 1982, Hariri participated in the Geneva and Lausanne conferences, which attempted unsuccessfully to put an end to the conflict in his native country. He has also used his enormous wealth to support philanthropic projects in Lebanon, including student loans through the Hariri Foundation, the creation of an Islamic Institute of Higher Education in Sidon, the reconstruction of war-damaged areas of Beirut and Tripoli and the building of a medical, educational and sporting complex in the south. In 1989 he endorsed the Taïf agreement, negotiated in Saudi Arabia and providing a political framework for ending the Lebanese civil war.

A general election in August and October 1992, held to implement the Taïf agreement and with a substantial Syrian military presence still in place, opened the way for Lebanese President Elias Hrawi to offer Hariri the premiership on 22 October. The deal which was effectively struck at this time, and which also involved, crucially, the endorsement of newly elected National Assembly speaker and Shi'a Muslim leader Nabih Berri, proved to be a basis for a period of comparative peace and economic revival, albeit with Syria continuing to be closely involved.

Hariri formed a second government in 1996 after parliamentary elections in August and October, at which his own nonconfessional list won most of the Beirut seats and in all some 20 seats in the 128-member National Assembly (with pro-Hariri candidates winning a substantial proportion of the rest). The success of his list and of his various allies was a triumph for Hariri, notwithstanding the claims that it was achieved, with strong Syrian backing, by the use of some overtly political strategies (such as the drawing of electoral boundaries in Mount Lebanon to suit Druze leader Walid Joumblatt in return for the latter's support) and, allegedly, by the widespread buying of votes. Hariri's new government, whose membership had been discussed in advance with President Hafez al-Assad of Syria and was calculated to draw in all possible factions without including any of his personal adversaries, won a vote of confidence by 102 votes to 19 in November 1996.

Declining to take up the premiership in a new government following the election of President Emile Lahoud in October 1998, Hariri established himself as the principal opposition to the new prime minister Salim al-Hoss. Despite renewed initiatives in the peace process with neighbouring Israel, Hoss proved unable to maintain his popularity and in the August 2000 elections Hariri and his supporters achieved a significant victory, gaining around 100 seats in the National Assembly. Hariri's campaign had allegedly cost him a total of US$50 million. Since his return to power an alleged power-sharing deal with President Lahoud has done little to prevent increased tension between the two men.

LESOTHO

Full name: The Kingdom of Lesotho.

Leadership structure: The head of state is a hereditary monarch. The head of government is the prime minister, leader of the majority parliamentary party, who appoints the cabinet.

King: Letsie III   Since 7 Feb. 1996

Prime Minister: Bethuel Pakalitha Mosisili   Since 29 May 1998

Legislature: The legislature, the Parliament, is bicameral. The lower chamber, the National Assembly, has 120 members, elected for a five-year term. The upper chamber, the Senate, has 33 members, comprising 22 principal chiefs and 11 other members named by the king.

Profile of the King:

LETSIE III

King Letsie III replaced his father, King Moshoeshoe II, as head of state of Lesotho, after Moshoeshoe's death in a car crash in January 1996. Letsie had already ruled for four years in the early 1990s, but had then abdicated to allow the return to the throne of his father, who had been head of state from the time of Lesotho's full independence within the Commonwealth in 1966 until he was deposed in 1990.

The future King Letsie was born Prince David Mohato Seeiso on 17 July 1963 in Morija. He went to Iketsetseng private primary school in Maseru in 1968 and then to primary and secondary school in the UK, returning to Lesotho for vacations and spending much time at his father's cattle posts in the mountains. He attended the National University of Lesotho, graduating in 1984 with a degree in law. He then continued his studies at the universities of Bristol, Cambridge and London, studying English law, development and agricultural economics.

He became principal chief of Matsieng in 1989, and was installed by the military government as King Letsie in November 1990 following the dethronement of his father. Moshoeshoe had been effectively ousted in March, since when he had been ostensibly on sabbatical leave in the UK. Two years later, when Moshoeshoe returned to Lesotho, Letsie offered to step down in his favour, but this was opposed by the ruling military council. In a compromise formula

Moshoeshoe was accorded the status of head of the royal family, but with Letsie still designated as monarch.

A return to civilian rule, and the holding of elections in March 1993, brought the Basotho Congress Party to power under Ntsu Mokhehle. Amid unrest and continuing coup rumours, Letsie attempted a decisive intervention, announcing on 17 August 1994 that he had removed the Mokhehle government and was calling fresh elections. He was immediately challenged by the mobilization of a large protest demonstration, precipitating a crisis which was eventually resolved only with mediation by Botswana, Zimbabwe and South Africa. Letsie agreed in September to reinstate Mokhehle and to abdicate in favour of his father. The necessary legislation was approved and Moshoeshoe returned to the throne on 25 January 1995, with Letsie reverting to the status of crown prince. However, a year later Moshoeshoe was killed in a car crash. Letsie succeeded to the throne three weeks after his death on 7 February 1996, and his coronation took place on 31 October 1997.

In 2000 Letsie married South African commoner Karabo Motšoeneng, and they now have one daughter. He announced before his wedding that, unlike many other African kings and chiefs, he intends to have only one wife.

Profile of the Prime Minister:

Bethuel Pakalitha **MOSISILI**

Bethuel Pakalitha Mosisili leads the ruling Lesotho Congress for Democracy (LCD). A career academic and examiner for a number of universities in the southern African region, he has been a member of the National Assembly and a cabinet minister since 1993. He was appointed prime minister in May 1998.

Bethuel Pakalitha Mosisili was born on 14 March 1945 near Qacha's Nek, eastern Lesotho. He married Mathalo Mosisili and they had four children, one of whom was shot and killed in 2002. He began his studies in 1966 at the University of Botswana, Lesotho and Swaziland (UBLS) in Roma, near the capital Maseru. A year into his course he joined the Basotho Congress Party (BCP). In July 1970, soon after graduating, he was imprisoned for his political affiliations.

Released from the maximum-security prison in November 1971, Mosisili was ordered not to leave the Mafeteng Reserve in the west of the country for a year. While under this restriction he found work teaching at local schools and was deputy headmaster at one until June 1973. His freedom restored, he went back to Roma to become an assistant lecturer in African languages at UBLS.

To further his training, Mosisili travelled to the USA in 1975 to study education at the University of Wisconsin, to South Africa in 1977 to gain another degree from the University of South Africa, and finally to Simon Fraser University, Canada, where he received a master's degree in 1982. In the meantime he had become a full lecturer in Lesotho in 1976 when UBLS had transformed into the National University of Lesotho. During the 1980s he travelled the region as a senior lecturer and external examiner, working at a number of universities in Lesotho and South Africa until 1992.

Direct military rule ended in Lesotho in 1993 and Mosisili took the opportunity to move from academia into politics. He was elected to the National Assembly to represent the Qacha's Nek constituency. The BCP had won a landslide victory and Mosisili was appointed minister of education and training, sports, culture and youth affairs (the portfolio was later restyled as education and manpower development). In February 1995 he was promoted to deputy prime minister—a post which had been vacant since the assassination of Selometsi Baholo in 1994—and minister of home affairs and local government.

Divisions within the ruling BCP prompted Prime Minister Ntsu Mokhehle in 1997 to form the LCD as the new ruling party. Mosisili was elected to replace Mokhehle as leader of the LCD in February 1998 and led the party to a landslide victory in the 1998 elections. He was appointed prime minister and minister of defence and public service in May. The party's success provoked mass unrest which led to the intervention of South African troops in September. Mosisili clashed with King Letsie over their arrival, and suggested that the king had sheltered opposition activists in the palace grounds during the disturbances, adding to the air of instability. In three days of violence 47 civilians were killed. The government agreed to hold early elections within 18 months.

Over the course of the next four years Mosisili oversaw the prosecution of those involved in the September 1998 violence, charging the opposition leaders of the time with high treason. The elections originally scheduled for mid-2000 were persistently postponed and were finally held in May 2002. The LCD won a sizable majority, securing 61 of the first 62 seats to declare for the 120-seat National Assembly. Mosisili was appointed for a new term on 4 June 2002.

LIBERIA

Full name: The Republic of Liberia.

Leadership structure: The head of state is a directly elected president. The president's term of office is six years, renewable once only. The head of government is the president, who appoints the cabinet.

President: Charles Taylor   Since 3 Aug. 1997

Legislature: The legislature is bicameral. The lower chamber, the House of Representatives, has 64 members, directly elected for a six-year term. The upper chamber, the Senate, has 26 members, elected for a nine-year term. Both chambers were elected for the first time in July 1997.

Profile of the President:

Charles **TAYLOR**

Charles Taylor is a member of Liberia's traditional elite group descended from freed American slaves, who ruled unchallenged between 1847 and 1980. After Samuel Doe's coup ended that supremacy, Taylor came to prominence as the leader of a guerrilla insurgency against the Doe regime. He seized power in 1990, but was not elected as president until 1997, the country having been embroiled meanwhile in a protracted civil war.

Charles Taylor (who subsequently adopted the middle name Ghankay) was born in 1948. He studied economics in the USA. In 1979 President William R. Tolbert appointed him director of Liberia's state General Services Agency, but Taylor switched allegiance in April 1980 to support Samuel Kanyon Doe in the bloody coup by which the latter seized power. A member of the Doe administration until 1983, Taylor later fled to the USA, however, amid allegations that he had embezzled government funds, and was arrested there in May 1984. He escaped from custody and returned to Africa.

In late December 1989 Taylor led an incursion of the National Patriotic Front of Liberia (NPFL) from neighbouring Côte d'Ivoire into Nimba province with the aim of overthrowing Doe. Advancing south and west, he seized control of the capital Monrovia in July 1990, deposed and killed Doe in September and declared himself president. During the civil war which followed Taylor was seen as an ally of Libya by the USA and was opposed by the Nigerian government, which had supported the Doe regime. The Economic Community of West African States

(ECOWAS) dispatched to Liberia an Economic Community Ceasefire Monitoring Group (ECOMOG) peacekeeping force. In 1992 ECOMOG drove Taylor out of the diamond-rich western part of Liberia, but failed in an attempt to gain control of Monrovia later that year.

Fighting between different factions continued while various parties sought unsuccessfully to secure a peace agreement that would hold. Eventually an ECOWAS summit, chaired by the then Nigerian president Gen. Sani Abacha, was convened in Nigeria in July 1996 and on 26 August Taylor was among those signing a renewed peace accord. This provided among other things for a new six-member transitional Council of State of which Taylor was a member.

Legislative and presidential elections were eventually held on 19 July 1997. Taylor, who owns a radio station and three newspapers, successfully dominated the election campaign and his National Patriotic Party secured 49 out of the 64 seats in the House of Representatives. In the presidential election he won over 70% of the vote, his closest rival being Ellen Johnson-Sirleaf who secured just over 9%.

Taylor was sworn in as president on 3 August 1997, when he pledged to set up commissions to protect human rights and assist reconciliation, and declared his priorities to be agriculture, health and education. His regime, however, has remained autocratic and stands accused of persistent human rights' violations and the suppression of political opposition. Its cross-border involvement in a wider pattern of regional conflict led to the imposition of UN sanctions. A renewed upsurge in fighting inside Liberia in 2002 prompted Taylor to impose a state of emergency (which he officially lifted later in the year), and to ban all political activity in April 2002. A supposed peace conference in August made little impact, as the main rebel faction explicitly refused to deal with Taylor himself.

LIBYA

Full name: The Great Socialist People's Libyan Arab Jamahariyah.

Leadership structure: The head of state is the 'leader of the revolution'. Executive power is held by the General People's Committee. The General People's Congress appoints the Committee's members, and decides on its structure. The Congress also has its own administrative secretariat.

'Leader of the Revolution':

Col. Moamer al-Kadhafi	Since 2 March 1979
(seized power on 1 Sept. 1969)	

Secretaries-General of the General People's Committee:

Mohammad Ahmed al-Manqoush	29 Dec. 1997—1 March 2000
Mubarak al-Shamikh	Since 1 March 2000

Legislature: The legislature is unicameral. The sole chamber, the General People's Congress (Mu'tamar al-Sha'ab al-'Am), has 750 members, appointed by local 'basic people's congresses' for a three-year term.

Profile of the 'Leader of the Revolution':

Col. Moamer al-**KADHAFI**

Moamer al-Kadhafi is a maverick pan-Arabist, quick to attack anything he sees as Western imperialism and Zionism, and with a special talent for the inflammatory gesture. His regime has attracted particularly strong condemnation from the USA because of Kadhafi's support for foreign liberation, anti-government and terrorist groups. Latterly he has been less in the spotlight. An Islamic reformist as opposed to a fundamentalist, he sees himself as an innovative thinker, aiming to develop a new kind of model for participative democracy in Libya—but retaining the apparatus for strict control of dissident activity.

Moamer al-Kadhafi was born in the Sirte region in 1942, one of three children in a bedouin family. He attended a Koranic elementary school and the high school at Sebha, where his early involvement in politics led to his expulsion. He used a false birth certificate to enrol in another school in Misrata, then studied history and politics at university in Benghazi.

Kadhafi's enthusiasm for the pan-Arabist cause was fired by President Nasser in neighbouring Egypt. In 1963, despite being known as a political activist, he was nevertheless accepted into the Royal Libyan Military Academy in Benghazi. Graduating in 1965, he was commissioned as an officer in the signals corps in Benghazi. A four-month training course in Beaconsfield, England, increased his knowledge of military signalling and armoured vehicle gunnery—and his dislike of the British.

Within the armed forces Kadhafi built up his clandestine Free Officers' Movement, the group that he would lead in a bloodless coup in 1969 to overthrow the conservative regime of King Idris. The intended coup date, twice deferred, was finally set for the early morning of 1 September. Kadhafi was already known to Western intelligence agencies and there has been speculation that they must have known something of his plans. When the date came the preparations worked smoothly and efficiently, and military and governmental installations in Benghazi and Tripoli were taken over with little bloodshed. Kadhafi made his first broadcast as head of the new regime within a few hours, and King Idris went into exile. Kadhafi's take-over reportedly pre-empted plans by more senior officers for a coup of their own.

Kadhafi became commander-in-chief of the armed forces, set up a Revolutionary Command Council with himself as president, and, from 1970 to 1972, also held the posts of prime minister and minister of defence. In 1976 he took the military rank of major-general but continued to use the title of colonel. He relinquished all official positions in 1979, styling himself thereafter 'leader of the revolution'.

Economic, social and political changes after the coup, based on Kadhafi's brand of 'natural socialism', included attempts to redistribute the country's oil wealth more equitably, and nationalization of foreign-owned banks, insurance companies, factories and oil companies. (Some liberalization of the economy did begin in the late 1980s, as did the development of steel manufacturing to reduce the country's near-total dependence on oil revenue.) Wage labour was declared to be abolished and workers were instead deemed to be partners in industrial ventures.

Instead of building a single-party state through mass membership of the Arab Socialist Union, Kadhafi embarked on the more idiosyncratic project of creating a structure for popular participation through a system of basic people's congresses and committees, with the parliament or General People's Congress at the centre. This was embodied in the 1977 Constitution of what was henceforth known officially as the Great Socialist People's Libyan Arab Jamahariyah. The *Green Book*, published in three volumes between 1976 and 1979, contains Kadhafi's thoughts on what he describes as his "third universal theory" spanning socialism, Islam, development and political systems.

Kadhafi's pan-Arabist aspirations, and his inclination to seek solidarity and involvement with regimes elsewhere which he identified as progressive, led him

310

into several declarations of union between Libya and other Arab and African states. Pan-Arabism also underlay his initial enthusiasm for the Arab Maghreb Union, formed in 1989 with Algeria, Mauritania, Morocco and Tunisia. His relations with neighbouring Egypt in particular have been tense, while his commitment to the Palestinian cause, something of an article of faith, has involved supporting 'rejectionist' factions and criticizing the mainstream Palestine Liberation Organization's 'sell-outs' to Israel.

Palestinian groups are only some among many causes to receive his backing, others including the British miners' union in its long strike in 1985, the Irish Republican Army, and leftist radicals in many African countries. Kadhafi has himself survived a number of assassination attempts and attempted coups, and has withstood (and bolstered his own defiant image as a result of) actions to 'punish' his regime on more than one occasion. The UK broke off diplomatic relations in 1984 over the shooting of a woman police officer at the Libyan embassy in London, and in 1986 the USA launched an air strike on Tripoli and Benghazi after a bomb attack on a West Berlin nightclub frequented by US servicemen. The bomb explosion on a Pan Am airliner over Lockerbie in Scotland in December 1988 was also laid at Kadhafi's door, leading to a long dispute about the extradition of suspects from Libya and the imposition of UN sanctions. This eventually moved towards resolution with a complex arrangement in 1999 under which two Libyans were tried under Scottish law in the Netherlands.

Col. Moamer al-Kadhafi is married to Safiya al-Kadhafi. They have five children, and their family also includes a number of adopted children, one of whom was killed in the 1986 US air strike against Tripoli. Kadhafi has a reclusive aspect in his character and has been prone to spending long periods in a tent in the desert.

During the 1990s Kadhafi kept a lower profile, notably remaining relatively silent during the Gulf War in 1991. He has attempted to forge a role as the champion of pan-Africanism. Since the 1990s Kadhafi's regime has been displaced by others as the main targets of Western hostility, and in April 1999 Libya was even taken off the US government's list of countries deemed to support international terrorism. However US president George W. Bush did add Libya to his nebulous 'axis of evil' states sponsoring terrorism in May 2002. Improvements in external relations included the establishment of diplomatic links with the Vatican in 1997, and Libya has the support of both the Organization of African Unity (now the African Union) and the Arab League for the lifting of sanctions.

Profile of the Secretary-General of the General People's Committee:

Mubarak al-**SHAMIKH**

Mubarak al-Shamikh is an independent. He was a long-term member of the General People's Committee (GPC) before being appointed its secretary-general in a major structural shake-up.

Mubarak Abdallah al-Shamikh was born in 1950. Before being appointed secretary-general of the GPC he had served at the head of a number of ministries from the 1980s onward. These included the communications and transport secretariat which he held until 1990, the utilities portfolio which he took on in 1992, and the combined housing and utilities secretariat which he held from 1994.

Leader of the Revolution Col. Moamer al-Kadhafi reorganized the GPC in March 2000, stripping many of its ministries and devolving responsibility to regional government. Shamikh was appointed secretary-general. His role, although formally considered equivalent to a prime minister, is largely nominal in the face of Kadhafi's personal power.

LIECHTENSTEIN

Full name: The Principality of Liechtenstein.

Leadership structure: The head of state is a constitutional and hereditary prince. The head of government is the leader of the cabinet, which is appointed by the prince, on the proposal of the Parliament.

Reigning Prince: Hans-Adam II   Since 13 Nov. 1989
                        von und zu Liechtenstein
                        (regent from 26 Aug. 1984)

Heads of Government: Mario Frick   15 Dec. 1993—5 April 2001

                         Otmar Hasler   Since 5 April 2001

Legislature: The legislature is unicameral. The sole chamber, the Parliament (Landtag), has 25 members, directly elected for a four-year term.

Profile of the Reigning Prince:

HANS-ADAM II von und zu Liechtenstein

Prince Hans-Adam II succeeded formally as 'reigning prince' of Liechtenstein upon the death of his father Prince Franz Josef II in 1989. An economics graduate with a business management background, he had already exercised the official powers of head of state, but without the title, for five years.

Hereditary Prince Hans-Adam was born on 14 February 1945. He went to the Schottengymnasium in Vienna, Austria, and completed his education in Switzerland, obtaining a diploma in national economy from the University of St Gallen in 1969. He worked briefly for a bank in London, before moving on to act as manager of the Prince of Liechtenstein Foundation from 1970 to 1981, during which time he was entrusted with the management and administration of the Royal House's property.

On 26 August 1984 Hans-Adam's elderly father passed all his official duties over to him as the representative of the head of state. When Franz Josef died on 13 November 1989 Hans-Adam became head of state in his own right.

Prince Hans-Adam married Countess Marie Kinsky von Wchinitz und Tettau in 1967. They have three sons and one daughter, their eldest son and heir apparent being Prince Alois, born in 1968.

Profile of the Head of Government:

Otmar **HASLER**

Otmar Hasler is a former secondary school teacher, and is a leading figure in the centre-left Progressive Citizens' Party (Fortschrittliche Bürgerpartei—FBP). On his inauguration as prime minister in April 2001 he pledged to continue many of the policies of his centre-right predecessor, Mario Frick.

Otmar Hasler was born on 28 September 1953. He graduated in teaching from the University of Fribourg, Switzerland, and began teaching at the secondary school in Eschen, northern Liechtenstein, in 1979. He is married to Traudi Hasler-Hilti and they have four children.

Hasler began his political career in 1989 when he was elected to Parliament for the FBP. Four years later, in 1993, he was appointed as a vice president of the legislature, a role he retained until becoming prime minister in 2001, apart from a two-year term as president of the legislature in 1995–97.

In 1993 he was elected president of the FBP, a post he held for two years, after which he remained a member of the party's presidium. Following the 1997 elections his party had its first spell out of government for 59 years, but after a four-year period in opposition it won an overall (albeit narrow) majority in legislative elections held in February 2001. Hasler was invited to form a government, and secured parliamentary approval two months later for his cabinet, which was drawn entirely from his own party in view of the decision by the rival centre-right Patriotic Union not to join a coalition.

LITHUANIA

Full name: The Republic of Lithuania.

Leadership structure: The head of state is a president, directly elected by universal adult suffrage. The president's term of office is five years, renewable once only. The head of government is the prime minister, who is appointed by the president with the approval of the Parliament.

President:	Valdas Adamkus	Since 26 Feb. 1998
Prime Ministers:	Andrius Kubilius	3 Nov. 1999—26 Oct. 2000
	Rolandas Paksas	26 Oct. 2000—20 June 2001
	Eugenijus Gentvilas (acting)	20 June 2001—3 July 2001
	Algirdas Brazauskas	Since 3 July 2001

Legislature: The legislature is unicameral. The sole chamber, the Parliament (Seimas), has 141 members, directly elected for a four-year term.

Profile of the President:

Valdas **ADAMKUS**

Valdas Adamkus had only just taken up residence in Lithuania at the time of his election to the presidency, having spent most of his adult life in the USA where he worked in the Environmental Protection Agency (EPA). He stood as a pro-market, independent candidate, with his nomination supported by the Lithuanian Centre Union, then the third-largest party in Parliament.

Valdas Adamkus was born on 3 November 1926 in Kaunas, Lithuania. As a teenager he joined the nationalist resistance, opposing both his country's forcible absorption into the Soviet Union in 1940, and its subsequent wartime occupation by Nazi Germany. During the Nazi occupation he ran an underground newspaper, but as Soviet troops advanced once again from the east he joined an anti-Soviet detachment supplied by the Nazis which fought for Lithuanian independence. When the Red Army took control of the country in 1944, he left Lithuania and fled to Germany.

Five years later he emigrated to the USA, where he found a job teaching Lithuanian, German, Polish and Russian at a US army school in Kansas. In 1951 he married another Lithuanian-born exile, Alma Adamkiene; they have no children.

Having moved to Chicago (where there is the largest Lithuanian community outside Lithuania), Adamkus completed a degree in civil engineering at the Illinois Institute of Technology. He joined the Republican Party and campaigned to prevent US recognition of the Soviet annexation of Lithuania, but had to cease party political activity when he started working for the US EPA in 1971. The following year he was on an EPA delegation to Lithuania, his first of a number of such visits to Eastern Europe. In 1981 he was promoted to EPA district administrator for the mid-west region.

During his time in the USA Adamkus was a leading member of the Lithuanian–American literary group Santara-Sviesa. In 1991, after Lithuania had gained independence from the Soviet Union, he applied for Lithuanian citizenship, and in 1994 he registered as a resident of the town of Šiauliai.

In October 1997 Adamkus gave up his job at the EPA and returned permanently to Lithuania, having been chosen in July as presidential candidate for the Lithuanian Centre Union (although he was not himself a member of any political party). During the three-month campaign he toured much of the country, seeking to demonstrate that he had sufficient experience of Lithuanian affairs. He received greatest support outside Vilnius, whereas in the capital academics disliked his anglicized language and he was criticized for being too pro-Western, giving rise to concerns that he would upset relations with neighbouring Russia.

The first round of voting, contested by seven candidates on 21 December 1997, saw Adamkus take second place with 28% of the vote, against 45% for Arturas Paulauskas, who was backed by the former communists including outgoing president Algirdas Brazauskas. In the runoff on 4 January 1998, Adamkus, supported by a broad centre-right coalition, secured a narrow victory with just 50.4% of the vote. Paulauskas claimed that irregularities had occurred but the electoral commission was satisfied, and Adamkus was duly sworn in on 26 February. As required by Lithuanian law, he immediately began the procedure to give up his US citizenship.

Although he proved to be a popular president, Adamkus had to handle a delicate political situation when a Social Democratic coalition headed by Brazauskas gained ground to become the largest bloc in the legislative elections of October 2000. Having initially invited the centre-right to form a minority government under Rolandas Paksas, he had to go back to the Social Democrats when Paksas's coalition collapsed the following June, and invite Brazauskas to form a government instead.

Seeking a second term as president, Adamkus headed the poll on the first round on 22 December 2002, although he faced an unexpectedly strong challenge from Paksas. Both went through to the second round due on 5 January 2003.

Profile of the Principal Challenger for the Presidency:

Rolandas **PAKSAS**

Rolandas Paksas is an engineer and former stunt pilot and has twice been mayor of Vilnius. Although formerly a member of the Homeland Union (Lithuanian Conservatives) (Tevynes Sąjunga (Lietuvos Konservatoriai)—TS(LK)), Paksas has led two successive right-of-centre liberal parties and had two short-lived terms as prime minister, in May–October 1999 and October 2000–June 2001. His resignations only helped to increase his high popularity rating and in December 2002 he forced President Valdas Adamkus to a second round of presidential elections scheduled for 5 January 2003.

Rolandas Paksas was born on 10 June 1956 in Telšiai, in what was then the Lithuanian Soviet Socialist Republic within the Soviet Union. He is married to Laima, an engineer and economist, and they have two young children. The couple were named Pair of the Year by a popular Lithuanian magazine in 1998.

Having gained a diploma from the Vilnius Institute of Civil Engineering (now the Vilnius Gediminas Technical University) in 1979, Paksas headed for Leningrad (now St Petersburg) in Russia. While studying at the Leningrad Institute of Civil Aviation, Paksas taught as a flying instructor. Once he graduated in 1984 he joined the Soviet Union's national aerobatics team and flew Sukhoi aircraft in competitions around the world. He was twice named Soviet champion. In 1989 he returned to Lithuania where he was chairman of the Vilnius flying club and the aviation department of the Voluntary Defence Service until 1992. He continued to fly in aerobatics competitions and was Lithuanian champion on several occasions.

As a democratic Lithuania emerged in 1992, Paksas reverted from flying to civil engineering. For five years he chaired the profitable construction and renovation company Restako. Politics drew him away from commerce in 1996 when he joined the TS(LK) which swept to power in November that year. As a TS(LK) candidate he entered municipal elections for the capital's council in 1997 and was elected for his first term as mayor of Vilnius. His rapid rise in conservative politics continued the following year when he joined the party's executive board.

In 1999 the TS(LK) prime minister, Gediminas Vagnorius, was forced to resign and the popular Paksas, completing his three-year rise in conservative politics, was nominated in his place. He was confirmed as the country's premier in May and opinion polls suggested he was the second most popular politician in the country behind President Adamkus. However, his patriotism undermined his position when he openly condemned a government move to sell, effectively at a loss, a 33% share in the country's Mazeikiu Nafta oil refinery to the US company Williams International. He staked his job on his opposition to the deal and lost. His resignation in October 1999 brought even greater public support for him.

For the first part of 2000 Paksas worked as a special adviser to the president and abandoned the increasingly unpopular TS(LK) in favour of founding his own

Lithuanian Liberal Union (Lietuvos Liberalu Sąjunga—LLS). He was elected as mayor of Vilnius yet again and re-entered the Parliament in October after fresh elections which saw a crushing defeat for the TS(LK). Concern that a government of the victorious Social Democrats could affect the country's economic prospects led President Adamkus to overlook them in favour of Paksas and his LLS. Paksas took office as prime minister once again on 26 October 2000. However, his coalition government only lasted eight months before collapsing amidst recriminations over Paksas's privatization and tax plans.

Paksas led a rebellion against his own party in early 2002 and formed the Liberal Democratic Party (Liberalu Demokratu Partija—LDP) from disaffected members. His centrist politics and his enormous popularity tipped him as a major contender in that year's presidential elections. His 19.7% in the first round held on 22 December took him through to a runoff against the incumbent President Adamkus, set for 5 January 2003.

Profile of the Prime Minister:

Algirdas **BRAZAUSKAS**

Algirdas Brazauskas steered Lithuania to independence from the Soviet Union in 1990 as the country's last Communist ruler and went on to be elected its first democratic president (1993–98). He returned to power as prime minister in 2001 at the head of the Lithuanian Social Democratic Party (Lietuvos Socialdemokratu Partija—LSDP) at a time of worsening economic problems, after the collapse of a minority right-of-centre government created after the October 2000 elections to keep his party out of power. His pledge to continue his predecessor's economic reforms, while also pursuing more socially oriented policies, was derided as impractical by many in the business community.

Algirdas Mykolas Brazauskas was born in Rokiškis on 22 September 1932, in what was then the nominally independent republic of Lithuania. He moved with his family to the town of Kaisiadorys, just east of Kaunas, soon after. Lithuania became a part of the Soviet Union in 1940 and Brazauskas attended the Soviet Kaunas Polytechnic Institute, graduating in 1956 having specialized in hydrotechnology. His first assignment was as senior engineer on the Kaunas hydroelectric power project. In 1958 he married Julia Styraite, a medical doctor, and they had two daughters before divorcing in the late 1990s. In 2002 he married hotelier Kristina Butrimiene.

Having spent eight years chairing the Energy Building Trust Board, Brazauskas shifted directly into the Soviet administration when he was appointed minister for the building material industry in 1965. Two years later he was made deputy chairman of the state planning committee. With the backing of a degree in economics gained in 1974, he was made secretary for economic affairs to the central committee of the ruling Communist Party of Lithuania (Lietuvos Komunistu Partijos—LKP) in 1977 where he stayed for a further ten years.

As the movement for democratization swept the Soviet Union Brazauskas, notwithstanding his association with the regime, was at the forefront of the awakening of Lithuanian nationalism, and initially received the backing of the popular Sajudis independence movement. During a decisive split within the LKP in 1988, Brazauskas was elected first secretary—the most senior position in Lithuania. In this role he led the LKP, and the country at large, away from its ties to Moscow and established an independent Lithuanian party in 1989, retaining the position of first secretary. In the final days of Lithuania's communist era in 1990 Brazauskas transformed the party into the Lithuanian Democratic Labour Party (Lietuvos Demokratine Darbo Partija—LDDP). He was duly elected its chairman, as well as becoming deputy prime minister of the newly independent Lithuania.

In the country's first legislative elections for the new Parliament in 1992 the LDDP scored a surprise victory to emerge as the largest single party. From November of that year Brazauskas served as chairman of the Parliament and thus acting president of Lithuania. In the first direct elections for a head of state Brazauskas emerged the victor with 60% of the vote and was sworn in as president on 25 February 1993. In accordance with the new constitution he suspended his membership of the LDDP. As president he presided over the government's decisions to seek closer ties with the West and to undertake the painful process of market reforms. During his five-year term Lithuania's economy became one of the success stories of the post-Soviet Baltic, although public support for the left-wing government deteriorated.

The LDDP was heavily defeated at the polls in 1996 by the new Homeland Union (Lithuanian Conservatives), and in 1997 Brazauskas announced he would not stand for re-election. His chosen successor was beaten in the subsequent presidential election in 1997–98 by the right-of-centre candidate Valdas Adamkus. In opposition Brazauskas returned to lead the LDDP. As a series of right-wing coalitions came and went between 1998 and 2000 Brazauskas rallied the left-wing opposition behind his own popular image. The A. Brazauskas Social Democratic Coalition won the greatest share of seats in the October 2000 legislative elections but was controversially overlooked by President Adamkus who turned instead to a multiparty minority coalition of the centre-right.

In 2001 Prime Minister Rolandas Paksas was compelled to resign by a revolt within his coalition over his privatization and pension reform plans. Brazauskas was called on in June to form a government based on his LSDP—formed from the merger of a party of the same name and the LDDP in January 2001—and the centre-left New Union (Social Liberals). It took office on 3 July. Reflecting the concerns of industry chiefs, President Adamkus warned Brazauskas that he would be watching the leftist government closely, and would intervene if it appeared to be jeopardizing the country's chances of joining the European Union (EU) and the North Atlantic Treaty Organization (NATO).

LUXEMBOURG

Full name: The Grand Duchy of Luxembourg.

Leadership structure: The head of state is a hereditary grand duke. The head of government is the prime minister, chosen by the grand duke on the basis that the prime minister must command the support of the Chamber of Deputies. The prime minister appoints the Council of Ministers.

Grand Dukes: Jean   12 Nov. 1964—7 Oct. 2000
(lieutenant-representative from 4 May 1961)

Henri   Since 7 Oct. 2000
(lieutenant-representative from 4 March 1998)

Prime Minister: Jean-Claude Juncker   Since 20 Jan. 1995

Legislature: The legislature is unicameral. The sole chamber, the Chamber of Deputies (Chambre des Députés/Châmber vun Députéirten), has 60 members, directly elected for a five-year term. There is also a Council of State, nominated by the monarch and comprising 21 members, which acts as the supreme administrative tribunal and has some legislative functions.

Profile of the Grand Duke:

HENRI

Grand Duke Henri succeeded as grand duke of Luxembourg on 7 October 2000, after the abdication of his father, Grand Duke Jean. Educated in political sciences, Henri follows his father's lead in championing the environment and social causes. As head of state he is constitutional monarch and executive authority is exercised on his behalf by the prime minister.

Henri Albert Gabriel Félix Marie Guillaume d'Aviano was born in Betzdorf in southeast Luxembourg on 16 April 1955, the second child of Crown Prince Jean and Princess Joséphine-Charlotte of Belgium. His father became grand duke after the voluntary abdication of the popular Grand Duchess Charlotte in 1964, making Henri, as his eldest son, the heir apparent. Henri attended primary school in Luxembourg and speaks English, French and German, as well as Luxembourgish. He passed the European baccalaureate in France in 1974 before travelling to the UK where he entered the Royal Military Academy at Sandhurst in 1975.

On passing out of Sandhurst Henri went to Switzerland where he studied political sciences at the University of Geneva. Having graduated in 1980, he married Cuban-born fellow student Maria Teresa Mestre on 14 February 1981; they have five children, the eldest of whom, Prince Guillaume, born on 11 November 1981, is heir apparent.

Henri's studies also took him to the USA and he continued to travel extensively thereafter, promoting Luxembourg's economy as an honorary chairman of the Board of Economic Development. He served as a member of the Council of State from 1980 to 1998, accustoming himself to the working of the country's government, and since 1998 has been a member of the International Olympic Committee.

The prince's interest in social issues led him to create the Mentor Foundation, in co-operation with the World Health Organization (WHO), to help combat solvent abuse among the young. He is also a member of the Charles Darwin Foundation for the Galapagos Islands, and chairman of its Luxembourg branch. Like his father, Henri is a keen sportsman with a particular interest in outdoor pursuits. He enjoys skiing, sailing, swimming and shooting, in particular.

In March 1998 Henri's father appointed him lieutenant-representative to take over his active duties as head of state and announced in December 1999 that he would abdicate in favour of his son in the following year. At an abdication ceremony on 7 October 2000 Henri was named grand duke.

Profile of the Prime Minister:

Jean-Claude **JUNCKER**

Jean-Claude Juncker, who trained as a lawyer, has been active throughout his career as a member of the Christian Social People's Party (Chrëschtlich Sozial Volkspartei—CSV), which ruled in coalition with the Luxembourg Socialist Workers' Party (Lëtzebuergesch Sozialistesch Arbechterpartei—LSAP) from 1984 to 1999. He held a variety of ministerial posts before becoming prime minister in 1995, in which post he replaced his CSV colleague Jacques Santer when Santer left to take up the presidency of the European Commission.

Born in Redange-sur-Attert, Luxembourg, on 9 December 1954, Jean-Claude Juncker received his secondary education in Clairefontaine, Belgium. He attended the University of Strasbourg from 1975 and graduated with a degree in public law in 1979, gaining admittance to the Luxembourg Bar in February 1980. He is married to Christiane Frising; they have no children.

From 1979 until 1985 he was president of the youth wing of the CSV and was also the party's parliamentary secretary from October 1979 until December 1982, when he was appointed state secretary for labour and social affairs.

Following the June 1984 general election, which brought the CSV–LSAP coalition to power under Santer's premiership, Juncker was named as minister of labour and minister in charge of the budget from July. As a result he presided over meetings of social affairs and budget ministers of the Council of Ministers, during Luxembourg's presidency of the European Communities for six months in 1985.

Re-elected to parliament in the June 1989 general election he was given responsibility for labour and finance in Santer's cabinet. As such he was instrumental in preparing a draft treaty on economic and monetary union during Luxembourg's presidency of the European Communities in the first half of 1991 which was later to form part of the Maastricht Treaty on European Union. The July 1991 collapse of the Bank of Credit and Commerce International, the holding company and a subsidiary of which were incorporated in Luxembourg, focused attention on Luxembourg's banking secrecy laws. In response to these concerns Juncker introduced legislation two years later requiring banks to notify cases of suspected money laundering and permitting such deposits to be seized.

Juncker retained his cabinet posts after the June 1994 general election. He was also elected president of the CSV in 1990 and president of the European Union of Christian Democratic Workers in 1993, retaining both posts until his appointment as prime minister on 20 January 1995. As prime minister he also holds the key post of minister of finance, although he has gradually relinquished his other ministerial responsibilities, notably for labour and employment. The June 1999 elections saw both the existing governing coalition parties lose seats, although Juncker's CSV remained the largest party in the Chamber of Deputies, and on 7 August 1999, having formed a new right-of-centre coalition with the Democratic Party of Luxembourg, he was sworn in for a further term as prime minister.

Juncker was a governor of the World Bank from 1989 until 1995 and, as minister of finance, is currently a governor of the European Investment Bank, the European Bank for Reconstruction and Development and the International Monetary Fund. In 2002 he began to be mentioned as a possible successor to Wim Duisenberg as governor of the European Central Bank. A firm believer in European integration, he has also been a vice president of the European People's Party.

THE FORMER YUGOSLAV REPUBLIC OF MACEDONIA

Full name: The Republic of Macedonia.

Leadership structure: The head of state is the president, directly elected by universal adult suffrage. The president's term of office is five years. The head of government is the prime minister, who is appointed by the president. Ministers are elected by, but not members of, the Assembly.

President:	Boris Trajkovski	Since 15 Dec. 1999
Prime Ministers:	Ljubčo Georgievski	30 Nov. 1998—1 Nov. 2002
	Branko Crvenkovski	Since 1 Nov. 2002

Legislature: The legislature is unicameral. The sole chamber, the Assembly (Sobranie), has 120 members, directly elected for a four-year term.

Profile of the President:

Boris **TRAJKOVSKI**

Boris Trajkovski is a former lawyer who achieved notoriety as deputy foreign minister, during the 1999 crisis in neighbouring Kosovo, by aligning himself with popularist sentiment against the international community. Later that year he stood successfully for the presidency, although confirmation of his victory came only after a controversial rerun of a runoff election which was itself surrounded by accusations of fraud. His appointment was disputed by opposition parties and international observers.

Boris Trajkovski was born on 25 June 1956 in the eastern town of Strumica in what was then the Yugoslav Republic of Macedonia. He graduated from Skopje University with a law degree in 1980 and worked for a number of years as a lawyer for a construction company. He is a committed Methodist Christian and for 12 years headed the Yugoslavian Methodist youth organization. Since Macedonia's independence he has led the executive committee of the Methodist Church of Macedonia. He is married with a son and daughter.

In 1992 he joined the centrist Internal Macedonian Revolutionary Organization–Democratic Party for Macedonian National Unity (Vnatrešno-Makedonska Revolucionerna Organizacija–Demokratska Partija za Makedonsko Nacionalno

Edinstvo—VMRO–DPMNE), and chaired its foreign relations commission for six years, as well as being adviser to the mayor of Skopje in the municipal district of Kisela Voda from 1997 to 1998. He then entered the national government as deputy foreign minister following the VMRO–DPMNE victory in legislative elections in December 1998. In this role he spoke out against Western criticism of Macedonia's refugee policies during the war in neighbouring Kosovo in 1999 and called instead for international aid.

In presidential elections held later that year Trajkovski trailed in the first round to the Social Democratic Alliance of Macedonia candidate, Tito Petkovski. The runoff was fraught with irregularities: although he appeared victorious, Trajkovski was met with public calls for fresh elections. A partial rerun was called in December and Trajkovski managed to win 96% of the vote in constituencies where the initial poll had been cancelled due to irregularities. Observers from the Organization for Security and Co-operation in Europe (OSCE) announced "serious concerns" about the result and domestic opposition politicians accused Trajkovski of unfairly mobilizing gangs of ethnic Albanians to cast multiple votes and intimidate opposition supporters.

Profile of the Prime Minister:

Branko **CRVENKOVSKI**

Branko Crvenkovski is a former computer engineer. His party, the Social Democratic Alliance of Macedonia (Socijaldemokratski Sojuz na Makedonije—SDSM), evolved from the former ruling League of Communists during the breakup of Yugoslavia and is closely aligned with ex-president Kiro Gligorov, describing itself as standing in the European democratic tradition and supporting the transformation to a market economy. First appointed prime minister in September 1992, Crvenkovski remained in office at the head of a coalition government following the 1994 elections. Out of office for four years from November 1998, he returned to power following the 2002 elections.

Born on 12 October 1962 in Sarajevo, Branko Crvenkovski graduated in 1986 with a degree in computer science and automation from the faculty of electrical engineering at Skopje University. He is married with one son and one daughter.

After a period as head of department at the computer engineering company Semos in Skopje, in 1990 Crvenkovski became a representative in the Assembly of the Republic of Macedonia (at that time part of the Socialist Federal Republic of Yugoslavia), and was elected as president of its commission for foreign political affairs and relations. As such he was closely involved in Macedonia's moves towards independence from Yugoslavia, which was declared in November 1991 and eventually fully recognized when the country secured membership of the UN in April 1993 under the name of the Former Yugoslav Republic of Macedonia (FYRM).

The former communist party was reborn as the SDSM at its party congress in April 1991, and Crvenkovski was elected as its president. In August 1992 he was put forward by the SDSM as prime minister-designate. Installed by President Gligorov, his government was formally elected by the Assembly on 4 September. He was reappointed as prime minister on 20 December 1994, following the general election held in October–November that year, heading a coalition of his own SDSM (the largest party in the Assembly), the Liberal Party, the Party for Democratic Prosperity and the Socialist Party of Macedonia.

An increase in tensions between the majority Macedonian population and the ethnic Albanian minority, and a barely avoided financial scandal involving a 'pyramid investment scheme', resulted in Crvenkovski's coalition losing elections four years later to the political right. Crvenkovski himself was, however, re-elected to the Assembly. Over the next few years ethnic tensions increased dramatically and boiled over into outright civil war in 2001. Crvenkovski took the SDSM into a 'government of national unity' in May, which was maintained for long enough to achieve the signing of a peace accord with the Albanian rebels. Having then taken the party back into opposition in November, Crvenkovski criticized the slow pace of the government in its implementation of the accord.

In elections held on 15 September 2002 Crvenkovski led the SDSM, under the Together for Macedonia (Za Makedonija Zajedno—ZMZ) coalition, back into power. The ten-party umbrella group gained 41% of the vote and formed a new government with the ethnic Albanian Democratic Union for Integration.

MADAGASCAR

Full name: The Republic of Madagascar.

Leadership structure: The head of state is a president, directly elected by universal adult suffrage. The president's term of office is five years. The president appoints the prime minister. Under the 1998 amendments to the constitution, the prime minister may be selected from a party which has a minority of seats in the National Assembly. The prime minister is head of government and appoints the other members of the Council of Ministers.

Presidents: Adml. Didier Ratsiraka 9 Feb. 1997—5 July 2002

(presidency in dispute between 22 Feb. and 5 July 2002)

Marc Ravalomanana Since 22 Feb. 2002

Prime Ministers under Ratsiraka:

Tantely René Gabrio Andrianarivo 23 July 1998—31 May 2002

Jean-Jacques Rasolondraibe (interim) 31 May 2002—5 July 2002

Prime Minister under Ravalomanana:

Jacques Sylla Since 26 Feb. 2002

Legislature: The legislature, the Parliament, is bicameral. The lower chamber, the National Assembly (Antenimierampirenena), has 160 members, directly elected for a five-year term. The upper chamber, the Senate (Antenimieramdoholana), has 90 members, two-thirds of them elected by an electoral college, the remainder nominated by the president, all for a six-year term.

Profile of the President:

Marc **RAVALOMANANA**

Marc Ravalomanana is one of Madagascar's wealthiest businessmen thanks to the success of the dairy produce company he founded in the 1970s. Mayor of the capital from 1999, he challenged long-time president and former dictator Didier Ratsiraka in the presidential elections two years later. Accusations of poll-rigging in Ratsiraka's favour, and Ravalomanana's assertion that he had won in the first round, led to a six-month political struggle which often threatened to spiral into full-scale civil war. Although he was officially sworn in as president on 6 May 2002, it took two more months for his victory to be fully accepted.

Marc Ravalomanana was born on 12 December 1949 in Imerinkasinina near the capital, Antananarivo. His family was part of the country's minority Protestant community and he attended religious schools in his home village before travelling to Sweden to attend secondary school at another religious institution. He is now deputy chairman of Madagascar's Protestant Church.

When he returned to Madagascar in the 1970s he set up his own small-scale business, producing home-made yoghurt which he sold from the back of a bicycle with the help of his wife Lalao. Within two years he had successfully applied for a loan from the World Bank, with the support of the Protestant Church, to build his first factory. His company, Tiko, is now Madagascar's biggest home-grown business, with a virtual monopoly on dairy and vegetable oil products, and Ravalomanana himself is a dollar millionaire. He has one daughter and three sons.

In 1999 Ravalomanana decided to divert his energies into politics, and ran successfully as an independent candidate in the mayoral elections for Antananarivo. Famously deriding the city's "filth and anarchy", he set about a massive sanitation and centralization campaign. His policies were exceptionally popular in the capital. Buoyed by this experience he registered to compete in the presidential elections in 2001.

Official results from the first round in December suggested that a second round was necessary between Ravalomanana and incumbent president Ratsiraka. Claiming that he had in fact won outright, Ravalomanana rejected this count and refused to participate in the second round, which had been scheduled for February 2002.

A six-month conflict began, in which over 30 people were killed in violent clashes between rival supporters. Ratsiraka retreated to his coastal stronghold of Toamasina while Ravalomanana was blockaded in Antananarivo, where he declared himself president on 22 February 2002. In April a recount of the disputed vote showed that Ravalomanana was indeed the rightful winner, and he was officially inaugurated on 6 May. By the end of June he had received international recognition; Toamasina, the last city claiming allegiance to Ratsiraka, was taken in early July and the former president fled into self-exile in France.

Among Ravalomanana's immediate tasks as head of state was to tackle government corruption. To this end, and no doubt also to reward the loyalty of his appointed government, he raised the pay of his ministers tenfold and promised similar raises to other civil servants "bit by bit".

Profile of the Prime Minister:

Jacques **SYLLA**

Jacques Sylla is an independent lawyer. He served as foreign minister in the 1990s under Madagascar's then president Albert Zafy. Appointed prime minister by presidential claimant Marc Ravalomanana on 26 February 2002, he was confirmed in the post in May.

Jacques Hugues Sylla was born in 1946 on the island of Sainte-Marie (Nosy Boraha) which lies off the coast of eastern Toamasina province. He trained as a lawyer in the late 1960s. Sylla is married to Yvette Rakoto and they have four children.

He began his political career in earnest in August 1993, when the opposition Forces Vives won legislative elections, allowing the country's first democratically elected president, Albert Zafy, to appoint a new cabinet. Sylla was nominated foreign minister and held that post until Zafy was impeached and failed to win re-election in 1996. Former dictator Didier Ratsiraka's return to power ended Sylla's role in government for the next five years.

When a fresh power struggle gripped the island following the presidential elections in December 2001, Sylla played an important role in the associated legal process, as head of the Toamasina section of the National Committee of Election Observers. Already appointed prime minister in the alternative cabinet drawn up by Ravalomanana in February 2002, he was among the 15 lawyers who attested in April to Ravalomanana's first-round victory. He remained head of Ravalomanana's cabinet once the latter's position was legitimized in May. Sylla's position has quite probably been strengthened by the fact that he is from the same ethnic *côtier* group as ousted president Ratsiraka, providing the new government with a sense of truly national representation.

MALAWI

Full name: The Republic of Malawi.

Leadership structure: The head of state is a president, directly elected by universal adult suffrage. The president's term of office is five years, renewable once only. The head of government is the president.

President: Bakili Muluzi   Since 21 May 1994

Legislature: The legislature is unicameral. The sole chamber, the National Assembly, has 193 members (expanded from 177 at the 1999 elections), directly elected for a five-year term.

Profile of the President:

Bakili **MULUZI**

Bakili Muluzi came to power in the country's first multiparty presidential and legislative elections, marking the end of three decades of restrictive and personalized rule by Hastings Kamuzu Banda. A rich Muslim businessman, he had been a government minister under Banda but left the sole and ruling Malawi Congress Party (MCP) in 1983. Nearly a decade later he founded the United Democratic Front (UDF), and then stood successfully against Banda in the 1994 elections. Re-elected in 1999, he courted controversy in 2002 by seeking a change in the constitution to allow himself the chance of a third term.

Bakili Muluzi was born on 17 March 1943 in Machinga, southern Malawi. He was educated at Thisted Technical School in Denmark from 1972 to 1973 and at Bolton College of Further Education in the UK in 1973, graduating with a diploma in the administration of technical education. On his return to Malawi later that year, he was appointed principal of Nasawa Technical College in Chiradzulu District. He is married with seven children.

Muluzi was active in the MCP as a regional party secretary from 1959, becoming secretary-general and administrative secretary in 1975, when he was elected to parliament for Machinga. He was appointed parliamentary secretary at the ministry of youth and culture in 1976, was minister of education from 1976 to 1977, and minister without portfolio between 1977 and 1982. However, in 1982 he was demoted to the post of minister of transport and communications. Fearing persecution by President Banda for gaining too much influence in the party, Muluzi resigned from the MCP and the government.

329

Thereafter he worked for several years in a number of commercial jobs, as deputy head of the National Chamber of Commerce, and in the Road Transport Association. In 1992, as international aid was suspended because of Banda's poor human rights record, Muluzi formed the UDF, the first opposition group set up amid the growing demands for democratic reforms. Facing widespread protests and international pressure, Banda agreed to allow a referendum on single-party rule, which produced a 63% 'no' vote when it eventually took place in June 1993.

On 17 May 1994 the first multiparty legislative and presidential elections were held. Muluzi was one of five presidential candidates and won 47.3% of the vote, against 33.6% for Banda. Muluzi's UDF, which had its power base in the populous south of the country, also secured the largest number of seats in the National Assembly, subsequently forming a coalition government with the Alliance for Democracy (Aford).

Having promised to give high priority to human rights issues, upon his election as president Muluzi immediately freed political prisoners and closed three prisons which had reportedly been used as torture centres. He also worked to reconcile divisions between his own UDF, Aford and the MCP, which threatened to paralyse the National Assembly. In April 1997 the MCP agreed to end a ten-month boycott of the Assembly, while Muluzi offered to remove flaws in the 1995 Constitution and prevent such problems arising again.

Muluzi and the UDF were re-elected on 15 June 1999. The elections were praised by international observers as "free and fair" but were rejected by the MCP and Aford. Although Muluzi had gained 51% of the vote, the opposition complained that this did not exactly translate to a majority of the electorate even though turnout had been a spectacular 94%. Meanwhile, divisions within the UDF reopened with rival congresses being held in August 2000—and with a majority of the party's Assembly delegates supporting Muluzi's rival, party vice president John Tembo. Muluzi struck out at 'corruption' in his government by dismissing the cabinet en masse that November, but this was not enough to prevent foreign donors from suspending aid.

By 2002 Muluzi was looking to secure himself an unconstitutional third term in office—in a manner similar to a number of other recent African leaders. Opposition was great and Muluzi banned rallies denouncing the plan, describing himself as a "good dictator" in the process. A private member's bill to amend the constitution accordingly was defeated to much surprise in July, prompting Muluzi to begin formulating an official government bill. The bill had not been debated in the National Assembly by the end of the year.

MALAYSIA

Full name: The Federation of Malaysia.

Leadership structure: The head of state is the *yang di-pertuan agong* (supreme head of state), elected by the nine hereditary Malay rulers of Peninsular Malaysia from among their own number. The head of state's term of office is five years. The head of government is the prime minister, who is appointed, with the cabinet, by the head of state.

Supreme Heads of State (*Yang di-Pertuan Agongs*):

Salehuddin Abdul Aziz ibni al-Marhum Hisamuddin Alam	26 April 1999—21 Nov. 2001
Mizan Zainal Abidin ibni al-Marhum Sultan Mahmud (acting from 8 Oct. 2001)	21 Nov. 2001—13 Dec. 2001
Syed Sirajuddin ibni al-Marhum Syed Putra Jamalullail	Since 13 Dec. 2001

Prime Minister: Mahathir Mohamed   Since 16 July 1981

Legislature: The legislature, the Parliament (Parlimen), is bicameral. The lower chamber, the House of Representatives (Dewan Rakyat), has 193 members, directly elected for a five-year term. The upper chamber, the Senate (Dewan Negara), has 69 members, serving a six-year term; each of the Legislative Assemblies of the states of Malaysia elects two members of the Senate, and the remaining 43 members are nominated by the head of state.

Profile of the Supreme Head of State (*Yang di-Pertuan Agong*):

Syed **SIRAJUDDIN** ibni al-Marhum Syed Putra Jamalullail

Tuanku Syed Sirajuddin was raja of the Malay state of Perlis before being elevated on 13 December 2001 to yang di-pertuan agong (supreme ruler of Malaysia). Having received education and military training in the UK, he abandoned a career in the army to concentrate on administration in Perlis. Although as head of state he is also commander-in-chief of the Malaysian armed forces, his role is purely ceremonial.

Syed Sirajuddin ibni al-Marhum Syed Putra Jamalullail was born on 16 May 1943 in Arau, Perlis, in the far northwest of Malaysia, the second of the ten children of the raja of Perlis. He began his education at a local preparatory school before entering the British colonial education system in 1950. Nine years later he travelled to the UK to complete his studies at the private Wellingborough School near Leicester. He was inaugurated as *raja muda* (crown prince) on 30 October 1960, while still at school.

After secondary school Sirajuddin began officer training in the UK in January 1964, at the Royal Military Academy in Sandhurst, from which he passed out as a second lieutenant in December 1965. He immediately returned to Malaysia and served in the reconnaissance force in Sabah, Sarawak and Pahang. Although he retired from active military service in December 1969, having attained the rank of lieutenant, he continued to serve in the army reserves in Perlis, as a captain from 1970 to 1972. As well as now being commander-in-chief of the national forces, he is also colonel of the Perlis reserve regiment.

His father died on 16 April 2000 and Sirajuddin, who had been acting as regent, was made full raja the next day. He was officially inaugurated in this office on 7 May. His role in Perlis is effectively as a figurehead and traditional leader and as such he is patron of various nongovernmental organizations there. Among them is the Tuanku Syed Putra Foundation which helps students from the state to pursue higher education. He is also chancellor of Universiti Sains Malaysia. He takes an active interest in sport in the region and is president of the Putra Golf Club and was chairman of the Perlis Football Association until 1995.

When the ruling *yang di-pertuan agong*, the sultan of Selangor, died in November 2001, the traditional conference of rulers from the nine Malay kingdoms elected Sirajuddin to be his replacement on 13 December. His official coronation as the 12th *yang di-pertuan agong* of Malaysia took place on 25 April 2002.

Sirajuddin married Tuanku Fauziah binti Tangka Abdul Rashid, a princess from the ruling houses of Terengganu and Kelantan, on 15 February 1967. She is now the patron of the Malaysian Girl Guides Association. Their eldest son, Tuanku Syed Faizuddin Putra, born on 30 December 1967, was on 12 October 2000 made *raja muda* of Perlis, where he is currently acting as regent.

Profile of the Prime Minister:

MAHATHIR Mohamed

Prime Minister Mahathir Mohamed, a doctor before he entered full-time politics, has a reputation as the most vocal proponent of 'Asian values' in political and economic development. Rejecting Western criticisms of authoritarianism, he also denounced international speculators for engineering the 'Asian crisis' of 1997, and was bitterly critical of world financial organizations for responding inadequately. Despite vocal demands for his resignation, accusations of corruption, and a bruising conflict with his former deputy Anwar Ibrahim, he led the governing coalition to a further electoral victory in December 1999.

Mahathir Mohamed was born on 20 December 1925, the son of a headmaster, in Alor Setar in the state of Kedah in northwest Malaysia, which was then a British protectorate. Having completed his schooling there, at Sultan Abdul Hamid College, he enrolled at the King Edward VII College of Medicine in the University of Malaya in Singapore, where he completed his medical training, going on to be a government medical officer from 1953 to 1957. He set up in private practice in 1957. Mahathir married another doctor, Siti Hasmah, in 1956; they have had four sons and three daughters.

He joined the United Malays National Organization (UMNO) upon its formation in 1946, while still a student, and sat on the party's supreme council and held a seat in the House of Representatives between 1964 and 1969. In that year he lost his seat at the May general election, but attracted notice by publishing a controversial (and subsequently banned) book, criticizing the then prime minister Tunku Abdul Rahman for his handling of an outbreak of communal rioting in the aftermath of the election. Restored to the party supreme council in 1972, he was appointed as a senator the following year, but in 1974 returned to the House of Representatives, holding his seat there ever since.

Mahathir held ministerial posts between 1974 and 1981, at education and then at trade and industry, and was in addition deputy prime minister from 1976. He rose at the same time in the party leadership, becoming one of three UMNO vice presidents in 1975, deputy president in 1978, and president in 1981. He took over the leadership of the government in July 1981, as prime minister and also minister of defence, and has led the National Front government since that time; the National Front, in which the UMNO is the main constituent, was returned to power in successive general elections in 1982, 1986, 1990, 1995 and 1999.

Mahathir risked the charge of ethnic Malay chauvinism in the early stages of his political career and, once in government, emphasized the need for development policies to focus especially on the indigenous Malay people or *bumiputras*. Having thereby done much to create a Malay middle class, he can claim to have redressed an imbalance in the ethnic mix, and now tries to appeal to a wider notion of nationalism embracing also the more prosperous Chinese and other minority groups.

Domestically, Mahathir is known for his forceful approach. He dismisses the accusation of authoritarianism, regarding his own grip on power as beneficial in terms of the political stability it provides. This claim became increasingly difficult for him to justify, however, in the turbulent climate of 1998 and 1999, when—effectively for the first time—he faced a sustained opposition campaign calling for his retirement. The crisis was fuelled by his sudden dismissal in September 1998 of the man widely assumed to be his heir apparent, Deputy Prime Minister and Finance Minister Anwar Ibrahim. Anwar's subsequent prosecution on charges of sexual misconduct was backed up by lurid allegations but widely condemned as political manipulation of the judicial system. Anwar had begun to distance himself from Mahathir earlier in the year, favouring a more accommodating stance vis-à-vis the International Monetary Fund (IMF) over economic reforms and expenditure cuts, and he fought back against his dismissal and prosecution by denunciations of Mahathir for corruption and demands that he resign. Until this point, the only serious challenges to Mahathir's leadership had taken the form of contests for the UMNO presidency, which he had overcome in 1987 and successfully forestalled in 1998. Apart from the speculation about his health aroused when he underwent heart surgery in 1989, there had been little question, until the conflict with Anwar, that he would choose the time of his own departure.

Internationally, Mahathir was a driving force behind regional integration in the Association of South East Asian Nations (ASEAN) and the wider Asia–Pacific Economic Co-operation forum (APEC). He helped to popularize the concept of the 'tiger economies' of the region, characterized until the economic crisis of 1997 by dramatic rates of growth and industrialization, but also came under criticism for the emphasis on high-profile projects, many but by no means all of them now suspended, in his Malaysia 2020 vision of an industrialized society. The abrupt ending of the boom in 1997 may have had its origins in the unsustainability of much of the export-led growth, and weaknesses in financial and corporate regulation, but Mahathir also took it as a personal affront and a calumny on the 'Asian model'. He famously traded insults with international investment fund manager George Soros, whose actions he attacked as typifying the immorality and destructiveness of financial speculators, and has remained trenchant in his criticisms of international organizations such as the IMF and the World Bank for not doing more to avert such crises or, more recently, to help Malaysia and other countries to recover from them.

In September 2000 Mahathir handed over many of his duties to his deputy Abdullah Ahmad Badawi ahead of a full handover of power at the end of his current term in office in 2004. Mahathir said he would concentrate more on party matters, leaving government-related affairs to Abdullah. He surprised the world on 22 June 2002 when he tearfully made the announcement that he would step down from power in late 2003.

MALDIVES

Full name: The Republic of Maldives.

Leadership structure: The head of state is a president, elected by the People's Assembly and confirmed by national referendum. The president's term of office is five years. The head of government is the president, who appoints and presides over the cabinet.

President: Maumoon Abdul Gayoom — Since 11 Nov. 1978

Legislature: The legislature is unicameral. The sole chamber, the People's Assembly (People's Majlis), has 50 members. Two members are directly elected from each of the provinces (atolls) and from Malé, the capital, and the remaining eight members are appointed by the president, all for a five-year term.

Profile of the President:

Maumoon Abdul **GAYOOM**

Maumoon Abdul Gayoom, a former lecturer in Islamic studies, became president of the Maldives in November 1978 and has been re-elected on four successive occasions for further five-year terms. Gayoom's dominance in the family-based nonparty political system was challenged, however, by a coup attempt in 1988 and a bid by his brother-in-law Ilyas Ibrahim for nomination for the presidency in 1993, while an educated younger generation began pressing for increased freedoms. His re-election was endorsed by referendum most recently in October 1998.

Gayoom was born in the capital, Malé, on 29 December 1937. Following early schooling in Malé he went to al-Azhar University in Cairo, Egypt, where he graduated with a degree in Islamic studies and a diploma in education, going on to gain a master's degree in Islamic studies in 1966. He then embarked on an academic career, becoming a lecturer in Islamic studies and philosophy at Abdullahi Bayero College, Nigeria, and returning to the Maldives to teach at Aminiya School from 1971 to 1972.

In the 1970s he became successively manager of the government's shipping department, director of the telecommunications department, special undersecretary in the office of the prime minister, deputy ambassador to Sri Lanka and undersecretary at the ministry of external affairs. In June 1976 he was appointed permanent representative at the UN. He then took on a cabinet post as minister of transport, holding this job until the 1978 presidential elections when long-serving president Ibrahim Nasir stood down.

Nominated by the People's Assembly, Gayoom was endorsed by a 92.9% vote in the popular ballot in that election. His nomination for successive terms has usually been uncontested, although in 1993 Ilyas Ibrahim's rival candidacy attracted some support in the Assembly. He was re-elected most recently with a 90.9% endorsement in a national referendum held on 16 October 1998, having been unanimously selected by the Assembly from among five candidates.

Gayoom took over the defence and national security portfolios in 1982, and since November 1993 he has also been minister of finance and of the treasury. His dependence on good relations with India was underlined when he had to be rescued by Indian intervention after a coup attempt in 1988. In the 1990s he has become better known internationally for drawing attention to the threat posed by global warming to small island states.

Gayoom, who was made a Knight Grand Cross of the Order of St Michael and St George in October 1997, is married to Nasreena Ibrahim and they have two sons and two twin daughters.

MALI

Full name: The Republic of Mali.

Leadership structure: The head of state is a president, directly elected by universal adult suffrage. The president's term of office is five years. The president appoints the prime minister, who is head of government and appoints the other members of the Council of Ministers.

Presidents:	Alpha Oumar Konaré	8 June 1992—8 June 2002
	Amadou Toumani Touré	Since 8 June 2002
Prime Ministers:	Ibraham Boubacar Keita	4 Feb. 1994—15 Feb. 2000
	Mandé Sidibé	15 Feb. 2000—18 March 2002
	Modibo Keita	18 March 2002—9 June 2002
	Ahmed Mohamed Ag Hamani	Since 9 June 2002

Legislature: The legislature is unicameral. The sole chamber, the National Assembly (Assemblée Nationale), has 147 members, directly elected for a five-year term, renewable once only.

Profile of the President:

Amadou **TOUMANI TOURÉ**

Gen. (retd) Amadou Toumani Touré is an independent who led the country to multiparty democracy in 1992 in the wake of a coup. He turned to international politics and conflict resolution after handing power over to his democratically elected successor, Alpha Oumar Konaré, but returned to office in 2002 after winning a landslide victory with the backing of over 40 political parties.

Amadou Toumani Touré, now popularly known as 'ATT', was born on 4 November 1948 in Mopti in what was then colonial French Sudan. After a local education Touré joined the Malian armed forces in 1969, a year after a successful coup by Gen. Moussa Traoré. Toumani Touré is married and has two children.

Rising through the ranks of the army, Toumani Touré became a lieutenant in 1972 and a captain in the parachute battalion in 1978. In that year he was also appointed commander of Traoré's presidential guard. He stepped down from the guard and attained the rank of lieutenant-colonel in 1986. A rising tide of popular discontent with Traoré was sparked in 1991 by his attempt to suppress an uprising by the northern Tuareg people, and by heavy-handed policing of growing political demonstrations. On 26 March 1991 Toumani Touré organized a coup to overthrow the aging president and placed himself at the head of a Transitional Committee for the Salvation of the People—effectively president.

Keen to relinquish his hold on power, Toumani Touré organized a National Reconciliation Council which approved a new multiparty democratic constitution. In April 1991 he also appointed a civilian, Soumana Sacko, as prime minister. Despite a failed countercoup in July his government convened fresh presidential and legislative elections in early 1992. On 8 June 1992 Toumani Touré handed over power to Konaré and the Alliance for Democracy in Mali (Alliance pour la Démocratie au Mali—ADEMA) which had won a majority in the National Assembly. For the next ten years Toumani Touré stayed away from Malian politics, acting instead as a prominent mediator in regional conflicts, notably in Burundi and the Central African Republic. He was also involved in charities promoting children's welfare.

By 2001 the ADEMA government had become mired in accusations of corruption. Opposition parties began to flourish and Toumani Touré resigned his army commission (by now he had become a general) in September in order to qualify for the May 2002 presidential contest. He was elected in the second round with an overwhelming 65% majority, having received the backing of around 40 political parties, many of which coalesced in the Hope 2002 movement (Espoir 2002) which went on to gain the largest single share of seats in the July elections. Having traded heavily on his political independence, Toumani Touré hinted that he would largely follow the policies of Konaré.

Profile of the Prime Minister:

Ahmed Mohamed Ag **HAMANI**

Mohamed Ag Hamani is an independent economist who served as a minister in the government of former dictator Moussa Traoré. He was working as Malian ambassador to the UK and Belgium when he was nominated as prime minister in June 2002.

Ahmed Mohamed Ag Hamani was born in 1941 and trained as an economist and statistician. He is married to Habiba Mint Rachid. A former heavy smoker, he has since given up, having received surgery following a heart attack in April 2000. At one time a cabinet minister under former military dictator Traoré, holding the portfolios of youth and sports and tourism, he returned to government when newly re-elected president Amadou Toumani Touré appointed him prime minister on 9 June 2002. This brought him back from a diplomatic career in which he had been high commissioner at the Senegal River Development Organization and, from March 2001, Mali's ambassador in Europe, based in Brussels.

MALTA

Full name: The Republic of Malta.

Leadership structure: The head of state is a president, elected by the House of Representatives. The president's term of office is five years, renewable once only. The president appoints the prime minister and, on the latter's advice, the other members of the government. The prime minister is head of government. The cabinet is responsible to parliament.

President:	Guido de Marco	Since 4 April 1999
Prime Minister:	Eddie Fenech Adami	Since 6 Sept. 1998

Legislature: The legislature is unicameral. The sole chamber, the House of Representatives (Kamra Tad-Deputati), has 65 members, directly elected for a five-year term by universal adult suffrage. However, if a party gains a majority of votes in a general election, without winning a majority of seats in the House, extra seats are created until that party holds a majority of one seat.

Profile of the President:

Guido DE MARCO

Guido de Marco is a criminal lawyer by training and a full professor who continues to lecture on the subject. He is a long-serving member of the Nationalist Party (Partit Nazzjonalista—PN), sitting in every parliament from 1966 to 1999, and holding senior cabinet office when the party was in government between 1987 and 1996 and again after 1998. As foreign minister, and latterly as president, he was an active supporter of Malta's application for membership of the European Union (EU).

Guido de Marco was born in Valletta on 22 July 1931. He was educated in Malta at St Joseph High School and St Aloysius College before attending the Royal University of Malta. He graduated with a degree in philosophy, economics and Italian in 1952 and earned a degree in law in 1955. He retained his links with the university (known from 1974 simply as the University of Malta) as an active lecturer and professor of criminal law. He is married to Violet Saliba, and together they have three grown children all in the legal profession.

After training to be a lawyer de Marco worked as a Crown Counsel from 1964 to 1966, when he ran for parliament as a candidate for the PN. In 1967 he was elected to the parliamentary assembly of the Council of Europe where he served for almost 20 years.

In 1972 de Marco was appointed as secretary-general of the PN and went on to become the party's deputy leader from 1977 to 1999 when he resigned to take up the presidential nomination. From 1972 to 1987 the PN remained in opposition in the House of Representatives, fighting against the controversially narrow majority held by the Malta Labour Party (MLP). In general elections in 1987 the PN was brought back into power and Prime Minister Eddie Fenech Adami appointed de Marco as deputy prime minister and minister of the interior and justice. As interior minister, de Marco attended various summits and international gatherings.

De Marco switched portfolios from the interior to the foreign ministry in 1990 and immediately submitted Malta's application to join the European Community (later the EU). Later that year he was elected as president of the UN General Assembly for its 45th annual session in which time he visited both North and South Korea, and oversaw their admission to the UN in 1991. As foreign minister he worked to promote Malta's special position, as mediator between Europe and the Mediterranean, within the Organization for Security and Co-operation in Europe (OSCE) and the UN.

The PN suffered an electoral defeat at the hands of the MLP in 1996 and de Marco was appointed as the shadow minister of foreign affairs and had to stand back as the MLP froze the application process for membership of the EU. In early elections in 1998 the PN staged a dramatic recovery to regain power and de Marco was reappointed as foreign minister. On his return to the ministry he immediately reactivated Malta's application to the EU, which became his campaign base for the presidential election. With the support of the PN members, the House of Representatives elected him as president in April 1999. In December 2002 Malta was among ten countries invited to join the EU in May 2004.

Profile of the Prime Minister:

Eddie FENECH ADAMI

Eddie Fenech Adami, who became prime minister for the second time in September 1998, had already held that office from 1987 to 1996 and had led the Nationalist Party (Partit Nazzjonalista—PN) since 1977. A lawyer by training, he was elected to the House of Representatives in 1969. When he first came into government he undertook to overturn years of socialist policies in Malta.

Edward Fenech Adami was born in Birkirkara on 7 February 1934, the son of a customs officer. He was educated at St Aloysius College before attending the Royal University of Malta in the 1950s. He graduated with a degree in economics and classics before returning to study law. He was called to the Bar in 1959. A keen journalist, he edited the weekly *Il-Poplu* from 1962 to 1969. In 1965 he married Mary Sciberras, and together they have five children.

In 1961 Fenech Adami joined the PN national executive and served as assistant secretary-general from 1962 to 1975. He was elected to parliament in 1969 and has held a seat ever since. From 1975 he acted as president of the administrative and general councils of the PN. Elected to lead the party in 1977 after its electoral defeat by the Malta Labour Party (MLP), he set about reforming the PN during a period in opposition which was to last for ten years.

Seeking to adapt to a more socially conscious electorate, Fenech Adami's reforms attracted a new party membership that was notably more youthful. His support grew to the extent that in the general election of 1981 the PN won a majority of votes but a minority of seats. This bitter defeat caused years of disruption in parliament with Fenech Adami leading a campaign of civil disobedience and repeated boycotts of parliamentary sessions from 1981 to 1983. A constitutional amendment agreed in 1987 enabled a party with a popular majority to assume 'bonus' seats in the House of Representatives if necessary to form a majority. In that year's election the PN won 31 out of 65 elected seats, and acquired four bonus seats, allowing it to form a government.

As leader of the party, Fenech Adami was appointed as prime minister and began a series of political reforms to restructure Malta after 16 years of socialist government. Industries were deregulated and some privatized. The government was able to record nine successive years of positive economic growth, during which it was returned for a second term in 1992. Fenech Adami brought the country ever closer to the European Union (EU) and as part of this drive introduced value-added tax (VAT) in 1996. It proved an unpopular move and the PN found itself back in opposition after defeat in an early election in that year.

Fenech Adami was returned to the premiership after only two years in opposition following unwelcome increases in taxation by the MLP government, whose decision to call a snap election in September 1998 backfired when the PN won by a margin of 4.8% of the vote. Enjoying the luxury of the biggest PN majority since the Second World War (albeit only with 35 seats in the 65-seat House of Representatives), Fenech Adami promptly reinstated VAT, and he and the then foreign minister Guido de Marco reactivated Malta's application for EU membership, which had been frozen under the MLP. In December 2002 Malta was among ten countries invited to join the EU in May 2004.

MARSHALL ISLANDS

Full name: The Republic of the Marshall Islands.

Leadership structure: The head of state is a president, elected by the Parliament from among its members. The president is also head of government and appoints the cabinet.

Presidents: Imata Kabua   22 Jan. 1997—10 Jan. 2000

                         Kessai Note   Since 10 Jan. 2000

Legislature: The legislature is unicameral. The sole chamber, the Parliament (Nitijela), has 33 members, directly elected for a four-year term. There is also a 12-member Council of Chiefs (Council of Iroij), composed of traditional leaders (*iroijlaplap*), with consultative authority on matters relating to land and custom and which advises the cabinet.

Profile of the President:

Kessai **NOTE**

Kessai Note, the third president of the Marshall Islands, has a long record as a member of the Parliament, and was elected as its speaker three times. An influential critic of the previous heads of state, Amata and Imata Kabua, he is supported in government by a slim majority held by the United Democratic Party (UDP).

Kessai Hesa Note was born in 1950 on Jabat island, one of the smallest of the 24 inhabited atolls that make up the Marshall Islands group. At that time the Marshall Islands were part of the UN Trust Territory of the Pacific. Note went to school first on Ebeye island and then to the Marshall Islands' High School on Majuro, before attending Vudal College, Papua New Guinea, between 1971 and 1974, where he witnessed much of that country's transition to independence, achieved in 1975.

Returning to Majuro, he worked in the agriculture office of the Trust Territory administration, but did not become involved in the Marshalls' separation movement until his election to the Constitutional Convention in 1977. This body oversaw the drafting of the new constitution, which came into effect in 1979.

Note then was recommended to be the parliamentary candidate for his home island of Jabat. With an area of only 0.22 sq km, Jabat has a population recorded in 1999 as just 95, and Note has faced no opposition in holding on to its seat since his first election in 1980.

The Marshall Islands were dominated for almost two decades by Amata Kabua, the high ranking traditional chief of Majuro atoll, who held the presidency from 1979 until his death in 1996 when he was succeeded by his cousin, the chief of Kwajalein atoll, Imata Kabua. Note was a strong critic of their rule and a thorn in the executive's side, serving on both the High Court and the Supreme Court. His ability to oppose the government increased greatly in his three terms from 1987 as speaker of the Parliament. From this position he became an active counterweight to both the Kabua administrations, successfully pushing through a proposal to outlaw gambling. In September 1999 Note oversaw the country's very first no-confidence vote against a head of state. Although the motion failed, Kabua's days in power were numbered. In the run-up to the presidential elections on 3 January 2000, in which Note proposed to stand, the Parliament had first to elect a new speaker. The resounding defeat of Kabua's preferred candidate, at the hands of the UDP's Litokwa Tomeing, sent shock waves through the executive and Kabua declined to stand in the presidential contest. Note's election, all the more spectacular as he thus became the first commoner to win the presidency, was achieved on a strong anti-corruption platform calling for a major reform of government.

Among Note's policies are opposition to the storage of nuclear or other toxic wastes on the uninhabited atolls, and a crackdown on the corruption of the Kabua regime. He is also keen to increase productivity among civil servants, who, he complained, often work for only an hour and a half a day. A year into his administration Note survived the country's second no-confidence vote, brought by opposition senators led by Kabua, winning 19 votes in his favour in the 33-seat Parliament. Among his opponents' complaints was Note's apparent unwillingness to tackle the delicate subject of land rental with the USA. Note also faces strong criticism for his relationship with the controversial Reverend Sun Myung Moon, self-proclaimed messiah and founder of the Unification Church (Moonies).

MAURITANIA

Full name: The Islamic Republic of Mauritania.

Leadership structure: The head of state is a president, directly elected by universal adult suffrage. The president's term of office is six years. The president appoints the prime minister, who is designated head of government.

President: Maaouya ould Sid' Ahmed Taya   Since 18 April 1992
(seized power on 12 Dec. 1984)

Prime Minister: Cheikh el-Avia ould Mohamed Khouna   Since 16 Nov. 1998

Legislature: The legislature, the Parliament (Barlamane), is bicameral. The lower chamber, the National Assembly (Jamiya-al-Wataniya), has 81 members, directly elected for a five-year term. The upper chamber, the Senate (Majlis al-Chouyoukh), has 56 members of whom three represent Mauritanians living abroad, indirectly elected for a six-year term, one-third renewed every two years.

Profile of the President:

Col. (retd) Maaouya ould Sid' Ahmed **TAYA**

Col. (retd) Maaouya ould Sid' Ahmed Taya, who first seized power in a military coup in 1984 and then introduced a multiparty system in 1991, was elected to the presidency for successive six-year terms in January 1992 and December 1997. A northerner and career army officer, he had taken part in an earlier coup in 1978, and launched his 1984 coup after being demoted from the prime ministership. His Democratic and Social Republican Party (Parti Républicain Démocratique et Social—PRDS) dominates the National Assembly.

Maaouya ould Sid' Ahmed Taya was born in 1941 into a small northern tribal group in Atar, Adrar. He went to high school in Rosso, before starting his military training: he graduated as an officer after three years at the French Military School, and then attended the Military High Academy and the French War Academy. From 1976 to 1978 he was chief of military operations, then deputy chief of staff under the country's first president, Moktar ould Daddah. In 1978 he was involved in a successful coup, and was subsequently appointed commander of the garrison at Bir Mogkreïn in the north and then minister of defence, at a time when the army was fighting the Polisario Front in neighbouring Western Sahara.

The new military regime installed a Military Committee for National Salvation (Comité Militaire pour le Salut National—CMSN), of which Taya became a member in 1979; he was also appointed commander of the national gendarmerie and minister in charge of permanent security. The following year he became minister of mines and energy and then, on 26 April 1981, prime minister and minister of defence. However, by March 1984 the then president Lt.-Col. Mohammed Khouna ould Haidalla, perceiving Taya as a dangerous political rival, demoted him to the post of chief of staff of the armed forces and assumed Taya's government posts himself. The president's fears were realized in December 1984 when Taya led a bloodless coup and declared himself president and prime minister as well as chairman of the CMSN.

Shortly after seizing power Taya pulled Mauritania out of the conflict in Western Sahara and recognized the independence of the Polisario's Sahrawi Arab Democratic Republic. This initially raised tensions with Morocco, although diplomatic relations were restored and a ceasefire declared the following year. Domestically, Taya's main problems stemmed from tensions between Maures like himself who form the ruling elite, and the majority black population who are ethnically kin to the Senegalese peoples. His regime was accused of political oppression, executing opponents on charges of coup plotting, and repression of discontent especially in the south; cross-border friction erupted in 1989 when Senegalese resentment flared up and forced an exodus of Maures from that country.

Having first promised elections back in 1986, Taya's regime eventually held a referendum in 1991 which approved a new multiparty constitution. By July six parties had been legalized, including Taya's PRDS, and on 24 January 1992 Taya was elected president with just over 62% of the popular vote in a poll against three other candidates. Opposition parties, however, rejected the result and boycotted the subsequent legislative elections. On 18 April Taya was inaugurated as president but did not retain the post of prime minister. Two years later he dropped his military title to emphasize the return to civilian rule.

On 12 December 1997 Taya was re-elected as president, with 90% of the vote against four other candidates, but with opposition groups complaining of widespread multiple voting by presidential supporters. Taya brushed aside the allegations. In October 1999, in an unexpected move, he re-established the country's links with Israel and later banned the pro-Iraqi Ba'athist National Vanguard Party. Some observers claimed that the realignment was a cynical ploy to improve relations with the USA, a major aid donor. In October 2000 Taya quashed growing political opposition from the Union of Democratic Forces–New Era, dissolving the party altogether. Nonetheless, 15 parties contested the October 2001 elections which included a "dose of proportional representation". The PRDS easily won re-election although Taya's opponents gained considerable ground. In January 2002 Taya ordered the dissolution of the new Action for Change party.

Profile of the Prime Minister:

Cheikh el-Avia ould Mohamed **KHOUNA**

Cheikh el-Avia ould Mohamed Khouna is a member of the Democratic and Social Republican Party (Parti Républicain Démocratique et Social—PRDS). Trained in aquiculture, he first joined the government in 1995 and was prime minister for two years. He was out of office only briefly, returning in mid-1998 as foreign minister for four months before being reappointed to the prime ministership.

Cheikh el-Avia ould Mohamed Khouna was born in 1956 in Amourj, in the deserted southeastern corner of Mauritania, but went on to specialize in fisheries issues as a student at the Hassan II Institute for Agriculture and Breeding in Rabat, Morocco, between 1978 and 1982.

In February 1995 Khouna was appointed to the government as minister of fisheries and maritime economy. At the end of the year he was nominated to be prime minister and took up office in January 1996. He held the post for two years before being replaced in December 1997 following the re-election of President Maaouya Taya.

Remaining close to the government, Khouna was appointed to the office of the presidency before he was brought back into the cabinet as minister of foreign affairs and co-operation in July 1998. In November that year he was reappointed as prime minister. The PRDS was re-elected in October 2001 and Khouna was confirmed in office. He aims to promote a liberal economy and to address environmental issues.

MAURITIUS

Full name: Republic of Mauritius.

Leadership structure: The head of state is a president, elected by the National Assembly. The president's term of office is five years. The head of government is the prime minister, the leader of the majority party in parliament. The Council of Ministers is appointed by the president on the advice of the prime minister.

Presidents:	Cassam Uteem	1 July 1992—15 Feb. 2002
	Angidi Chettiar (acting)	15 Feb. 2002—18 Feb. 2002
	Arianga Pillay (interim)	18 Feb. 2002—25 Feb. 2002
	Karl Offmann	Since 25 Feb. 2002
Prime Ministers:	Navinchandra Ramgoolam	27 Dec. 1995—15 Sept. 2000
	Sir Anerood Jugnauth	Since 16 Sept. 2000

Legislature: The legislature is unicameral. The sole chamber, the National Assembly, has 70 members directly elected by universal adult suffrage. The members serve for a five-year term.

Profile of the President:

Karl **OFFMANN**

Karl Offmann is a leading member of the ruling Militant Socialist Movement (Mouvement Socialiste Militant—MSM). He is a career politician, having held cabinet office in four separate roles spanning more than 20 years. His appointment as president by the National Assembly in February 2002 followed the resignation of two previous heads of state over a contentious anti-terrorism bill.

Karl Auguste Offmann was born on 25 November 1940 into the island's minority Roman Catholic community. He has been closely involved with left-leaning Catholic groups, including the Young Christian Workers movement from 1957 to 1970. He is married to Danielle and has two sons. His early education was entirely on Mauritius where he graduated in mechanical engineering from the Technical College in Floréal in 1963.

After graduating Offmann found work in the Mauritian press, working as a manager at the Sentinelle Ltée until 1979, before becoming director of the Père Laval printing works. In 1983 he mixed his publishing life with his burgeoning political career, becoming director of *Le Socialiste*. He had first dabbled in politics in 1976 and won a seat in parliament in June 1982, representing the socialists in the central Curepipe constituency.

Under the stewardship of Prime Minister Anerood Jugnauth, Offmann was repeatedly appointed to the cabinet, beginning in 1983 as minister of economic planning and development. Between then and the MSM's legislative defeat in 1995 he served as minister of local government and co-operatives (1984–86), reform institutions (1986–87), social security and national solidarity (1986–87 and 1991–94) and labour and industrial relations (1994–95). He was also government chief whip for three years (1988–91).

Offmann was elected as president of the MSM in 1995 as it moved into opposition, and remained part of its politburo and national secretariat when he gave up the presidency in 2000.

In 2002, as the USA began recruiting allies in its 'war on terror', governments around the world responded by passing anti-terrorist laws aimed at increasing police powers. In February the incumbent and veteran Mauritian president, Cassam Uteem, resigned in disgust over the government's own anti-terrorism act. He was succeeded by Vice President Angidi Chettiar, who again resigned over the same law just three days later. The bill was eventually passed into law by an interim head of state, Chief Justice of the Supreme Court Arianga Pillay, leaving the post of president vacant. In elections on 25 February the National Assembly chose Offmann to fill the role.

Profile of the Prime Minister:

Sir Anerood **JUGNAUTH**

Anerood Jugnauth is a barrister and veteran politician, who was prime minister from 1982 to 1995 and was returned to office in 2000. Made a member of the (UK) Privy Council in 1987, he was knighted in 1988, and received the French Legion of Honour in 1990.

Anerood Jugnauth was born on 29 March 1930 in Palma. He was educated at the Church of England School in Palma, and then at Regent College, Quatre Bornes. He studied at Lincoln's Inn, UK, from 1951 and was called to the Bar in 1954. He is married to Sarojani Devi Ballah, with two children, and he speaks English, French, Hindi, Bhojpuri and Creole.

In 1963 Jugnauth first became a member of the Legislative Assembly (redesignated as the National Assembly in 1992 when Mauritius became a republic within the Commonwealth). In 1965 he was appointed minister of state for development, a post he occupied until 1967, when he became minister of labour. Between 1967 and 1969 he was a district magistrate, becoming Crown Counsel in 1969, Senior Crown Counsel in 1971 and Queen's Counsel in 1980.

In 1969 he was a cofounder, along with Paul Bérenger, of the Militant Mauritian Movement (Mouvement Militant Mauricien—MMM), and as president of the MMM between 1973 and 1982 became leader of the opposition in 1976. In 1982 the MMM formed a coalition government with the Mauritian Socialist Party (Parti Socialiste Mauricien—PSM) and Jugnauth became prime minister, with Bérenger as minister of finance. In 1983 he broke with Bérenger and the MMM to form the Militant Socialist Movement (Mouvement Socialiste Militant— MSM), which incorporated the PSM. This break in the coalition ended the government's majority and fresh elections were held in August. The MSM remained the dominant party in the coalition governments of 1983–87 and 1987– 91, and 1991–95, and Jugnauth retained the premiership. In addition, during the 1980s he at various times held the ministerial portfolios of finance, defence, internal security and reform institutions, information, interior and exterior communications with the outer islands, justice and was attorney general. Two attempts were made on Jugnauth's life, one in November 1988 and the other in March 1989, which he attributed to narcotics traffickers.

In November 1995 the government was defeated in a vote in the National Assembly on a constitutional amendment to provide primary education in oriental languages. Jugnauth dissolved the Assembly, elections were held in December, and a new government was formed by an alliance of the MMM and the Mauritius Labour Party of Navinchandra Ramgoolam, with the MSM completely unrepresented in the Assembly. Within five years this catastrophic defeat was reversed and the MSM returned to power, in September 2000, winning over three-quarters of the seats. Jugnauth, as its leader, was duly called upon to form another government.

MEXICO

Full name: The United Mexican States.

Leadership structure: The head of state is a president, directly elected by universal adult suffrage. The president's term of office is six years; presidential candidates must not have held public office in the six months prior to the election. The head of government is the president, who appoints the cabinet.

Presidents: Ernesto Zedillo   1 Dec. 1994—30 Nov. 2000

                        Vicente Fox   Since 1 Dec. 2000

Legislature: The legislature, the Congress of the Union (Congreso de la Unión), is bicameral. The lower chamber, the Chamber of Deputies (Cámara de Diputados), has 500 members, directly elected for a three-year term. The upper chamber, the Senate of the Republic (Senado de la República), has 128 members, directly elected for a six-year term.

Profile of the President:

Vicente **FOX**

Vicente Fox's election as president ended 71 years of rule by the Institutional Revolutionary Party (Partido Revolucionario Institucional—PRI), while his centrist National Action Party (Partido Acción Nacional—PAN) swept the PRI from power in concurrent legislative elections. He is a rural businessman who received his commercial training when he headed Coca-Cola's operations in Latin America in the late 1970s, and his political education as governor of Guanajuato state. Fox's plain talking, cowboy-dressing style was much criticized by opponents as lacking in substance. He has promised to soften the country's 'harsh' capitalism with a 'third way'.

Vicente Fox Quesada was born in Mexico City on 2 July 1942 but was soon taken home to the San Cristóbal ranch in Guanajuato state in central Mexico. He was raised in the rural community and has kept closely in touch with his agricultural roots throughout his career. He studied business administration at the Ibero-American University, in Mexico City, then went to Harvard in the USA to get a diploma in management skills, and returned to Mexico in 1965 to work for the Coca-Cola Company as a 'route supervisor'.

After three years of travelling around the country on delivery trucks Fox was appointed as the company's youngest ever regional manager. He continued to work his way up the ranks, to become manager for the company's operations in Mexico and Latin America in 1975. During his four years in this position Fox ensured that Coca-Cola replaced its main international rival, Pepsi, as the dominant supplier of soft drinks in Mexico.

In 1979 Fox abandoned management in the multinational to direct his family's Guanajuato-based agricultural enterprise, Gruppo Fox (GF). As well as ranching, GF engaged in various types of agro-industrial activities, and even shoe making, a speciality of the area. Fox has maintained an active role in agriculture and his family farm in the central state exports vegetables to Europe, Japan and the USA, as well as rearing cattle and ostriches for the domestic market. While managing GF, Fox developed an association with the opposition PAN, and began to write political articles for national and state newspapers.

In elections in 1988 Fox won a seat in the Federal Chamber of Deputies as a PAN candidate. Three years later he stood in gubernatorial elections for Guanajuato state but was defeated by PRI candidate Ramón Aguirre. However, popular discontent with the result forced Aguirre from office, leaving a PAN member as interim governor. Fox won fresh elections in 1995. His governorship of Guanajuato was widely seen as a major success and provided the training ground for his later bid for the presidency. Under his leadership there was greater investment in the state and a marked improvement in education.

Fox, who has married twice (most recently to Marta Sahagún in July 2001) and has four children, made much of his rural roots during his campaign for president in 1999–2000, even pledging to continue wearing cowboy boots and jeans if elected. His abrasive manner towards his opponents, labelling the PRI candidate Francisco Labastida a "sissy", won support among the rural voters. However, his detractors accused him of carrying no real conviction with his pledge to perform a "new economic miracle". Although he was an extremely popular candidate, there can be little doubt that dissatisfaction with 71 years of PRI rule played a major role in his electoral victory in the July 2000 poll. He gained a convincing 43.5% of the vote, leaving Labastida with only 37%.

Promises of an inclusive consensus government were confounded when the PRI rejected Fox's invitation to join a broad-based coalition, and political rivalry between the PRI and PAN has dominated elections at all levels. Among Fox's campaign pledges had been a promise to recommence negotiations with Zapatista rebels from the southern state of Chiapas and within weeks of his inauguration he ordered the first major troop withdrawals from the state. Despite this gesture, however, the Zapatistas continued to press for further concessions. Elsewhere Fox's popularity has begun to fall as he has done little to achieve his "economic miracle", stymied as he is by the global economic slowdown which has particularly affected the USA, Mexico's main trading partner. In January 2002 he dismantled the now defunct agrarian policy which had once been the cornerstone of the PRI regime, and promised to properly codify land claims to end decades of disputes.

FEDERATED STATES OF MICRONESIA

Full name: The Federated States of Micronesia.

Leadership structure: The head of state is a president, elected by the Congress. The president's term of office is four years. The head of government is the president, who is responsible to the Congress. The cabinet is appointed by the president.

President: Leo Falcam   Since 12 May 1999

Legislature: The legislature is unicameral. The sole chamber, the Congress of the Federated States of Micronesia (FSM), has 14 members, ten senators directly elected for a two-year term and four 'at large' senators (one from each state) who are elected for a four-year term. Both president and vice president must be chosen from among the 'at large' senators.

Profile of the President:

Leo **FALCAM**

Leo Falcam, who was vice president prior to his election to the presidency in May 1999, was educated in the USA and served in the Micronesian embassy in Washington D.C. after a career in the US-controlled administration of the UN Trust Territory of the Pacific Islands.

Leo Falcam was born on the island of Pohnpei (known as Ponape until 1984) on 20 November 1935, in what was then Japanese-controlled territory. After the Second World War, and Micronesia's transition from Japanese colony to UN Trust Territory, Falcam went to Hawaii, USA, to study sociology, and then to a postgraduate course at the Woodrow Wilson School of Public and International Affairs at Princeton University in New Jersey.

In 1975 Falcam was appointed as chairman of the Ponape delegation to the Micronesian Constitutional Convention. From here he began his political career in the office of the high commissioner of the (US-controlled) Trust Territory administration while maintaining his links with his home state as district administrator for Ponape. In 1979 the Trust Territory splintered into the independent Federated States of Micronesia (FSM) and the Marshall Islands.

Representing the new government, Falcam returned to the USA in the early 1980s and served as the country's first liaison officer in Washington D.C. He chaired the Ponape Constitutional Convention from 1983 until the introduction of the new constitution the following year (under which the island's name was changed to Pohnpei). He then became the first postmaster-general for the FSM, and the chairman of the national bank. He also sat on the board of trustees for the Pohnpei Agriculture and Trade School. In 1987 he was elected to the FSM Congress and served successive governments in various roles before becoming senator-at-large for Pohnpei and vice president of the country.

In the election held by the Congress in May 1999 Falcam defeated the incumbent FSM president Jacob Nena. Under his administration the FSM renegotiated its Compact of Free Association with the USA, maintaining defence and security ties, and promoting economic aid and development. During 2000 Falcam's government had to weather the economic effects of an embargo on all exports to the US territories of Guam and the Northern Mariana Islands, prompted by an outbreak of cholera on Pohnpei.

MOLDOVA

Full name: The Republic of Moldova.

Leadership structure: The head of state is a president, hitherto directly elected by universal adult suffrage, but, under the constitutional amendment of 2000, now elected by the Parliament. The president's term of office is four years. The president nominates a prime minister and a government. The prime minister is head of government, although the president may preside over Council of Ministers meetings on matters of particular importance. A referendum held on 23 May 1999, under the terms of which the president would also be head of government, was ruled invalid on 3 November 1999 by the Constitutional Court. In July 2000 Parliament overruled the president to amend the constitution to increase the powers of the executive.

Presidents:	Petru Lucinschi	15 Jan. 1997—7 April 2001
	Vladimir Voronin	Since 7 April 2001
Prime Ministers:	Dumitru Braghiş	21 Dec. 1999—19 April 2001
	Vasile Tarlev	Since 19 April 2001

Legislature: The legislature is unicameral. The sole chamber, the Parliament (Parlamentul), has 101 members, directly elected for a four-year term.

Profile of the President:

Vladimir **VORONIN**

Vladimir Voronin is a charismatic former baker, who worked his way up through the ranks of the Moldovan Communist hierarchy for thirty years, reaching the presidency (to the considerable alarm of foreign investors) in 2001 ten years after the country gained independence upon the breakup of the Soviet Union. Despite campaigning against the presidential system in the late 1990s, he has attempted to increase the position's power since his election. He has also tried, so far in vain, to break the deadlock over the separatist Transdniestria region where he himself was born.

Vladimir Nikolayevich Voronin was born on 25 May 1941 in Corjova (Korzhevo), a village in the Chişinau (Kishinev) district but now within the breakaway Transdniestrian Republic. At the time, Moldova had been incorporated into the Soviet Union, as it was once again in 1944 (after a period of

Soviet retreat before Hitler's armies). In 1958 Voronin enrolled at the Chişinau Consumer Co-operation College and graduated in 1961 to become manager of a bakery in Criuleni, on the Dniester River. He moved on in 1966 to become the director of a municipal bakery in the town of Dubossary across the river.

Voronin, who is married with two children, retrained in 1971 as an economist at the Moscow Food Industry Institute and then returned to Moldova to begin work within the republican branch of the Communist Party. Between then and 1989 he was an active party official in Dubossary, in the western border town of Ungeny, and in Bendery (back on the Dniester). He also became a deputy in the Moldovan Supreme Soviet (parliament) in 1980 and retrained as a political scientist at the Academy of Social Sciences, graduating in 1983.

Entering the Moldovan government as minister of internal affairs in 1989 (and given the rank of major-general), he left the government before it declared Moldovan independence in 1991 and spent two years out of the limelight, studying law. During this time he was also a reservist in the Russian police force. In 1993 he returned to mainstream Moldovan politics. He helped to co-ordinate the rebirth of the Moldovan Communist Party (Partidul Comunistilor din Republica Moldova—PCRM) and was elected its first secretary at the December 1994 party congress.

When Voronin stood as the party's candidate in the 1996 presidential elections, he came third out of nine with just over 10% of the vote. Two years later, in the country's third legislative elections, the PCRM secured 40 seats in Parliament, Voronin's among them. Within Parliament, Voronin led the PCRM in campaigns against the weak presidential system and the country's increasingly painful economic reforms. Constitutional amendments in 2000 saw Parliament take over responsibility for electing the president, but after repeated failures by any candidate to gain a victory, the legislature was dissolved. Legislative elections in February 2001 produced a dramatic and overwhelming PCRM victory. With 71 seats in the 101-seat chamber, the party's deputies had no difficulty in electing Voronin to the presidency in a ballot held on 4 April.

As president, Voronin has personally led renewed negotiations with the self-proclaimed president of separatist Transdniestria, Igor Smirnov, although these talks have achieved few tangible results to match their many headlines. Voronin has also proven eager to expand his own constitutional powers. It has even been suggested that he intends to merge the presidency with the premiership. His appointment of the independent businessman Vasile Tarlev as prime minister leaves him as the most influential member of the PCRM in government. The choice of Tarlev, coupled with his own pledges of commitment to a market economy, have gone some way to placate reformists and foreign investors alarmed by his postelection proclamation that "I have been, am, and will remain a Communist". Nevertheless, his government has distanced Moldova from Western Europe and he has even expressed interest in making the country a third member of a proposed Russia–Belarus union.

Profile of the Prime Minister:

Vasile **TARLEV**

Vasile Tarlev was inaugurated as prime minister of Moldova on 19 April 2001. Five times the Chişinau Businessman of the Year at the head of the sweet and chocolate giant Bucuria, he had no affiliation to any political party, and his appointment signalled the new Communist government's intention to maintain a free-market economy after its sweeping electoral victory in early 2001. His position is somewhat undermined by the efforts of Communist President Vladimir Voronin to strengthen his own role.

Vasile Pavlovich Tarlev, who is now married with two children, was born into the ethnic Bulgarian community in Bascalia in the extreme south of Soviet-controlled Moldova on 9 October 1963, and worked in the village as a tractor and goods vehicle driver before being conscripted into the Soviet army in 1981. He returned to work as a driver, moving in this capacity to the Pushkin Theatre in Chişinau (Kishinev), until 1985 when he enrolled with the technology faculty of the Chişinau Polytechnic Institute.

On graduation Tarlev found employment in the capital with the Bucuria confectionery firm as a mechanic, and steadily worked his way up the company. By the time of Moldovan independence in 1991 he was chief engineer, and within a further four years he had become director-general of Bucuria and been elected chairman of the National Producers' Association. He was first awarded the accolade of "Businessman of the Year" by the Chişinau city authorities in 1996 and held the title for four successive years.

In 1998 Tarlev was awarded a doctorate in technical studies and entered government service as a member of President Petru Lucinschi's Supreme Economic Council. This experience, along with his prominent role at the head of Bucuria, made Tarlev an attractive choice for prime minister in April 2001 for the newly elected President Voronin, eager to convince foreign donors that his communist government would not derail the country's post-Soviet economic reforms. Tarlev's lack of political affiliation also helped counter the concern that the Communists' parliamentary majority would be used to swamp the government with party apparatchiks. His lack of a power base in the party was another reason for Voronin to favour him, avoiding the emergence of a powerful party rival.

As prime minister, Tarlev has pledged to continue the free-market policies of his predecessors but did criticize the method of previous privatizations. Under his stewardship the country has already been welcomed into the World Trade Organization (WTO) and the Balkan Security Pact.

MONACO

Full name: The Principality of Monaco.

Leadership structure: The head of state is a hereditary prince. The head of government is the minister of state, nominated by the prince from a list of three French diplomats submitted by the French government.

Prince:	Rainier III	Since 9 May 1949
Ministers of State:	Michel Lévêque	3 Feb. 1997—5 Jan. 2000
	Patrick Leclercq	Since 5 Jan. 2000

Legislature: The legislature is unicameral. The sole chamber, the National Council (Conseil National), has 18 members, directly elected by universal adult suffrage for a maximum five-year term. The chamber will be enlarged to 24 members at the elections due in early 2003.

Profile of the Prince:

RAINIER III

Prince Rainier has been head of state for longer than any other current incumbent in the world save for King Bhumibol of Thailand. He gave up his absolute powers in 1962, but as sovereign retains significant authority and represents Monaco in its relations with foreign powers, signing and ratifying treaties. His marriage to film star Grace Kelly ensured that he and his family retained a place of particular prominence in the celebrity-obsessed media.

Born on 31 May 1923, Rainier inherited the throne at the age of 25. He succeeded his grandfather Prince Louis II through the female line, being the son of Prince Louis's daughter Princess Charlotte and of Prince Pierre de Polignac. Before Louis's death Rainier had fought in the French army as a volunteer during the Second World War and was awarded the War Cross, followed in 1947 by the Cross of the Legion of Honour.

In 1951, two years after his accession to the throne, Prince Rainier signed the Franco-Monégasque convention of friendship and mutual administrative assistance, one of a series of conventions on which relations between the principality and France are now based. In 1962 he reformed the constitution, which had first been promulgated in 1911 by Albert I, and abrogated his absolute powers. In 1966 he led Monte Carlo's centenary celebrations and has since then

357

presided over Monaco's successful development as a tax haven and exclusive tourist destination for the international jet set. However, the country's status as a tax haven has prompted international criticism in recent years. In an unusual outburst in response, Prince Rainier threatened in October 2000 to declare the principality's sovereignty and break off relations with France after it had demanded a change in Monaco's tax laws and other financial regulations.

Prince Rainier married the US film star Grace Patricia Kelly on 18 April 1956, and they had three children, Princess Caroline, Prince Albert (the heir to the throne) and Princess Stephanie. Princess Grace died in a car crash in 1982 while driving in the hills above Monaco.

Profile of the Minister of State:

Patrick **LECLERCQ**

Patrick Leclercq was sworn in as minister of state for the principality of Monaco on 5 January 2000. His role is effectively as chief administrator in the tiny state and he heads a four-member cabinet. He was chosen by the ruling monarch Prince Rainier III from a list of three French diplomats presented by the French government, and had previously served for many years as an ambassador for France.

Patrick Leclercq was born in Lille, northern France, on 2 August 1938. He graduated from the Ecole Libre des Sciences Politiques (now the Paris Institute of Political Studies) before attending the elite state-run Ecole Nationale d'Administration. From here he began a long career in diplomacy. He has been married twice and has a total of three children.

Between 1971 and 1976 Leclercq acted as first secretary at France's permanent mission to the UN in New York, USA. He returned to Paris in 1978 where he was appointed as a deputy manager in the foreign ministry and went on to fill the role of diplomatic counsellor in the office of President Valéry Giscard d'Estaing. After the 1981 change of government, he was posted in 1982 to Canada where he served as consul-general in Montréal until 1985. He then took up his first ambassadorial position, in Jordan. In 1989 he was appointed as director of France's diplomatic efforts in the Middle East and north Africa, and he went on to become ambassador to Egypt (1991–96) and then to Spain (1996–99).

On 28 December 1999 Prince Rainier chose Leclercq, from the traditional list presented by the French government, as minister of state in place of Michel Lévêque who retired a few days later. In October 2000 Prince Rainier, angered at continued French insistence on economic reform, put Leclercq in an awkward position when he threatened to declare Monaco's unilateral sovereignty and break loose from its constitutional ties with France.

MONGOLIA

Full name: Mongolia.

Leadership structure: The head of state is a president, directly elected by universal adult suffrage. The president's term of office is four years. The head of government is the prime minister, who is elected by the State Great Hural and appoints a cabinet.

President: Natsagyn Bagabandi   Since 20 June 1997

Prime Ministers: Rinchinnyamyn Amarjargal   30 July 1999—26 July 2000

                        Nambariyn Enkhbayar   Since 26 July 2000

Legislature: The legislature is unicameral. The sole chamber, the State Great Hural (Ulsyn Ikh Khural), has 76 members, directly elected for a four-year term.

Profile of the President:

Natsagyn **BAGABANDI**

Natsagyn Bagabandi is a Moscow-trained food technologist and long-standing member of the Mongolian People's Revolutionary Party (MPRP), which was the sole ruling party until the 1990s. He chaired the State Great Hural between 1992 and 1996, before standing as MPRP candidate for the presidency. His convincing victory over outgoing President Punsalmaagyn Ochirbat of the Democratic Union Coalition (DUC) in May 1997 was won on a platform of slowing the pace of Mongolia's market reforms and boosting spending on social programmes. Until the MPRP's victory in the 2000 legislative elections he had to work in 'cohabitation' with a DUC government.

Born on 22 April 1950, in Zavkhan province, Natsagyn Bagabandi was educated in the Soviet Union, studying at the Food Technological Institute in Moscow. After completing his education he worked in a food factory from 1972. Three years later he returned to Mongolia, continuing to work in the food industry.

Becoming active in politics in the 1970s, he made steady progress in the MPRP, serving on the central committee from 1980 onward and becoming its deputy president in 1992, at the time of the country's retreat from communism. Also in 1992, when the MPRP won an overwhelming victory in Mongolia's first multiparty elections, Bagabandi was elected to represent his native province in the State Great Hural. He was chairman of the Hural for the next four years, and during this time made official visits to Russia, China and Japan, broadening parliamentary links.

In the June 1996 legislative elections the MPRP suffered a serious defeat and the DUC won 50 of the 76 seats in the Hural. The new government brought in a radical programme of privatization and free-market reforms, with the aim of moving Mongolia rapidly from a centralized to a market economy, but leading initially to sharp increases in the cost of living and in unemployment.

In January 1997, when the MPRP decided at its 22nd congress to drop its Marxist–Leninist ideology in favour of 'democratic socialism', the moderate Bagabandi was an obvious choice as chairman of the party. In the presidential elections on 18 May 1997 he won 60.8% of the vote. The DUC government remained in office for a further three years, however, in an uncertain form of 'cohabitation' with Bagabandi, and lacking the required two-thirds majority to overturn any presidential veto.

The situation was reversed dramatically in legislative elections in July 2000 when the MPRP virtually eradicated the DUC (which by 2002 had merged to become part of the Mongolian National Democratic Party). With the backing of the government Bagabandi was able to secure re-election in May 2001 with 58% of the vote.

Profile of the Prime Minister:

Nambariyn **ENKHBAYAR**

Nambariyn Enkhbayar became prime minister after his Mongolian People's Revolutionary Party (MPRP) won a sweeping victory in the 2000 legislative elections, returning to power after its first four years in opposition. He has worked hard to transform the MPRP (the former ruling communists) into a modernist centre-left party, distancing it from its Soviet heritage. His style is often likened to that of UK prime minister Tony Blair.

Nambariyn Enkhbayar was born on 1 June 1958 in Ulan Bator, the capital of what was then the Mongolian People's Republic. He went to school in the city before travelling to the neighbouring Soviet Union to attend the prestigious Moscow Institute of Literature. After graduating in 1980 he returned to Mongolia and joined the Mongolian Writers' Union (MWU) as an interpreter–editor.

During the course of the 1980s Enkhbayar rose up the hierarchy of the MWU, becoming chief secretary in 1990 as well as vice president of the Mongolian Interpreters' Union. In 1985 he joined the MPRP, and made the transition to a government role with relative ease, serving in 1990–92 as the first deputy chairman of the government committee on culture and art. In the country's first democratic elections in 1992 Enkhbayar won a seat in the State Great Hural, and was appointed to be minister of culture.

The MPRP suffered a crushing defeat at the hands of the Democratic Union Coalition (DUC) in the general elections of June 1996. Enkhbayar lost his parliamentary seat, as did many of his colleagues. Splits then began to emerge within the MPRP between the communist old guard and the reformist faction eager to reinvent the party. As a reformist, Enkhbayar was elected as general secretary in July, and after the election of the party chairman Natsagyn Bagabandi as president in 1997, he was appointed to succeed him as chairman. He re-entered the Hural through a by-election for Bagabandi's vacant seat. One of his first actions as leader of the opposition was to initiate a motion of censure against the DUC government, setting the tone for the next three years. In 1998 he led the MPRP in a boycott of the Hural, returning only to pass a motion of no confidence in the beleaguered administration. In all, Enkhbayar faced three successive prime ministers across the parliamentary floor before general elections in July 2000 returned the transformed MPRP to power with an overwhelming majority, controlling 95% of the seats in the Hural.

On winning the election, Enkhbayar made it clear that he and his party were not "communist monsters" and would press ahead with a "third way" of industrial privatizations coupled with generous social spending. Enkhbayar has tried consciously to emulate modern Western leaders in style. He associates with popular musicians and dresses according to modern fashion in an attempt to shake off the dusty image of communist-era bureaucrats. To this end he has even hired an image consultant from a UK firm. However, his grand programme of modernization depends heavily on international aid, and in reality the country is still struggling to recover from the crippling winter of 1999/2000.

Nambariyn Enkhbayar is married and has three children. He is fluent in Russian and English and took a year out in 1986 to study English literature at the University of Leeds in the UK; he has translated into Mongolian some of the works of, among others, Charles Dickens, Aldous Huxley and Virginia Woolf.

MOROCCO

Full name: The Kingdom of Morocco.

Leadership structure: The head of state is a hereditary constitutional monarch. The head of government is the prime minister, appointed by the king. The prime minister appoints the cabinet.

King:	Mohammed VI	Since 23 July 1999
Prime Ministers:	Abderrahmane el-Youssoufi	4 Feb. 1998—9 Oct. 2002
	Driss Jettou	Since 9 Oct. 2002

Legislature: The legislature, the Parliament (Barlaman), is bicameral. The lower house, the House of Representatives (Majlis al-Nuwab), has 325 members, directly elected for a five-year term. The upper house, the House of Councillors (Majlis al-Mustasharin), has 270 representatives from local authorities, professional organizations and the 'salaried classes', indirectly elected for nine years, with one-third of its members elected every three years.

Profile of the King:

MOHAMMED VI

Mohammed succeeded to the throne on the death of his father King Hassan II in July 1999. Although royal iconography is prevalent everywhere in Morocco, he stated his intention of pursuing a constitutional monarchy, taking King Juan Carlos of Spain as a model for his own role. Although he has fostered his image as a modernizer and a reformer, he has proceeded cautiously, while sometimes using the more traditional direct means of government to introduce reforms.

Mohammed was born on 21 August 1963, in Rabat, and educated at the Collège Royale, and the faculty of judicial, economic and social sciences at the University Mohammed V, Rabat. Under his father he had very limited direct political involvement, although he did chair the organizing committee for the Ninth Mediterranean Games, held in Casablanca in 1982, and the following year led the Moroccan delegation to both the Seventh Summit of Non-Aligned Nations in New Delhi (India) and the Tenth Franco-African Conference at Vittel (France). In 1985 he was appointed co-ordinator of administration and services for the armed forces, and he was promoted to the rank of general in 1994.

Propelled into the centre of political life by the death of King Hassan in mid-1999, Mohammed concentrated on fulfilling public engagements during the first few months of his reign, but did mark a departure from his father's policy by meeting the son of the former Berber leader Abdelkarim Khattari during a visit to the north in October 1999. The first real indication of major change came in November when he dismissed the authoritarian minister of the interior, Driss Basri, who had been close to King Hassan. The following March he launched his National Action Plan, which included provision for extending the rights of women, although this has proven fraught with difficulties in view of the powerful opposition of Islamic fundamentalists.

While some of Mohammed's efforts in the sphere of human rights promotion have been applauded, such as his opening of the first Arab human rights training centre in Rabat in April 2000, his intolerance of criticism in the media has caused concern. In late 2000 journalists and newspapers were prosecuted for printing stories critical of the military and the ruling socialist government. Similarly, he inaugurated the Royal Institute for Amazigh (Berber) Culture in July 2001 but has been forthright in restating his country's claim to Western Sahara. Following elections in September 2002, Mohammed replaced the previous Socialist prime minister with the nonparty Driss Jettou.

In a notable break with tradition Mohammed publicly announced his July 2002 marriage to computer engineer Salma Bennani, now Princess Lalla, before it happened, and agreed to stage a televised public ceremony.

Profile of the Prime Minister:

Driss **JETTOU**

Driss Jettou is an independent technocrat and a career politician. Having served as commerce and industry minister with varying responsibilities throughout much of the 1990s, he was appointed prime minister by King Mohammed VI on 9 October 2002 following general elections.

Driss Jettou was born on 24 May 1945 in El Jadida on the Atlantic coast of what was then the Spanish colony of Morocco. After studying in nearby Casablanca he graduated in physics and chemistry in 1966, and completed his education in 1968 with a diploma in business management from Cordwainers College in London, UK. He has headed a number of commercial federations, including the Moroccan Federation of Leather Industries and the Moroccan Association of Exporters. He is married and has four children.

When King Hassan II appointed a nonparty government in 1993, he included Jettou as commerce and industry minister. Jettou held this portfolio for five years, adding in July 1994 the portfolios of foreign trade (although only until February 1995) and artisans.

In 1998, when the Socialist Union of Popular Forces (Union Socialiste des Forces Populaires—USFP) formed a government after the legislative elections, Jettou was excluded from office, but he returned to the cabinet on 19 September 2001, this time as interior minister under USFP prime minister Abderrahmane el-Youssoufi.

In legislative elections held on 27 September 2002 the USFP and its right-of-centre ally Istiqlal remained the largest parties in the House of Representatives despite an increase in support for Islamist parties. However, King Mohammed VI retired the veteran Youssoufi and turned instead to Jettou as a prominent nonpartisan figure to head his new government.

MOZAMBIQUE

Full name: The Republic of Mozambique.

Leadership structure: The head of state is a president, directly elected by universal adult suffrage. The president's term of office is five years, renewable no more than twice consecutively. The president is head of government, and appoints the Council of Ministers, including a prime minister to assist the president in the leadership of the government.

President: Joaquim Alberto Chissano   Since 6 Nov. 1986

Prime Minister: Pascoal Mocumbi   Since 16 Dec. 1994

Legislature: The legislature is unicameral. The sole chamber, the Assembly of the Republic (Assembléia da República), has 250 members, directly elected for a five-year term.

Profile of the President:

Joaquim Alberto **CHISSANO**

Joaquim Chissano, who first became president under the single-party regime in November 1986, has twice been re-elected (in 1994 and 1999) under the 1990 multiparty constitution. Chissano was a guerrilla leader in the struggle for independence from Portugal, and cofounder of the Mozambique Liberation Front (Frente da Libertação de Moçambique—FRELIMO), taking over as leader on the death in 1986 of Samora Machel.

Joaquim Alberto Chissano was born on 22 October 1939 in Malehice, Chibuto district, Gaza province, into a wealthy and influential family. His traditional name is Dambuza. He was one of the first black pupils to attend the grammar school founded by the Portuguese in Lourenço Marques (now Maputo) and was president of the Nucleus of African Secondary Students of Mozambique in 1959–60. He went to Portugal in 1960 to study medicine at university, but left secretly the following year to join the liberation forces. In 1962 Chissano cofounded FRELIMO, becoming secretary to the movement's president. He joined the war as a guerrilla in 1964 and became FRELIMO representative in Tanzania in 1968–74. He is married with four children.

Chissano participated in the 1974 Lusaka negotiations between FRELIMO and the Portuguese government which established a framework for a rapid transition to independence. Samora Machel, the FRELIMO leader who was to become the first postindependence president of Mozambique, appointed him as prime minister of the interim government during this period, and as minister of foreign affairs for the first decade after independence. He became a member of the People's Assembly in 1977, and a major-general in the Mozambican armed forces in 1980. When Machel died in a plane crash in 1986, the central committee of the party elected Chissano as president and commander-in-chief in his place.

As president, Chissano oversaw the drafting of a multiparty constitution in 1990 and the signing in 1992 of the UN-brokered peace agreement which signalled the end of the civil war between the (former Marxist) FRELIMO and the South African-backed Mozambique National Resistance Movement (Resistência Nacional Moçambicana—RENAMO). As part of that agreement, multiparty elections for the presidency and the renamed legislature, the Assembly of the Republic, were eventually held in October 1994. Chissano won the presidential poll with 53% of the vote against 33% for RENAMO leader Afonso Dhlakama.

Chissano's chief task at this time was to rebuild a country devastated by the civil war, which had left 900,000 dead and one million refugees. He successfully oversaw the process of demobilization, although the government had problems reasserting its authority in central districts. In 1995 Mozambique joined the Commonwealth, the first state to do so which was neither anglophone nor a former British colony.

Presidential and legislative elections were held simultaneously on 3–5 December 1999, bringing re-election for Chissano, with 52.3% of the vote against Dhlakama, and victory to FRELIMO in the legislative poll. International observers noted some logistical problems but pronounced the votes free and fair. RENAMO disagreed, leading to a protracted dispute with the government which was not even interrupted by the terrible flooding which struck the south of the country in early 2000. By December of that year, however, RENAMO had ended its boycott of parliament, dropped threats to form a parallel government and finally recognized the re-election of Chissano. Chissano pledged in December 2001 that he would not seek a third term in office, as many other African leaders were doing, but would step down at the end of his current term in 2004.

Profile of the Prime Minister:

Pascoal **MOCUMBI**

Pascoal Mocumbi, with a background in medicine, worked in Mozambique in obstetrics and gynaecology and in smallpox eradication, and initially entered the government as minister of health, moving only in 1987 to the foreign ministry (and seven years later to the premiership). He has been a member of the Mozambique Liberation Front (Frente da Libertação de Moçambique—

FRELIMO) since its formation during the country's struggle for independence. A practising Christian, he is a member of the Presbyterian Church.

Pascoal Mocumbi was born in Lourenço Marques (now Maputo) on 10 April 1941, the son of Manuel Mocumbi Malume and Leta Alson Cuhle. His traditional name is Mahykete. He received his primary education at the mission school in Inharrime, Inhambane province, and between 1953 and 1960 attended secondary school at the Liceu Salazar in Maputo. He went to Lisbon Medical University in 1960–61 and then to the University of Poitiers, France, until 1963 for further medical study. He became involved in student politics in the late 1950s, joining the Nucleus of African Secondary Students in Mozambique, and in 1961 he was a founder member of the National Union of Mozambique Students, later serving as the organization's secretary-general and vice president.

In 1962 he interrupted his studies in Europe to take part in the creation of FRELIMO in exile in Tanzania, becoming a member of the central committee and also head of information and propaganda. He later served as the FRELIMO permanent representative to Algeria, from 1965 to 1967. He resumed his studies at the University of Lausanne in 1967, and in 1970 he married Adelina Isabel Bernardino Paindane Mocumbi; they have six children.

Having gained his medical diploma in 1973, and completed his medical internship in Switzerland in 1975, he returned to Mozambique to become a doctor of obstetrics and gynaecology at Maputo Central Hospital, and director of the José Macamo Hospital in 1975–76. He then held a series of medical posts, and was involved in the National Vaccination Campaign to eradicate smallpox.

He joined the government as minister of health in 1980, holding the post until 1987, during which time he established a programme of primary care mother-and-baby clinics. As foreign minister from 1987 until 1994, he faced the complexities of relations with neighbouring countries then supporting the Mozambique National Resistance (Resistência Nacional Moçambicana—RENAMO) rebel group. After a protracted series of talks, a UN-brokered peace agreement was signed in October 1992. He became prime minister after the 1994 presidential and legislative elections, with the main task of economic reconstruction after the years of conflict, a task made more difficult by the devastating floods of 2000. He was reappointed following FRELIMO's electoral victory in the December 1999 legislative elections.

MYANMAR

Full name: Union of Myanmar (formerly Burma).

Leadership structure: The de facto head of state under the military regime is the chairman of the SPDC (State Peace and Development Council), formerly the State Law and Order Restoration Council (SLORC) until 15 November 1997. The head of government is the prime minister, who is also the chairman of the SPDC, and who appoints the members of the government.

Chairman of SLORC/SPDC: Senior Gen. Than Shwe   Since 23 April 1992
(prime minister since 24 April 1992)

Legislature: The unicameral 485-member Constituent Assembly elected in 1990 has not been allowed to meet.

Profile of the Chairman of the SPDC:

Senior Gen. **THAN** Shwe

Senior Gen. Than Shwe, a career soldier from the generation which joined the military after Burma's independence in 1948, is head of state by virtue of his office as chairman of the ruling military council which seized power in 1988. It was he who announced in April 1991 the military regime's refusal to accept the results of the 1990 elections, declaring the election winners, the National League for Democracy (NLD), "subversive" and "unfit to rule".

Born on 2 February 1933, in Kyaukse, Mandalay division, Than Shwe attended secondary school before becoming a postal clerk. Joining the military officers training school in 1953, he rose to the position of army general.

In 1985 he became deputy commander-in-chief of the army under Gen. Saw Maung. After Saw Maung seized power in 1988 and became chairman of the State Law and Order Restoration Council (SLORC), Than Shwe became deputy chairman and commander-in-chief of the army. Burma was officially renamed the Union of Myanmar in 1989.

Than Shwe took over the defence ministry in March 1992 and was appointed on 23 April of that year to head the ruling military council in succession to Saw Maung, who was replaced on grounds of health. Than Shwe was in addition named as prime minister the following day, and retained control of the defence portfolio.

He is generally seen as a hard-liner, although in recent years he has ordered the release of a number of political prisoners, including members of the pro-democracy NLD and (in late 2001) its leader, Aung San Suu Kyi, the winner of the 1991 Nobel Peace Prize. Increasingly pragmatic in his approach, Than Shwe realizes that Myanmar can only receive foreign aid if it is willing to make some changes—hence his redesignation of the SLORC in 1997 as a State Peace and Development Council (SPDC).

By accepting the need for some reform, however, his regime faces stronger opposition from pro-democracy supporters. In the meantime, with a military government and no officially recognized opposition party, most opposition is met with heavy repression.

NAMIBIA

Full name: The Republic of Namibia.

Leadership structure: The head of state is a president, directly elected by universal adult suffrage. The president's term of office is five years, normally renewable once only, but a constitutional amendment passed by Parliament on 19 November 1998 allowed Sam Nujoma to stand for a third term of office at the elections in 1999. The president is also head of government. The president appoints the prime minister and other members of the cabinet.

President:	Sam Nujoma	Since 21 March 1990
Prime Ministers:	Hage Geingob	21 March 1990—28 Aug. 2002
	Theo-Ben Gurirab	Since 28 Aug. 2002

Legislature: The legislature, the Parliament, is bicameral. The lower chamber, the National Assembly, has 72 members, directly elected for a five-year term. Six additional nonvoting members may be appointed by the president. The upper chamber, the National Council, has 26 members, indirectly elected by the Regional Councils from among their members for a six-year term.

Profile of the President:

Sam **NUJOMA**

Sam Nujoma, so far the only president Namibia has had since independence in 1990, was the leading figure in his country's long struggle for the ending of South African control. He has been head of the South West Africa People's Organization of Namibia (SWAPO) for more than four decades, most of that period having been spent in exile engaged in ceaseless international lobbying while simultaneously pursuing the armed struggle.

Samuel Daniel Shafiishuna Nujoma was born on 12 May 1929 in Etunda village in Ongandjera district in northern Namibia (then known as South West Africa, and administered by South Africa as a League of Nations mandated territory since the ending of German colonial rule in the First World War). Nujoma is from the Ovambo ethnic group, the largest in Namibia, and was one of ten children in a family of subsistence farmers. He himself is now married with four children.

Nujoma attended the Finnish mission school in Okahao (1937–45) before leaving for Windhoek. While working for the South African Railways, Nujoma attended night school at St Barnabas, studying for his junior certificate by correspondence with the Trans-Africa Correspondence College in South Africa.

Nujoma began political life when he sought to mobilize workers in Windhoek, for which he lost his job. In 1959 he became leader of the Ovamboland People's Organization, the nucleus of what became SWAPO. Arrested for organizing resistance to apartheid-style forced township removals, he went into exile in 1960. In New York, USA, as president of the newly founded SWAPO, he lobbied the UN General Assembly, demanding an end to South African rule (which derived from a mandate originally entrusted to South Africa by the League of Nations). He was the Namibian representative at the founding of the Non-Aligned Movement in Belgrade in 1961 and two years later in Addis Ababa at the founding of the Organization of African Unity (OAU—now the African Union).

Nujoma was arrested again in March 1966 when attempting to return to Namibia, and was deported to Zambia, where SWAPO began to mobilize its forces and to obtain weapons to smuggle into Namibia. For over two decades Nujoma was to be preoccupied with the armed struggle on the one hand, and ceaseless international lobbying efforts on the other. He was awarded the Lenin Peace Prize in 1973, the Ho Chi Minh Peace Award in 1988, and the Indira Gandhi Peace Prize in 1990.

The first leader of an African nationalist movement to address the UN Security Council, in 1971, Nujoma also led the SWAPO team in negotiations in 1977–78 involving the UN, South Africa and the southern African front-line states. The resulting UN Security Council Resolution 435 envisaged Namibia's independence by 1978. Implementation of this resolution was delayed for over ten years, repeatedly stalled by South Africa as a protracted military struggle developed, extending from Namibia to encompass the continuing civil war in Angola.

When a ceasefire agreement was eventually signed, SWAPO won a majority in elections for a Constituent Assembly in 1989. Nujoma was elected unanimously by the Assembly on 16 February 1990 to be the first president of the Republic of Namibia. He was sworn in by UN secretary-general Javier Pérez de Cuéllar on the day the country achieved independence, 21 March 1990. He was re-elected for successive further terms in nationwide ballots in December 1994 and in November–December 1999, winning three-quarters of the vote on both occasions.

While Nujoma's drive to increase the participation of women in government has been applauded, his vitriolic attacks on homosexuality have drawn condemnation from around the world. In April 2001 he ordered authorities to identify and arrest all homosexuals, who he has said should be either deported or sent to prison. He has also begun to exert a moral influence over television broadcasting, calling for an end to the screening of "criminal" violent movies and banning in September 2002 the broadcast of foreign-made programmes. Instead Namibian television now shows only programmes which portray the country in a positive light.

Profile of the Prime Minister:

Theo-Ben **GURIRAB**

Theo-Ben Gurirab is a member of the central committee and politburo of the ruling South West Africa People's Organization of Namibia (SWAPO) and is popularly seen as one of the founding fathers of Namibian independence. He represented the Namibian independence movement at the UN during 27 years of exile before returning to serve as the country's first foreign minister. He was shifted from the foreign ministry after 12 years to take up his appointment as prime minister in 2002.

Theo-Ben Gurirab was born on 23 January 1939 in Usakos, in what was then the South African-controlled territory of South West Africa. After qualifying as a teacher at the Augustineum College in nearby Okahandja in 1960, Gurirab fled the growing oppression of black people imposed by South African rule in the territory, and arrived in Tanzania in 1962.

Having been awarded a UN fellowship, Gurirab went to the USA in 1963 to continue his education at Temple University in Philadelphia, Pennsylvania. He graduated in political science in 1969 and stayed on to study international relations at postgraduate level. Throughout his university career he also represented SWAPO, which was to become engaged in an armed struggle for the liberation of South West Africa. He was made one of SWAPO's three associate representatives to the UN and the Americas in 1964, and its chief representative upon his final graduation from Temple in 1971. He is married, with four children.

Gurirab was a major voice in raising awareness about Namibia's plight and was appointed SWAPO's secretary for foreign affairs in 1986. He went on to become the group's permanent observer at the UN. He was central to the drafting of UN Resolution 435 (1978), a key text calling for the country's full independence.

As apartheid began to crumble in South Africa, Gurirab was among the first of SWAPO's exiled leaders to return to Namibia in 1989 where he helped arrange the lasting ceasefire between SWAPO and the South African government. He was elected to Namibia's transitional Constituent Assembly later that year and was appointed foreign minister in the first independent government in March 1990.

As foreign minister, Gurirab continued to champion Namibia's cause on the world stage. He represented the country in 1995 at the Organization of African Unity (OAU—now the African Union) and was involved with the formation of the organization's conflict resolution body. He also cofounded the African–Latin American Initiative. In 1999 he returned to New York to serve as president of the UN's General Assembly. Also of note was his role in negotiating the return from South Africa to Namibia of Walvis Bay and other disputed territories in 1994. In 2000 his responsibilities were increased in the cabinet when he was given the information and broadcasting portfolios. Two years later he was appointed prime minister in a surprise reshuffle.

NAURU

Full name: The Republic of Nauru.

Leadership structure: The head of state is a president, elected by Parliament from among its members for a three-year term. The head of government is the president, who is responsible to Parliament. The cabinet is appointed by the president.

Presidents:	Rene Harris	28 April 1999—19 April 2000
	Bernard Dowiyogo	19 April 2000—30 March 2001
	Rene Harris	Since 30 March 2001

Legislature: The legislature is unicameral. The sole chamber, the Parliament, has 18 members, directly elected for a three-year term.

Profile of the President:

Rene **HARRIS**

Rene Harris, an Australian-educated businessman, has held a seat continuously in the island-country's Parliament since 1977. Since his election in March 2001 his position as president (which he also held in 1999–2000) has remained extremely precarious; Nauru's small Parliament has a propensity to cut short presidential careers with votes of no confidence.

Rene Harris was born on 11 November 1947, at which time Nauru was a UN Trust Territory administered by Australia. It gained independence in 1968. Educated at one of Australia's most prestigious schools, Geelong College in Victoria, Harris remains a dedicated fan of the Geelong Australian-rules football team. He is married to Roslyn and they have five children.

A member of Parliament for the Aiwo constituency since 1977, Harris also had a successful business career with the Nauru Phosphate Corporation (although the country's phosphate deposits are expected to run out in 2003). Beginning as a labour officer in 1979, he worked his way up to become assistant personnel manager in 1981 and ultimately chairman of the board from 1992 to 1995. In the meantime he had also sat on numerous parliamentary committees and was deputy speaker of Parliament in 1978 and 1986 and also full speaker in 1986.

The incumbent president, Bernard Dowiyogo, was ousted in a vote of no confidence in April 1999 and Harris was appointed by Parliament in his place.

Following legislative elections in April 2000 Harris was reappointed, but resigned almost immediately when he came into conflict with the new Parliament speaker. Dowiyogo returned to become president until he was ousted over a financial scandal in March 2001. Harris was then returned to office with a 9–6 vote in his favour. However, by the end of 2002 his position had become precarious. His budget for 2003 had been blocked by Dowiyogo's supporters and he faced growing criticism for his support for the Australian 'Pacific solution' to its own immigration problem—namely housing over 1,000 refugees in Nauru in return for economic aid.

Profile of the Previous President:

Bernard **DOWIYOGO**

Bernard Dowiyogo is Nauru's longest-serving parliamentary member, and has also been its president on five separate occasions between 1976 and 2001. A qualified lawyer, Dowiyogo favours an active world role for Nauru and was the first head of state to openly support separatists in Papua, Indonesia, in 1999.

Bernard Dowiyogo was born on 14 February 1946. Like many Nauruans, Dowiyogo forged strong links with Australia, which administered Nauru as a UN Trust Territory until 1968. He went to school in Ballarat, Victoria, and to the Australian National University in Canberra where he studied law, and he is a keen follower of Australian-rules football.

On qualifying as a lawyer Dowiyogo returned to Nauru and entered the island's Parliament in 1973. He took on the leadership of the newly formed Nauru Party and was elected as Nauru's president in 1976. He replaced the island's first head of state, Hammer DeRoburt, whose supporters then made it difficult for him to pass legislation and forced the holding of fresh legislative and presidential elections in November 1977: Dowiyogo narrowly secured re-election. In the course of his long career he was president in December 1976–April 1978, December 1989–November 1995, November 1996, June 1998–April 1999 and April 2000–March 2001. On this last occasion he was ousted in a vote of no confidence based on allegations that the Russian mafia had become involved in the country's much-criticized tax-free banking system.

Most recently Dowiyogo has attacked the incumbent President Harris for accepting an influx of asylum seekers from Australia in return for financial aid, and his supporters helped to block the 2003 budget at the end of 2002.

NEPAL

Full name: The Kingdom of Nepal.

Leadership structure: The head of state is the king. Executive power is vested in the king and the Council of Ministers. The prime minister is formally appointed by the king, but must be able to command a parliamentary majority.

Kings:	Birendra Bir Bikram Shah Dev	31 Jan. 1972—1 June 2001
	Dipendra Bir Bikram Shah Dev	1 June 2001—4 June 2001
	Gyanendra Bir Bikram Shah Dev (regent from 2 June 2001)	Since 4 June 2001

Prime Ministers:	Krishna Prasad Bhattarai	31 May 1999—22 March 2000
	Girija Prasad Koirala	22 March 2000—26 July 2001
	Sher Bahadur Deuba	26 July 2001—4 Oct. 2002
	vacant	4 Oct. 2002— 11 Oct. 2002
	Lokendra Bahadur Chand	Since 11 Oct. 2002

Legislature: The legislature, the Parliament (Sansad), is bicameral. The lower chamber, the House of Representatives (Pratinidhi Sabha), has 205 members, directly elected for a five-year term. The upper chamber, the National Council (Rastriya Sabha), has 60 members, ten of them nominated by the king, and 50 indirectly elected, for a six-year term, with one-third renewed every two years.

Profile of the King:

GYANENDRA Bir Bikram Shah Dev

King Gyanendra has a reputation as a conservative hard-liner but became more popularly known before he ascended the throne as the champion of conservation programmes. He also has various commercial interests. He came to power on 4 June 2001 after the massacre of the reigning royal family by the then crown prince, Dipendra. He has already used the authority which the constitution allows him, but which his predecessor Birendra had not used since the democratization of 1990, to take on executive powers briefly in October 2002.

Prince Gyanendra Bir Bikram Shah Dev was born on 7 July 1947 in Kathmandu. He was briefly crowned king in November 1950, when he was just three years old, during a power struggle between his own grandfather, King Tribhuvan, and the government of Prime Minister Mohan Shamsher Rana. He was removed from the throne on 7 January 1951 when Tribhuvan returned from exile in India. Gyanendra graduated from St Joseph's College, India, in 1966 and from the Tribhuvan University, Kathmandu, in 1969. He married Komal Rajya Laxmi Rana on 2 May 1970. They have two children. Their controversy-seeking son Prince Paras was declared crown prince and heir to the throne in November 2001.

Once a keen hunter, Gyanendra became chairman in 1982 of the King Mahendra Trust for Nature Conservation, whose most important responsibility is for the Annapurna Conservation Area Project, created in 1986 at the centre of the Himalayas as the country's largest nature reservation. Gyanendra is also an honorary member of the World Wide Fund for Nature (WWF). Along with his conservation work he has a number of commercial interests, including a hotel in Kathmandu, a tea estate in the east of the country and a cigarette factory. He was a key opponent of King Birendra's failed attempt to have the members of the royal family shed their business interests.

On 1 June 2001 Crown Prince Dipendra gunned down his father King Birendra, his mother Queen Aishwarya and seven other family members in an apparent drunken rage before turning his automatic weapon on himself. Although fatally injured, Dipendra became king upon Birendra's death. Gyanendra, whose own wife was one of only two survivors of the Narayanhiti Palace massacre, was not present at the time and now found himself next in line to the throne. He was rushed to Kathmandu to act as regent for Dipendra, who died three days later, whereupon Gyanendra was automatically named as the next monarch. Confusion over the details of the massacre and the deep popularity of Birendra, in contrast to the general mistrust cast on Gyanendra, led to an overflow of conspiracy theories and days of widespread unrest.

Although he is generally regarded as 'a safe pair of hands' for the Nepalese monarchy in the face of an intensifying Maoist guerrilla campaign, Gyanendra's conservative leanings and willingness to become personally engaged in politics make it unlikely that he will recover the popularity enjoyed by his brother. For a week in early October 2002 Gyanendra assumed executive powers for himself after his prime minister had called for a postponement of general elections. Although the move was strictly in line with the constitution it represented an unprecedented interference from the throne since the implementation of democracy in 1990.

Profile of the Prime Minister:

Lokendra Bahadur **CHAND**

Lokendra Bahadur Chand is a cofounder and leader of the right-wing National Democratic Party/Chand (NDP/Chand). A prominent royalist and a published author and poet, he had served as prime minister on three separate occasions before he was personally appointed prime minister by King Gyanendra on 11 October 2002.

Lokendra Bahadur Chand was born on 15 February 1940 in the far-western district of Baitadi. He completed his secondary education in India and then studied law in the northern Indian town of Dehra Dun, graduating in 1966. His connections with India remain strong. He has also written several short stories and poems in Hindi as well as Nepali. He is married and has four sons and three daughters.

A loyal royalist, Chand's political career extends back into the late 1960s and he was chairman of the nonparty legislature under the absolutist *panchayat* system run by King Birendra. He was first appointed prime minister in July 1983 and served for almost three years. He stepped down in March 1986 amid growing opposition in the legislature to the *panchayat* system. His second period in office lasted a mere two weeks in April 1990, in the very final days of *panchayat*. In the subsequent multiparty system he was a cofounder of the NDP. However, it split in 1997 and each faction briefly led broad coalitions. Chand was prime minister at the head of his faction, with the support of the Communist Party of Nepal–Unified Marxist–Leninist, from March to October 1997.

In elections in 1999 Chand lost his seat in the House of Representatives and returned to his writing. The then prime minister Sher Bahadur Deuba even launched a book of Chand's poetry in 2001. The following year the country's political system fell into crisis. Deuba quarrelled with his own Nepali Congress party and failed to prepare the country for elections in November 2002. Gyanendra dismissed the government on 4 October and took personal control for a week before appointing Chand as his prime minister in an interim technocratic government drawn from smaller, pro-monarchy parties, pending the calling of elections.

NETHERLANDS

Full name: The Kingdom of the Netherlands.

Leadership structure: The head of state is a constitutional monarch. The head of government is the prime minister, who is responsible to the States-General. The Council of Ministers is appointed by royal decree, on the advice of the prime minister.

Queen:	Beatrix	Since 30 April 1980
Prime Minister:	Wim Kok	22 Aug. 1994—22 July 2002
	Jan Peter Balkenende	Since 22 July 2002

Legislature: The legislature, the States-General (Staten-Generaal), is bicameral. The lower chamber, the Second Chamber (Tweede Kamer), has 150 members, directly elected for a four-year term. The upper chamber, the First Chamber (Eerste Kamer), has 75 members, indirectly elected for a four-year term.

Profile of the Queen:

BEATRIX

Queen Beatrix of the Netherlands succeeded to the throne following the abdication of her mother, Queen Juliana. As queen she is also head of state of Aruba and of the Netherlands Antilles, represented on each by a governor. Her role is ceremonial, although views which she has expressed on environmental and social issues in particular have had some political impact.

Beatrix Wilhelmina Armgard was born at the Soestdijk Palace in Baarn on 31 January 1938, the eldest of the three daughters of Juliana and Prince Bernhard. Following the German invasion in May 1940 she was taken to England and on to Ottawa, Canada, for the duration of the Second World War. On her return to the Netherlands she continued her primary education, and received her grammar school certificate in 1956. When she had reached her 18th birthday earlier that year, she had become a member of the Council of State. In the same year she entered the University of Leiden, studying sociology, jurisprudence, economics, constitutional law and international affairs. She passed her final doctoral degree examination in July 1961.

Beatrix's interests include sculpture, painting, dramatic art and ballet. She enjoys riding and sailing, is patron of the National Fund for the Prevention of

Poliomyelitis and also supports, among others, charities assisting handicapped children. Queen Beatrix married Claus von Amsberg, a former German diplomat, on 10 March 1966, the nationality of her husband causing adverse reactions in some circles at the time. Prince Claus died in October 2002. They had three sons, the heir to the throne being Prince Willem-Alexander, born in 1967.

Profile of the Prime Minister:

Jan Peter **BALKENENDE**

Jan Peter Balkenende, leader of the conservative Christian Democratic Appeal (Christen Democratisch Appèl—CDA), is a graduate in law and a university teacher who only entered parliament in 1998. As prime minister he headed the shortest-lived government in the country's history, a three-party coalition which included the anti-immigrant Pim Fortuyn List (Lijst Pim Fortuyn—LPF), and which collapsed in October 2002. Balkenende remained in post pending the outcome of fresh elections. Renowned for his staunch Christianity, Balkenende bears a striking resemblance to the children's literary character Harry Potter.

Jan Peter (also spelled Pieter) Balkenende was born on 7 May 1956 in the southwestern Dutch town of Kapelle, near Goes. He graduated in history and then law from the Free University of Amsterdam in 1982. For the nest two years he advised the Netherlands Universities Council on legal affairs. He was awarded his doctorate in law in 1992 and since 1993 has taught Christian social thought on society and economics at the university. He chairs the Association of Christian Lawyers and has held executive positions in Christian broadcasting companies. He married Bianca Hoogendijk in 1996 and they now have one child.

After graduating in 1982 Balkenende began his political career on the municipal council of Amstelveen, on the outskirts of Amsterdam. His association with the Christian democrats was formalized in 1984 when he began serving in the CDA's policy institute. He became leader of the Amstelveen CDA group in 1994. These roles were left behind in May 1998 when he was successfully elected to the Second Chamber. His rise within the party was then meteoric. He emerged victorious in October 2001 from a tumultuous internal leadership contest. Just seven months later he led the party to its first election win in eight years. After two months of negotiations he formed a somewhat unlikely coalition with the LPF and the right-wing People's Party for Freedom and Democracy in July 2002.

Balkenende's dramatic rise to power was rapidly overshadowed by an even more dramatic fall. The LPF, catapulted to popularity by the assassination nine days before polling of its charismatic founder Pim Fortuyn, quickly became mired in internal disputes which prompted the coalition's premature collapse just three months later on 16 October. It had been the shortest-lived government in recent Dutch history. Balkenende remained in office as caretaker pending fresh elections expected early in the new year.

NEW ZEALAND

Full name: New Zealand.

Leadership structure: The head of state is the British sovereign, styled 'Queen of New Zealand, and of Her other Realms and Territories, head of the Commonwealth, Defender of the Faith', and represented by a governor-general who is a New Zealander appointed on the advice of the New Zealand government. The head of government is the prime minister, who, with the cabinet, is appointed by the governor-general on the advice of the House of Representatives and responsible to it.

Queen:	Elizabeth II	Since 6 Feb. 1952
Governors-General:	Sir Michael Hardie Boys	21 March 1996—22 March 2001
	Dame Sian Elias (acting)	22 March 2001—4 April 2001
	Dame Silvia Cartwright	Since 4 April 2001
Prime Minister:	Helen Clark	Since 10 Dec. 1999

Legislature: The legislature is unicameral. The sole chamber, the House of Representatives, has 120 members, directly elected for a three-year term. Under a new electoral system first implemented in October 1996, there are 61 members from single-member constituencies, six from Maori constituencies, and 53 allocated from party lists.

Profile of the Governor-General:

Dame Silvia **CARTWRIGHT**

Dame Silvia Cartwright is a qualified lawyer and prominent advocate for women's rights. She was New Zealand's first female High Court judge in 1993 and is the second woman (following Dame Cath Tizard in 1990–96) to hold the post of governor-general.

Silvia Rose Poulter was born on 7 November 1943 in Dunedin on the southeast coast of New Zealand's South Island. She graduated in law from the local University of Otago in 1966, was admitted as a solicitor in 1967 and as a barrister in 1968. She married fellow lawyer Peter Cartwright in 1969. He is now chairman of the Broadcasting Standards Authority.

Silvia Cartwright joined the private law firm Harkness Henry & Co. in 1971 where she specialized in family law. She was made a district and family court judge in 1981; eight years later she became the country's first ever female chief district court judge, and was also made a dame commander of the order of the British Empire. In 1993 she moved up to be a High Court judge, another groundbreaking step for a woman.

Concurrent with her judicial career, Sylvia Cartwright championed the cause of female equality. She reached the national consciousness in 1987 when she headed an inquiry into treatment for cervical cancer at the National Women's Hospital in Auckland. The inquiry prompted widespread reforms in treatment and has since become known by her name. She also sought to promote equality in the judicial system as convenor of the Judicial Working Group on Gender Equity. From 1993 to 2000 she raised her profile to the international level when she was a member of the UN committee seeking to oversee compliance with the UN Convention on the Elimination of All Forms of Discrimination Against Women (CEDAW).

In August 2000 Dame Sylvia Cartwright was nominated by Queen Elizabeth II to be her next representative as head of state in New Zealand. She took over accordingly as governor-general following the retirement of Sir Michael Hardie Boys on 22 March 2001. (During the brief period between his retirement and her inauguration on 4 April, the functions of the governor-general were formally exercised in an acting capacity by the chief justice, Dame Sian Elias.) It attracted considerable attention internationally that at this time women held the five highest offices in New Zealand (head of state, governor-general, chief justice, prime minister and leader of the opposition).

Profile of the Prime Minister:

Helen **CLARK**

Helen Clark has led two minority governments since first becoming prime minister—a coalition with the Alliance party from 1999 to 2002, and with the Progressive Coalition since the July 2002 elections. A farmer's daughter and former student activist, she was a university lecturer in politics before entering parliament in 1981. Although she can point to a career in which she has held responsibility at every level in the New Zealand Labour Party (NZLP), her approach to politics has been described as lacking in charisma and strongly academic.

Helen Elizabeth Clark was born in Hamilton in 1950, the daughter of a farmer from the rural Waikato district on North Island. She was educated at boarding school in Auckland, where she admits to having been painfully shy, before attending the University of Auckland to study politics.

She began her active involvement in politics by joining the Labour Party in 1971 and was active in student societies against the Viet Nam War and apartheid in South Africa. She graduated with a master's degree in 1974 with a thesis on rural political behaviour. She lectured on political studies at the university from 1973 until her election to the House of Representatives on behalf of the Mount Albert constituency in 1981.

Clark became a member of the Labour executive in 1978 and represented the party at congresses of the Socialist International in 1976, 1978, 1983 and 1986. Following Labour's electoral victory in 1984 Clark was convenor of a government committee on external affairs and security. Further success at the polls in 1987 led to her appointment as minister, holding the conservation and housing portfolios. Two years later she switched these for the ministries of health and labour and was promoted to deputy prime minister in August 1989. Through this influential position Clark chaired numerous cabinet committees until in 1990 Labour's disastrous economic experiments led to defeat at the polls and a return to opposition.

From 1990 until 1993 Clark was deputy leader of the opposition. When she replaced Mike Moore in December 1993 as leader of the Labour Party, she thereby became leader of the opposition in parliament.

The 1996 elections, held under a newly introduced system of proportional representation, almost saw a return to power for Labour. This was forestalled when a coalition was put together at the last moment by the incumbent National Party (NP) and its small splinter party New Zealand First (NZF)—but not before the holding of premature celebrations in the Labour camp, and the publication of an issue of *Time* magazine featuring Clark on the cover as New Zealand's first female prime minister. This distinction went instead, the following year, to the NP's Jenny Shipley.

By the time of the next elections, in November 1999, the government's difficulties and the internal fractiousness of the NP–NZF coalition had provoked a swing of popular support back to Labour. The party took 38.7% of the national vote and secured 49 of the 120 seats in the House of Representatives, enabling Clark to form a minority government in coalition with the Alliance party. In addition to the prime ministership she also took on the arts, culture and heritage portfolio.

Clark pledged to return the nation to "basic New Zealand values" of fairness, opportunity and social equality, along with increases in taxation. Although never an outspoken republican, in the months following her election she stated that for New Zealand replacing the monarchy was inevitable. She has also backtracked on years of opposition to the idea of a single Australian–New Zealand dollar, suggesting that, like republican status, this too might be merely a matter of time. Among other policies she has cut the New Zealand armed forces—grounding the combat wing of the air force altogether.

Splits within the Alliance party over the government's support for the war in Afghanistan in late 2001 prompted Clark to call early legislative elections for 27 July 2002. Labour increased its share of the vote to 41.3%, giving it 52 seats. Clark formed a new minority coalition with the left-of-centre Progressive Coalition, receiving support from the liberal United Future party and co-operation from the Green Party.

Helen Clark is married to Peter Davis but made a conscious decision not to have children, stating that she valued her "personal space and privacy too highly". Her personal space is occupied with studying politics, classical music, cross-country skiing, and an appreciation of good Chardonnay wine.

NICARAGUA

Full name: The Republic of Nicaragua.

Leadership structure: The head of state is a president, directly elected by universal adult suffrage. The president's term of office is five years. A president may not serve two consecutive terms, but may stand for re-election in a later election. Close relatives of the incumbent president may not stand for election as president. The head of government is the president, who is responsible to the National Assembly. The cabinet is appointed by the president.

Presidents:	Arnoldo Alemán	10 Jan. 1997—10 Jan. 2002
	Enrique Bolaños	Since 10 Jan. 2002

Legislature: The legislature is unicameral. The sole chamber, the National Assembly (Asamblea Nacional), has 90 members directly elected for a five-year term. In addition, any presidential or vice-presidential candidate who receives nationally at least as many votes as the average of the winning percentages in each regional electoral district, but is not successful in being elected president or vice president, instead becomes a member of the National Assembly.

Profile of the President:

Enrique **BOLAÑOS**

Enrique Bolaños is a successful businessman and a former leader of the conservative Liberal Constitutionalist Party (Partido Liberal Constitucionalista—PLC). An outspoken critic of the left-wing 1980s Sandinista regime, he was persecuted and imprisoned but refused to leave the country. Since running for election in November 2001 he has distanced himself from his former running mate and scandal-tainted predecessor Arnoldo Alemán.

Enrique Bolaños Geyer was born on 13 May 1928 in Masaya, near Managua. His younger brother Nicolas is now a member of the rival Conservative Party of Nicaragua. Enrique married Lila T. Abaunza, also from Masaya, in 1949 and they had five children, although one son has since died. Bolaños graduated in industrial engineering from the Jesuit-run St Louis University in Missouri, USA.

Back in Nicaragua from 1952, Bolaños developed the family farming business, creating one of the country's largest cotton-growing firms. By 1978 the Bolaños-Geyer family company was producing 5% of the country's cotton. In 1979 the revolutionary Sandinista regime confiscated the company and nationalized the cotton industry. Bolaños refused to go into exile, as many of the previous regime's entrepreneurs had done, and instead faced the wrath of the left-wing government for his voluble criticism. He spent a period in jail. During the 1980s, while civil war raged, he headed various business groups, including the Nicaragua Chamber of Industry and the Central American Institute of Business Administration, where he had also previously studied management. He took to writing, producing critical articles and books including *How are we doing?* (1982) and the *Ideas for All* column.

In 1996 Bolaños was chosen as the PLC's candidate for vice president, as the running mate of Managua mayor Arnoldo Alemán. The pair were successfully elected in October, and took office in January 1997. As vice president he struggled to promote government transparency. By the end of its term in 2001 the Alemán regime had become embroiled in corruption scandals, raising the prospect of a Sandinista victory at the polls. Bolaños resigned as vice president and began to distance himself from Alemán in order to take on the PLC nomination for president. In the November election he defeated the Sandinista candidate, former president Daniel Ortega, by taking 56% of the vote. He took office on 10 January 2002.

As president, Bolaños has found it necessary to put further space between himself and Alemán, and opened an investigation into his predecessor over an alleged million-dollar fraud. His efforts were lambasted by the PLC in August 2002 when it accused him of pursuing a personal vendetta against party leader Alemán, which has split the party into factions.

NIGER

Full name: The Republic of Niger.

Leadership structure: The head of state is a president, directly elected by universal adult suffrage. The head of government is the prime minister, who is appointed from the parliamentary majority.

President:	Mamadou Tandja	Since 22 Dec. 1999
Prime Ministers:	Ibrahim Hassane Mayaki	27 Nov. 1997—3 Jan. 2000
	Hama Amadou	Since 3 Jan. 2000

Legislature: The legislature is unicameral. The sole chamber, the National Assembly (Assemblée Nationale), has 83 members. Following legislative elections in November 1999, a new Assembly was sworn in on 26 December, for a five-year term.

Profile of the President:

Mamadou **TANDJA**

Mamadou Tandja started his career as a professional solider, and came into government as a result of the military coup against President Hamani Diori in April 1974. He was twice an unsuccessful candidate in presidential elections, in 1993 and 1996, before his victory in 1999. He has a reputation for being both thorough and hardworking.

Mamadou Tandja was born in 1938 in the southeastern part of the country. He joined the armed forces and took part in the 1974 coup, after which he became interior minister. He rose to the rank of lieutenant-general before retiring to civilian life.

In July 1991 he became leader of the National Movement for a Development Society (Mouvement National pour la Société de Développement—MNSD-Nassara) in succession to President Ali Saïbou, and stood as the MNSD-Nassara candidate in the 1993 presidential elections when Saïbou himself declined to take part. Despite winning the greatest share of the vote in the first round, he lost in the runoff to Mahamane Ousmane.

The 1990s were a time of considerable unrest, and in April 1994 Tandja was briefly detained after an anti-government protest, when many members of the opposition were arrested and prosecuted. In the next election, held in 1996 (following a coup in January and the formation of a transitional government), Tandja was again an unsuccessful candidate, this time losing to Brig.-Gen. Ibrahim Barre Maïnassara, the coup leader and head of the transitional government.

In 1999 the pattern of military coup followed by a return to elected government was repeated, but on this occasion without the coup leader being himself a candidate for the presidency. Polling took place in two rounds, on 17 October and 24 November. Tandja, standing once again as the MNSD-Nassara candidate, won the runoff against Mahamadou Issoufou of the Nigerien Party for Democracy and Socialism, and the MNSD-Nassara also gained a majority in the concurrent election to the National Assembly. He took office on 22 December.

Profile of the Prime Minister:

Hama **AMADOU**

Hama Amadou had a career in broadcasting before becoming private secretary to successive presidents in the 1980s and early 1990s. A leading figure in the National Movement for a Development Society (Mouvement National pour la Société de Développement—MNSD-Nassara), he was first appointed as prime minister in February 1995. Ousted in the military coup the following January, he returned to office four years later following his party's success in the presidential and legislative elections of November 1999.

Hama Amadou, a former managing director of the Niger Broadcasting Board, established himself as an influential political figure as a result of his posts as private secretary to Presidents Seyni Kountché (1974–87) and Ali Saïbou (1987–93) and also secretary-general, and then president, of MNSD-Nassara, the pro-military party originally founded by Saïbou prior to the adoption of a multiparty constitution.

Amadou was out of government from 1993 as a result of the electoral victory that year of the Democratic and Social Convention (Convention Démocratique et Sociale—CDS-Rahama). He was reluctantly appointed as prime minister on 17 February 1995, however, by the CDS-Rahama leader President Mahamane Ousmane, who had resorted to calling early legislative elections only to see his party suffer losses at the hands of the MNSD-Nassara. The turbulent period of 'cohabitation' which ensued was brought to an end by the military coup of January 1996. A constitutional referendum held in May 1996 prepared for a return to elected government, but, with the MNSD-Nassara out of power for nearly four years, Amadou did not return to office until after its November 1999 election victory. In the intervening period, he was briefly detained after being arrested on 1 January 1998 and accused of involvement in a coup attempt. He was appointed prime minister by the incoming President Tandja in January 2000.

NIGERIA

Full name: The Federal Republic of Nigeria.

Leadership structure: The head of state is an elected president. The president's term of office is four years, renewable once only. The head of government under the 1999 Constitution is the president, who names a cabinet or Federal Executive Council, which must be approved by the Senate.

President: Gen. (retd) Olusegun Obasanjo Since 29 May 1999

Legislature: The legislature, the National Assembly, is bicameral. The lower chamber, the House of Representatives, has 360 members and the upper chamber, the Senate, has 109 members, both elected for four-year terms.

Profile of the President:

Gen. (retd) Olusegun **OBASANJO**

Olusegun Obasanjo was a leading figure in the 1975 coup which ousted Gen. Gowon. He won credit by returning the country to civilian rule in 1979. Concentrating thereafter on an international role, he was nevertheless arrested under the autocratic regime of Gen. Sani Abacha in 1995 and imprisoned for three years, emerging to campaign for, and win, the presidency in the 1999 elections. A rarity among Nigerian rulers in that he is not seen as personally corrupt, he has tried to steer his federal government away from direct confrontation with Islamists in the north; he is himself a Christian southerner from the Yoruba ethnic group.

Olusegun Obasanjo was born on 6 March 1937 in Abeokuta, Ogun State, in the southwest of the country, and was educated at the Baptist Boys' High School in Abeokuta. He enlisted in the Nigerian army in 1958, and trained in the UK at Mons Officers Cadet School, Aldershot, the Royal College of Military Engineering, Chatham, and the School of Survey, Newbury. In 1958 and 1959 he served in the fifth battalion, Nigerian army, in Kaduna and the Cameroons, and in the 1960s he was posted to the UN peacekeeping force in Congo. Promoted through the ranks to colonel by 1969, he fought in the civil war against the Biafra secessionists, and received the surrender from the Biafran army in 1970.

He first entered the government in January 1975, as federal commissioner for works and housing, and the same year was appointed chief of staff. He was a member of the Supreme Military Council which took control of the country in

July 1975, after the incumbent president Gen. Gowon had refused to set any agenda for a return to civilian rule. The Supreme Military Council appointed Brig. Murtala Mohammed as president, but in February 1976 he was assassinated and replaced by Obasanjo as both head of state and commander-in-chief of the armed forces. Obasanjo presided over the return to civilian elected government in September 1979, when he retired from the army (with the rank of general) to his poultry farm.

Although appointed a member of the advisory Council of State in 1979, he pursued a more international role for the next two decades, with a series of appointments notably at the UN Educational, Scientific and Cultural Organization (UNESCO) and the World Health Organization (WHO). In 1980 he was a member of the Independent Commission on Disarmament and Security, and in 1985 he cochaired the Eminent Persons Group on South Africa. He also founded the Africa Leadership Forum in 1987 and was involved in mediation efforts in Namibia, Angola, Sudan, South Africa, Mozambique and Burundi. In 1991 he was a candidate for the post of secretary-general of the UN. He served as an official observer in elections in Angola (1992) and Mozambique (1994), and until 1999 was chairman of the advisory council of Transparency International, the organization campaigning against corruption in business and public life.

In 1995 he became involved in domestic politics once more when he was among 43 people arrested and charged with treason, for an alleged plot against the then military ruler, President Sani Abacha. Obasanjo was given a 15-year prison sentence, but was released in 1998. Selected as the presidential candidate of the People's Democratic Party (PDP) for elections in 1999, he emerged as the victor in the 27 February poll, his party having won a parliamentary majority in the legislative elections the previous week. He took office at the end of May, and a month later he swore in a new civilian government, leaving northerners aggrieved at the loss of the preponderance of power they had enjoyed under military rule.

His presidency has had to contend with a marked rise in Islamic fundamentalist influence in the Muslim north, where eight states adopted *shari'a* (Islamic law), a divisive issue over which Obasanjo has been very guarded in his public responses.

Obasanjo's published works include *My Command* (an account of the Nigerian civil war, published in 1979), *Africa Embattled* (1988), *Constitution for National Integration and Development* (1989), *Africa: Rise to Challenge* (1993) and *This Animal Called Man* (1999). He had two sons and four daughters by his first wife, Oluremi Akinbwon, and is now married to Stella Abebe.

NORWAY

Full name: The Kingdom of Norway.

Leadership structure: The head of state is a constitutional monarch. The head of government is the prime minister, who is responsible to Parliament. The Council of State is appointed by the prime minister.

King:	Harald V	Since 17 Jan. 1991

Prime Ministers:	Kjell Magne Bondevik	17 Oct. 1997—17 March 2000
	Jens Stoltenberg	17 March 2000—19 Oct. 2001
	Kjell Magne Bondevik	Since 19 Oct. 2001

Legislature: The legislature is unicameral. The sole chamber, the Parliament (Storting), has 165 members, directly elected for a four-year term. When dealing with legislative matters the Parliament divides itself into two bodies, the upper chamber (Lagting) and the lower chamber (Odelsting).

Profile of the King:

HARALD V

King Harald V came to the throne in 1991 following the death of his father King Olav V, having taken over his official duties the previous year, and having served a 33-year apprenticeship as crown prince. As a young man he studied political science at Balliol College, Oxford, and he is noted as an Olympic sailor. His marriage to a commoner in 1968 was extremely popular with the Norwegian people.

Harald was born on 21 February 1937, at Skaugum, the estate which is still the home of the royal family. He was baptized on 31 March 1937 in the palace chapel. With the Nazi invasion in 1940, the royal family fled into exile and he spent most of the war years living in the USA near Washington D.C. He returned to Norway after liberation in 1945, attending Smestad primary school until 1950 and the Oslo cathedral school until 1955, taking his upper secondary diploma in science. Between 1956 and 1957 he attended the cavalry officers' candidate school at Trandum, and then the military academy where he remained until graduation in 1959. He has the rank of general in the army and the air force and admiral in the navy.

On 21 September 1957 he took his place beside his father, King Olav V, in the Council of State following the death of his grandfather, King Håkon VII. He was made crown prince, taking the oath to the constitution on 21 February 1958.

Harald studied political science at Balliol College, Oxford, UK, between 1960 and 1962, and subsequently devoted much time to foreign visits and the promotion of Norwegian business interests abroad. He took over his father's official duties after King Olav suffered a stroke in June 1990. He came to the throne on his father's death on 17 January 1991, and was sworn in as king four days later.

King Harald married Sonja Haraldsen on 29 August 1968. They have one daughter, Princess Märtha Louise, born in 1971, and one son, Crown Prince Håkon, who was born in 1973. Håkon is the heir to the throne, although legislation passed in May 1990 gives equal succession rights to both sexes thereafter.

Profile of the Prime Minister:

Kjell Magne **BONDEVIK**

Kjell Magne Bondevik, a priest in the (Lutheran) Church of Norway, first became prime minister of Norway in October 1997, heading a minority coalition government including his right-of-centre Christian Democratic Party (Kristelig Folkeparti—KrF). Out of office between March 2000 and October 2001, he then formed another minority coalition government. Bondevik himself has retained a seat in parliament since 1973 and held cabinet office in the mid-1980s and in 1989–90, when he was foreign minister.

Kjell Magne Bondevik was born on 3 September 1947 in Molde, a coastal town west of Trondheim. He was active in the KrF party youth movement, the Young Christian Democrats (Kristelig Folkepartis Ungdom—KrFU), becoming its deputy leader in 1968 and leader from 1970 to 1973. From 1972 to 1973 he was a municipal councillor in Nesodden and a member of the municipal school board. He was also state secretary in the office of the prime minister during the same period. He entered the Parliament for the first time in 1973, after four years as an alternate member, and has represented his native county, Møre and Romsdal, ever since.

Pursuing his theological studies, Bondevik gained a degree from the free faculty of theology at the University of Oslo in 1975. In 1979 he was ordained as priest in the (Lutheran) Church of Norway. Kjell Magne Bondevik is married to Bjørg née Rasmussen, and they have three children.

Within the KrF he was party deputy chairman between 1975 and 1983, and in addition leader of the parliamentary party between 1981 and 1983, in which year he became party chairman. He retained the party chairmanship for 12 years (being succeeded in 1995 by Valgerd Svarstad Haugland), and was in addition leader of the parliamentary party between 1986 and 1989 and again from 1993 onward. In the course of his career, when not holding a ministerial post, he has sat on the parliamentary standing committees on the Church and education (1973–77), on finance (1977–83), on foreign affairs (1986–89), on defence affairs (1990–93) and once again on foreign affairs (1993–97). Between 1983 and 1986 he was minister of Church and education, and in 1989 he became minister of foreign affairs, in the short-lived centre-right minority coalition government of the conservative Jan Syse which held power until October 1990. As foreign minister, Bondevik, an opponent of membership of the European Union (EU), conducted Norway's negotiations with the EU on the formation of the European Economic Area (EEA), which were eventually concluded in October 1991.

Bondevik became prime minister in the government appointed on 17 October 1997 as a result of lengthy coalition negotiations in the aftermath of the election held on 15 September. The KrF and its Agrarian and Liberal coalition partners had won an aggregate of only 26.1% of the vote and held less than a quarter of the seats in the Parliament, and Bondevik's prime ministership thus began amid much speculation as to how long his government might survive. Concerns were heightened when he took three weeks' leave at the end of August 1998 for 'stress'. Lacking a parliamentary majority, Bondevik was forced by the far-right Progress Party (Fremskrittpartiet—FrP) to abandon tax increases in order to pass the 1999 budget.

In March 2000 Bondevik became the first Norwegian prime minister to resign over an environmental issue. His government had lost a no-confidence motion over the proposed postponement of plans to build new gas-fired power stations. Bondevik nominated the Norwegian Labour Party (Det Norske Arbeiderparti—DNA), the largest party in Parliament, to take over in a single-party minority government.

However, public sympathies were steadily swinging to the right and by the time of the September 2001 legislative elections the DNA recorded its worst result in over 100 years while the parties of the right performed well—although the KrF itself slightly decreased its representation. After a tentative DNA minority government collapsed, Bondevik was asked to head a right-wing minority coalition from 19 October. His KrF dominates, but is supported by the conservative Høyre (now the second-biggest party) and the liberal Venstre, with parliamentary backing again from the FrP (the third-biggest party). The influence of the FrP forced Bondevik in December 2002 to introduce tax cuts in the 2003 budget in the face of a threatened vote of no confidence.

OMAN

Full name: The Sultanate of Oman.

Leadership structure: The head of state is the sultan, who is also head of government, advised by the cabinet and the Consultative Council.

Sultan:	Qaboos bin Said al-Said	Since 23 July 1970
	(prime minister from 2 Jan. 1972)	

Legislature: Legislation is by decree of the sultan, advised by the 83-member Consultative Council (Majlis al-Shoura). The Council was directly elected for the first time in September 2000, when successful candidates included two women. Election is by electoral college in each province, with a total of 175,000 electors, made up of men and women 'of standing' in the community. The Council has a three-year mandate. On 16 December 1997 Sultan Qaboos appointed for the first time the 41 members of a new Council of State (Majlis al-Dawlah), which was intended to serve as "a positive contributor to constructive co-operation between the government and the citizens".

Profile of the Sultan:

QABOOS bin Said al-Said

Sultan Qaboos has ruled Oman since July 1970, when he deposed his father Said bin Taimur. Qaboos took control with the support of the armed forces and several members of the royal family after the alleged deterioration in the former sultan's health. As sultan he is in effect an absolute monarch, and his rule is authoritarian but paternalistic, combining a conservative perspective with cautious modernization to the extent of holding direct elections to the advisory Consultative Council in 2000.

Qaboos bin Said al-Said, who remains unmarried, was born in Şalalah, in the southern province of Dhofar, on 18 November 1940. He is the latest heir to the Bu Said dynasty, the Ibadi Muslim clan which has ruled Oman since the 18th century; the sultanate of Muscat and Oman formally gained independence from the UK in 1951. Qaboos was educated privately in England and trained as an officer at the Royal Military Academy, Sandhurst, from 1960, including a one-year tour of duty with a British infantry battalion stationed in West Germany. Before returning to Oman he studied local government with Bedfordshire County Council for almost 12 months. In Şalalah, from 1966, he studied Islamic history and culture under the guidance of his father.

Qaboos justified the 1970 coup in Ṣalalah with reference to a need to modernize and develop Oman's international relations, and has maintained a consistently pro-Western stance, while also developing contacts within the Arab world and among the other conservative Gulf sheikhdoms. He framed a series of five-year plans, designed to create a modern infrastructure in Oman, which nevertheless remains relatively little developed and dependent on oil for its prosperity. Since coming to power he has been minister of foreign affairs and minister of defence, and he has also had the role of prime minister since 1972.

He established in 1981 an appointed Consultative Council, which in 1991 became an indirectly elected body and in 2000 was directly elected for the first time. The creation of a second chamber, the advisory Council of State, took effect with appointments made by Qaboos at the end of 1997, pursuant to a decree he had issued on 6 November 1996 which forms the Basic Statute of the State (and which, among other things, also clarifies the royal succession).

PAKISTAN

Full name: The Islamic Republic of Pakistan.

Leadership structure: Under the 1973 Constitution, the head of state is a president, elected by Parliament, for a five-year term of office. Although the October 1999 coup did not entail any change in this nominal position, Gen. Pervez Musharraf dismissed Muhammad Rafiq Tarar on 20 June 2001 and assumed the presidency himself.

Musharraf also retained until November 2002 the position of chief executive, which he had assumed at the time of the coup. Following the October 2002 elections the post of head of government passed to the newly appointed prime minister. The prime minister is nominated by and responsible to Parliament, and appoints the cabinet.

Prior to those elections the extension of Musharraf's presidency for a further five years had been approved in a referendum on 30 April 2002, and on 21 August 2002 Musharraf announced changes to the constitution giving him the right to dismiss an elected Parliament. More changes to the constitution were made in November 2002 giving the president the power to take legislative powers if no party could achieve a majority in Parliament.

Presidents:	Muhammad Rafiq Tarar	1 Jan. 1998—20 June 2001
	Gen. Pervez Musharraf	Since 20 June 2001
Chief Executive:	Gen. Pervez Musharraf (seized power on 12 Oct. 1999)	15 Oct. 1999—23 Nov. 2002
Prime Minister:	Mir Zafarullah Jamali	Since 23 Nov. 2002

Legislature: The Parliament (Majlis al-Shoora) was suspended following the 1999 coup, and dissolved on 20 June 2001, as were the provincial assemblies. The following year elections were held and the parliament reinstated. It consists of a National Assembly with 342 members (including ten elected by non-Muslim minorities and 60 elected women) and a Senate with 100 members (88 elected by the provincial assemblies, eight chosen by tribal agencies, and four elected by the National Assembly), both houses having five-year terms.

Profile of the President:

Gen. Pervez **MUSHARRAF**

Gen. Pervez Musharraf was head of the Pakistani army before staging the bloodless coup which brought him to power as 'chief executive' in October 1999. His reputation in the armed services and his vow to sweep away 'sham' democracy initially gave him high approval ratings. However, by the time he assumed the role of president in June 2001, his support in the country had dropped to less than 25%. He met a self-imposed deadline to reintroduce a democratically elected parliament by October 2002, while guaranteeing his own position by extending his presidential mandate and increasing his constitutional powers.

Pervez Musharraf was born on 11 August 1943 in New Delhi, the capital of what was then British-controlled India. His family was relatively wealthy and his father served in the colonial government's foreign service. As Muslims they migrated to Karachi, in what had become East Pakistan, soon after the partition of India in 1947, managing to avoid the violent scenes that accompanied the later exodus. As an Urdu-speaking migrant from India, Musharraf is known in Pakistan as a *mohajir*. His father, Syed Musharaff-ud-Din, transferred to the foreign ministry of the fledgling Pakistani state and was despatched to Turkey in 1949, taking his family with him. Musharraf spent seven years in Ankara and is consequently fluent in Turkish, as well as professing great admiration for that country's military founder, Gen. Mustafa Kemal Atatürk.

The family returned to Pakistan in 1956 and Musharraf was educated at two prestigious, and originally Christian-run, schools before travelling to the UK to attend the Royal College of Defence Studies. He received a commission in the artillery in 1964 having graduated finally from the Pakistan Military Academy. He first saw action on the field during the first India–Pakistan war of 1965, for which he received a medal for gallantry. After that war he volunteered to join the Special Service Group 'commandos', and he led a commando company during the second India–Pakistan war in 1971. Meanwhile he had married Sehba Fareed in 1968; they have two children.

Over the next 20 years Musharraf held various positions in the army, including leading artillery regiments, infantry brigades and an armoured artillery division. In 1991 he was promoted to major-general and given command of an infantry division. Four years later he rose to be lieutenant-general and took control of a prestigious strike corps.

In October 1998 Musharraf achieved the rank of full general and was appointed chief of army staff. He is only the second *mohajir* to head the Pakistani army. Some observers suggested that the then prime minister Nawaz Sharif had specifically appointed Musharraf because of his background; reasoning that a *mohajir* would find it harder to build up popular support and would consequently pose no threat to the government. However, the very next year Musharraf and

Sharif quarrelled over Pakistan's military activities in the disputed region of Kashmir. When Sharif attempted to dismiss Musharraf in October 1999, the general responded by staging a military coup on 12 October. He had Sharif imprisoned before suspending multiparty politics and the country's constitution, installing himself as chief executive on 15 October.

In the beginning the coup received widespread public support as it was seen to overthrow a corrupt regime. However, despite pledges to restore full democracy by 2003, Musharraf lost the majority public confidence he initially enjoyed. Particularly sensitive was his support, against a strong current of Islamist opinion in the country, for the US-led 'war on terrorism' and the associated armed intervention which ousted the *taliban* regime in neighbouring Afghanistan.

On 20 June 2001 he assumed the presidency, while maintaining his role as chief executive and head of the armed forces. His term in office was extended for another five years following the approval of a controversial referendum held in April 2002, and later that year he reinstated the constitutional powers of the presidency, just two months before legislative elections. Under these changes he has the power to dissolve Parliament and alter the constitution.

Legislative elections held on 10 October 2002 were won by the pro-presidential Pakistan Muslim League/Quaid (PML/Q) but saw significant support go to the previous ruling parties and Islamists. Making sure that he would avoid 'cohabitation' with an opposition-led government, Musharraf stretched out the period for coalition talks by over a month and then, to ensure the accession of Mir Zafarullah Jamali of the PML/Q, altered the boundaries for prime ministerial qualification by suddenly including previous state premiers, as long as they had only ruled in an 'acting' capacity. Musharraf himself was inaugurated for another five-year presidential term on 16 November 2002. Although he officially handed over the reins of government to Jamali a week later, he remains firmly in control of the regime.

Profile of the Prime Minister:

Mir Zafarullah **JAMALI**

Mir Zafarullah Jamali is a member of the pro-presidential Pakistan Muslim League/Quaid (PML/Q). A career politician and an avid supporter of field hockey, Jamali is the first person from Baluchistan to rise to high office in Pakistan. He is generally seen as politically moderate but lightweight, having only served in minor roles in federal government. His selection as prime minister on 21 November 2002 ended four years of nonparty rule by President Pervez Musharraf, and came after weeks of political jockeying among the newly elected parties.

Mir Zafarullah Khan Jamali was born in 1944 in Rowjhan, in the impoverished southwestern province of Baluchistan. His family were notable landowners and have been active in politics for generations. He himself now has five children.

Jamali graduated from Government College in Lahore and received a master's degree in history from the University of the Punjab. He was first involved with politics as early as 1964 when he worked as bodyguard and driver to Fathima Jinnah, sister of Pakistani founding hero Muhammad Ali Jinnah. Since the late 1970s he has been a promoter of field hockey and represented Pakistan at international college level. He went on to serve as chief selector of the national squad for more than 20 years.

In the 1970s Jamali joined the Pakistan People's Party (PPP) of then prime minister Zulfikar Ali Bhutto and in 1977 he helped lead the party to victory in the Baluchistan provincial assembly. He was appointed minister of information in the provincial government. In July that year he quit the party after Gen. Zia-ul Haq staged a military coup. His career took off under Gen. Zia, and he was intermittently in the federal cabinet between 1981 and 1988. In 1985 Jamali joined the Pakistan Muslim League (PML) and was only just passed over for the position of prime minister. Instead he served under Prime Minister Muhammad Khan Junejo as minister of water and power.

In 1988 Jamali returned to Baluchistan to briefly hold the post of acting chief minister there with a precarious one-seat majority. He was reappointed to the post for a short while in 1990 and again in 1996. In the meantime he was elected to the National Assembly in 1993 and again in 1996.

Three years later, in October 1999, Gen. Pervez Musharraf staged a popular coup, ousting PML prime minister Nawaz Sharif and suspending the Parliament. In 2001 Jamali joined the PML/Q faction which had given its support to Musharraf and in 2002 he was elected to the newly reopened National Assembly. For over a month the PML/Q (which had won the greatest single share of seats) battled with the PPP and the Islamic Muttahida Majlis-e-Amal group to try and create a workable coalition. Musharraf tipped the scales in favour of the PML/Q and Jamali was approved as prime minister on 21 November with the valuable support of ten rogue PPP parliamentarians, and inaugurated on 23 November. Before his appointment, however, President Musharraf had changed the constitution to ensure that real government power rested in his own hands.

PALAU

Full name: Republic of Palau.

Leadership structure: The head of state is a president, directly elected by universal adult suffrage. The president's term of office is four years, renewable once only. The constitution also provides for an advisory body to the president which is composed of the paramount chief of each of the country's 16 separate states. The head of government is the president. The cabinet is appointed by the president.

Presidents:	Kuniwo Nakamura	1 Jan. 1993—19 Jan. 2001
	Tommy Remengesau	Since 19 Jan. 2001

Legislature: The legislature, the National Congress (Olbiil era Kelulau), is bicameral. The lower chamber, the House of Delegates, has 16 members, directly elected for a four-year term. The upper chamber, the Senate, has 14 members, elected for a four-year term. Members of both houses are elected as independents.

Profile of the President:

Tommy **REMENGESAU**

Tommy Remengesau's inauguration as president of Palau in January 2001 followed his election on 7 November 2000 when he was backed by outgoing president Kuniwo Nakamura. Educated in the USA, he had been vice president since 1993, and his appointment represents little change in previous policy, seeking greater economic development for Palau.

Thomas Esang Remengesau Jr was born in Palau, then a district of the UN Trust Territory of the Pacific Islands, on 28 February 1956. He studied as a postgraduate at the State University, Michigan, USA, after graduating from the state's Grand Valley University in the late 1970s. He returned to the Micronesian islands in 1980 and began work as an administrator and planner at the Palau Bureau of Health Services. He married Debbie Mineich and they have two sons and two daughters. He is a keen fisherman and has been All-Micronesian Grand Champion twice.

In 1981 Remengesau was appointed public information officer at the newly created autonomous Palau legislature, the National Congress. In 1984, though still only in his twenties, he decided to run for a seat in the Senate. He surprisingly received the most votes out of the 14 candidates vying for the three seats of the northeastern Badelboab constituency. He spent eight years in the Senate, gradually earning the respect of the older generation of politicians.

In popular elections held in 1992 Remengesau was elected vice president and took on the role of administration minister. Two years later the country entered into a compact of free association with the USA and became fully independent, the last of the US-administered Trust Territories to make this step. He served a second elected term as vice president from 1998 to 2001.

President Nakamura, whose second term was due to end in January 2001, could not stand for re-election and strongly supported Remengesau's candidacy to replace him. Remengesau won the November election with 52% of the vote, defeating his only rival, Peter Sugiyama. He inherited a determined policy to rescue the country from its dependence on US financial assistance, and promised to introduce an economic advisory council made up of private business interests to help him achieve his aims.

PALESTINE

Leadership structure: Yassir Arafat was elected as executive president of the Palestinian Legislative Council on 20 January 1996, and sworn in on 12 February 1996. He is often accorded the status of head of state internationally, although a formal declaration of Palestinian statehood has not been made. As president of the Council he is also head of the government, the Palestinian National Authority (PNA), and appoints the cabinet, which is accountable to the legislature.

President: Yassir Arafat   Since 12 Feb. 1996
(chairman of PNA from 5 July 1994)

Legislature: The legislature is unicameral. The sole chamber, the Palestinian Legislative Council (PLC, Majlis al-Tashri'i), has one seat reserved for the Palestinian president, and 88 constituency members. On election in 1996 all members of the PLC were given automatic membership of the Palestine National Council (PNC), which is the governing body of the Palestine Liberation Organization (PLO).

Profile of the President:

Yassir **ARAFAT**

The Palestinian guerrilla leader Yassir Arafat's transformation to elder statesman was widely celebrated when he shared the 1994 Nobel Peace Prize with Israeli government leaders for their contribution to the Israel–Palestine peace process. Latterly, however, his stock has fallen sharply. Still the object of fierce hatred among large sections of the Israeli public, and much diminished by ill health, he has seen hopes for the peace process lost amid violent conflict, and stands accused by more radical Palestinians of compromising their cause, while Israeli and US governments condemn his continuing leadership role as an obstacle to negotiation.

Mohammed Abdel-Raouf Arafat al-Qudwa al-Hussein was born on 24 August 1929 in Cairo, Egypt. He was nicknamed Yassir, meaning 'easy', and spent most of his childhood in Jerusalem, living with his uncle after the death of his mother when he was four. In 1944 he joined the League of Palestinian Students. Aged only 17, he began procuring weapons for an anticipated battle for Palestinian territory. During the Arab–Israeli conflict which surrounded the creation of the state of Israel, Arafat fought with forces backing the grand mufti of Jerusalem, and in 1948 he fled to Cairo, one of some three-quarters of a million Palestinian Arabs left stateless. He began studies in engineering at Cairo University.

In 1952 he joined the Muslim Brotherhood and Union of Palestinian Students, of which he became president. At the outbreak of the Suez crisis in 1956, he participated in the Egyptian army. Moving to Kuwait that year, he worked as an engineer before founding his own company.

In 1957 Arafat cofounded Fatah (the Palestine National Liberation Movement) and other underground organizations which mounted several attacks on Israel. In 1968 Arafat and Fatah received international publicity when they fought off Israeli troops who had entered Jordan. Fatah soon became linked with the umbrella Palestine Liberation Organization (PLO), becoming its dominant faction. Arafat was himself elected as PLO chairman in 1969 and has retained this post ever since. From this time the PLO moved from a stand of pan-Arabism to an increasing preoccupation with the cause of a specifically Palestinian nationhood. Arafat and the PLO won wide international recognition as "the sole legitimate representative of the Palestinian people", the UN voting in 1974 (after Arafat addressed the General Assembly) to give the PLO observer status and to recognize the Palestinians' claim to self-determination.

Forced out of Jordan in 1970, the PLO switched its main activities to bases in Lebanon, from where it continued to carry out raids against Israel until it was again driven out, this time to Tunisia, by the Israeli forces which invaded Lebanon in 1982.

On 15 November 1988 an independent state of Palestine was proclaimed, at a meeting of the PLO's 'parliament', the Palestine National Council, in Algiers. The territory of Palestine was defined as comprising the West Bank and the Gaza Strip, at that time in the throes of a popular uprising or *intifada* against Israeli occupation. Arafat went on to declare before the UN that the PLO renounced terrorism, and that it supported the right of all parties to live in peace. This declaration, going much of the way to meeting the Israeli complaint that the PLO opposed its right to existence as a state, led to an expansion in the international recognition of the PLO, and was a diplomatic success for Arafat. The following year, he was elected president of Palestine by the central council of the Palestine National Council, although a period of diplomatic setbacks followed, with the PLO's standing in the West in particular suffering from Arafat's backing for the Iraqi side in the 1991 Gulf War. The outlook for Arafat appeared particularly bleak at this time—although on a personal level 1991 was the year of his marriage to Suha Tawil. The impetus within Palestinian nationalism appeared to be passing from his essentially secular vision, to the radical Islamic groups and younger activists in the *intifada*, where stone-throwing youths repeatedly confronted Israeli security forces in a sustained bid to make the territory ungovernable. The following year, on 7 April 1992, Arafat was involved in a plane crash in Libya, and later had a blood clot removed from his brain. A deterioration in his health became more pronounced in the ensuing years, fuelling rumours of his impending retirement and speculation that he had Parkinson's disease.

US-led negotiations launched in Madrid in 1991, aiming to set in motion a comprehensive Middle East peace process, bore little positive fruit in respect of the Palestinian issue. Matters did progress, however, after secret negotiations, when in 1993 the Oslo agreement laid down a 'land for peace' formula. Arafat's own international standing increased significantly when, in recognition of the importance of the Oslo agreement, he, Shimon Peres and Yitzhak Rabin won the 1994 Nobel Peace Prize. Israeli forces withdrew from Jericho, and Arafat returned at last to Palestinian territory, as chairman of a Palestinian National Authority (PNA) set up under the 1993 peace agreement.

On 20 January 1996 Arafat was overwhelmingly elected first president of the PNA's legislative body, the 88-seat Palestinian Legislative Council (PLC). He took office on 12 February. He was widely regarded, and treated, as head of state of the Palestinian territory in the Gaza Strip and those areas of the West Bank from which the Israelis withdrew.

He held off, however, from a formal declaration of Palestinian statehood, recognizing that this could be an inflammatory step and prejudicial to the continuing—even if apparently deadlocked—talks with Israel. Arafat resisted the temptation to abandon the 'peace process', despite the evident lack of any real commitment to progress on the part of the right-wing Israeli government led by Binyamin Netanyahu from May 1996. Arafat saw no real alternative but to cultivate support internationally, receive signs of US favour, which culminated in US president Bill Clinton's visit to Gaza in late 1998, and await a change in the Israeli stance. Meanwhile he came under fire from critics within the Palestinian movement for the way he kept a firm grip on political control in the Palestinian self-government area, and the extensive use of his police force to suppress dissent.

The peace process picked up pace in 1999 with the election in Israel of the relatively more conciliatory Ehud Barak as prime minister. By early September 2000 Arafat and the PNA were preparing plans for a full declaration of statehood. By the end of that month, however, the cycle of violence had resumed, marking the beginning of the current *intifada*. The spur was the visit on 28 September by the Israeli right-winger Ariel Sharon to the holy al-Haram al-Sharif/Temple Mount site in Jerusalem.

When Sharon was elected Israeli prime minister in February 2001, he immediately hardened his government's stance towards Arafat in particular. For his part, Arafat attempted to distance the PNA from the violence of the *intifada*, calling for an end to stone-throwing children provoking Israeli soldiers, and latterly condemning suicide bomb attacks. However, he has increasingly lost his influence over the militant organizations Hamas and Islamic Jihad, which have reflected and led the hardening of popular Palestinian sentiment with a series of suicide bombings and attacks on Israeli civilian and military targets.

Arafat's personal standing has also been battered from the outside. The international press backed Arafat's unrequited desire to attend Christmas Eve celebrations in Bethlehem in December 2001, but the Israeli government and increasingly its US ally began pursuing a personal attack on Arafat. In April–May and September 2002 this onslaught had its most dramatic moments when Arafat was besieged by Israeli tanks in his Ramallah headquarters. Sharon has since strengthened his position against Arafat, insisting that he poses an obstacle to negotiations and that he must be removed as Palestinian leader. From June 2002 Sharon has been backed in this position by US president George W. Bush.

PANAMA

Full name: The Republic of Panama.

Leadership structure: The head of state is a president, directly elected by universal adult suffrage. The president's term of office is five years, not renewable. The final stage of a bill to allow the re-election of a president was passed in May 1998, but was heavily defeated in a referendum on 30 August 1998. The head of government is the president, who is responsible to the Legislative Assembly. The cabinet is appointed by the president.

President: Mireya Moscoso   Since 1 Sept. 1999

Legislature: The legislature is unicameral. The sole chamber, the Legislative Assembly (Asamblea Legislativa), has 71 members, directly elected for a five-year term.

Profile of the President:

Mireya **MOSCOSO**

Mireya Moscoso, Panama's first female president, is the widow of Arnulfo Arias, who was president himself three times before a coup in 1968 instigated 21 years of military rule. Although not considered a seasoned politician, she has led the Arnulfista Party (Partido Arnulfista—PA) since its formation in 1991. While her critics call her a housewife without adequate academic qualifications, her supporters see her as an able administrator in touch with the populace. In the first few months of her presidency in 1999 she oversaw Panama's assumption of control over the Panama Canal and has promised to maintain its efficient functioning as an international seaway.

Mireya Elisa Moscoso Rodríguez was born in Panama City on 1 July 1946. After completing her secondary education she began work as a secretary in 1963 before joining the unsuccessful electoral campaign of Arnulfo Arias Madrid, the Authentic Panamanian Party (Partido Panameñista Auténtico—PPA) leader, the following year. Arias had been president twice before, and had twice been deposed before completing his term. Despite an age difference of 44 years the two developed a close relationship which continued beyond the election, when Arias appointed Moscoso as sales manager at his coffee-producing firm.

In 1968 Arias again contested the presidential election. Although he was victorious he was once more forcibly deposed, this time by a military coup led by

Gen. Omar Torrijos, who then exiled Arias and his supporters. Moscoso joined Arias in exile in the USA, and a year later they were married. During her 13 years in the USA Moscoso earned her only professional qualification, a degree in interior design from the Miami Dade Community College.

Arias suffered a heart attack and died in 1988, seven years after returning to Panama. Moscoso became leader of her late husband's party, although two factions broke off to form new parties. The US-led overthrow of the military dictator Gen. Noriega opened the way for a return to civilian rule. The PPA, relaunched in 1991 as the PA, with Moscoso as its president, and maintaining the populist stance of the Arias years, quickly established itself as the main opposition to the ruling Revolutionary Democratic Party (Partido Revolucionario Democrático—PRD). The 1994 presidential elections, the first since 1968, saw Moscoso mount a strong challenge on a platform promising to tackle poverty, health care and education. Only narrowly defeated, she spent five years in opposition and stood again, this time successfully, in 1999. She took 44.9% of the vote, giving her a convincing margin over the PRD candidate Martín Torrijos, son of the late Gen. Torrijos who had overthrown her husband.

Moscoso became president at a significant moment in Panama's history. In December 1999 control of the Panama Canal was handed to the government along with real estate worth around US$4,000 million. Maintenance of the canal's political neutrality and operational status are issues of ongoing concern to Moscoso's administration, as is capitalizing on the canal's economic potential. Demand for shipping through the canal is expected to surpass current capacity in 2010.

Mireya Moscoso was married for a second time to businessman Ricardo Gruber, but they divorced in 1997. She runs her own successful coffee plantation in the country and has one adopted son, Ricardo.

PAPUA NEW GUINEA

Full name: Papua New Guinea.

Leadership structure: The head of state is the British sovereign, styled 'Queen of Papua New Guinea, and of Her other Realms and Territories, head of the Commonwealth'. She is represented by a governor-general elected by Parliament and formally appointed by the queen as head of state for a six-year term. The head of government is the prime minister, appointed by the governor-general on the proposal of the National Parliament. The National Executive Council is appointed on the proposal of the prime minister.

Queen:	Elizabeth II	Since 6 Feb. 1952
Governor-General:	Sir Silas Atopare	Since 20 Nov. 1997
Prime Ministers:	Sir Mekere Morauta	14 July 1999—5 Aug. 2002
	Sir Michael Somare	Since 5 Aug. 2002

Legislature: The legislature is unicameral. The sole chamber, the National Parliament, has 109 members, directly elected for a five-year term.

Profile of the Governor-General:

Sir Silas **ATOPARE**

Sir Silas Atopare, elected on 13 November 1997 and appointed formally by the queen and sworn in on 20 November, is the country's seventh governor-general.

Silas Atopare was born in 1951. He was a member of parliament for the Eastern Highlands province and secretary-general of the Papua New Guinea Smallholder Coffee Growers' Association before his election as governor-general in 1997. He is married to Lady Agatha Atopare, and is a member of the Seventh-day Adventist Church, part of a sizable community of Adventists in the Eastern Highlands region.

Atopare emerged as the victor in a lengthy process of parliamentary balloting for a new governor-general, after his predecessor Sir Wiwa Korowi had failed to win the two-thirds majority which is required by the constitution if an incumbent governor-general is to be re-elected to serve a second term. In the final ballot, held on 13 November, Atopare won 54 votes against 44 for Evangelical Lutheran Church leader Sir Getake Gam.

Profile of the Prime Minister:

Sir Michael **SOMARE**

Sir Michael Somare, a former teacher, heads the National Alliance (NA) party after years as a prominent member of the Papua New Guinea United Party (Pangu Pati). He is known in Papua New Guinea (PNG) variously as 'the chief', 'the old man', and the 'father of the nation' as he led the country to independence in 1975 and became its first prime minister thereafter. His face can now even be found on the 50 kina bank note, the country's largest denomination bill. He has held the post of premier a total of three times—in 1975–80, in 1982–85 and since August 2002.

Michael Thomas Somare was born in Rabaul on the eastern tip of New Britain Island on 9 April 1936, although his family had originally come from the East Sepik region of the northern PNG mainland. He learnt basic Japanese when the country was partially occupied by Japanese forces in the Second World War. He trained to be a teacher at Sogeri Education Centre in the 1950s and taught at various schools from 1956 before becoming deputy headmaster at Talidig Primary School in Madang after further training.

Switching from teaching in 1962, Somare joined the department of information at Wewak as a broadcast officer. In 1965 he married Veronica Bula Kaiap and they now have five children. In the same year he received further education at the Port Moresby Staff College before going on air in 1966 as a radio journalist. In 1967 he joined Pangu Pati, standing as the party's candidate the following year for the East Sepik constituency, which he won and which he has held in every subsequent election. Pangu emerged victorious in the 1972 elections and Somare, by now its leader, was charged with putting together the country's first coalition government with himself as chief minister.

Independence from Australia was achieved in 1975, with Somare becoming the first prime minister. He remained in office for most of the following decade, with a two-year break in 1980–82 when he was leader of the opposition following a vote of no confidence. The objectives of cutting back government spending, and introducing a fairer distribution of the country's considerable potential wealth, were goals which he (in common with all prime ministers since that time) signally failed to achieve, obstructed by the political hierarchy's ingrained business interests and the exploitation of the country's resources by foreign firms.

In the elections of 1982 Pangu gained the largest parliamentary majority ever attained in PNG. The lack of a structured opposition, however, actually hindered Somare's government, as rival factions within Pangu itself arose to counter the government's policies. Somare was eventually ousted as prime minister in 1985 after a protracted leadership struggle and his second no-confidence vote.

Once again leader of the opposition, he failed to lead Pangu back to power in the 1987 elections and was forced out as party leader in 1988. However, shifts in the precarious balance of power in Papuan politics enabled Somare to return to government as foreign minister to the man who had succeeded him as Pangu leader, Prime Minister Rabbie Namaliu. He was knighted in 1991 and in 1995 he was appointed governor of his home province of East Sepik.

In and out of the party leadership in the 1990s, he was definitively ousted in 1997 when his party membership was terminated by the Pangu parliamentary caucus. In response he formed his own party, the NA. Two years later in July 1999 the party was brought into the ruling coalition, and Somare returned to the foreign ministry. However, the relationship between Prime Minister Sir Mekere Morauta and Somare was far from smooth. By the end of 1999 he had been made Bougainville minister (in which capacity he concluded the March 2000 Loloata Understanding, consolidating the two-year-old ceasefire with guarantees of the island's autonomy), but had lost the foreign ministry and instead now doubled as mines minister.

As Somare's rivalries with Morauta became increasingly overt, he ceased to be a member of the cabinet in late 2000, and a complete breach between them in May 2001 saw the NA return to opposition. In June 2002, after 12 days of chaotic legislative elections, the NA emerged as the largest single party (although with only 19 out of the 109 seats) and Somare was asked to become prime minister for a third time. He took office on 5 August. His first policy moves were to call a halt to the previous administration's privatization programme and to cancel PNG's involvement in the Australian government's 'Pacific Solution' to its own immigration problem. His government quickly admitted that the country faces bankruptcy if spending is not drastically reduced.

PARAGUAY

Full name: The Republic of Paraguay.

Leadership structure: The head of state is a president, normally elected directly by universal adult suffrage. The president's term of office is five years, not renewable. The head of government is the president, who is responsible to congress. The Council of Ministers is appointed by the president.

President:　　　　Luis González Macchi　　　　Since 28 March 1999

Legislature: The legislature, Congress (Congreso), is bicameral. The lower chamber, the Chamber of Deputies (Cámara de Diputados), has 80 members, directly elected for a five-year term. The upper chamber, the Senate (Senado or Cámara de Senadores), has 45 members, also directly elected for a five-year term.

Profile of the President:

Luis **GONZÁLEZ MACCHI**

Luis González Macchi has been president of Paraguay since being hurriedly sworn in on 28 March 1999 to replace President Raúl Cubas Grau who resigned earlier that day. Vice President Luis María Argaña had been assassinated five days beforehand, so González Macchi, as president of Congress, was constitutionally the next in line. A lawyer by training, González Macchi spent most of his career working for the International Labour Organization (ILO) in various foreign postings.

Luis Angel González Macchi was born on 13 December 1947 in Asunción, where he attended school and went on to study law at the National University. In 1970 he won a scholarship to study management in Madrid, Spain, and from 1972 he worked for the Paraguayan ministry of justice and work. González Macchi spent almost 20 years attached to the ILO and working for its Latin and South American office in various missions ranging from Jamaica in 1972, to Honduras in 1979, and Brazil in 1989. In this capacity he also spent time in the USA in 1981. He is married to Susana Galli and together they have two daughters.

González Macchi has long been a member of the National Republican Association–Colorado Party (Asociación Nacional Republicana–Partido Colorado—ANR–PC) and from 1993 to 1998 he served as president of the Congress before events in 1999 thrust him to the top of the political hierarchy.

410

At this time President Cubas faced impeachment over the charge that he had repaid the powerful but controversial Gen. Lino Oviedo for the latter's electoral support by annulling his prison sentence. Vice President Argaña, who led the calls to impeach Cubas, had been well placed to take over as president himself, until he was gunned down publicly on 23 March. Five days after Argaña's assassination, Cubas tendered his resignation and González Macchi, next in line by virtue of his office as president of the Congress, was sworn in as president of the republic on the same day. In his inaugural address he promised to put an end to the "violence, terror and persecution" that had dogged his predecessors' tenures but for a moment his own position was decidedly insecure and he faced the possibility of fresh elections. González Macchi rode the moment with confidence, announcing a four-year programme for national economic recovery in April, before the Supreme Court had ruled that he was able to serve out the rest of Cubas's term in office which expires in 2003.

In March 2000, when angry protests at the government's handling of the economy broke out in Asunción, González Macchi attempted to pacify the crowd by making an unexpected appearance in a public square to address the demonstrators. The ploy ended in his humiliation, however, as the demonstrators forced him to flee. Two months later González Macchi was forewarned of a coup attempt on 18 May, which had intended to capitalize on popular anti-government sentiment. The warning gave him the chance to ensure the support of most of the military command, who went on to rout the insurgents. In June Oviedo was arrested in Brazil, but now lives there in exile after an extradition request from Paraguay in connection with Argaña's death was rejected.

Since then the country's economic health has worsened and González Macchi's popularity has plummeted. From August 2000 he had to contend with an opposition vice president, Julio César 'Yoyito' Franco. He has also had to face strong public protest over the faltering economy, declaring a state of emergency after riots in July 2001, fuelled by the financial chaos in neighbouring Argentina. In August that year González Macchi dismissed calls to step down, even from within his own ANR–PC. The following year presidential elections were called for April 2003, and Franco resigned in order to present his own candidacy. In December 2002 González Macchi dismissed a vote for his impeachment in the Chamber of Deputies as political manoeuvring and optimistically promised that it would be defeated in the Senate the following month.

PERU

Full name: The Republic of Peru.

Leadership structure: The head of state is a president, directly elected by universal adult suffrage. The president's term of office is five years, renewable once only. The head of government is the president, who is responsible to the Congress of the Republic. The Council of Ministers is appointed by the president.

Presidents:	Alberto Fujimori	1 July 1990—21 Nov. 2000
	Valentín Paniagua	22 Nov. 2000—28 July 2001
	Alejandro Toledo	Since 28 July 2001

Presidents of the Council of Ministers:

	Alberto Bustamante Belaúnde	10 Oct. 1999—29 July 2000
	Federico Salas Guevara	29 July 2000—19 Nov. 2000
	vacant	19 Nov. 2000—25 Nov. 2000
	Javier Pérez de Cuéllar	25 Nov. 2000—28 July 2001
	Roberto Dañino	28 July 2001—12 July 2002
	Luis Solari	Since 12 July 2002

Legislature: The legislature is unicameral. The sole chamber, the Congress of the Republic (Congreso de la República), has 120 members, directly elected for a five-year term. The term of the Congress elected in April 2000 was reduced on 5 October 2000, so as to expire on 26 July 2001, and thus enable early legislative elections to be held at the same time as the presidential elections.

Profile of the President:

Alejandro **TOLEDO**

Alejandro Toledo, leader of the Perú Posible (PP) party, is Peru's first president of Amerindian descent. His life has been a real rags-to-riches story. A soccer scholarship to the USA lifted him from poverty and opened a path leading eventually to international consulting. He failed to make much of an impact in presidential elections in 1995, but in 2000 he led opposition to the corruption of President Alberto Fujimori, and the following year he won the presidential election on the second round in June. Since then his promises of an economic turnaround have not been fulfilled and his popularity has sunk dramatically.

Alejandro Celestino Toledo Manrique was born on 28 March 1946 in the small Andean village of Cabana in Ancash province. He was one of 16 children in a poor family of mixed Amerindian descent. The Toledo family joined the migration of Amerindians to Peru's developing ports in the 1950s and settled in Chimbote. The economic migrants became known as *cholo*, a name Toledo now bears with pride. He was put to work polishing shoes and selling soft drinks. He eventually found employment as a newspaper correspondent on *La Prensa* in Chimbote, where he interviewed many high-ranking politicians of the day. His intelligence was noted and he was helped by the US Peace Corps to gain a soccer scholarship to Stanford University, California, in 1965.

Toledo's studies in economics were supported by part-time jobs including teaching and semiprofessional soccer playing. His undergraduate studies were completed at the University of San Francisco and he returned to Stanford in 1970 where he obtained a doctorate in human resources economics in 1976. While at Stanford he met Eliane Karp, a Belgian-born Jewish American who had studied the Amerindian people of Peru, and they married in 1979. They have one daughter, Chantal. From his time in the USA Toledo is now fluent in English while, from her studies, Eliane is fluent in the Amerindian language Quechua.

Between 1976 and 1985 Toledo took on various jobs around the world. Moving from the USA to Paris, France, and then to Geneva, Switzerland, he found employment as an academic and as an adviser to the UN, the World Bank, the International Labour Organization (ILO) and the Organization for Co-operation and Economic Development (OECD) among others. He returned to Peru in 1985 and took up a position as director of the government-run Sur Medio y Callao bank. He also taught at the Business Management School for Graduates in Lima. Six years later he became a visiting researcher at the Institute for International Development at Harvard University.

Toledo's political career began in 1994 when he established País Posible, the forerunner to PP. He stood in the next year's presidential elections against incumbent President Fujimori but came a poor third behind Fujimori and the popular former UN chief Javier Pérez de Cuéllar, receiving barely 3% of the vote. Stung by the defeat, he returned to the Business Management School and nurtured plans for a comeback in 2000, reforming his party into the PP in 1999. His reinvigorated campaign in that year was based on a more populist platform. His appeal as a successful *cholo* was aided by the prominence given to his wife Eliane, and the popular association of European brides with social advancement. His fiery, populist rhetoric was also enhanced by Eliane's ability to give campaign speeches in Quechua. He encountered vilification, however, from Fujimori, who accused him of abusing cocaine in the 1980s as well as fathering an illegitimate child.

In the first round of voting in April 2000, Fujimori claimed to have taken 49% of the vote, fractionally short of a simple majority. Accusing his rival of blatant fraud, Toledo withdrew from the second round held in May, which Fujimori therefore won uncontested. Toledo fomented popular anger at such a 'victory' and formed the opposition Democratic Alliance for National Unity in July. Domestic unrest, international pressure and high-profile corruption scandals forced Fujimori to step down from office before the end of the year, and fresh elections were scheduled.

Toledo only narrowly won the presidential election on the second round in June 2001, taking 52% of the vote against former president Alan García Pérez. He took office on 28 July. Within months he was facing popular protest over the continuing poor state of the economy. He pursued his liberal economic agenda, although he tempered it with the announcement in October of an ambitious public works scheme called 'To Work', and himself took a voluntary 33% pay cut the following month. However, his unsuccessful privatization policies provoked such violent protest in June 2002 that he was forced to declare a state of emergency in the southern city of Arequipa.

In October 2002 Toledo finally admitted that he had indeed fathered an illegitimate child in the late 1980s and agreed to pay US$100,000 to his second daughter, Zarai. The paternity suit actually increased the president's flagging popularity in macho-oriented Peruvian society.

Profile of the President of the Council of Ministers:

Luis **SOLARI**

Luis Solari is a founding member of the ruling Perú Posible (PP) party and was minister of health in the first cabinet formed by President Alejandro Toledo in 2001. Having worked as a medical doctor, specializing in internal medicine, he had found common cause with Toledo and helped establish PP and its predecessor, País Posible.

Luis María Santiago Eduardo Solari de la Fuente was born into a Roman Catholic family of Italian descent in Lima on 28 January 1948. After studying locally, and at the St Louis de Conzague School in Paris, France, he studied internal medicine and surgery at the National University of San Marcos in Lima. He is married and has two children.

Between 1974 and 1994 Solari worked as a doctor and consultant in a variety of institutions, specializing in internal medicine and the study of demography. This included work for the Peruvian Red Cross in the late 1970s as well as teaching at San Marcos, and consultancy at the Lima Institute of Ophthalmology and at the Dutch embassy. He was also involved in work for the Catholic Church in Peru, and his achievements were recognized by the Vatican when he was awarded the title 'commander' in 1997.

In 1994 Solari teamed up with Toledo and was a founder member of País Posible, for which he was secretary-general in 1995. He helped to run Toledo's ultimately unsuccessful presidential campaign that year, and remained at his side in the aftermath. País Posible was transformed into PP and Solari again became secretary-general in 1999, in the run-up to the next presidential elections. Toledo was beaten once more, although this time the result was controversial and the consequent political crisis ultimately led to the downfall of the incumbent, President Alberto Fujimori. Toledo and PP won fresh elections held in 2001. Solari was elected to Congress and was appointed health minister in Toledo's new cabinet. He lost his cabinet position amid government infighting in January 2002, but returned that July as president of the Council Of Ministers, a post effectively equivalent to that of prime minister.

415

PHILIPPINES

Full name: The Republic of the Philippines.

Leadership structure: The head of state is a president, directly elected by universal adult suffrage. The president's term of office is six years, not renewable. The head of government is the president. The cabinet is appointed by the president.

Presidents:	Joseph Estrada	30 June 1998—19 Jan. 2001
	Gloria Macapagal Arroyo	Since 20 Jan. 2001

Legislature: The legislature, the Congress (Kongreso), is bicameral. The lower chamber, the House of Representatives (Kapulungan ng mga Kinatawan), has at most 250 members, 204 directly elected and the rest (up to 20%) from party and minority-group lists, for a three-year term. The upper chamber, the Senate (Senado), has 24 members, directly elected for a six-year term (with half falling due for re-election every three years).

Profile of the President:

Gloria Macapagal **ARROYO**

Gloria Arroyo is the daughter of former president Diosdado Macapagal. She was popular enough to win the greatest personal majority in Philippine history when she was re-elected to the Senate in 1995. Vice president from 1998, she led the opposition to the corruption of then president Joseph Estrada in 2000 and replaced him after the country's second demonstration of 'people power' in January 2001. She has made herself a key US ally in southeast Asia and has attempted to reinvigorate the country's liberal economic reforms. She faces strong political opposition and has already had to move to pre-empt attempts to oust her by force.

Gloria Macapagal was born on 5 April 1947 in Manila and voluntarily split her childhood between there and her grandmother's hometown of Iligan, on the southern island of Mindanao. She began her further education with a two-year course at Georgetown University, USA, where she was a contemporary of future US president Bill Clinton. Returning to the Philippines, she graduated with a degree in commercial science from the Assumption Convent in Manila and then a master's degree in economics from the Ateneo de Manila University. Her working life began as a teacher at the Convent. She is married to the lawyer and businessman Jose Miguel Tuason Arroyo and they have three children.

In the early 1980s, persuaded to develop her career further, Arroyo returned to university to study for a doctorate in economics at the University of the Philippines. Following the first 'people power' movement in 1986, Arroyo entered the government of President Corazon Aquino as an assistant secretary in the ministry of trade and industry. She was later promoted to undersecretary. In 1992 she ran successfully for a seat in the Senate and in 1995 she was re-elected with 16 million votes—the largest personal mandate in Philippine history.

After considering seeking the presidency in the 1998 elections, Arroyo decided instead to set her sights on the vice presidency (for which there is a separate ballot under the Philippine system), standing as an independent. The 13 million votes she received was the highest number ever cast for a vice-presidential or presidential candidate. Her victory gave her the post of vice president in the administration headed by Joseph Estrada, the former action-movie star whose populist campaign had brought him success in the presidential poll. Although their politics were quite seriously at odds, Estrada also appointed her secretary of social welfare and development in his cabinet.

As serious accusations of corruption began to emerge against Estrada, his position became increasingly untenable, despite his immense popularity especially in rural areas. He was finally accused outright in 2000 of accepting US$8.5 million from illegal gambling syndicates.

Arroyo distanced herself from his regime at this point by resigning from the social welfare and development department, but voiced concern that her support for impeachment would be improper, as she would clearly gain politically from the president's removal. However, in October 2000 she cast her doubts aside and formed the anti-Estrada United Opposition. Estrada was impeached in December, found guilty and dismissed from office on 19 January 2001 after a massive protest against him on the streets of Manila. Arroyo was inaugurated as president the following day.

Despite the strong showing of support for her in the capital, Arroyo's position since her inauguration has been far from secure. Within a week there were rumours of an imminent military coup. In May, following Estrada's eventual arrest, violent demonstrations forced Arroyo to declare a week-long 'state of rebellion' in the capital. Three senators were arrested for plotting to overthrow her. Less than a year later, in January 2002, Arroyo warned that unnamed groups were actively attempting to destabilize her government.

Arroyo's main policy platforms have been based on her contrast to Estrada's populist flamboyance. She has targeted cronyism and corruption while promising to put back on track the economic liberalization programmes of Estrada's predecessor, Fidel Ramos. Her support for the USA after the 11 September 2001 terrorist attacks has gained her that country's increased support, while her attempts to deal firmly and diplomatically with Muslim separatists in Mindanao have won praise from the international community as a whole. However, extremists pose one of the biggest threats to her administration, with bombing campaigns in Mindanao and across the country continuing during 2002.

That year she joined the ruling Lakas ng (Power of) EDSA–National Union of Christian Democrats (Lakas–NUCD), becoming party chairman. She announced in December that she would not stand for re-election as president in 2004.

POLAND

Full name: The Republic of Poland.

Leadership structure: The head of state is a president, directly elected by universal adult suffrage. The president's term of office is five years, renewable once only. The head of government is the chairman of the Council of Ministers (prime minister), who is appointed by the Diet on the basis of a motion made by the president. The Council of Ministers is appointed by the Diet.

President:	Aleksander Kwaśniewski	Since 23 Dec. 1995
Prime Ministers:	Jerzy Buzek	31 Oct. 1997—19 Oct. 2001
	Leszek Miller	Since 19 Oct. 2001

Legislature: The legislature, the National Assembly (Zgromadzenie Narodowe), is bicameral. The lower chamber, the Diet (Sejm), has 460 members, directly elected for a four-year term. The upper chamber, the Senate (Senat), has 100 members, elected for a four-year term.

Profile of the President:

Aleksander **KWAŚNIEWSKI**

Aleksander Kwaśniewski is an ex-communist whose election to the presidency in 1995 caused some alarm, especially in the USA. However, he represents a younger generation of pragmatic reformers in the party, the heir of which is now a part of the Democratic Left Alliance (Sojusz Lewicy Demokratycznej—SLD). An economist by training and editor of party youth publications, he was a junior minister in the last communist governments of the late 1980s and was active in the 1989 round-table debates on introducing a multiparty system. He led the reformed communist party from 1990 until his election as president.

Aleksander Kwaśniewski was born in the northwestern town of Białogard on 15 November 1954. After attending high school in Białogard, he graduated from the University of Gdańsk with a degree in transport economics. He was an energetic political activist in the student socialist youth union, joined the then ruling communist party, the Polish United Workers' Party (Polska Zjednoczona Partia Robotnicza—PZPR), in 1977, edited the official student weekly paper in 1981–84 and was editor-in-chief of the youth daily *Sztandar Mlodych* in 1984–85. Kwaśniewski is married to Jolanta née Konty and they have one daughter.

In November 1985 Kwaśniewski joined the Council of Ministers and had special responsibility for youth affairs. By 1987 he had become chairman of the committee for youth and physical education and in October 1988 he was appointed head of the government sociopolitical committee. The following year he took part in the round-table debates on the creation of a pluralist system, held between February and April. After these talks had opened the way for partially free elections, and the PZPR had entered a Solidarity-led coalition government, the party held an extraordinary congress in January 1990 and reconstituted itself as the Social Democracy of the Republic of Poland (Socjaldemokracja Rzeczypospolitej Polskiej—SdRP), with the youthful Kwaśniewski a forward-looking choice as its first chairman.

Kwaśniewski was elected in 1991 to sit as a deputy in the Diet, the lower chamber in what had become a bicameral parliament. For two years from November 1993 he chaired the parliamentary constitutional committee and gained a reputation for seeking consensus in the interests of political unity. This even extended to giving his initial support to the conclusion of a concordat between Poland and the Vatican, to which many in his party were openly hostile. Kwaśniewski also sat as a member of the foreign affairs committee and the economic policy, budget and finance committee.

In the 1995 presidential election, Kwaśniewski led in the first round on 5 November with just over 35% of the vote, narrowly ahead of the incumbent Lech Wałęsa in a field of 13 candidates. The runoff two weeks later was again close, Kwaśniewski winning with 51.7%. He was sworn in on 23 December, after the constitutional tribunal had ruled against Wałęsa's attempt to have him disqualified for allegedly misleading the voters about his electoral qualifications by claiming a postgraduate degree.

As president, Kwaśniewski committed himself to promoting national consensus—a promise sorely tested the following year by the issue of abortion. (He eventually signed into law a bill permitting terminations but only within the early period of a pregnancy.) He also expressed his support for continuing economic reforms and concluding the formulation of a democratic constitution (which finally took effect in October 1997), and backed Poland's applications for membership of the European Union (EU) and the North Atlantic Treaty Organization (NATO). Although both membership quests ultimately proved successful in 2002, with membership of both expected in 2004, Kwaśniewski has strongly argued the case for preventing foreigners from buying Polish agricultural land.

In August 2000 Kwaśniewski was exonerated of any involvement with the communist-era secret police, clearing his candidature for the October presidential election. He was successfully re-elected in the first round of voting on 9 October with 53.9% of the vote against 11 opponents.

Profile of the Prime Minister:

Leszek **MILLER**

Leszek Miller is chairman of the socialist Democratic Left Alliance (Sojusz Lewicy Demokratycznej—SLD). Briefly a politburo member in the ruling Polish United Workers' Party (Polska Zjednoczona Partia Robotnicza—PZPR) at the very end of the communist era, and holder of various ministerial posts in the 1990s, he is renowned for standing up for the record of the former communist government, and also for his intention to distance the Polish State from the Roman Catholic Church. However, he is now a strong advocate of free-market economics and European integration.

Leszek Miller was born on 3 July 1946 in Żyrardów, just west of Warsaw. He is married to Aleksandra and has one son. He left school at 17 and worked for seven years as an electrician in the linen industry in his home town. He began his political career in 1969 when he joined the ruling communist PZPR. He held various administrative posts within the party while also studying political science at the Higher School of Social Sciences in Warsaw.

Rising rapidly within the PZPR, Miller was appointed secretary of the party committee in his home province of Skierniewice in 1986 and had become a member of the politburo by 1989. After sitting on the transitional 'round table' in 1989, he was a founder member the following year of the reformed-communist Social Democracy of the Republic of Poland (Socjaldemokracja Rzeczypospolitej Polskiej—SdRP), which became part of the SLD alliance in the newly democratized Poland.

In 1991, in the first democratic elections since the collapse of communism, Miller was elected to the National Assembly. Appointed minister of labour and social policy in 1993, he was minister-head of the office of the Council of Ministers in 1996 before becoming interior minister in 1997. In these roles he was instrumental in negotiating the Roman Catholic Church's status in Poland.

Following the SLD's electoral defeat in 1997 Miller served on various parliamentary committees, and was nominated as a goodwill ambassador for the UN Children's Fund (UNICEF) in 2000. Meanwhile the SLD had transformed itself into a single political party in 1999 and elected Miller as its first chairman. Rejuvenated, the party went on to score a significant victory in legislative elections in 2001 against a deeply unpopular conservative government. Miller was appointed prime minister in October. He has since inaugurated a four-year economic plan to increase public spending while simultaneously encouraging entrepreneurship. His government has also been told that Poland can expect to join the European Union (EU) in 2004.

PORTUGAL

Full name: The Republic of Portugal.

Leadership structure: The head of state is a president, directly elected by universal adult suffrage. The president's term of office is five years, renewable once only. The head of government is the prime minister, who is appointed by the president. The Council of Ministers is appointed by the president on the advice of the prime minister.

President:	Jorge Sampaio	Since 9 March 1996
Prime Ministers:	António Guterres	29 Oct. 1995—6 April 2002
	José Manuel Durão Barroso	Since 6 April 2002

Legislature: The legislature is unicameral. The sole chamber, the Assembly of the Republic (Assembléia da República), has 230 members, directly elected for a four-year term.

Profile of the President:

Jorge **SAMPAIO**

Jorge Sampaio is a lawyer and former mayor of Lisbon, and a one-time student activist agitating for an end to the Salazar regime. He began his second five-year term as president of Portugal in March 2001. He was the candidate of the Socialist Party (Partido Socialista—PS).

Jorge Fernando Branco de Sampaio was born on 18 September 1939 in Lisbon. The son of a doctor, he spent part of his schooldays in England, and went to Lisbon University in 1956 to study law. His political career began at this time and he led student protests against the dictatorship of António de Oliveira Salazar. He went on to defend other opponents of the regime as a young lawyer in Lisbon.

After the 'Carnation Revolution' in 1974 he initially supported the small Movement of the Socialist Left, but distanced himself from the movement when it began to adopt Marxist policies. In 1978 he joined the PS, led by Mário Soares, and was elected as a parliamentary deputy in the 1979 general election and in subsequent elections. Throughout, Sampaio has maintained a strong commitment to the defence of human rights and from 1979 to 1984 served on the Council of Europe's Commission for Human Rights in Strasbourg. In 1987 he was elected president of the PS parliamentary party; he became PS secretary-general in 1989, but was replaced in 1992 by António Guterres.

In December 1989 Sampaio was elected mayor of Lisbon, a post to which he was re-elected in 1994. He lives in Lisbon with his second wife, and has one son and one daughter.

The election of a socialist government in October 1995, and Sampaio's election as president on 14 January 1996, when he won 53.8% of the vote, brought to an end a decade of Portuguese politics dominated by socialist Soares as president and centre-right Social Democratic Party (Partido Social Democrata—PSD) leader Aníbal Cavaco Silva as prime minister. However, while Sampaio remained highly popular, the PS government rapidly lost support as the country's economy failed to improve. A plan to increase fuel prices prompted a general strike organized by the Communist and Socialist trade union federation in May 2000. Sampaio easily won re-election in the January 2001 presidential election, gaining 55.8% of the vote in the first round, but he has been in 'cohabitation' with a PSD government since April 2002.

Profile of the Prime Minister:

José Manuel **DURÃO BARROSO**

José Manuel Durão Barroso leads the centre-right Social Democratic Party (Partido Social Democrata—PSD). Originally an academic, he was foreign minister in the 1980s and early 1990s, and took over the leadership of the PSD in 1999. He successfully led it out of opposition in 2002 in early legislative elections sparked by the party's earlier landslide victory in local elections.

José Manuel Durão Barroso was born in Lisbon on 23 March 1956. Throughout his childhood and education, Durão Barroso was exposed to the often violent repression of the conservative dictatorship in control of the country at that time, and he became interested in politics from an early age. In 1969, aged only 13, he helped distribute pamphlets for the opposition Electoral Democratic Commission. The beginning of his university career in 1974 coincided with the 'Carnation Revolution'. He graduated in law from the University of Lisbon, where he met his future wife, Margarida Sousa Uva. They now have three children.

After graduation Durão Barroso remained in academia, beginning work as an assistant at the University of Lisbon. He went on to receive postgraduate qualifications in social sciences from Geneva University, Switzerland, and Georgetown University, USA. He published many political articles and taught at a number of foreign institutions. In 1980 he joined the PSD when it formed the party of power in the transitional government.

In 1985 Durão Barroso was elected to the Assembly of the Republic and was appointed assistant secretary of state for home affairs in the PSD's minority government. The party went on to win an outright majority in 1987 and Durão Barroso was also appointed secretary of state for foreign affairs. He remained attached to the latter portfolio, becoming foreign minister in 1992, until the defeat of the PSD in 1995. During this time he oversaw the normalization of Portugal's relations with its former colonies. Among his major achievements was facilitating the 1990 Bicesse Agreement which temporarily brought peace to Angola, and campaigning for the independence of East Timor.

Forced into opposition in 1995, Durão Barroso maintained his seat in the Assembly but turned his attention back to his academic career. He once again became a visiting scholar at Georgetown University. He also headed the department of international relations at the University of Lusíada until 1999 when he was elected leader of the PSD.

Campaigning against the incumbent government's economic policies, he led the party to a sweeping victory at local polls in December 2001, taking 160 of the available 308 city councils, including Lisbon. Durão Barroso himself was elected president of the municipal assembly of Valpaços, in the north of the country. The stinging defeat proved too much for the ruling Socialist Party government which resigned soon after.

In fresh elections held in March 2002 the PSD took around 40% of the vote, securing the largest share of seats. Durão Barroso was appointed prime minister on 6 April at the head of a coalition with the smaller People's Party.

QATAR

Full name: The State of Qatar.

Leadership structure: The head of state is an amir. The amir is head of government and appoints the other members of the Council of Ministers, including the prime minister.

Amir: Sheikh Hamad bin Khalifa al-Thani   Since 27 June 1995

Prime Minister: Sheikh Abdullah bin Khalifa al-Thani   Since 29 Oct. 1996

Legislature: There is no legislature. The amir announced plans on 16 November 1998 to establish an elected parliament, setting up a committee to draft a constitution accordingly. There is a 35-member Advisory Council.

Profile of the Amir:

Sheikh **HAMAD** bin Khalifa al-Thani

Sheikh Hamad acceded to power on 27 June 1995, ousting his father, Sheikh Khalifa, in a bloodless coup to become amir of Qatar. A Sandhurst-trained officer and head of his country's armed forces since 1972, he had played a major role in modernizing army units and in increasing armed forces personnel.

Born in 1950 in Doha, Hamad bin Khalifa al-Thani attended primary and secondary schools there before joining the Royal Military Academy, Sandhurst, from which he passed out in 1971. He joined the Qatari armed forces and was appointed commander of the First Mobile Battalion with the rank of major, a rank he held until his promotion to major-general and appointment as commander-in-chief of the armed forces in February 1972.

On 31 May 1977 he was named as heir apparent and first entered the government as minister of defence, while remaining as commander-in-chief of the armed forces. In May 1989 he was appointed chairman of the Higher Council for Planning, a position considered to be vital in the building of a modern state. He also chaired the Higher Council for Youth Welfare from its establishment in 1979 until September 1991, when the General Authority for Youth and Sports was established and a full-time chairman appointed.

Sheikh Hamad's takeover of power on 27 June 1995, while his father was abroad, was overwhelmingly supported by the armed forces and cabinet, and welcomed by neighbouring states. It was apparently motivated by disagreements when

Sheikh Khalifa sought to resume closer control of the government, having effectively passed over its management to Sheikh Hamad three years earlier.

On becoming amir, Sheikh Hamad also became prime minister, but held this post for only a year. In 1996 he issued an amiri decree to amend the Basic Temporary Amended Statutes of the Rule of the State, in order to separate the role of amir and the post of prime minister, to which he then appointed his brother Sheikh Abdullah.

Profile of the Prime Minister:

Sheikh **ABDULLAH** bin Khalifa al-Thani

Sheikh Abdullah is the younger brother of Qatar's ruling amir, Sheikh Hamad. Prior to the creation of the post of prime minister in October 1996, he had headed the country's Olympic committee from 1979 and run the interior ministry from 1989.

Abdullah bin Khalifa al-Thani was born in Doha on 25 December 1956 into Qatar's ruling Thani clan. His father, Sheikh Khalifa, became amir in 1972, and Abdullah's eldest brother Hamad took the title for himself in 1995. As a member of the ruling royal family, Sheikh Abdullah had a privileged upbringing. After a local education, he went to the UK to attend the prestigious Royal Military Academy at Sandhurst, from which he passed out as an officer in December 1976.

On his return to Qatar, Sheikh Abdullah served in the military in various senior posts until 1989. By the end of his military career he had achieved the rank of lieutenant-colonel and was assistant commander-in-chief of the armed forces. He also sought to foster the country's sporting aspirations, establishing the Qatar Olympic Committee in March 1979 and heading it for the next ten years.

In 1989 Sheikh Abdullah was appointed to his father's government as interior minister. In July 1995 he took on the additional role of deputy prime minister in the new government formed after his brother's coup. The following year Amir Sheikh Hamad amended the constitution to separate the roles of head of state and head of government. He appointed Sheikh Abdullah as prime minister on 29 October 1996, while retaining him also as interior minister (although he relinquished the latter post in January 2001). Sheikh Abdullah chairs the cabinet, but real power remains with his brother.

ROMANIA

Full name: Romania.

Leadership structure: The head of state is a president, directly elected by universal adult suffrage. The president's term of office is four years, renewable once only. The head of government is the prime minister, who is appointed by the president. The cabinet is appointed by the prime minister.

Presidents:	Emil Constantinescu	29 Nov. 1996—20 Dec. 2000
	Ion Iliescu	Since 20 Dec. 2000
Prime Ministers:	Mugur Isarescu	21 Dec. 1999—28 Dec. 2000
	Adrian Nastase	Since 28 Dec. 2000

Legislature: The legislature, the Parliament of Romania (Parlamentul României), is bicameral. The lower chamber, the House of Deputies (Camera Deputaţilor), has 345 members (with 18 seats reserved for minorities), directly elected for a four-year term. The upper chamber, the Senate (Senatul), has 140 members, directly elected for a four-year term.

Profile of the President:

Ion **ILIESCU**

Ion Iliescu's victory at the December 2000 presidential elections marked his return to power after four years in opposition. An ex-communist himself, he clashed with the autocratic dictator Nicolae Ceauşescu in the 1970s, and managed to ride the tide of the collapse of Ceauşescu's regime at the end of 1989, becoming Romania's first democratically elected president the following year. His two terms as president were notable for increasing economic hardship and the state-sanctioned use of violence against demonstrators. Since then he has toned down his leftist politics and embraced European integration.

Ion Iliescu was born on 3 March 1930 in the rural town of Olteniţa, southeast of Bucharest near the border with Bulgaria. He joined the Romanian Communist Party (Partidul Comunist Român—PCR) in the last years of the Second World War while still a schoolboy in Bucharest. After the end of the war, under the new communist regime, Iliescu studied at the Bucharest Polytechnic Institute. He married Elena, an engineer specializing in metallurgy, in 1951. After graduating, he went to Moscow, to the Energy Institute, where he specialized in water management and ecology. When he returned to Romania he began work in 1955 as a designer-engineer at the Energy Engineering Institute in Bucharest.

Iliescu's political activism flourished in the postwar years. He helped found the Union of High School Students' Association in 1948 and the Romanian Union of Student Associations (RUSA) in 1956. Both were based on Western student unions, and the first was dissolved for neglect of Marxist ideologies. His presidency of the RUSA, on the other hand, later helped him into his first ministerial post, in charge of the youth affairs portfolio in 1967.

His rise within the PCR, where he became a junior member of the central committee in 1965, a full member three years later and a member of the secretariat in 1971, came to an abrupt halt in 1972 when he came into conflict with Ceauşescu because of his open opposition to the leader's proposed 'cultural revolution'. Shunted into the vice chairmanship of Timiş county council, and then moved again in 1974 to the county council in the far-northeastern city of Iaşi, he was subsequently placed under close surveillance by Ceauşescu's secret police, the Securitate, as an 'intellectual deviant'. The posts he held from 1979 to 1989, at the National Water Resources Council and then as director of the Technical Publishing House, did, however, bring him back to Bucharest and keep him in contact with the disparate elements which emerged in 1989 in opposition to the Ceauşescu regime.

When open revolt broke out in December 1989, Ceauşescu quickly lost the backing of the military and was summarily tried and executed. Iliescu's name was chanted in the streets and the emerging National Salvation Front (Frontul Salvarii Nationale—FSN), a collection of generals, artists, and outcast party members from the previous regime, nominated him as interim president. Although the FSN was initially seen as a liberator from Ceauşescu's totalitarianism, it soon gathered opponents. The decision not to insist on the dissolution of the PCR, and the resolve that the FSN would contest elections itself (contrary to previous pledges), built up a strong anti-FSN movement, often resulting in street violence between political rivals. In this climate Iliescu won presidential elections held in May 1990 with a convincing 80% of the vote.

President Iliescu's new regime failed to lift the country from its desperate economic situation and was characterized by violent unrest. In June 1990 he made a television appeal for miners to come to Bucharest to put down anti-government demonstrations, resulting in a pitched battle in the capital. By 1992 the pace of free-market reforms had created chaos in the country. Iliescu, who distanced himself as president from the prime minister's more zealous free-market economics, was re-elected president in a second-round victory in October that year, and his new Democratic National Salvation Front (Frontul Democrat al Salvarii Nationale—FDSN) gained a significant proportion of seats in both houses of Parliament. However, he came to rely increasingly on the support of extremist parties in Parliament, including the ultranationalist Greater Romania Party (Partidul România Mare—PRM). By the time of general elections in

November 1996 support for Iliescu and the renamed Social Democracy Party of Romania (Partidul Democratiei Sociale din România—PDSR) was at a low ebb, and he was defeated in the second round by opposition leader Emil Constantinescu.

Having entered the Senate on behalf of the PDSR, Iliescu spent the next four years as a vocal critic of the centrist governments of Constantinescu, as they battled with the same economic pressures and civil unrest with which his own regime had struggled. Public support for centrist politics declined to the extent that the presidential contest in 2000 proved to be a head-to-head race between Iliescu and the far-right PRM leader, Corneliu Vadim Tudor. Iliescu comfortably won in the second round in December. In line with the constitution, he stepped down in January 2001 as leader of the PDSR, which had also been victorious in legislative elections, in favour of the leading party reformer and new prime minister Adrian Nastase. The party was transformed into the Social Democrat Party (Partidul Social Democrat—PSD) in June after it merged with the former communist (and originally anti-Iliescu) Romanian Social Democratic Party.

Profile of the Prime Minister:

Adrian **NASTASE**

Adrian Nastase, a respected professor of law, has strong connections with western Europe, particularly with France. He has sat in the House of Deputies since the first post-Ceauşescu elections in 1990, and is seen as a champion of the more liberal faction in the governing Social Democrat Party (Partidul Social Democrat—PSD). As prime minister he has had to overcome rumours of his imminent dismissal on a regular basis.

Adrian Nastase was born on 22 June 1950 in Bucharest. He was educated in the city and graduated from the University of Bucharest with a degree in law in 1973. On completing his course he was appointed as a research fellow at the Bucharest Institute of Legal Research and re-entered the university, this time at the faculty of sociology. A year before completing his postgraduate studies in 1978 he was nominated as an associate professor in international law. He was awarded a doctorate in the subject in 1987 and was made a full professor in 1990. Meanwhile, in 1986, he married Daniela Miculescu, the daughter of a Communist government minister, and they now have two sons.

Nastase established close links with the West while Romania was still a Communist country. In 1980 he was a visiting fellow to the UN Educational, Scientific and Cultural Organization (UNESCO) and the International Peace Institute in Oslo, Norway, and in 1984 he acted as director of studies at the International Institute of Human Rights in Strasbourg, France. He has encouraged ties between Romania and the West as a member of the board at the Institute for East–West Studies in New York, USA, since 1991. His special relationship with

France has been fostered through his position as an associate of international law at the prestigious Sorbonne University, in Paris, which he has held since 1994, and his membership of the International Assembly of Francophone Parliamentarians. He has authored over 240 papers and articles and a number of texts on international law and human rights.

Following the collapse of the Communist regime of Nicolae Ceauşescu in 1989, Nastase was elected to the House of Deputies in 1990 and was appointed by President Iliescu as foreign minister. In Iliescu's second term, beginning in 1992, Nastase was chairman of the House of Deputies. He followed Iliescu into the newly formed Social Democracy Party of Romania (Partidul Democratiei Sociale din România—PDSR) and sat on the party's executive from its creation in 1993. During this time he also continued to lecture in international law and took up professorships at various Bucharest institutions.

Following the PDSR's crushing electoral defeat in 1996, Iliescu turned to Nastase to help reform the stricken party. Nastase, now vice chairman of the House of Deputies, secured an agreement with Iliescu in 1997 to manage the reconstruction as the party's vice president in exchange for a guarantee of the premiership in any future PDSR government. The rigours of transition to a free-market economy took its toll on popular support for the centrist government in the late 1990s, and the PDSR returned to power in November 2000, with Iliescu regaining the presidency. True to his word, he nominated Nastase as prime minister, heading a government which substantially retained the policies of its predecessor, insofar as Nastase pledged to draw the country further down the path of European integration and economic reform. He replaced Iliescu as leader of the PDSR in January 2001 and the party was transformed into the PSD in June.

RUSSIAN FEDERATION

Full name: The Russian Federation (Russia).

Leadership structure: The head of state is a president, directly elected by universal adult suffrage. The president's term of office is four years, renewable only once consecutively. The president appoints (subject to parliamentary approval) the chairman of the Council of Ministers. The president is, however, entitled to chair sessions of the Council.

President: Vladimir Putin Since 7 May 2000
(acting from 31 Dec. 1999)

Chairmen of the Council of Ministers:

Vladimir Putin 16 Aug. 1999—7 May 2000
(acting from 9 Aug. 1999)

Mikhail Kasyanov Since 17 May 2000
(acting from 7 May 2000)

Legislature: The legislature, the Federal Assembly (Federalnoye Sobraniye), is bicameral. The lower chamber, the State Duma (Gosudarstvennaya Duma), has 450 members, directly elected for a four-year term. The upper chamber, the Council of the Federation (Soviet Federatsii), has 178 members (two representatives from each member of the Russian Federation). The individual members' terms vary according to the electing region.

Profile of the President:

Vladimir **PUTIN**

Vladimir Putin was little known when Boris Yeltsin made him prime minister in 1999, and was then propelled into the presidency by Yeltsin's unexpected resignation at the end of that year. Unaffiliated to any political party, he spent the majority of his career working as a KGB agent. As acting head of state he pursued the domestically popular war in Chechnya with determined ferocity, and with the Russian economy in an apparent state of recovery he won a convincing first-round victory in presidential elections in March 2000. Since then he has gambled on further military action in Chechnya and has been forced to play down a rising cult of personality.

Vladimir Vladimirovich Putin was born on 7 October 1952 in Leningrad (now St Petersburg). His grandfather was Lenin's cook and from a young age Putin expressed a desire to serve the state by working as a spy. In 1975 he graduated from the law department of Leningrad's State University and was immediately recruited by the Committee for State Security (Komitet Gosudarstvennoy Bezopasnosti—KGB). Little is known of the details of his secret service career other than that he spent most of his time in East Germany following his transfer there in 1984. By the time he left active service in 1990 he had reached the rank of colonel. He is married to Lyudmila, and they have two children.

Returning to Leningrad (renamed St Petersburg the following year), Putin began work as an adviser on international affairs to the State University and the city council in 1990 and quickly made his name in city politics under his old law professor and mentor, the reformist mayor Anatoly Sobchak. Putin became a deputy mayor and worked as the chairman of the committee on foreign relations from 1994 to 1996. He instigated a series of successful export quotas designed to generate funds to tackle the city's acute shortages, which had followed hard on the heels of the Soviet Union's collapse in 1991. After Sobchak was defeated in mayoral elections in 1996, Putin moved to Moscow to pursue a governmental career in the Kremlin. In 1997 he was appointed as head of the control department, deputy manager of property and deputy administrator for the presidential department; in the latter role he was an influential adviser to President Yeltsin on matters concerning Russia's regional policy.

In July 1998 President Boris Yeltsin promoted Putin to be head of the KGB's successor, the Federal Security Service (Federal'naya Sluzhba Bezopasnosti—FSB). In this role his main mandate was economic espionage and cracking down on illegal foreign trading. By March 1999 he had added the role of secretary of Yeltsin's security council and was heavily involved in the dispute with the North Atlantic Treaty Organization (NATO) over Kosovo.

On 9 August Boris Yeltsin named Putin as his new prime minister and endorsed him as his preferred presidential heir. Putin's lack of high-powered political experience made him an unusual choice for the role of prime minister, the fourth since March 1998. From his first day Putin showed what his approach would be, taking a hard line on separatism in the Caucasus, no matter the international response, while leaving the economic policies of his predecessor largely unchanged to minimize domestic upheaval. Rebels in Dagestan were crushed with remorseless swiftness, and in October Putin masterminded an invasion of Chechnya. Despite initial media cynicism, this soon won him the rating of Russia's most popular politician, as Russian troops made steady advances on the Chechen capital Grozny. He was also building an impressive base of support in the Duma, with the newly formed pro-Putin grouping Unity making sizable gains in legislative elections in December.

The drama climaxed on 31 December 1999 when Yeltsin publicly announced his resignation and personally nominated Putin as his interim replacement. As acting president, Putin became solely responsible in the public's eye for the continuing Chechen war which persistently overran its 'imminent' end, and he quickly sought to soften his authoritarian image. A hastily drawn together collection of interviews was published as an autobiography, and much was made of his concerns for animal welfare with the release of his email correspondence with the famous ex-film-star activist Brigitte Bardot. Despite mounting international criticism of the war, Putin retained his lead over other Russian politicians and clinched the presidency in the first round of elections in March 2000 with 52.9% of the vote. His nearest rival, the Communist Gennady Zyuganov, received less than 30%.

One of his first acts as president-elect was to talk of the "dictatorship of the law" while recommitting his administration to the Chechen war. While some Russian writers talked of a "modernized Stalinism", others suggested that in Russia "dictatorship" was not seen as inherently bad. Fears abroad were allayed when Putin assembled an economic think tank comprising the four men considered the most liberal and pro-market on the Russian scene. He also rejected outright the Communist Party's demand that it be included in the new cabinet in proportion to its size in the Duma. Confirming his nonparty style of politics, Putin made it clear that his chosen ministers would have to leave their party affiliations at the door when they entered his government. Putin was inaugurated on 7 May.

Domestically, Putin has consolidated his power with a fierce war on the 'oligarchs' of the Yeltsin era and a concerted centralization of control over the country's vast infrastructure. In the Duma he has enabled the growth of Unity into a full political party which, through mergers and defections, has become a rival in size to the Communists.

The end of Putin's political honeymoon can be firmly identified as August 2000 and the sinking of the *Kursk* nuclear-powered submarine with the loss of all 118 sailors aboard. His hesitation over whether to involve foreign countries in the ultimately doomed rescue effort, and his failure to cancel a vacation on hearing the news, severely damaged his personal standing in Russian eyes. Despite this setback, however, many observers noticed a rapidly growing cult of personality forming around the president. While his name and image proliferate in popular culture, the rise of the Moving Together pro-Putin youth group, whose members often claim to idolize Putin and his personal traits, has caused some to worry greatly.

Internationally, Putin's position was revolutionized by the 11 September 2001 terrorist attacks on the USA. Where once he was openly criticized by the West over the war in Chechnya (which he grandly and somewhat falsely declared to be "over" in April 2002), Putin was suddenly welcomed by US president George W. Bush and his allies as a combatant against terrorism. Putin quickly capitalized on this change, toning down previous criticism of the USA's controversial National Missile Defence system, and shelving suspicion of NATO expansion in the Baltics to move instead to participation, through the NATO–Russia Council, from May 2002. His publicly cordial relations with Bush became less convincing towards the end of 2002, however, as Putin became a vocal doubter over the justification for a US-led war on Iraq.

Profile of the Chairman of the Council of Ministers:

Mikhail **KASYANOV**

Although he did not formally become prime minister until May 2000, Mikhail Kasyanov was effectively running the cabinet from early January, when he was appointed as first deputy prime minister by Vladimir Putin, the erstwhile premier who had just become acting president. Kasyanov's career at the centre of national economic policy, and his distinct lack of political ambition, were prime considerations for Putin who was keen to focus on Russia's economic problems and secure his own position as president. Kasyanov is not affiliated with any political party, although there have been persistent rumours about his connections with various business 'oligarchs'.

Mikhail Kasyanov was born on 8 December 1957 in the southern Moscow suburb of Solntsevo. During his education he attained a fluency in English which set him in good stead for negotiating with international investors in later years. He attended the Moscow Institute of Civil Engineering before joining the Soviet Gosplan economic planning agency where he completed his studies. He stayed in Gosplan for nine years until 1990.

In 1990 Kasyanov transferred to the new Russian economics ministry, working notably on foreign relations for three years, as the Soviet Union collapsed, before crossing over to the finance ministry in 1993. There he quickly worked his way from deputy minister to first deputy minister and achieved cabinet rank as minister of finance in May 1999. On New Year's Eve that year Boris Yeltsin announced his resignation and appointed his prime minister, Putin, as acting head of state. Within weeks Putin filled the vacuum beneath him by raising Kasyanov to the role of deputy prime minister, effectively head of the government until a new president could be elected and choose a new cabinet. Kasyanov maintained his position as minister of finance.

In February 2000 Kasyanov achieved a major triumph when he successfully negotiated with the London Club of private international investors to overhaul Russia's Soviet-era debts and had US$10,000 million written off entirely. For this achievement he has become known as 'Mr Debt'. In the following month, with the presidential election looming, Kasyanov was quick to ensure that the Russian economy showed none of the chronic tendencies it had developed under President Boris Yeltsin. Pensions were paid and civil servants' back payments were cleared, while Kasyanov also managed to balance steady foreign debt payments against an expensive war in Chechnya.

His detractors pointed to his apparent association with Russian tycoon Boris Berezovsky, one of the so-called 'oligarchs' who assumed excessive influence under President Yeltsin's administration. For his part, Kasyanov defiantly denied having any such ties, promoting his loyalty to President Putin and to Putin's crusade against financial corruption in Russia. Once Putin had been inaugurated on 7 May 2000, it was only ten days before Kasyanov was ratified by the Duma as prime minister.

Since then Kasyanov has continued on his relatively successful path in rehabilitating the Russian economy and in August 2002 it was announced that the country's living standards had crept back above the pre-1998 crisis level. However, it has also been noted that the accumulation of wealth in the new Russia has been far from equitable. The wage gap yawns wider than ever and 50% of the economy still operates on the black market. Kasyanov's successes have been magnified by his happily subordinate position to President Putin. Posing no threat politically he has survived many rumours of his imminent dismissal.

RWANDA

Full name: The Republic of Rwanda.

Leadership structure: The head of state is a president. The president's term of office is five years, renewable once only. The period of political transition was extended to 2003 in July 1999. The president appoints the Council of Ministers, whose head is the prime minister.

Presidents: Pasteur Bizimungu   19 July 1994—23 March 2000

         Maj.-Gen. Paul Kagame   Since 22 April 2000
         (interim from 23 March 2000)

Prime Ministers: Pierre-Célestin Rwigyema 31 Aug. 1995—8 March 2000

         Bernard Makuza   Since 8 March 2000

Legislature: The legislature is unicameral. The sole chamber, the Transitional National Assembly (Assemblée Nationale de Transition), has 74 members, appointed in 1994 for a five-year term, which was extended in July 1999 for a further four years.

Profile of the President:

Maj.-Gen. Paul **KAGAME**

Paul Kagame grew up in Uganda and has close connections with the Ugandan president Yoweri Museveni. He fought in the guerrilla struggle through which Museveni came to power, and then with the Rwandan Patriotic Front (Front Patriotique Rwandais—FPR) which finally overthrew the ethnic Hutu-dominated genocidal regime in the Rwandan capital Kigali in 1994. He himself is a Tutsi, but has stated his preference for being called Rwandan rather than Tutsi. In power he has retained a reputation for not being associated with corruption.

Paul Kagame was born in October 1957 in Gitarama prefecture, central Rwanda, to Deogratius and Asteria Rutagambwa. In 1960 his family went into exile to avoid growing Hutu violence towards the Tutsi people. Kagame went to primary and secondary school in Uganda, and from there to Makarere University, where he joined Yoweri Museveni in the overthrow of Milton Obote, and was appointed Museveni's chief of intelligence.

Kagame stayed in Uganda, becoming a senior officer in the Ugandan army in the late 1980s. In 1990 he attended staff and command courses at Fort Leavenworth, Kansas, USA, and then returned to Uganda to take up his role as military chief of the largely Tutsi FPR.

The FPR launched its military campaign from Uganda in October 1990. Almost four years of fighting followed before the FPR made its final assault on the Rwandan capital, Kigali, in June–July 1994. The FPR was included in the 'government of national unity' sworn into office in July, and Kagame was appointed vice president and minister of defence. In 1998 Kagame was elected FPR chairman.

President Pasteur Bizimungu resigned from office on 23 March 2000. Kagame, as his deputy, was appointed interim president by the Supreme Court. He was formally elected president by the Transitional National Assembly just under a month later, with 81 of the 86 votes cast. He was inaugurated on 22 April, the first Tutsi head of state since 1959.

Kagame holds a diploma in professional management and business studies from the Open University (UK). He married Jeanette Nyiramongi in 1989, and they have four children.

Profile of the Prime Minister:

Bernard **MAKUZA**

Bernard Makuza, who was born on 30 September 1961, is a member of the Hutu-dominated Democratic Republican Movement (Mouvement Démocratique Républicain—MDR). He was Rwanda's ambassador to Germany before he was appointed prime minister on 8 March 2000 following the resignation of Pierre-Célestin Rwigyema.

Makuza's new government, announced on 19 March, was the first since 1994 in which the parties were not represented in accordance with the 1993 Arusha peace accords. This controversial lineup provoked the resignation of President Pasteur Bizimungu on 23 March, but Makuza remained in post under his successor Paul Kagame.

ST KITTS AND NEVIS

Full name: The Federation of St Kitts and Nevis (also known as St Christopher and Nevis).

Leadership structure: The head of state is the British sovereign, styled 'Queen of St Christopher and Nevis, and of Her other Realms and Territories, Head of the Commonwealth', and represented by a governor-general who is appointed on the advice of the St Kitts prime minister. The head of government is the prime minister, who is responsible to the National Assembly and is appointed by the governor-general. The cabinet is appointed by the governor-general.

Queen:	Elizabeth II	Since 6 Feb. 1952
Governor-General:	Sir Cuthbert Sebastian	Since 1 Jan. 1996
Prime Minister:	Denzil Douglas	Since 4 July 1995

Legislature: The legislature is unicameral. The sole chamber, the National Assembly, has 15 members, 11 directly elected for a five-year term, a speaker and three members appointed by the governor-general in accordance with the wishes of the prime minister and leader of the opposition.

Profile of the Governor-General:

Sir Cuthbert **SEBASTIAN**

Sir Cuthbert Sebastian is the second governor-general of St Kitts and Nevis. He trained in Canada as a doctor, later specializing in obstetrics and gynaecology (for which he trained in Scotland), and was for many years the chief medical officer at the general hospital in St Kitts.

Cuthbert Montraville Sebastian was born on 22 October 1921 and was educated at Basseterre Boys' Elementary School, teaching the younger boys for the last few years he was there. In 1939 he joined the St Kitts-Nevis Defence Force and started work as a learner dispenser at Cunningham hospital. Four years later he finished his training as a chemist and druggist and was promoted to medical sergeant. In 1944 he qualified as a laboratory technician. He then joined the Royal Air Force, serving as a rear gunner until the end of the war.

In 1945 Sebastian was appointed senior dispenser and steward (hospital administrator) at Cunningham hospital, where he remained for the next five years.

He then went to study medicine in Canada, graduating from Mount Allison University and going on to Dalhousie Medical School, where he gained his doctorate in 1958 as well as a master's degree in surgery. Having obtained licences from the Nova Scotia Medical Board and the Canadian Medical Council, he returned to St Kitts, becoming captain-surgeon of the Defence Force and working as a general practitioner for four years in many parts of St Kitts, Nevis and Anguilla.

In 1962 he decided to specialize in obstetrics and gynaecology and he attended the Dundee Royal Infirmary in Scotland for the next four years. On his return to St Kitts in 1966 he was appointed medical superintendent and obstetrician gynaecologist at Cunningham hospital and again took up the post of captain-surgeon of the Defence Force, which he held until 1980. In 1967 he moved to the new Joseph N. France general hospital and was made chief medical officer three years later.

In 1975, during a visit by the prince of Wales to St Kitts, Sebastian was appointed as his local physician. Two years later he accompanied the then prime minister, Robert L. Bradshaw, to London for Queen Elizabeth II's Silver Jubilee, acting as his aide-de-camp and personal physician. He continued to practise medicine until he was appointed to the governor-generalship in January 1996.

Profile of the Prime Minister:

Denzil **DOUGLAS**

Denzil Douglas became prime minister of St Kitts and Nevis following the general election in July 1995. A doctor and former president of the country's medical association, he is the leader of the moderate left-of-centre Labour Party.

Born on 14 January 1953, Denzil Llewellyn Douglas holds three degrees—in medicine, surgery and science—from the University of the West Indies. After a two-year internship at the General Hospital in Port of Spain, Trinidad, he returned to St Kitts and Nevis in 1986 to practise as a family physician. He served as president of the St Kitts-Nevis Medical Association until 1989. In March of that year he was elected to the National Assembly as one of only two successful candidates of the Labour Party (which had been the dominant party for decades under British rule but had lost its majority at the last pre-independence elections, held in 1980). Shortly after the 1989 election Douglas took over as party leader.

Within the broader regional context, the situation on Haiti was a major issue in 1990, in which Douglas became involved through his participation in a National Democratic Institute, sending a delegation to Haiti to demonstrate international support for its transition to democracy. Later that year he joined the mission led by former US president Jimmy Carter which acted as an international observer group at the Haitian general election.

Under Douglas's leadership the Labour Party in the early 1990s recovered much of its former support on St Kitts, the main island, and won four of the eight St Kitts seats at the November 1993 general election, but was kept in opposition by a coalition which included the three members from Nevis. (Labour has consistently been critical of the overrepresentation of Nevis proportional to its population, an attitude which made secession appear a more attractive option to the inhabitants of the smaller island when a Labour government did come to power in 1995.)

An early general election was held in 1995, the government having been severely weakened by the political repercussions of a crime wave related to drugs trafficking, to the extent that a 'national unity forum' had provided for all-party involvement in key decision-making in an interim pre-election period. The poll in July was a major victory for Douglas, with his Labour Party winning 58.8% of the vote and a clear parliamentary majority, and he was sworn in as prime minister on 4 July 1995.

In his first term of office, the Douglas government was preoccupied largely with the Nevis secession issue, which became particularly acute when the prime minister's initiative on constitutional reform was rebuffed by the Nevis legislature in a unanimous vote for secession in October 1997. The issue was only silenced when a referendum on secession failed on 10 August 1998 when the vote in favour fell just short of the necessary two-thirds majority.

Hoping to capitalize on a historic corruption scandal concerning the previous government, Douglas called early legislative elections for March 2000. Labour won all eight seats on St Kitts although its overall share of the vote fell slightly, to 53.9%. The biggest issue in his second term in office has been the international community's perception that St Kitts and Nevis had become a centre for money laundering. A tightening of financial regulations saw the country removed from a blacklist of suspect states in June 2002.

ST LUCIA

Full name: St Lucia.

Leadership structure: The head of state is the British sovereign, styled 'Queen of St Lucia, and of Her other Realms and Territories, Head of the Commonwealth', and represented by a governor-general who is appointed on the advice of the St Lucian prime minister. The head of government is the prime minister, who is responsible to Parliament and is appointed by the governor-general on the advice of Parliament. The cabinet is appointed by the governor-general.

Queen:	Elizabeth II	Since 6 Feb. 1952
Governor-General:	Dame Pearlette Louisy	Since 17 Sept. 1997
Prime Minister:	Kenny D. Anthony	Since 24 May 1997

Legislature: The legislature, the Parliament, is bicameral. The lower chamber, the House of Assembly, has 17 directly elected members and an appointed speaker, all serving a five-year term. The upper chamber, the Senate, has 11 members, six nominated by the government, three by the opposition and two by the governor-general.

Profile of the Governor-General:

Dame Pearlette **LOUISY**

Dame Pearlette Louisy, the first woman governor-general of St Lucia, is a former teacher and principal of a tertiary education college in the capital, Castries.

Calliopa Pearlette Louisy was born on 8 June 1946 in the small village of Laborie on the south coast of the island. She attended St Joseph's Convent School in Castries and went on to the University of the West Indies (UWI) in Barbados, graduating in English and French in 1969. By 1975 she had obtained a master's degree in linguistics from the Université Laval in Québec, Canada. Between periods of study she taught in Castries, where she was a college principal in the 1980s and also national correspondent to the Agence de Co-opération Culturelle et Technique, a position she held for ten years.

In 1986 she moved to the Sir Arthur Louis Community College at The Morne, Castries, as dean of the division of arts, science and general studies, a position she held for six years before her promotion to vice principal and (in 1996) principal of the college. By 1994 she had obtained a doctoral degree in higher education from the University of Bristol, UK. From 1996, until her appointment as governor-general the following year, she was secretary and treasurer of the Association of Caribbean Tertiary Institutions in addition to her role as college principal.

During her career Dame Pearlette Louisy has written a number of papers and spoken frequently on a range of issues in tertiary education; she has also written several publications on learning the Creole language.

Profile of the Prime Minister:

Kenny D. ANTHONY

Kenny Anthony, a teacher and barrister, taught law at the University of the West Indies (UWI) before being elected leader of the St Lucia Labour Party (SLP) in May 1996 and leading his left-of-centre party to victory in the election the following year.

Kenny Davis Anthony was born on 8 January 1951. Educated at the Vieux Fort Senior Secondary School and then the St Lucia Teachers' College, he went on to study government and history at UWI, graduating in 1976. He began a teaching career at the Castries Anglican Primary School, moving later to the Vieux Fort Senior Secondary School. From 1978 to 1979 he was a part-time tutor at the St Augustine Campus of the UWI in Trinidad.

Anthony held ministerial office briefly in the SLP government of Allan Louisy between 1980 and 1981. He was initially appointed, in July 1979, as a special adviser in the ministry of education and culture, but was not able to take the post of minister at this stage because he held no seat in the House of Assembly, and was too young to be eligible for appointment to the Senate. Legislation to reduce the qualifying age from 30 to 21 was passed in time for him to take office as minister of education from December 1980, but he resigned the following March, disillusioned with the rampant factional disputes within the ruling party.

Resuming his studies, this time in law, Anthony completed his degree and master's degree at UWI and studied for his doctorate (awarded in 1988) at the University of Birmingham in the UK. Called to the Bars of St Lucia and Barbados, he was lecturer in law at the Cave Hill campus of UWI in Barbados and head of the law teaching department there from 1989 to 1993. In October 1993 he was appointed director of the Caribbean justice improvement project in the faculty of law at Cave Hill. He is married to Rose Marie Belle Antoine-Anthony, a Trinidadian and senior law lecturer at UWI, and has three children.

In March 1996 Anthony was seconded from UWI as general counsel to the secretariat of the Caribbean Community (Caricom) at Georgetown, Guyana, but resigned a month later to contest the election for the leadership of the SLP at the party convention in April and took up the party leadership in May. In a landslide victory at the general election on 23 May 1997 the SLP (in opposition since 1982) won 16 of the 17 elected seats in the House of Assembly. Anthony thereupon took office as prime minister.

Four-and-a-half years later the party slipped slightly, to 14 seats, after elections held on 3 December 2001. Anthony's government has been struggling against international pressure to reform its financial regulations following criticism that the country serves as a centre for money laundering. He has also been eager to take part in the move to create a Caribbean Court of Justice separate from the Privy Council in London which remains the highest court of appeal for the region's Commonwealth members.

ST VINCENT AND THE GRENADINES

Full name: St Vincent and the Grenadines.

Leadership structure: The head of state is the British sovereign, styled 'Queen of St Vincent and the Grenadines, and of Her other Realms and Territories, Head of the Commonwealth', and represented by a governor-general who is appointed on the advice of the prime minister. The head of government is the prime minister, who is responsible to the House of Assembly and is appointed by the governor-general on the advice of the House of Assembly. The cabinet is appointed by the governor-general on the advice of the prime minister.

Queen:	Elizabeth II	Since 6 Feb. 1952
Governors-General:	Charles Antrobus	1 June 1996—3 June 2002
	Monica Dacon (acting)	3 June 2002—2 Sept. 2002
	Frederick Ballantyne	Since 2 Sept. 2002
Prime Ministers:	James Mitchell	30 July 1984—27 Oct. 2000
	Arnhim Eustace	27 Oct. 2000—29 March 2001
	Ralph Gonsalves	Since 29 March 2001

Legislature: The legislature is unicameral. The sole chamber, the House of Assembly, has 21 members, 15 directly elected for a five-year term and six senators appointed by the governor-general.

Profile of the Governor-General:

Frederick **BALLANTYNE**

Fred Ballantyne is a US-trained doctor, leading hotelier and general entrepreneur. He was appointed governor-general on 2 September 2002 after the sudden death of his predecessor.

Frederick Nathaniel Ballantyne was an only child born to one of St Vincent's first hoteliers. He became an integral part of the family business and in 1980, while still in his early twenties, he and his compatriot Vidal Browne amassed US$370,000 to buy the 14-hectare Young Island and its luxury hotel complex, off the St Vincent coast. He continues to own and run Young Island as well as a number of other tourist ventures.

Travelling to the USA, Ballantyne was trained as a medical doctor at Syracuse University in New York. After graduating he found work at Montréal General Hospital, Canada, and Rochester General Hospital in New York. He returned to the Caribbean to serve as chief of medicine and medical director for the newly built Kingstown General Hospital in St Vincent. He worked at the hospital for 14 years, while also acting as assistant dean of clinical studies at the medical school at St George's University in Grenada. Although now retired from medical practice he continues to volunteer at Kingstown and remains in charge of visiting medical specialists, whom he accommodates on Young Island.

Moving from general practice to public life, Ballantyne served as chief medical officer for St Vincent and the Grenadines for seven years into the mid-1990s. In February 1998 he was appointed president of the international branch of Dimethaid, a Canadian-based company specializing in developing methods for the 'transdermal delivery' of drugs. He was also appointed deputy director of the Windward Islands Research and Education Foundation in 2001.

In June 2002 Governor-General Charles Antrobus died, leaving the position vacant. Three months later Ballantyne was appointed in his place after the interim administration of Monica Dacon, the country's first female governor-general.

Profile of the Prime Minister:

Ralph **GONSALVES**

Ralph Gonsalves leads the centre-left Unity Labour Party (ULP). A former university lecturer who retrained as a lawyer, he is popularly known as 'Comrade Ralph' for his left-wing views. He entered the House of Assembly in 1994 and was appointed prime minister in March 2001 after the ULP won a landslide victory in elections.

Ralph Everard Gonsalves was born on 8 August 1946 in Colonarie, St Vincent. He graduated in economics from the University of the West Indies (UWI) in 1969 and stayed on for a master's degree in government studies, completed in 1971. He continued his university career by successfully defending a doctorate in government studies at the University of Manchester in the UK in 1974.

Returning to the Caribbean to lecture in government and politics at UWI, he also became directly involved in politics, leading the United People's Movement in 1979–82. Meanwhile studying law, he was called to the Bar at Gray's Inn, London, in 1981.

For the next 20 years Gonsalves combined an active career as a lawyer at the Eastern Caribbean Supreme Court with work as an activist for the political opposition to the ruling conservative New Democratic Party (NDP). In this capacity he raised his public profile as a weekly columnist and writer on political issues.

In 1994 Gonsalves was elected to the House of Assembly as deputy leader of the resurgent ULP. Four years later he was elected to head the party, and in 1999 he became leader of the opposition. Two years later a ULP electoral victory ended 17 years of NDP-rule, and Gonsalves was appointed prime minister in March 2001.

SAMOA

Full name: The Independent State of Samoa (formerly Western Samoa).

Leadership structure: The head of state is an elective monarch or *o le ao o le malo*. The next *o le ao o le malo* will be elected by the Legislative Assembly and will have a five-year term of office. The head of government is the prime minister, who is appointed by the *o le ao o le malo* on the recommendation of the Legislative Assembly. The cabinet is appointed by the prime minister.

O le Ao o le Malo:	Susuga Malietoa Tanumafili II (ruling jointly until 5 April 1963)	Since 1 Jan. 1962
Prime Minister:	Tuilaepa Sailele Malielegaoi	Since 24 Nov. 1998

Legislature: The legislature is unicameral. The sole chamber, the Legislative Assembly (Fono), has 49 members, elected for a five-year term. The right to stand for election is confined to members of the *matai* (elected clan leaders).

Profile of the *o le Ao o le Malo*:

Susuga Malietoa **TANUMAFILI II**

Malietoa Tanumafili II has been monarch since independence in 1962. Although his office is an elective one, he holds it for life, unaffected by the constitutional amendment defining the term of future monarchs as five years.

Tanumafili was born on 4 January 1913 and was educated in New Zealand at St Stephen's College, Auckland, and Wesley College, Pukekohe. He succeeded to the title of Malietoa (head of one of the four Samoan royal families) on the death of his father in 1940. In the same year he was appointed *fautua* (adviser) to the New Zealand governor of Western Samoa.

Tanumafili was one of the prominent Samoan leaders in the period leading up to independence in 1962. In 1958 he joined the New Zealand delegation to the UN, and was joint chairman of the working committee on independence and the constitutional convention in 1959. At the end of 1961, when the country achieved independence from New Zealand administration, he was appointed joint head of state. The death of Tupua Tamasese Mea'ole the following year left him as sole head of state, a post he holds for life. Celebrations held in 1990 marked his 50-year jubilee of continuous service to the government and people of the country.

Tanumafili has been married twice. With his first wife Lili Tunu, whom he married in 1940, he had five children, one of whom died in 1985. He has no children with Tiresa Patu Tauvela Hunter, whom he married in 1962.

Profile of the Prime Minister:

TUILAEPA Sailele Malielegaoi

Tuilaepa Sailele Malielegaoi leads the Human Rights Protection Party (HRPP). A career politician, he trained as an economist and briefly represented Samoa at the European Economic Community. He first entered government in 1982 and was appointed prime minister in November 1998 after veteran leader Tofilau Eti Alesana resigned. Tuilaepa has sought to strengthen the economy through modernization.

Tuilaepa Sailele Malielegaoi was born on 14 April 1945 in Lepa, on the southeastern tip of 'Upolu. At that time the islands constituted the New Zealand-controlled colony of Western Samoa. After a local early education, Tuilaepa travelled to New Zealand to attend St Paul's College in Auckland. He stayed in that city throughout the 1960s and attended Auckland University where he studied commerce. He obtained a degree in 1968, and the following year he became the first Samoan to receive a master's degree.

Returning to what was now independent Western Samoa, Tuilaepa worked in the treasury department based in Apia in the 1970s. In 1978 he departed for Brussels, Belgium, to take up a financial position in the European Economic Community, but returned two years later when he was elected to the Legislative Assembly for the first time, representing the Lepa constituency for the newly created HRPP. Initially he also continued to work for a private accountancy firm.

Under Prime Minister Tofilau, the first HRPP premier, Tuilaepa was appointed as minister of economic affairs, transport and civil aviation, and as associate minister of finance in 1982. In 1984 he was promoted to head the finance ministry. Although removed from office in 1985, he returned as finance minister in 1988. Three years later he was appointed deputy prime minister, as well as minister of finance, tourism, trade commerce and industry.

Through the 1990s resentment over Tofilau's increasingly autocratic and self-serving administration began to erode the HRPP's popularity. Under great pressure to resign, Tofilau eventually stepped down in 1998, officially citing health concerns. Tuilaepa was appointed in his place. He also took on the foreign affairs and treasury, inland revenue and customs portfolios.

As prime minister, Tuilaepa has sought to sweep away the cronyism which had blossomed under Tofilau, and has taken a firm grip of the economy. The HRPP was re-elected in 2001 and the government outraged the opposition by getting itself reappointed without the usual parliamentary debate.

SAN MARINO

Full name: The Republic of San Marino.

Leadership structure: The heads of state are two captains-regent, elected by the Great and General Council. The term of office of the captains-regent is six months. The joint heads of government are the captains-regent, who are responsible to the Great and General Council. The Congress of State is elected by the Great and General Council.

Captains-Regent:	Marino Bollini & Giuseppe Arzilli	1 Oct. 1999—1 April 2000
	Gian Marco Marcucci & Maria Domenica Michelotti	1 April 2000—1 Oct. 2000
	Enzo Colombini & Gianfranco Terenzi	1 Oct. 2000—1 April 2001
	Luigi Lonfernini & Fabio Berardi	1 April 2001—1 Oct. 2001
	Alberto Cecchetti & Gino Giovagnoli	1 Oct. 2001—1 April 2002
	Antonio Lazzaro Volpinari & Giovanni Francesco Ugolini	1 April 2002—1 Oct. 2002
	Giuseppe Maria Morganti & Mauro Chiaruzzi	Since 1 Oct. 2002

Legislature: The legislature is unicameral. The sole chamber, the Great and General Council (Consiglio Grande e Generale), has 60 members, directly elected for a five-year term.

Profiles of the Captains-Regent:

Giuseppe Maria **MORGANTI**

Giuseppe Maria Morganti is a publisher and former member of the San Marino Communist Party (Partito Comunista Sammarinese—PCS). He was first elected in 1993 to the Great and General Council, where he has sat since 2001 as part of the Party of Democrats (Partito dei Democratici—PD) group.

Giuseppe Maria Morganti was born in San Marino on 12 March 1955. He began studying business and economics at the University of Modena, in neighbouring Italy, in 1974 but his degree was interrupted in 1977.

Having joined the Groups of the New Left in 1974, Morganti first had a (junior) government post as secretary to the deputy minister for industry and artisans in 1979, when the PCS was part of a coalition government with the Socialist Party of San Marino (Partito Socialista Sammarinese—PSS). In 1981 he joined the PCS itself. During the 1980s Morganti also worked in publishing with positions in the management of a local newspaper. Since 1983 he has managed the Sammarinese publishing company AIEP Editore. He married Maurizia Zonzini, who works for the San Marino Bank, in 1986 and they have four children.

Morganti was elected to parliament in 1993 and became a member of the centre-left PD when it was formed in 2001. He also served on a government working group on San Marino's relations with the European Union (EU). Morganti was elected captain-regent in September 2002 and took up his post on 1 October.

Mauro **CHIARUZZI**

Mauro Chiaruzzi is a member of the executive of the dominant ruling Socialist Party of San Marino (Partito Socialista Sammarinese—PSS). A trained pharmacist, he entered the Great and General Council at the June 2001 elections and had thus been in parliament for little over one year when he was elected captain-regent.

Mauro Chiaruzzi was born in 1952. Like many Sammarinese he attended university in neighbouring Italy, where he studied pharmacology at the nearby University of Urbino. He continues to work in the pharmacy of San Marino's State Hospital. Chiaruzzi is married to Paola and they have three children.

Chiaruzzi's political life began in the early 1980s when he joined the United Socialist Party at a time when San Marino boasted the only government in Western Europe to contain a communist party. In 1984 he was elected to a two-year term as castle-captain (head of the local government) for the Castle of Fiorentino. In 1998 he was appointed as a co-ordinator in the ministry of health and social security.

In the legislative elections held in 2001 Chiaruzzi won his parliamentary seat for the PSS. As a member of the party's executive he holds a number of important positions at the head of parliamentary commissions. He was elected captain-regent in September 2002 and took up his post on 1 October.

450

SÃO TOMÉ AND PRÍNCIPE

Full name: The Democratic Republic of São Tomé and Príncipe.

Leadership structure: The head of state is a president, directly elected by universal adult suffrage. The president's term of office is five years, renewable once only. The president appoints the prime minister, who is head of government and who proposes the other members of the cabinet.

Presidents:	Miguel Trovoada	3 April 1991—3 Sept. 2001
	(deposed temporarily in Aug. 1995)	
	Fradique de Menezes	Since 3 Sept. 2001
Prime Ministers:	Guilherme Pósser da Costa	30 Dec. 1998—18 Sept. 2001
	Evaristo Carvalho	26 Sept. 2001—26 March 2002
	Gabriel Costa	26 March 2002—7 Oct. 2002
	Maria das Neves	Since 7 Oct. 2002

Legislature: The legislature is unicameral. The sole chamber, the National Assembly (Assembléia Nacional), has 55 members, directly elected for a four-year term. An eight-member regional council, established in April 1995, looks after the affairs of the island of Príncipe.

Profile of the President:

Fradique **DE MENEZES**

Fradique de Menezes is a successful businessman and former diplomat. Once a member of what was then the sole and ruling party, the São Tomé Liberation Movement (Movimento de Libertação de São Tomé e Príncipe—MLSTP), he was briefly foreign minister, but left the party in 1990 claiming growing ideological differences. Despite the MLSTP's majority in parliament, he defeated its candidate in the second round of presidential elections in July 2001, when he was supported by the Independent Democratic Action (Acção Democrática Independente—ADI) party.

Fradique Bandeira Melo de Menezes was born in Água-Têlha on 21 March 1942 to a Portuguese father and a São Toméan mother. Until 2001 he held the citizenship of both countries, potentially jeopardizing his future political aspirations. He was educated abroad and, after a year's military service, graduated from the Higher Institute of Applied Psychology in Lisbon, Portugal, and in human sciences from the University of Brussels, Belgium. He is a widower.

São Tomé gained independence in 1975 as a Marxist single-party state and in that year de Menezes returned and found work as a teacher, and later in the ministry of agriculture. His experience of living and working in Europe inclined him towards diplomacy and in 1981 he was despatched to London, UK, to head the São Tomé and Príncipe commercial delegation. Two years later he switched to Brussels to act as São Tomé's ambassador to Belgium, Germany, Holland, Italy, Luxembourg, Norway, Sweden, the European Communities, the Food and Agriculture Organization (FAO) and UN Educational, Scientific and Cultural Organization (UNESCO).

De Menezes returned to São Tomé once again in 1986, when he was appointed foreign and co-operation minister by the Marxist president Manuel Pinto da Costa. He remained co-operation minister when the portfolios were split the following year, but soon handed in his resignation, citing "incompatibility" with the government. He left the cabinet in a reshuffle in January 1988 and in 1990 he left the MLSTP altogether.

For the rest of the 1980s and 1990s, as the country emerged as a multiparty democracy, de Menezes headed a successful cocoa-producing company. As president, he has retained the idea that agriculture forms the basis of the country's economy, despite the potential from new found oil wealth. Between 1987 and 1994 he chaired the São Tomé chamber of commerce.

In presidential elections in 2001 de Menezes challenged the ruling MLSTP, which had been returned to power in legislative elections in 1994. He received the backing of the main opposition ADI, which had supported his predecessor, and outgoing president, Miguel Trovoada. During the campaign the MLSTP unsuccessfully challenged his candidature on the grounds of his former dual citizenship. Although there was some confusion in the close-run first round, de Menezes won a clear but slim majority in the second stage, despite an all-time low voter turnout of only 62%. He was inaugurated as the country's third president on 3 September 2001.

Profile of the Prime Minister:

Maria **DAS NEVES**

Maria das Neves is a member of the ruling São Tomé Liberation Movement (Movimento de Libertação de São Tomé e Príncipe—MLSTP). An economist by training, she first entered the cabinet as economy minister in 1999.

Maria das Neves Ceita Batista de Sousa was born in 1958. She trained as an economist, and went on to work for both the UN Children's Fund (UNICEF) and the World Bank, for which she acted as alternate-governor for São Tomé. Brought into the cabinet as economy minister in January 1999, she became head of a 'superministry' encompassing economy, agriculture, fisheries and trade in May 2000.

The newly elected president, Fradique de Menezes, excluded the MLSTP from government when he was inaugurated in September 2001. However, the party's superior showing in legislative elections in March 2002 forced the president to invite them back into government, and das Neves was appointed minister of trade, industry and tourism in April. In October 2002 de Menezes reshuffled his cabinet after a dispute over military appointments, and das Neves became São Tomé's first ever female prime minister.

SAUDI ARABIA

Full name: The Kingdom of Saudi Arabia.

Leadership structure: The head of state is a king, who is also head of government in his capacity as prime minister, and who appoints the Council of Ministers.

King and Prime Minister:

> Fahd ibn Abd al-Aziz al-Saud   Since 13 June 1982
> (custodian of the two holy mosques since 1986)

Legislature: There is no legislative assembly. The Consultative Council (Majlis al-Shoura), appointed every four years, now has 120 members.

Profile of the King:

FAHD ibn Abd al-Aziz al-Saud

King Fahd is a conservative absolute monarch and one of the richest people in the world, with an immense family fortune derived from the country's oil wealth. Governing according to Islamic law, he has also shown his determination to protect his mainly Sunni Muslim kingdom and its Wahhabi orthodoxy from the turbulence of radical Islamic fundamentalism. He adopted in 1986 an additional official title to denote his religious role, the custodian of the two holy mosques. He has been frail since a stroke in 1995, and the country faces the possibility of a period of change under his most likely successor.

Prince Fahd ibn Abd al-Aziz was born in 1923 in Riyadh, the eldest of the seven sons of King Abd al-Aziz ibn Saud, founder of the Saudi state in the modern period, and his favourite wife, Hassa. He graduated from the Scientific Institute in Mecca (Makkah). In 1953 he was appointed (Saudi Arabia's first) minister of education, and introduced a series of five-year development plans in an attempt to improve his country's education system. In 1962 he became minister of the interior, and by 1967 was second deputy prime minister. In March 1975, on the accession to the throne of his half-brother Khaled, Fahd was appointed crown prince and deputy prime minister. As crown prince he was the effective ruler of the country and oversaw the implementation of successive five-year development plans.

Since his own accession to the throne on 13 June 1982, following Khaled's death, Fahd has continued to take responsibility himself for the country's subsequent development plans, emphasizing the growth of the private sector. On 1 March 1992 he introduced a Basic Law for the System of Government, and later that year restructured the Consultative Council. He has introduced new laws governing the administration of the Saudi provinces and the Council of Ministers.

King Fahd has long taken an active interest in Saudi Arabia's international position. In 1977, he met with US officials to discuss solutions to the Arab–Israeli conflict, and in 1981 he outlined his own Eight-Point Peace Plan, which became the basis for the Fez Declaration. He called in 1985 for increased US intervention in the Middle East.

The 1991 Gulf conflict, arising from the Iraqi invasion of Kuwait the previous year, sent shock waves through the conservative monarchies of the region. Fahd permitted the US-led allied forces to operate from Saudi Arabia, a decision strongly criticized by radicals elsewhere in the Arab world (and denounced especially by Osama bin Laden's al-Qaida terrorist group), but the tight grip which his regime maintains on domestic affairs effectively prevented the expression of any dissent. In 1992 Fahd donated emergency relief funds to Bosnia and established a Supreme Committee for the Collection of Donations for the Muslims of Bosnia.

Accounts vary as to the number of King Fahd's children—between six and nine sons and either four or five daughters. The first of his three wives, Princess Anud, and their eldest son, Faisal, both died in 1999. His half brother, Prince Abdullah, has been crown prince since Fahd came to the throne and took charge in 1995–96 when Fahd was described officially as resting, having reportedly suffered a stroke. Fahd has been significantly weakened ever since this illness, giving rise to repeated speculation about the succession, which intensified when he underwent hospital treatment again in Riyadh in March and August 1998. However, he was discharged from hospital on 18 August 1998 after a team led by a US surgeon had reportedly successfully completed an operation to remove his gall bladder. Prince Abdullah undertook a world tour the following month, apparently designed to raise his profile internationally, which encouraged speculation about competition between factions of the royal family. Prince Abdullah has since gone on to take the principal role in the state's affairs.

SENEGAL

Full name: The Republic of Senegal.

Leadership structure: The head of state is a president, directly elected by universal adult suffrage for a five-year term (reduced from seven years under the 2001 constitutional amendments), with a limit of two terms. The president appoints the prime minister, who then proposes the other members of the Council of Ministers. The president is designated head of government.

Presidents:	Abdou Diouf	1 Jan. 1981—1 April 2000
	Abdoulaye Wade	Since 1 April 2000
Prime Ministers:	Mamadou Lemine Loum	3 July 1998—1 April 2000
	Moustapha Niasse	1 April 2000—3 March 2001
	Mame Madior Boye (acting)	3 March 2001—5 Nov. 2002
	Idrissa Seck	Since 5 Nov. 2002

Legislature: The legislature is unicameral, since the abolition of the upper house, the Senate, under the 2001 constitutional amendments. The sole chamber, the National Assembly (Assemblée Nationale), has 120 members, directly elected for a five-year term.

Profile of the President:

Abdoulaye **WADE**

Abdoulaye Wade is a veteran opposition politician, who was elected president for a seven-year term in 2000, at his fifth attempt. His main policy has been opposition to the Socialist Party (Parti Socialiste—PS), in power since independence in 1960, and in particular to its former leader, ex-president Abdou Diouf. He is known as a devout Muslim, a political liberal and a free marketeer, and he describes himself as a "committed pan-Africanist".

Abdoulaye Wade was born on 29 May 1926 in St Louis and was educated in Senegal and France. He graduated in law from the faculty of law and economics in Dijon, France, in 1955, trained at the Bar in Besançon between 1955 and 1957, and gained a doctorate in law and economics from Grenoble in 1959. In 1960 he was appointed assistant lecturer at the University of Dakar, a post he left in 1966, and he spent the following year in research in Boston, USA. He returned to France in 1967 for university posts in Paris, before becoming professor and later dean of the law and economics faculty at the University of Dakar. He is a barrister at the Court of Appeal in Dakar, a member of the International Academy of Comparative Law in Stockholm, Sweden, and a member of the International Academy of Trial Lawyers. He is married to Viviane, a French-born Catholic, and they have two children.

In 1974 he founded the Senegalese Democratic Party (Parti Démocratique Sénégalais—PDS), and has been the party's secretary-general ever since. He was elected to parliament in 1978, and was the unsuccessful PDS candidate in the presidential elections of 1978, 1983, 1988 and 1993. During the 1980s Wade was in outright conflict with the government: he was arrested in July 1985 and held for several days for taking part in an 'unauthorized demonstration', and again after the February 1988 elections, when public protests over the election results led to charges relating to the country's internal security, and he was given a one-year suspended sentence. The following year he left Senegal for France, returning in February 1990.

In the 1990s he continued to oppose Diouf and the PS, but in April 1991 accepted the post of minister of state as one of four PDS representatives in the government. He resigned in October 1992 in order to contest the 1993 presidential elections. In October 1993 he was charged with complicity in the murder earlier that year of Babacar Sèye, president of the Constitutional Council, and a few months later he was also facing charges in connection with violence at a demonstration protesting against the January 1994 devaluation. He was taken into custody awaiting trial. The charges in connection with Sèye's murder were dropped in May, but he remained in detention. He began a hunger strike in June, was released in July, and the charges in connection with the riots were subsequently dropped.

In January 1995 he held a private meeting with Diouf, at which he and the PDS were invited to rejoin the government, and he became minister of state to the president. In the presidential election held in February 2000 the first round was inconclusive, although Diouf emerged as the leading contender. In the runoff election in March five of the original eight candidates transferred their support to Wade, including Moustapha Niasse, who later became Wade's first prime minister, and Wade gained a 17% margin over Diouf. Traditionally Wade and the PDS drew the major part of their support from urban areas, but the 2000 elections, in which Wade's main campaign promise was simply for "change", indicated that they had made inroads into the rural vote as well. During his first year in office Wade presided over the drafting of a new constitution, which was endorsed in a referendum. In April 2001 fresh legislative elections were held, and the newly formed Sopi (Change) coalition, in which the PDS was the largest member party, won 89 of the 120 seats in the National Assembly. The PS gained only ten seats, behind the Alliance of Progressive Forces, led by Niasse, with 11.

Wade has chaired many international conferences on law and the problems of development, and has written many publications on economics, law and politics, with a special interest in development issues.

Profile of the Prime Minister:

Idrissa **SECK**

Idrissa Seck is a key member of the ruling Senegalese Democratic Party (Parti Démocratique Sénégalais—PDS). Having served in a broad coalition government in the mid-1990s, he is a close ally of President Abdoulaye Wade and headed the presidential office before being appointed prime minister on 5 November 2002.

Idrissa Seck was born in Thiès in 1959. He is married and now has four children. His connection to the PDS began at the young age of 15. He graduated from the Institute of Political Studies in Paris, France, and then went to the USA to attend Princeton University, New Jersey. After graduating he found work as a business consultant with the international firm PricewaterhouseCoopers in 1986. After six years Seck left PricewaterhouseCoopers to form his own consultancy firm, ACG Afrique, in 1992.

During the 1980s he had formed a close alliance with PDS chief Abdoulaye Wade, and had played a major role in Wade's ultimately unsuccessful bid for the presidency in 1988. In March 1995 the then president, Abdou Diouf of the Socialist Party, brought the opposition PDS into government and appointed Seck as his minister of commerce, handicrafts and industrialization. The party remained in the power-sharing agreement for three years before withdrawing in March 1998 in order to contest legislative elections that May. It refused to enter a new coalition following the Socialist victory and Seck returned to consultancy, this time starting a new company, IS Development.

Seck returned as campaign manager for Wade for the 2000 presidential election. Leading the Sopi (Change) coalition, Wade overcame more than 40 years of Socialist rule to win the presidency. Seck was appointed minister of state without portfolio in the new PDS-dominated government. He also directed the president's office and continued as deputy secretary-general of the PDS. The party won a landslide victory in the 2001 legislative elections. Early in 2002 Seck was elected mayor of Thiès.

In September of that year, the navy-operated *Joola* ferry sank at sea en route from Ziguinchor to Dakar, killing 970 people. The scale of the tragedy called for a political response and Wade dismissed the government of Prime Minister Mame Madior Boye on 4 November. The next day he appointed Seck to fill the vacancy.

SEYCHELLES

Full name: The Republic of Seychelles.

Leadership structure: The head of state is a president, directly elected by universal adult suffrage. The president's term of office is five years, with a maximum of three consecutive terms. The head of government is the president. The Council of Ministers is appointed by the president.

President: France Albert René   Since 5 June 1977

Legislature: The legislature is unicameral. The sole chamber, the National Assembly, has up to 34 members, 23 members directly elected for a five-year term and up to 11 members allocated on a proportional basis.

Profile of the President:

France Albert **RENÉ**

France Albert René first became president of Seychelles a year after independence and has ruled continuously since then, managing the transition from a one-party state to the current system of multiparty elections which he first held (and won) in 1993.

France Albert René was born on Mahé on 16 November 1935. Having completed his early education in Seychelles, he travelled to Switzerland, and then the UK, in order to complete his education at St Mary's College, Southampton, and at King's College, London. He qualified in law at the Middle Temple in a record five months and was called to the Bar in 1957, subsequently returning to Seychelles, where he practised in the capital, Victoria, and was also involved in the trade union movement.

In June 1964 René founded and led the Seychelles People's United Party—later the Seychelles People's Progressive Front (SPPF)—and was elected to the Seychelles Legislative Assembly in a by-election in 1965. He directed the governmental committee for three years from 1967. In 1970 he was the leader of the opposition in the Assembly, campaigning for the return of several islands, for universal suffrage, and for national independence. In 1974 René was re-elected to the Legislative Assembly, becoming the minister of works and land development in 1975.

On 29 June 1976 Seychelles gained independence. René became prime minister (1976–77) in a coalition government with the Seychelles Democratic Party,

459

whose leader James Mancham became president. However, one year later René deposed Mancham in an almost bloodless coup on 4–5 June 1977, while the president was attending a Commonwealth summit in London. As president and commander-in-chief, René ran a single-party state in which the newly formed SPPF, of which he was president, was defined as having the leading role. Besides being head of state, René retained several ministerial posts himself.

At an extraordinary SPPF congress in December 1991, in line with the trends sweeping Africa, René announced the introduction of a multiparty democracy and inaugurated a period of constitutional reform. At the same congress he was unanimously re-elected secretary-general of the party. In the first multiparty presidential election, held on 23 July 1993, René was returned to office with 59.5% of the vote compared with 36.7% for his closest rival, Mancham, and in the concurrent legislative elections to the new National Assembly the SPPF won an absolute majority of seats. René was re-elected for a third term in early elections held in August–September 2001 with 54.2% of the vote. His most significant opponent, Wavel Ramkalawan, unsuccessfully challenged the result but his Seychelles National Party made major gains in legislative elections held on 6 December 2001, reducing the SPPF to 23 out of 34 seats in the National Assembly.

France Albert René has been married three times: to Karen Handley in 1956, to Geva Adam in 1975, and to Sarah Zarquani in 1993. He has three children.

SIERRA LEONE

Full name: The Republic of Sierra Leone.

Leadership structure: Under the 1991 Constitution the head of state is a president, directly elected by universal adult suffrage. The head of government (under the 1991 Constitution) is the president, who is responsible to the Parliament. The cabinet is appointed by the president.

President: Ahmed Tejan Kabbah   Since 29 March 1996
(in exile from 25 May 1997 to 10 March 1998)

Legislature: The legislature is unicameral. The sole chamber, the Parliament, has 112 members directly elected for a five-year term, and 12 members indirectly elected to represent the 12 provincial districts.

Profile of the President:

Ahmed Tejan **KABBAH**

Ahmed Kabbah is a barrister and former UN official who won the 1996 presidential elections as the candidate of the Sierra Leone People's Party (SLPP). Forced into exile by a coup in May 1997 but restored to office the following March, he entered a power-sharing agreement with the rebel Revolutionary United Front (RUF) in 1999 in an attempt to end the decade-long civil war, but the violence continued and he found himself dependent on UK military intervention to repel advancing RUF forces the following year. A ceasefire in 2001 allowed him to confirm his position at the polls in May 2002.

Ahmed Tejan Kabbah was born on 16 February 1932 in Pendembu, Kailahun district. Although he is himself a Muslim, he went to the country's oldest Catholic school, St Edward's in Freetown. He completed his education in Wales, first at Cardiff College of Technology and Commerce and then at University College, Aberystwyth, where he completed a degree in economics before joining the colonial administrative service in 1959.

Kabbah was an assistant district commissioner in the Bombali, Moyamba, Kono and Kambia districts before transferring to Freetown as deputy permanent secretary in the ministry of social welfare. Promoted to permanent secretary, he then worked at the ministry of trade and industry and the ministry of education. In 1965 he married Patricia Lucy Tucker, a Catholic former teacher from southern Sierra Leone who was working in the prime minister's office, and together they

461

went to London in 1968 to study law. They subsequently had a daughter and three sons. She died in May 1998.

Called to the Bar at Gray's Inn in London, Kabbah moved to the UN in New York on completion of his barrister's examinations, as deputy chief of its West African Division. He headed the UN Development Programme (UNDP) missions in several southern African states between 1973 and 1981, when he was promoted to deputy personnel director, then director of UNDP's division of administration and management.

In the 1996 presidential elections he won 35.8% of the vote in the first round on 26–27 February and 59.5% in the runoff on 15 March. Polling was disrupted by the rebel RUF and some 27 people were killed. Kabbah was sworn in on 29 March.

Kabbah was forced to flee to Guinea on 25 May 1997 following a coup led by Lt.-Gen. Johnny Koroma. Kabbah, however, retained recognition internationally as the lawful president, representing Sierra Leone in this capacity at the Commonwealth heads of government meeting in Edinburgh in October 1997. The Economic Community of West African States (ECOWAS) dispatched to Sierra Leone an Economic Community Ceasefire Monitoring Group (ECOMOG) peacekeeping force. Its intervention eventually resulted in his restoration as president on 10 March 1998.

Back in power, Kabbah returned his attention to peace negotiations with the RUF. He signed the Lomé peace deal with RUF leader Foday Sankoh in July 1999, but this was undermined by a return to full-scale violence in May 2000. Peace was finally achieved in January 2002 after the intervention in 2001 of the UK armed forces on the side of the government. Kabbah was resoundingly re-elected on 14 May 2002 with 70.1% of the vote, and was inaugurated for his second full term six days later. In parallel legislative elections the SLPP gained a commanding majority while the RUF's new political party failed to win a single seat.

SINGAPORE

Full name: The Republic of Singapore.

Leadership structure: The head of state is a president, directly elected by universal adult suffrage. The president's term of office is six years. The head of government is the prime minister, who is appointed by the president. The cabinet is appointed by the president.

President:	Sellapan Rama Nathan	Since 1 Sept. 1999
Prime Minister:	Goh Chok Tong	Since 28 Nov. 1990

Legislature: The legislature is unicameral. The sole chamber, the Parliament, has 84 directly elected members, and up to six extra members from opposition parties (depending on their share of the vote) elected for a five-year term. Up to nine members may also be nominated for two-year terms by the government.

Profile of the President:

Sellapan Rama **NATHAN**

S.R. Nathan was declared the winner of the 1999 presidential election on 18 August after all other candidates had been deemed ineligible to run. A long-serving government minister and head of the state media empire, The Straits Times Press, Nathan is the second ethnic Indian to be president of the city-state since its independence from Malaysia in 1965. Under constitutional changes in 1991 the office of president became a mostly ceremonial role, but with powers to check government actions including the use of the state's vast reserves.

Sellapan Rama Nathan was born in Singapore on 3 July 1924 and was educated in the city. Before he had completed his primary studies he began working and put himself through secondary education on a self-study course. In 1954 he graduated from the University of Malaya, which was then based in Singapore, with a diploma in social studies. He is a Hindu and has been prominent in Singapore–India relations, cofounding the Singapore Indian Development Association. Nathan is married to Urmila Nandey and they have one daughter and one son.

In 1955 Nathan began working for the civil service as a medical social worker and the following year he was appointed seamen's welfare officer at the ministry of labour. From 1962 he began a long association with the labour research unit when he was appointed as assistant director. He went on to become a full director of the unit until February 1966 when he was transferred to the foreign ministry of the newly independent state. There he rose rapidly to become deputy secretary before being transferred to the ministry of home affairs, where he was appointed acting permanent secretary in 1971. Later that year he switched to become permanent secretary in the defence ministry, in which role he was noted for taking part in a commando operation to disarm hijackers on board a ship in Singaporean waters in 1974. For his actions he was awarded the meritorious service medal. In 1979 he returned to the foreign ministry as its first permanent secretary.

Nathan switched from politics to the press in February 1982 when he left the foreign ministry to become executive chairman of the Straits Times Press, at the behest of the then prime minister, Lee Kuan Yew. Over the next six years he spread his commercial activities wide, acting as director for a number of publishing and media companies in Singapore, as well as continuing his connection to the Japanese engineering company Mitsubishi, for which he had begun working in 1973.

In 1988 Nathan was appointed high commissioner to Malaysia. Two years later he went to the USA as Singaporean ambassador, and remained there until June 1996. When he returned he was appointed ambassador-at-large and also became director of the Institute of Defence and Strategic Studies, a defence think tank based at the Nanyang Technological University. He resigned from both positions to stand as president in 1999, and was elected to that office on 18 August 1999, as the only candidate, with the full support of Lee Kuan Yew (who had stepped down as prime minister in 1990, but remained powerful as senior minister). Nathan was inaugurated on 1 September.

Profile of the Prime Minister:

GOH Chok Tong

Goh Chok Tong, an economist, first entered parliament in 1976. He is a long-standing member of the governing People's Action Party (PAP), and gained extensive ministerial experience while being groomed for the premiership. He took over from his predecessor, Lee Kuan Yew, as prime minister in November 1990 and as PAP secretary-general in late 1992. Goh represents a 'second generation' in Singapore politics which has never fully stamped its authority on the government, and Lee remains a powerful force as senior minister while his son, Lee Hsien Loong, is part of the rising 'third generation', holding one of the two deputy premierships.

Goh Chok Tong was born in Singapore on 20 May 1941. He was educated at the Raffles Institution between 1955 and 1960 and then went to the University of Singapore, graduating in economics in 1964. In 1966 he went to Williams College in the USA, where he gained a master's degree in developmental economics. Goh Chok Tong is married to Tan Choo Leng, a solicitor, and they have twin children, a son and a daughter.

Between 1964 and 1969 Goh was an administrative officer in the Singapore Administrative Service. In 1969 he joined Neptune Oriental Lines (the national shipping company) as planning and projects manager, and was managing director from November 1973 to September 1977. In 1977 he began his involvement with the trade union movement, and in 1987, after holding a number of trade union posts, he was awarded the Medal of Honour by the National Trades Union Congress.

He was first elected to Parliament in December 1976, representing the Marine Parade constituency, one of several new constituencies with an electorate of public housing residents. He has been a member of the PAP central executive committee since 1979, holding the positions of assistant secretary-general and, since 1992, secretary-general. From 1977 until 1990 he held a succession of ministerial portfolios, notably those of trade and industry, health and defence. In 1985 he became first deputy prime minister, in addition to his responsibilities as minister of defence. On 28 November 1990 he became prime minister, also retaining the defence portfolio until 1991.

Goh's PAP, which has had a parliamentary majority continuously since 1959, won a sweeping victory in the general election in January 1997, the opposition parties contesting only 36 of the 83 parliamentary seats and winning only two. The election was regarded by Goh as a ringing endorsement of his government's performance and a decisive rejection of "Western-style liberal democracy" in favour of the more authoritarian Singaporean model. His views were further endorsed when the number of uncontested seats for the 2001 elections assured the PAP yet another term in office before elections were even held in November. A novel device in the country's resultant 'unique' democratic system was Goh's order that 20 PAP members should act on a revolving basis as a People's Action Forum to take the place of an official opposition to the government. On 23 November 2001, in his inauguration speech for his new term in office, Goh promised to hand over to a "new crew" at some point during his current term.

SLOVAKIA

Full name: The Slovak Republic.

Leadership structure: The head of state is a president, directly elected for the first time in May 1999. The president's term of office is five years, renewable once only. The head of government is the prime minister, who is appointed by the president. The cabinet is appointed by the president on the recommendation of the prime minister.

President:	Rudolf Schuster	Since 15 June 1999

Prime Minister:	Mikuláš Dzurinda	Since 30 Oct. 1998
	(acting president until 15 June 1999)	

Legislature: The legislature is unicameral. The sole chamber, the National Council of the Slovak Republic (Národná Rada Slovenskej Republiky), has 150 members, directly elected for a four-year term.

Profile of the President:

Rudolf **SCHUSTER**

Rudolf Schuster was inaugurated as the first directly elected president of Slovakia on 15 June 1999. Three-time mayor of the eastern city of Košice, he is also a film maker and writer, who as president has continued his output of both fiction and nonfiction works.

Rudolf Schuster was born in Košice on 4 January 1934 in what was then eastern Czechoslovakia. He began training as an engineer at the Slovak Technical University in Bratislava under the newly installed Communist regime. He graduated in 1959 and began work as a designer at the Regional Agricultural Planning Institute in the city in 1960. Schuster received an honorary doctorate in ecology from the Košice Technical University in 1984. In the course of his studies he has learned four foreign languages: English, German, Hungarian and Russian.

After leaving the Planning Institute and working as an assistant at the Slovak Academy of Sciences, Schuster began a 12-year career at the Eastern Slovakia Iron Works in 1962. He joined the Slovak Communist Party (Komunistická Strana Slovenska—KSS) in 1964. On leaving the iron works, where he had become technical assistant to the managing director, he joined the Košice City

Council in 1982 and was appointed in 1983 as mayor of the city (a post to which he was re-elected in 1994 and 1998). From 1986 he was a member of the KSS central committee.

After the 'velvet revolution' of 1989, which overthrew the Communist regime, he was made speaker of Slovakia's National Council, and in 1990 he was posted to Canada as ambassador for the new democratic Czechoslovakia. He returned two years later as the country fragmented into its two constituent republics, and was appointed to the ministry of foreign affairs in the independent Slovakian government in 1993.

After founding the pro-market Party of Civic Understanding (Strana Obcianskeho Porozumenia—SOP) in 1998, Schuster re-entered the National Council in elections in October of that year. Since March the National Council had been unable to agree on a new president, and Prime Minister Vladimír Mečiar had taken on the powers of the executive in the interim. Following the legislative elections, the Slovak Democratic Coalition (Slovenska Demokraticka Koalicia—SDK) co-opted the SOP and other small parties to prevent Mečiar and his party from returning to government. The constitution was amended by the new administration, whose leader Mikuláš Dzurinda as prime minister was now acting as president in the interim, to provide direct presidential elections. Schuster was nominated by the SDK, and defeated Mečiar in the second round of the poll in May 1999 with 57.2% of the vote. He took office on 15 June.

As president, Schuster was obliged to resign his positions as mayor of Košice and as chairman of the SOP. He campaigned strongly for Slovakia's proposed entry to the European Union (EU) and the North Atlantic Treaty Organization (NATO), despite strong domestic criticism of the bombing campaign against Yugoslavia. His relationship with the National Council was marked by clashes over his derogatory remarks about the Roma, a significant minority within Slovakia, and his continued pride in the country's Communist past. Most significant of these battles has been over the assumption of presidential powers by the government during his serious illness in 2000. His criticism of the constitutional action was described by Dzurinda as "unfortunate", but the two men have avoided direct confrontation. Schuster was treated for his condition in neighbouring Austria and spent the latter part of 2000 convalescing in Košice from where he resumed most of his duties.

Rudolf Schuster is married to Irena and has two children. He is a prolific writer and film maker and collects cinematographic equipment. In his position as a prominent politician he has made a number of documentaries and, in particular, travelogues from across the world. He has written 15 books, including histories of eastern Slovakia, novels, and plays, and has continued writing since his inauguration. In December 1999 he provoked strong government opposition over plans to publish a work on contemporary Slovakian politics.

Profile of the Prime Minister:

Mikuláš **DZURINDA**

Mikuláš Dzurinda has been prime minister of Slovakia since 30 October 1998. An ardent advocate of pro-market economics, he was brought to power at the head of a broad-based right-of-centre coalition which set integration with the West among its top priorities. Rifts within the coalition led Dzurinda to form a new party, the Slovak Democratic and Christian Union (Slovenská Demokratická a Krestanská Unia—SDKU), which went on to form a new conservative coalition after the September 2002 elections. He briefly held executive powers prior to the election of President Rudolf Schuster in 1999 and during his serious illness in 2000.

Mikuláš Dzurinda was born in Spišský Štvrtok, in the central mountain district of Spišská Nová Ves, on 4 February 1955. He is now married with two children. A student at the University of Transport and Communications in Žilina from 1974, he began working at the city's transport research institute in 1979, having graduated the previous year. In 1980 he moved to the Slovak capital, Bratislava, to work in the information technologies section of the Czechoslovak State Transport agency. From 1988 he headed the agency's automated controls section.

In 1991 Dzurinda began his political career in the emergent democracy and was appointed deputy transport minister in the Slovakian government. In elections in 1992, preceding independence, Dzurinda entered the National Council. He was affiliated to the Christian Democratic Movement and was appointed its vice chairman with responsibility for economic policy in 1993. Strong resistance to attempts by the authoritarian Prime Minister Vladimír Mečiar to weaken opposition parties led to the formation of the Slovak Democratic Coalition (Slovenská Demokratická Koalícia—SDK) in 1997, with Dzurinda as its unofficial head, a role formalized in July 1998. Mečiar's Movement for a Democratic Slovakia (Hnutie za Demokratické Slovensko—HZDS) remained the largest single party in parliament by just one seat in elections held that October. Unable to find coalition partners it was left to Dzurinda and the SDK to form a new broad centre-right coalition and Dzurinda was duly appointed prime minister. One of his first tasks was to sweep away the Mečiar regime. The corruption-prone police force was overhauled and amnesties granted to those involved in high-level scandals were quickly withdrawn (although the Constitutional Court later overruled Dzurinda's right to revoke the amnesties).

With an eye constantly on the objective of European integration, Dzurinda was quick to start reforming the economy to meet international criteria and 'catch up' with neighbouring states already in membership discussions with the European Union (EU). In November 1998 he secured an agreement establishing a committee to identify the key areas in need of reform. Negotiations for Slovakia's entry began in March 2000, and the country was invited in December 2002 to become a full member from May 2004, the same year that it has also been invited to join the North Atlantic Treaty Organization (NATO).

Along with changes to the economy, a priority for the new government was the introduction of direct elections for the presidency. Since early 1998 the post had been left vacant due to parliamentary disagreements, with the prime minister wielding executive powers in the interim. The election of the pro-Western Rudolf Schuster in May 1999 was seen as a positive step towards integration. However, when Schuster fell seriously ill in 2000 Dzurinda was roundly criticized by the opposition, and Schuster himself, for quickly adopting executive powers along with the speaker of the National Council. Schuster resumed his full duties towards the end of the year.

The disunity of the SDK government quickly became a cause for concern. Tensions were heightened when Dzurinda's ardent pro-NATO stance forced colleagues to give grudging support to the bombing campaign against Yugoslavia in 1999. The cracks in the coalition deepened and in January 2000 Dzurinda spearheaded the formation of a new political group, the SDKU, but insisted it would not become a separate group in parliament for the rest of its term. Despite vocal opposition from within and without the ruling coalition, Dzurinda survived a vote of no confidence in April 2000, and a referendum calling for early elections failed to attract sufficient public support in November. The SDKU was finally transformed into a full party in November 2001 and Dzurinda was elected its leader.

Although the HZDS still retained its position as the largest single party after the September 2002 elections, it again failed to form a ruling coalition. Dzurinda's SDKU came in second in a field dominated by new parties. He cobbled together a new conservative four-party coalition, successfully excluding both the authoritarian HZDS and the populist Direction Party–Third Way, which had taken the third-largest share of seats on its electoral debut.

SLOVENIA

Full name: The Republic of Slovenia.

Leadership structure: The head of state is a president, directly elected by universal adult suffrage. The president's term of office is five years. The head of government is the prime minister, who is nominated by the president, and elected by the National Assembly. The prime minister appoints a cabinet, which must be approved by the National Assembly.

Presidents:	Milan Kučan	Since 10 May 1990
	(president of the state presidency until 22 Dec. 1992)	
	Janez Drnovšek	Since 23 Dec. 2002
Prime Ministers:	Janez Drnovšek	14 May 1992—3 May 2000
	Andrej Bajuk	3 May 2000—1 Dec. 2000
	Janez Drnovšek	1 Dec. 2000—23 Dec. 2002
	Anton Rop	Since 23 Dec. 2002

Legislature: The legislature is unicameral. The sole chamber, the National Assembly (Državni Zbor), has 90 members, directly elected for a four-year term. The National Council (Državni Svet), with 40 indirectly elected members, has an advisory role.

Profile of the President:

Janez **DRNOVŠEK**

Before his election as president at the end of 2002, Janez Drnovšek had been prime minister for almost the whole decade of Slovenia's existence as an independent state. An economist by training, he led the Liberal Democracy of Slovenia (Liberalna Demokracija Slovenije—LDS) party, which was a major element in successive coalition governments. He stepped down as party leader in order to become president.

Janez Drnovšek was born on 17 May 1950 in Celje, some 60 km northeast of Ljubljana. He obtained a doctorate in economics at the University of Maribor, near the Austrian border, in 1986, with a thesis entitled *The International Monetary Fund and Yugoslavia.* Having completed his education, he worked first with a construction company, then as chief executive of a branch of Ljubljanska

Bank and finally as adviser on economic affairs at the Yugoslav embassy in Egypt. He is the author of numerous articles in the area of finance, and speaks many languages including English, German, Italian, French and Spanish. He is married and has two children.

Drnovšek first emerged as a prominent political figure in 1989, as the then Socialist Federal Republic of Yugoslavia (SFRY) began to enter the period of its fragmentation into its constituent republics. He was elected as the Slovenian representative to the collective SFRY presidency, standing as an independent and defeating the communist candidate in the first genuinely contested election of its kind. Between 1989 and 1990 he was president of the presidency under its principle of annual rotation between republics. In this capacity he headed the Non-Aligned Movement and chaired the Non-Aligned Summit in Belgrade in September 1989. In October 1990, however, he withdrew from the SFRY presidency, protesting over its manipulation by its new Serbian president.

The progressive disintegration of Yugoslavia from the late 1980s was dramatically accelerated when Slovenia and Croatia simultaneously declared independence on 25 June 1991; federal Yugoslav troops failed in their attempt to reverse these declarations by military action. Drnovšek was the main Slovenian negotiator with the Yugoslav People's Army in talks brokered by European Community intermediaries, which resulted in a ceasefire agreement in July and the international recognition of independent Slovenia (and Croatia) by early 1992.

Drnovšek was a founder of the LDS, a secular centre-left party which, in the December 1992 general election, won the highest number of seats in parliament. Drnovšek had by this time already been prime minister for seven months, having been appointed after the collapse in April of Slovenia's first postindependence government led by Lojze Peterle. He required the support of four other parties to form a coalition in January 1993. During his first period in office Drnovšek focused on the economic transformation of the country to a free-market system.

A general election in November 1996 increased the parliamentary representation of the LDS from 22 to 25 out of 90 seats but gave the centre-right opposition Slovenian Spring grouping control of 45 seats. It was only in March 1997 that Drnovšek eventually succeeded in forming a four-party coalition, having failed in his bid to create a 'national unity' government. However, this was then undermined in March 2000 when two of the parties agreed to merge and withdraw from the government. Without a parliamentary majority Drnovšek was forced to resign. In opposition he gained in popularity, especially as the replacement government of Andrej Bajuk struggled against a hostile parliament.

In legislative elections held on 15 October 2000 the LDS won an impressive 34 seats becoming by far the biggest party in the National Council. Weeks of negotiations led to the formation of a new four-party coalition.

Throughout Drnovšek's career as prime minister, Slovenia's closer integration with western Europe was the key priority. In March 1994 Slovenia joined the

Partnership for Peace programme of the North Atlantic Treaty Organization (NATO), but was left out of the first round of NATO expansion announced in mid-1997. In June 1996 Drnovšek signed an association agreement with the European Union (EU) and negotiations for membership began in November 1998. Invitations of membership of both bodies from 2004 were received in November and December 2002 respectively.

Amid growing speculation Drnovšek confirmed in October 2002 that he would seek the presidency in elections held on 10 November. Campaigning while still in office as prime minister, he was forced to a runoff on 1 December against former chief prosecutor, and independent candidate, Barbara Brezigar. In the event, Drnovšek was victorious, gaining 56.5% of the vote. He handed over the role of prime minister, and leadership of the LDS, to his finance minister Anton Rop and was inaugurated on 23 December.

Profile of the Prime Minister:

Anton **ROP**

Anton Rop is president of the ruling Liberal Democracy of Slovenia (Liberalna Demokracija Slovenije—LDS). Trained as an economist, he advised the newly independent country's government from 1992 before joining the cabinet himself in 1996. He was made prime minister following the election of the incumbent Janez Drnovšek as president in December 2002.

Anton Rop was born in Ljubljana on 27 December 1960. He graduated in economics from Ljubljana University in 1984 and became an assistant director of the Slovene Institute for Macroeconomic Analysis and Development in 1985, specializing in assessment of privatization policies and government expenditure. In this role, Rop gave advice on economic policy to the newly independent government of Slovenia after its secession from Yugoslavia in 1992, and helped to draft legislation. In 1993 he was appointed state secretary for privatization at the ministry of economic relations and development. The ruling coalition under Prime Minister Drnovšek was restructured in early 1996 and Rop was appointed minister of labour, family and social affairs on 7 February. He held the post until Drnovšek was briefly ousted in mid-2000.

Out of government during the premiership of the conservative Andrej Bajuk, Rop returned in Drnovšek's new cabinet which took office in December 2000, this time as finance minister. In this role he helped the country secure its reputation as a stable, central European economy. In October 2002 Slovenia was among ten countries picked for inclusion in the 2004 expansion of the European Union (EU).

When Drnovšek was elected president on 1 December 2002, Rop was his immediate choice as successor in the role of prime minister. He was inaugurated in this role on 23 December and has become leader of the LDS.

SOLOMON ISLANDS

Full name: The Solomon Islands.

Leadership structure: The head of state is the British sovereign, styled 'Queen of the Solomon Islands, and of Her other Realms and Territories, Head of the Commonwealth', and represented by a governor-general who is chosen by Parliament. The head of government is the prime minister, who is elected by members of Parliament from among their number. The cabinet is appointed by the governor-general on the recommendation of the prime minister.

Queen:	Elizabeth II	Since 6 Feb. 1952
Governor-General:	Sir John Lapli	Since 7 July 1999
Prime Ministers:	Bartholomew Ulufa'alu	30 Aug. 1997—30 June 2000
	Manasseh Sogavare	30 June 2000—17 Dec. 2001
	Sir Allan Kemakeza	Since 17 Dec. 2001

Legislature: The legislature is unicameral. The sole chamber, the National Parliament, has 50 members, directly elected for a four-year term.

Profile of the Governor-General:

Sir John **LAPLI**

Sir John Ini Lapli is an Anglican priest. He served as provincial premier in the eastern Solomon Islands throughout the troubled 1990s and became governor-general in July 1999. During his time in the ceremonial post the country has tentatively emerged from a two-year civil war but remains under the shadow of the threat of national bankruptcy.

John Ini Lapli was born in 1955. He studied at Selwyn College on the main Solomon Island of Guadalcanal before travelling to New Zealand to train as a priest. He entered the priesthood after graduating from St John's Theological College in Auckland, where he also taught other students from 1982 to 1983. In 1985 he taught at a rural training centre in the Solomons and in that year he married his wife, Helen; they now have three sons and one daughter.

After a year spent as a parish priest in 1986, Lapli worked briefly as a Bible translator in 1987–88. After that he took on a political role when he was appointed as premier of Temotu Province which covers the Santa Cruz Islands in the east of the country. He remained in this post for 11 years before being recommended as the next governor-general. Although his role is largely ceremonial, Lapli was called upon to fulfil his duties in declaring fresh elections in June 2000 at the height of the civil war. Although peace has largely returned to the country, the new government faces bankruptcy, and effective autonomy has been declared in the remote provinces, including Temotu.

Profile of the Prime Minister:

Sir Allan **KEMAKEZA**

Sir Allan Kemakeza has led the ruling People's Alliance Party (PAP) since 2001. Originally a policeman, he entered politics in 1989 and has represented his home constituency of Savo/Russells ever since. Despite controversy over the destination of compensation payments for the two-year civil conflict, which saw him sacked as deputy prime minister in August 2001, he was elected prime minister four months later after the PAP was victorious in general elections. The issue of compensation still plagues Kemakeza and threatens to bankrupt the country.

Allan Kemakeza was born in 1951 in Panueli village on Savo Island, to the north of Honiara. After a local education he enlisted in the Royal Solomon Islands Police Force in 1972 when the country was still a colony of the UK. (Independence was achieved in 1978.) He remained in the force for 17 years, rising to the rank of assistant superintendent. During his police career he attended policing courses in the UK and Australia. In the late 1980s he worked closely with the Solomons' first governor-general, Sir Baddeley Devesi.

In 1989 Kemakeza resigned his commission and entered politics. He won a seat in the National Parliament representing Savo and the Russell Islands. Solomon Mamaloni, the leader of the PAP, was elected prime minister for a second time and he appointed Kemakeza as minister of housing and government services. Kemakeza's political career remained linked to that of Mamaloni throughout the 1990s. The government coalition was defeated in 1993, but Mamaloni returned in 1995 and Kemakeza was appointed minister of forests, environment and conservation. Mamaloni was defeated again in elections held in 1997 and Kemakeza found himself out of ministerial office once more.

Ethnic tensions between the indigenous Guadalcanal, or Isatabu, islanders and immigrants from neighbouring Malaita Island exploded in 1998 into full-scale civil war. In June 2000 the conflict came to a head when the Malaita Eagle Force kidnapped Prime Minister Bartholomew Ulufa'alu, and a new government was formed under opposition leader and former finance minister Manasseh Sogavare. Kemakeza was reappointed to the cabinet, this time as deputy prime minister and, most importantly, minister for peace and national reconciliation. He approached the role with gusto, falling back on his experience in the police and engaging the rebels face-to-face. He proved pivotal in organizing peace talks, which eventually produced the breakthrough Townsville Peace Accord, and he received a knighthood for his efforts. Under the terms of the accord, Kemakeza supervised the creation of a fund to pay compensation for damages caused during the conflict.

In August 2001 Kemakeza was publicly sacked by Sogavare for paying himself compensation for property on Savo which had been looted by rebels. He had already been forced to admit in July that claims had outstripped the US$25 million fund provided by Taiwan. Nonetheless, he denied any wrongdoing and suggested that Sogavare was instead attempting to secure his own position in government. In elections in December the PAP, of which Kemakeza had become party leader, regained its position as one of the Solomon Islands' main political parties, emerging as the largest single party in the National Parliament. Kemakeza was duly elected prime minister.

SOMALIA

Full name: Somalia.

Leadership structure: Dominated through the 1990s by conflict between rival warlords, Somalia has had since August 2000 a Transitional National Assembly (inaugurated in neighbouring Djibouti but subsequently moved to the Somali capital, Mogadishu), and a president elected by that assembly. The president named a prime minister that October, and the prime minister in turn named an interim government a month later. Powerful warlords have refused to recognize this regime, as have secessionists in Somaliland (in the north), which declared independence in 1991, and in Puntland, which declared its autonomy in 1998 pending the formation of a federal system of national government.

Presidents:	*vacant*	26 Jan. 1991—27 Aug. 2000
	(since overthrow of Siyad Barre regime)	
	Abdulkassim Salat Hassan	Since 27 Aug. 2000
	(transitional)	
Prime Ministers:	*vacant*	26 Jan. 1991—8 Oct. 2000
	(since overthrow of Siyad Barre regime)	
	Ali Khalif Galayadh	8 Oct. 2000—28 Oct. 2001
	(transitional)	
	Osman Jama Ali	28 Oct. 2001—12 Nov. 2001
	(acting)	
	Hassan Abshir Farah	Since 12 Nov. 2001
	(transitional)	

Legislature: The 'Transitional National Assembly' inaugurated in Djibouti on 13 August 2000, which later transferred to Mogadishu, has 245 members.

Profile of the President:

Abdulkassim **SALAT HASSAN**

Abdulkassim Salat Hassan was an associate of former President Siyad Barre in the 1980s. He has a reputation as sympathetic to radical Muslim politics, but he has also indicated his willingness to appoint women in his administration, and favours a pluralist democratic system and the free market.

476

Abdulkassim Salat Hassan was aged 58 when appointed president in 2000. He is a former deputy prime minister and was minister of the interior during the regime of Siyad Barre (1969–91). After the overthrow of Siyad Barre in January 1991, Salat Hassan went into exile in Egypt, later returning to work with grassroots organizations for peace.

Salat Hassan was chosen as transitional president at the conference in Arta, Djibouti, in August 2000. He entered Mogadishu to popular acclaim later in the month, but members of his government have received death threats, and one minister was shot dead. Salat Hassan's authority is not recognized by Somaliland or Puntland, which together account for about one-third of Somalia's population.

Salat Hassan speaks Somali, Arabic, Italian, English and Russian.

Profile of the Prime Minister:

HASSAN ABSHIR Farah

Hassan Abshir Farah is a close associate of President Abdulkassim Salat Hassan and comes originally from the breakaway region of Puntland. He cochaired the Arta conference in 2000 which formulated the transitional national government (TNG), and has been a member of the cabinet ever since. He was appointed prime minister on 12 November 2001 after a vote of no confidence in his predecessor.

Hassan Abshir Farah was born in 1945 in Garoowe, now the capital of the self-declared republic of Puntland. He is a member of the Ise Mahmud subclan of the Majerten. He unofficially represents the breakaway region in the TNG. He began his political career under the rule of Somali dictator Siyad Barre (1969–91). During this time he was mayor of the capital Mogadishu, governor of Middle Shabelle and Bakol, and Somali ambassador to Japan and later to Germany. He was working in Germany when the Siyad Barre government collapsed in 1991.

When the northeastern tip of the country declared autonomy as the Puntland State in July 1998, Hassan Abshir identified at first with the secessionists, becoming 'interior minister'. He served self-declared Puntland president Abdullahi Yusuf Ahmad until 2000 when he travelled to nearby Djibouti to cochair the national reconciliation conference in Arta. As a result of the conference (which was repudiated by the Puntland secessionists), the TNG was established and eventually took control of Mogadishu. Hassan Abshir was appointed minister of minerals, water and resources.

In October 2001, amid general dissatisfaction at the lack of progress made by the TNG, the then prime minister Ali Khalif Galayadh was ousted in a vote of no confidence. Two weeks later Hassan Abshir, noted as a close associate of President Salat Hassan, was appointed in his place. His position has been undermined by his own ill health; he was hospitalized for complications arising from his diabetes in April 2002.

SOUTH AFRICA

Full name: The Republic of South Africa.

Leadership structure: The head of state is a president, elected by the National Assembly. The president's term of office is five years, renewable once only. The head of government is the president, who is responsible to Parliament. The cabinet is appointed by the president.

President: Thabo Mbeki   Since 16 June 1999

Legislature: The legislature, the Parliament, is bicameral. The lower chamber, the National Assembly (Volksraad), has 400 members, directly elected for a five-year term. The upper chamber, the National Council of Provinces, has 90 members, indirectly elected (ten for each of the nine provinces) for a five-year term.

Profile of the President:

Thabo **MBEKI**

Thabo Mbeki, who succeeded the renowned South African leader Nelson Mandela as the country's second post-apartheid president, had worked in exile during the apartheid years as a representative of the African National Congress (ANC), and was central to the negotiations which brought the apartheid regime to an end in 1990. A one-time student activist and lifelong socialist who completed his university education in the UK in the mid-1960s, Mbeki benefited from Mandela's endorsement in becoming his successor. As president he has faced a rising tide of crime and lawlessness in the country's inner cities, and the serious threat of the AIDS epidemic.

Thabo Mvuyelwa Mbeki was born on 18 June 1942 in Idutywa, Transkei. His parents were both civil rights activists. His father, Govan Mbeki, was a leading figure in the local ANC and headed the movement's Youth League (ANCYL) which Thabo joined in 1956. After receiving his primary education in Idutywa and Butterworth, Thabo went on to high school in Alice, Ciskei, from where he was expelled in 1959 for taking part in student strikes. He completed his secondary education from home and studied for British 'A-level' qualifications between 1960 and 1961. His British education extended to include a correspondence degree course in economics with the University of London, from 1961 to 1962, and eventually full enrolment at the University of Sussex, where he received a master's degree in economics in 1966.

Mbeki's political radicalism began when he joined the ANCYL. In the early 1960s he was actively involved in various underground activities, including a student strike against the move to take South Africa out of the Commonwealth in 1961. In the same year he was elected as Secretary of the African Students' Association (ASA). With the apartheid government stepping up its counter insurgency measures (which dealt the ASA a fatal blow, and led to the arrest and life imprisonment of Govan Mbeki), Thabo Mbeki, along with many other young activists, was urged to leave the country by the ANC. In 1962 he travelled first to Southern Rhodesia (modern Zimbabwe) and then via Tanganyika (modern Tanzania) to the UK.

After completing his master's degree in 1966, Mbeki formalized his activism by working for the ANC's London office from 1967 to 1970. In 1970 the ANC, which was still essentially a revolutionary organization, sent Mbeki to undergo military training with its international ally, the Soviet Union. The following year Mbeki returned to Africa to work at the office of the revolutionary council of the ANC in Lusaka, Zambia, as an assistant secretary.

For the next seven years Mbeki travelled through southern Africa as a representative of the ANC and worked to establish foreign departments, earning himself the unofficial title of ANC 'foreign minister'. During this period he married the businesswoman and active feminist Zanele Dlamini in 1974. Together they have two fully grown children. A third child born before 1974 was reported as missing in the 1980s.

From 1973 to 1974 Mbeki worked in Botswana, before moving on to Swaziland. In both countries he worked to strengthen the ANC infrastructure in southern Africa, and in 1975 he was appointed to the movement's National Executive Committee (NEC). From 1976 to 1978 he played the same role in Nigeria until returning to Lusaka to work in the office of the ANC president, Oliver Tambo.

From 1984 to 1990 Mbeki was deeply involved in the ANC's transition from revolutionary force to democratic movement, and was vital in the discussions with the white minority government. In these years he worked through various ANC roles: as the director of the movement's department of information and publicity, secretary for presidential affairs, and member of the political and military councils. He has been credited with doing much to turn the international community against apartheid, and so to facilitate the regime's crippling isolation. He also led ANC delegations in significant communication with South African representatives, including a meeting with members of the country's business community at Mfuwe, Zambia, in 1985, and with the Institute for a Democratic Alternative for South Africa at Dakar, Senegal, in 1987. The crowning achievement of this period of tense negotiation came in 1989 when Mbeki joined other high level members of the ANC in direct secret talks with the South African government which led to the lifting of the ban on the ANC.

From that point onward, Mbeki worked closely on the negotiations leading to the adoption of South Africa's interim nonracial constitution in 1993, in which year he was also elected as chairperson of the ANC. After the first democratic elections in 1994, newly elected President Mandela appointed Mbeki as his deputy and thereby singled him out as his ultimate successor. Three years later Mbeki took over the presidency of the ANC and his position seemed set, although to the public he was still largely an unknown. To win hearts as well as minds, Mbeki embarked on a process to humanize the public's image of a cold efficient ruler whose only known habits were pipe-smoking and reading English poetry and economic tomes. Obliged to engage the populace, he swapped formal suits for the more colourful approach already used by Mandela.

Mbeki had sufficient success in cultivating this new image to see the ANC under his leadership reaffirmed as the dominant power in South Africa at the June 1999 elections, when it won two-thirds of the vote and 266 seats in the 400-seat National Assembly. The Assembly duly elected Mbeki as president and he was inaugurated on 16 June 1999. As president he confirmed his commitment to the ANC's policy of steady reform, while urging a faster pace to combat social and economic crises.

Mbeki's international image suffered greatly following a speech in April 2000 in which he expressed personal doubt over the accepted connection between the HIV virus and AIDS, an enormous problem in southern Africa where 50% of the youth are expected ultimately to succumb to the disease. Mbeki vociferously opposed what he called "Western solutions" to a "uniquely African catastrophe". He has also lost face with the West through his support for Zimbabwean president Robert Mugabe.

SPAIN

Full name: The Kingdom of Spain.

Leadership structure: The head of state is a constitutional monarch. The head of government is the president of the government (prime minister), who is appointed by the king. The Council of Ministers is appointed by the king on the recommendation of the president of the government.

King: Juan Carlos I de Borbón   Since 22 Nov. 1975
                           (acting from 30 Oct. 1975)

President of the Government:
                          José María Aznar López   Since 6 May 1996

Legislature: The legislature, the Cortes (Cortes Generales), is bicameral. The lower chamber, the Congress of Deputies (Congreso de los Diputados), has 350 members, directly elected for a four-year term. The upper chamber, the Senate (Senado), has 259 members, 208 directly elected and 51 indirectly elected, for a four-year term.

Profile of the King:

JUAN CARLOS I de Borbón

Juan Carlos I was proclaimed king of Spain in November 1975, following the death of Gen. Francisco Franco, whose right-wing dictatorship dated from his military uprising in 1936 at the onset of the civil war. The country had become a republic in 1931, but Franco declared it in 1947 to be a monarchy (without a monarch), and designated Juan Carlos as heir to the throne in 1969. Spain is now a parliamentary monarchy, and the duties of the king are mainly ceremonial, although Juan Carlos has gained considerable moral authority by showing his commitment on occasions of crisis to upholding the constitution.

Juan Carlos de Borbón y Borbón was born on 5 January 1938 in Rome. Initially educated in Italy, Switzerland and Portugal, Juan Carlos first went to Spain at the age of ten, when Franco announced his wish to groom him as his successor. He completed his schooling at the San Isidro School in Madrid in 1954, then studied at the army, navy and air force academies, and finally in 1961 studied law and economics at Madrid's Complutense University. In 1962 he went to live at the Palacio de la Zarzuela, on the outskirts of Madrid. In July 1969 Franco officially designated the prince as his successor.

Juan Carlos became provisional head of state on 30 October 1975, in the last weeks of Franco's terminal illness, and was formally declared king on 22 November, becoming also commander-in-chief of the armed forces and head of the Supreme Council of Defence. In his first message to the nation as king he expressed his intent to restore democracy and to become king of all Spaniards, without exception. He hastened reform in July 1976 by appointing a new head of government, Adolfo Suárez, and supporting him at critical junctures thereafter. Multiparty elections in June 1977 were followed by a referendum in December 1978 to approve a new constitution. This constitution was ratified by the king, who also supported the progressive devolution of powers to the regions.

Meanwhile in May 1977 his father, the count of Barcelona, transferred his dynastic rights to Juan Carlos, together with his position as head of the Royal Household. (He had ruled out his own reinstatement by refusing to swear allegiance to the principles of the Franco period.)

In February 1981, when a group of Civil Guards stormed the parliament building, Juan Carlos acted swiftly to secure the loyalty of other branches of the armed forces and thus restore the democratic process. His actions earned him widespread respect both within the armed forces and among the wider population. Since then he has assumed a more traditional role as constitutional monarch, touring every continent and addressing many international organizations, including the UN. He has had a particular impact in relations with Latin America, emphasizing the common cultural community.

Juan Carlos married Princess Sofía of Greece on 14 May 1962 in Athens. They have three children, Princess Elena, Princess Cristina and Prince Felipe.

Profile of the President of the Government:

José María **AZNAR** López

José Aznar is a lawyer and former tax inspector from Madrid and a long-standing member of the conservative Popular Alliance (Alianza Popular—AP) and its successor, the Popular Party (Partido Popular—PP). As PP leader since 1991, he has worked to modernize it as a party of the moderate centre-right. The PP's narrow victory in the March 1996 general election marked the end of 13 years of socialist government and enabled Aznar to form a minority government. His economic successes in his first term earned the PP enough support to win an overall majority in elections in March 2000.

José María Aznar López was born in Madrid on 25 February 1953, into a family connected to the Falange nationalist party of Gen. Francisco Franco, although Aznar subsequently distanced himself from that regime. He trained as a lawyer at the Complutense University in Madrid, graduating in 1979, and went to work as a tax inspector, rising to the position of state inspector of finance for the Castilla y

León region. He is married to Ana Botella and they have two sons and one daughter.

Aznar first entered politics in 1978 when he joined the regional section of the AP at Logroño. He became general secretary of the regional party the following year and in 1982 was elected to the Congress of Deputies for Ávila and as general secretary of the AP, retaining both posts until 1987 when he was elected premier of the Castilla y León autonomous region.

In January 1989 at the AP's ninth national congress the party renamed itself as the PP, electing Manuel Fraga Iribarne as its president and Aznar as vice president. In September of that year Aznar was elected to head the PP list for the 1989 general election. From this period onward Aznar served as a parliamentary deputy for Madrid. Although the PP was defeated at the national level, Aznar helped to record a notable success for his party two months later in overturning a socialist majority in the regional parliament of Galicia.

Two years later he became president of the party in place of the veteran Fraga, but in the 1993 general election the PP again failed to unseat the socialist government. Aznar was also involved in the conservative movement at European and international level, as vice president of the European People's Party and European Democratic Union, and of the UK-based International Democrat Union.

In the general election on 3 March 1996 Aznar's PP won 156 out of the 350 seats in parliament, overtaking the socialists (with 141 seats) as the largest party. After protracted negotiations Aznar eventually secured the support of three regionalist parties and was sworn in on 6 May at the head of a centrist cabinet dominated by conservative, Roman Catholic figures.

In his first term he implemented spending cuts in order to contain government spending, reduce the public debt and enable Spain to meet the economic convergence criteria which allowed it to join the eurozone and adopt the euro in place of the peseta with full effect from 1 January 2002. Economic success was cited as the principal reason why Aznar and the PP performed so well in legislative elections held on 12 March 2000. The PP unexpectedly secured a simple majority, with a total of 183 seats.

In his second term Aznar has sought to increase his international standing. He toured extensively in Asia in mid-2000 to promote Spain's economic ties in the region, and was, in July that year, the first European leader to visit Algeria since the beginning of the civil conflict there in 1992. Within Europe he has been a champion of the conservative right. When he took over the rotating presidency of the European Union (EU) for the first half of 2002, he announced that the US-led 'war on terrorism' would become the Union's focus and towards the end of the year he pledged his support to the USA's threat of war on Iraq. This last stance put him increasingly at odds with Spanish public opinion.

At home Aznar has been preoccupied with continuing troubles in the Basque country. He personally joined anti-violence demonstrations in Madrid and Barcelona in late 2000. He has also tackled the perennial issue of immigration. Since authorities complained of being overwhelmed by the number of illegal migrants in mid-2000, he has introduced tough new laws making it easier to expel immigrants. The government was criticized by Human Rights Watch for the state of detention centres in the Canary Islands.

In January 2002 Aznar was reappointed leader of the PP but announced that he would not seek a further term as president of the government.

SRI LANKA

Full name: The Democratic Socialist Republic of Sri Lanka.

Leadership structure: The head of state is a president, directly elected by universal adult suffrage. The president's term of office is six years. The president appoints the cabinet, may choose to hold any portfolio in it, and presides over its meetings. The prime minister, a member of the cabinet, is likewise appointed by (and may be dismissed by) the president.

President: Chandrika Bandaranaike Kumaratunga   Since 12 Nov. 1994

Prime Ministers: Sirimavo Bandaranaike   14 Nov. 1994—10 Aug. 2000

                       Ratnasiri Wickremanayake   10 Aug. 2000—9 Dec. 2001

                       Ranil Wickremasinghe   Since 9 Dec. 2001

Legislature: The legislature is unicameral. The sole chamber, the Parliament, has 225 members, directly elected for a six-year term.

Profile of the President:

Chandrika Bandaranaike **KUMARATUNGA**

Chandrika Bandaranaike Kumaratunga is, uniquely, the daughter of two former prime ministers—and also the widow of an assassinated 'rising star'. In office as prime minister from August 1994, but switching within months to the executive presidency, she modified the leftist agenda of her People's Alliance to promote neoliberal policies, but failed to deliver her promise of ending Sri Lanka's protracted ethnic conflict. She has latterly become a critic of the peace process as pursued by the government of the rival United National Party (UNP), with which she has had to 'cohabit' since the December 2001 legislative elections.

Chandrika Bandaranaike was born in Colombo on 29 June 1945, and was educated initially at St Bridget's Convent in the capital. Her father Solomon Bandaranaike founded the Sri Lanka Freedom Party (SLFP), leading it to electoral success and becoming prime minister, but was assassinated in 1959. Her mother Sirimavo Bandaranaike, propelled into politics as his widow, took over the party leadership prior to an election campaign in 1960 which resulted in her becoming the first woman in the world to be elected as prime minister. Sirimavo Bandaranaike held that office from 1960 to 1965 and from 1970 to 1977, but was later banned from taking any active part in politics on grounds of abuse of power;

she nevertheless remained the power behind the scenes at the SLFP throughout its nearly two decades in opposition.

Chandrika, meanwhile, spent the latter part of the 1960s in France, training in political journalism with *Le Monde* in Paris, completing degrees in law and political science, and going on to gain a doctorate in development economics. This served as preparation for a subsequent career which encompassed teaching and lecturing, research and work in land reform. Between 1972 and 1976, while her mother was head of government, she helped run the Land Reforms Commission of Sri Lanka, and she then worked as an expert consultant for the UN Food and Agriculture Organization (FAO) until 1979. During this period she published a book entitled *The Janawasa Movement: Future Strategies for Development in Sri Lanka*. She chaired the Janawasa Commission in the late 1970s and carried out research projects in the fields of food policy, political violence and agrarian reform. In 1974 she became a member of the executive committee of the SLFP's Women's League.

After 1977, with the SLFP cast out into the political wilderness, Chandrika Bandaranaike pursued her press and publishing career, as chairman and managing director from 1977 to 1985 of the Sinhalese daily newspaper *Dinakara*. By 1980, the year in which her mother was deprived of her political rights, Chandrika was playing a greater role in working to rebuild the fortunes of the SLFP, as a member of both its executive and its working committee. Factional disputes, however, conducted in an atmosphere of heightened tension following the outbreak of what was to become a protracted civil war with the minority ethnic Tamil separatists in the north and east, led to the formation of a separate left-wing socialist Sri Lanka Mahajana (People's) Party (SLMP) in January 1984. Chandrika was closely involved with this new party, whose moving spirit was the film idol Vijaya Kumaranatunga whom she had married in 1978. While he was its national organizer, she was the party's first vice president, and from 1986 to 1988 its president. Together they had two children.

On 16 February 1988 Vijaya Kumaranatunga was shot dead in Colombo. His killing, like other political attacks at this time, was attributed not to Tamil separatists but to Sinhalese extremists. The widowed Chandrika (who later dropped one of the syllables of her late husband's name, calling herself Chandrika Bandaranaike Kumaratunga) went abroad for three years, attending the Institute of Commonwealth Studies at the University of London as a research fellow, but returned once again to Sri Lanka in 1991.

Realizing the futility of an opposition weakened by factional divisions, Chandrika Kumaratunga was instrumental in forming in early 1993 a broader left-wing People's Alliance, encompassing both the SLFP and the United Socialist Alliance (a grouping of which Chandrika's SLMP had been a member since 1988). In May 1993 this People's Alliance recorded a notable victory in Western province (which included the capital, Colombo) when elections were held for provincial councils. Chandrika Kumaratunga was sworn in on 21 May as chief minister of

Western province. Another of the obstacles to effective opposition unity was removed later that year when her brother and sometime rival Anura Bandaranaike resigned from the SLFP. The general election in August 1994 saw her campaigning as the Alliance leader, with the leadership of the SLFP itself being retained by her mother (whose political rights had been restored in 1986). Their victory on 16 August opened the way for Kumaratunga to become prime minister, and she was duly sworn in three days later.

Following on her general election victory, Kumaratunga secured the Alliance's nomination to stand three months later in elections for the country's presidency, the top executive post since a constitutional change in 1978. She won a record 62% of the vote in the November 1994 presidential poll, and was inaugurated for a six-year term on 12 November. Her mother Sirimavo Bandaranaike, despite having harboured her own ambitions for the top job, instead accepted the subordinate role of prime minister. Kumaratunga has since postponed the idea of abolishing the executive presidency and reverting to a prime ministerial form of government.

Kumaratunga based her 1994 presidential campaign, like the Alliance's general election campaign, around her pledge to restore peace to Sri Lanka. This entailed seeking a rapid end to the ethnic conflict which had divided the majority Sinhalese and minority Tamil populations for over a decade. She launched several initiatives over the succeeding years in efforts to negotiate with the Tamil separatists, pursuing a far-reaching devolution policy to assist in this. However, the initial optimism encouraged by a truce in January 1995 was soon lost amid renewed violence, and, beginning with a major army offensive in July 1995, Kumaratunga has repeatedly shown herself prepared to use force in efforts to break the Tamil separatists' military resistance in the north. In 1998, with the fighting still continuing, her government attempted to tighten its grip with the imposition of a formal ban on the main Tamil separatist organization, followed by press controls on reporting of the war and, later in the year, the declaration of a state of emergency.

Early presidential elections were called for 21 December 1999 amid a worsening in the conflict. On 18 December Kumaratunga survived an assassination attempt by a suspected Tamil suicide bomber, in which 21 people were killed and 150 injured, including the president, who suffered damage to her right eye. Her subsequent victory in the presidential election, with 51.1% of the vote, was partly attributed to public sympathy, while the opposition also claimed widespread fraud and intimidation.

Kumaratunga's mother stepped down as prime minister in August 2000, and died that October. Kumaratunga's personal loss was compounded by the loss of a key and powerful ally in Parliament. Nonetheless, public sympathy was again on the president's side and, along with a breakthrough military victory in the ongoing war, the People's Alliance won the greatest share of seats in Parliament in the 13 October 2000 poll. Kumaratunga was forced to form a government with moderate

Tamil and Muslim parties while the opposition complained bitterly once more of electoral fraud and state-sponsored violence.

From then on Kumaratunga's position was increasingly undermined. Her relatively weak parliamentary base was exacerbated by the failure of her peace plans offering limited autonomy for the Tamils. She was forced to dissolve Parliament altogether from July 2001 in order to avoid a vote of no confidence. Her parliamentary majority crumbled when 12 members of the People's Alliance defected as soon as the house was reconvened in October. Snap elections were called for December 2001.

In that poll, conducted amid serious violence, the opposition United National Party fell just short of winning an outright majority. It formed a coalition with the main Muslim party, and Kumaratunga was forced to enter into 'cohabitation' with UNP leader Ranil Wickremasinghe as prime minister. Since then the two have been at loggerheads, with Wickremasinghe scoring a massive early victory by negotiating a permanent ceasefire with the Tamil rebels on 21 February 2002. This has left the president apparently sidelined, with the prime minister taking on near executive powers. She has resorted to criticizing the rapid progress of the peace talks for giving too much to the rebels.

Profile of the Prime Minister:

Ranil WICKREMASINGHE

Ranil Wickremasinghe is leader of the conservative United National Party (UNP) and is a career politician. After studying law he entered government in his late twenties and was proclaimed Sri Lanka's youngest prime minister in 1993 at the age of 34. He led the opposition in fiery exchanges with President Kumuratunga in the early 2000s before the UNP won the December 2001 legislative elections. In his second term as prime minister, as well as restarting the country's privatization campaign, he has overseen negotiations with the Tamil Tiger rebels to end the 19-year civil war.

Ranil Wickremasinghe was born in Colombo on 24 March 1949 into a prestigious family of government advisers and publishers. He studied law at the University of Sri Lanka in the late 1960s and early 1970s, qualifying as an attorney of the Supreme Court in 1972. Although he had been active in student politics, he practised law until 1977 when he was elected to parliament as a UNP member.

Wickremasinghe was appointed deputy minister of foreign affairs in the government of Prime Minister Junius Richard Jayawardene. The next year, as Jayawardene was elected president, Wickremasinghe was promoted to full ministerial level as minister of youth affairs and employment. In 1980 he also took on the responsibility of the education ministry. In these positions he inaugurated the first all-island Youth Development Programme and oversaw the introduction of computers into Sri Lankan schools. Meanwhile civil war broke out in 1983 between the Sinhalese majority and the Tamil minority.

In 1989 Jayawardene was succeeded by Ranasinghe Premadasa as president and Wickremasinghe was appointed as leader of Parliament, as well as remaining in the cabinet as minister of industries. The next year he was also made minister of science and technology. In this capacity he unveiled the Strategy for Industrialization which saw the creation of investment promotion zones and designated industrial estates, as well as fostering the development of information technology. He also increased his public profile as the government's chief media spokesman from 1991.

Premadasa was assassinated in May 1993, and in the subsequent reshuffling Wickremasinghe was appointed prime minister. He led the government for a year until legislative elections were held in mid-1994. Consigned by the polls to the opposition, Wickremasinghe became leader of the UNP and determined to restructure the party in order to regain its popularity. He married his wife Maithree, a lecturer in English, in 1995.

As the official leader of the opposition, Wickremasinghe challenged the pace of economic liberalization under the government appointed by President Kumaratunga and unsuccessfully ran against her for the presidency in December 1999, gaining 43% of the vote behind Kumaratunga's winning 51%. Over the course of 2000 and 2001 Wickremasinghe stepped up his opposition to the president, focusing on her belligerent approach to the ongoing civil war. Wickremasinghe failed to lead the UNP to victory over the ruling People's Alliance in legislative elections in October 2000, coming second again. After six months of co-operation with the government Wickremasinghe redoubled his opposition when Kumuratunga suspended Parliament in July 2001. He personally led MPs in breaking into Parliament and led violent demonstrations later in the year.

The UNP returned to power in snap elections in December, falling just short of an outright majority and forming a coalition with the main Muslim party. Wickremasinghe, becoming prime minister for the second time, immediately implemented a more conciliatory stance towards the rebel Tamil Tigers, securing a cessation in hostilities from them on 24 December. A permanent ceasefire on 21 February 2002 marked an end to almost 19 years of civil war. Wickremasinghe became the first prime minister to visit the front line of the war when he travelled to Jaffna in March. Despite remarkable progress in talks, Wickremasinghe faces criticism for 'surrendering Sri Lanka's sovereignty' in deals with the rebels. On the economic front he has restarted the privatization programme frozen by the previous government in 2001.

SUDAN

Full name: The Republic of the Sudan.

Leadership structure: The head of state is a president, directly elected by universal adult suffrage. The president's term of office is five years. The head of government is the president. The cabinet is appointed by the president.

President: Lt.-Gen. Omar Hassan Ahmad al-Bashir   Since 16 Oct. 1993
               (seized power on 30 June 1989)

Legislature: The legislature is unicameral. The sole chamber, the National Assembly (Majlis Watani), has 400 members directly elected for a four-year term.

Profile of the President:

Lt.-Gen. Omar Hassan Ahmad al-**BASHIR**

Lt.-Gen. Bashir, a career soldier from the north, was a major-general when he launched his 1989 coup. He sought democratic legitimacy for his rule in a nonparty presidential election in March 1996, defeating a large number of relatively unknown opponents, and held elections again in December 2000, when he secured a further term. His regime is dominated by Islamic fundamentalists through the ruling party, which recently changed its name from National Islamic Front (NIF) to National Congress (NC). Bashir's expressions of desire for an end to conflict with the (mainly Christian) south have begun to be translated into a peace process.

Omar Hassan Ahmad al-Bashir was born in 1935. Educated in Khartoum, the capital, he was a soldier in the Sudanese army from 1960, having trained in Egypt and Malaysia. He fought for the Egyptians in the Yom Kippur war against Israel in 1973, and was involved also in the Sudanese government's long conflict with southern rebels, who resist attempts to make Sudan an Islamic state ruled by *shari'a* (Islamic law).

On 30 June 1989 Bashir staged a coup, ousting the government of Sadiq al-Mahdi and dissolving parliament. He appointed himself chairman of the Revolutionary Command Council for National Salvation (RCC), prime minister (a position he still holds) and minister of defence. He also banned political parties and suspended the constitution, imprisoning many government members and releasing soldiers implicated in previous military coup attempts. Still at war with rebel groups in southern Sudan, his regime became increasingly committed to the introduction of *shari'a* throughout the country, an objective kept in the forefront by the political dominance of the National Islamic Front (NIF).

In 1993 the RCC announced a return to civilian rule, after appointing Bashir as president and consolidating the power of the National Islamic Front. Nonparty elections for a president and a new National Assembly were held in March 1996 but were boycotted by the major opposition factions which had formed a National Democratic Alliance (NDA) based in Asmara, Eritrea. Forty independent candidates stood and, amid outcries of irregularities, Bashir was elected president for a five-year term with 76% of the vote. The NIF won the majority of seats in the Assembly. Elections in December 2000 produced a similar outcome. Bashir was re-elected with 86.5% of the vote and the newly renamed NC gained a majority of over 75% in the Assembly. Again the opposition boycotted the polls, although Bashir had made overtures to the NDA and the Umma party, led by Mahdi, which he had allowed back into the country in March 2000. A splinter of Umma then joined the government outright in July 2002.

Arguably the greatest challenge to Bashir has been the ongoing civil war with the rebel Sudan People's Liberation Army (SPLA) in the south. A number of peace agreements have been drafted and rejected, while innumerable ceasefires have been implemented only to be broken within days. A state of emergency declared by Bashir in December 1999 has been consistently extended in what has become an annual event. Nonetheless, a breakthrough was heralded in July 2002. Although fighting did not diminish, key stumbling blocks were apparently overcome. Under the 2002 proposals, the south of the country will hold a referendum on possible independence in 2008 after six years of legislative autonomy, and during that time *shari'a* will not be extended to non-Muslims.

Under the Bashir regime, diplomatic links have been severed with neighbouring countries which Sudan accuses of aiding the southern rebels, among them Eritrea. Other states have offered assistance in providing a base for peace talks, including Ethiopia, Kenya and, from 2001, Egypt.

Bashir was among the first world leaders to offer condolences after the 11 September 2001 attacks on the USA. The same month saw the lifting of the five-year-old UN sanctions against Sudan, which had been accused by the USA and other countries of harbouring Islamist terrorists. Later that year, however, Bashir was quick to condemn the US-led war in Afghanistan as unfairly targeting Muslims. The Sudan Peace Act passed by the USA in October 2002 gave the US president the power to impose sanctions in response to nonassistance from the Sudanese government.

SURINAME

Full name: The Republic of Suriname.

Leadership structure: The head of state is a president, elected (along with the vice president) by the National Assembly or, if the required two-thirds majority is not achieved, by a broader United Peoples' Conference (UPC) convened for the purpose and including district and local council representatives. The president's term of office is five years. The head of government is the president. The cabinet is appointed by the president. The vice president also holds the post of prime minister and leads the cabinet.

| **Presidents:** | Jules Wijdenbosch | 15 Sept. 1996—12 Aug. 2000 |
| | Ronald Venetiaan | Since 12 Aug. 2000 |

Vice Presidents/Prime Ministers:

| | Pretaapnarian Radhakishun | 15 Sept. 1996—12 Aug. 2000 |
| | Jules Ajodhia | Since 12 Aug. 2000 |

Legislature: The legislature is unicameral. The sole chamber, the National Assembly (Nationale Assemblee), has 51 members, directly elected for a five-year term.

Profile of the President:

Ronald **VENETIAAN**

Ronald Venetiaan leads the New Front (Nieuwe Front—NF) coalition. A prominent figure in Suriname's relatively recent return to democracy, he was president for the first time from 1991 to 1996. He was re-elected to the post in August 2000 after a landslide victory at the polls for the NF.

Runaldo Ronald Venetiaan was born on 18 June 1936 in Paramaribo. He went to the Netherlands in the 1950s to study mathematics and physics at the University of Leiden, receiving a doctorate in mathematics in 1964. He is married to Liesbeth Vanenburg and they have four children.

In 1964 Venetiaan returned to Suriname, where he worked as a mathematics teacher at the University Preparatory and Teacher Training Colleges. He ran the mathematics department from 1965 and in 1969 he was appointed headmaster of Algemene Middelbare School. During his teaching career he had begun working with the political left and in 1973 he was called to government as minister of education under Prime Minister Henck Arron.

After the military coup led by Lt.-Col. Desi Bouterse in 1980, Venetiaan returned to full-time teaching as a lecturer in mathematics. He re-engaged with politics as a research adviser to the general statistics bureau in 1985 and as chairman of the advisory board of the Suriname National Party (Nationale Partij Suriname—NPS) from 1987. He was returned to the education ministry following the reappointment of Arron after fresh elections in 1988.

Venetiaan remained education minister through the second military coup and until fresh elections were held in 1991. These were won by the NF coalition, which included the NPS, and after the poll Venetiaan was nominated as the coalition's candidate for president; he was successfully elected in September. As president he consolidated the country's democracy, purging the government of military control and replacing Bouterse, who had become commander-in-chief of the armed forces. He also instituted a Structural Adjustment Programme which involved unpopular but largely successful economic austerity measures. In addition he oversaw the end of the six-year Maroon insurgency in 1992.

Legislative polls in 1996 saw the NF lose its majority in the National Assembly, although it remained the largest party. Amid protracted coalition talks, Venetiaan faced Jules Wijdenbosch in presidential elections. Neither candidate could achieve the two-thirds majority to secure election so a United People's Conference was convened, which elected Wijdenbosch as president. Two factions then split from the NF and agreed to join Wijdenbosch's coalition on condition that Bouterse was excluded from the government.

For the next four years Venetiaan led the NF in opposition. The grouping rode to a significant victory in early elections held in 2000, retaking a majority in the National Assembly, and Venetiaan was once again elected president.

Profile of the Vice President:

Jules AJODHIA

Jules Ajodhia is a member of the United Reform Party (Verenigde Hervormings Partij—VHP). Trained as a lawyer, he has been Ronald Venetiaan's running mate in elections since 1991, thereby holding office as vice president and prime minister in 1991–96 and again from 2000.

Jules Rattankoemar Ajodhia was born into the country's large Hindu community on 27 January 1945. He attended the Suriname Law School in the 1960s and qualified in the subject from the University of Suriname in 1970. From the age of 17 he had worked in the office of the procurator-general and from 1973 he acted as a district commissioner. During this period he joined the VHP and became chairman of the Prekash football club. He is married to Lucia Baldew and they have three children.

In 1988 he joined the government of Prime Minister Henck Arron as justice minister and worked alongside his cabinet colleague Venetiaan. The two then teamed up in 1991 to present a joint ticket for fresh presidential elections, with Ajodhia as vice president. They were elected by the National Assembly in September. As vice president, Ajodhia was also prime minister.

Following the parliamentary elections of 1996, the Venetiaan–Ajodhia team was defeated in the contest for the presidency, and Ajodhia returned to law as a lecturer at the University of Suriname. Four years later, amid public protest at the economic decline suffered by the country during the rule of President Jules Wijdenbosch, Ajodhia and Venetiaan teamed up once more and were elected again in August 2000.

SWAZILAND

Full name: The Kingdom of Swaziland.

Leadership structure: The head of state is the king. The head of government is the prime minister who is appointed by the king. The king also appoints the cabinet, in consultation with the prime minister.

King: Mswati III Since 25 April 1986

Prime Minister: Barnabas Sibusiso Dlamini Since 26 July 1996

Legislature: The legislature, the Parliament (Libandla), is bicameral. The lower chamber, the House of Assembly, has 65 members (55 directly elected, ten appointed by the king), serving for a five-year term. The upper chamber, the Senate, has 30 members (ten elected by the House of Assembly, 20 appointed by the king), also serving for a five-year term.

Profile of the King:

MSWATI III

Mswati III was crowned king of Swaziland on 25 April 1986, becoming the youngest reigning monarch in the world at the age of 18. His father, King Sobhuza II, had died four years previously and a power struggle had ensued during the regency, with the result that Mswati was invested as king earlier than planned. He has strengthened the royal powers and rules mainly by decree, despite pressure for more democratization.

Prince Makhosetive (as he was known before his coronation) was born on 19 April 1968. He was educated in Swaziland and then in England, at Sherborne public school and the Royal Military Academy, Sandhurst. His father died when he was 14 and Queen Dzeliwe, one of the royal wives, was appointed regent with the task of governing together with the Liqoqo, the traditional advisory council.

The following year she was ousted by members of the Liqoqo and replaced by Queen Ntombi, Makhosetive's mother. On the same day, 10 August 1983, Makhosetive was declared heir to the throne which, according to custom, he could not ascend until he was 21. A month later the Liqoqo requested that he return from school in England in the hope that his presence would reduce the unrest in the country.

Over the next three years the power struggle continued, with the result that the coronation was brought forward and held on 25 April 1986. The following month the newly enthroned King Mswati abolished the Liqoqo, and in May 1987 he charged 12 government officials with sedition for their alleged involvement in the dethronement of Queen Dzeliwe and the subsequent intrigue. In September of that year he dissolved Parliament. Fresh elections were held in November under a system whereby the electorate could vote for candidates nominated by local councils.

On his 21st birthday Mswati assumed the full powers and responsibilities of the paramount chief, but there were already demands for multiparty elections and the restriction of the monarchy to a ceremonial position. In October 1992 he again dissolved parliament, appointed a Council of Ministers and with their help agreed to rule by decree until multiparty elections could be held. However, political parties have still not been legalized. Elections were held to the House of Assembly in September–October 1993 and again in October 1998, but the Assembly does not have full legislative powers and can only debate government policy and advise the king.

Mswati's response to growing pressure within the region for a degree of democratization has been limited. After an eight-day protest in January 1996 he agreed to begin talks on the future of the monarchy but refused to consider giving up his powers. Delays on political reforms caused significant social unrest again in 1997, when he appointed a constitutional review commission. The conclusion of this commission, published in August 2001, was that the majority of Swazis actually wanted to see the king's powers extended rather than restricted—a conclusion fiercely contested by pro-democracy groups and trade unions.

Profile of the Prime Minister:

Barnabas Sibusiso **DLAMINI**

Barnabas Sibusiso Dlamini trained as an industrial chemist, accountant and economist, and first entered the cabinet in 1984. He worked for the International Monetary Fund (IMF) for four years in the 1990s prior to his appointment as prime minister in July 1996.

Barnabas Sibusiso Dlamini was born on 15 May 1942. He was awarded a US government scholarship to study at the University of Wisconsin, USA, in 1966–69, and graduated with a degree in chemistry and mathematics from the University of South Africa in 1969. He gained a further degree in economics and accounting from New York University, USA, in 1976 and an MBA (master's degree in business administration) in financial management in 1982. He is married and has five children.

Dlamini joined the Swaziland Iron Ore Development Company in 1969, becoming the company's chief chemist in 1972 and its metallurgical superintendent in 1977. The next year he began working for Coopers and Lybrand, qualified as a chartered accountant, and was made a partner in 1983. Between 1984 and 1992 he was a partner in a Swazi firm of chartered accountants. He joined the IMF as alternate executive director in 1992, and two years later became executive director, representing a group of 21 African countries.

He entered politics in 1978 as a senator, and became a member of the House of Assembly in 1983. Between 1984 and 1992 he was minister of finance, and after his four years' service at the IMF he was appointed prime minister by King Mswati in July 1996. After the July 1998 elections he was confirmed in office on 13 November 1998 and sworn in a week later at the head of a reshuffled government.

SWEDEN

Full name: The Kingdom of Sweden.

Leadership structure: The head of state is a constitutional monarch. The head of government is the prime minister, who is responsible to Parliament. The cabinet is appointed by the prime minister.

King: Carl XVI Gustaf   Since 15 Sept. 1973

Prime Minister: Göran Persson   Since 17 March 1996

Legislature: The legislature is unicameral. The sole chamber, the Parliament (Riksdag), has 349 members, directly elected for a four-year term.

Profile of the King:

CARL XVI GUSTAF

Carl XVI Gustaf, the 74th king of Sweden, belongs to the Bernadotte dynasty, which has been on the throne since 1818. At the time of his accession in 1973 he was only 27, the youngest ever Bernadotte monarch. His style is unostentatious, in the manner of Scandinavian constitutional monarchies, and he is noted for his commitment to environmental protection, exemplified by his presidency of the Swedish branch of the World Wide Fund for Nature (WWF).

Carl XVI Gustaf was born on 30 April 1946 at the Haga Palace, the fifth child and only son of Hereditary Prince Gustaf Adolf, who was killed in a plane crash the following year. Carl Gustaf was educated privately, initially at the royal palace in Stockholm, after which he went on to Broms school and Sigtuna boarding school, where he matriculated in 1966. He then did two-and-a-half years of military service, training in the army, navy and air force. He passed his naval officer examination in 1968. His military training was later supplemented by a management course at the national defence college and commissioned service on board ships of the Swedish navy. In 1968 and 1969 the crown prince studied history, sociology, political science, financial law and economics at Uppsala University. Later he also studied economics at Stockholm University.

Under a programme designed to give him experience of the local, national, and international political scene, he was attached to Sweden's permanent mission to the UN in New York and then spent time in London, UK, at Hambros Bank and at the Swedish embassy and chamber of commerce. When his grandfather King Gustaf VI Adolf died on 15 September 1973, Carl Gustaf became king.

In addition to his interest in conservation and environmental protection, he has been active representing Sweden at international events, and was made honorary president of the World Scout Foundation in 1977.

King Carl XVI Gustaf is married to Queen Silvia, née Sommerlath, the daughter of a German businessman. They met at the 1972 Munich Olympic games where she was working as an interpreter and hostess. They have two daughters and one son. Their eldest child, Crown Princess Victoria, born in 1977, is heir to the throne under the 1980 Act of Succession, which now stipulates that the title passes to the monarch's eldest child regardless of sex.

Profile of the Prime Minister:

Göran **PERSSON**

Göran Persson became prime minister in succession to his social democratic colleague Ingvar Carlsson, whom he had previously served as finance minister. Two days before becoming prime minister, Persson also assumed the leadership of the Swedish Social Democrats (Socialdemokratiska Arbetarepartiet—SAP). He worked as an administrator in adult education before entering Parliament in 1979, since when his political career has involved him in a variety of posts at both the national and local level.

Göran Persson was born on 20 January 1949 in Vingåker. He left secondary school with a certificate in engineering in 1969, and went on to the University College of Örebro until 1971. In that year he took up the first of a number of administrative posts in adult education, and became organizing secretary of the SAP youth league, having first joined the party's youth wing at the age of 15. Between 1972 and 1975 he was a member of the board of the SAP youth league. He did his military service between 1973 and 1974.

He was first elected to Parliament in 1979, after two years as full-time chairman of the Katrineholm board of education. He left Parliament in 1985 to return to local politics, as municipal commissioner in Katrineholm, a post he held for four years. Between 1989 and 1991 he was minister at the ministry of education with responsibility for comprehensive and upper schools, adult education and public education.

Re-elected to Parliament in 1991, he was chairman of the parliamentary standing committee on agriculture from 1991 to 1992, a member of the parliamentary standing committee on industry from 1992 to 1993 (and also party spokesperson for industrial policy issues), and vice chairman of the parliamentary standing committee on finance (1993–94). He was chairman of the SAP district organization in Sörmland from 1992 to 1996, and between 1993 and 1996 he was a deputy member of the SAP executive committee.

When the SAP returned to power after the September 1994 general election, Persson was appointed minister of finance. In this post he introduced tough austerity measures in 1995 to tackle the economic recession which had beset the country since the early 1990s. He was also a strong supporter of Swedish participation in the single European currency, following Sweden's accession to the European Union in January 1995.

Persson became prime minister on 17 March 1996, his predecessor Carlsson having announced in August 1995 his intention of resigning the premiership which he had held for most of the last ten years. Persson's government's first major controversy came over the commitment to the decommissioning of all nuclear power stations in Sweden by 2010, as had been approved by referendum in 1980. Persson confirmed in early 1997 that his government would close two of Sweden's 12 nuclear reactors by 2001. In May 2001 he became the first Western leader to travel to North Korea to meet that isolated country's leader, Kim Jong Il.

The SAP and Persson were re-elected on 15 September 2002, winning 144 seats in the 349-seat Parliament. He continues to rule the country with a minority government, relying on support in Parliament from the Left Party and the Greens. Adopting the euro has been part of the SAP's official party policy since 2000, but Persson declined from holding a referendum on the issue in his previous term; he has now promised to do so in September 2003.

Göran Persson filed for divorce from his wife Annika in December 2002. He has two children from a previous marriage.

SWITZERLAND

Full name: The Swiss Confederation.

Leadership structure: The head of state is a president, elected annually by the Federal Assembly from the members of the Federal Council. The president's term of office is one year. The president chairs the Federal Council (Bundesrat; Conseil Fédéral; Consiglio Federale), which has joint responsibility for government. The Federal Council is chosen by the Assembly from its members after every general election, and serves for four years.

Presidents:	Adolf Ogi	1 Jan. 2000—31 Dec. 2000
	Moritz Leuenberger	1 Jan. 2001—31 Dec. 2001
	Kaspar Villiger	1 Jan. 2002—31 Dec. 2002
	Pascal Couchepin	Since 1 Jan. 2003

Legislature: The legislature, the Federal Assembly (Bundesversammlung; Assemblée Fédérale; Assemblea Federale), is bicameral. The lower chamber, the National Council (Nationalrat; Conseil National; Consiglio Nazionale), has 200 members, directly elected for a four-year term. The upper chamber, the Council of States (Ständerat; Conseil des Etats; Consiglio degli Stati), has 46 representatives directly elected within each canton for a four-year term.

Profile of the President:

Pascal **COUCHEPIN**

Pascal Couchepin is a member of the Radical Democratic Party (Freisinnig-Demokratische Partei der Schweiz—FDP; Parti Radical-Démocratique Suisse—PRD). A career politician, and long-time mayor of Martigny, he was brought into the federal cabinet as economy minister in 1998 and elected for the 2003 presidency in December 2002.

Pascal Couchepin was born in Martigny on 5 April 1942. He is married and has three children. He graduated in law from the University of Lausanne and established his own private law practice in 1968.

In the same year Couchepin began his political career and was elected as a councillor in Martigny. Eight years later he was appointed deputy mayor of the town and became mayor in 1984. In the meantime he had been elected to the National Council in 1979 and was head of his party's parliamentary group from

1989 to 1996. In March 1998 he was elected to the Federal Council as economics minister and consequently stood down as mayor of Martigny.

Couchepin has sat on the board of a number of private companies in the energy, mechanical engineering and telecommunications industries. He has also been president of the Valais Association for Physically and Mentally Disabled Persons, and supports the Swiss Multiple Sclerosis Society.

In December 2001 Couchepin was elected from among the federal councillors to be vice president for 2002, a post which is rotated every year and which usually leads on to the holder being elected president for the following year. He began his one-year tenure as president in January 2003.

SYRIA

Full name: The Syrian Arab Republic.

Leadership structure: The head of state is a president, elected by parliament for a seven-year term and confirmed by referendum. The head of government is the president. The Council of Ministers is appointed by the president.

Presidents:	Hafez al-Assad (seized power on 15 Oct. 1970)	14 March 1971—10 June 2000
	Abd al-Halim Khaddam (acting)	10 June 2000—17 July 2000
	Bashar al-Assad	Since 17 July 2000
Prime Ministers:	Mahmoud al-Zubi (acting from 7 March 2000)	1 Nov. 1987—20 March 2000
	Mohammad Mustafa Miro	Since 20 March 2000

Legislature: The legislature is unicameral. The sole chamber, the People's Council (Majlis al-Sha'ab), has 250 members, directly elected for a four-year term.

Profile of the President:

Bashar al-**ASSAD**

Bashar al-Assad was proclaimed president of Syria in 2000 following the death of his father, President Hafez al-Assad, who had ruled the country since 1970. An ophthalmologist by training, Bashar had only been groomed for the succession after the accidental death of his elder brother Basil in 1994. Since then he has proceeded through a crash course in leadership. His attempts at liberalization have been slow and steady, with the focus on economic rather than political reform. His administration is supported by the all-powerful Renaissance Arab Socialist Party (Hizb al-Ba'ath al-Arabi al-Ishtriraki—Ba'ath), of which he is also leader.

Bashar al-Assad was born in Damascus on 11 September 1965. He was the third child of Gen. Hafez al-Assad and was educated at one of the city's elite Franco-Arab schools, al-Hurriyet. From 1982 he began his studies in medicine at Damascus University; he graduated as a general practitioner six years later. He first specialized in ophthalmology at a military hospital before going to the UK in 1992 to pursue his professional qualifications in London.

The death of Bashar's elder brother Basil in a car crash in 1994 changed Bashar's life dramatically. The fast-living Basil had long been brought up as Hafez's successor and was a man much in his father's mould. Bashar, on the other hand, is described as shy and reserved, and at first refused his father's demands to return from the UK to prepare as the future leader of his country.

Processed through the military academy at Homs, a necessary process in view of the domination of Syrian politics by the military, Bashar was a colonel by January 1999. Meanwhile he also began to be sent on official visits to neighbouring states. He is thought to have played a key role in the accession of Gen. Emile Lahoud as president in Lebanon in 1998, and reportedly referred to Iraqi dictator Saddam Hussein as a "beast", while on a tour of Kuwait. At home he spearheaded a 'clean hands' campaign to root out corruption in the regime. Many senior army officers and members of the intelligence organization, all possible obstacles to his succession, were forced to resign. His role in politics was formalized in March 2000 when he advised his ailing father on the formation of a new government under Prime Minister Mohammad Mustafa Miro.

Throughout this period Bashar insisted that he had no presidential ambitions. However, when Hafez eventually died on 10 June 2000, Bashar was immediately nominated as the new leader of the Ba'ath party, the constitution was hastily altered lowering the minimum age for a president from 40 to 34 (Bashar's age), and he was promptly promoted to lieutenant-general and chief of staff of the armed forces. His succession as president was endorsed by an overwhelming 97% of the electorate in a popular referendum held on 10 July.

Modernization of the economy has ranked high on Bashar's agenda. A raft of reforms issued in December 2000 included the reintroduction of private banks for the first time since 1963, and the creation of a stock market. He is also keen to promote new media. As chairman of the Syrian Computer Society he encouraged the growth of Internet usage in the country despite the hesitations of his father. In November 2000 he also promised to modernize the press laws and permitted the circulation of political papers by parties other than the Ba'ath. A general air of new freedoms has evoked small-scale criticism of the regime in the People's Assembly and has encouraged some unusually outspoken journalism.

Hopes for a quick thawing of relations with Israel were soon dispelled when he reiterated his father's demands for the return of the Golan Heights as a precondition for any talks. However, before the situation deteriorated on the West Bank in late 2000, he did suggest he was willing to restart negotiations when the Israeli government was ready.

Known affectionately as 'Doctor', Bashar is noted for his close physical resemblance to his father, but his personality is very different. Described as bookish, his interests include photography and cycling. His time in London and his fluency in English and French are at the heart of his apparent pro-Western image. Bashar al-Assad married Asma al-Akhras, a UK-born computer specialist, at a secret ceremony at the end of December 2000. They now have one son.

Profile of the Prime Minister:

Mohammad Mustafa **MIRO**

Mohammad Mustafa Miro is a member of the ruling Renaissance Arab Socialist Party (Hizb al-Ba'ath al-Arabi al-Ishtriraki—Ba'ath). He was governor of three different towns, including the country's second-biggest urban centre, Aleppo, before he was appointed prime minister on 13 March 2000 and took office a week later.

Mohammad Mustafa Miro was born in 1941 in al-Tal near Damascus. Little is known about his early life. He studied at Damascus University and holds a doctorate in Arab literature and humanitarian sciences. He was also closely involved with the Arab Teachers' Union, of which he has been secretary-general for cultural affairs and publications. He is a widower with five children. His wife died in a car accident in the mid-1990s.

In 1980 Miro was appointed governor, or mayor, of the southern town of Dar'a on the country's border with Jordan. He was there for six years before crossing the Syrian desert to take up the same position in the town of al-Hasakah, in the northeast of the country. In 1993 he was promoted to become governor of Aleppo, the country's second city. In this capacity he was integral to Syria's dealings with neighbouring Turkey and is said to have maintained good relations despite regional tensions.

In March 2000 Miro was appointed to government as prime minister. Following the death of President Hafez al-Assad in June, Miro was promoted within the Ba'ath party and was retained as premier by Assad's son and successor, Bashar al-Assad. In December 2001 he was charged with forming a new cabinet in an apparent effort to stimulate economic reforms.

TAIWAN

Full name: The Republic of China.

Leadership structure: The head of state is a president, directly elected by universal adult suffrage. The president's term of office is four years, renewable once only. The head of government is the premier, who is appointed by the president. The Executive Yuan is responsible to the Legislative Yuan.

Presidents:	Lee Teng-hui	13 Jan. 1988—20 May 2000
	Chen Shui-bian	Since 20 May 2000
Premiers:	Vincent Siew	1 Sept. 1997—20 May 2000
	Tang Fei	20 May 2000—3 Oct. 2000
	Chang Chun-hsiung (acting from 4 Oct. 2000)	6 Oct. 2000—1 Feb. 2002
	Yu Shyi-kun	Since 1 Feb. 2002

Legislature: The legislature is now effectively unicameral. The Legislative Yuan (Li-fa Yuan) has 225 members (176 directly elected, 49 elected proportionately by party) serving a three-year term. The National Assembly (Kuo-min Ta-hui) has transformed itself into a largely ceremonial 300-member body, convening ad hoc when required and appointed proportionally by the parties represented in the Legislative Yuan.

Profile of the President:

CHEN Shui-bian

Chen Shui-bian's inauguration as the tenth president of Taiwan broke 50 years of domination by the nationalist Kuomintang (KMT). As a major opposition figure he was mayor of Taipei from 1994 to 1998. Determined to succeed from humble origins, he is intolerant of ideology and even his own wife has described him as "a bore". His authoritarian nature led to serious conflict in late 2000 with the Legislative Yuan, which was at that time dominated by the KMT. The 2001 legislative elections changed this situation to Chen's advantage, with the KMT losing ground and his Democratic Progressive Party (DPP) becoming the largest party.

Chen Shui-bian was born in 1950 to poor native tenant farmers in Hsi-chuang, Tainan province, in the south of the island (known then as Formosa). He was a weak infant so his parents did not immediately register his birth; his identification certificate shows his date of birth as 18 February 1951. Chen's family borrowed money to send him through school and he is famed for his remarkable academic achievements, reportedly coming first at every level from primary school to university. He entered the National University in 1969 and, after changing course the following year, graduated with a degree in law in 1974. He went on to join the Formosan International Marine and Commercial Law Office as an attorney specializing in maritime law.

Chen Shui-bian met Wu Shu-chen, the daughter of wealthy doctors, while at university, and they eloped to marry in 1975. Wu followed her own political career and won great public sympathy when she was knocked down by a farm vehicle in 1985 in what is rumoured to have been a politically motivated assassination attempt. Since then she has been paralyzed from the waist down. She is a close adviser to her husband and often makes appearances at political rallies. They have two children.

It was the Kaohsiung Incident of 1979 which provided Chen with his first taste of politics. The editors of *Formosa* magazine, to which he was affiliated, were charged with sedition and rioting after their attempts to hold an anti-KMT rally erupted in violence in Kaohsiung. Chen defended them in court, despite his lack of relevant experience and the heavy odds against them. He lost the case in 1980 but was inspired to enter politics as an opponent of the KMT's prolific use of martial law. He became the youngest ever city councillor in Taipei in 1981 and stayed on the council for four years.

The tables turned against Chen in 1985 when *Formosa* magazine, of which he was now chairman, was sued for libel; on losing the case, he left the magazine and resigned from the city council. He was defeated in an attempt to seek office in his rural birthplace and an appeal against the libel conviction failed. He was sent to Tucheng penitentiary for eight months. On release from prison Chen joined the DPP, which had emerged following a relaxation in martial law in 1987. His wife Wu had entered the Legislative Yuan in 1986 on the back of popular anger at his own imprisonment, and Chen served as her office manager. In 1989 he was elected to the Legislative Yuan himself and was a leading member of the DPP's parliamentary bloc. He became the first opposition politician to hold the chairmanship of the National Defence Committee.

After two terms in the Legislative Yuan, Chen became the first democratically elected mayor of Taipei in 1994, having benefited greatly from a divisive split of traditional votes between the KMT and the New Party (NP). Despite his strong anti-KMT image, Chen showed himself to value pragmatism above consistency and chose to work alongside proven KMT administrators. As mayor, Chen is remembered for greatly improving the city's transport network and business profile, but also for pursuing unpopular and ruthless right-wing cleanup campaigns. A crackdown on Taipei's sex industry was harshly executed, with no provisions for the welfare of the many sex workers, while in the creation of two city parks Chen evicted all the residents of 'Kangleh village'. The justifications for some of the measures implemented by his administration were overturned later in courts of appeal. An alliance between the KMT and the NP led to Chen being voted from office in 1998.

Losing the post of mayor at this time proved fortuitous for Chen in that it freed him to run for the presidency at a time when the DPP had been struggling to find a high-profile representative. Moreover, the ruling KMT's support was being drained by the defection of the popular James Soong, who then stood as an independent candidate. Chen campaigned on a platform of opposition to years of KMT corruption and he countered mainland Chinese threats of imminent war with reassurances to his supporters that he no longer advocated immediate sovereignty. He was elected the first non-KMT president of Taiwan in March 2000 with 39.3% of the vote. The KMT's Lien Chan came a poor third. Chen took office on 20 May.

For the first 18 months of his presidency, Chen had to face the hostility of a KMT-dominated Legislative Yuan. An attempt to promote a sense of national consensus failed when his KMT prime minister Tang Fei resigned after four months. The nationalists were particularly angered by Chen's proposal to scrap a KMT-initiated nuclear power plant project. However, massive displays of anti-nuclear feeling, and popular support for Chen, muted opposition calls for his recall.

Legislative elections on 1 December 2001 put Chen in a far more commanding position when the KMT lost its majority for the first time in Taiwanese history. Although the DPP became the largest single party, it failed to secure an outright majority and the KMT and other opposition groups were unmoved by Chen's call for a 'unity' coalition. In an effort to 'stabilize' democracy, Chen took over as leader of the DPP in July 2002.

Relations with China under Chen have seen remarkable progress. The two countries now have an unprecedented level of contact, with transport links being progressively opened every year. Tensions remain, of course, and the occasional use of undiplomatic language by Chen has provoked sabre rattling from the mainland.

Profile of the Premier:

YU Shyi-kun

Yu Shyi-kun is a cofounder and senior member of the pro-presidential Democratic Progressive Party (DPP). A leading advocate of the pro-democracy Tang Wai movement as early as the 1970s, he is a close associate of President

Chen Shui-bian and has served as campaign manager for many DPP and other figures. Despite resigning as vice premier over the Pachang River disaster in July 2000, Yu returned to the cabinet just months later and took office as prime minister in February 2002.

Yu Shyi-kun was born on 25 April 1948 in the village of Taiho in Taiwan's northeastern Ilan County. His family were tenant farmers and, following the death of his father in 1961, Yu was forced to abandon his school studies to help run the family farm. He resumed his education at the age of 19. While at school he made connections with the Tang Wai pro-democracy movement in Ilan; he joined the Youth Party and worked closely with its founder Kuo Yu-hsin, who was a leading figure in Tang Wei. After graduating from high school he completed his military service and attended the Chih Lee College of Business before finding work at the Cathay Trust Company in Taipei. He married Yang Pao-yu in 1978 and they have two sons.

While working in the capital, Yu continued to support the Tang Wai movement in Ilan. As part of this connection with the pro-democracy movement, he acted as Ilan bureau chief for the dissident *Formosa Magazine*. He escaped the ruling nationalist (Kuomintang—KMT) government's crackdown following the 1979 Kaohsiung Incident and went on to become a senior figure in the Tang Wai movement while its leaders languished in prison. He was elected to the provincial assembly in 1981 and to the Legislative Yuan in 1983. Deciding to complete his education, he obtained a degree in political science from Tunghai University in 1985. A year later he helped to cofound the DPP with Chen Shui-bian and was elected to the new party's central committee. He left the party in 1990 after being elected as a magistrate in Ilan.

After concentrating on local politics in Ilan for much of the 1990s, Yu returned to Taipei in 1997 at the invitation of the city's then mayor, and Yu's former colleague, Chen. For the remaining year of Chen's tenure there, Yu headed the capital's Rapid Transit Corporation. When Chen stepped down as mayor in 1998, Yu left the city administration too and took up the post of secretary-general of the DPP. In this role he oversaw a series of high-level election campaigns culminating in Chen's election as president in 2000. As a reward, and to counterbalance the appointment of the nationalist Kuomintang candidate Tang Fei as prime minister, Yu was made vice premier in May 2000.

In July 2000 four people were killed during the Pachang River incident, which was blamed on an inefficient emergency response. Chen rejected the proffered resignation of Tang, and instead Yu was forced to step down. He spent six months as an associate professor of 'cultural administration' before returning to the cabinet in early 2001 as head of the president's office. Following the DPP's election success in late 2001, a fully pro-presidential cabinet was made possible in early 2002; Yu was appointed to head it on 21 January and took office on 1 February.

TAJIKISTAN

Full name: The Republic of Tajikistan.

Leadership structure: The head of state is a president, directly elected by universal adult suffrage. The president's term of office is seven years, and not renewable, in accordance with the constitutional amendments approved by referendum on 26 September 1999. The head of government is the president. The Council of Ministers is appointed by the prime minister.

President: Imomali Rakhmanov   Since 16 Nov. 1994
(chairman of Supreme Soviet from 19 Nov. 1992)

Prime Minister: Akil Akilov   Since 20 Dec. 1999

Legislature: The legislature is bicameral. The lower chamber, the Assembly of Representatives (Majlisi Namoyandagon), has 63 members, directly elected for a five-year term, and the upper chamber, the National Assembly (Majlisi Milli), has 33 members, 25 indirectly elected and eight appointed by the president, for a five-year term.

Profile of the President:

Imomali **RAKHMANOV**

Imomali Rakhmanov has been in power in Tajikistan, amid conditions of civil war, since late 1992, and was confirmed in office as president by elections held in November 1994, when a new constitution was also adopted by referendum. An ex-communist, he was seen when he came to power as pro-Russian, and is a former ally of ex-president Rakhmon Nabiyev. He has promoted close links with the Karimov regime in neighbouring Uzbekistan.

Imomali Rakhmanov was born on 5 October 1952 in Dangara in the Kulob district of southern Tajikistan. He graduated in economics from Tajik State University, then worked as an electrician, salesman, government secretary and chairman of a trade union committee. Rising up the Communist Party system, from 1988 he was director of collective farms in the Kulob region, and in 1992 became chairman of the executive committee of the Kulob regional soviet (i.e. council). He is married and has nine children.

Following Tajikistan's declaration of independence in 1991 and the disintegration of the Soviet Union, the new state faced a period of civil war in which the former communist authorities were ranged against an Islamic fundamentalist opposition. The Islamic forces briefly gained the upper hand in September 1992, but the ex-communists regained control of the capital, Dushanbe, in December. Rakhmanov, chosen the previous month as chairman of the Supreme Soviet, thereupon formed a new government. His authority was effectively preserved by the intervention of a Russian-led peacekeeping force intended to prevent the re-escalation of the conflict.

In the presidential elections of 6 November 1994, held amid conditions of continuing civil war, Rakhmanov won 58.3% of the vote, according to the official results, against 35% for the former prime minister, Abdumalik Abdullajanov, whose supporters complained of alleged vote-rigging.

Although he had kept the Islamists from power, Rakhmanov faced the continuing threat of violence, with insurgents operating by infiltration from neighbouring Afghanistan. Amid continuing conflict and the open violation of ceasefire agreements, a proposal to create a National Reconciliation Council was agreed in December 1996. Over the course of the next two years, a stumbling peace process was interrupted by flashes of violence. Rakhmanov himself was wounded in April 1997 when a grenade was thrown at his feet, killing two other people and injuring 60. A final agreement, first drafted in January 1997, led to the eventual return of peace by early 1999, with members of the United Tajik Opposition sitting in a new interim government. A referendum in September 1999 approved the extension of future presidential terms from five to seven years ahead of presidential elections in November.

On 6 November 1999 Rakhmanov claimed to have won 97% of the vote in the presidential election. The opposition expressed profound suspicion at the size of his victory and the Organization for Security and Co-operation in Europe (OSCE), which had refused to observe the poll at all, claimed widespread irregularities. Similar complaints surfaced following legislative elections on 27 February 2000. The pro-presidential People's Democratic Party of Tajikistan (PDPT) won an outright majority, securing Rakhmanov's position. Human rights organizations continue to accuse Rakhmanov of autocratic practices. Economically, the country has suffered from devastating droughts, while prices for basic goods spiralled when Rakhmanov introduced a new currency, the somoni, in October 2000.

Profile of the Prime Minister:

Akil **AKILOV**

Akil Akilov is a member of the People's Democratic Party of Tajikistan (PDPT). Trained as an engineer under the Soviet regime, he entered the independent Tajikistani government in 1994 and was elevated to prime minister in 1999.

Akil Gaibullayevich Akilov was born on 2 February 1944 in the northern city of Leninabad (modern-day Khujand) in what was then the Tajik Soviet Socialist Republic. After qualifying as an engineer from the Moscow Institute of Construction and Engineering, he found work in Leninabad on a number of construction projects. From 1976 he also officially worked within the structure of the ruling Communist Party.

Akilov served the government of the newly independent Tajikistan from 1993 as construction minister, and also as deputy prime minister from 1994. From 1996 to 1999 he was first deputy governor of the Leninabad region. After the presidential elections in November 1999, he was brought back into the cabinet in December as prime minister.

TANZANIA

Full name: The United Republic of Tanzania.

Leadership structure: The head of state is a president, directly elected by universal adult suffrage. The president's term of office is five years, renewable once only. The head of government is the president, who is responsible to the National Assembly. The cabinet is appointed by the president.

President:	Benjamin Mkapa	Since 23 Nov. 1995
Prime Minister:	Frederick Tluway Sumaye	Since 28 Nov. 1995

Legislature: The legislature is unicameral. The sole chamber, the National Assembly (Bunge), has 280 directly elected members serving five-year terms and five members chosen by the House of Representatives of Zanzibar. The attorney general has a seat ex officio. Since February 2000 the president has had powers to appoint up to ten members to the National Assembly.

Profile of the President:

Benjamin **MKAPA**

Benjamin Mkapa took office as president of Tanzania in November 1995 after the country's first multiparty presidential and legislative elections the previous month. A former journalist and for many years foreign minister, he was the candidate of the Revolutionary Party (Chama Cha Mapinduzi—CCM), the former sole and ruling party.

Benjamin William Mkapa was born on 12 November 1938 in Ndanda near Masasi in the southeast of what was then Tanganyika. Mkapa was educated locally and then went to Uganda to complete his studies, obtaining a degree in English from Makerere University in 1962. He is married with two sons.

Mkapa began his career as a civil servant, working briefly as an administrative officer in Dodoma and Dar es Salaam and then as a foreign service officer from 1963. He joined the ruling party, the Tanganyika African National Union, which was later renamed as the CCM after the 1977 merger with the ruling party of Zanzibar.

Switching from the civil service to journalism, Mkapa was managing editor of the party-owned newspapers *The Nationalist* and *Uhuru* from 1966. *The Nationalist* merged with *The Standard* to form the state-owned *Daily News* in 1972 and

Mkapa remained as managing editor. He was a founding director of the Tanzania News Agency (Shihata) in 1976.

In 1974 he was appointed press secretary to the president. In 1976 he was made high commissioner to Nigeria. The following year he joined the cabinet as minister of foreign affairs until 1980, when he was appointed minister of information and culture. Two years later he returned to the diplomatic service as high commissioner to Canada and the USA in 1982–83, before returning to Tanzania, once again to the post of minister of foreign affairs between 1984 and 1990. He was minister of information and broadcasting in 1990–92 and minister of higher education, science and technology in 1992–95.

Mkapa represented Nanyumbu in the National Assembly for ten years from 1985, until his election as president in October 1995. This poll, held concurrently with the legislative elections, was the first since the transition from a single-party state to a multiparty democracy in 1992. Mkapa had only narrowly won the nomination as CCM candidate at the party congress, but the strength of the party was sufficient to ensure him a wide margin of victory in the nationwide poll. Organization of the elections was chaotic at times and opposition parties alleged electoral fraud, but the High Court eventually declared Mkapa to have won with 61.8% of the vote. He was subsequently re-elected on 29 October 2000 with an increased 71.7% of the vote, having narrowly avoided death in a freak traffic accident three weeks previously. In concurrent legislative elections the CCM gained a massive 82% of seats in the National Assembly.

As president, Mkapa has had to contend with political violence in the island province of Zanzibar, and international criticism for the purchase of a US$40 million air traffic system from the UK in 2002. More positively, he has pledged to reintroduce free primary education with a parallel recruitment drive for teachers.

Profile of the Prime Minister:

Frederick Tluway **SUMAYE**

Frederick Sumaye is a former carpenter whose only governmental experience was in the ministry of agriculture prior to being named as prime minister in 1995. Like President Benjamin Mkapa, who appointed him immediately after winning the presidency, he is a member of the Revolutionary Party (Chama Cha Mapinduzi—CCM), the former sole party and still the country's dominant political organization. Sumaye, too young to have been involved in the independence movement of the 1950s, has a reputation for competence rather than charisma, but despite his low profile he is considered a possible successor to Mkapa as president.

Frederick Tluway Sumaye was born on 29 May 1950 in Hanang in the Arusha region. He attended the Ilboru Secondary School in Arusha and trained as a carpenter, going on later to study agricultural engineering. He is married to Esther Sumaye.

A member of the ruling CCM who now holds a seat on the party's national executive, Sumaye first entered parliament at the October 1985 elections, representing his native Hanang constituency. He has been re-elected on successive occasions in 1990, 1995 and, most recently, November 2000,

Sumaye's first government post was as deputy minister of agriculture, to which he was appointed in December 1990 by the then president Ali Hassan Mwinyi. He rose to full ministerial rank in the same department before being named in November 1995 as prime minister by the incoming president Benjamin Mkapa in a reorganization of the cabinet following that year's elections.

He was reappointed to the premiership by Mkapa on 17 November 2000, again following the simultaneous presidential and legislative elections held on 29 October. Foreign Minister Jakaya Kikwete is generally regarded as Sumaye's most likely rival for the presidency when Mkapa's second and final term ends in 2005.

THAILAND

Full name: The Kingdom of Thailand.

Leadership structure: The head of state is a king. The head of government is the prime minister, who is responsible to the House of Representatives. The cabinet is appointed by the prime minister.

King:	Bhumibol Adulyadej (Rama IX)	Since 9 June 1946

Prime Ministers:	Chuan Leekpai	9 Nov. 1997—18 Feb. 2001
	Thaksin Shinawatra	Since 18 Feb. 2001

Legislature: The legislature, the National Assembly (Rathasapha), is bicameral. The lower chamber, the House of Representatives (Saphaphuthan-ratsadon), has 500 members, directly elected for a four-year term. Under the 1997 Constitution (which expanded the membership of the House from 393 to 500 members), 400 of them are elected in single-member constituencies and 100 from party lists. The 200-member upper chamber, the Senate (Wuthisapha), which was formerly appointed, is directly elected on a nonparty basis, with a six-year term.

Profile of the King:

BHUMIBOL Adulyadej (Rama IX)

King Bhumibol has been king of Thailand for well over half a century and is the world's longest-reigning current monarch, his official royal title being King Rama IX. He is a highly influential figure, revered as semidivine by some of his subjects, although he rules as a constitutional monarch.

Bhumibol Adulyadej was born on 5 December 1927 in the USA, in Cambridge, Massachusetts. The youngest of the three children of Prince and Princess Mahidol of Songkla, at the time of his birth he was not expected ever to become king, and there was little mention of his birth in the newspapers in Bangkok. His early education was in Bangkok, but in 1934 his widowed mother took her children to Switzerland to continue their education. He attended the Gymnase Classique Cantonal in Lausanne, Switzerland, and graduated in political science and law from Lausanne University.

Bhumibol acceded to the throne in June 1946, aged 18, succeeding his elder brother, Ananda Mahidol, who had been found shot dead. He was formally crowned on 5 May 1950 as King Rama IX, the ninth ruler of the Chakri Dynasty.

Much of his energy has latterly been devoted to the Chaipattana (Victory in Development) Foundation, which he set up in 1987 and of which he is president. It enables funds to be made immediately available to the king for urgent projects without need for approval by the government, as was formerly necessary. One of the earliest and better known projects funded by the foundation has been the Chaipattana Aerator machine, and in 1993 a patent was granted to the king for the invention of the Chaipattana Aerator Model RX-2. Other projects include the lessening of traffic congestion and better flood control. Aside from his skill in engineering, the king has a keen interest in jazz music and cartography.

He married Mom Rajawongse Sirikit Kitiyakara, daughter of Prince Chandaburi Suranath, on 28 April 1950. He and Queen Sirikit have one son, Crown Prince Maha Vajiralongkorn, born in 1952, and three daughters.

Profile of the Prime Minister:

THAKSIN Shinawatra

Thaksin Shinawatra is a flamboyant multimillionaire who founded and heads the ruling party Thais Love Thais (Thai Rak Thai—TRT). Trained as a policeman, he began a telecommunications business in 1982 which became one of the country's largest firms, making him one of Thailand's richest men. Brought into government in the mid-1990s, he was ousted in 1997 and formed TRT in 1998. Charges of corruption did not prevent him winning elections in January 2001 and were ultimately dropped. He is noted for initiatives such as the 'million baht village' rural investment scheme and efforts to get government ministers to relax by taking them on train journeys for 'mobile cabinet meetings'.

Thaksin Shinawatra was born on 26 July 1949 in the northern city of Chiang Mai. He has had a close association with the distinct northern cultural movement and has headed a number of groups dedicated to it, including the Northerners' Association of Thailand. His family (the family name is Shinawatra, although he is always referred to by his given name as Thaksin) operated a successful silk firm which diversified into buses and cinemas, giving him a taste of business management from an early age. Nonetheless, he found his vocation in the police force and graduated from the Police Cadet Academy in 1973. He married Khunying Potjaman Damapong in 1974 and the couple now have three children.

Winning a scholarship from the government, Thaksin travelled to the USA to study for a master's degree in criminal justice at the Eastern Kentucky University in Richmond. After graduating in 1974 he went on to the Sam Houston State University in Huntsville and received his doctorate in the same subject in 1978. He returned to Thailand to teach at the police academy and had risen to the rank of lieutenant-colonel by the time he left in 1987. In the interim he and his wife had founded a telecommunications company in 1982 that would grow eventually into the powerful Shin Corporation.

The company signed a contract with the police department to supply computer software in 1982 and Thaksin was able to resign his commission in 1987 to become full-time head of the firm, which went on to market a pager service and even a homegrown satellite communication system. In 1990 he signed a 20-year contract with the Telephone Organization of Thailand for a monopoly on mobile phone services. He was nominated by the Association of South East Asian Nations (ASEAN) as 'businessman of the year' in 1992. When he was invited in 1994 to enter the government he undertook to 'cleanse' himself for public service and resigned from all his positions within the Shin Corporation.

In 1994 he was appointed foreign minister and was affiliated to the Moral Force (Palang Dharma—PD) party. He was elevated to deputy prime minister and PD leader in 1995 and was charged with resolving the terrible traffic problems experienced by Bangkok. Although, somewhat predictably, he failed in his grand aims, he was retained as a deputy prime minister in the next government formed in 1997, but was forced from the cabinet later that year after its collapse. Soon after it had lost its position of power, the PD fell apart.

The following year Thaksin resolved to return to government and formed the enigmatic, populist TRT in July 1998. Promising to lead the country from its financial malaise by investing over US$1,000 million in the rural economy and clearing banks' bad debts, he led the TRT to a massive electoral victory in the polls in January 2001.

Thaksin's future as prime minister was briefly in question owing to a charge of failing to declare his personal assets. His successful defence was that he had forgotten about his decision to divulge his fortune into the hands of trusted family servants. (He was eventually acquitted of the charges in August 2001.) Soon after he came to power in February he was almost dramatically removed in March when a plane he was about to board exploded on the runway. Early claims of terrorism were later discounted by proof of a malfunction. In April 2001 Thaksin was overtaken as the country's richest man by his own son.

TOGO

Full name: The Republic of Togo.

Leadership structure: The head of state is a president, directly elected by universal adult suffrage. The president's term of office is five years. In December 2002 the National Assembly passed a constitutional amendment which would allow the president to seek re-election with no limit on the number of consecutive terms. The head of government is the prime minister, who is appointed by the president. The prime minister, in consultation with the president, appoints the other members of the Council of Ministers.

President: Gen. Gnassingbé Eyadéma — Since 14 April 1967
(seized power on 13 Jan. 1967)

Prime Ministers: Eugene Koffi Adoboli — 21 May 1999—31 Aug. 2000

Agbéyomè Messan Kodjo — 31 Aug. 2000—29 June 2002

Koffi Sama — Since 29 June 2002

Legislature: The legislature is unicameral. The sole chamber, the National Assembly (Assemblée Nationale), has 81 members, directly elected for a five-year term.

Profile of the President:

Gen. Gnassingbé **EYADÉMA**

Gen. Eyadéma, the former soldier and author of a bloodless coup in January 1967, has retained power ever since, despite a nominal conversion to multipartyism in the 1990s. His re-election as president in 1993, and again in 1998, drew vociferous opposition protests over intimidation, manipulation and fraud. Eyadéma justifies his regime for having maintained continuity of government and economic stability, although his use of repressive force has caused rifts with Western aid donors. A constitutional amendment in December 2002 allows him to seek further presidential terms without limit.

Etienne Eyadéma (who took the Kabyè name Gnassingbé in May 1974) was born on 26 December 1937 in the village of Pya, in the region of Kabyè in northern Togo. Entering the French colonial army as a teenager in 1953, he saw action in Benin (then known as Dahomey), Indochina, Algeria and Niger. However, following Togo's independence in 1960, he returned to his country in 1961. He was made adjutant in 1961, captain in 1963 and lieutenant-colonel in 1965, when he was also appointed army chief of staff.

In January 1967 he led a bloodless army coup against Nicolas Grunitzky's provisional government. In April 1967 he dissolved the Committee of National Reconciliation which had been set up, and appointed his own government, taking the posts of president and minister of national defence. In 1969 he formed the sole ruling Rally of the Togolese People (Rassemblement du Peuple Togolais—RPT), remaining its leader ever since. In 1972 he was confirmed as president in a national referendum in which he ran unopposed. In 1979 he declared a third republic and a transition to more civilian rule with a mixed civilian and military cabinet. A new constitution in 1980 provided for a National Assembly as a consultative body. He was re-elected for a third consecutive seven-year term in December 1986 with 99.5% of the vote in another uncontested election.

Between 1989 and 1991 there were clashes in Togo between anti-government demonstrators and security forces. Eyadéma agreed, under pressure, to the holding of a national conference on multipartyism. An interim constitution was drafted which provided for a one-year transitional regime followed by free elections and the formation of a new government. During the transitional period Eyadéma continued as chief of state, supposedly with limited powers, but he increased his role once again when the transition period was extended to the end of 1992. In a national referendum in 1992 voters overwhelmingly supported the new constitution, thus initiating Togo's fourth republic. In the presidential election on 25 August 1993 Eyadéma won 96% of the votes cast. The election was boycotted by opposition parties and he was once again unopposed.

Eyadéma has survived a number of assassination attempts. He faced an opposition majority in the legislature after elections in 1994, but the lack of opposition unity assisted the president in his determination to make his own government appointments. In mid-1996 the RPT regained a parliamentary majority by winning several seats in by-elections, while Eyadéma strengthened his grip by appointing a new prime minister and reshuffling the cabinet.

Presidential elections on 21 June 1998 were quickly mired in controversy after Eyadéma abruptly cancelled vote counting when it became apparent that he had fallen into second place. The then minister of the interior took over responsibility for the counting and Eyadéma was declared the winner with 52.1% of the vote. The announcement prompted violence in Lomé and condemnation from the international community. He continued to defy opposition pressure over the affair and the RPT swept to re-election in March 1999 amid an opposition boycott. Eyadéma's international image was damaged further when the human rights group Amnesty International accused his government of persecuting and killing opponents following the 1998 election.

Some political stability was restored when Eyadéma pledged in July 1999 not to stand again in 2003. In return, the opposition recognized his re-election and agreed to take part in fresh legislative elections. These polls were delayed by wrangling over the appointment of an electoral commission and, later, by protest at the arrest of senior opposition figures. After the government had at one point hinted that the vote would be put off until early 2003, elections were finally called for 27 October 2002. Yet again the opposition boycotted the vote and the RPT won a massive majority. Despite his 1999 pledge and the continuing anger of his opponents, Eyadéma pushed through a constitutional amendment on 30 December 2002 allowing him to stand for re-election the following year.

Gnassingbé Eyadéma is married to Badagnaki Eyadéma. His son Faure Gnassingbé is considered a possible successor, while other sons Ernest, Rock and Kpatcha Gnassingbé have been, respectively, head of the presidential guard, president of the national football federation and head of the development of the free trade zone. Gnékélé Gnassingbé, the daughter of Eyadéma and Badagnaki, has been placed in charge of her father's campaign for re-election in 2003.

Profile of the Prime Minister:

Koffi **SAMA**

Koffi Sama is a leading figure in the ruling Rally of the Togolese People (Rassemblement du Peuple Togolais—RPT). Originally trained as a vet, he worked in agricultural administration, and first entered the government in 1981. He was appointed prime minister on 29 June 2002.

Koffi Sama was born in 1944 in Amoutchou in eastern Togo. In 1966 he went to Toulouse, France, to study veterinary medicine at the French National Veterinary School. Specializing in hygiene, he graduated with a doctorate in 1972. He is now married with a family.

After returning to Togo in 1972, Sama held a number of positions in agricultural administration, beginning as head of the division of rural and industrial breeding and ending as director-general of the national office of abattoirs and refrigeration. In 1981 he entered the government as minister of youth, sports and culture. He left the cabinet in 1984 and was appointed regional director of rural development and the maritime region in 1986. From 1990 to 1996 he was director-general of the Togo Cotton Society.

In 1996 Sama was reappointed to the cabinet as minister of health. Three years later he was switched to the ministry of national education and research. While holding this latter portfolio he was made secretary-general of the RPT in December 2000. In June 2002, with fresh elections unexpectedly convened, President Gnassingbé Eyadéma dismissed the incumbent administration and appointed Sama as prime minister in a new cabinet. The RPT was re-elected in a landslide victory on 27 October 2002, in the face of an opposition boycott, and Sama retained his position.

TONGA

Full name: The Kingdom of Tonga.

Leadership structure: The king of Tonga is hereditary head of state. An appointed 11-member Privy Council functions as a cabinet, presided over by the king. The prime minister is head of government.

King:	Taufa'ahau Tupou IV	Since 16 Dec. 1965
Prime Ministers:	Baron Vaea	22 Aug. 1991—3 Jan. 2000
	Prince Ulukalala Lavaka Ata	Since 3 Jan. 2000

Legislature: The legislature is unicameral. The sole chamber, the 30-member Legislative Assembly (Fale Alea), consists of the king, Privy Council, nine hereditary nobles (elected by their peers) and nine popularly elected representatives. Elected representatives hold office for three years.

Profile of the King:

TAUFA'AHAU Tupou IV

Taufa'ahau Tupou IV, the son of the late Queen Salote Tupou III, became the king of Tonga in 1965. Australian-educated, a keen mathematician and a Wesleyan lay preacher, he is a direct descendant of King George Tupou I, who is considered to be the founder of modern Tonga.

Crown Prince Siaosi Taufa'ahau Tupoulahi was born on 4 July 1918 in the royal palace in Tonga. He was the first monarch to receive a Western education, attending Newington College and Sydney University in Australia, graduating both in the arts and law. His mother appointed him minister of education in 1943, and soon afterwards he established a teacher training college and revised the Tongan alphabet; in 1947 he founded the Tonga High School. In 1944 he was made minister of health, a post he held until he became premier in 1949. While premier he was also responsible for foreign affairs and for agriculture.

Taufa'ahau succeeded to the throne on 16 December 1965 on the death of his mother. His coronation was held on 4 July 1967. He is a member of the International Mathematics Association. He is a lay preacher of the Free Wesleyan Church, and holds a special position giving him the conditional right to appoint an acting president of the Church. Between 1970 and 1973 he was chancellor of the South Pacific University.

King Taufa'ahau and his wife Queen Halaevalu Mata'aho, who married in 1947, have three sons and one daughter. Their eldest child Crown Prince Tupouto'a is heir to the throne and their third son Prince Ulukalala Lavaka Ata has been prime minister since 2000.

Profile of the Prime Minister:

Ulukalala **LAVAKA ATA**

Prince Ulukalala Lavaka Ata was appointed by his father King Taufa'ahau Tupou IV as Tonga's prime minister for life on 3 January 2000. His appointment took the country by surprise as it was widely expected that his elder brother Crown Prince Tupouto'a would be appointed. A staunch conservative and an opponent of the democratic movement which Tupouto'a has championed, Lavaka Ata is constitutionally subordinate to his father who appoints the cabinet.

Prince 'Aho'eitu' Unuaki'otonga Tuku'aho was born into the ruling Ha'a Havea clan on 12 July 1959. He was the fourth child, and third son, of the then Crown Prince Siaosi Taufa'ahau Tupoulahi, who ascended the throne of Tonga on 16 December 1965. He was granted the titles Ulukalala and Lavaka Ata in 1989. As a member of the royal family he completed a commission as a naval officer. The prince married Heuifanga Nanasipau'u, daughter of Baron Vaea of Houma (who was Tonga's prime minister from 1991 to 2000), on 11 December 1982. Lavaka Ata holds two university degrees at master's level, the second of them (a degree in international relations from the small, private University of Bond in Australia) awarded as recently as 1999.

In 1998 Lavaka Ata was appointed to the cabinet by his father to fulfil the role of minister of foreign affairs and defence. This post had been vacated by his elder brother Tupouto'a, who had resigned from politics to pursue his various business interests after quarrelling with the king over proposed democratic reforms, including the abolishment of the permanent premiership.

The continuing dispute left Lavaka Ata in a position, as a supporter of Taufa'ahau's authoritarian rule, to take over the premiership in 2000. Lavaka Ata cancelled his plans to pursue a doctoral degree in Australia when the king finally accepted the long-proffered resignation of the aging Baron Vaea, and appointed Lavaka Ata in his stead. Lavaka Ata retained the foreign affairs and defence portfolios, and also has ministerial responsibilities for agriculture and fisheries and for civil aviation and communications.

Lavaka Ata's opposition to change is reflected in his connections with the conservative Wesleyan Church, in which he is a lay preacher like his father. Whereas his elder brother looked set to question their father's powers of appointment and rule, Lavaka Ata has been happier to accept the status quo in the country, confounding the hopes of the younger generation.

TRINIDAD AND TOBAGO

Full name: The Republic of Trinidad and Tobago.

Leadership structure: The head of state is a president, elected by an electoral college comprising both houses of Parliament. The president's term of office is five years. The head of government is the prime minister, who is responsible to Parliament. The Council of Ministers is appointed by the prime minister.

President:	Arthur N. Robinson	Since 19 March 1997
Prime Ministers:	Basdeo Panday	9 Nov. 1995—24 Dec. 2001
	Patrick Manning	Since 24 Dec. 2001

Legislature: The legislature, the Parliament of Trinidad and Tobago, is bicameral. The lower chamber, the House of Representatives, has 36 members, directly elected for a five-year term. The upper chamber, the Senate, has 31 members, appointed by the president on the advice of the prime minister and leader of the opposition for a five-year term. Tobago's legislature is a unicameral House of Assembly with 15 members, 12 of them elected and three chosen by the House for a four-year term.

Profile of the President:

Arthur N. **ROBINSON**

Arthur Robinson, long the dominant political figure on the island of Tobago, had been part of Trinidad and Tobago's first postindependence government in 1962, and was prime minister in 1985–91, before his election to the largely ceremonial role of president in 1997. A lawyer by training, he also has a degree from Oxford in philosophy, politics and economics.

Arthur Napoleon Raymond Robinson was born on 16 December 1926. Having taken an external law degree with London University, Robinson went to the UK in 1951, passed his Bar examinations and graduated in philosophy, politics and economics from St John's College, Oxford. Returning to Trinidad and Tobago in 1955, he practised as a lawyer from 1957 to 1961, and was first elected to the Federal Parliament of the West Indies in 1958. He married Patricia Jean Rawlins in 1961, and they have a son and a daughter.

Robinson was one of the founders of the People's National Movement (PNM) which led Trinidad and Tobago to independence in 1962. At various times between 1962 and 1970, when he resigned from the PNM, he served as minister of finance, of external affairs, and as deputy prime minister to Eric Williams.

In the course of his long political career, Robinson campaigned from the mid-1970s to the mid-1980s for the devolution of power to Tobago, and sought to access UN funds to reduce local poverty. He was also, in 1971, consultant to the Foundation for the Establishment of an International Criminal Court, a cause for which he has campaigned ever since. He chaired the Democratic Action Congress from 1971 until 1986, when he was instrumental in its merger with other opposition parties to form the National Alliance for Reconstruction (NAR).

As the NAR's leader, he was sworn in as prime minister after its sweeping success in the 1986 legislative elections. In a dramatic incident in July 1990, he was briefly held hostage in the parliament building by militant Black Muslims as part of an attempted coup. Robinson's government was unpopular because of its reliance on severe austerity measures to address its economic problems, and in the December 1991 legislative elections he was one of only two NAR members to retain their seats. Taking responsibility for this crushing defeat, Robinson resigned the party leadership.

From November 1995 until his election as president in February 1997, he returned to government (in which the NAR was a junior coalition partner) as minister extraordinaire for Tobago, the UN and international organizations, and adviser to the prime minister.

Robinson's presidency has been characterized by conflict between himself and the previous United National Congress (UNC) prime minister, Basdeo Panday. In January 2000 Robinson refused to endorse the dismissal of two Tobagan senators, claiming it would harm interisland relations. The ensuing public row between himself and Panday, including accusations of defamatory remarks and the cessation of their weekly meetings, did little to provide political stability.

The situation worsened in January 2001 when Robinson refused to approve the appointment of seven cabinet ministers as they had not won seats in the December 2000 legislative elections. Analysts argued that while Robinson had accused Panday of dictatorship over the nominations, it was the president who was inflating his own constitutional role. His clear preference for the PNM was made apparent when, after fresh elections in December 2001 which produced a historic tie between the PNM and the UNC, he chose PNM leader Patrick Manning as prime minister. Panday, who had agreed to abide by Robinson's decision, condemned the appointment.

Robinson remained in office after his term was due to expire in March 2002 because the House of Representatives proved consistently unable to agree on a speaker, and therefore could not convene to elect a new president.

Profile of the Prime Minister:

Patrick **MANNING**

Patrick Manning leads the right-of-centre People's National Movement (PNM). Originally trained as a geologist, he entered government service in the early 1970s and went on to have a prominent political career. He was prime minister from 1991 to 1995 and regained power in 2001 amid unprecedented political wrangling.

Patrick Augustus Mervyn Manning was born on 17 August 1946 in San Fernando, western Trinidad. After leaving school in 1965 he spent a year as a refinery operator with the oil giant Texaco in Pointe-à-Pierre, just to the north of San Fernando. He travelled to Jamaica in 1966 to study geology at the University of the West Indies, and returned to Point-à-Pierre in 1969 to apply his new knowledge in the service of his former employer. Two years later he swapped geology for the world of politics and was elected to represent San Fernando East constituency for the PNM. He married Hazel Anne-Marie Kinsale in 1972 and they have two sons.

Between 1971 and 1978 Manning served as a parliamentary secretary for various ministers in the PNM governments of the time. He shuttled between the ministry of petroleum, the prime minister's office and ended at the ministry of works, transport and communications. In 1978 he was appointed to the cabinet as a junior minister in the ministry of finance, and added a position in the prime minister's office in 1979. He became a full minister for the first time in 1981 as minister of information and minister of industry and commerce. He went on to serve as minister of energy and natural resources from 1981 to 1986.

Since 1987 Manning has been leader of the PNM. As such he led it in opposition until its triumphal return to power in 1991. His policies as prime minister of economic liberalization and privatization brought praise and investment from abroad, but failed to captivate the electorate. The PNM was forced from power once again in 1995 and Manning returned to his post as leader of the opposition. The party fared badly in the 2000 elections, as the centre-left United National Congress (UNC) climbed to a simple majority.

The UNC majority proved fragile, however, and in December 2001 fresh elections were held which resulted in an unprecedented tie of 18 seats each for the PNM and the UNC. President Arthur Robinson was left to choose the premier and plumped for Manning, much to the anger of the UNC. Manning agreed to hold fresh elections within the year. In October 2002 the PNM was returned with an indisputable majority of its own and Manning was reconfirmed as prime minister.

TUNISIA

Full name: The Republic of Tunisia.

Leadership structure: The head of state is a president, directly elected by universal adult suffrage. The president's term of office is five years. A referendum, held on 26 May 2002, approved changes to the constitution to allow the incumbent president to seek a fourth term in 2004, which also necessitated raising the maximum permitted age of candidates. The head of government is the president, who is responsible to the Chamber of Deputies. The Council of Ministers is appointed by the president.

President:	Zine el-Abidine Ben Ali	Since 7 Nov. 1987
Prime Minister:	Mohammed Ghannouchi	Since 17 Nov. 1999

Legislature: The legislature is unicameral. The sole chamber, the Chamber of Deputies (Majlis al-Nuwaab), has 182 members, directly elected for a five-year term. The May 2002 referendum approved the formation of a second chamber.

Profile of the President:

Zine el-Abidine **BEN ALI**

Gen. Zine el-Abidine Ben Ali is a former military and intelligence specialist, and only the second president of Tunisia since independence in 1956. Having taken over in 1987 when Habib Bourguiba was deposed on grounds of senility, he was confirmed in power in successive direct elections in 1989, 1994 and 1999. On each occasion he was credited with over 99% of the vote, even though on the third occasion he faced nominal opposition from two other candidates.

Zine el-Abidine Ben Ali was born in Hammam Sousse on 3 September 1936. He was expelled from secondary school for political activism. Initially trained in electronics at the military academy in Saint-Cyr in France, he was later educated in all aspects of military intelligence at the artillery school in Châlons-sur-Marne (France) and at the senior intelligence school in Maryland (USA). Unlike Bourguiba, who was an agnostic, Ben Ali is a practising Muslim, even though his training and policies are primarily Western in orientation. He is married with three daughters.

He began his working career as a military officer, and was the director of Tunisia's military intelligence security department from 1964 to 1974. For the

527

next three years he was attaché to Spain and Morocco with general responsibility for defence, military and naval matters. By 1977 he had risen to the position of director-general of national security and was responsible for curbing protests by striking workers in 1978 and bringing under control an uprising by Islamic fundamentalists in the mining town of Gafsa in January 1980. Later that year, however, he was removed from his post and sent as ambassador to Poland.

In 1984 he entered the cabinet as minister of national security, and in 1986 was appointed secretary-general of the ruling Destour Socialist Party (Parti Socialiste Destourien—PSD), which had been the sole legal political party from 1964 until 1981. From 1986 until he commenced his presidency, Ben Ali was minister of the interior and from October 1987 he was also prime minister. His assumption of the presidency on 7 November 1987, in a move backed by the military, signalled the first change in executive power since Bourguiba had led Tunisia to independence in 1956.

In 1988 Ben Ali changed the name of the PSD to the Constitutional Democratic Rally (Rassemblement Constitutionnel Démocratique—RCD) as part of a process which sought to reflect a climate of increased openness and legitimacy. He has since been re-elected with massive majorities in April 1989, March 1994 and most recently in October 1999, while the RCD has consistently won the vast majority of seats in the Chamber of Deputies. The most recent (1999) poll was the first to be contested by other candidates, but nonetheless Ben Ali secured 99.45% of the vote. The quasi-unanimity of his endorsements has been tainted by the frequent arrest-release-rearrest of opposition pro-democracy activists.

In September 2001 the RCD defied the constitution to nominate the president to stand for a fourth term in office in 2004. In order to legitimize his candidacy, Ben Ali organized the country's first ever referendum on 26 May 2002, in which 99% of voters approved abolishing the three-term limit and raising the maximum age for presidents from 70 to 75 years of age. The referendum also included provisions to introduce a second parliamentary chamber and pledges to improve human rights.

Ben Ali has been criticized for failing to introduce a genuinely pluralist form of politics in Tunisia, and for his harsh treatment of Islamic fundamentalist groups. Mindful of the turmoil in neighbouring Algeria, he has maintained a hard line in an attempt to preserve stability and thus ensure continued income from tourism, the country's largest source of foreign currency earnings.

Profile of the Prime Minister:

Mohammed **GHANNOUCHI**

Mohammed Ghannouchi is a leading member of the ruling Constitutional Democratic Rally (Rassemblement Constitutionnel Démocratique—RCD). A career politician and economist, he entered the ministry of planning in 1966 and was first appointed to the cabinet in 1987. His appointment as prime minister in November 1999 was seen as confirming the government's commitment to economic liberalization.

Mohammed Ghannouchi was born near Sousse on 18 August 1941. He graduated from the Tunis University of Law, Political Sciences and Economics (now the University of Tunis III) with a degree in economics in 1966 and went straight to work for the ministry of planning. Ten years later he was appointed general director of planning.

In 1987, after Gen. Zine el-Abidine Ben Ali had assumed power as prime minister, Ghannouchi was inducted into government as minister of planning. From 1989 he was also minister of finance, and minister of national economy and finance from 1990. A year later he was made simply minister of finance and in 1992 his role was specialized as minister of international co-operation and foreign investment. For the rest of the 1990s Ghannouchi was crucial to Tunisia's negotiations with international financial institutions such as the World Bank, the International Monetary Fund (IMF) and the European Union (EU). Consequently he gained international exposure and a reputation for supporting liberal economics. In 1995 he oversaw the signing of a free trade zone agreement with the EU.

Following the re-election of President Ben Ali and the RCD in 1999, Ghannouchi was appointed prime minister on 17 November. His nomination sent a clear message to the international community that Tunisia was eager to embrace the economic policies of the West.

TURKEY

Full name: The Republic of Turkey.

Leadership structure: The head of state is a president, elected by the Turkish Grand National Assembly. The president's term of office is seven years, not renewable. Parliament rejected various proposals submitted in February 2000 to make the presidency directly elected, and to enable a president to serve two five-year terms. The head of government is the prime minister, who is appointed by the president. The cabinet is appointed by the prime minister.

Presidents:	Süleyman Demirel	16 May 1993—16 May 2000
	Ahmet Necdet Sezer	Since 16 May 2000
Prime Ministers:	Bülent Ecevit	11 Jan. 1999—18 Nov. 2002
	Abdullah Gül	Since 18 Nov. 2002

Legislature: The legislature is unicameral. The sole chamber, the Turkish Grand National Assembly (Türkiye Büyük Millet Meclisi), has 550 members, directly elected for a five-year term.

Profile of the President:

Ahmet Necdet **SEZER**

Ahmet Sezer, a judge by training and chief of the Constitutional Court from 1998 until May 2000, was then chosen as a last-minute apolitical candidate to succeed the popular Süleyman Demirel as president. A reserved and uncharismatic figure, he is only the fourth civilian to hold this largely ceremonial post, and the first holder to be neither a general nor a politician. From the beginning he has stressed his commitment to democracy and urged reforms to help Turkey head towards membership of the European Union (EU).

Ahmet Necdet Sezer was born in Afyon in west-central Anatolia on 13 September 1941. He attended secondary school in the town before heading to Ankara in 1958 to study law. He graduated with a degree from the University of Ankara in 1962 and began his career as a judge in the city in the same year. After completing a period in the Land Forces Academy as part of his military service, he moved to the town of Dicle in the southeast near the border with Syria, where he again worked as a judge. In the 1970s Sezer was back in Ankara after being appointed as a supervisory judge at the High Court of Appeals. He returned to the capital's university and received a master's degree in civil law in 1978. Five years later he was elected to be a full judge at the High Court of Appeals and served in this capacity for a further five years.

Sezer, who is married with three children, was appointed by the president in 1988 to work in the Constitutional Court and by 1998 he was the court's chief justice. His reputation as a no-nonsense advocate of secular democracy was forged in this role when he pronounced a ban on the main Islamic party of the time in 1998. He has since stressed his strong belief that a secular state is a "must for democracy". He also made a strongly worded speech in April 1999 calling for profound constitutional changes to the military-dictated constitution which has been in place since a coup in 1980. His pleas centred on Turkey's much condemned policies limiting freedom of speech and expression.

When President Demirel's seven-year term expired in early 2000, the prime minister, Bülent Ecevit, made a last-minute plea to maintain a sense of continuity and harmony in the Grand National Assembly by allowing him to serve on for a second term. Only when this failed did Sezer's name arise as a suitable nonpartisan replacement. Despite his public popularity, a number of politicians questioned his lack of political experience. After failing to win the necessary majorities in the first two votes, due largely to protest voting from deputies, Sezer was eventually elected in May 2000 by 330 of the Assembly's 550 possible votes.

Within hours of his election Sezer made his first public comments and immediately called for further and faster political reform, stating that "democracy and democratic values" were essential in creating a "social state of law". He has also urged greater economic reforms based on an inspection of public spending and rates of inflation in an attempt to redress disparities in income. Essentially Sezer's main task is to help to align Turkey with the policies of the EU to enable the country's eventual admission.

Profile of the Prime Minister:

Abdullah **GÜL**

Abdullah Gül is deputy leader of the pro-Islamist Justice and Development Party (Adelet ve Kalkinma Partisi—AK). A trained economist, he returned from a career with the Islamic Development Bank in 1991 to engage in domestic politics. He was prominent in both the Welfare Party (Refah Partisi—RP) and then the Virtue Party (Fazilet Partisi—FP), successively banned as unconstitutionally Islamist in 1998 and 2001 respectively, before helping to found the ostensibly secular AK in 2001. Following the AK's November 2002 election victory, he became prime minister in lieu of party leader Recep Tayyip Erdogan who is banned from politics.

Abdullah Gül was born in the central city of Kayseri on 29 October 1950. The city sits in Turkey's conservative heartland and his father unsuccessfully ran for parliament in 1973 for the Islamist movement of future prime minister Necmettin Erbakan. In the meantime Gül had graduated in economics from the University of Istanbul in 1971 and stayed on there to pursue postgraduate qualifications, and eventually a doctorate in 1983. His studies included a two-year stay in the UK at universities in London and Exeter. He is married and has three children.

In 1983 Gül went to Saudi Arabia to take up a position as an economics expert at the Islamic Development Bank in Jeddah. He stayed there for eight years before returning to Turkey in 1991, when he became an associate professor and was successfully elected to parliament for the Welfare Party. Two years later he was elected deputy leader in charge of foreign affairs. In this role he travelled the world, raising his profile and expounding the party's policies abroad. In 1995 Gül was re-elected to parliament on the back of a significant victory for Welfare. Although the party was initially kept from power, it entered government in 1996 and Gül was appointed minister of state for foreign affairs under Prime Minister Erbakan.

Fearing for the country's secular constitution, the army ousted the Welfare government in 1997 and Erbakan was banned. The Islamist political movement, reconstituted as the Virtue Party, was forced to reflect on its approach and Gül emerged as a prominent champion of the modernist wing. He renounced overt Islamic politics and accepted that Erbakan had made mistakes in his approach. In 1999 Gül was re-elected to parliament and in 2000 he contested the party leadership, representing the reformists. He came within 60 votes of winning the internal ballot. The party was banned in June 2000 for its apparent anti-secularism and the Islamist camp split firmly in two. The moderates, including Gül, established the AK in August and abandoned all calls for the establishment of an Islamic political society. Gül was made its deputy leader behind Erdogan.

The AK's popularity was boosted by Erdogan's high profile and by the failures of the incumbent right-wing government. In November 2002 it won a spectacular outright majority at the polls. Gül was called upon to become prime minister, as Erdogan remained banned for previous militant comments. However, it was clear that the AK leader would exert considerable influence, and would take over the premiership himself if he succeeded in overturning his ban. Gül has pledged to make Turkey's application to join the European Union (EU) his main priority.

TURKMENISTAN

Full name: Turkmenistan.

Leadership structure: The head of state is a president, directly elected by universal adult suffrage. Under the constitution the president's term of office is five years, renewable once only, but the term of incumbent president Saparmurad Niyazov has been extended indefinitely. The head of government is the president, who appoints the Council of Ministers.

President: Saparmurad Niyazov   Since 27 Oct. 1990
               (chairman of Supreme Soviet from 19 Jan. 1990)

Legislature: The legislature is unicameral. The sole chamber, the Parliament (Majlis), has 50 members, directly elected for a five-year term. The People's Council (Khalk Maslakhaty), which is the supreme representative and supervisory body (but not legislative or executive), includes 50 directly elected members, the 50 members of the Parliament, ten appointed members and a varying number of ex officio members.

Profile of the President:

Saparmurad **NIYAZOV**

Saparmurad Niyazov, the first elected president of the Turkmenistan republic within the Soviet Union, remained in office as the republic moved to independence with the collapse of the Soviet system. An engineer by training, he was previously the first secretary of the Communist Party of Turkmenistan (CPT) in 1985–90. Since independence he has promoted a cult of personality, and had his term of office extended first for five years and then indefinitely. In February 2001 Niyazov promised that presidential elections would be held in 2010.

Saparmurad Niyazov was born on 18 February 1940 and grew up in the capital, Ashkhabad. His father died in the Second World War, and in 1948 he lost most of his remaining close family in the Ashkhabad earthquake. He is now married and has one son and one daughter.

Niyazov studied physics and mathematics at the Leningrad Polytechnic School in 1962–66, and graduated as a power engineer. From 1959 to 1967 he was a member of the All-Union Central Trade Union Council, working as an instructor for mineral prospecting works in Turkmenistan. From 1967 to 1970 he worked at the Bezmeinskaya hydroelectric power station.

In 1962 Niyazov joined the CPT, and by 1970 he had risen to the position of instructor, then department head, within its central committee. He was first secretary of the CPT central committee for Ashkhabad in 1980–84, and in 1985 was appointed first secretary for Turkmenistan, the highest party post in the republic. In this capacity, like the 14 other first secretaries of the republics making up the Soviet Union, Niyazov was brought into the politburo of the Communist Party of the Soviet Union (CPSU) in the major restructuring of that organ in July 1990.

Niyazov became chairman of the Turkmenistan Supreme Soviet, in effect the republic's head of state, in January 1990. He held the republic's new directly elective presidency as a result of elections in October 1990 when he won what was recorded as 98.3% of the vote, and became commander-in-chief of the armed forces. The CPT was renamed in 1991 as the Democratic Party of Turkmenistan (DPT), with Niyazov continuing as its chairman. In the first elections held after full independence, in June 1992, he was confirmed in his post as president with 99.5% of the vote.

Closing his grip on power, Niyazov has instituted a grandiose cult of personality. In 1993 the Parliament conferred upon him the title Turkmenbashi—'father of the Turkmen people'. Among the monuments to the president in Ashkhabad is a 12-metre-high construction featuring a revolving gold-plated statue of Niyazov which permanently faces the sun. His guide to life, the *Ruhnama*, was adopted as a 'national code' in October 2001 and is now required reading for university applicants, while the Parliament debated conferring the additional title of 'prophet' on him that year. Behind the flamboyance lies an increasingly apparent tendency for authoritarianism and isolation.

Politically Niyazov has tried to make his position unassailable. A referendum in January 1994 on a five-year extension (until 2002) of his term in office was approved with a recorded 99.9% endorsement. This was superseded on 28 December 1999 when the Parliament unanimously voted to remove the limit to the length of his term in office altogether. To counterbalance these moves, Niyazov declared in February 2001 that he would step down before he turns 70 in 2010. Opposition to him is growing. Although political debate is seriously curtailed, certain exiled figures have appeared as potential rivals. On 25 November 2002 gunmen opened fire on the president's motorcade in the capital and Niyazov immediately blamed 'foreign' sources, principally his former foreign minister Boris Shikhmuradov. After a public confession Shikhmuradov was arrested on 29 December.

TUVALU

Full name: Tuvalu.

Leadership structure: The head of state is the British sovereign, styled 'Queen of Tuvalu, and of Her other Realms and Territories, Head of the Commonwealth', and represented by a governor-general who is appointed on the advice of the Tuvaluan prime minister. The head of government is the prime minister, who is elected by MPs from among their number. The cabinet is appointed by the governor-general on the advice of the prime minister.

Queen:	Elizabeth II	Since 6 Feb. 1952
Governor-General:	Sir Tomasi Puapua	Since 26 June 1998
Prime Ministers:	Ionatana Ionatana	27 April 1999—8 Dec. 2000
	Lagitupu Tuilimu (acting)	8 Dec. 2000—24 Feb. 2001
	Faimalaga Luka	24 Feb. 2001—14 Dec. 2001
	Koloa Talake	14 Dec. 2001—2 Aug. 2002
	Saufatu Sopoanga	Since 2 Aug. 2002

Legislature: The legislature is unicameral. The sole chamber, the Parliament of Tuvalu (Palamene o Tuvalu), currently has 15 members, directly elected for a four-year term. The constitution stipulates a minimum of 12 members, with more added by Act of Parliament to account for changes in population and boundaries of each electoral district, and any other special circumstances.

Profile of the Governor-General:

Sir Tomasi **PUAPUA**

Sir Tomasi Puapua is a qualified doctor, and has been one of the country's most prominent political figures since independence. He was prime minister in the 1980s and a senior figure in Parliament during the 1990s, until his appointment as governor-general in 1998. Two weeks before his inauguration in June as governor-general he received a knighthood in the queen's birthday honours for "services to medicine, politics and the community".

Tomasi Puapua was born on 10 September 1938, in what was then the British colony of the Ellice Islands. He was educated locally before heading to the British colony of Fiji where he attended the Fiji School of Medicine. He completed his training as a doctor at the University of Otago in Dunedin, southeastern New Zealand. Once qualified he worked as a practitioner. He married Riana Tabokai, from neighbouring Kiribati (then known as the British-administered Gilbert Islands), in 1971 and they have four children.

Puapua began a career in politics in the newly autonomous government of Tuvalu in the late 1970s. He stood successfully as one of the two representatives from the central island of Vaitupu.

As Tuvalu passed from autonomy to full independence in 1978, Puapua served as minister for the civil service administration and local government, and as minister of foreign affairs. His growing political profile secured him the nomination as prime minister when the first premier, Toaripi Lauti, stepped down in 1981 amid an alleged corruption scandal. Puapua won the vote in September that year and was re-elected in 1985. During his term in office he unsuccessfully backed efforts to edge the country towards republicanism. A referendum on the issue was soundly defeated in 1986.

Puapua was ousted as premier in elections in 1989 by his major political rival Bikenibeu Paeniu. After four years in opposition Puapua once again contested the prime ministerial election in 1993. Both he and Paeniu received six votes in the 12-seat Parliament, leading to two months of political deadlock until Puapua agreed to step down in favour of parliamentary speaker Kamuta Latasi, who went on to win the next vote in December. Puapua took on the vacant role of speaker and presided as such until his nomination as governor-general in 1998. In 1996 he joined a group of high-level parliamentarians who withdrew their support for Latasi, thereby returning Paeniu to power for another 18 months.

As governor-general, Puapua has pleaded to the industrialized world to consider the consequences of global warming for oceanic nations such as Tuvalu.

Profile of the Prime Minister:

Saufatu **SOPOANGA**

Saufatu Sopoanga, whose election as prime minister was achieved by the slimmest of majorities with eight votes in his favour and seven against in the parliament on 2 August 2002, had been finance minister in the outgoing parliament. He made a name for himself at the UN summit on sustainable development in Johannesburg the following month with his measured but eloquent advocacy of effective measures to combat global warning, in sympathy with other island states whose very existence is menaced—like Tuvalu's—by rising ocean levels.

Saufatu Sopoanga was born on 22 February 1952 in Nukufetau atoll. He began work in the colonial administration of the then Ellice Islands in 1973, acting as a permanent secretary to various ministries between 1975 and 1995. During this time he also studied development administration at various institutions in the UK, receiving postgraduate qualifications from the South Devon Technical College, Torquay, in 1978, and the University of Manchester in 1992. He was awarded a master's degree from the University of Liverpool in 1993. Sopoanga is married and has one son and three daughters.

From 1996 Sopoanga acted as a state secretary, the highest position in the Tuvaluan civil service. He retired from the service in October 2000 and successfully contested a seat in Parliament in 2001. His predecessor as prime minister, Koloa Talake, then brought him into the cabinet as finance minister in December 2001. After Talake lost his seat in the parliamentary elections of 25 July 2002, Sopoanga defeated the opposition candidate Amasone Kilei in the parliamentary vote to choose Talake's successor. On taking office, Sopoanga (who also holds the foreign affairs and labour portfolios) said he wanted to draw up a development plan for the country in an effort to improve health and education.

As prime minister, Sopoanga has spoken eloquently about the danger posed by global warming to his country and others like it. Warning that inaction on the issue could see Tuvalu disappear beneath the ocean within 50 years, he told delegates at the Johannesburg summit: "We want our nation to exist for ever and ever and not to be drowned because of the greed of the industrialized world." He has strongly criticized the USA and Australia for their opposition to mandatory targets on cutting 'greenhouse gas' emissions, which were stipulated in the international Kyoto protocol agreement as a first step to bringing man-made global warming under control.

On the domestic political front, Sopoanga has also given support to the idea of a referendum on future constitutional arrangements, including the possibility of Tuvalu becoming a republic and adopting a system of direct election of the head of government. He favours this as offering a better prospect of stable leadership than the current system whereby the prime minister is elected—and can as readily be ousted—by the notoriously fractious Parliament.

UGANDA

Full name: The Republic of Uganda.

Leadership structure: The head of state is a president, directly elected by universal adult suffrage. The president's term of office is five years. The president is also head of government and appoints the cabinet.

President:	Yoweri Museveni	Since 29 Jan. 1986
	(took power on 26 Jan. 1986)	
Prime Minister:	Apollo Nsibambi	Since 6 April 1999

Legislature: The legislature is unicameral. The sole chamber, the Parliament, has 276 members, serving a five-year term. Of these, 214 are elected by constituencies and 62 are elected indirectly to represent particular groups including women, youth and the disabled. Cabinet ministers who are not already members of the Parliament are ex officio members of it, as is the vice president.

Profile of the President:

Yoweri **MUSEVENI**

Yoweri Museveni presides over a nonparty system based on his National Resistance Movement (NRM), and was most recently re-elected as president in March 2001. He originally came to prominence in the Tanzanian-backed intervention in 1979 to remove the regime of Idi Amin. Soon rebelling once more, against the dictatorial rule of Milton Obote, he waged a five-year guerrilla struggle, culminating in the ousting in 1986 of a military regime which had deposed Obote the previous year. Since then Museveni is credited not only with having restored peace in the strife-ridden country, but also with having done much to revive the economy.

Yoweri Kaguta Museveni was born in 1944 in Ntungamo in southwest Uganda. He studied locally before reading political science, economics and education at Dar es Salaam University in Tanzania in 1967–70. Closely linked during his student days with the Marxist guerrilla Front for the Liberation of Mozambique, he also chaired the University Students' African Revolutionary Front, a pan-Africanist and anti-colonialist organization.

Returning to Uganda, he worked briefly as a research assistant at the office of President Milton Obote, until Gen. Idi Amin overthrew the government in 1971.

Museveni fled back to Tanzania, where in 1973 he married a fellow Ugandan and fellow Christian, Janet Kataaha; they have one son and three daughters. While teaching at Moshi Co-operative College in Tanzania, Museveni set up an exile Front for National Salvation. This organization grew to the point where it could claim a fighting strength of up to 9,000, and in 1979 it was part of the ad hoc coalition which launched a bid to overthrow Amin. Heavily backed by Tanzanian forces, the Uganda National Liberation Front succeeded in driving out Amin. Museveni served briefly as defence minister in an interim government and vice chairman of a subsequent military commission pending the holding of a general election in 1980.

Museveni stood as a candidate of the Uganda Patriotic Movement in the 1980 election, but returned to guerrilla resistance when Obote's Uganda People's Congress hijacked the poll with blatant ballot-rigging to ensure its own victory. Museveni spent the next five years waging a gradually growing insurgency, as founder and leader of the National Resistance Army (NRA), against the Obote regime. Effectively without external support, his guerrilla forces gained ground in the south and west. When the NRA was unable to reach an agreement with the military government that had toppled Obote in mid-1985, it began a rapid advance towards the capital, Kampala, where in January 1986 the government of Gen. Tito Okello collapsed. Museveni took power himself on 26 January, ans was sworn in as president and minister of defence three days later.

In power, Museveni continued to project himself as a 'freedom fighter'. While urging national reconciliation, he had also to contend with continuing violence in the north in particular for the first years of his rule. Although his NRM-based regime emphasized nonalignment internationally, Museveni established sufficient credibility with foreign aid donors to attract sustained backing from the World Bank for economic reconstruction work. He built up regional links particularly through the southern African Preferential Trade Area, and was chairman in 1990–91 of the Organization of African Unity (OAU—now the African Union).

A new constitution, the product of lengthy consultation over two years, came into effect in 1995, providing for an elective presidency and a mainly elective Parliament. Museveni won the presidential election on 9 May 1996, campaigning with the slogan "No Change" and taking almost 75% of the vote against two other candidates. The legislative elections held on a nonparty basis in late June of the same year produced an assembly in which the president's supporters held a clear majority. Just over 90% of voters backed the No Change formula again in a referendum held on 29 June 2000, despite opposition calls for a boycott.

The presidential election campaign in 2000–01 was a tense race between Museveni and Kizza Besigye. The opposition accused the government of intimidation. Museveni's campaign was aided by an increase in regional tensions and rumours that Besigye had received illegal funding from the 'hostile' regime in neighbouring Rwanda. In the event, Museveni was resoundingly re-elected with 69.3% of the vote on 12 March 2001, with Besigye receiving only 27.8%.

International observers echoed opposition unease over the level of pre-electoral intimidation. Pro-Museveni candidates went on to win a majority in the June legislative elections. By the end of 2001 Museveni had established a committee to evaluate alternatives to the movement system, including full democracy.

Museveni's second term has been dominated by the re-intensification of the conflict in the north of the country with the brutal Lord's Resistance Army and a rebellion in the west in 2000. In response Museveni has dropped plans to cut defence spending in favour of funding an improvement of the armed forces and a crackdown on corruption in the military. He has also pushed for the withdrawal of Ugandan troops from the neighbouring Democratic Republic of the Congo (DRC), where his own brother was named by the UN in 2001 on a list of people accused of plundering the DRC's resources under cover of war.

Profile of the Prime Minister:

Apollo **NSIBAMBI**

Apollo Nsibambi has an academic background in economics and political science, working on issues of governance and development in Africa. He was one of a key group of Baganda intellectuals whose support for Yoweri Museveni helped swing this ethnic constituency, Uganda's largest, behind the president in the 1996 elections. He joined the cabinet shortly afterwards, rising within three years to the premiership.

Apollo Nsibambi was born on 27 November 1938. He gained a degree in economics from London, UK, in 1964, a master's degree in political science from Chicago, USA, in 1966 and a doctorate from Nairobi, Kenya, in 1984. He taught political science in higher education, becoming a professor, head of department, and in 1993 dean of the faculty of social sciences at Makerere University in Kampala, as well as director of the Makerere Institute of Social Research and vice chairman of the Council of the Christian University of East Africa. It was at Makerere that he met his wife Rhoda, who taught there for over 30 years; she died in 2001, leaving four daughters.

Unlike many teachers and intellectuals who went into exile during the violence of the Amin regime and the long years of civil war, Nsibambi remained in Uganda, working in higher education, throughout the 1970s and 1980s. He also had some experience in government, as minister of constitutional and political affairs and human rights in the regional government of the kingdom of Buganda, before serving as a delegate on the Uganda Constituent Assembly in 1994. Following the 1996 elections, in which the king of Buganda and intellectual leaders such as Nsibambi were influential in swaying the sizable Baganda vote behind Museveni, he was appointed in July 1996 to the Ugandan government as minister of public service. In May 1998 he became minister of education and sports, and in April 1999 Museveni appointed him prime minister.

UKRAINE

Full name: Ukraine.

Leadership structure: The head of state is a president, directly elected by universal adult suffrage. The president's term of office is five years. The president appoints the Council of Ministers, which is chaired by the prime minister as head of government.

President:	Leonid Kuchma	Since 19 July 1994
Prime Ministers:	Viktor Yushchenko	22 Dec. 1999—29 May 2001
	Anatoliy Kinakh	29 May 2001—21 Nov. 2002
	Viktor Yanukovych	Since 21 Nov. 2002

Legislature: The legislature is unicameral. The sole chamber, the Supreme Council (Verkhovna Rada), has 450 members, directly elected for a four-year term.

Profile of the President:

Leonid **KUCHMA**

Leonid Kuchma is a former engineer and manager in the weapons industry and space research. A Communist Party member in the Soviet era, he presented himself after Ukraine's independence in 1991 as an advocate of rapid transition to a free-market economy. As prime minister in 1992–93 he encountered strong opposition from the parliament and eventually resigned. Returning to contest the presidency and defeat the incumbent Leonid Kravchuk in 1994, he has become increasingly authoritarian during his years in power.

Leonid Danylovych Kuchma was born on 9 August 1938 in the village of Chaikyne, in the Chernihiv region. In 1960 he graduated as a mechanical engineer from the University of Dnipropetrovsk. He spent the next 32 years working at the Pivdenmash machine-building factory, the Soviet Union's largest weapons manufacturer, rising to become managing director in 1986. From 1966 to 1975 he was also the technical manager at Baikonur cosmodrome in Kazakhstan, the centre of the Soviet space programme. Kuchma is married with one daughter.

Having joined the Communist Party in 1960, Kuchma was secretary of the party at the Pivdenmash factory from 1975 until 1982. In March 1990 he was elected to the Ukrainian Supreme Soviet and served as a member of the parliamentary committee on defence and state security. The abortive coup in Moscow in August 1991 prompted the banning of the Communist Party of Ukraine, from which Kuchma resigned, and a declaration of independence by the Ukrainian Supreme Soviet, which was endorsed in a referendum the following December. In 1992 Kuchma retired from his directorship of the Pivdenmash factory and, on 27 October, was appointed as Ukraine's second postindependence prime minister.

Initially granted special powers to rule by decree for six months, in order to tackle the country's economic crisis, he introduced rapid and radical reforms, involving privatization, severe cuts in government spending, and anti-corruption measures. These were popular with centrist and right-wing parties but opposed by the former communists and in May parliament refused to renew Kuchma's powers. Over the ensuing weeks Kuchma repeatedly sought to resign as prime minister and this was eventually accepted on 21 September 1993. In December he was appointed president of the Ukrainian Association of Industrialists and Entrepreneurs, a post he held until July 1994.

In the first round of the presidential elections, held on 26 June 1994, Kuchma came second, behind the incumbent president Kravchuk. He was supported by the Interregional Reform Bloc, which had been founded in January as a less nationalistic party than that of Kravchuk. In the runoff on 10 July Kuchma won 52.1% of the vote. The swing was due to support from the revived communist party and among ethnic Russians, especially in industrial areas.

As president he began a programme based on market reform, review of the electoral system, and better relations with Russia. Again his radical approach was disliked both by the communists and within his own party, as he had promised a slower pace during his campaign. Tensions between Kuchma and parliament eventually resulted in June 1995 in a constitutional agreement under which Kuchma undertook not to hold a referendum on his powers, in exchange for the presidential right to appoint a wider range of officials without parliamentary approval and to issue decrees with legislative force.

These increased powers were eventually approved by parliament in June 1996. That December, amid widespread unrest over nonpayment of wages, Kuchma issued two decrees increasing his powers still further and making the internal, foreign, defence and information ministers directly responsible to the president. Tensions between president and government have persisted, with Kuchma making repeated government changes in an effort to ensure implementation of economic reforms.

In foreign policy Kuchma has sought to develop closer relations with Russia, which went through a period of particular tension following the disintegration of the Soviet Union in 1991 because of disputes over the ownership of the Black Sea fleet and, more importantly, sovereignty over Crimea. In May 1997 he and the then Russian president Boris Yeltsin signed a treaty of friendship, co-operation and partnership resolving these differences and confirming Crimea as part of Ukraine.

In presidential elections in October–November 1999 Kuchma was re-elected in the second round with 57.7% of the vote. The result was reluctantly accepted by the international community which had viewed the campaign with deep suspicion. Kuchma was accused of having wielded his powers to ensure state funding and blanket media coverage for his own campaign. In between the two rounds, governors of regions which had broadly supported his opponent, the Communist Petro Symonenko, found themselves summarily dismissed.

Despite his 1995 pledge to not hold a referendum on his constitutional powers, Kuchma organized just such a vote for April 2000. Just under 85% of participants in the poll approved an increase in the scope of his role, including the creation of a presidentially appointed second parliamentary chamber and the power for Kuchma to dissolve parliament altogether if parties fail to form a working majority. Yet again observers cast doubt on the results. Although opposition began to focus in 2000–01 around Deputy Prime Minister Yulia Timoshenko (who Kuchma proceeded to sack in January 2001), the greatest threat to Kuchma's presidency came from the mysterious death of the independent journalist Georgy Gongadze. Rumours that Kuchma had been personally involved in ordering Gongadze's murder provoked repeated mass demonstrations in Kiev for much of 2001–02. There were even taped recordings of him calling for the reporter to be "dealt with". Attempts by the government to declare that the 'spontaneous' crime had been committed by two now deceased 'hooligans' has not calmed the general disquiet. Kuchma now even faces calls from parliament and the Supreme Court for him to face charges connected to Gongadze's death and other politically motivated crimes.

On 31 March 2002 the opposition 'Our Ukraine' led by Viktor Yushchenko, who had been prime minister in 1999–2001, won a slim victory in legislative elections, beating the pro-Kuchma 'For a United Ukraine' into second place in the Supreme Council. The USA led the international community in deriding the poll as poorly organized and flawed. Kuchma has since urged the parties to form a coalition government and has even suggested handing back some of the powers he has accrued.

Profile of the Prime Minister:

Viktor **YANUKOVYCH**

Viktor Yanukovych is an independent. Trained as a mechanical engineer, he was governor of the politically turbulent but economically vital eastern region of Donetsk before being appointed prime minister on 21 November 2002. He is seen as a hard-line politician and, significantly, a close ally of President Leonid Kuchma.

Viktor Fedorovych Yanukovych was born on 9 July 1950 in Yenakiyevo, in the eastern Donetsk region. Ukraine was then an integral part of the Soviet Union. When he was later appointed prime minister he disclosed that in 1968 he had been detained briefly in a juvenile correction camp for an undisclosed crime, and that he was found guilty in 1970 of 'medium' assault, though he did not say if he was imprisoned at all for this later misdemeanour. He is now married and has two children.

In 1969 Yanukovych began his career as a metalworker at the Yenakiyevo metallurgical works. After working at the plant for seven years, he moved on to find greater responsibility at larger engineering firms in the region and between 1976 and 1996 he was director-general of Donbastransremont and Ukrvuhlepromtrans (both state-run), and the Donetsk Regional Association of Motor Transport. During this time he also studied for a qualification in mechanical engineering at the Donetsk Polytechnic Institute, graduating in 1980.

Yanukovych switched from business management to politics in 1996 when he was appointed deputy governor of the Donetsk region with special responsibility for industry. In March 1997 he was made full governor. Over the course of his five and a half years in office he earned a reputation for being capable, but hard-line. From June 1998 he was also a member of the Donetsk regional council, of which he was chairman from May 1999.

Over the course of 2002 President Kuchma faced increasing hostility from the public and from the international community. Amid a smouldering row over the alleged sale of military hardware to Iraq and the murder of a journalist, Kuchma dismissed his entire government on 16 November and appointed Yanukovych as prime minister five days later. It was speculated that Yanukovych, as an apparent staunch ally of Kuchma, would protect the president from future prosecution.

UNITED ARAB EMIRATES

Full name: The United Arab Emirates.

Leadership structure: The head of state is a president. The president and vice president are elected by the Supreme Council of Rulers (comprising the hereditary rulers of the UAE's seven constituent emirates) from among its members. The president's term of office is five years. The head of government is the prime minister, who is appointed by the president. The Council of Ministers is appointed by the president.

President: Sheikh Zayed bin Sultan al-Nahyan   Since 2 Dec. 1971

Prime Minister: Sheikh Maktoum bin Rashid al-Maktoum Since 20 Nov. 1990

Legislature: The Federal National Council (Majlis Watani Itihad), which is unicameral and has 40 members, appointed for a two-year term, is a consultative body. It considers legislation proposed by the Council of Ministers.

Profile of the President:

Sheikh **ZAYED** bin Sultan al-Nahyan

Sheikh Zayed bin Sultan al-Nahyan has been ruler of Abu Dhabi since 1966. and was a prime mover in the creation of the United Arab Emirates (UAE) in 1971. He then became, and has remained, its president—the post being in theory elective among the seven emirs, but remaining in practice in his hands as ruler of the largest emirate.

Zayed bin Sultan al-Nahyan was born around 1918 (the date is uncertain) in the Jahili fortress at the Al Ain oasis. From 1946 to 1966 he acted on behalf of his brother, the then ruler of Abu Dhabi, Sheikh Shakhbut, as governor of Al Ain and the surrounding eastern province. In 1966 he succeeded Sheikh Shakhbut as ruler of Abu Dhabi. Sheikh Zayed has many wives and children. First Lady Sheikha Fatima bint Murabak has been president of the Abu Dhabi Women's Society since 1975.

In the circumstances created by the British withdrawal from the Gulf (announced in 1968 and completed in 1971), and the separate independence of Bahrain and Qatar, Sheikh Zayed pressed successfully for the creation of a closer union between the emirates then known as the Trucial States, and this was formalized with the creation on 2 December 1971 of the UAE, with himself as president. The sheikhs, like most UAE citizens, are Sunni Muslim, and under Sheikh Zayed the country has retained a conservative Islamic social code, but oil has brought wealth and rapid development, contact with a Western expatriate community, and an influx of construction workers. Sheikh Zayed, noted for his 'hands on' leadership style, has responded to criticism about the lack of democratic representation by reviving an advisory Federal National Council.

Sheikh Zayed's foreign policy has been based around co-operation among the Gulf states (with whom he helped to set up the Gulf Co-operation Council in 1981), promoting Arab unity, membership of the Non-Aligned Movement, and a broadly pro-Western orientation. Although in the 1991 Gulf War he made bases available for US-led allied forces, to help drive Iraqi troops out of Kuwait, Sheikh Zayed has opposed the maintenance of UN sanctions against Iraq. His main security concern has been relations with Iran, particularly since a dispute over offshore islands in the Gulf flared up in the early 1990s.

As a major shareholder in the Bank of Credit and Commerce International (BCCI), Sheikh Zayed was badly affected by the bank's spectacular collapse in 1991, both financially (he had provided a large amount of money in an unsuccessful effort to save the bank) and in terms of damage to his prestige as the long investigation and closure of the bank continued to generate publicity through to the mid-1990s.

Profile of the Prime Minister:

Sheikh **MAKTOUM** bin Rashid al-Maktoum

Sheikh Maktoum took over as UAE prime minister, UAE vice president and ruler of Dubai—the second-largest of the seven emirates which make up the UAE—upon the death of his father in 1990. The Cambridge-educated Sheikh Maktoum, who is also known internationally for his involvement in horse racing, had previously held the office of prime minister for eight years from 1971, before standing down to allow his father to take the post.

Maktoum bin Rashid al-Maktoum, born in 1941, is the eldest of four brothers. When his grandfather Sheikh Saeed died in 1958, his father became ruler of Dubai and he was made crown prince of Dubai. He was appointed in 1960 as chairman of the Dubai lands department, established to deal with the legalities of land and property ownership. Between 1961 and 1964 he studied in the UK at the University of Cambridge. Sheikh Maktoum married in 1971.

Upon the creation of the UAE in 1971, when Sheikh Zayed al-Nahyan and Sheikh Rashid al-Maktoum (as the rulers of Abu Dhabi and Dubai respectively) were elected as the UAE's first president and vice president, Sheikh Maktoum was appointed as prime minister. They were re-elected, and he was reappointed, at the end of their initial five-year term.

During this period Sheikh Zayed, supported in the main by the smaller emirates, had worked towards greater centralization, giving rise to growing concern in Dubai about Abu Dhabi becoming too dominant. In April 1979 Sheikh Maktoum resigned as prime minister to boost the position of his father, Sheikh Rashid, who took on the post himself with Maktoum as his deputy.

As crown prince of Dubai, Sheikh Maktoum succeeded automatically as ruler of Dubai when his father died on 7 October 1990. The following month he was elected formally by the Supreme Council of Rulers as UAE vice president, and appointed by the president, Sheikh Zayed, as prime minister.

Sheikh Maktoum's brother Sheikh Mohammed was appointed crown prince of Dubai in January 1995 and is also minister of defence in the UAE government. Another brother, Sheikh Hamdan, is the UAE minister of finance and industry. The fourth brother, Sheikh Ahmed, is a military commander. The four brothers rule Dubai in what has been described as a collegiate system.

UNITED KINGDOM

Full name: The United Kingdom of Great Britain and Northern Ireland.

Leadership structure: The head of state is a constitutional monarch. The sovereign is styled 'of the United Kingdom of Great Britain and Northern Ireland and of Her other Realms and Territories Queen, Head of the Commonwealth, Defender of the Faith'. The head of government is the prime minister, who is responsible to Parliament. The cabinet is appointed by the prime minister.

Queen:	Elizabeth II	Since 6 Feb. 1952
Prime Minister:	Tony Blair	Since 2 May 1997

Legislature: The legislature, the Parliament, is bicameral. The lower chamber, the House of Commons, currently has 659 members, directly elected for a maximum five-year term. The future of the upper chamber, the House of Lords, was the subject of a Royal Commission report published on 20 January 2000. An interim measure approved by the House of Lords on 26 October 1999, provided that some 650 hereditary peers would no longer have seats as of right. On 5 November 1999, they elected 75 of their number to the House, which also includes over 500 life peers, certain senior judges, 26 bishops of the Church of England, two ceremonial posts held by hereditary peers, and 15 deputy speakers elected by the whole House from among the hereditary peers.

Profile of the Queen:

ELIZABETH II

Elizabeth II succeeded to the throne on the death of her father George VI in 1952. Her coronation took place on 2 June 1953. She had been named as heir presumptive in 1936 following the death of her grandfather George V and the abdication of her uncle Edward VIII. She is also the head of the navy, air force and army, head of the Church of England and head of the Commonwealth, in which capacity she is titular head of state of Antigua and Barbuda, Australia, the Bahamas, Barbados, Belize, Canada, Grenada, Jamaica, New Zealand, Papua New Guinea, the Solomon Islands, St Kitts and Nevis, St Lucia, St Vincent and the Grenadines and Tuvalu.

Elizabeth Alexandra Mary of Windsor was born in London on 21 April 1926, the first child of George VI and Queen Elizabeth (who were then the duke and duchess of York). She spent most of her early childhood in the London area, and was educated mainly by private tutors in French, art, music, law and constitutional history. In October 1940 she gave her first public broadcast in a message to the children of Britain and the Commonwealth. In 1944, during the Second World War, she was appointed a counsellor of state and had her first formal experience as future monarch while the king was at the front in Italy. She had joined the war effort as a member of the Auxiliary Territorial Service (ATS).

In 1947 she made her first formal visit abroad, to South Africa. Her special dedication to the Commonwealth was re-emphasized when she came to the throne in 1952, her father's death occurring and being announced while she was on a state visit to Kenya, and a year after her coronation she resumed her tour of the Commonwealth, at a time when many colonies and territories were pushing for independence from British rule.

Her long reign has been characterized by far-reaching changes in the public face of the British monarchy and its relationship with the nation. As an institution, the monarchy has faced increasing scrutiny in terms of the cost to the public and whether it yields 'value for money', accompanied by pressure to streamline the civil list. The queen is present at numerous public occasions, maintains the traditional weekly audience with the prime minister, and sees all cabinet papers and a daily summary of events in Parliament. Besides being head of the Church, she is the patron of many societies and institutions. Her coronation ceremony was the first to be televised, and was broadcast worldwide by radio, and she marked her silver jubilee in 1977 (celebrated in popular events and parties around the country) by an extensive tour of the UK and the Commonwealth. Her golden jubilee, celebrated in 2002, was generally accounted a great popular success.

Elizabeth married Prince Philip in November 1947. The son of Prince and Princess Andrew of Greece and Denmark, he was naturalized a British subject and created duke of Edinburgh. They have three sons, one daughter and six grandchildren. Their eldest child, the prince of Wales and heir to the throne, is Prince Charles, born in 1948. The life of the royal family has been conducted under intense, and ever growing, media attention. The wedding of Prince Charles and Lady Diana Spencer in 1981 was immensely popular with the public. Princess Diana's glamour did much to change public expectations of the monarchy away from the family-centred ideal and the concepts of impartial service to the nation with which Elizabeth had grown up. While she herself continued to personify this ideal, it was undermined by the failure of the marriages of three of her children. The separation of Prince Charles and Princess Diana in 1992, the separation of the queen's second son from his wife and the formalization of her daughter's divorce in the same year, and the coincidence of a destructive fire at the queen's Windsor Castle residence, led her to describe 1992 in a famous phrase as her "annus horribilis". In 1997 a wave of public emotion and grieving over the death of Princess Diana in a car crash in Paris fuelled further criticism that the queen and the royal family held too much to tradition in such a moment and were too reserved and out of touch with the 'mood of the nation'.

From this low point the public perception of the monarchy and the queen herself has rebounded. The year 2002, her golden jubilee, began with more personal grief. Her sister Princess Margaret died on 9 February from a stroke and her mother Queen Elizabeth, the enormously popular 'Queen Mum', died on 30 March. The resulting public sympathy added extra significance to the summer's golden jubilee celebrations.

Profile of the Prime Minister:

Tony **BLAIR**

Tony Blair swept to power in the 1997 elections after revamping the old socialist Labour Party into a centrist 'New Labour'. He has introduced devolution to the UK, come near to achieving a lasting peace in Northern Ireland and championed the idea of public–private partnerships as a third alternative to nationalization and privatization. In 2001 he secured a second full term, unprecedented for a Labour government. His critics accuse him of excessive reliance on presentation and 'spin', of dodging crucial issues of integration in the European Union (EU), and of subservience in his close relationship with right-wing US president George W. Bush.

Anthony Charles Lynton Blair was born on 6 May 1953 in Edinburgh. For three years in the mid-1950s his family lived in Australia. After their return, his father, a law lecturer, industrial tribunal chairman and later a failed candidate for the Conservative (Tory) Party, held a university post in Durham, where the young Blair attended Durham Cathedral School. He finished his education at Fettes College, Edinburgh, before attending Oxford University, where he studied law at St John's College, graduating in 1975.

During his time in Oxford, Blair was lead singer and bass guitarist in a college rock band called Ugly Rumours, and he then worked briefly in Paris as a bartender and insurance clerk before resuming his legal training. Called to the Bar at Lincoln's Inn in 1976, he practised as a barrister until 1983, specializing in employment and industrial law. Tony Blair met Cherie Booth when they were both working in the barristers' chambers headed by Alexander (Derry) Irvine, later the lord chancellor. He and Cherie married in 1980; she is now a Queen's Counsel, and the couple have four children, born in 1984, 1986, 1989 and 2000. The youngest, Leo, was the first child born to a serving UK prime minister in over 150 years. Blair has been a committed Christian since his student days, his religious faith being an integral element in his political beliefs. A member of the Anglican Church, he also frequently attends mass in the Roman Catholic Church to which his wife belongs, and in which their children have been brought up.

Blair joined the Labour Party in 1975 and was elected to Parliament for the first time in June 1983, the year Labour suffered its heaviest defeat in its history. He held his seat, in the traditionally safe Labour constituency of Sedgefield in County Durham, at successive elections in 1987, 1992, 1997 and 2001.

Between 1984 and 1994, when Blair became Labour Party leader, he held a series of posts as 'shadow' spokesman, representing Labour (as the official opposition in Parliament) on issues dealt with by a specific government department. From 1984 to 1987 he was treasury spokesman, with special responsibility for consumer affairs and the City (London's financial sector). From 1987 to 1988 he was trade and industry spokesman. In 1988 he was elected to the shadow cabinet, becoming shadow secretary of state for energy, and then for employment (1989–92), in which role he forged a new industrial relations policy ending Labour's support for the so-called 'closed shop' or compulsory union membership in particular workplaces. After the Labour defeat in the 1992 election Blair was promoted to shadow secretary of state for home affairs under a new party leader, John Smith.

Shortly after the 1992 election defeat, Blair and Gordon Brown, the then shadow chancellor of the exchequer (i.e. shadow minister of finance), visited the USA on a fact-finding mission, holding discussions with Democratic Party campaign chiefs to discuss tactics for getting the Labour Party elected to government. In September that year Blair was elected to Labour's national executive committee, the ruling body of the party. He led the drive to turn Labour into a mass membership party (whereas in the past the Labour membership had been dominated by affiliated trade unions, wielding 'bloc' votes at party conferences proportionate to their size). By 1997 Labour had more than 400,000 individual members, making it one of the fastest-growing parties in Europe. Since then, however, numbers have fallen during its six years in power to around 270,000.

In May 1994 Labour leader John Smith died suddenly of a heart attack. An election for the leadership and deputy leadership of the party followed. Blair put himself forward as a candidate for the leadership, despite what was reportedly an earlier informal understanding between himself and Gordon Brown that he would back a Brown candidacy if the leadership became vacant. Rumours concerning a so-called 'gentleman's agreement' between the two continue to haunt Blair, prompting a public rejection from him in September 2001 of the idea that he had at one time agreed to step down after one term in office in favour of Brown. In the event, it was Brown who stood aside in the 1994 contest and Blair came top of the poll, ahead of John Prescott (who became deputy leader).

Tony Blair thus became Labour leader on 21 July 1994 at the age of 41, the youngest leader of the party in its history. This youthful image helped him to create the concept of 'new Labour'. The party has been centralized, with discipline tightened ferociously, indeed to such an extent that Blair was labelled a 'control freak' by members of his own party within a year in office. One of his first acts of party reform was to abolish Clause IV in the party constitution, on the nationalization of the key elements of the economy. He went on to lead his Labour Party to a landslide victory in the 1 May 1997 general election against a tired and scandal-plagued Conservative government. After 18 years of Tory rule, the first Labour administration to hold power since 1979 took office amid a wave of optimistic enthusiasm.

In his first term as prime minister Blair made good use of his unprecedented 419-seat majority in Parliament to introduce radical reforms. In Northern Ireland he achieved what appeared to be his greatest victory. After a committed negotiation process the Good Friday Agreement was signed by the various parties in the troubled province in April 1998, and in June that year the Northern Ireland Assembly was inaugurated providing the region with its own government for the first time in 25 years. Unfortunately the Assembly has since been closed down as the peace process has floundered. Elsewhere, a government white paper on devolution for Scotland and Wales was published in July 1997 and elections to a separate Scottish Parliament and a Welsh Assembly were held in May 1999.

Politically, Blair has championed the now global concept of the 'third way', essentially the yoking of free-market economics with social welfare considerations, promoted by public–private sector partnership and guided by consultation with 'stakeholder' groups. With the help of the 'iron chancellor', as played by Brown, Blair's policies have helped the UK maintain relatively high growth and record low unemployment despite the onset of a slowdown in the global economy. In his first term this success was partly buoyed by the 'dotcom' bubble of Internet start-up companies. A particular achievement was the introduction of the minimum wage in April 1999.

Despite these successes, the high popularity with which Blair entered government began to fade. Certain key election pledges were seen to have been avoided. Businesses complained of an increase in red tape rather than a reduction. In hospitals the controversial use of mixed-sex wards has continued, while the decrepitude of the health service in general remains one of the major issues in UK politics. In education Blair's policy of introducing tuition fees for university students promoted a vicious backlash and was modified in his second term. But perhaps the biggest challenge to Blair's authority came from a spontaneous one-week blockade of fuel depots by the so-called 'fuel protestors' in September 2000 which brought the country to a standstill. Despite public support for the protest, Blair refused to give in to the protestors' demands for fuel-tax cuts, showing his ability to ride out periods of unpopularity with dogged resistance.

The strongest criticism in the first term was reserved for the use of 'spin', which has been mobilized by Blair in order to turn the Labour Party into a modern, media-savvy organization. Far from endearing the government's message to the public, the over use of this glossy approach to public relations has seen a marked drop in trust and a rise in scepticism. The Conservative opposition has made much of this issue, accusing Blair of hiding behind his media machine in order to evade key issues such as whether the UK should join the eurozone and adopt the euro currency. For his part, Blair has repeatedly stated that he is waiting for the country to pass Chancellor Brown's five economic tests before a vote will be held on joining the euro.

Labour won an unprecedented second full term in office on 7 June 2001, winning 413 seats—a slightly reduced majority—with 40.7% of the vote. However, the success was tainted by the lowest turnout since 1918—at only 59.4%—and seemed unremarkable in the face of a lacklustre campaign led by the far from charismatic Conservative leader William Hague.

In Blair's second term in office his popularity fell further. His support for the principle of public–private partnerships as an alternative to full privatization has drawn considerable criticism in the face of patients seeking health care abroad and the ongoing debate about the poor standard of wages for health professionals. By the end of 2002 he was also facing a critical stand-off with the firefighters' union, one of the last old-style monopoly trade unions, which took high-profile strike action over pay and conditions.

By far the biggest criticism Blair has drawn in recent years is for his apparently subservient stance towards the 'special relationship' with the USA. As recently as 1999 he had appeared to aspire to equal status on the world stage alongside the then US president Bill Clinton, despite the huge real power disparity. This was most evident in Blair's high-profile role in the decision to mount a sustained aerial bombardment of Yugoslavia, in a bid to halt its persecution of ethnic Albanians in Kosovo. Since the 11 September 2001 attacks on the USA, however, Blair's solidarity with George W. Bush as US president has led him to follow Bush's foreign policy agenda with few signs that he is even a modifying influence. Although military intervention in Afghanistan proved more successful than many had feared, the hawkish Bush/Blair stance towards Iraq in 2002 over enforcing the elimination of weapons of mass destruction placed Blair at odds with a resolutely anti-war movement. Observers noted that the gap between the government and public opinion on this issue was one of the largest in recent UK political history.

UNITED STATES OF AMERICA

Full name: The United States of America.

Leadership structure: The head of state is a president, chosen (technically) by an electoral college which is elected state by state by universal adult suffrage. The president's term of office is four years, with a maximum of two consecutive terms. The head of government is the president. The cabinet is appointed by the president, subject to confirmation by the Senate.

| **Presidents:** | Bill Clinton | 20 Jan. 1993—20 Jan. 2001 |
| | George W. Bush | Since 20 Jan. 2001 |

Legislature: The legislature, the Congress, is bicameral. The lower chamber, the House of Representatives, has 435 members, directly elected for a two-year term. The upper chamber, the Senate, has 100 members, elected for a six-year term; one-third of the membership is up for election every two years.

Profile of the President:

George W. **BUSH**

George W. Bush was inaugurated as the 43rd president of the USA after the most closely fought and hotly contested election in decades. He is only the second US president in history to fail to secure a majority of the popular vote. Son of the former president George Bush, he was governor of Texas from 1994, overseeing more executions there than in any other state. Renowned during his election campaign for verbal gaffes and a painful ignorance of international affairs, George 'dubya' Bush now seeks to lead a global 'war on terrorism' in response to the 11 September 2001 attacks in New York and Washington D.C.

George Walker Bush was born on 6 July 1946 in New Haven, Connecticut. His father took the family to Odessa in oil-rich Texas after he himself had graduated from the prestigious Yale University in 1948. The Bush dynasty has since been tied to the twin drives of politics and oil. George W. Bush's grandfather, Prescott Bush, who remained in the northeast, was a moderate, pro-civil rights Republican senator for Connecticut between 1952 and 1962.

After primary school George W. Bush was sent to Phillips Academy, an elite high school in Andover, Massachusetts, in 1961. Following in his father's footsteps he then attended Yale, where he studied history from 1964, but did not achieve academic distinction. A staunch conservative, he chose to avoid political debate on the hot issues of the day, including civil rights and the Viet Nam War. Facing the prospect of the draft after graduating in 1968, he enrolled in the elite Texas Air National Guard, an opportunity to spend two years learning to fly fighter planes, as well as to discharge his military service obligations in the comparative safety of Texas.

Having been active in all of his father's political campaigns in the 1960s, George W. Bush drifted thereafter into what he described as his "nomadic" years between 1970 and 1973. Dabbling in politics and mixing various jobs with periods of unemployment, playing sport, partying and flying, he lacked direction until he decided to return to full-time education in 1973 and got into Harvard University in Cambridge, Massachusetts, for an MBA (master's degree in business administration) course. After graduating in 1975, he went back to Texas and the oil business, establishing Bush Exploration that year. The company failed to turn major profits and was rescued from financial ruin on two separate occasions. After the second bailout in 1986, Bush was left as a consultant for the Harken Energy Corporation. In the meantime he had married Laura Welch, a former teacher and librarian from Texas, in 1977 and their twin daughters had been born in 1981.

Bush ran in his first election campaign in 1978, competing unsuccessfully for a seat in the House of Representatives. His father, however, was seeing his political fortunes change for the better. After a spell as head of the Central Intelligence Agency (CIA), Bush Sr was elected in 1980 to be vice president under Ronald Reagan, and (after two terms) was selected by the Republican Party to run for president in 1988. Bush Jr was enrolled to write speeches for his father in this campaign and moved with his young family to Washington D.C.

After his father's election as the 41st US president, Bush returned to Texas. Turning this time not to oil but to his childhood love for baseball, he mobilized support among family friends and oil magnates to form a consortium of investors to purchase the Texas Rangers team in 1989. In the 1990s his fortunes rebounded. He had given up his increasingly prominent vices of drinking and smoking and was 'born again' into the conservative Christian faith. In 1994 he set his eyes upon the gubernatorial elections for Texas. Riding high on the Rangers' success and his father's high approval rating following the 'victorious' conclusion of the Gulf War, he defeated the incumbent, Democrat Ann Richards. His campaign had focused on education and legal reform and he had won a convincing 54% majority. His re-election four years later was even more spectacular, making him the first two-term Republican governor of Texas, with an unprecedented 69% majority.

As governor of Texas, Bush is most famous for the rate of executions in the state—the highest in the country. Almost half of the lethal injections conducted since the death penalty's introduction there in 1977 were carried out under Bush's governorship in the late 1990s. He claims to have only spent an average of 15 minutes considering each case. Generally his terms in Texas were characterized by strict conservatism, with the abolition of parole for violent offenders, a cut in government spending accompanied by large tax cuts and an encouragement to faith-based charities to take up welfare provision. These were policies he was to bring with him to the presidency.

Success in Texas led Bush to the Republican nomination for the presidential campaign of 2000 against the incumbent Democrat vice president, Al Gore. Despite revelations about a previous arrest for drink-driving, several prominent gaffes, and the remarkable US economic boom under outgoing President Bill Clinton, the election proved one of the closest ever fought. It ended in a series of legal claims and counterclaims revolving around hand recounts in the crux state of Florida—the governor of which was Bush's elder brother, Jeb. The Supreme Court finally ruled in favour of the Republicans, banning further recounts and effectively handing Bush the presidency.

The first year of Bush's presidency prompted frustration from liberals around the world. Within days of his inauguration he had stepped firmly into controversy by re-imposing a Reagan-era ban on the government funding of foreign family-planning campaigns which promoted abortion. His pro-life stance prompted suspicion that he might promote a pro-life judge to the Supreme Court when a position became vacant, threatening the legality of abortion altogether. He also blurred the divisions between state and religion by proposing direct funding of faith-based charities. In international affairs he made good on his election pledge to refocus the country's foreign policy on the Americas, at the cost of making his administration appear parochial, stepping away from the Kyoto Protocol on greenhouse gas emissions, shunning the formation of an International Criminal Court, and allowing US–Chinese relations to deteriorate badly over the course of 2001.

Even though Bush's cabinet was the most ethnically diverse ever appointed, it was immediately criticized by the political opposition as containing renowned conservative hard-liners, including former Gulf War military commander Colin Powell as secretary of state, Condoleezza Rice as national security adviser, Donald Rumsfeld as secretary of defence and, most notably, his father's erstwhile defence secretary Dick Cheney as vice president.

The horror of 11 September 2001, when thousands were killed by terrorists flying hijacked passenger jets into the World Trade Center in New York and the Pentagon in Washington D.C., was to prove the making of George W. Bush's presidency. Despite initial criticism when he was rushed into hiding on the day itself, the president emerged as the nation's champion. Where once his lack of verbal finesse had attracted ridicule, his plain speaking, all-American vocabulary now appeared tailor-made to comfort a shocked and deeply frightened populace. The sense of a nation under siege was boosted by a spate of mysterious anthrax attacks designed to target high-ranking officials. Just nine days after 11 September Bush launched his 'war on terrorism'. Afghanistan, and its Islamic *taliban* regime, became the first target for refusing to hand over suspected terrorist mastermind Osama bin Laden. Bush asserted dramatically on 6 November, in a joint press conference with French president Jacques Chirac, that the nations of the world would be "held accountable for inactivity" and were "either with us or against us in the fight against terror". US-led intervention in Afghanistan tilted the balance decisively against the *taliban* and a new regime was successfully installed, albeit at a cost of more lives than were lost in the 11 September attacks.

Although many countries gave their support for the 'war on terrorism' in its initial stages, many have since expressed reservations, especially over the apparent focus on Islamic extremists rather than terrorism in general. Bush's denunciation of an 'axis of evil' states who sponsored terrorism, the oddly assorted trio of the officially secular (though largely Muslim) Iraq, the Islamic theocracy of Iran and the Stalinist dictatorship of North Korea, did little to change this perception—especially since, with regard to the Israeli–Palestinian conflict, Bush maintained US support for the right-wing Israeli prime minister Ariel Sharon.

Within the USA, however, Bush enjoyed a period where he appeared almost immune to criticism. His domestic political agenda received a major boost when the Republicans achieved historic election victories in the mid-term congressional polls in November 2002. The first president in 50 years to see his party gain in the mid-terms, Bush now had majority support in both houses of Congress that he needed to implement his ambitious trillion-dollar tax-cutting programme. To many Americans, the serious downturn in the US economy spelled more of a threat to the president's popularity than the looming prospect of war in Iraq.

URUGUAY

Full name: The Eastern Republic of Uruguay.

Leadership structure: The head of state is a president, directly elected by universal adult suffrage for a five-year term. The president is also head of government, responsible to the General Assembly, and appoints the Council of Ministers.

Presidents: Julio María Sanguinetti   1 March 1995—1 March 2000

                      Jorge Batlle Ibáñez   Since 1 March 2000

Legislature: The legislature, the General Assembly (Asamblea General), is bicameral. The lower chamber, the Chamber of Representatives (Cámara de Representantes), has 99 members, directly elected for a five-year term. The upper chamber, the Chamber of Senators (Cámara de Senadores), has 31 members, 30 elected for a five-year term and one ex officio member (the vice president).

Profile of the President:

Jorge **BATLLE** Ibáñez

Jorge Batlle is the fourth member of his family to be president. Previously a Chamber of Representatives deputy and twice a senator, Batlle heads the Colorado Party (Partido Colorado—PC) and maintains his majority in parliament through a coalition with the Blanco party. He was elected on a strongly liberal economic ticket, urging further reductions in public spending and deregulation to stimulate Uruguay's volatile economy.

Jorge Luis Batlle Ibañez was born on 25 October 1927. His great-grandfather, great-uncle and father were all presidents of Uruguay. In 1943 he became a journalist for Radio Ariel and, with the exception of a study period in London in 1947, continued to work for the station until 1976, including acting as its director. He also wrote for the daily newspaper *Acción* from 1948 to 1973, eventually becoming its editor.

Batlle, who is married to Mercedes Menafra and has two children, also began his political career during this period, after obtaining his qualifications as a legal advocate from the Montevideo Faculty of Law and Sciences in 1956. He was elected as a deputy for the PC in 1958 and re-elected in 1962. He went on to become the party's secretary-general but was banned from politics by the military dictatorship of 1973 to 1984, though he was still a leading figure in the PC's

Unidad y Reforma (mainstream) faction. Due to Batlle's ban, Julio Sanguinetti officially led the party to victory in the 1984 legislative and presidential elections, following the end of the junta's rule, and Batlle had to settle for election as senator. He was elected to preside over the General Assembly in its efforts to supervise the restoration of democracy to Uruguay. He also headed Uruguay's delegation at the UN in 1986.

By 1989 the PC's Unidad y Reforma faction had split, with Batlle and Sanguinetti each heading one splinter. In internal party elections Batlle defeated Sanguinetti's Vice President Enrique Tarigo to claim the nomination as the party's presidential candidate. He came second in the national vote and led the PC into opposition where he secured the party four ministerial posts in a deal with the ruling Blanco party. In 1994 Batlle was elected to the Senate for a second time and ran for president once again.

By the late 1990s Batlle was playing the role of elder statesman as a co-ordinator of the Constitution Reform Project, a representative for his country at the 50th anniversary of Israel and again at the UN in 1998. He fought and won the tight November 1999 presidential election against the surprisingly strong challenge of the socialist candidate, Tabaré Vázquez, who led the field in the first round. Batlle, who was inaugurated on 1 March 2000, is reliant on his allies in the Blanco party to ensure a majority in both of the parliamentary chambers where the PC is only the second-biggest party.

UZBEKISTAN

Full name: The Republic of Uzbekistan.

Leadership structure: The head of state is a president, directly elected by universal adult suffrage. The president's term of office under the 1992 Constitution was normally five years, renewable once only, but the term was extended to seven years under constitutional amendments in 2002. The president appoints the prime minister and the cabinet, which is chaired by the prime minister.

President:	Islam Karimov	Since 24 March 1990
Prime Minister:	Utkur Sultanov	Since 21 Dec. 1995

Legislature: The legislature is unicameral. The sole chamber, the Supreme Council (Oliy Majlis), has 250 members, directly elected for a five-year term. Legislation to create a second chamber was passed by parliament on 12 December 2002. The new chamber will come into being in 2004 after the expiry of the current term of the present parliament.

Profile of the President:

Islam **KARIMOV**

Islam Karimov is a former engineer who rose through the Uzbek state planning committee (Gosplan) to senior government and party roles under the communist regime, becoming first secretary of the Communist Party of Uzbekistan in 1989. He has been president of Uzbekistan since March 1990, when it was a republic of the former Soviet Union, and had his position endorsed in a popular vote in December 1991, following the declaration of independence that August. A March 1995 referendum extended his term of office to the year 2000, when he was re-elected against token opposition in a poll dismissed by international observers as neither free nor fair.

Islam Karimov was born on 30 January 1938 in Samarkand and was raised in a Soviet orphanage. After completing his schooling he attended the Central Asian Polytechnic and Tashkent Economics Institute, gaining diplomas in mechanical engineering and economics. He began his working career in 1960 in the Tashkent agricultural machinery plant. The following year he moved to Tashkent's aviation factory as senior design engineer where he worked for five years. He is married to Tatyana Karimova and they have two daughters.

Having joined the Communist Party of the Soviet Union (CPSU) in 1964, Karimov became a member of the state planning committee (Gosplan) of Uzbekistan in 1966, rising from senior specialist in the scientific department to be its vice chairman. He was appointed finance minister in the Uzbek Council of Ministers in 1983, and by 1986 was its deputy chairman. For the next three years he was first secretary of the Kashkadarinsk region committee. During 1989 to 1991 he was first secretary of the Communist Party of Uzbekistan and also a member of the Congress of People's Deputies of the Soviet Union. In 1990 Karimov, together with the party first secretaries of the other republics, became a member of the CPSU politburo as part of the restructuring of that body.

On 24 March 1990 he was elected by the republican Supreme Soviet as president of the Uzbek Soviet Socialist Republic, a newly created position, as the republics began moving towards independence. However, he supported moves by the then Soviet president Mikhail Gorbachev to prevent the complete disintegration of the Union. When the breakup of the Union became a fait accompli following the August 1991 attempted coup in Moscow, Karimov resigned from the CPSU politburo but was reluctant to see the party itself dissolved.

Uzbekistan followed its neighbouring states by declaring independence on 31 August, and joined the Commonwealth of Independent States (CIS) on 21 December, but it was not until 29 December that a referendum was held to give formal popular confirmation to its independence. On the same day, Karimov was confirmed as president of the new republic for a five-year term. He was credited with winning 86% of the vote against one other candidate, while the main secular nationalist opposition grouping Birlik (Unity) was debarred from contesting the election on the grounds that it was not formally a political party.

On 26 March 1995 a referendum extended Karimov's term of office until 2000, reputedly with 99.6% support from a turnout of 99.3%, and he was subsequently re-elected in the 9 January 2000 poll with an official result of 91.2% of the vote. Both the USA and the Organization for Security and Co-operation in Europe (OSCE) condemned the poll for having no candidates from opposition parties. Two years later, in January 2002, 90% of voters apparently approved the extension of Karimov's term in office even further, from five years to seven, in an equally condemned referendum. The relevant constitutional amendment was passed by the Supreme Council in April.

The former communists, renamed the People's Democratic Party (PDP), remain the dominant political organization in Uzbekistan. The 1992 Constitution gives formal backing to multipartyism, and Karimov resigned the chairmanship of the PDP in 1996 to present himself in a nonparty light, but Birlik remained subject to a ban imposed in 1992, and human rights organizations have been critical of the restrictions placed on political freedoms by the Karimov regime. In elections held on 5 and 19 December 1999, while the PDP emerged as the largest single party, nonpartisans took the lion's share of seats in the Supreme Council. The two opposition parties in existence had been barred from participating in the vote.

Although Karimov is himself a Muslim, like the majority of the population, his regime has taken a firm stand against Islamic fundamentalists. He is an advocate of the unification of the former Soviet republics in central Asia, and has seen some progress achieved in this direction with Kazakhstan and Kyrgyzstan, but is less enthusiastic about participating in an 'inner core' of the Russian-dominated CIS. In the economic sphere his regime has retained characteristics of the centrally planned command economies of the Communist era rather than pursuing a rapid transition to a free-market system. The development of the oil and gas resources of the region, however, has resulted in the conclusion of a number of joint ventures with foreign companies.

Profile of the Prime Minister:

Utkur SULTANOV

Utkur Sultanov has an electrical engineering background, worked in the aviation and defence industry during the Soviet era prior to Uzbekistan's independence in 1991, and then took charge of the ministry of foreign economic relations before becoming prime minister in 1995. He is a member of the People's Democratic Party (PDP), the restructured former ruling communist party led by President Karimov, which dominates the Supreme Council.

Utkur Tukhtamuradovych Sultanov was born on 14 July 1939 in Tashkent. He graduated from the Tomsk Polytechnical Institute in 1964, having worked as an electrician and mechanic at the Tomsk plant of cutting metals the previous year. He then began a period of 21 years working for the Tashkent Aviation Industrial Association, rising steadily through different departments to become deputy chief engineer and then deputy director-general. He left the Association in 1985, and became head of the Vostok scientific production unit, remaining there until 1991. He is married with one daughter.

In 1991 Sultanov became chairman of the state committee for foreign trade and international relations, and in 1992 he was appointed to head the newly created ministry for foreign economic relations, with the rank of deputy prime minister. In this role he focused on attracting foreign investment, in particular in the gold-mining sector, and on manpower development, sending trainees to work in financial institutions in the West. He also set targets for achieving self-sufficiency in energy and for reducing dependence on imported food.

On 21 December 1995 Sultanov was appointed prime minister, replacing Abdulkhashim Mutalov. No official reason was given for Mutalov's resignation, which reportedly was a consequence of a bad harvest. During Sultanov's time in office he has gained a reputation as a good administrator and has raised his international profile with a number of foreign visits.

VANUATU

Full name: The Republic of Vanuatu.

Leadership structure: The head of state is a president, elected by an electoral college. The president's term of office is five years. The head of government is the prime minister, who is elected by Parliament. The Council of Ministers is appointed by the prime minister.

President:	Fr John Bani	Since 24 March 1999
Prime Ministers:	Barak Sope	25 Nov. 1999—13 April 2001
	Edward Natapei	Since 13 April 2001

Legislature: The legislature is unicameral. The sole chamber, the Parliament, has 52 members, directly elected for a four-year term.

Profile of the President:

Fr John **BANI**

Fr John Bani was appointed as the fifth president of Vanuatu on 24 March 1999. A cleric by training, he was a close aide to the independence leader Fr Walter Lini, and was a committed socialist throughout the 1970s. Bani no longer has any official party affiliation.

John Bennett Bani was born on 1 July 1941 on the eastern island of Pentecost in what was then the New Hebrides, a colonial territory under joint French and British rule. He spent most of his early life on the island and was raised in the minority Anglican Christian faith. He went to nearby New Zealand to study theology and trained as a parish priest, returning in 1971.

In the late 1970s Bani became involved in politics and worked closely with the independence movement. With the future prime ministers Walter Lini and Donald Kalpokas, he helped to found a separatist newspaper from which they urged the decolonization of the archipelago. From 1979 to 1980 Bani worked as director of rural development, youth and sport in the ruling Our Land Party (Vanua'aku Parti—VP) government. At the end of this period the country achieved independence as Vanuatu.

In March 1999 the parliamentary electoral college chose Bani over 21 other contenders as president in succession to Jean-Marie Leye, amid accusations that the leaders of the main parties had come to a political compromise over a suitable candidate. In the first round of voting Bani had received only two votes, but he won 43 of the possible 54 votes in the second round. On his election Bani called for unity among the political parties and people of Vanuatu.

Profile of the Prime Minister:

Edward **NATAPEI**

Edward Natapei heads the centre-left Our Land Party (Vanua'aku Pati—VP) and is generally considered as one of the few 'nice guys' in ni-Vanuatu politics. Speaker of Parliament in the late 1990s, he led the opposition to Prime Minister Barak Sope before replacing him in April 2001.

Edward Nipake Natapei was born in 1954 on the far southeastern island of Futuna. He studied business in Fiji and found work for a trust company and the Co-operatives Federation before entering politics in 1982. He is married with three children and is an active member of the Presbyterian Church, for which he chairs a finance committee.

In 1982 the parliamentary representative for Futuna quarelled with the then prime minister, Walter Lini, and resigned his seat. Natapei was elected in his place and has been a member of Parliament ever since. In 1987 he served in Lini's cabinet as minister of health and was promoted to the foreign ministry in 1991. Between 1996 and 1999 he held the constitutionally powerful role of parliamentary speaker. In this position he came to act as president for three weeks in March 1999 following the ouster of President Jean-Marie Leye.

The 1999 elections resulted in the temporary exclusion of the VP from power, and from 2000 Natapei was the official leader of the opposition in Parliament. Challenging the corruption of Prime Minister Sope, however, he called a successful vote of no confidence in April 2001, and as a result was elected prime minister in Sope's place.

VATICAN CITY

Full name: The State of the Vatican City.

Leadership structure: The head of state is the pope, bishop of Rome and head of the Roman Catholic Church, who is elected for life by a conclave comprising members of the Sacred College of Cardinals. The administrative affairs of the Vatican City are conducted by a Pontifical Commission, appointed by the pope.

Pope: John Paul II   Since 16 Oct. 1978

Secretary of State: Cardinal Angelo Sodano   Since 2 Dec. 1990

Legislature: None.

Profile of the Pope:

JOHN PAUL II

John Paul II (Karol Wojtyła) is the first Polish pope in history and the first non-Italian pope since 1523. Known worldwide through his many foreign trips, he is the author of a best-selling popular book as well as numerous papal encyclicals. On Catholic moral doctrine he has sought to stem the growing acceptance of more liberal ideas on such issues as birth control, abortion, homosexuality and the ordination of women. A convinced anti-communist, he has also developed a critique of global capitalism and the operation of the free market, concerned that it fails to guarantee the global good and the exercise of economic and social rights.

Karol Jozef Wojtyła, the son of Polish army officer Karol Wojtyła and schoolteacher Emilia Kaczorowska, was born on 18 May 1920 in Wadowice, Poland, where he received his early education. His mother died in 1929, followed by his brother three years later.

He was confirmed in May 1938 and commenced his studies at the Jagellonian University in Kraków in October. During the Second World War he worked in a variety of manual jobs, earning the name 'worker cardinal', and from 1942 studied secretly for the priesthood in Kraków. During these years he was reputedly active in UNIA, the Christian democratic underground organization, while some authorities have testified that he helped Jews find refuge from the Nazis.

Wojtyła was ordained to the priesthood on 1 November 1946. In 1948, after two years of study in Rome, he received a degree in theology from the Angelicum. He returned to Kraków in 1948, working as a parish priest first in Niegowić, near Gdów, and then at St Florian's, in the Kraków diocese. In 1953 he received a doctorate in philosophy from the Jagellonian University in Kraków. He taught moral theology there from 1952 to 1958 and at Lublin from 1954, before he was appointed auxiliary bishop in Kraków in 1958. In 1963 he was nominated as the archbishop of Kraków, and was formally installed on 13 January 1964. Pope Paul VI, whom he had impressed with his 1960 book *Love and Responsibility* setting out his conservative Catholic views on marriage, appointed him a cardinal in June 1967. He became pope on 16 October 1978 (and simultaneously head of state of the Vatican City, the sovereign ministate created under the 1929 Lateran treaty), by virtue of his election by the Sacred College of Cardinals. He took the name John Paul II.

In the context of the political upheavals of the times, the pope was treated by many in his native Poland as a symbol of freedom against the power of the communist state, and his visits to Poland in the ensuing years accordingly took on a special significance. He has also made strong criticisms of the arms trade and the use of the death penalty, on human rights grounds. He used a special message before World Peace Day on 1 January 1999 to reinforce his concern about the pernicious effects of consumerism, sounding the alarm about the neglect of the common good, and of economic and social rights, under global free-market capitalism.

Theologically, however, he is a conservative, espousing an exclusively male priesthood, while opposing birth control, homosexuality and extramarital sex. It was especially his stance against birth control, and his implacable hostility to abortion, which placed his doctrinal leadership at odds with more radical proponents of 'liberation theology'. Pope John Paul II has come to be seen, by many Catholics as well as non-Catholics, as an obstacle in the way of the Church providing moral guidance more practically attuned to the challenges of social conditions and development in the third world. He reaffirmed his authority, however, with a May 1994 apostolic letter rejecting the ordination of women, and a mid-1998 apostolic letter on 'obligatory teachings' across a wide range of issues of morality and faith. All practising Catholics were required to show obedience to these teachings, and an existing 1989 oath pledging the clergy and theologians to follow the Vatican line has been strengthened by being incorporated into Canon Law.

This aspect of John Paul II's papacy, stressing the papal authority to pronounce infallibly on matters of doctrine, is one side of his dual image. The other side is his personal accessibility and his efforts to find ways of speaking directly to ordinary Catholics, as with the publication in 1994 of his best-selling book, *Crossing the Threshold of Hope*. In addition to his personal charisma, he has shown an instinct for the telling gesture and his papacy has been notable for the large number of new saints he has canonized, some of them highly controversial. He has also nominated the greatest number of cardinals at any one time—37 on 21 January 2001. He has survived two assassination attempts, the first in May 1981 in St Peter's Square, Rome, when he was shot and wounded by a Turkish gunman named Mehmet Ali Agça (whom he later visited in prison and reportedly forgave), and the second a year later in Fátima, Portugal.

John Paul II is the most well-travelled pontiff of all time. His frequent foreign excursions have been undertaken with evident enthusiasm, drawing huge crowds to open air masses or just to cheer him in his famous 'popemobile'. His high-profile trip to Cuba in early 1998 was the 81st in a series encompassing almost every region of the world.

It was the year 2000, however, when he really started to tread new ground. In March that year he began a 'message of peace' tour to the Middle East and over the following two years he toured extensively around the Mediterranean tracing the footsteps of St Paul. He used the trip to emphasize what is one of his main aims as leader of the Catholic Church: to promote closer ties to other world religions. On 6 May 2001 he became the first pope to enter a mosque. He prayed for a resolution to the Israeli–Palestinian conflict at the famous 8th-century Umayyad mosque in Syria, which contains the tomb of St John the Baptist. The pilgrimage took him on a controversial tour of Orthodox Greece and ended with a stay at the Catholic island-state of Malta.

The Vatican City's establishment of full diplomatic relations with Israel in June 1994 was hailed as a landmark in efforts made by John Paul II to move the Catholic Church towards reconciliation with the past victims of discrimination and intolerance, although a 1998 statement on the Church's behaviour towards the Jews disappointed those who had hoped to see Catholicism accept partial responsibility for the Holocaust. In October 1998 his 13th encyclical, *Fides et Ratio*, included explicit recognition of the great contributions made by non-Christian philosophy to contemporary thought and faith, and in March 2000 he made a general apology for violence and persecution committed in the course of the last two millennia in the name of the Church.

Since 1994 a major factor in John Paul II's papacy has been his own rapidly deteriorating health. The Italian surgeon who took care of him in that year later admitted that, in his opinion, the pope has the degenerative neural condition, Parkinson's disease. Until that year he was noted for his vigour and robust appetite, had been a keen sportsman and was also strongly interested in the theatre, for which he has written several plays. Over the following years, however, he became visibly and audibly frail. In November 2001 he was forced to cancel a planned trip to the South Pacific, and instead sent the first 'virtual' apology to the people of the region for the conduct in the region of Roman Catholic missionaries and bishops, who have been accused in the past of sexually abusing members of their congregations.

Profile of the Secretary of State:

Cardinal Angelo **SODANO**

Angelo Sodano's career in the Catholic Church has been divided between Latin America and the Vatican. An Italian who was first ordained in 1950, he became a cardinal in May 1991, the year after his appointment as secretary of state—in which capacity he is the papal representative in the civil government of the State of the Vatican City.

Angelo Sodano was born on 23 November 1927 in Isola d'Asti, southwest of Turin, in the family of an Italian parliamentary deputy. He studied theology and canon law in Rome at the Pontifical Gregorian University, the Pontifical Lateran University and the Pontifical Ecclesiastical Academy, and was ordained in 1950. From 1959 to 1968 he worked in the office of the Vatican secretary of state and in papal nunciatures in Ecuador, Uruguay and Chile. From 1968 to 1977 he worked in the Vatican council for the public affairs of the Church, before being nominated by Pope Paul VI in November 1977 as apostolic nuncio in Chile and being invested as titular archbishop of Nova di Cesare in January 1978. Between 1988 and 1989 he was secretary of the council for public affairs of the Church, and for the following year he was secretary for relations with states.

He was appointed secretary of state by Pope John Paul II in December 1990, as successor to Cardinal Casaroli. He became a cardinal on 29 May 1991 and received the church of Santa Maria Nuova. In January 1994 he was made titular bishop of Albano. On 23 April 1997 he was nominated the papal legate for the 46th international eucharistic congress in Wrocław, Poland. He was the pope's personal representative at the funeral of Mother Teresa on 13 September 1997, where he read the funeral mass.

VENEZUELA

Full name: The Bolivarian Republic of Venezuela.

Leadership structure: The head of state is a president, directly elected by universal adult suffrage. Under the 1999 Constitution, the president's term of office is six years, renewable once consecutively. The head of government is the president. The Council of Ministers is appointed by the president.

Presidents:	Col. (retd) Hugo Chávez Frías	2 Feb. 1999—12 April 2002
	Pedro Carmona Estanga	12 April 2002—13 April 2002
	Diosdado Cabello (acting)	13 April 2002—14 April 2002
	Col. (retd) Hugo Chávez Frías	Since 14 April 2002

Legislature: Under the 1999 Constitution, the new unicameral National Assembly (Asamblea Nacional) has 165 members, directly elected for a five-year term.

Profile of the President:

Col. (retd) Hugo **CHÁVEZ** Frías

Col. Hugo Chávez is a charismatic advocate of the ill-defined 'Bolivarian revolution', and was once jailed for two years following a failed coup attempt in 1992. As president, pursuing his centralizing 'third way', he launched head-on struggles with the legislature, the Supreme Court and the trade unions. Having rewritten the constitution during his first year in power, he was re-elected for a six-year term on 30 July 2000. Despite strong parliamentary support from his own Movement of the Fifth Republic (Movimiento V (Quinta) República—MVR), his government faces crippling strike action amid a worsening economic crisis.

Hugo Rafael Chávez Frías was born on 28 July 1954 in Sabaneta in the western state of Barinas. His parents, both schoolteachers, sent him to the Venezuelan Military Academy in Caracas in the mid-1960s. He graduated with a degree in Military Sciences and the rank of second lieutenant in 1975. Staying on at the academy throughout the next 15 years, he specialized and excelled in the study of engineering and military armour. After receiving a master's degree in politics from the Simón Bolívar University in 1990, he trained to become a commando and reached the rank of colonel in 1992. Hugo Chávez is married, for the second time, to María Isabel Rodríguez. He has a total of five children.

In 1982 Chávez had formed the Revolutionary Bolivarian Movement (Movimiento Bolivariano Revolucionario—MBR), based on the principles of South American independence hero Simón Bolívar, and he had dedicated his life to 'redeeming' Venezuela. On 4 February 1992 he led an armed rebellion against the troubled social-democratic regime of President Carlos Andrés Pérez Rodríguez. Hundreds of rebels were killed in the action and Chávez was captured. He spent two years in jail from where he remained a prominent opposition figure but did little to affect the regime. The military hierarchy denounced Chávez for his role in the attempted coup and the US government barred him from ever entering the USA.

President Pérez was forced from office amid charges of corruption in 1993 and his successor, Rafael Caldera Rodríguez, pardoned Chávez the following year. Once free Chávez set about furthering his revolutionary cause, establishing the MVR in 1997 and drawing increasing popular support among the poor. Acquiring political backing from several other leftist parties under the umbrella of the Patriotic Pole (Polo Patriótico—PP), he headed into the November–December 1998 elections confident of victory. His outspoken leftist politics put fear into business leaders and the Caracas stock exchange, which plummeted in the face of pro-Chávez opinion polls. However, he toned down the Bolivarian rhetoric in the run-up to the presidential poll, promising to encourage foreign investment and introduce business-friendly policies such as guarantees for investors' rights and a hard line on government corruption.

The 1998 elections saw the PP gaining 34% of the vote, shattering the traditional pattern of party voting in Venezuela, while Chávez himself won a convincing 56% in the presidential poll—the largest majority since the 1950s. The peaceful conduct of the voting swayed previously hostile opinions. The army, opposition regional governors and the stock market all expressed confidence in the new president, and the USA even offered to extend him a visa should he want to apply.

The honeymoon soon passed as Chávez attempted to realize his promises of rewriting the constitution, with the intention of strengthening the presidency and reorganizing the legislature. He threatened to rule by decree if the Congress did not respond to his calls for its dissolution. A referendum in April 1999 (marred by a low turnout of under 40%) approved his proposal to create a new transitional Constituent Assembly, which by August had voted to strip Congress of its powers. In December Chávez renamed the country the Bolivarian Republic of Venezuela as part of the new constitution.

Chávez began 2000 effectively ruling by decree, with the Constituent Assembly winding up its operations ahead of scheduled elections. His popularity among urbanized Venezuelans ebbed away through the year as continuing low wages and his struggle with the trade unions drew thousands of protestors onto the streets of Caracas. Nonetheless, he was re-elected with 59.5% of the vote in presidential elections held on 30 July 2000, and the MVR entered the newly created National Assembly in August with 76 of its 165 seats. The new Assembly soon approved Chávez's Enabling Act in November 2000, granting him one year's licence to rule by decree in areas of economic, social and technological policy—ostensibly to lighten the burden on the legislature.

Over the course of 2001 opposition to Chávez began to coalesce around the traditionally conservative pillars of Venezuelan society: business leaders, the Roman Catholic Church and the army. Large-scale protests both for and against the president were common sights in the capital and elsewhere. True to his word, Chávez rescinded his emergency powers on 14 November, rushing through a handful of decrees to beat the deadline on the day itself. However, handing power back to the government and parliament, which was increasingly preoccupied with infighting within the PP, failed to quiet his opponents. On 10 December 2001 the country's first general strike in 40 years was called by the Fedecámaras chamber of commerce.

Chávez's position was seriously undermined in March 2002 when trade unions gave their support to the protestors, calling for further industrial action to overthrow Chávez after several senior military figures had either resigned or given their outspoken support to the opposition. Another general strike was called for 9 April, during which 16 protestors were killed by police, prompting senior military officers to launch a bloodless coup three days later. Chávez agreed to resign and business leader Pedro Carmona was appointed in his place. However, the coup was brought down by a ground swell of pro-Chávez support in the capital. After massive counterdemonstrations, and the refusal of some sectors of the military to join the coup, Chávez was airlifted back to the presidential palace and reinstated within 48 hours. Aware of the strong support his opponents had been able to marshal, Chávez announced a general amnesty and called for negotiations.

Unbowed by the failure of the April coup, the opposition rebounded quickly. Demonstrations numbering in the thousands had returned to the capital by May. By October competing rallies were drawing around a million people each. Chávez claimed a coup plot had been foiled later that month and took personal control of the police in Caracas in November, on the grounds that the ranks of the municipal security forces had "fallen into anarchy". On 2 December a one-day general strike began. By the end of the year it had become an ongoing industrial lockdown, slashing production in the country's vital oil industry amid daily calls for Chávez's resignation. Chávez dismissed the strike out of hand and hoped to sit out the action, knowing that another military coup was unlikely.

VIET NAM

Full name: The Socialist Republic of Viet Nam.

Leadership structure: The head of state is a president, elected by the National Assembly. The president's term of office is five years. The head of government is the prime minister, who is responsible to the National Assembly. The cabinet is appointed by the National Assembly.

President:	Tran Duc Luong	Since 24 Sept. 1997
Prime Minister:	Phan Van Khai	Since 25 Sept. 1997

General Secretaries of the Communist Party of Viet Nam:

Le Kha Phieu	29 Dec. 1997—22 April 2001
Nong Duc Manh	Since 22 April 2001

Legislature: The legislature is unicameral. The sole chamber, the National Assembly (Quoc Hoi), has 500 members, directly elected for a five-year term.

Profile of the President:

TRAN Duc Luong

Tran Duc Luong, a former engineer who is generally described as a technocrat and pragmatist, came into government only in 1987 and first joined the politburo of the ruling Communist Party of Viet Nam (CPV) in 1996, the year before he became president. His elevation was part of a 'generation change' in the Vietnamese leadership, where the key figures are the triumvirate of president, prime minister and general secretary of the CPV.

Tran Duc Luong was born on 5 May 1937 in the central province of Quang Ngai. He studied engineering at Hanoi Mining and Geology University and in the Soviet Union, and worked in the General Directorate for Geology, where he was general director from 1979 until 1987. He chaired the science and technology committee of the National Assembly, and in 1987 was appointed as a vice chairman of the Council of Ministers, with responsibility for industry, external economic relations, capital construction, transport and communications. Tran headed Viet Nam's delegation to the USA in 1994, which laid foundations for the normalization of relations a year later. He joined the CPV politburo in 1996, when he ranked 12th of its 19 members.

With President Le Duc Anh, Prime Minister Vo Van Kiet and CPV General Secretary Do Muoi all due to stand down ahead of the 1997 party congress because of old age and poor health, the renewal of the leadership was a major issue for debate throughout the year. Tran was nominated for the presidency in September 1997 by the CPV central committee, and confirmed as president by the National Assembly the same month. At the CPV annual congress in April 2001 he was promoted within a revised politburo to be second in the party hierarchy behind the new CPV general secretary, Nong Duc Manh. Later that year, in August, he made a landmark visit to South Korea. On 25 July 2002 Tran was re-elected president of Viet Nam for a second five-year term, receiving 97% of the parliamentary vote.

Profile of the Prime Minister:

PHAN Van Khai

Phan Van Khai was a close adviser to Vo Van Kiet, his predecessor as prime minister. His career up to that point had centred more on economics than on politics, especially on the issue of administrative reform. One of two new members of the ruling 'triumvirate' appointed at the September 1997 National Assembly session (together with President Tran Duc Luong), he is a strong advocate of measures to attract foreign investment, and his appointment was generally welcomed in Western business circles as confirming Viet Nam on the path to economic restructuring.

Phan Van Khai was born on 25 December 1933 in the Cu Chi district near Saigon (now Ho Chi Minh City). He took part in the anti-French resistance in the south of the country from 1947 to 1954, and moved to North Viet Nam following the partition of the country. In 1960 he joined the Communist Party of Viet Nam (CPV) and was sent to Moscow where he studied at the National Institute of Economics. On his return, he worked with North Viet Nam's state planning commission until 1972, before being sent to South Viet Nam as a member of the Liberation Movement, the North's underground provisional government. In 1974 he went to Hanoi as deputy director of the committee for reunification.

On the reunification of Viet Nam in 1976, Phan returned to Ho Chi Minh City, becoming a member of the local CPV committee, and vice president, later president, of the state planning commission for the city. Rising through the ranks of the party, he was promoted to permanent member and then deputy secretary of the local CPV committee. In 1984 Phan was put forward for membership of the central committee of the CPV, and two years later he became president of the people's committee (i.e. mayor) of Ho Chi Minh City.

In 1989 Phan was chosen to head the influential state planning commission, joining the 19-member CPV politburo as its eighth-ranking member. In 1991 he was appointed first deputy prime minister, and as such, was identified as the most likely successor to the old and ailing prime minister, Vo Van Kiet, in speculative discussions which lasted so long that they had the effect of slowing down the country's economic reform process. His nomination for the premiership by the CPV's central committee (the real centre of power) was formally endorsed by a vote of the newly elected National Assembly in September 1997.

Before his elevation to the premiership, Phan had overseen, as minister in charge of the economy, Viet Nam's transition in the late 1980s from a communist, centrally planned economy towards an open market economy, halving to some 6,000 the number of state enterprises as part of a policy known as *doi moi* (renovation). As prime minister, he announced in late October 1997 that the reform of loss-making state-owned enterprises was of "fundamental importance", although a core of 300 companies, either essential utilities or "purely profit-generating enterprises", would continue to receive preferential state support. In his new role Phan also shared the responsibility of dealing with endemic corruption, a major issue in the restructuring process, although there was a history of corruption charges against members of his family. The Asian economic crisis of 1997–98 reduced the scope of Phan's reforms and his government has since aimed at more moderate growth, although the country continues to perform relatively strongly against its competitors. In 2000 Phan oversaw the introduction of policies designed specifically to boost foreign investment and also the opening of the country's first stock exchange. In February 2002 the CPV voted to allow its members to participate in private business ventures.

At the April 2001 CPV congress Phan was repositioned as the third most powerful member of the party's politburo, behind the new general secretary, Nong Duc Manh, and President Tran Duc Luong. A year later, on 25 July 2002, he was re-elected as prime minister with 90% of the parliamentary vote.

Profile of the General Secretary of the Communist Party of Viet Nam:

NONG Duc Manh

Nong Duc Manh is a former forest ranger who has been a member of the Communist Party of Viet Nam (CPV) since 1963. He first became a member of the ruling politburo in 1991. His election as general secretary in April 2001 was seen as a boost to the reformist wing of the party, although Nong has excelled at keeping out of party infighting.

Nong Duc Manh was born on 11 September 1940 in the far north in what was then known as Bac Thai province (now Bac Can province). A member of the Tay ethnic minority, he was rumoured to be the illegitimate son of revolutionary leader Ho Chi Minh. Whatever his parentage his family background was poor and he is said to have been forced to wait until he was 11 to start his education. He is credited with joining the revolution in 1958, when he also began attending the

Hanoi Agro-Forestry High School, and the CPV in 1963, a year after beginning work as a forestry worker in Bac Thai.

Being a party member enabled Nong to serve in administrative positions and from 1963 to 1980 he worked at various levels in the forestry and agricultural industries in the north. During this period he also travelled to Hanoi once more to attend a one-year Russian language course, before studying forestry at the Leningrad Forestry Institute in the then Soviet Union between 1966 and 1971. He also studied at the Nguyen Ai Quoc Party School from 1974 to 1976. By the time he left forestry work in 1980 he had become director of the forestry service in Bac Thai province.

Following the end of the ten-year Viet Nam War with the USA in 1975, Nong entered politics as a member of the provincial CPV committee in Bac Thai. He moved into the CPV machinery on a full-time basis in 1980 when he was elevated to deputy chairman of the Bac Thai People's Committee. Working his way up in the local party, he was elected as a member of the CPV central committee in May 1989. Later that year he entered the National Assembly in a by-election and two years after that he entered the party politburo for the first time as an alternate member.

Nong was re-elected to his politburo post in 1996 and became a full member in 1997. He chaired the National Assembly from 1992 until his election as CPV general secretary at the party congress in April 2001, replacing the more conservative Le Kha Phieu. In this role he became the third member of the country's ruling triumvirate, but ranking higher in the party hierarchy than his colleagues, President Tran Duc Luong and Prime Minister Phan Van Khai, who had both been in post for four years.

YEMEN

Full name: The Republic of Yemen.

Leadership structure: The head of state is a president, directly elected for the first time in September 1999. The president's term of office is seven years under the new constitutional amendments, renewable once only. The head of government is the prime minister, who is appointed by the president. The Council of Ministers is appointed by the president on the advice of the prime minister.

President: Field Marshal Ali Abdullah Saleh   Since 22 May 1990
(president of Yemen Arab Republic from 18 July 1978 until unification; chairman of presidential council to 1 Oct. 1994)

Prime Ministers: Abd al-Karim Ali al-Iryani   14 May 1998—31 March 2001
(acting from 29 April 1998)

Abd al-Qadir Bajammal   Since 31 March 2001

Legislature: Under the constitutional amendments approved in February 2001, the legislature remains unicameral. The House of Representatives (Majlis al-Nuwab) has 301 members, directly elected for a six-year term under the constitutional amendments. The amendments created in addition a Shura Council, replacing the previous Consultative Council, with 111 members appointed by the president to advise on issues of fundamental importance in Yemeni society.

Profile of the President:

Field Marshal Ali Abdullah **SALEH**

Ali Abdullah Saleh, head of state since unification in 1990, is a soldier from the Sana region who began his army career as a noncommissioned officer (NCO). He took part in the 1974 military coup in the Yemen Arab Republic (YAR) and in 1978 he succeeded to the YAR presidency, in which capacity he was a leading advocate of unification with the People's Democratic Republic of Yemen (PDRY, also South Yemen). The approval of the new constitution in May 1991, and the defeat of a secessionist rebellion in the south in July 1994, enabled him to consolidate his position, and he was re-elected for further five-year terms in 1994 and 1999.

Ali Abdullah Saleh was born around 1942 in Beit al-Ahmar, near Sana. He is married and has several children. His own primary education took place in a local

Koranic school and it was through the armed forces, which he joined in 1958, that he obtained his subsequent training as well as his commitment to republicanism. He began attending the army's NCO school in 1960, and participated in preparations among fellow NCOs for the 1962 revolution, which ousted the ruling Zaidi Islamic theocracy and installed a republican military regime. A year later he entered the Armor school for further military training. He fought, and was wounded several times, in the civil war between Saudi-back royalists and republicans, which ended in 1970 with a republican victory. He rose to be battalion commander and then Armor brigade commander, and commander in Taiz province.

In 1974 Saleh participated in an army coup in the YAR. Between 1974 and 1978 he was part of the military government of Taiz province. In July 1978, following the assassination of President Ahmed Hussein al-Ghashmi, he was brought into a four-member presidential council and almost immediately elected by the parliament as president of the YAR and commander-in-chief of the armed forces. Promoted in September 1978 to the rank of colonel, he was re-elected in 1983 and 1988 to further terms as president and commander-in chief.

Upon unification in May 1990 Saleh was elected chairman of the presidential council (i.e. president) of the Republic of Yemen. His initial 30-month transitional term was extended pending delayed parliamentary elections, but in October 1993 the new House of Representatives confirmed his position. Under his leadership the government sought to modernize the country, building schools and hospitals and embarking on a literacy campaign to transform a society hitherto dominated by conservative clan allegiances. His failure to criticize Iraq's invasion of Kuwait in 1990 resulted in a temporary halt to foreign aid, and strained relations with neighbouring Saudi Arabia to the north.

Saleh has had to contend with continuing tensions between Islamist and secular groups, and between regions. A brief but intense civil war erupted in 1994, ending with the defeat of 'southern' secessionists. Saleh was re-elected as president by the House of Representatives in October 1994, the president's powers having been greatly enhanced by amendments to the constitution, and in April 1997 his General People's Congress (GPC) secured an absolute majority of seats in the republic's second general election, thus consolidating his hold on power. In December 1997 he was promoted to the rank of field marshal.

In the first direct presidential elections in Yemen, held on 23 September 1999, Saleh was re-elected with a resounding 96.3% of the vote. His only opponent was a member of the GPC who stood as an independent. Opposition groups decried the lack of a plausible alternative to Saleh. In a referendum held on 20 February 2001 Saleh's term in office was extended from five to seven years as part of constitutional amendments.

In October 2000 a suicide bomber attacked the USS *Cole* in Aden harbour, killing 17 US personnel. Since that time, in answer to the US suspicion that the state of lawlessness in much of the country's interior is exploited as a safe haven by Islamist terrorists, Saleh has made a bold stand in favour of US policy, further alienating Islamist groups. From late 2001, with the advent of the US-led 'war on terrorism', Saleh has ordered military strikes by Yemeni and US forces against suspected terrorist cells in his own country. Despite this co-operation, relations with the USA are sensitive, and have been harmed by a number of incidents including an attack on a French tanker in October 2002 and the discovery in December that Saleh's government had purchased scud missiles from North Korea.

Profile of the Prime Minister:

Abd al-Qadir **BAJAMMAL**

Abd al-Qadir Bajammal is a senior member of the ruling General People's Congress (GPC). A member of the government of the former People's Democratic Republic of Yemen (PDRY, also South Yemen), he joined the unified administration in 1990 and backed the incumbent government in the 1994 civil war. He was foreign minister before being made prime minister in March 2001.

Abd al-Qadir Abd al-Rahman Bajammal was born on 18 February 1946 in the southern Hadhramaut region. He went to Egypt to study and graduated in commerce from Cairo University in 1974. While at the university he had chaired the Arab Nationalist Students' Union in 1969. He returned to Yemen and taught economics at Aden University between 1978 and 1980, in what was then the PDRY. He was a member of the Yemen Socialist Party.

In 1978 he joined the government of the PDRY as deputy minister of industry and became deputy minister of planning and chairman of the oil and mineral resources authority in 1980. Five years later he was appointed minister of minerals. When the two Yemens were unified in 1990, Bajammal joined the GPC led by the former Yemen Arab Republic leader and now president of the unified state, Ali Abdullah Saleh. From 1991 to 1994 he served as chairman of the Free Zone Authority.

During the 1994 civil war Bajammal backed the Saleh government. In May of that year he was appointed deputy prime minister, a post he retained until 2001, adding the foreign affairs portfolio to his responsibilities from 1998. In March 2001, in the country's first major cabinet reshuffle in four years, Bajammal was appointed prime minister to replace the long-overworked Abd al-Karim Ali al-Iryani. His new cabinet was sworn in on 4 April.

YUGOSLAVIA

Full name: The Federal Republic of Yugoslavia.

Leadership structure: The Federal Republic of Yugoslavia (FRY), still in existence at the end of 2002, consisted of the two republics of Serbia and Montenegro which were in the process of adopting a confederal constitution, redefining their relationship. Under the FRY structure the federal head of state was a president. Amendments to the constitution in 2000 had established that the president was directly elected for a four-year term with the possibility of re-election. Serbia and Montenegro also each had an elected president. The head of government was the prime minister, responsible to the Federal Assembly, and required not to be from the same republic as the president. The ministers were appointed by the prime minister.

Federal Presidents:	Slobodan Milošević	23 July 1997—7 Oct. 2000
	Vojislav Koštunica	Since 7 Oct. 2000
Federal Prime Ministers:		
	Momir Bulatović	20 May 1998—4 Nov. 2000
	Zoran Zizić	4 Nov. 2000—24 July 2001
	Dragiša Pešić	Since 24 July 2001
Presidents of Serbia:	Milan Milutinović	29 Dec. 1997—29 Dec. 2002
	Nataša Mićić (acting)	Since 29 Dec. 2002
Prime Ministers of Serbia:		
	Mirko Marjanović	18 March 1994—24 Oct. 2000
	Milomir Minić	24 Oct. 2000—25 Jan. 2001
	Zoran Djindjić	Since 25 Jan. 2001
Presidents of Montenegro:		
	Milo Djukanović	15 Jan. 1998—25 Nov. 2002
	Filip Vujanović (acting)	Since 25 Nov. 2002
Prime Ministers of Montenegro:		
	Filip Vujanović	5 Feb. 1998—25 Nov. 2002
	Milo Djukanović	Since 26 Nov. 2002

Legislature: The legislature of the FRY, the Federal Assembly (Savezna Skupština), was bicameral. The lower chamber, the Chamber of Citizens (Veće Gradjana), had 138 members (108 members from Serbia and 30 from Montenegro), directly elected for a four-year term. The upper chamber, the Chamber of Republics (Veće Republika), had 40 members (20 from Serbia and 20 from Montenegro). Under the 2000 amendments to the constitution, the Chamber of Republics was directly elected for a four-year term.

Profile of the Federal President:

Vojislav **KOŠTUNICA**

Vojislav Koštunica, head of the small Democratic Party of Serbia (Demokratska Stranka Srbije—DSS), emerged from relative obscurity as the standard bearer of the Democratic Opposition of Serbia (Demokratska Opozicija Srbije—DOS) for presidential elections in 2000 and became president of Yugoslavia after a popular uprising prevented the incumbent, Slobodan Milošević, from 'stealing' victory. Free from any connection with the Milošević regime, he was described as a 'soft' nationalist in the 1970s. He had, however, sided with the extreme right during the early 1990s, and in 1999 loudly condemned the West's bombing of Yugoslavia over oppression in Kosovo.

Vojislav Koštunica was born in Belgrade, Serbia, in 1944. A year after his birth Marshal Tito established a communist federal republic in Yugoslavia. Koštunica attended the University of Belgrade's faculty of law from the mid-1960s, achieving a master's degree in 1970 and a doctorate in 1974. He is married to fellow lawyer Zorica Radović.

Koštunica's nationalist politics jarred with the Tito regime. He was eventually dismissed from the Belgrade law faculty over his support for prominent critics of Tito's 1974 federal constitution, which Serb nationalists resented for giving Kosovo and Vojvodina autonomous status within Serbia. When offered a professorship at the same institute in 1989 he famously refused.

From 1974 Koštunica worked at the Institute for Social Sciences in Belgrade and was briefly its director in the mid-1980s. During this period he also edited several well-respected political and legal journals including *Law and Social Sciences Archive* and *Philosophy and Society*. His doctoral thesis, on institutionalized opposition in capitalist political stystems, was also published as a book along with further writings on law and politics. He mixed nationalism with advocacy of human rights and was prominent on the Board for the Protection of the Freedom of Thought and Expression. In 1989, with civil unrest mounting and nationalism gaining popularity, Koštunica put his theories into practice and cofounded the Democratic Party (Demokratska Stranka—DS). In elections in 1990 he won a seat in the lower house of the Federal Assembly which he held through consecutive elections until 1997.

He left the DS in 1992, considering its stance during Yugoslavia's civil war to be insufficiently pro-Serb. Instead he created the DSS and has been its president ever since. By 1993 the DSS was on the very fringe of Serbian politics, becoming known as the 'van party' on the basis that all of its supporters could fit in one van. Koštunica earned the dubious honour of being lumped among the pro-war bloc in parliament for his continual attacks on the various Western-proposed peace plans, and for his support for the extreme nationalist Radovan Karadžić and the rebellious Bosnian Serbs, although he condemned the excessive violence of the various paramilitary groups.

Hostility to Milošević grew in strength after the Yugoslav defeat in Kosovo in 1999, and when Milošević unexpectedly called a presidential election the disparate opposition parties turned to Koštunica in July 2000 as a unifying candidate free from the taint of the corrupt regime. He proved himself an able politician, despite lacking the charisma of the other candidates, and under the slogan "no to the White House [USA], no to the White Castle [Milošević government]" he won popularity among Serbia's dissatisfied but still proudly nationalistic populace. After the electoral commission admitted having been ordered to falsify the results of the elections, a wave of mass demonstrations on 5 October forced Milošević to resign. Final results confirmed Koštunica's first-round victory with 50% of the vote ahead of Milošević's 37%.

This 'October revolution' opened the way for Yugoslavia to rejoin the international community and Koštunica was hailed as a champion of democracy. Famously eschewing the trappings of power, he could still be seen driving through the streets of Belgrade in his battered old Yugo car. The old pro-Milošević infrastructure slowly dissolved and a new government was formed in November. However, Koštunica proved to be as consistent as ever and continued to condemn outside interference. With Montenegro no longer effectively participating in the federal structure, Koštunica attempted to establish his role as the pre-eminent power in Serbia. He easily overshadowed the Milošević-era Serbian president, Milan Milutinović, but found himself unable to dominate the Serbian government formed by Zoran Djindjić after the DOS won the December 2000 elections to the republican legislature.

In January 2001 Koštunica sent shock waves through the DOS when he met with Milošević to discuss the issues of the day, and openly condemned the war crimes tribunal for the former Yugoslavia as a "monstrous institution". His most important political relationship, with the Serbian government, worsened considerably after Djindjić took office on 25 January 2001. The two men clashed almost instantly. The main bone of contention became the Serbian government's level of co-operation with the West, particularly over the indictment of suspected war criminals. When Milošević himself was arrested on 1 April, and extradited on

28 June, tensions were magnified. Divisions were played out in the machinations of the Serbian parliament.

In June 2002 Koštunica took his DSS out of the DOS coalition altogether after its members were expelled from the Serbian parliament for failing to attend sessions. Formally cut off from the Serbian government (which wielded much more importance in Yugoslavia than the federal authority), Koštunica multiplied his opposition to Djindjić. He horrified the international community when he reportedly said that the ethnic Serb Republic (Republika Srpska) in neighbouring Bosnia was only temporarily separated from Serbia. As the constituent parts of the Federal Republic of Yugoslavia voted over the course of the year to dissolve the union in favour of a looser confederation of 'Serbia and Montenegro', Koštunica's position became somewhat that of a lame duck. Eager to remain influential in the new state's political life, he declared on 26 August 2002 that he would stand in the Serbian presidential elections due in October.

Although Koštunica led in both rounds of the elections, held on 30 September and 13 October, voter turnout failed to pass the necessary 50% barrier, making the poll null and void. Again he led the field in the rerun on 8 December, but again fewer than half of the electorate bothered to cast their ballots. By the end of the year the Serbian presidency had passed to the speaker of the Serbian parliament, Nataša Mićić, while Koštunica's position as Yugoslav president looked set to have only a few more months of relevance. He has already stated that he will continue in his efforts to become head of state of Serbia.

Profile of the Federal Prime Minister:

Dragiša **PEŠIĆ**

Dragiša Pešić is a leading member of the nationalist Socialist People's Party of Montenegro (Socijalistička Narodna Partija Crne Gore—SNPCG). A financial expert since the 1970s, he began his political career in the municipal government of the Montenegrin capital, Podgorica, in 1989, and was first elected to the Federal Assembly in 1996. Before his appointment as federal prime minister in 2001 he had held the finance portfolio for three years.

Dragiša Pešić was born in Danilovgrad, central Montenegro (then an integral part of Yugoslavia), on 8 August 1954. He is married to the flautist Lela Pešić and they now have two children. He graduated in economics from the University of Sarajevo in 1977 and remained in Bosnia and Herzegovina (also part of Yugoslavia at that time) for five years, working as a financial expert for the private company, Vatrostalna, based in Zenica. Returning to Montenegro in 1982, he found similar work with the Podgorica-based company, Industriaimport.

Pešić began his political career in 1989 as president of the municipal government in the Montenegrin capital, representing the Democratic Party of Socialists of

Montenegro (Demokratska Partija Socijalista Crne Gore—DPSCG) of which he was a director. Re-elected for a second term in Podgorica, he was also elected to the Yugoslav Federal Assembly in 1996 and was appointed federal finance minister in 1998 after he sided with the pro-Yugoslav faction of the DPSCG, which went on to become the SNPCG.

The position of federal prime minister became vacant in mid-2001 after the incumbent Zoran Zizić resigned over the extradition of former dictator Slobodan Milošević. Pešić was appointed in his place after the SNPCG leader Momir Bulatović rejected the post. The role of Yugoslav prime minister is under review as the federation is replaced by the confederal entity 'Serbia and Montenegro'.

Profile of the Acting President of Serbia:

Nataša **MIĆIĆ**

Nataša Mićić is a member of the tiny Civic Alliance of Serbia (Gradjanski Savez Srbije—GSS), part of the ruling Democratic Opposition of Serbia (Demokratska Opozicija Srbije—DOS) coalition. A human rights lawyer before the fall of Milošević, she became the youngest and first woman speaker of the Serbian parliament in 2001. As speaker she became acting president of Serbia on 29 December 2000, again as the first woman to hold the post, when elections to replace the departing Milan Milutinović were voided by low voter turnout.

Nataša Mićić was born on 8 November 1965 in Užice in western Serbia. She is married and has one child. After graduating in law from Belgrade University she began practising law in 1998 and is the legal representative for the Association of Independent Electronics Media.

In the final years of the Milošević regime, Mićić's offices in Užice became the focal point of the local branch of the pro-democracy Otpor movement. When the DOS finally came to power in October 2000, Mićić was elected deputy speaker of the Serbian parliament. In 2001, when the incumbent Dragan Maršićanin was forced from his position during wranglings between the Serbian government and the Yugoslav President Vojislav Koštunica, Mićić was constitutionally elevated to become speaker. The conflict between Koštunica and Serbian Prime Minister Zoran Djindjić created a great deal of tension in the chamber and Mićić had everything from abuse to a glass of water thrown in her face during its turbulent sessions.

Over the course of two separate polls to elect a new president in late 2002, the Serbian electorate registered its disillusionment with mainstream politicians by largely avoiding the ballot boxes. The low turnout forced a cancellation of the polls. Consequently, when President Milutinović's term expired on 29 December, Mićić was drafted in to fill the vacancy as the holder of the next highest-ranking position in the Serbian hierarchy. Fresh elections for the post were expected before the dissolution of Yugoslavia into a confederation of its two remaining constituent republics in early 2003.

Profile of the Prime Minister of Serbia:

Zoran **DJINDJIĆ**

Zoran Djindjić leads the right-wing Democratic Party (Demokratska Stranka— DS) and has been prime minister of Serbia since 25 January 2001, in the country's first post-Milošević government. His efforts to exert his own constitutional power over the federal government have brought him into conflict with Federal President Vojislav Koštunica. He is seen as a distinctly pro-Western, pro-reform prime minister and has been adept at political manoeuvring to maintain his precarious position. Once Yugoslavia is dissolved in early 2003 his post is likely to gain in power.

Zoran Djindjić was born on 1 August 1952 in Bosanski Šamac, in what is now part of the Republika Srpska in Bosnia and Herzegovina. He graduated in philosophy from the University of Belgrade in 1974 and has written many articles on philosophy and politics. He has also received a doctorate from the University of Konstanz, Germany. He is married to Ružica and they have two children.

Active in the student pro-democracy movement in Yugoslavia, Djindjić was jailed for a year for his activities. During the 1980s he also coedited the journal of the philosophical society, *Teorija*. He briefly taught philosophy at the University of Novi Sad before cofounding the DS in 1989. He was elected the party's president in 1994. A prominent member of the DS in the Serbian parliament from 1990 and in the Federal Assembly from 1993, he briefly led the opposition Zajedno bloc in 1996–97. For seven months from February to September 1997 he was also the first noncommunist mayor of Belgrade.

In June 2000 Djindjić was appointed co-ordinator of the pro-democracy Alliance for Change and led the DS into the Democratic Opposition of Serbia (Demokratska Opozicija Srbije—DOS) that year. The DOS swept to victory in the Serbian elections in December 2000 and he was appointed prime minister in January 2001. Of the clashes between himself and Koštunica, few have rivalled that engendered in June 2001 when he exerted his power to overrule the Constitutional Court to have Slobodan Milošević extradited to the International Criminal Tribunal for the former Yugoslavia in The Hague.

Djindjić and Koštunica traded insults and accusations in the runup to the Serbian presidential elections in late 2002. These polls were headed by Koštunica, but were repeatedly voided due to low voter turnout. It has been speculated that Djindjić actively sought to keep Koštunica from the post in order to render him politically redundant once Yugoslavia was finally dissolved in early 2003.

Djindjić was internationally embarrassed in October 2002 when it emerged that the state-run arms industry had recently sold weapons to Iraq.

Profile of the Acting President of Montenegro:

Filip VUJANOVIĆ

Filip Vujanović is a moderate member of the centre-left Democratic Party of Socialists of Montenegro (Demokratska Partija Socijalista Crne Gore—DPSCG). He served in the Montenegrin government as justice minister and interior minister before becoming prime minister in 1998 in succession to Milo Djukanović. When the latter then sought to reclaim his role in late 2002, Vujanović became acting president and stood in abortive presidential elections. Further polls were expected in early 2003.

Filip Vujanović was born on 1 September 1954 in Belgrade. He graduated in law from the city's university in 1978 and began work in the district attorney's office in Belgrade before moving to Podgorica, the capital of his ancestral homeland, Montenegro, in 1981. He is married to Svetlana, and has two daughters and a son. After working in the city's district court in the 1980s, Vujanović was registered as the youngest lawyer in the attorney's chamber in 1989. He became a well-known figure in 1992 when he represented the then President of Montenegro, Momir Bulatović, in his lawsuit against detractors. In March 1993 he was appointed to Djukanović's cabinet as justice minister and later moved to the interior ministry in 1996, in which position he remained in the next Djukanović cabinet inaugurated later that year. Following Djukanović's electoral success as president in January 1998, he was appointed prime minister of Montenegro on 5 February and was reconfirmed in the post on 2 July 2001.

As the demise of Yugoslavia loomed in late 2002, Djukanović sought to maintain a position of power in the new confederal structure and pre-emptively resigned as president on 25 November in order to take over from Vujanović as prime minister. In his role as speaker of the Montenegrin parliament, Vujanović took over as acting president, and stood for the post in early elections on 22 December. Despite winning a decisive majority of 86% of the vote, the poll was ultimately rejected as it had failed to attract the necessary minimum of 50% of the electorate. A fresh election was expected in early 2003.

Profile of the Prime Minister of Montenegro:

Milo DJUKANOVIĆ

Milo Djukanović stood down in November 2002 as president of Montenegro, a position he had held for almost five years. He did so because the post was about to lose its significance, in structural changes accompanying the passage from federal Yugoslavia to a looser confederation of 'Serbia and Montenegro'. Instead he resumed the post of Montenegrin prime minister, which he had held from 1991 to early 1998. Although he belongs to the former communist Democratic Party of Socialists of Montenegro (Demokratska Partija Socijalista Crne Gore—DPSCG), Djukanović is generally considered a pro-Western reformer.

Milo Djukanović is the son of a High Court judge and was born on 15 February 1962 in the industrial town of Nikšić where he went to school. He studied economics at Titograd University (now the University of Montenegro), where he first became involved in politics, joining the League of Communists of Yugoslavia (LCY) in 1979. He is married to Lidija and they have one son.

By the age of 24 Djukanović had been appointed to the party's central committee. In 1989–90, when Slobodan Milošević secured first the chairmanship of the collective presidency of Serbia and then in 1990 the Serbian presidency itself, Djukanović at first supported him, and was rewarded with the post of prime minister of Montenegro in January 1991.

However, over the course of the wars in the ensuing five years, Djukanović became a firm opponent of Milošević, accusing the Serbian dictator of corruption and the destruction of Yugoslavia for his own ends. In 1996 he gave his support to the Serbian protest movement and the DPS (the successor to the LCY in Montenegro) split into two factions, one led by him and the other by the then Montenegrin president, Momir Bulatović. Djukanović reportedly blamed Milošević for the continuation of international sanctions against Yugoslavia, and wanted to improve Montenegro's relations with Western countries to ensure that they were lifted.

In the first round of the October 1997 presidential election in Montenegro none of the eight candidates achieved an absolute majority, although both Djukanović and Bulatović secured well over 40%. When Djukanović won the 19 October runoff by a narrow margin, Bulatović claimed that irregularities had occurred, demanded new elections, and threatened not to stand down as president, but international observers declared the elections valid.

As president, Djukanović slowly began the process of wresting control of the republic away from the federal authorities in Belgrade. His desire for full independence for Montenegro has been openly opposed by the West, which fears sparking a further round of pro-independence violence in other parts of the Balkans. During the 1999 Kosovo conflict Djukanović declared Montenegro's neutrality, sparing the country from bombardment by Western warplanes. In the aftermath there was widespread fear that Milošević would punish Djukanović by engineering his overthrow.

The hope that the ouster of Milošević in October 2000 would dampen Djukanović's separatist ambitions was dashed when he rejected the plans of the new Yugoslav president Vojislav Koštunica to reform the existing federation. In November that year he confidently declared that "Yugoslavia does not exist", echoing the famous statement by the Croat leader Stipe Mesić which heralded the collapse of the former socialist state in 1991. However, support for secession in Montenegro is finely balanced, and coupled with the international community's reluctance, Djukanović has had to accept a compromise reform of Yugoslavia. Under plans for the new state of 'Serbia and Montenegro', the smaller republic will have the option to vote for full secession in 2005 and Djukanović has made it clear that he intends to exercise this option.

In order to remain relevant in the structure of the new state, Djukanović resigned as Montenegrin president on 25 November 2002. Instead he became the republic's constitutionally more powerful prime minister. The incumbent premier, Filip Vujanović, became acting president in his capacity as speaker of the Montenegrin parliament.

ZAMBIA

Full name: The Republic of Zambia.

Leadership structure: The head of state is a president, directly elected by universal adult suffrage. Under the 1991 Constitution, the president's term of office is five years, renewable once only. The head of government is the president. The cabinet is appointed by the president.

Presidents:	Frederick Chiluba	2 Nov. 1991—2 Jan. 2002
	Levy Mwanawasa	Since 2 Jan. 2002

Legislature: The legislature is unicameral. The sole chamber, the National Assembly, has 150 members directly elected, up to eight nominated by the president, and a speaker, all having a five-year term.

Profile of the President:

Levy **MWANAWASA**

Levy Mwanawasa is leader of the Movement for Multiparty Democracy (MMD). A well-respected lawyer, he is often referred to as 'Mr Injunction' in a reference to his fight against corruption. Although opposition parties admitted that there was no trace of corruption around Mwanawasa himself, his decisive election in December 2001 was viewed with deep suspicion by domestic and international observers. He is a keen farmer who spends the summer months 'on leave' inspecting work on his three farms.

Levy Patrick Mwanawasa, the second of ten children, was born on 3 September 1948 in the city of Mufulira. He graduated in law from the University of Zambia in 1973, having been vice president of its students' union. He worked part-time with the private law firm Jaques & Partners while he completed his training at the Law Practice Institute in Lusaka, and transferred to the firm's Ndola office when he was called to the Zambian Bar in 1975. Two years later he left to form his own practice.

Mwanawasa & Company was tremendously successful and Mwanawasa was made vice chairman of the Zambian Law Association in 1982–83, the first University of Zambia-educated lawyer to head the association. In 1985 he was appointed solicitor general of Zambia. He returned to private practice the following year. In 1988 he married fellow lawyer Maureen Kakubo and they have four children. Mwanawasa also has two children from an earlier marriage. He is a committed Christian, having been baptized again in 1977, while Maureen was a Jehovah's Witness before being excommunicated in 2001 because of the family's involvement in politics.

Operating at the highest level of his profession, Mwanawasa successfully defended Lt.-Gen. Christon Tembo against charges of involvement in a coup plot against the Kaunda regime in 1989. Tembo went on to become a leading member of the MMD and ultimately Zambia's vice president before leading a party split in 2001.

In the meantime, Mwanawasa had joined the MMD on the country's return to multiparty democracy in 1991 and was appointed as the party's deputy leader. He gained a seat in the National Assembly amid the MMD's election victory that year and was nominated as vice president in November. The following month he suffered serious head injuries in a mysterious car accident and was hospitalized in South Africa for three months. Opponents later suggested that his injuries were causing him to slur his speech, giving him the unkind nickname 'Cabbage'.

Mwanawasa's reputation as incorruptible was strengthened greatly in 1994 when he resigned as vice president in disgust at the abuse of power he had witnessed in his own office. Between then and 2001 he avoided mainstream politics and returned to private legal practice, although he made an unsuccessful bid to be MMD leader in 1996.

Over the course of 2001 the MMD was split asunder over the failed attempt by incumbent President Frederick Chiluba to stand for an unconstitutional third term. Mwanawasa was selected as its presidential candidate in August, having been made party leader in March. The official results of the December 2001 elections, giving him the presidency and the MMD a parliamentary majority, were derided by the new and popular opposition and also questioned by observers from the European Union (EU). Since becoming president in January 2002, Mwanawasa has attempted to sweep aside the controversy of his election. As part of this aim, he has distanced himself from his former guardian Chiluba, and removed the former president's immunity from prosecution in order to pursue charges of corruption against him.

ZIMBABWE

Full name: The Republic of Zimbabwe.

Leadership structure: The head of state is a directly elected president. The president's term of office is six years. The head of government is the president. The cabinet is appointed by the president.

President: Robert Mugabe   Since 31 Dec. 1987
                    (prime minister from 18 April 1980)

Legislature: The legislature is unicameral. The sole chamber, the Parliament, has 150 members, 120 directly elected for a five-year term, 20 appointed by the president, and ten traditional chiefs.

Profile of the President:

Robert **MUGABE**

Robert Mugabe is a veteran of the long guerrilla struggle for independence and against white minority rule. He led the more left-wing of the two main African nationalist movements at the 1979 Lancaster House conference, which established the framework for independence and majority rule. Effectively in power ever since, he now stands accused of ruthlessness in eliminating opponents, abuse of human rights, large-scale repression and the manipulation of elections. The violence unleashed in a populist drive to redistribute white-owned farmland contributed to his regime being shunned internationally, and to dire problems of food shortage for ordinary Zimbabweans.

Robert Gabriel Mugabe was born on 21 February 1924 at Kutama Mission in Zvimba. A member of the country's majority Shona ethnic group, he had a Christian upbringing in mission schools, where he then became a teacher himself. He obtained a degree in history and English from the University of Fort Hare in South Africa in 1951. Returning to teaching, he worked in mission schools, in government schools in Salisbury (now Harare) and Gwelo, and at teacher training college from 1955. He did an external degree with the University of London at this time, graduating in economics in 1958. In that year he went to Ghana to lecture at St Mary's Teacher Training College in Takoradi, but returned in 1960 to chair the inaugural congress of the National Democratic Party (NDP). Chosen as NDP secretary for information and publicity, he began his long involvement in full-time African nationalist politics. Mugabe married Sarah Francesca Hayfron in April 1961. After her death in 1992 he married a second time, in August 1996, to Grace Marufu. Together they have three children; the oldest two were born while he was still married to Sarah.

The proscription of the NDP in December 1961 prompted its leaders to reorganize as the Zimbabwe African People's Union (ZAPU). Joshua Nkomo, the erstwhile NDP president, headed the new party, of which Mugabe was a cofounder, acting secretary-general, publicity secretary and editor of *The People's Voice*. ZAPU was soon banned in its turn, however, in September 1962. A split and realignment in the nationalist movement led to Mugabe becoming secretary-general in 1963 of a new Zimbabwe African National Union (ZANU), led by Rev. Ndabaningi Sithole.

Mugabe was detained from December 1963 until March 1964, and then imprisoned for over ten years, from August 1964 until December 1974, for his political activities. Imprisonment reinforced his political solidarity with fellow nationalist detainees, while he also completed three further academic degrees during this period. In 1975 he escaped to Mozambique, where he set about reinvigorating the armed liberation struggle as leader of ZANU's armed wing, the Zimbabwe African National Liberation Army.

Mugabe was at this point isolated in opposing a ceasefire with the white minority regime of Prime Minister Ian Smith, which had unilaterally declared independence, as Rhodesia, ten years previously in 1965. The better known African nationalist leaders—Nkomo of ZAPU and Sithole of ZANU—favoured attending talks with Smith under the umbrella of the African National Council (ANC), formed in 1971 by Bishop Abel Muzorewa to co-ordinate internal opposition when the British government was considering an earlier constitutional proposal. Mugabe's stance split ZANU into internal and external wings, but was vindicated by the failure of the latest round of talks with the Smith regime. Nkomo and he set up a Patriotic Front (PF) alliance in 1976 between ZAPU and ZANU, pledging to fight on to achieve genuine black majority rule. Sithole began to be marginalized, leading a separate faction when Mugabe was elected president of ZANU at the party's congress-in-exile in Mozambique in 1977.

The Patriotic Front held together in rejecting a subsequent internal settlement, in which Smith and Muzorewa were the main participants, and in boycotting the 1978 elections held to legitimize their formula. The guerrilla struggle, backed by the key African 'front-line' states, was stepped up, until the internal regime agreed to attend a constitutional conference convened by the British government at Lancaster House in London in September 1979. Mugabe performed impressively as leader of ZANU in a joint Patriotic Front delegation, and the pre-independence general elections held in March 1980 proved a triumph for him and his party (renamed as ZANU–PF). He became prime minister, leading the country to independence as Zimbabwe on 18 April 1980, and announcing a policy of national reconstruction aimed at restoring peace and stability.

In power, Mugabe initially avoided alienating the international business community and the white minority, making only gradual moves towards the redistribution of wealth which he had propounded as a Marxist guerrilla leader, and keeping within the terms of the agreed constitutional settlement (although he launched more far-reaching proposals for the compulsory acquisition of white-owned land in 1992, 1997 and 2000). The main conflict in the 1980s was not with the white minority but with his former allies in ZAPU. Under a state of emergency which remained in force until 1990, Mugabe used troops with great ruthlessness in 1983–84 to crush resistance in Matabeleland, the main Ndebele-populated heartland of ZAPU support. The massacres at this time, and the detention and alleged torture of dissident opponents, were accompanied by the strengthening of ZANU–PF's political dominance. Elections in 1985 gave the party an increased majority, and by the end of the decade the abolition of the reserved white seats in parliament and the merger of ZAPU into the ruling party left it with little more than nominal opposition. Mugabe himself advocated the creation of a single-party state, but in 1991 he announced that he was abandoning plans to implement this.

Meanwhile Mugabe had moved over from the post of prime minister to the newly created executive presidency on 31 December 1987. Unopposed as first holder of the post, he was re-elected in March 1990 with just under 80% of the vote against one other candidate. In 1991 he hosted the Commonwealth heads of government meeting in Harare. This summit broadened his international profile, Zimbabwe's main role having hitherto been as a front-line state in the anti-apartheid struggle and the confrontation with South African-backed forces in Namibia, Angola and Mozambique. In November 1995 Mugabe became the chairman of the Group of 15 developing countries. His aspiration to an 'elder statesman' role on the international stage was fatally compromised, however, by the criticisms levelled at his regime over human rights and the restriction of political opposition, compounded by his intemperate denunciations of homosexuality on a number of occasions. He was re-elected president on 16–17 March 1996, although his victory was undermined by a turnout of only 31% and no real opposition; both Muzorewa and Sithole, although named on the ballot papers, withdrew in protest over restrictive electoral laws and alleged intimidation.

Domestic opposition to Mugabe crystallized in January 2000 when the Movement for Democratic Change (MDC) held its first party convention. Since then it has risen to become the biggest threat to the Mugabe regime. Its first victory was the defeat of a referendum in February aimed at increasing Mugabe's powers. However, the entire situation in the country was electrified when Mugabe ushered in a revitalized campaign later that month to redistribute the large farm estates owned almost exclusively by wealthy white farmers. The invasion of squatters was led by the semiofficial 'war veterans' movement, which used blatant intimidation to force white families and their workers from their farms. This movement prompted the West to turn its back on Mugabe, halting aid and giving open support to the MDC, but it encouraged support from the former African 'front-line' states, particularly South Africa. However, the war veterans themselves appeared to be beyond government control and were occasionally ordered to rein in their violent enthusiasm, which soon included the murders of white farmers and MDC supporters. Mugabe himself declared the country's wealthy white minority as its greatest enemy.

Mugabe held on to power in the 24–25 June 2000 legislative elections, despite a strong showing by the MDC on its electoral debut. The European Union (EU) derided the violent polls as "neither free nor fair" and dropped all development aid in March 2001, before imposing travel restrictions on Mugabe and his ministers in February 2002. Over the course of 2000–02 Mugabe continued to tolerate the violence of the war veterans, while persecuting MDC voters and white farmers. High on his list of enemies was MDC leader Morgan Tsvangirai. During the run-up to presidential elections on 13 March 2002, Tsvangirai was accused of treason in a last ditch effort to derail his growing support. Mugabe's re-election with 54% of the vote was immediately contested by the MDC and split the international community along Western and African lines once again. Later in the month the Commonwealth even suspended Zimbabwe for 12 months after reluctant support from South Africa and Nigeria. By the end of 2002 it was claimed that Mugabe had sanctioned the targeted refusal of food aid to regions which had supported the MDC in elections, and felt compelled to illegalize insulting gestures made towards his motorcade.

APPENDIX: CONTACT DETAILS

Afghanistan

Office of the President
Kabul
Tel.:   +93 25889
http://afghangovernment.com/

Albania

Office of the President
Tirana
Tel.:   +355 4 228313
Fax: +355 4 233761
Email: presec@presec.tirana.al
http://president.al/

Office of the Prime Minister
Tirana
Tel.:   +355 4 228210
Fax: +355 4 227888
www.albgovt.gov.al/

Algeria

Office of the President
Présidence de la République
el-Mouradia
BP Alger Gare
Algiers
Tel.:   +213 21 691515
Fax: +213 21 606628
www.el-mouradia.dz/

Office of the Prime Minister
rue Docteur Saâdane
Algiers
Tel.:   +213 21 732300
Fax: +213 21 717929

Andorra

Spanish Embassy
    (Delegation of Bishop of Urgel)
Carrer Prat de la Creu 34
Andorra la Vella
Fax: +376 868500

French Embassy
    (Delegation of President of France)
Carrer les Canals 38
Andorra la Vella
Tel.:   +376 820239
www.coprince-fr.ad/

Office of the President of the Executive
    Council
Carrer Prat de la Creu 62–64
Andorra la Vella
Tel.:   +376 875700
Fax: +376 822882
www.andorra.ad/govern/

Angola

Office of the President
Protocolo de Estado
Futunga de Belas
Luanda
Tel.:   +244 2 350409
www.angola.org/

Office of the Prime Minister
Palácio do Povo
Luanda

Antigua and Barbuda

Office of the Governor-General
Government House
St John's
Tel.:   +1 268 462 0003
Fax: +1 268 462 2566
Email: govg@candw.ag
www.antiguagov.com/office.htm

Office of the Prime Minister
Queen Elizabeth Highway
St John's
Tel.:   +1 268 462 4956
Fax: +1 268 462 3225
Email: primeminister@lesterbird.com
www.antiguagov.com/pm.htm

Argentina

Office of the President
Balcarce 50
1064 Buenos Aires
Tel.:   +54 11 4344 3600
Fax: +54 11 4331 1398
Email: scyc@presidencia.gov.ar
www.presidencia.gov.ar/

Armenia

Office of the President
Marshal Baghramian Street 26
375077 Yerevan
Tel.:   +374 1 52 02 04
Fax: +374 1 52 15 51
Email: web@president.am
www.president.am/

Office of the Prime Minister
Government House
1 Republic Square
375010 Yerevan
Tel.:   +374 1 52 03 60
Fax: +374 1 15 10 35
www.gov.am/en/

Australia

Office of the Governor-General
Government House
Dunrossil Drive
Yarralumla ACT 2600
Tel.:   +61 2 6283 3533
Fax: +61 2 6283 3760
Email: governor-general@gg.gov.au
www.gg.gov.au

Office of the Prime Minister
3–5 National Circuit
Barton ACT 2600
Tel.:   +61 2 6271 5111
Fax: +61 2 6271 5414
Email: firstname.surname@dpmc.gov.au
www.dpmc.gov.au/

Austria

Office of the Federal President
Hofburg
1010 Vienna
Tel.:   +43 1 534 220
Fax: +43 1 535 6512
Email: thomas.klestil@hofburg.at
www.hofburg.at/

Office of the Federal Chancellor
Ballhausplatz 2
1014 Vienna
Tel.:   +43 1 531 150
Fax: +43 1 535 0338
Email: praesidium@bka.gov.at
www.austria.gv.at/

Azerbaijan

Office of the President
Istiklal Street 19
370066 Baku
Tel.:   +994 12 92 79 06
Fax: +994 12 98 08 22
Email: root@lider.baku.az
www.president.az/

Office of the Prime Minister
Lermontov Street 63
370066 Baku
Tel.:   +994 12 95 75 28
Fax: +994 12 98 97 86

Bahamas

Office of the Governor-General
Government House
Government Hill
PO Box N-8301
Nassau
Tel.:   +1 242 322 1875
Fax: +1 242 322 4659
www.bahamas.gov.bs/bahamasweb/home.nsf

Office of the Prime Minister
Sir Cecil Wallace-Whitfield Centre
Cable Beach
PO Box CB-10980
Nassau
Tel.:   +1 242 327 5826
Fax: +1 242 327 5806
Email: info@opm.gov.bs
www.opm.gov.bs/index.php

Bahrain

Office of the King
The Amiri Court
Rifa'a Palace
PO Box 555
Manama
Tel.:   +973 666 666
Fax: +973 663 070

Office of the Prime Minister
Government House
Government Road
PO Box 1000
Manama
Tel.:   +973 252 556
Fax: +973 246 585

Bangladesh

Office of the President
Bangabhaban
Dhaka 1000
Tel.:   +880 2 831 2066
Fax: +880 2 956 6242

Office of the Prime Minister
Old Sangshad Bhaban
Tejgaon
Dhaka
Tel.:   +880 2 811 5100
Fax: +880 2 811 3244
Email: pm@pmobd.org
www.bangladeshgov.org/pmo/index.htm

Barbados

Office of the Governor-General
Government House
St Michael
Tel.:   +1 246 429 2646
Fax: +1 246 436 5910

Office of the Prime Minister
Government Headquarters
Bay Street
St Michael
Tel.:   +1 246 436 6435
Fax: +1 246 436 9280
Email: info@primeminister.gov.bb
www.primeminister.gov.bb/

Belarus

Office of the President
Dom Urada
ulitsa K. Marksa 38
220016 Minsk
Tel.:   +375 172 226006
Fax: +375 172 260610
Email: contact@president.gov.by
www.president.gov.by/

Office of the Prime Minister
House of Government
Independence Square
220010 Minsk
Tel.:   +375 172 226905
Fax: +375 172 226665
Email: contact@president.gov.by
Email: cm@mail.belpak.by

Belgium

Office of the King
Palais Royal/Koninklijk Paleis
rue de Bréderode
B-1000 Brussels
Tel.:   +32 2 551 20 20

Office of the Prime Minister
16 rue de la Loi – Wetstraat
B-1000 Brussels
Tel.:   +32 2 501 02 11
Fax: +32 2 512 69 53
http://premier.fgov.be/

Belize

Office of the Governor-General
Belize House
Belmopan
Tel.:   +501 8222521
Fax: +501 8222050

Office of the Prime Minister
New Administrative Building
Belmopan
Tel.:   +501 8222346
Fax: +501 8223323
Email: primeminister@belize.gov.bz
www.belize.gov.bz/pm/welcome.shtm

Benin

Office of the President
BP 1288
Cotonou
Tel.:   +229 30 02 28
Fax: +229 30 06 36

Bhutan

Office of the King
Tashichhodzong
Thimpu
Tel.:   +975 2 322521
Fax: +975 2 322079

Office of the Chairman of the Cabinet
Thimpu
Tel.:   +975 2 321437
Fax: +975 2 321438

Bolivia

Office of the President
Palacio de Gobierno
Plaza Murillo
La Paz
Tel.:   +591 2 2430700
Fax: +591 2 2391216
www.presidencia.gov.bo/

Bosnia and Herzegovina

Office of the President
Musala 5
71000 Sarajevo
Tel.:   +387 3366 4941
Fax: +387 3347 2791

Office of the Prime Minister
Vojvode Putnika 3
71000 Sarajevo
Tel.:   +387 3366 4941
Fax: +387 3344 3446

Office of the High Representative
Emerika Bluma 1
71000 Sarajevo
Tel.:   +387 3328 3500
Fax: +387 3328 3501
www.ohr.int/

Botswana

Office of the President
Private Bag 001
Gaborone
Tel.:   +267 3950800
Fax: +267 3950888
Email: op.registry@gov.bw
www.gov.bw/

Brazil

Office of the President
Palacio do Planalto
Praça dos Três Poderes
70150-900
Brasília DF
Tel.:   +55 61 211 1221
Fax: +55 61 226 7566
Email: casacivil@planalto.gov.br
www.planalto.gov.br/

Brunei

Office of the Sultan
Istana Nurul Iman
BA1000
Bandar Seri Begawan
Tel.:   +673 2229988
Email: pro@jpm.gov.bn
www.bruneisultan.com/

Bulgaria

Office of the President
2 Dondukov Boulevard
Sofia 1000
Tel.:   +359 2 983 38 39
Email: president@president.bg
www.president.bg/

Office of the Prime Minister
1 Dondukov Boulevard
Sofia 1000
Tel.:   +359 2 85 01
Fax: +359 2 980 20 56
Email: primeminister@government.bg
www.government.bg/

Burkina Faso

Office of the President
BP 7030
Ouagadougou
Tel.: +226 30 66 30
Fax: +226 31 05 78
www.presidence.bf/presidence/index.php

Office of the Prime Minister
BP 7027
Ouagadougou
Tel.: +226 32 48 89
Fax: +226 31 47 61
www.primature.gov.bf/republic/
    fgouvernement.htm

Burundi

Office of the President
Bujumbura
Tel.: +257 226063
Fax: +257 227490
www.burundi.gov.bi/htm/president.htm

Cambodia

Office of the King
Phnom Penh

Office of the Prime Minister
Phnom Penh

Cameroon

Office of the President
Palais de l'Unité
Yaoundé
Tel.: +237 223 40 25
www.camnet.cm/celcom/homepr.htm

Office of the Prime Minister
c/o the Central Post Office
Yaoundé
Tel.: +237 223 57 50
Fax: +237 223 57 50
Email: spm@spm.gov.cm
www.spm.gov.cm/

Canada

Office of the Governor-General
Rideau Hall
One Sussex Drive
Ottawa ON K1A 0A1
Fax: +1 613 990 7636
Email: info@gg.ca
www.gg.ca/

Office of the Prime Minister
#309-S Centre Block
House of Commons
111 Wellington Street
Ottawa ON K1A 0A6
Tel.: +1 613 992 4211
Fax: +1 613 995 0101
Email: pm@pm.gc.ca
http://pm.gc.ca/

Cape Verde

Office of the President
Presidência da República
CP100
Plateau
Praia
São Tiago
Tel.: +238 61 26 69
Fax: +238 61 43 56

Office of the Prime Minister
Palácio do Governo
CP 16
Avenida Cidade Lisboa
Praia
São Tiago
Tel.: +238 61 05 13
Fax: +238 61 30 99

Central African Republic

Office of the President
Palais de la Renaissance
Bangui
Tel.: +236 61 03 23
www.rca-gouv.net/etoile.html

Office of the Prime Minister
Bangui
www.rca-gouv.net/etoile.html

Chad

Office of the President
BP 74
N'Djamena
Tel.:   +235 51 44 37
Fax: +235 51 45 01

Office of the Prime Minister
N'Djamena
Tel.:   +235 52 63 39
Fax: +235 52 45 40

Chile

Office of the President
Palácio de la Moneda
Santiago
Tel.:   +56 2 690 4000
Fax: +56 2 698 4656
www.presidencia.cl/

China

Office of the President
Beijing

Office of the Premier
Beijing
Tel.:   +86 10 6207 2370
Fax: +86 10 6205 3995
Email: gov@mail.ctca.com.cn
www.gov.cn/

Chinese Communist Party
Beijing
Email: master@ccp.org.cn
www.ccp.org.cn/

Colombia

Office of the President
Palácio de Nariño
Carrera 8a
No 7–26
Santafé de Bogotá
Tel.:   +57 1 562 9300
Fax: +57 1 336 1128
www.presidencia.gov.co/

Comoros

Office of the President
BP 521
Moroni
Tel.:   +269 74 4814
Fax: +269 74 4829
www.presidence-uniondescomores.com/

Democratic Republic of the Congo

Office of the President
Mont Ngaliema
Kinshasa
Tel.:   +243 12 313 12

Republic of the Congo

Office of the President
Palais du Peuple
Brazzaville
Tel.:   +242 810235
Fax: +242 814557
Email: collgros@altanet.fr
www.congo-brazza.com/

Office of the Minister of State
Brazzaville
Tel.:   +242 815239
Fax: +242 813348

Costa Rica

Office of the President
Casa Presidencial
Apartado 10.089
San José 1000
Tel.:   +506 225 3211
Fax: +506 253 9676
www.casapres.go.cr/

Côte d'Ivoire

Office of the President
01 BP 1354
Abidjan 01
Tel.:   +225 20 21 02 88
Fax: +225 20 21 34 25
Email: lepresident@pr.ci
www.vlada.cz/index.win.htm

Office of the Prime Minister
Boulevard Angoulvant
01 BP 1533
Abidjan 01
Tel.:   +225 20 31 50 06
Fax: +225 20 22 18 33

Croatia

Office of the President
Pantovčak 241
Zagreb
Tel.:   +385 1 456 51 91
Fax: +385 1 456 52 99
Email: ured@predsjednik.hr
www.predsjednik.hr/

Office of the Prime Minister
Trg svetog Marka 2
10 000 Zagreb
Tel.:   +385 1 456 92 01
Fax: +385 1 630 30 19
Email: premijer@vlada.hr
www.vlada.hr/

Cuba

Office of the President
Havana
www.cubagob.cu/

Cyprus

Office of the President
Presidential Palace
Demosthenis Severis Avenue
1400 Nicosia
Tel.:   +357 22 661333
Fax: +357 22 663799
Email: grafio-proedrou@cytanet.com.cy
www.cyprus.gov.cy/

Turkish Republic of Northern Cyprus

Office of the President
(Lefkoşa)
Mersin 10
Turkey

Office of the Prime Minister
(Lefkoşa)
Mersin 10
Turkey
Tel.:   +90 392 22 83141
Fax: +90 392 22 75281
Email: pressdpt@brimnet.com
www.cm.gov.nc.tr/

Czech Republic

Office of the President
Prazsky Hrad
119 08 Prague 1
Tel.:   +420 2 2437 1111
Fax: +420 2 2437 3300
www.hrad.cz/

Office of the Prime Minister
nábřeží Eduarda Beneše 4
110 00 Prague 1
Tel.:   +420 2 2400 2111
Fax: +420 2 2481 0231
Email: www@vlada.cz
www.vlada.cz/index.win.htm

Denmark

Office of the Queen
The Lord Chamberlain's Office
Det Gule Palæ
Amaliegade 18
1256 Copenhagen K
Tel.:   +45 33 40 10 10
Email: hofmarskallatet@konghuset.dk
www.kongehuset.dk/

Office of the Prime Minister
Christiansborg
Prins Jørgens Gard 11
1218 Copenhagen K
Tel.:   +45 33 92 33 00
Fax: +45 33 11 16 65
Email: stm@stm.dk
www.stm.dk/

Djibouti

Office of the President
BP 6
Djibouti
Tel.:   +253 350201

Office of the Prime Minister
BP 2086
Djibouti
Tel.:　　+253 351494
Fax:　　+253 355049

Dominica

Office of the President
Government Headquarters
Morne Bruce
Roseau
Tel.:　　+1 767 4482 054
Fax:　　+1 767 4498 366

Office of the Prime Minister
Government Headquarters
Kennedy Avenue
Roseau
Tel.:　　+1 767 4482 401 ext. 3300
Fax:　　+1 767 4488 960
Email:　pmoffice@cwdom.dm

Dominican Republic

Office of the President
Palacio Nacional
Calle Moisés García
Santo Domingo DN
Tel.:　　+1 809 686 4771
Fax:　　+1 809 688 2100
www.presidencia.gov.do/

East Timor

Office of the President
Dili
www.gov.east-timor.org

Office of the Prime Minister
Dili
Tel.:　　+670 390 312210
Email:　info@gov.east-timor.org
www.gov.east-timor.org

Ecuador

Office of the President
Palacio Nacional
García Moreno 1043
Quito
Tel.:　　+593 2 2216 300

Egypt

Office of the President
al-Etehadia Building
Heliopolis
Cairo
Tel.:　　+20 2 245 9816
www.presidency.gov.eg/

Office of the Prime Minister
Sharia Majlis al-Sha'ab
Cairo
Tel.:　　+20 2 355 3192
Fax:　　+20 2 355 8016
Email:　primemin@idsc.gov.eg
www.misrnet.idsc.gov.eg/

El Salvador

Office of the President
Alameda Dr Manuel Enrique Araújo
Km. 6
San Salvador
Tel.:　　+503 271 1555
Fax:　　+503 271 0850
www.casapres.gob.sv/

Equatorial Guinea

Office of the President
Malabo

Office of the Prime Minister
Malabo

Eritrea

Office of the President
PO Box 257
Asmara
Tel.:　　+291 1 12 21 32
Fax:　　+291 1 12 51 23

Estonia

Office of the President
Weizenbergi 39
15050
Tallinn
Tel.:　　+372 631 6202
Fax:　　+372 631 6250
Email:　sekretar@vpk.ee
www.president.ee/

Office of the Prime Minister
Stenbock House
Rahukohtu 3
15161
Tallinn
Tel.:   +372 693 5701
Fax: +372 693 5994
Email: peaminister@rk.ee
www.peaminister.ee/

Ethiopia

Office of the President
PO Box 1031
Addis Ababa
Tel.:   +251 1 51 10 00
Fax: +251 1 55 20 41

Office of the Prime Minister
PO Box 1031
Addis Ababa
Tel.:   +251 1 55 20 44
Fax: +251 1 55 20 20
www.ethiospokes.net/

Fiji

Office of the President
Government Buildings
PO Box 2513
Suva
Tel.:   +679 3314 244
Fax: +679 3301 645
www.fiji.gov.fj/president/index.shtml

Office of the Prime Minister
Government Buildings
PO Box 2353
Suva
Tel.:   +679 3211 201
Fax: +679 3306 034
Email: pmsoffice@connect.com.fj
www.fiji.gov.fj/cabinet/prime_minister.shtml

Finland

Office of the President
Mariankatu 2
FIN-00170
Helsinki
Tel.:   +358 9 661 133
Email: presidentti@tpk.fi
www.tpk.fi/

Office of the Prime Minister
Snellmaninkatu 1A
PO Box 23
FIN-00023
Helsinki
Tel.:   +358 9 16001
Fax: +358 9 1602 2165
Email: firstname.surname@vnk.fi
www.vn.fi/vnk/

France

Office of the President
Palais de l'Elysée
55–57 rue du Faubourg Saint Honoré
75008 Paris
Tel.:   +33 1 42 92 81 00
Fax: +33 1 47 42 24 65
www.elysee.fr/

Office of the Prime Minister
Hôtel Matignon
57 rue de Varenne
75700 Paris
Tel.:   +33 1 42 75 80 00
Fax: +33 1 45 44 15 72
Email: premier-ministre@premier-
    ministre.gouv.fr
www.premier-ministre.gouv.fr/

Gabon

Office of the President
BP 546
Libreville
Tel.:   +241 72 20 30

Office of the Prime Minister
BP 546
Libreville

Gambia

Office of the President
State House
Banjul
Tel.:   +220 227 208
Fax: +220 227 034
Email: info@statehouse.gm
www.statehouse.gm/

Georgia

Office of the President
Rustaveli 29
300002 Tbilisi
Tel.: +995 32 99 74 75
Fax: +995 32 99 96 30
Email: office@presidpress.gov.ge
www.presidpress.gov.ge/

Office of the State Minister
Ingorokva 7
380018 Tbilisi
Tel.: +995 32 93 59 07
Fax: +995 32 98 23 54

Germany

Office of the Federal President
Schloß Bellevue
Spreeweg 1
10557 Berlin
Tel.: +49 30 2000 0
Fax: +49 30 2000 1999
Email: poststelle@bpra.bund.de
www.bundespraesident.de/

Office of the Federal Chancellor
Schloßplatz 1
10178 Berlin
Tel.: +49 30 4000 0
Fax: +49 30 4000 1818
Email: bundeskanzler@bundeskanzler.de
www.bundesregierung.de/

Ghana

Office of the President
The Castle
Osu
PO Box 1627
Accra
Tel.: +233 21 665 415
www.ghana.gov.gh/

Greece

Office of the President
17 Odos Stissichorou
106 74 Athens
Tel.: +30 210 728 3111
Fax: +30 210 724 8938

Office of the Prime Minister
Maximos' Mansion
19 Hrodou Attikou
106 71 Athens
Tel.: +30 210 671 7732
Fax: +30 210 671 5799
Email: mail@primeminister.gr
www.primeminister.gr/

Grenada

Office of the Governor-General
Government House
St George's
Tel.: +1 473 440 2401
Fax: +1 473 440 6688

Office of the Prime Minister
Ministerial Complex
6th Floor
St George's
Tel.: +1 473 440 2255
Fax: +1 473 440 4116
Email: gndpm@caribsurf.com
www.spiceisle.com/gndpm/

Guatemala

Office of the President
Palacio Nacional
6a Calle y 7a Avenida
Zona 1
Guatemala City
Tel.: +502 221 4428
www.concyt.gob.gt/sectpub/presi/

Guinea

Office of the President
Conakry
Tel.: +224 44 11 47
Fax: +224 41 52 82
www.guinee.gov.gn/1_bienvenue/
    president.htm

Office of the Prime Minister
Cité des Nations
Conakry
Tel.: +224 44 10 70
www.guinee.gov.gn/1_bienvenue/ministre.htm

Guinea-Bissau

Office of the President
Bissau

Office of the Prime Minister
Avenida Unidade Africana
CP 137
Bissau
Tel.: +245 211308
Fax: +245 201671

Guyana

Office of the President
New Garden Street
Georgetown
Tel.: +592 225 1330
Fax: +592 226 9969

Office of the Prime Minister
Wight's Lane
Kingston
Georgetown
Tel.: +592 226 6955
Fax: +592 225 7573

Haiti

Office of the President
rue Champ-de-Mars
Port-au-Prince
Tel.: +509 228 2128
Fax: +509 228 2320
www.palaishaiti.net/

Office of the Prime Minister
Villa d'Accueil
Delmas 60
Museau
Port-au-Prince
Tel.: +509 245 0007
Fax: +509 245 1624

Honduras

Office of the President
Casa Presidencial
Boulevard Juan Pablo II
Tegucigalpa
Tel.: +504 239 1515
Fax: +504 231 0097

Hungary

Office of the President
Kossuth Lajos tér 1–3
1055 Budapest
Tel.: +36 1 441 4000

Office of the Prime Minister
Kossuth Lajos tér 1–3
1055 Budapest
Tel.: +36 1 441 4000
Fax: +36 1 268 3050
www.kancellaria.gov.hu/

Iceland

Office of the President
Stadastadur
Sóleyjargata 1
150 Reykjavík
Tel.: +354 540 4400
Fax: +354 562 4802
Email: forseti@forseti.is

Office of the Prime Minister
Stjórnarrádshúsinu vid Lækjargötu
150 Reykjavík
Tel.: +354 560 9400
Fax: +354 562 4014
Email: postur@for.stjr.is
www.stjr.is/for

India

Office of the President
Rashtrapati Bhavan
New Delhi 110 004
Tel.: +91 11 23015 321
Fax: +91 11 23017 290
Email: poi_gen@rb.nic.in
http://presidentofindia.nic.in/

Office of the Prime Minister
South Block
New Delhi 110 011
Tel.:   +91 11 23012 312
Fax: +91 11 23016 857
http://pmindia.nic.in/

Indonesia

Office of the President
Istana Merdeka
Jakarta
Tel.:   +62 21 331 097

Iran

Office of the Spiritual Leader
Tehran

Office of the President
Palestine Avenue
Azerbaijan Intersection
Tehran
Tel.:   +98 21 6161
Email: khatami@president.ir
www.president.ir/

Iraq

Office of the President
Presidential Palace
Karradat Mariam
Baghdad
Email: uruk@uruklink.net
www.uruklink.net/iraq/

Ireland

Office of the President
Áras an Uachtaráin
Phoenix Park
Dublin 8
Tel.:   +353 1 6772 815
Fax: +353 1 6710 529
Email: webmaster@aras.irlgov.ie
www.irlgov.ie/aras/

Office of the Prime Minister
Government Buildings
Upper Merrion Street
Dublin 2
Tel.:   +353 1 6624 422
Fax: +353 1 6789 791
Email: webmaster@taoiseach.irlgov.ie
www.irlgov.ie/taoiseach/

Israel

Office of the President
3 Hanassi Street
Jerusalem 92188
Tel.:   +972 2 670 7211
Fax: +972 2 561 0037

Office of the Prime Minister
PO Box 187
3 Kaplan Street
Kiryat Ben-Gurion
Jerusalem 91919
Tel.:   +972 2 670 5555
Fax: +972 2 651 2631
Email: webmaster@pmo.gov.il
www.pmo.gov.il/

Italy

Office of the President
Palazzo del Quirinale
00187 Rome
Tel.:   +39 06 46991
Fax: +39 06 46992384
www.quirinale.it/

Office of the Prime Minister
Palazzo Chigi
Piazza Colonna 370
00187 Rome
Tel.:   +39 06 67791
Fax: +39 06 6783998
www.palazzochigi.it/

Jamaica

Office of the Governor-General
King's House
Hope Road
Kingston 10
Tel.:   +1 876 927 6424
Fax: +1 876 927 4561

Office of the Prime Minister
Jamaica House
1 Devon Road
Kingston 6
Tel.: +1 876 927 9941
Fax: +1 876 929 0005
Email: pmo@opm.gov.jm
www.cabinet.gov.jm/

Japan

Imperial Household Agency
1-1 Chiyoda
Chiyoda-ku
Tokyo 100-8111
Tel.: +81 3 3213 1111
Fax: +81 3 3282 1407
Email: information@kunaicho.go.jp
www.kunaicho.go.jp/eindex.html

Office of the Prime Minister
1-1-6 Nagata-cho
Chiyoda-ku
Tokyo 100-8968
Tel.: +81 3 3581 2361
Fax: +81 3 3581 1910
www.sorifu.go.jp/english/index.html

Jordan

Office of the King
Royal Palace
Amman
Tel.: +962 6 4637 341
www.kingabdullah.jo/

Office of the Prime Minister
PO Box 1577
Amman
Tel.: +962 6 4641 211
Fax: +962 6 4642 520
Email: prime@pm.gov.jo
www.pm.gov.jo/

Kazakhstan

Office of the President
11 Beybitshilik Street
473000 Astana
Tel.: +7 317 2152000
Fax: +7 317 2326182
www.president.kz/

Office of the Prime Minister
11 Beybitshilik Street
473000 Astana
Tel.: +7 317 2323104
Fax: +7 317 2323003

Kenya

Office of the President
Harambee House
Harambee Avenue
PO Box 30510
Nairobi
Tel.: +254 20 227 411 (up to 31 July
2003, then +254 20 2227 411)
www.officeofthepresident.go.ke/

Kiribati

Office of the President
PO Box 68
Bairiki
Tarawa
Tel.: +686 21183
Fax: +686 21145

North Korea

Supreme People's Assembly
Mansoudong Central District
Pyongyang
Tel.: +850 2 18 111
Fax: +850 2 381 2100

Office of the National Defence Commission
Pyongyang

Office of the Premier
Pyongyang

South Korea

Office of the President
Cheong Wa Dae
1 Sejong-no Jongno-gu
Seoul
Tel.: +82 2 770 0011
Fax: +82 2 770 0344
www.cwd.go.kr/

607

Office of the Prime Minister
77 Sejong-no
Jongno-gu
Seoul
Tel.:   +82 2 720 2006
Fax: +82 2 720 3571
Email: president@cwd.go.kr
www.opm.go.kr/

Kuwait

Office of the Amir
PO Box 799
13008 Safat
Kuwait City
Tel.:   +965 539 6144
Fax: +965 534 7696

Office of the Prime Minister
PO Box 4
Safat
Kuwait City
Tel.:   +965 539 0217
Fax: +965 539 0430

Kyrgyzstan

Office of the President
Government House
720000 Bishkek
Tel.:   +996 312 212466
Fax: +996 312 218627
Email: office@mail.gov.kg
www.president.kg/

Office of the Prime Minister
Government House
720000 Bishkek
Tel.:   +996 312 225656
Fax: +996 312 218627
www.gov.kg/prime.htm

Laos

Office of the President
Sethathirath Road
Vientiane
Tel.:   +856 21 214210
Fax: +856 21 214208

Office of the Prime Minister
Lane Xang Avenue
Vientiane
Tel.:   +856 21 213652
Fax: +856 21 213560

Latvia

Office of the President
Pils lauk 3
Riga
Tel.:   +371 7377 548
Fax: +371 7325 800
Email: chancery@president.lv
www.president.lv/index.php

Office of the Prime Minister
Brivibas bulvaris 36
Riga 1520
Tel.:   +371 7332 232
Fax: +371 7286 598
Email: vk@mk.gov.lv
www.mk.gov.lv/lv

Lebanon

Office of the President
Presidential Palace
Baabda
Beirut
Tel.:   +961 1 387200
Fax: +961 5 922400
Email: president_office@presidency.gov.lb
www.presidency.gov.lb/

Office of the Council of Ministers
Grand Sérail
rue des Arts et Métiers
Sanayeh
Beirut
Tel.:   +961 1 862001
Fax: +961 1 865630
www.rafikhariri.net

Lesotho

Office of the King
PO Box 524
Maseru 100
Tel.:   +266 22322170
Fax: +266 22310083
Email: sps@palace.org.ls

Office of the Prime Minister
PO Box 527
Maseru 100
Tel.:   +266 22311000
Fax: +266 22310444
www.lesotho.gov.ls/ministers/
    mndefence.htm

Liberia

Office of the President
Executive Mansion
Capitol Hill
PO Box 9001
Monrovia
Tel.:   +231 224961
Email: emansion@liberia.net

Libya

Office of the Leader of the Revolution
Secretariat of the General People's
    Committee
Tripoli
Tel.:   +218 21 48210
Email: greenbook2001@yahoo.com

Office of the Secretary-General
Secretariat of the General People's
    Committee
Tripoli
Tel.:   +218 21 48210

Liechtenstein

Office of the Prince
Schloß Vaduz
FL-9490
Vaduz
Tel.:   +423 2321212
Fax: +423 2326862
www.fuerstenhaus.li/

Office of the Head of Government
FL-9490
Vaduz
Tel.:   +423 2366111
Fax: +423 2366022
www.firstlink.li/regierung/

Lithuania

Office of the President
S. Daukanto apylinke 3
Vilnius 2008
Tel.:   +370 526 28986
Fax: +370 521 26202
Email: info@president.lt
www.president.lt/

Office of the Prime Minister
Gedimino prospekt 11
Vilnius 2039
Tel.:   +370 521 21088
Fax: +370 521 27452
Email: kanceliarija@lrvk.lt
www.lrvk.lt/

Luxembourg

Office of the Grand Duke
Palais Grand-Ducal
Marché-aux-Herbes
L-1728 Luxembourg-Ville
Tel.:   +352 47 487 41

Office of the Prime Minister
Hôtel de Bourgogne
4 rue de la Congrégation
L-2910 Luxembourg-Ville
Tel.:   +352 4781
Fax: +352 46 1720
Email: me@me.smtp.etat.lu
www.gouvernement.lu/

Macedonia

Office of the President
11 Oktomvri bb
91000 Skopje
Tel.:   +389 91 113 318
Fax: +389 91 112 643
www.president.gov.mk/

Office of the Prime Minister
Ilindenska bb
91000 Skopje
Tel.:   +389 91 115 389
Fax: +389 91 112 561
Email: office@primeminister.gov.mk
www.primeminister.gov.mk/

Madagascar

Office of the President
BP 955/1310
Ambohitsirohitra
101 Antananarivo
Tel.:   +261 20 2227474

Office of the Prime Minister
BP 248
Mahazoarivo
101 Antananarivo
Tel.: +261 20 2225258
Fax: +261 20 2235258

Malawi

Office of the President
Government Offices
Private Bag 302
Lilongwe 3
Tel.: +265 1 782 655
Fax: +265 1 782 095
Email: opc@malawi.gov.mw
www.malawi.gov.mw/opc/opc.htm

Malaysia

Office of the Head of State
Istana Negara
50500 Kuala Lumpur
Tel.: +60 3 2078 8332

Office of the Prime Minister
Jalan Dato' Onn
50502 Kuala Lumpur
Tel.: +60 3 2072 1957
Fax: +60 3 2698 4172
Email: ppm@smpke.jpm.my
www.smpke.jpm.my/

Maldives

Office of the President
Medhuziyaaraiy Magu
Malé 20-05
Tel.: +960 323701
Fax: +960 325500
Email: webmaster@presidencymaldives.
gov.mv
www.presidencymaldives.gov.mv

Mali

Office of the President
BP 1463
Koulouba
Bamako
Tel.: +223 2 22 80 30
Fax: +223 2 22 01 29

Office of the Prime Minister
Quartier du Fleuve
BP 97
Bamako
Tel.: +223 2 22 55 34
Fax: +223 2 22 85 83

Malta

Office of the President
The Palace
Valletta CMR 02
Tel.: +356 21 221221
Fax: +356 21 241241

Office of the Prime Minister
Auberge de Castille (Kastilja)
Valletta CMR 02
Tel.: +356 21 242560
Fax: +356 21 252752
www.magnet.mt/ministries/opm/

Marshall Islands

Office of the President
PO Box 2
MH 96960 Majuro
Tel.: +692 625 3445
Fax: +692 625 4020
Email: presoff@ntamar.com

Mauritania

Office of the President
Présidence de la République
BP 184
Nouakchott
Tel.: +222 5252 317
www.mauritania.mr/

Office of the Prime Minister
Présidence de la République
BP 184
Nouakchott
www.mauritania.mr/

Mauritius

Office of the President
State House
Reduit
Port Louis
Tel.: +230 454 3021
Fax: +230 464 5370
Email: statepas@intnet.mu
http://ncb.intnet.mu/presiden.htm

Office of the Prime Minister
Government House
Port Louis
Tel.: +230 201 2850
Fax: +230 208 7907
Email: secab@intnet.mu
http://ncb.intnet.mu/pmo.htm

Mexico

Office of the President
Los Pinos
Colonia San Miguel Chapultepec
11850 Mexico DF
Tel.: +52 55 5277 7455
Fax: +52 55 5510 3717
www.presidencia.gob.mx/

Federated States of Micronesia

Office of the President
PO Box PS-5
3 Palikir
96941 FM Pohnpei
Tel.: +691 320 2228
Fax: +691 320 2785
www.fsmgov.org/bio/falcam.html

Moldova

Office of the President
Ştefan cel Mare 154
Chişinau
Tel.: +373 2 234 793
Fax: +373 2 245 089

Office of the Prime Minister
Piaţa Marii Adunari Naţionale 1
227033
Chişinau
Tel.: +373 2 233 092
Fax: +373 2 242 696

Monaco

Office of the Prince
Palais de Monaco
Place du Palais
BP 518
98015 Monaco
Tel.: +377 93 25 18 31
Fax: +377 93 30 26 26
www.gouv.mc/

Office of the Minister of State
Place de la Visitation
BP 522
98015 Monaco
Tel.: +377 93 15 80 00
Fax: +377 93 15 82 17
Email: centre-info@gouv.mc
www.gouv.mc/

Mongolia

Office of the President
State Palace
Sukhbaatar Square 1
Ulan Bator 12
www.mongol.net/president/

Office of the Prime Minister
State Palace
Sukhbaatar Square 1
Ulan Bator 12
Tel.: +976 11 310011
Fax: +976 11 323501
www.pmis.gov.mn/cabinet

Morocco

Office of the King
Palais Royal
Rabat
Tel.: +212 37 760122

Office of the Prime Minister
Al Méchouar
Essaid
Rabat
Tel.: +212 37 761763
Fax: +212 37 769995
www.pm.gov.ma/

Mozambique

Office of the President
Avenida Julius Nyerere 1780
Maputo
Tel.:   +258 1 491121
Fax: +258 1 492065
www.mozambique.mz/governo/presiden.htm

Office of the Prime Minister
Praça da Marinha
Maputo
Tel.:   +258 1 426861
Fax: +258 1 426881
Email: dgpm.gov@teledata.mz
www.mozambique.mz/governo/mocumbi.htm

Myanmar

Office of the Chair of the SPDC
15–16 Windermere Park
Rangoon
Tel.:   +95 1 282445
www.myanmar.com/

Namibia

Office of the President
State House
Private Bag 13339
Windhoek
Tel.:   +264 61 220 010
Fax: +264 61 221 780
Email: angolo@op.gov.na
www.op.gov.na/

Office of the Prime Minister
Private Bag 13338
Windhoek
Tel.:   +264 61 287 9111
Fax: +264 61 226 189
www.opm.gov.na/

Nauru

Office of the President
Government Offices
Yaren
Tel.:   +674 444 3100
Fax: +674 444 3199

Nepal

Office of the King
Narayamhity Royal Palace
Durbar Marg
Kathmandu
Tel.:   +977 1 4413 577

Office of the Prime Minister
Central Secretariat
Singha Durbar
Kathmandu
Tel.:   +977 1 4228 555
Fax: +977 1 4227 286
Email: info@pmo.gov.np
www.pmo.gov.np/

Netherlands

Office of the Queen
Paleis Noordeinde
PO Box 30412
2500 GK
The Hague
www.koninklijkhuis.nl/

Office of the Prime Minister
Binnenhof 20
Postbus 20001
2500 EA
The Hague
Tel.:   +31 70 356 4100
Fax: +31 70 356 4683
www.postbus51.nl/

New Zealand

Office of the Governor-General
Government House
Wellington
Tel.:   +64 4 389 8055
Fax: +64 4 389 5536
www.gov-gen.govt.nz/

Office of the Prime Minister
Executive Wing
Parliament Buildings
Wellington
Tel.:   +64 4 471 9998
Fax: +64 4 473 7045
www.beehive.govt.nz/

Nicaragua

Office of the President
Avenida Bolívar y dupla sur
Managua
Tel.: +505 228 2803
Fax: +505 228 6771
www.presidencia.gob.ni/

Niger

Office of the President
Palais Présidentiel
Niamey
Tel.: +227 722 381
www.presidence.ne/

Office of the Prime Minister
Niamey
Tel.: +227 722 698

Nigeria

Office of the President
Federal Secretariat
Shehu Shagari Way
Abuja
Tel.: +234 9 2341 010
Fax: +234 9 2341 733
Email: ssa@nopa.net
www.nopa.net/

Norway

Office of the King
Det Kongelige Slott
0010 Oslo
Tel.: +47 22 04 87 00
Fax: +47 22 04 87 90
www.kongehuset.no/

Office of the Prime Minister
Akersgaten 42
PO Box 8001 Dep.
0030 Oslo
Tel.: +47 22 24 90 90
Fax: +47 22 24 95 00
Email: postmottak@smk.dep.no
http://odin.dep.no/smk/

Oman

Office of the Sultan
Royal Palace
Muscat
Tel.: +968 738 711
Fax: +968 739 427
www.diwan.gov.om

Pakistan

Office of the President
Constitution Avenue
Islamabad
Tel.: +92 51 922 0136
Fax: +92 51 920 3938
Email: psecyp@isb.paknet.com.pk

Office of the Prime Minister
Islamabad
Tel.: +92 51 922 2666
Fax: +92 51 920 4632
http://na.gov.pk/Intro_PM.htm

Palau

Office of the President
PO Box 100
PW 96940
Koror
Tel.: +680 488 2702
Fax: +680 488 1725
Email: roppressoffice@palaunet.com

Palestine

Office of the President
Gaza
Tel.: +970 8 2824670
Fax: +970 8 2822365
www.gov.ps/

Panama

Office of the President
Palacio Presidencial
San Felipe
Panamá
Tel.: +507 227 4062
Fax: +507 227 0076
www.presidencia.gob.pa/

Papua New Guinea

Office of the Governor-General
Government House
PO Box 79
Konedobu
Tel.:   +675 321 4466
Fax: +675 321 4543

Office of the Prime Minister
Morauta Haus
PO Box 639
Waigani
Tel.:   +675 327 6713
Fax: +675 327 6696
Email: primeminister@pm.gov.pg
www.pm.gov.pg/pmsoffice/pmsoffice.nsf

Paraguay

Office of the President
Palacio de Lopez
Asunción
Tel.:   +595 21 441 889
Fax: +595 21 493 154
www.presidencia.gov.py/

Peru

Office of the President
Plaza Mayor 5
Cercado de Lima
Lima 1
Tel.:   +51 1 426 6770
Fax: +51 1 426 6770
www.pres.gob.pe/

Office of the Council of Ministers
Avenida 28 de Julio no 878
Miraflores
Lima 18
Tel.:   +51 1 446 9800
Fax: +51 1 444 9168
Email: postmast@pcm.gob.pe
www.pcm.gob.pe/

Philippines

Office of the President
Malacanang Palace
J.P. Laurel Street
San Miguel 1005
Manila
Tel.:   +63 2 564 1451
Fax: +63 2 929 3968
Email: opnet@ops.gov.ph
www.opnet.ops.gov.ph/

Poland

Office of the President
ulica Wiejska 10
00-902 Warsaw
Tel.:   +48 22 695 2900
Fax: +48 22 695 2257
www.prezydent.pl/

Office of the Prime Minister
aleje Ujazdowskie 1/3
00-583 Warsaw
Tel.:   +48 22 694 6000
Fax: +48 22 625 2637
Email: cirinfo@kprm.gov.pl
www.kprm.gov.pl/

Portugal

Office of the President
Presidência da República
Palácio de Belém
1300 Lisbon
Tel.:   +351 213 637 141
Fax: +351 213 636 603
Email: presidente@presidenciarepublica.pt
www.presidenciarepublica.pt/

Office of the Prime Minister
Presidência do Conselho de Ministros
Rua Professor Gomes Teixeira
1399-022 Lisbon
Tel.:   +351 213 927 600
Fax: +351 213 927 615
Email: relacoes.publicas@pcm.gov.pt
www.portugal.gov.pt/

Qatar

Office of the Amir
PO Box 923
Doha
Tel.:   +974 446 2300
Fax: +974 436 1212
www.diwan.gov.qa/

Office of the Prime Minister
Doha

Romania

Office of the President
Cotroceni Palace
Bulevard Geniului 1
76238 Bucharest
Tel.:   +40 21 410 0581
Fax: +40 21 312 1179
Email: procetatean@presidency.ro
www.presidency.ro/

Office of the Prime Minister
Piaţa Victoriei 1
71201 Bucharest
Tel.:   +40 21 614 3400
Fax: +40 21 222 5814
Email: premier@gov.ro
www.guv.ro/

Russian Federation

Office of the President
Staraya ploshchad 42
Moscow
Tel.:   +7 095 206 2511
Fax: +7 095 206 5173
http://president.kremlin.ru/

Office of the Council of Ministers
Krasnopresenskaya 2
Moscow
Tel.:   +7 095 925 3581
Fax: +7 095 205 4219
www.gov.ru/

Rwanda

Office of the President
BP 15 Kigali
Tel.:   +250 584085
Fax: +250 584390
Email: presirep@rwanda1.com
www.rwanda1.com/government/presindex.html

Office of the Prime Minister
Kigali
Tel.:   +250 585444
Fax: +250 583714

St Kitts and Nevis

Office of the Governor-General
Government House
Basseterre
Tel.:   +1 869 465 2315

Office of the Prime Minister
Government Headquarters
Basseterre
Tel.:   +1 869 465 0297
Fax: +1 869 465 1001
Email: chiefsec@caribsurf.com
www.stkittsnevis.net

St Lucia

Office of the Governor-General
Government House
The Morne
Castries
Tel.:   +1 758 452 2481
Fax: +1 758 453 2731
www.stluciagovernmenthouse.com/

Office of the Prime Minister
Greaham Louisy Administrative Building
The Waterfront
Castries
Tel.:   +1 758 452 79880
Fax: +1 758 453 7352
Email: pmoffice@candw.lc
www.stlucia.gov.lc/primeminister/

St Vincent and the Grenadines

Office of the Governor-General
Government House
Old Montrose
Kingstown
Tel.:   +1 784 456 1111
Fax: +1 784 457 9710

Office of the Prime Minister
Administrative Centre
Bay Street
Kingstown
Tel.:   +1 784 456 1111
Fax: +1 784 457 2152
Email: pmosvg@caribsurf.com

Samoa

Office of the Head of State
Government House
Vailima
Apia
Tel.:   +685 20438
www.samoa.ws/govtsamoapress/
    head_of_state.htm

Office of the Prime Minister
PO Box 193
Apia
Tel.:   +685 21500
Fax: +685 21504
Email: pmdept@ipasifika.net

San Marino

Office of the Captains Regent
Palazzo Pubblico
47031 San Marino
Tel.:   +378 882259

São Tomé and Príncipe

Office of the President
Praga do Pouo
São Tomé
Tel.:   +239 221 020

Office of the Prime Minister
Praça Yon Gato
CP 302
São Tomé
Tel.:   +239 222 890
Fax: +239 221 670

Saudi Arabia

Office of the King
Riyadh
Tel.:   +966 1 401 4576
Email: kfb@saudinf.com
www.kingfahdbinabdulaziz.com/

Senegal

Office of the President
avenue Léopold Sédar Senghor
BP 168
Dakar
Tel.:   +221 8231 088
Fax: +221 8218 660
www.gouv.sn/institutions/president.html

Office of the Prime Minister
Immeuble Administratif
avenue Léopold Sédar Senghor
Dakar
Tel.:   +221 8231 088
Fax: +221 8225 578
www.gouv.sn/

Seychelles

Office of the President
PO Box 55
State House
Victoria
Mahé
Tel.:   +248 224155
Fax: +248 225117

Sierra Leone

Office of the President
State House
Independence Avenue
Freetown
Tel.:   +232 22 232101
Fax: +232 22 231404
Email: info@statehouse-sl.org
www.statehouse-sl.org/

Singapore

Office of the President
Istana
Orchard Road
238823 Singapore
Tel.:   +65 6737 5522
Fax: +65 6737 9896
Email: istana_general_office@istana.gov.sg
www.istana.gov.sg/

Office of the Prime Minister
Istana Annexe
Orchard Road
238823 Singapore
Tel.:   +65 6235 8577
Fax: +65 6732 4627
Email: pmo_hq@pmo.gov.sg
www.pmo.gov.sg/

Slovakia

Office of the President
Štefánikova ulica 1
81104 Bratislava - Hrad
Tel.:   +421 2 5441 7121
Fax: +421 2 5443 0683
Email: informacie@prezident.sk
www.prezident.sk/

Office of the Prime Minister
Námestie Slobody 1
81370 Bratislava
Tel.:   +421 2 5729 5111
Fax: +421 2 5249 7595
Email: tio@government.gov.sk
www.government.gov.sk/

Slovenia

Office of the President
Erjavčeva 17
1000 Ljubljana
Tel.:   +386 1 478 1205
Fax: +386 1 478 1357
Email: vlada@gov.si
www.sigov.si/up-rs/

Office of the Prime Minister
Gregorčičeva 20
1000 Ljubljana
Tel.:   +386 1 478 1000
Fax: +386 1 478 1721
www.sigov.si/pv/

Solomon Islands

Office of the Governor-General
Honiara

Office of the Prime Minister
PO Box G1
Honiara
Tel.:   +677 21863
Fax: +677 26088

Somalia

Office of the President
People's Palace
Mogadishu
Tel.:   +252 1 723

Office of the Prime Minister
Mogadishu

South Africa

Office of the State President
Private Bag X1000
0001 Pretoria
Tel.:   +27 12 319 1500
Fax: +27 12 319 1569
Email: president@po.gov.za
www.gov.za/dept/president/

Spain

Office of the King
Palacio de la Zarzuela
28071 Madrid
Tel.:   +34 91 599 2424
Fax: +34 91 599 2525
www.casareal.es/casareal/

Office of the President of the Government
Complejo de la Moncloa
Edificio Consejo
28071 Madrid
Tel.:   +34 91 335 3535
Fax: +34 91 335 3338
www.la-moncloa.es/

Sri Lanka

Office of the President
Republic Square
Colombo 01
Tel.:   +94 1 248 010
Email: info@presidentsl.org
www.priu.gov.lk/execpres/presecretariat.html

Office of the Prime Minister
58 Sir Ernest de Silva Mawatha
Colombo 07
Tel.:   +94 1 575 317
Fax: +94 1 437 017
Email: prime_minister@sltnet.lk
www.gov.lk/pm/office.htm

Sudan

Office of the President
Khartoum
Tel.: +249 11 779426
www.sudan.net/gov.shtml

Suriname

Office of the President
Onafhankelijkheidsplein
Paramaribo
Tel.: +597 472 841
Fax: +597 475 266
www.sr.net/users/burpres/

Office of the Vice President
Dr S Redmondstraat
1st floor
Paramaribo
Tel.: +597 474 805
Fax: +597 472 917

Swaziland

Office of the King
Lozitha Palace
Private Bag 1
Kwaluseni
Tel.: +268 51 84022
Fax: +268 51 85028
www.swazi.com/king/king.html

Office of the Prime Minister
PO Box 395
Mbabane
Tel.: +268 40 42251
Fax: +268 40 43943
Email: ppcu@realnet.co.sz
www.swazi.com/government/

Sweden

Office of the King
Kungliga Slottet
Slottsbacken
111 30 Stockholm
Tel.: +46 8 789 8500
www.royalcourt.se/

Office of the Prime Minister
Rosenbad 4
103 33 Stockholm
Tel.: +46 8 405 1000
Fax: +46 8 723 1171
Email: webmaster@primeminister.ministry.se
http://statsradsberedningen.regeringen.se/

Switzerland

Office of the President
Bundeshaus West
3003 Bern
Tel.: +41 31 332 2111
Fax: +41 31 322 3706
www.admin.ch/

Syria

Office of the President
Mouhajreen
Presidential Palace
Abu Rumanch
Al-Rashid Street
Damascus
Tel.: +963 11 2231 112
www.assad.org/

Office of the Prime Minister
Shahbandar Street
behind Central Bank
Damascus
Tel.: +963 11 2226 001
Fax: +963 11 2233 373

Taiwan

Office of the President
Chiehshou Hall
122 Chungking South Road
Section 1
Taipei
Tel.: +886 2 2311 3731
Fax: +886 2 2314 0746
Email: public@mail.oop.gov.tw
www.president.gov.tw/index_e.html

Office of the Premier
1 Chunghsiao East Road
Section 1
Taipei
Tel.:   +886 2 2356 1500
Fax: +886 2 2394 8727
Email: eyemail@eyemail.gio.gov.tw
www.ey.gov.tw/

Tajikistan

Office of the President
prospect Rudaki 80
734023 Dushanbe
Tel.:   +992 372 210 418
Fax: +992 372 211 837

Office of the Prime Minister
prospect Rudaki 80
734023 Dushanbe
Tel.:   +992 372 215 110
Fax: +992 372 211 510

Tanzania

Office of the President
The State House
Magogoni Road
PO Box 9120
Dar es Salaam
Tel.:   +255 22 211 6898
Fax: +255 22 211 3425

Office of the Prime Minister
Magogoni Road
PO Box 3021
Dar es Salaam
Tel.:   +255 22 211 2850
Fax: +255 22 211 3439

Thailand

Office of the King
The Grand Palace
Bangkok 10200
Tel.:   +66 2 221 1151
www.kanchanapisek.or.th/

Office of the Prime Minister
Government House
Thanon Nakhon Pathom
Bangkok 10300
Tel.:   +66 2 280 3693
Fax: +66 2 280 0858
www.pmoffice.go.th/

Togo

Office of the President
Palais Présidentiel
ave de la Marina
Lomé
Tel.:   +228 221 2701
Fax: +228 221 1897
Email: presidence@republicoftogo.com
www.republicoftogo.com/

Office of the Prime Minister
Lomé
Tel.:   +228 221 1564
Fax: +228 221 2040
Email: info@republicoftogo.com

Tonga

Office of the King
PO Box 6
Nuku'alofa
Tel.:   +676 25064
Fax: +676 24102

Office of the Prime Minister
PO Box 62
Hala Taufa'ahau
Nuku'alofa
Tel.:   +676 24644
Fax: +676 23888
Email: pmomail@pmo.gov.to
www.pmo.gov.to/
        office_of_the_prime_minister.htm

Trinidad and Tobago

Office of the President
President's House
St Ann's
Port of Spain
Tel.:   +1 868 624 1261
Fax: +1 868 625 7950
Email: presoftt@carib-link.net

Office of the Prime Minister
Whitehall
Maraval Road
Port of Spain
Tel.:   +1 868 622 1625
Fax: +1 868 622 0055
Email: opm@trinidad.net
www.opm.gov.tt/

Tunisia

Office of the President
Palais Présidentiel
Tunis and Carthage
Tel.:   +216 71 260 348

Office of the Prime Minister
Place du Gouvernement
La Kasbah
1008 Tunis
Tel.:   +216 71 263 991
Fax: +216 71 569 205
Email: prm@ministeres.tn
www.ministeres.tn/

Turkey

Office of the President
Cumhurbaşkanlıgı Köşkü
Cankaya
Ankara
Tel.:   +90 312 468 5030
Fax: +90 312 427 1330
Email: cankaya@tccb.gov.tr
www.cankaya.gov.tr/

Office of the Prime Minister
Başbakanlık
Bakanlıklar
Ankara
Tel.:   +90 312 418 9056
Fax: +90 312 417 0476
www.basbakanlik.gov.tr/

Turkmenistan

Office of the President
Presidential Palace
ulitsa Karl Marxa 24
744000 Ashkhabad
Tel.:   +993 12 354534
Fax: +993 12 354388

Tuvalu

Office of the Governor-General
Vaiaku
Funafuti atoll
Tel.:   +688 20715

Office of the Prime Minister
Vaiaku
Funafuti atoll
Tel.:   +688 20716
Fax: +688 20819

Uganda

Office of the President
Parliament Buildings
PO Box 7168
Kampala
Tel.:   +256 41 254 881
Fax: +256 41 235 459
Email: info@gouexecutive.net
www.statehouse.go.ug/

Office of the Prime Minister
PO Box 341
Kampala
Tel.:   +256 41 258 721
Fax: +256 41 242 341

Ukraine

Office of the President
vulitsa Bankova 11
01220 Kiev
Tel.:   +380 44 291 5333
Fax: +380 44 293 1001
Email: questions@kuchma.gov.ua
www.kuchma.gov.ua

Office of the Prime Minister
vulitsa M. Hrushevskoho 12/2
01008 Kiev
Tel.:   +380 44 226 2289
Fax: +380 44 293 2093
Email: web@kmu.gov.ua
www.kmu.gov.ua

United Arab Emirates

Office of the President
Manhal Palace
PO Box 280
Abu Dhabi
Tel.:   +971 2 665 2000
Fax: +971 2 665 1962

Office of the Prime Minister
PO Box 12848
Dubai
Tel.:   +971 4 353 4550
Fax: +971 4 353 0111
www.uae.gov.ae/

United Kingdom

Office of the Queen
Buckingham Palace
London
SW1 1AA
Tel.:   +44 20 7930 4832
www.royal.gov.uk/

Office of the Prime Minister
10 Downing Street
London
SW1A 2AA
Tel.:   +44 20 7270 1234
www.pm.gov.uk/

United States of America

Office of the President
The White House
1600 Pennsylvania Ave NW
Washington D.C. 20500-0001
Tel.:   +1 202 456 1414
Fax: +1 202 456 1907
Email: president@whitehouse.gov
www.whitehouse.gov/

Uruguay

Office of the President
Edificio Libertad
Avenida Dr Luis Alberto de Herrera 3350
Montevideo
Tel.:   +598 2 487 2110
Fax: +598 2 480 9397
Email: presidente@presidencia.gub.uy
www.presidencia.gub.uy/

Uzbekistan

Office of the President
43 Uzbekistanskaya Street
700163 Tashkent
Tel.:   +998 71 239 5746
Fax: +998 71 239 5525
Email: presidents_office@press-service.uz
www.press-service.uz/

Office of the Prime Minister
Government House
700008 Tashkent
Tel.:   +998 71 239 8295
Fax: +998 71 239 8601
www.gov.uz/

Vanuatu

Office of the President
Private Mail Bag 100
Port Vila
Tel.:   +678 230 55
Fax: +678 266 93
www.vanuatugovernment.gov.vu/
       president.html

Office of the Prime Minister
Private Mail Bag 053
Port Vila
Tel.:   +678 224 13
Fax: +678 228 63
www.vanuatugovernment.gov.vu/
       primeminister.html

Vatican City

Office of the Pope
Palazzo Apostolico Vaticano
00120 Vatican City
www.vatican.va/

Secretariat of State
Palazzo Apostolico Vaticano
00120 Vatican City
Tel.:   +39 066982 83913
Fax: +39 066982 85255
Email: vati026@relstat-segstat.va

Venezuela

Office of the President
Palacio de Miraflores
Caracas 1010
Tel.:   +58 212 860 0811
Fax: +58 212 860 1101
Email: presidencia@venezuela.gov.ve
www.venezuela.gov.ve/

Viet Nam

Office of the President
Hanoi

Office of the Prime Minister
Hanoi

Communist Party of Viet Nam
1 Hoang Van Thu, Hanoi
Email: cpv@hn.vnn.vn
www.cpv.org.vn

Yemen

Office of the President
Zubairy Street
Sana
Tel.:   +967 1 273092

Office of the Prime Minister
Sana

Yugoslavia

Office of the Federal Presidency
Bulevar Mihajla Pupina 2
11 070 Belgrade
Tel.:   +381 11 311 3008
Fax: +381 11 301 5055

Office of the Federal Prime Minister
Bulevar Mihajla Pupina 2
11 070 Belgrade
Tel.:   +381 11 311 3548
Fax: +381 11 311 1019
www.gov.yu/

Office of the President of Serbia
Andrićev venac 1
11 000 Belgrade
Tel.:   +381 11 323 2915
Fax: +381 11 658 584

Office of the Prime Minister of Serbia
Nemanjina 11
11 000 Belgrade
Tel.:   +381 11 361 7719
Fax: +381 11 361 7609
www.srbija.sr.gov.yu/

Office of the President of Montenegro
Bulevar Blaža Jovanovića 2
81000 Podgorica
Tel.:   +381 81 242382
Fax: +381 81 242329
www.predsjednik.cg.yu/

Office of the Prime Minister of Montenegro
Jovana Tomaševića bb
81000 Podgorica
Tel.:   +381 81 242530
Fax: +381 81 242329
www.vlada.cg.yu/

Zambia

Office of the President
PO Box 30208
Lusaka
Tel.:   +260 1 260317
www.statehouse.gov.zm/

Zimbabwe

Office of the President
Munhumutapa Building
Samora Machel Avenue
Causeway
Harare
Tel.:   +263 4 707091
Fax: +263 4 734644

INDEX BY DATE OF TAKING POWER

	22 Oct.	Ange-Félix Patassé, President, Central African Republic	96
	4 Nov.	Jean Chrétien, Prime Minister, Canada	90
	17 Nov.	Sir Colville Young, Governor-General, Belize	52
1994	9 March	Lester Bird, Prime Minister, Antigua and Barbuda	16
	21 May	Bakili Muluzi, President, Malawi	329
	5 July	Yassir Arafat, President, Palestine	401
	19 July	Leonid Kuchma, President, Ukraine	541
	20 July	Aleksandr Lukashenka, President, Belarus	46
	22 July	Col. (retd) Yahya Jammeh, President, Gambia	185
	7 Sept.	Owen Arthur, Prime Minister, Barbados	44
	1 Oct.	Teburoro Tito, President, Kiribati	274
	12 Nov.	Chandrika Bandaranaike Kumaratunga, President, Sri Lanka	485
	7 Dec.	Marc Forné Molné, President of the Executive Council, Andorra	11
	16 Dec.	Pascoal Mocumbi, Prime Minister, Mozambique	366
1995	20 Jan.	Jean-Claude Juncker, Prime Minister, Luxembourg	321
	10 March	Costas Stephanopoulos, President, Greece	198
	13 April	Paavo Lipponen, Prime Minister, Finland	175
	17 May	Jacques Chirac, President of the Republic, France	177
	22 June	Keith Mitchell, Prime Minister, Grenada	202
	27 June	Sheikh Hamad, Amir, Qatar	425
	4 July	Denzil Douglas, Prime Minister, St Kitts and Nevis	439
	23 Nov.	Benjamin Mkapa, President, Tanzania	513
	28 Nov.	Frederick Tluway Sumaye, Prime Minister, Tanzania	514
	21 Dec.	Utkur Sultanov, Prime Minister, Uzbekistan	562
	23 Dec.	Aleksander Kwaśniewski, President, Poland	419
1996	1 Jan.	Sir Cuthbert Sebastian, Governor-General, St Kitts and Nevis	438
	22 Jan.	Costas Simitis, Prime Minister, Greece	199
	7 Feb.	Letsie III, King, Lesotho	304
	9 March	Jorge Sampaio, President, Portugal	422
	11 March	John Howard, Prime Minister, Australia	25
	17 March	Göran Persson, Prime Minister, Sweden	499
	24 March	Gen. Mathieu Kérékou, President, Benin	55
	29 March	Ahmed Tejan Kabbah, President, Sierra Leone	461
	6 May	José María Aznar López, President of the Government, Spain	482
	1 June	Sir Clifford Husbands, Governor-General, Barbados	43
	25 July	Maj. Pierre Buyoya, President, Burundi	79
	26 July	Barnabas Sibusiso Dlamini, Prime Minister, Swaziland	496
	1 Aug.	Ólafur Ragnar Grímsson, President, Iceland	224
	8 Aug.	Sir Daniel Williams, Governor-General, Grenada	201
	16 Aug.	Derviş Eroglu, Prime Minister, Turkish Rep. of Northern Cyprus	132
	19 Sept.	Peter Mafany Musonge, Prime Minister, Cameroon	87
	29 Oct.	Sheikh Abdullah, Prime Minister, Qatar	426
	26 Nov.	Artur Rasizade, Prime Minister, Azerbaijan	33
1997	3 Feb.	Michel Lévêque, Minister of State, Monaco	358
	19 March	Arthur N. Robinson, President, Trinidad and Tobago	524
	2 May	Tony Blair, Prime Minister, UK	550
	24 May	Kenny D. Anthony, Prime Minister, St Lucia	442
	20 June	Natsagyn Bagabandi, President, Mongolia	359

	16 June	Thabo Mbeki, President, South Africa	478
	1 July	Johannes Rau, Federal President, Germany	191
	7 July	Sir John Lapli, Governor-General, Solomon Islands	473
	8 July	Vaira Vike-Freiberga, President, Latvia	297
	12 July	Guy Verhofstadt, Prime Minister, Belgium	50
	23 July	Mohammed VI, King, Morocco	362
	11 Aug.	Bharrat Jagdeo, President, Guyana	211
	1 Sept.	Mireya Moscoso, President, Panama	405
	1 Sept.	Sellapan Rama Nathan, President, Singapore	463
	5 Oct.	Atif Mohammad Obeid, Prime Minister, Egypt	157
	7 Oct.	Adrienne Clarkson, Governor-General, Canada	89
	12 Oct.	Gen. Pervez Musharraf, President, Pakistan	396
	25 Oct.	Sérgio Vieira de Mello, UN Administrator, East Timor	148
	17 Nov.	Mohammed Ghannouchi, Prime Minister, Tunisia	528
	10 Dec.	Helen Clark, Prime Minister, New Zealand	381
	15 Dec.	Boris Trajkovski, President, Macedonia	323
	20 Dec.	Akil Akilov, Prime Minister, Tajikistan	511
	22 Dec.	Mamadou Tandja, President, Niger	386
2000	3 Jan.	Hama Amadou, Prime Minister, Niger	387
	3 Jan.	Prince Ulukalala Lavaka Ata, Prime Minister, Tonga	523
	5 Jan.	Patrick Leclercq, Minister of State, Monaco	358
	10 Jan.	Kessai Note, President, Marshall Islands	342
	14 Jan.	Alfonso Portillo Cabrera, President, Guatemala	204
	22 Jan.	Gustavo Noboa Bejarano, President, Ecuador	152
	27 Jan.	Ivica Račan, Prime Minister, Croatia	125
	4 Feb.	Wolfgang Schüssel, Federal Chancellor, Austria	29
	17 Feb.	Kumba Yallá, President, Guinea-Bissau	209
	18 Feb.	Stipe Mesić, President, Croatia	123
	1 March	Tarja Halonen, President, Finland	174
	1 March	Mubarak al-Shamikh, Sec.-Gen. of Gen. People's Comm., Libya	311
	1 March	Jorge Batlle Ibáñez, President, Uruguay	558
	8 March	Bernard Makuza, Prime Minister, Rwanda	437
	11 March	Ricardo Lagos Escobar, President, Chile	101
	20 March	Mohammad Mustafa Miro, Prime Minister, Syria	505
	1 April	Abdoulaye Wade, President, Senegal	456
	22 April	Maj.-Gen. Paul Kagame, President, Rwanda	436
	7 May	Vladimir Putin, President, Russia	431
	12 May	Andranik Markarian, Prime Minister, Armenia	23
	16 May	Ahmet Necdet Sezer, President, Turkey	530
	17 May	Mikhail Kasyanov, Chair of the Council of Ministers, Russia	434
	20 May	Chen Shui-bian, President of the Republic, Taiwan	506
	19 June	Ali Abu al-Ragheb, Prime Minister, Jordan	266
	17 July	Bashar al-Assad, President, Syria	503
	26 July	Nambariyn Enkhbayar, Prime Minister, Mongolia	360
	1 Aug.	Moshe Katsav, President, Israel	247
	4 Aug.	Ferenc Mádl, President, Hungary	220
	12 Aug.	Ronald Venetiaan, President, Suriname	492
	12 Aug.	Jules Ajodhia, Vice President/Prime Minister, Suriname	493
	16 Aug.	Hipólito Mejía Domínguez, President, Dominican Republic	146

Index: *Dates of Taking Power*

	3 Sept.	Fradique de Menezes, President, São Tomé and Príncipe	451
	10 Sept.	Laisenia Qarase, Prime Minister, Fiji	172
	20 Sept.	Mari Alkatiri, Prime Minister, East Timor	150
	8 Oct.	Arnold Rüütel, President, Estonia	165
	8 Oct.	Lt. Girma Wolde Giorgis, President, Ethiopia	167
	10 Oct.	Khaleda Zia, Prime Minister, Bangladesh	41
	10 Oct.	Gennady Novitsky, Prime Minister, Belarus	48
	19 Oct.	Kjell Magne Bondevik, Prime Minister, Norway	391
	19 Oct.	Leszek Miller, Prime Minister, Poland	421
	12 Nov.	Hassan Abshir Farah, Prime Minister, Somalia	477
	27 Nov.	Anders Fogh Rasmussen, Prime Minister, Denmark	139
	9 Dec.	Ranil Wickremasinghe, Prime Minister, Sri Lanka	488
	13 Dec.	Syed Sirajuddin, Yang di-Pertuan Agong, Malaysia	331
	17 Dec.	Sir Allan Kemakeza, Prime Minister, Solomon Islands	474
	21 Dec.	Avtandil Jorbenadze, State Minister, Georgia	190
	22 Dec.	Hamid Karzai, Transitional President, Afghanistan	1
	24 Dec.	Patrick Manning, Prime Minister, Trinidad and Tobago	526
2002	1 Jan.	Dame Ivy Dumont, Governor-General, Bahamas	34
	2 Jan.	Eduardo Alberto Duhalde, President, Argentina	19
	2 Jan.	Levy Mwanawasa, President, Zambia	588
	10 Jan.	Enrique Bolaños, President, Nicaragua	384
	22 Jan.	Georgi Purvanov, President, Bulgaria	73
	27 Jan.	Ricardo Maduro, President, Honduras	218
	28 Jan.	Siim Kallas, Prime Minister, Estonia	166
	28 Jan.	Imangali Tasmagambetov, Prime Minister, Kazakhstan	269
	1 Feb.	Yu Shyi-kun, Premier, Taiwan	508
	22 Feb.	Marc Ravalomanana, President, Madagascar	326
	25 Feb.	Karl Offmann, President, Mauritius	347
	26 Feb.	Jacques Sylla, Prime Minister, Madagascar	328
	15 March	Yvon Neptune, Prime Minister, Haiti	216
	6 April	José Manuel Durão Barroso, Prime Minister, Portugal	423
	14 April	Col. (retd) Hugo Chávez Frías, President, Venezuela	569
	3 May	Alfredo Atanasof, Cabinet Chief, Argentina	20
	3 May	Perry Christie, Prime Minister, Bahamas	35
	6 May	Jean-Pierre Raffarin, Prime Minister, France	180
	8 May	Abel Pacheco de la Espriella, President, Costa Rica	118
	20 May	Xanana Gusmão, President, East Timor	148
	26 May	Col. Assoumani Azali, President, Comoros	110
	27 May	Paddy Ashdown, High Representative, Bosnia and Herzegovina	63
	27 May	Péter Medgyessy, Prime Minister, Hungary	222
	30 May	Nikolay Tanayev, Prime Minister, Kyrgyzstan	293
	8 June	Amadou Toumani Touré, President, Mali	337
	9 June	Ahmed Mohamed Ag Hamani, Prime Minister, Mali	338
	12 June	Haroun Kabadi, Prime Minister, Chad	100
	29 June	Koffi Sama, Prime Minister, Togo	521
	12 July	Vladimír Špidla, Prime Minister, Czech Republic	137
	12 July	Luis Solari, President of the Council of Ministers, Peru	414
	22 July	Jan Peter Balkenende, Prime Minister, Netherlands	379
	24 July	Gen. (retd) Alfred Moisiu, President, Albania	4

INDEX OF PERSONAL NAMES

INDEX BY TYPE OF REGIME

Monarchies

Bahrain, Bhutan, Brunei, Jordan,
Kuwait, Monaco, Morocco, Oman,
Qatar, Saudi Arabia, Swaziland,
Tonga, United Arab Emirates

One-party states

China, Cuba, Iraq, North Korea,
Laos, Libya, Syria, Turkmenistan,
Viet Nam

Nonparty systems

Kiribati, Maldives, Micronesia,
Nauru, Palau, Tuvalu, Uganda

Transitional regimes

Afghanistan, Burundi, Eritrea,
Rwanda, Somalia

Presidential systems

Algeria	Djibouti	Liberia	Senegal
Angola	Dominican Rep.	Madagascar	Seychelles
Argentina	Ecuador	Malawi	Sierra Leone
Armenia	Egypt	Mali	Sudan
Azerbaijan	El Salvador	Mauritania	Taiwan
Belarus	Equatorial Guinea	Mexico	Tajikistan
Benin	Gabon	Mozambique	Tanzania
Bolivia	Gambia	Namibia	Togo
Botswana	Georgia	Nicaragua	Tunisia
Brazil	Ghana	Niger	Ukraine
Burkina Faso	Guatemala	Nigeria	United States
Cameroon	Guinea	Pakistan	of America
Chad	Guinea-Bissau	Panama	Uruguay
Chile	Guyana	Paraguay	Uzbekistan
Colombia	Haiti	Peru	Venezuela
Comoros	Honduras	Philippines	Yemen
Congo, Rep.	Kazakhstan	Romania	Zambia
Costa Rica	Kenya	Russia	Zimbabwe
Côte d'Ivoire	South Korea	São Tomé and	
Cyprus	Kyrgyzstan	Príncipe	

Parliamentary systems

Albania
Andorra
Antigua and
  Barbuda
Australia
Austria
Bahamas
Bangladesh
Barbados
Belgium
Belize
Bosnia and
  Herzegovina
Bulgaria
Cambodia
Canada
Croatia
Czech Republic
Denmark
Dominica

East Timor
Estonia
Ethiopia
Fiji
Finland
Germany
Greece
Grenada
Hungary
Iceland
India
Indonesia
Ireland
Israel
Italy
Jamaica
Japan
Latvia
Lebanon
Lesotho

Liechtenstein
Lithuania
Luxembourg
Malaysia
Malta
Marshall Islands
Mauritius
Moldova
Nepal
Netherlands
New Zealand
Norway
Papua New Guinea
Poland
Portugal
St Kitts and Nevis
St Lucia
St Vincent and
  the Grenadines
Samoa

San Marino
Singapore
Slovakia
Slovenia
Solomon Islands
South Africa
Spain
Sri Lanka
Suriname
Sweden
Switzerland
Thailand
Trinidad and
  Tobago
Turkey
United Kingdom
Vanuatu
Yugoslavia

Mixed presidential–parliamentary systems

Cape Verde, Central African Republic, France, Macedonia, Mongolia

Others

Congo, Dem. Rep. (military-based regime)
Iran (Islamic theocracy)
Myanmar (military-based regime)
Palestine (unrecognized state)
Vatican City (papal state)